Acclaim for David Margolick's

BEYOND GLORY

"Margolick goes beyond those loaded symbols to bring alive the complex characters of the fighters. . . . In a *Seabiscuit*-like turn, Margolick also captures what life was like in a very different time, when Americans were still struggling through the Depression and when they were just starting to come to terms with a burgeoning civil rights movement. And when a single sporting event could matter so much."   —*Sports Illustrated*

"Compelling. . . . Margolick deftly moves his characters on and off stage against a backdrop of increasing tension. . . . [He] provides a sense that by managing to unite disparate American interests behind a common cause and undermining the Aryan illusion of racial supremacy, Louis helped insure a nation for the fight ahead."
—*The Washington Post Book World*

"Engrossing. . . . Margolick's work reminds us where we stood in terms of race and freedom then, and makes us think about where we stand now."
—*The Pittsburgh Post-Gazette*

"A knockout punch. . . . History at its liveliest."   —*The Baltimore Sun*

"[Margolick] deserve[s] praise as much for [his] literary execution as for vividly reminding us of the night when the world held its breath waiting to find out who would come out on top in a boxing match."
—*The Boston Globe*

"Margolick does a wonderful job of recreating an era. . . . Books like *Beyond Glory* . . . remind us how transcendent a sport boxing can be."
—*The New York Times*

"Margolick's painstakingly researched book brings to life the ambiguities and tensions of the pre-war years. *Beyond Glory* is likely to remain the definitive account of the Louis/Schmeling encounters and why they mattered." —*The Daily Telegraph* (London)

"An illuminating study of the period as well as the match. . . . A meticulous account of how the boxers' lives were buffeted by the political chaos and racial segregation of their age." —*BusinessWeek*

"[Margolick] lets the argot of sportswriting in the 1930s tell the story. . . . [He] does a fine job of looking into the smaller ironies and ambiguities of a unique American life and the picture which emerges of complex American attitudes to race. . . . Margolick's definitive book does the event and the characters who lived it the justice they deserve." —*Irish Times*

"Brilliant and colorful. . . . The two principles are deftly drawn. . . . A great book, packed with great writing and memorable moments." —*The Flint Journal*

"This peerless account from heavyweight author David Margolick deftly evokes the times and skillfully puts the controversy into its rightful context." —*Scotland on Sunday*

"*Beyond Glory* [is] a breathless stew of narrative. . . . Thickly detailed." —*The Nation*

"Superb. . . . History at its liveliest. . . . Because of Margolick's book, the two men—and all they came to symbolize—seem alive again." —*The Charlotte Observer*

"A definitive work. . . . [Margolick] is a smooth and talented writer. . . . It might be hard for today's fans to understand why the fight . . . seemed so significant. . . . It was—and still is. *Beyond Glory* tells us why, brilliantly." —*The Washington Times*

"The most extensively researched book on Joe Louis ever written. . . . [Margolick] has done his homework and then some." —*The New York Post*

David Margolick

BEYOND GLORY

David Margolick is a longtime contributing editor at *Vanity Fair*, where he writes about culture, the media, and politics. He served as national legal affairs editor at *The New York Times*, where he wrote the weekly "At the Bar" column for seven years. He is the author most recently of *Strange Fruit: The Biography of a Song*. This is his fourth book. He lives in New York City.

7/18

TO A FAN-TAS-TIC
FATHER-IN-LAW,

WISHING YOU A HAPPY BIRTHDAY
AND MY THANKS & LOVE FOR
BEING SUCH A PAL!
LOVE,
DAVID

BOOKS BY DAVID MARGOLICK

Strange Fruit:
The Biography of a Song

At the Bar:
The Passions and Peccadilloes of American Lawyers

Undue Influence:
The Epic Battle for the Johnson & Johnson Fortune

Beyond Glory:
Joe Louis vs. Max Schmeling, and a World on the Brink

BEYOND GLORY

Joe Louis *vs.* Max Schmeling,
and a World on the Brink

David Margolick

VINTAGE BOOKS
A DIVISION OF RANDOM HOUSE, INC.
NEW YORK

To my mother and father

The Library of Congress has cataloged the Knopf edition as follows:
Margolick, David.
Beyond glory : Joe Louis vs. Max Schmeling, and a world on the brink /
David Margolick.
p.   cm.
Includes bibliographical references and index.
1. Boxing—Social aspects—History. 2. Nationalism and sports—History.
3. Louis, Joe, 1914–1981. 4. Schmeling, Max, 1905–2005.
5. Sports rivalries—History. I. Title.
GV1136.8.M37   2005
796.83'09043—dc22
2005045141

Vintage ISBN-13: 978-0-375-72619-4
Vintage ISBN-10: 0-375-72619-5

Author photograph © Elena Seibert
Book design by Virginia Tan

www.vintagebooks.com

CONTENTS

BEYOND GLORY

AUTHOR'S NOTE

PEOPLE IN THIS BOOK are occasionally quoted talking in dialect, as rendered by someone writing about them at the time. In the belief that contemporaneous documents are precious, and that the insights they provide, both deliberate and inadvertent, must take precedence over evolving standards of fairness or taste, all such quotes appear precisely as they did originally. Readers can be trusted, I believe, to decide for themselves how those quoted must have spoken.

Introduction

O
N THE MORNING OF JUNE 22, 1938, the *New York Journal-American* plastered an enormous cartoon across the front page of its sports section. "Ringside Tonight!" it was titled. It depicted a darkened stadium topped by a circle of flags silhouetted against the evening sky and enclosing a small, illuminated square. Inside that square were two tiny figures, one black, one white, heading toward each other with their arms raised, about to come to blows. Looking on was a mob of people discernible near the action, and visible in the distance only as tiny specks of light. And sitting by the ropes was a giant anthropomorphic globe, with oversize bug eyes and a furrowed brow superimposed over the lines of latitude and longitude. The orb held a small sign, which read, MAIN BOUT, JOE LOUIS, U.S. VS. MAX SCHMELING, GERMANY.

Had you picked up any other newspaper that day, in Berlin or London or Tokyo or Johannesburg or Moscow, the message would have been the same: something extraordinary was about to happen in New York City. Around ten p.m., a timekeeper would strike a small bell, and much of a world still unaccustomed to acting in unison would cease whatever it was doing and come to attention. In Yankee Stadium, nearly seventy thousand fans would lean forward in their seats; throughout the rest of the world, a hundred million people or more—the largest audience in history for *anything*—would gather around their radios. Everything else would suddenly cease to matter.

"Wars, involving the fate of nations, rage elsewhere on this globe," the *New York Mirror* had declared that morning, "but the eyes of the world will be focused tonight on a two-man battle in a ribbon of light stabbing the darkness of the Yankee Stadium." The *Angriff*, the mouthpiece of

Nazi propaganda minister Joseph Goebbels, had little in common with the *Mirror*, a tabloid read primarily by working-class American Jews. But regarding this point, the two newspapers agreed. "On this day," the *Angriff* observed, "two men will hold an entire world in the utmost tension." Twenty million Germans would join the sixty million Americans who would be listening, even though it would be three o'clock the next morning in Berlin when the gong sounded. Much of Germany would simply not go to bed. Five months before Kristallnacht, the Night of the Broken Glass—the pogrom that would signal the end of any remaining semblance of normal Jewish life in Germany—the Nazi state would experience what one newspaper called "The Night of the Bright Windows."

Unique among the sports, boxing seemed to crystallize the ethnic, racial, and political tensions of a culture. But even to veteran boxing writers, this fight, between a twenty-four-year-old black American and a German nine years his senior, between the world heavyweight champion and a former title holder—and the only man ever to beat him in his professional career—was unlike any other. It was not just black against white, which was combustible enough, but youth versus age; raw talent and instinct versus experience; freedom against fascism; and, in its own way, the Jews versus Adolf Hitler. Though everyone made a prediction, no one felt very confident about it; there were too many imponderables. Since the moment two years earlier when, in one of the greatest upsets in the history of sports, Max Schmeling had knocked out the purportedly unstoppable Joe Louis, people had savored the idea of a rematch. For months now, it had been analyzed from every possible angle. "The relative merits of each fighter from the size of the pupils of his eyes down to the manner in which he shuffles his feet when he walks have been mulled over in a million conversations," Richard Wright wrote in the *Daily Worker*, the official paper of the American Communist Party, which for all of its Marxist wariness of professional athletics was following the fight as closely as any publication. "Louis or Schmeling?" the great sportswriter Grantland Rice asked. "These two names beat upon your eardrums as steadily as the tom-toms of a Zulu tribe moving to a raid."

No single sporting event—even Jack Johnson's victory over Jim Jeffries in 1910, which sparked race riots throughout the United States, or anything in the 1936 Olympics in Berlin—had ever borne such worldwide weight. The fight implicated both the future of race relations and the prestige of two powerful nations. Each fighter was bearing on his shoulders more than any athlete ever had. "Louis represents democracy in its purest form: the Negro boy who would be permitted to become a world champion without regard for race, creed or color," a sportswriter from Boston had written that morning. "Schmeling represents a country which does not recognize this idea and ideal."

In a nation still racked by the Depression, people had spent nearly a million dollars for tickets, something that had happened in boxing only a few times before, and only during boom times. "Judges and lawyers, Representatives and Senators, Governors and Mayors, bankers and brokers, merchant princes and industrial giants, doctors, artists, writers, figures of prominence in the various fields of sports, champions of the past and present in the ring . . . stars of the stage and screen—everybody, it seems," would be at or near ringside that night, *The New York Times* predicted. But equally impressive were those in the bleachers, many of them black, who had dug down deep into their pockets and their cookie jars, sacrificed their relief checks, pawned the precious little they owned for the privilege of watching two distant specks do battle, and to be—at least for a little while—at what felt like the center of the universe.

By ten o'clock, the streets in most American cities would be utterly deserted. With open windows offering the only defense against summertime heat and humidity, the sounds of the fight would float out of homes and apartments, spilling out into the streets and reverberating around empty courtyards. In movie theaters and restaurants, at baseball games and dances, the fight would be piped in. Four months later, when Seabiscuit beat War Admiral, perhaps forty million Americans would be listening. Tonight, sixty million would be—nearly half of the country's population, more people than had ever heard one of Franklin D. Roosevelt's fireside chats. Of course, anyone missing the action on NBC could read plenty about it the next morning; by one estimate, more journalists would gather at Yankee Stadium than there had been in Versailles for the formal end of World War I.

One didn't need to be an anthropologist to know there had never been anything like it, or a soothsayer to know there would never be anything like it again. If Louis, the "Brown Bomber," lost, the energy and dynamism with which he had single-handedly revitalized an entire sport over the previous four years would quickly dissipate, and the crown would go to Nazi Germany, where it could sit until Hitler deigned to let it go. If Louis won, no rivalry on the horizon could possibly generate as much excitement. And with Europe and, inevitably, America, on the brink of war, the world would soon have more than prizefights on its mind.

• • •

THEN AS NOW, New York City was usually too sprawling and too imperturbable to bend very much to anything in its midst. The place swallowed up sporting events, no matter the magnitude. "World Series scarcely cause a crush on the subway," one sportswriter observed two days before the fight. "Olympic tryouts go on unheeded. International tennis matches are just murmurs in the city's roar. But even New York and all its millions wouldn't submerge this fight," he went on. "It dominated everything." By one count, the city had more visitors that week than at any time since the Democratic Convention of 1924. Hotels, restaurants, and nightclubs were jammed. More blacks had flooded into New York than at any time in its history; since all of Harlem's hostelries were filled, and since hotels downtown were either too expensive or too discriminatory, these visitors were sleeping in their cars. Whatever prosperity black America could muster in these worst of times was on display, either on wheels or on their backs or in the hands of bookies. "If Joe loses, and no one here even thinks that, so many tears will flow down Seventh and Lenox avenues that it will seem like a Mississippi River flood," the *Amsterdam News*, Harlem's principal newspaper, reported. "On the other hand, if Joe wins, more liquor will be consumed than there is in 'Ole Man Ribber.'"

As many as two thousand Germans had come to New York for the fight, most of them aboard mighty ocean liners like the *Bremen* or the *Europa*, swastikas flying from their masts. All were fired up by prefight coverage in the Nazi press, which predicted that Schmeling was simply too superior to Louis—both as a boxer and as a man—to lose. Schmeling had been boxing for more than ten years. Several times, his career had been declared over. But always, through skill, discipline, and tenacity, he had clawed his way back. And as the ground in his homeland trembled beneath him, he had displayed diplomatic footwork fancier than anything ever demanded of him in the ring, making the jarring transition from Weimar to Nazi Germany without a stumble, replacing friends who had fled—Jews, artists, intellectuals—with a new crop in better odor with the regime. How many people, after all, could say they had cabled congratulations to Franklin Roosevelt when he was elected president, and then, only a few months later, received a wedding present from Adolf Hitler?

The Führer had been a boon to German boxing. He had extolled it in *Mein Kampf* and insisted it be taught in German schools. What made for good fighters—courage, resolve, speed, cold-blooded calculation—made for good soldiers, too, he said. In Reich sports culture, the *Daily Worker* had wisecracked, boxing was second only to Jew-baiting in popularity. The Nazis initially had little use for professional athletes. They served the wrong gods: themselves. Schmeling, moreover, was dark and brooding and had an almost Asian cast, a far cry from the lithe and cheery Aryan blonds of Leni Riefenstahl's films. But Schmeling's ability to confound his critics, to rebound from defeat, to prevail by sheer force of character and will, embodied the Nazi vision of a renascent Reich. When he had beaten Louis two years earlier, the Nazis had embraced him. *Schmeling's Victory: A German Victory*, they titled the film of that fight, which was shown throughout Germany by Hitler's personal decree, to enormous audiences of rapturous fans. "The first nationally-sponsored heavy-weight," one American writer called Schmeling.

But placating Hitler and the Americans simultaneously was a challenge even for the nimble and malleable Schmeling. In the United States, boxing meant New York, and New York, in large part, meant Jews. The man who controlled the sport in New York, and who was promoting tonight's fight, was Jewish. Many boxers, including champions in several divisions, were Jewish. So were many of the trainers, writers, and suppliers, as well as an enormous number of fans. So, too, were most of the fight managers, including Schmeling's; this irritated the Nazis, but it was, they surely realized, the price they had to pay to do business in New York. For five years now, New York fans had looked warily upon Schmeling, and upon his insistence that he was a "sportsman" rather than a "politician" and that nothing was amiss back home. Many came to consider him as much a German product as Krupp steel, someone whose purses helped prop up a brutal but financially strapped regime, and they had boycotted his fights. The Nazis believed that Schmeling had deserved a title shot the previous year and that New York Jews had killed it, and it was hard to argue with either point. For a time, the fight's promoter talked of moving the bout to a venue where there were fewer Jews. But he ultimately decided that despite the political pressures, the Jews would come out to this fight anyway: they were too eager to see Louis slaughter Schmeling to stay away. This hatred only made Germany embrace Schmeling more tenaciously. On the morning of the fight, Hitler sent a telegram wishing him luck.

That Schmeling was fighting a black man, and on behalf of a regime for which race was paramount, upped the symbolic ante. All whites, the

Nazis asserted, were in Schmeling's corner—not just in Germany but in
the American South, Australia, South America, and South Africa. German commentators had repeatedly charged that the United States was
more concerned about retaining the heavyweight crown than about
upholding the honor of the white race, so the task had fallen to Germany.
That anyone could accuse a segregated and bigoted America of giving
people of color a break was almost comic. But Louis, only the second
black man ever to win the heavyweight title, and the first in twenty-two
years, had made himself indispensable—and, just as remarkably, largely
acceptable—to white America.

"I'M GOING TO SEE HEIFETZ," one man tells another. "Oh, yeah?" the second man replies. "Who's he fighting?"

It is an old gag, but it captures the power and reach of boxing in the
United States before World War II. Once, the fight game had been a sport
of back rooms and lowlifes, gamblers and thugs. But in the Jazz Age it had
become legal, respectable, glamorous, omnipresent. Its male, working-
class constituency expanded to the wealthy, to intellectuals, to women—
and in particular society women. Epic contests attracted tens of thousands
of people and, in two instances, more than one hundred thousand. The
kingdom called "Fistiana" reached into nearly every city, neighborhood,
and town; each had its own arenas, boxing clubs, and favorites. On any
given night in New York, fans could choose between a dozen fights in as
many venues, pitting Irishmen against Jews against Italians against Poles.
To the fighters, most of them immigrants or the children of immigrants,
boxing was both a way to tout one's origins and an avenue toward Ameri-
canization, or at least upward mobility. The world capital of Fistiana was
Jacobs Beach, the block of West Forty-ninth Street just east of Madison
Square Garden (then located on Eighth Avenue), where the managers,
matchmakers, ticket sellers, trainers, and pugs congregated. The area was
named for its reigning monarch, Mike Jacobs, the former ticket salesman
who now ran boxing at Madison Square Garden. Fistiana had its own
scribes, usually the best writers a paper had; floods and strikes, the journalist Heywood Broun once wrote, were for second stringers.

The Depression had knocked some oomph out of professional boxing,
as had the retirements of luminaries like Jack Dempsey and Gene Tunney. The sport sputtered as a series of less glamorous champions, Schmeling among them, quickly came and went. But a heavyweight title fight

was still the most lavish, anticipated spectacle in sports. Unlike baseball, football, hockey, golf, or tennis, it crossed all borders and classes. "Tonight's the night," the *New York Post* declared that afternoon, "when little shots rub elbows with big shots; clergymen discuss hooks and right crosses with gangsters and de-lovelies powder pert noses in $30 seats that their sweeties paid 100 bucks for."

If boxing brought classes together, it brought the races together, too. More than in almost any other segment of American life, fight crowds at heavyweight bouts had become integrated, at least since Joe Louis had come along, even if most blacks sat in the cheap seats. In the stadium, one black writer observed, the wall between the races was far thinner than in almost any church. And in the ring more than anywhere else, blacks had now come to believe they could be judged fairly. It hadn't always been so. If a black man was too good, Damon Runyon once wrote, whites wouldn't fight him, and if he was no good, well then, what good was he? Fights between blacks and whites were still rare enough—white boxers as recent and as eminent as Jack Dempsey had ducked all their black counter-parts—to have a name: "mixed bouts." Only a few years before Louis turned professional, a New York paper mistakenly called a white fighter black—and the fighter sued for libel.

But Louis was too good a boxer, and too good for boxing, to keep down. He was a precise and devastating puncher with both hands, and as Runyon himself noted, "the public loves a puncher, white, black, yellow or green." He invariably scored knockouts, clean and quick, ferocious and unequivocal. White America was vaguely embarrassed by its love of box-ing, but black America felt few qualms; for blacks, boxing offered a breach in the ghetto wall. "Fame and money are still more likely to come to the Negro of brawn and skill and gameness who knocks men down for a count of ten seconds than to his fellow athlete, to the scientist, scholar, actor, doctor, artist, labor leader, statesman, preacher, business man, inventor or judge," a landmark study of the time observed. The roped square, at least with Louis inside it, meant a square deal. "You can't Jim Crow a left hook" was how another great black boxer, Henry Armstrong, had put it. Boxing also offered the black man revenge with impunity. "The ring," Malcolm X was to write in his autobiography, "was the only place a Negro could whip a white man and not be lynched."

More had been written about Louis in the previous few years, Runyon speculated, than about anyone besides Charles A. Lindbergh. A midwest-ern professor asked his students to identify John L. Lewis, Joe Louis, and

Sinclair Lewis; few had heard of the labor leader or the author, but nearly all knew the Brown Bomber. (So popular had he become that sportswriters had recently started calling the New York Yankees the "Bronx Bombers.") Louis's appeal was no accident. By temperament and design, he had tried to be everything the much-vilified, still-controversial previous black titleholder, Jack Johnson, was not: dignified, gentle, self-effacing, unthreatening. While whites sometimes patronized him—"a big, superbly built Negro youth, who was born to listen to jazz music, eat a lot of fried chicken, play ball with the gang on the corner and never do a lick of heavy work he could escape," Bill Corum of the *New York Evening Journal* had written of him the previous year—they generally liked him, even below the Mason-Dixon Line. Once, southern exhibitors put Louis footage at the ends of newsreels, the easier to crop it out; now it was played, and applauded. One black columnist estimated as the Louis-Schmeling fight approached that two of three white southerners were pulling for Louis—partly, he admitted, because Schmeling was the most unpopular white man to take on a black man in the history of boxing. For Louis, then, much of the bigotry that afflicted America was briefly and selectively suspended. "There is not one iota of feeling that the Negro is an interloper, and that if we cannot have a white American at the top, the division is in the doldrums," Nat Fleischer wrote in the pages of his hugely influential publication, *Ring* magazine, a month before the fight. "Louis is an American, and a darn good one at that." As the sport's most tireless champion, and a New Yorker, and a Jew, Fleischer certainly overstated things. But a surprising number of Americans shared his views.

In black America, Louis was idolized as no one had ever been. Writers compared him to Booker T. Washington, the biblical David, and Jesus Christ. Black newspapers were filled with poems about him. Musicians composed songs about him. Preachers who had once deemed prizefighting crooked and unchristian extolled him from the pulpit; families hung pictures of him in their parlors. Even Jesse Owens, the only black athlete to rival him in fame and accomplishment, became in his exalted presence just another rabid fan. "Day by day, since their alleged emancipation, they have watched a picture of themselves being painted as lazy, stupid, and diseased," Richard Wright wrote. To black America, he went on, Louis "symbolized the living refutation of the hatred spewed forth daily over radios, in newspapers, in movies and in books about their lives." Louis let blacks everywhere think lofty and heretical thoughts; if he could shatter racial barriers, those barriers could not be so formidable. The sports pages put Louis's reach at seventy-six inches. In fact, it was global. But for all this, black America was hedging its bets. Louis had burned them once, when he lost to Schmeling in 1936, and besides, the black community never took anything, particularly anything good, for granted. The Harlem that one black visitor encountered before the fight was quiet and fearful, as if everyone were in prayer.

After showers earlier in the day, the weather in the Bronx had cleared. By five o'clock, five thousand people were waiting to buy general admission tickets for $3.50 apiece; a redcap was first in line, a cook, second. As darkness began to fall, thousands made their way to the stadium, "in purring limousines, grinding cabs, and up from the subway slots in great spouting geysers of humanity," wrote Bob Considine in the *New York Mirror*. From the window of her apartment in the Sugar Hill section of Harlem, Louis's young bride could see the giant stadium and watch the enormous procession making its way there by car and by bus and on foot. She would be listening to the fight on the radio. Shortly before ten, the fighters entered the ring. The NBC broadcaster Clem McCarthy was at the microphone when the referee, Arthur Donovan, summoned the two fighters and their seconds. Donovan asked the contestants how they felt, reviewed the dangers of low blows, warned their seconds not to step through the ropes while the fight was on. He then reminded the combatants of their responsibility, both to the crowd and to the unseen audience beyond, all of whom were expecting one of the greatest fights ever. "Now let's go," he concluded, "and may the best man win."

"The old slogan of boxing, 'May the best man win,' and she's about to start, with this Yankee Stadium packed to the doors!" McCarthy exclaimed. "Joe Louis in his corner, prancing, and rubbing his feet in the resin, and Max Schmeling standing calmly . . . and they're ready with the bell just about to ring."

And then the bell rang.

CHAPTER 1

Just Off the Boat

FIVE YEARS EARLIER, on the morning of April 14, 1933, the North German Lloyd liner *Bremen* had steamed into New York Harbor, with Max Schmeling aboard. The setting was spectacular—the mighty vessel, after its five-day crossing, making its way toward the Statue of Liberty, with the towers of lower Manhattan beckoning—but scarcely more epic, at least in the world of sports, than the events about to unfold. Schmeling would soon attempt something that had never been done: to regain the heavyweight crown. And his prospects looked good; after all, many believed he should never have lost it.

Schmeling, twenty-seven years old, had been coming to the United States for five years now, and the arrival ritual had grown routine. Meeting him aboard the ship would be the usual mob of fight reporters, who had commandeered a cutter to bring them there: all ten New York City newspapers had at least one boxing writer, as did the wire services, and there were emissaries from Boston, Philadelphia, Newark, and Chicago, to name just a few other cities with boxing correspondents of their own. Then there would be the photographers and newsreel boys, who would put Schmeling through the same staged scenes and make him utter the same wooden dialogue for the cameras. The previous June, Schmeling had lost the title to Jack Sharkey in a much-criticized decision. "We wuz robbed!" his fiery, outlandish manager, Joe Jacobs, had immortally declared afterward. But now Schmeling, with characteristic determination, had set out to win it back. And why not? He had already defied the odds three years earlier, when, in an equally disputed fight, he'd become the first European ever to win the heavyweight title.

A personable sort, Schmeling had long since come to know most of the reporters by name. They were friendly, irreverent types—smart alecks—likely to ask an impertinent question or two, but not to be too persistent or obnoxious about it; whatever edge they had was certain to be dulled by the good German beer Schmeling always brought with him. The floating press conference would then pull into the pier, where he would be greeted by a mob of fight fans coming to show their support or simply to glimpse a celebrity. Schmeling could easily have been unpopular; he'd won the title under the most debatable circumstances, spoke English with a heavy accent, and came from a country with which America had been at war only fifteen years earlier. After he'd beaten Sharkey for the title, he'd dragged his feet on a promised rematch, offending Americans and Germans alike. But when he lost the crown he'd been a gentleman, picking up an aura of martyrdom. Though he revealed only so much of himself, there always appeared to be something endearingly earnest about him.

And then there was the good fortune of his physical appearance. Schmeling looked uncannily like the man who epitomized boxing's golden era, the legendarily hard-hitting and much-missed Jack Dempsey, who'd retired only a few years earlier after producing all five of boxing's million-dollar "gates"—that is, fights where ticket sales went into seven figures. Schmeling had the same build, the same wavy, dark, slicked-down hair, the same heavy brows. Schmeling's style in the ring, though, was not the slashing, overwhelmingly aggressive assault Dempsey favored but something cooler, slower, more methodical—"Teutonic," as it was often described. And outside the ring he was as self-contained and calculating as Dempsey was gregarious.

Dempsey was promoting Schmeling's upcoming fight on June 8 in Yankee Stadium against a promising young California heavyweight named Max Baer, and was among those greeting Schmeling. The next day's papers would be filled with pictures of the two men together, wearing nearly identical suits and topcoats, all but daring readers to tell them apart. At the pier the confusion had already begun; an excited young woman broke through the crowd, grabbed Dempsey's hand, and tried to kiss it. "Oh, Max!" she cried. "You're wonderful!" Accompanying Schmeling on the voyage, as always, was Max Machon, his longtime German trainer. And just as predictably, greeting him at the pier was Joe Jacobs, the ever-present cigar jutting out of his mouth.

Schmeling tried to be boyish and lighthearted with the press, as if nothing had changed since his last visit to New York, the year before. Anyone bending over to inspect his lapel pin—"Athletic Club," it said—

got water spritzed into his eye. But Schmeling now faced more than the usual inquiries about the kind of shape he was in, how and where he planned to train, and the state of his punches. Three months earlier, Hitler had come to power in Germany. Almost instantly, life for Germany's 600,000 Jews had changed profoundly, and terrifyingly. Already, they were being banished from universities, public schools, symphony orchestras, the legal and medical professions. Jewish-owned newspapers, soon to be confiscated by the government, had to chronicle the mighty flow of anti-Jewish enactments. In but a couple of months, the dark ages had descended upon the German-Jewish community. It was hard to know whether the storm would pass, and while many Jews quickly left, far more stayed. But it was sobering indeed when the *Angriff* declared that Germany's Jews were done for, morally and commercially.

Nowhere was their fate followed more closely than in New York, a city with two million Jews of its own, many of them passionate fight fans with deep ties to Europe. Three weeks before Schmeling's arrival, 100,000 of them, including 20,000 Jewish veterans of World War I, had marched through the snow from the Lower East Side to city hall to protest events in Germany. Four days later, 22,000 of them rallied at Madison Square Garden, with 35,000 more on the streets outside. Such protests only fired up the Nazis further. By the time Schmeling boarded the *Bremen*, there had been a nationwide boycott of Jewish businesses in Germany, torchlight processions in support of the anti-Jewish measures, and paroxysms of violent anti-Semitism. "Hundreds of Jews have been beaten or tortured," the Berlin correspondent of the *New York Evening Post*, H. R. Knickerbocker, reported shortly before Schmeling steamed in. "Thousands of Jews have fled. Thousands of Jews have been, or will be, deprived of their livelihood." Germany's entire Jewish population, he wrote, was in a state of terror.

New York, by contrast, must have seemed the picture of tranquillity to Schmeling when he arrived. But it had also grown less receptive to him, more wary. The goodwill he had built up in the United States, like the goodwill he had established with the Nazis, was impressive but thin, and would require delicacy and dexterity to preserve. Schmeling faced two fights in America. The first, in the ring, was hard enough: Baer was a furious puncher who had beaten one rival to death and very nearly killed another. But Schmeling also faced the formidable challenge of placating the American fight public without offending the regime back home, of mollifying Jews and Nazis simultaneously.

• • •

TWELVE YEARS EARLIER, on July 2, 1921, fifteen-year-old Max Schmeling had stood outside a newspaper office in Cologne, following an account of Dempsey's fight against the Frenchman Georges Carpentier as it came across the wire from the United States. He rooted for Dempsey, not just because he liked him, but because he wanted the heavyweight championship to remain in America long enough to go there and get it. Afterward, Schmeling spent some of his meager earnings repeatedly watching films of the fight in a local theater. He convinced his father, a navigator on the Hamburg-America Line, to pay for some boxing lessons. Then young Max bought some used gloves and hung them over his bed.

Max Siegfried Adolph Otto Schmeling was born in Klein Luckow—a town in northern Germany eighty miles north of Berlin—on September 28, 1905, and grew up in Hamburg. He left school early and worked variously at an advertising firm, as a pipe fitter, and as a strong man in the circus. He flirted with soccer, but found himself drawn to boxing. Interest in the sport, which had been illegal and underground in Germany before World War I, had recently exploded. German soldiers had learned it as prisoners of war in Britain, or from the Americans who occupied their country once the war was over. In Weimar Germany as in the United States, the sport became a great passion not just of the working classes but also of artists and intellectuals, who saw in it something pure and manly, elemental and elegant, timeless and modern. When he visited Germany in 1926, Nat Fleischer was astounded to see how the country had embraced the sport. Germany had forty thousand amateur boxers, he pointed out, and if only a dozen stars emerged, they could soon menace American hegemony.

In Düsseldorf, then in Cologne, Schmeling spent most of his spare time in boxing clubs. It was in Cologne that he honed his distinctive style: methodical, scientific, and patient. He became well versed in the fundamentals of footwork, body movement, and defense; his style was to bide his time, study his opponent, and wait for openings rather than slug it out too early. His right was his money punch, his left, as someone later put it, merely something for holding his fork. Schmeling's personal code was regimented: a careful diet, no alcohol or tobacco, regular hours. When he'd go to the Roxy-Bar (a favorite hangout for Berlin's athletes and aesthetes), he'd always order fresh orange juice and "Café Hag"—that is, decaffeinated coffee. He was, as the German weekly *Box-Sport* once wrote, a *Musterknabe*—a prig. Nothing distracted him from his objective.

One of his fights came only four days after he'd crashed his motorcycle, killing his fourteen-year-old sister. He won.

Schmeling turned professional in 1924 and won nine of his first ten fights. But "professional" was a relative term: when *Box-Sport's* editor, Arthur Bülow, became his manager, Schmeling had only nine cents in his pocket. Dempsey visited Cologne in 1925, and Schmeling was one of three local boxers who fought him in two-round exhibitions. Fleischer, too, saw Schmeling there, and immediately cabled the majordomo of American boxing, Tex Rickard of Madison Square Garden, about him. In August 1926, Schmeling won the German light heavyweight championship in less than a minute. The following January, *Box-Sport* called him "our greatest hope" and extolled his "cold, sure eye, technique, brain and general ability." To his critics, Schmeling was almost too calculating; *Box-Sport* faulted him for what it called "an insufficient will to annihilate." But that June, before a frenzied, ecstatic crowd in Dortmund, he beat a Belgian, Fernand Delarge, for the European light heavyweight championship. For a country still traumatized by losing a war and in the throes of political and economic upheaval, it was an epic event. Moments after he knocked out the Italian Michele Bonaglia in January 1928, eight thousand fans stood up and sang "Deutschland über Alles."

Schmeling gained entry into elite German intellectual circles, meeting the filmmaker Josef von Sternberg, the artist George Grosz (for whom he became a model), the novelist Heinrich Mann, and other Weimar cultural figures. He relished the role. *"Künstler, schenkt mir Eure Gunst— Boxen ist auch 'ne Kunst!"* he wrote in the guest book of one artistic hangout: "Artists, grant me your favor—boxing is also an art!" That someone with his limited background and education could make himself comfortable in so alien a world was an early indication of Schmeling's extraordinary adaptability. Conversely, German society was showing its ability to adapt itself to him, to see in him whatever it wanted.

Even before meeting Schmeling or watching him in action, Paul Gallico, a sports columnist for the *New York Daily News*, a man who spoke German and read the German newspapers, began praising him and urging him to come to the United States. Schmeling had his lapses and his losses, which some attributed to his new and highfalutin life. But in April 1928, despite fracturing his thumb early in the fight, Schmeling outpointed Franz Diener for the German heavyweight championship. Now, America really beckoned; a cartoon in *Box-Sport* showed Schmeling "swimming after the dollar" across the Atlantic. That May, Schmeling, accompanied by Bülow, arrived in New York for the first time. His appearance rated only meager coverage in a few newspapers—all of which misspelled his name.

Schmeling's injured thumb precluded any immediate action. For months, he lived off the charity of Madame Hranoush Aglaganian Bey, a Constantinople-born grande dame who ran a famous training camp in Summit, New Jersey. Gradually Schmeling's idleness, poverty, and poor prospects soured him on Bülow, and Harry Sperber, a reporter for the *New Yorker Staats-Zeitung*, a German-American paper, urged Schmeling to find himself an American manager, someone familiar with boxing in New York and wily and aggressive enough to get him a few fights. Schmeling initially hired Nat Fleischer, who advanced him $250 to tide him over until his thumb healed. But everything changed when Joe Jacobs came by Madame Bey's to see one of his fighters. Before long, Jacobs had elbowed Bülow and Fleischer aside—a maneuver that earned him the nickname "Yussel the Muscle," "Yussel" being the Yiddish diminutive for Joseph.* (In one story, someone asked Schmeling where he got the three crisp $1,000 bills he was brandishing. "Joe Jacobs gave 'em to me," he said. "He told me to buy myself some cigars.") Schmeling believed the Jews controlled New York, and now he had someone to help him negotiate his way around the place. For Schmeling, it was the start of a long and bitter feud with Bülow, with whom he technically remained under contract. It was also the start of what was surely one of the most incongruous and tumultuous partnerships in the history of sports.

Jacobs, then in his early thirties, was the quintessential Broadway guy, a Damon Runyon character from whom even Damon Runyon, then writing a sports column for the Hearst newspapers, could pick up some pointers. His goal in life was to do everything with style. He was ever quick with the buck, the wisecrack, and the dames. No matter how strapped he might be, he wore tailor-made suits and striped shirts (all designed to make him look taller than his five feet two inches) and flashy shoes polished to a dazzling sheen. Then there was his omnipresent expensive cigar: he went through fifteen or twenty of them a day, and one could always gauge how flush he was by their pedigree. Reporters knew that Jacobs was always good for a snappy quote, and they clung to him. "If all the newspaper copy he inspired were stretched end to end, a blow would be dealt to the King's English from which it would never recover," Dan Parker, the sports columnist of the *New York Mirror*, once wrote. Even

*Fleischer wrote years later that Schmeling never repaid the $250.

when he wasn't trying to, Jacobs flirted with *Webster's*, or *Bartlett's*. There was that freezing day in Detroit when, violating all of his instincts and habits, he'd actually awakened early to attend the World Series. "I shudda stood in bed," he famously complained. Most of the time, Jacobs stayed in midtown Manhattan, within a block or two of Broadway; anywhere else (apart from the places where his fighters fought) he seemed to wilt. Rural things, like training camps and trees, either bored or frightened him, or tired him out. "It's too darned quiet to sleep," he once complained upon returning to civilization. Jacobs invariably slept late, often in one of the love nests he shared with his retinue of showgirls, chorines, models, and divorcées. Each of them—there might be half a dozen at a time, several of whom he supported—he would introduce as "my little wife." Someone once asked him if he was married. "Do you think I'm crazy?" he replied. Most days he'd get up as the sun went down, go for a shave, and emerge smelling, as someone once put it, like a fugitive from a florist shop. By eight-thirty or so in the evening, after checking in at his office, he'd have his "breakfast," perhaps at Lindy's. By midnight, after making further rounds, it would be time for "dinner." Then it was off to the nightclubs, though always within reach of a fight promoter in search of a deal. Once, peering sadly down Broadway as day broke, he groused, "Why do guys have to sleep at all?"

The columnist Westbrook Pegler once called Jacobs "a New York side-walk boy of the most conspicuous Jewishness." He wore it on his sleeve, but was forever trying to shed the coat, saying kaddish (the Jewish prayer for the dead) for his mother one minute, then eating a ham sandwich in a Broadway beanery the next. He had grown up in the Hell's Kitchen section of Manhattan, the son of a tailor. His father wanted him to be a rabbi, but young Joe gravitated toward boxing; while still in high school he had fighters on his payroll. In military service during World War I, he arranged bouts between rival companies, then promoted fights between soldiers to the general public. Within a few years, he'd landed a light heavyweight named Mike McTigue, who went on to become champion of the world. In October 1923 he brought McTigue, along with his own portable New York–based referee, to Columbus, Georgia, to fight a local hero named Young Stribling. When McTigue tried to back out at the last moment—he'd hurt his hand—local Ku Klux Klan members threatened to string up Jacobs and his fighter. By one account, Jacobs stood up to the bullies. "If you hang me, there will be some guys down here from New York that will blow this dump off the map," he warned. In another version of the story,

Jacobs saw two trees, one a mighty oak, the other a mere sapling. "You take the big tree," he told his boxer magnanimously. "The little one is all I want." In any case, the fight proceeded, and when, after ten rounds, Jacobs's referee called it a draw, the Klansmen filled the ring and forced him to name Stribling the winner. Three hours later, safely out of the Klan's reach, the referee reinstated the original decision. After that, Jacobs never ventured down South again; there were, he explained, too many trees there. Jacobs was fanatically devoted to his fighters, whom he championed unceasingly and ingeniously. When doctors said one of them had double pneumonia, Jacobs asked why they couldn't call it "triple pneumonia" instead: it would sound better in the papers, he explained, and besides, his man was a pretty big guy.

Having landed Schmeling, Jacobs paraded his new prized prospect around tirelessly. The heavyweight division was, as he liked to say, where most of the "coconuts" could be made. Some, including Schmeling himself, credited him with what became Schmeling's inapt but enduring nickname: "The Black Uhlan of the Rhine." While it had a nice ring to it, it bore little resemblance to reality; Schmeling had no connection whatever to the Uhlans (cavalry lancers in the Prussian army), was from nowhere near the Rhine, and only his hair was black. (The nickname is more generally attributed to Damon Runyon.) In November 1928, his hand now healed, Schmeling made his American debut, knocking out Joe Monte. The following January, with the crowd shouting "Dempsey! Dempsey!" he won a decision against Joe Sekyra. That earned him his first big fight, in February 1929, against Johnny Risko, who had once gone the distance with Gene Tunney. When Schmeling knocked him out in nine rounds before twenty-five thousand screaming fans, people began predicting he'd be heavyweight champion. Thanks to Schmeling, *Box-Sport* declared, American public opinion toward Germany had warmed up for probably the first time since the Armistice.

The victory raised the stakes in Schmeling's dispute with Bülow. During one hearing, the two men nearly came to blows; Bülow complained that Schmeling treated him like a dog. Despite Schmeling's efforts—he visited with the German ambassador in Washington and may even have attempted to see President Coolidge—the New York boxing commission ruled that Bülow was still Schmeling's manager, at least for the eighteen months remaining on their contract, and was entitled to a share of his income. Schmeling threatened to hang up his gloves for the duration. In the meantime, he returned to Germany, where twenty thousand people greeted him at the train station in Berlin. But he soon returned to America for a fight with another top contender, Paolino Uzcudun, the so-called Basque Woodchopper. Jacobs went into overdrive, writing a seventeen-part series on Schmeling for the *New York American*. Schmeling beat Uzcudun, and "all Berlin was frantic with joy," *The New York Times* reported. The excitement in the Fatherland, one newspaper there stated, resembled what had followed the great German victories of World War I. A Schmeling championship appeared so inevitable that one former title-holder, James J. Corbett, began to bemoan what it signaled about American boxing. In barely a year, Schmeling's purses topped $95,000, the fastest start for a boxer ever.

Schmeling's stubborn insistence on outlasting Bülow, though, meant remaining idle, which lost him admirers on both continents. But when he signed to fight Jack Sharkey on June 12, 1930, for the heavyweight crown — Tunney, the champion, had retired — the sniping largely stopped. Schmeling's arrival in New York on May 4, 1930, was almost regal, but he drew mixed reviews from the press. "He is quiet, modest, sincere (as far as one can tell)," wrote Frank Graham, the respected columnist of the *New York Sun*. Joe Williams of the *New York Telegram* disagreed, detecting "an insolence, an arrogance, and a latent meanness about him." Jacobs tried to smooth things over. But taking no chances, Yussel, visiting a Bronx synagogue to say kaddish for his father, threw in a prayer for Schmeling, too — that, as the Yiddish daily *Forverts* later put it, God should help his fighter "punch harder than the Lithuanian *sheygets* [Gentile]. To secure the heavenly bequest," it went on, "Jacobs flipped a couple of coins into the charity box." And God delivered, in a backhanded kind of way.

A crowd of eighty thousand gathered at Yankee Stadium for what was framed as a battle of nations. Schmeling wore the German national colors and was introduced as "the fighting son of the Fatherland." The applause was deafening, for German Americans, Austrians, and Germans (including Ernst Lubitsch, Josef von Sternberg, and Marlene Dietrich) filled the stands. Sharkey, whom the ring announcer called "the man on whom every American pins his faith," was then introduced, and traipsed around the ring with an American flag wrapped over his shoulders.

Schmeling, feeling under the weather, started out even more slowly than usual and lost the first two rounds. By the third, Sharkey felt he could knock him out at will, and restrained himself only to make Schmeling look bad. In Schmeling's corner, Jacobs was shoving smelling salts under his nose between rounds. Mindful of fouls — he'd been cautioned in the second round against low blows — Sharkey was shooting only at the head. But in the fourth round he saw an opening to Schmeling's body and went for it. It was a left, half hook and half uppercut. It landed, as someone later put it, with the sound of a cow pulling her foot out of the mud. But precisely where it landed, whether above or below the belt, will remain forever uncertain.

Schmeling recoiled. A stabbing pain shot through his body, he later said, and his legs buckled. Down he went, his hand clawing at his abdomen. He tried to get up, but felt "paralyzed." And that was fine with Jacobs. "Stay down, you idiot!" he shouted. "He fouled you!" The referee counted to five before the round ended, and Jacobs, "a screaming, dancing midge of a man," climbed through the ropes, rushed at him, and grabbed his arm. Foul! Foul! Disqualify him! he shrieked. The befuddled referee frantically consulted the two judges. One thought the punch was low; the other had missed it. The ring was in chaos. It was then that Arthur Brisbane, the powerful Hearst columnist sitting at ringside, stepped in. Schmeling had been fouled, he decreed, and unless he was declared the winner, boxing either was dead in New York or would be banned from the Hearst papers, which pretty much amounted to the same thing. The ring announcer, Joe Humphries, then walked over to Schmeling and lifted his limp left arm. "You're the champion, Max!" Jacobs shouted in his ear. Schmeling, who'd been doubled over with pain, "brightened up like a child seeing his Christmas tree for the first time."

Schmeling's mood quickly blackened, however, as the full ignominy of his "victory" became clear. No one had ever won the title on a foul before (and, because the rules were changed as a result of the ensuing outrage, no one ever would again). Fans filed out of the stadium disgustedly. In Schmeling's dressing room, Jacobs produced a dented protective cup, which some reporters suspected he had procured beforehand and made to look, as one writer put it, "as though an armored truck had struck it at full speed." (Far more persuasive was a medical report of a spasm in Schmeling's left testicle that suggested "a severe blow in that region.") Schmeling believed he'd been turning things around in the fight, and would have won had it gone the distance. But he promised Sharkey a rematch whenever he wanted one. "From the bottom of my heart I can only thank [the American people] for a fairness to a stranger in their land that has never been equaled in the history of sport," he told Paul Gallico of the *Daily News*, who had advised Schmeling that he'd be crazy not to accept the crown, even under such sullied circumstances. "I owe a debt to [them] and I swear to you that some day I will repay. And so, too, will my country."

It was not the only debt Schmeling incurred that night. Sitting behind a post in the mezzanine, covering the fight on a special woman's pass for a magazine called *Outlook and Independent,* the novelist Katherine Brush saw things more clearly than many men at ringside. "If anyone won the heavyweight championship of the world on June 12, 1930, it was Joey Jacobs, height about five feet 2, weight about 120 pounds," she wrote. Schmeling acknowledged as much. "You know, that *Yacobs*—I did not know that he could do that," Schmeling said. "I see him the way he runs around the ring and fights for me. And I don't forget that." Nor did he forget Jacobs's heavenly appeal. "I'm sure it helped me win the fight," he said. (Perhaps, the *Forverts* mused, the spirit of Jacobs's father had in fact come from the *yene velt*—the other world—and lowered Sharkey's fateful punch.) Though always tight with a buck, Schmeling, technically still represented by Bülow, gave Yussel $10,000 anyway, and arm in arm, the two men left Yankee Stadium. That fall, shortly after his contract with Bülow expired, Schmeling signed a pact with Jacobs, extending into 1935. The Nazi press, predictably, had few kind words for Yussel, calling him "this unpleasant, loud-mouthed American Jew." But with what even apolitical German boxing fans considered Jacobs's unsentimental, aggressive, and mercenary ways, he was foreign to German sensibilities long before his Jewishness came to loom so large.

There was some celebrating in Germany over Schmeling's triumph, but the overwhelming reaction was embarrassment. This was no way to win a championship; some fundamental German sense of fair play had been violated. "We're on our way to becoming the greatest sporting nation in the world if only we get hit often enough below the belt," one paper sneered. Schmeling became the butt of vicious jokes. When the fight films arrived in Berlin cinemas, audiences laughed uproariously. Introduced at a local boxing match, he encountered "a concert of boos and whistles"; pale and shaken, he promptly left the hall.

Reluctant to fight Sharkey again and unwilling to enter a ring until his contract with Bülow expired, Schmeling saw no action for months. The New York State Athletic Commission declared the crown vacant. Embarrassed German boxing officials begged Schmeling not to humiliate his country. An artist who'd once sculpted Schmeling lamented how he'd degenerated from a modest, curious, and sensitive young man into a self-centered penny-pincher. Newspapers across the political spectrum condemned him; one in Berlin called his evasions "a disgrace to German sport." The *Angriff* blamed it all on the "mean, impertinent, incompetent Jew" representing Schmeling. It also accused Schmeling of using Berlin's Jewish-owned newspapers as his personal mouthpiece. But when he finally signed up to defend his championship against Young Stribling, New York boxing officials decreed that Schmeling was still champ.

In late January 1931, Schmeling returned to the United States to begin a forty-city exhibition tour, designed to cash in on his championship and make a bit of money between fights. It was poorly attended, and Schmeling was rudely received. But in Cleveland that July, Schmeling knocked out Stribling, something no one else had done in 264 previous fights, and began turning perceptions around, both in the United States and in Germany. Schmeling canceled a scheduled fight against Primo Carnera, the gargantuan Italian, earning him yet more criticism, but in January 1932, he finally agreed to a June rematch with Sharkey. In the meantime, the first Schmeling biography, by Rolf Nürnberg, sports editor of the 12 *Uhr-Blatt* in Berlin, appeared. It depicted Schmeling as cold, unforgiving, disloyal, selfish, and cynical, someone who exploited those who helped him and rarely gave anything back to anyone. "Ruthlessness was the law; for sentimentality there was little room," Nürnberg wrote.

Schmeling returned to New York and began his training. One day Governor Franklin D. Roosevelt, about to embark on an epic campaign of his own, stopped by Schmeling's camp in Kingston, New York; along with everyone else, Schmeling was amazed when Roosevelt spoke to him in German. Seventy thousand fans showed up for the fight on June 21, at the Madison Square Garden Bowl in Long Island City. They saw a dull contest, in which Schmeling appeared to dominate. But Jacobs had sensed trouble from the outset; it was, he feared, payback time for the fiasco of the first fight. When it was over, Schmeling had lost a split decision. As soon as the announcement was made, a sepulchral Jacobs grabbed the microphone of the radio announcer and began shouting imprecations into it. The next day's newspapers rendered it variously: "He was robbed." "He was jobbed." "We were robbed." But another version prevailed, and quickly entered the English language: "We wuz robbed!" "The great Sharkey-Schmeling controversy now stands at one steal apiece," Gallico wrote.

In fact, opinions were divided, depending, among other things, on where one was sitting, or if one had seen only the films of the fight or had heard it on the radio. (Edward Zeltner of the *Mirror* studied the fight film and counted 634 punches for Sharkey to Schmeling's 539.) But if Schme-ling's win over Sharkey had really been a loss, this loss would become a colossal win. Americans could only pull so hard for a foreigner whose claim to the title had been tainted, who'd reneged on his promises, who'd fought the rematch, as the columnist Westbrook Pegler put it, like "some-one closing a deal, with a lawyer ever at his elbow." But in Germany, fans once again took Schmeling to their bosom. Fleischer pushed for a rubber match between the two, but Schmeling bridled at having to take the far smaller challenger's share, and in early January 1933 he signed to fight Max Baer instead. In the five years that were to pass before Schmeling got another shot at the title, he would come to realize how right Fleischer was. But three weeks later, Fleischer, Schmeling, and everyone else had something far more serious to ponder. Adolf Hitler now ruled Germany.

For the ever-pragmatic Schmeling, the new political situation must have seemed both disturbing and promising. On the one hand, many of Schmeling's artist and intellectual friends were enemies of the new Reich, or Jews, or both. On the other hand, Hitler, unlike prior German leaders, loved boxing. If, as he later declared during a party rally in Nuremberg, "the German boy of the future must be lithe and slender, swift as greyhounds, tough as leather, and hard as Krupp steel," boxing promised to become almost an official state sport. "There is no sport that cultivates a spirit of aggressiveness, that demands lightning-quick decisive-ness, that develops the body to such steely smoothness," Hitler had written in *Mein Kampf*. Had German intellectuals studied boxing instead of etiquette, he wrote, then "a German revolution of pimps, deserters and similar rabble [presumably the persons responsible for the Weimar democracy] never would have been possible."

But just where Schmeling would fit into the new order wasn't clear. No one embodied Nazi conceptions of steely physicality and iron disci-pline more than he, which is surely why Hitler commissioned a statue of him for the Reichssportfeld in Berlin, where the 1936 Summer Olympics would be staged. But with what the sportswriter Bob Considine described as "the high cheek bones of an Indian" and an "almost Neanderthal slope to his brow," his looks hardly matched the Nazi ideal, and his status as a professional didn't match, either; in collectivist Nazi culture, there was little room for self-interested mercenaries. In time, the propaganda value of professional athletes, and their usefulness as a source of scarce foreign capital, came to trump Nazi paeans to amateurism. But none of that was immediately apparent.

Then there was the Jewish question. Even before they came to power, in line with the more general contempt they expressed for Jewish influence in Germany, the Nazis assailed the degree to which Jewish managers, promoters, and bureaucrats dominated German boxing. They depicted these Jews as aliens (usually highlighting their eastern European origins), fat-cat exploiters of German youth who, while "incapable of performing even a single knee-bend on their flat feet," were still plenty able to pay young Aryan men a pittance for having their brains beaten out. More than two years before Hitler took power, the *Angriff* complained that Jews controlled the whole business, regulating only their corrupt, exploitative selves. Jacobs, though not German, was attacked as "a man from whom even his own kind turn away, a man at home in the most dangerous criminal circles in New York," a "dirty," "mean," "impertinent," "incompetent" Jew. He was blamed for making bad business deals for Schmeling, then for leaving him inactive for far too long. Always unmentioned, of course, was how he had talked Schmeling into the title.

The *Angriff* was far more outraged over Schmeling's relationship with Jacobs than anything Schmeling had ever done, but it viewed him warily, too. Incensed by what it considered Schmeling's democratic leanings—during an exhibition in 1929 Schmeling, along with Jacobs and his trainer Max Machon, had worn the black, red, and gold of the Weimar Republic—it attacked him for his disloyalty and his choice of associates: not just the "grubby" Jacobs, but also Machon, whom it described as a "spruced-up numbskull and toady." "The German people will accuse you, Herr Schmeling, of breaking your word, and the German people disapprove of you and this dirty Jacobs going around hawking the German name," it declared. This image of Schmeling as a poor sport and ingrate seemed to be the one thing upon which a Nazi newspaper and Schmeling's Jewish biographer, Nürnberg, could agree. But in the *Angriff*, as in other German papers, the antipathy toward Schmeling eased following the second Sharkey fight.

Now, as Schmeling prepared to take on Baer, the Nazis were in control, and no longer had to carp from the sidelines. *Box-Sport* did not instantly absorb the new order: in early March 1933 it ran a picture of the newly crowned German light heavyweight champion, a Jew named Erich Seelig (who also held the middleweight title), on its cover. But after that, change came swiftly. Indeed, it was a sign of the importance the Nazis assigned sports in general, and boxing in particular, that they campaigned to make boxing *judenrein*—free of Jews—before similar purges in all other sectors of German society. At a meeting on March 30, the deputy chairman of the Deutscher Reichsverband für Amateurboxen, the organization of German amateur boxers, declared that henceforth all Jews would be barred from the group. The next night, as Seelig prepared to defend one of his two titles, Nazi officials entered his dressing room to say that unless he left the country immediately, his family would be murdered. (He fled, and was promptly stripped of both his titles.) Around the same time, the organization of professional boxers, the Verband Deutscher Faustkämpfer, issued a sweeping order removing Jews entirely from its realm. "Finally, Finally! The VDF Purged of Jews," the *Angriff* exulted on April 4. *Box-Sport* printed the actual order, which made clear how extraordinarily all-encompassing it was. All Jews, even those who'd been baptized, were stricken from the group's membership rolls and forbidden to enter all association facilities; professional boxers were freed from all contracts with their Jewish managers; all licensed technical personnel were barred from working at any boxing events put on by "Jewish capital or Jewish persons." And, as if to demonstrate the gulf that was now to separate the German boxing establishment from anything Jewish, all German boxers were prohibited from using Jewish doctors, lawyers, and dentists.

The previously apolitical and tempered *Box-Sport* quickly adapted to the new era, suddenly enumerating all of the long-festering problems in its realm that it had somehow previously overlooked. The new measures were "a defensive action against the countless Jewish profiteers" in German professional boxing, it declared: German boxers trained, fought, and ruined their health, while Jewish promoters, managers, and "whatever else these blood-suckers call themselves" hovered in the background. Though certain boxers had done well under the old regime — Schmeling was mentioned — most couldn't even pay for their training, it asserted, while their Jewish backers always managed to enrich themselves. Respectable Germans who had done great service for German boxing had been marginalized, while "a clique of corrupt and unscrupulous profiteers" took care of one another. Instead of being regulated by trained, expert, independent, and honorable ethnic Germans, the brave young fighters of the Fatherland were dragged before "Jewish big-wigs and corrupt exploiters who know as much about boxing as a donkey knows about jumping rope." With the Jews gone, however, German boxing had lost its economic underpinnings, and *Box-Sport* called on the sport's brightest lights, Schmeling included, to stop "giving the cold shoulder to their homeland" and start fighting in Germany.

Under the new rules, Schmeling's fight against the purportedly Jewish Max Baer (he was not) on June 8 in New York could never have been held in Germany. But as was often to be the case, the Nazis could be pragmatic when they needed to be. They knew that to stay in the heavyweight picture, Schmeling had to take the best fights, and fighters, he could find. Prior to Schmeling's departure for the United States, Hitler summoned him to the Reich's chancellory. For Schmeling the encounter was a first—and an impressive, heartening one at that. To meet President Hindenburg, as he had tried to do, you had to be from nobility, and now here was Hitler, coming to *him*. "If anyone over there asks how it's going in Germany, you can reassure the doomsayers that everything is moving along quite peacefully," the Führer told him. Hitler was not at all the overwrought, comical character Schmeling had expected, but charming, calm, quietly confident. Goebbels and Göring were friendly, too. As Schmeling departed, Hitler told him to let him know if he ever needed anything. Schmeling turned out to be a faithful emissary, though it wasn't easy. The world had already changed too much for that.

Because sports and politics were considered strictly separate, or because no editors much cared, or because there were too many other horror stories coming out of Germany, or because it all seemed so far away, the purge of Jews from German boxing went unnoted in the sports pages of most American newspapers. Three weeks went by before *The New York Times* even mentioned it in a short, inconspicuous wire dispatch at the back of its sports section, beneath a banner headline about a horse show. The story got better play in papers such as the *Ironwood (Michigan) Daily Globe* than in the most important paper in the city with the largest population of Jews in the country. In Britain, too, the German edict excited little comment.* Only the French sports newspaper *L'Auto* gave it the attention it deserved, noting how it countered every effort to banish prejudice from sports. "It would be paradoxical to see Jews evicted from the 'Noble Art' exactly at the same time as Negroes are having their natural rights recognized all the way to the top, including in world title fights," it said. It expressed regret over such a political incursion into

*The British magazine *Boxing* initially said nothing about the ban, and when it finally did, its Berlin correspondent, H. V. Gunnell, blamed foreign Jews, and their "exaggerated and untruthful stories" about Nazi persecutions, for what had happened. Three weeks later he praised the anti-Jewish measures. In a guest column for *Box-Sport* in October

sports, particularly one aimed at a group that had produced so many champion boxers. But events in Germany inevitably seeped into American sports coverage. On March 27, the *New York Mirror* printed an extraordinary half-page notice in Yiddish—with no English translation—on its back page (the front page of the tabloid's sports section), urging people to rally that night in Madison Square Garden against "the decrepit medievalism that has darkened the skies of the Jewish people in the land of Goethe and Mendelssohn."

Pushing for boycotts of anything connected to the Nazis, some members of the Jewish War Veterans asked American immigration authorities to bar Schmeling. The day before Schmeling arrived, Congressman Emmanuel Celler, who represented the Flatbush section of Brooklyn, urged a boycott of the exhibition tour Schmeling was to take prior to the Baer fight. "We all know what would happen if the situation were reversed and a Jewish prize fighter like Maxie Rosenbloom or Max Baer were scheduled to enter the prize ring in Germany against Max Schmeling," he said.* So poisoned had the atmosphere in New York grown against Schmeling that Jacobs considered having him train in Montreal instead. Jacobs now served as Schmeling's Jewish shield: the *Daily News* reported that the "Delancey Street dandy" had neutralized anti-Schmeling sentiment by procuring letters from several rabbis. "There are many Hebrews here and they are bitter against Hitler and confuse every German with the Nazis, which is tough for Schmeling," Jacobs told a Montreal newspaper. "He is not a Nazi by any means, and not at all in sympathy with their propaganda." Schmeling, he insisted, was willing to box free for any Jewish charity, and had even accompanied him to synagogue.

When Schmeling arrived aboard the *Bremen* on that April day in 1933, with the horde of boxing writers awaiting him, he stepped into precisely the kind of atmosphere Jacobs feared. Though he spoke little English when he'd first come to New York, Schmeling had picked it up quite

---

1933, he wrote: "The fact that the new, great leader of the German people, Adolf Hitler, has spoken out precisely in support of boxing means not a little for this sport in Germany. Since the reorganized boxing authorities in Germany have weeded out the undesired elements that until recently have so hindered the development of boxing and so damaged the reputation of it, the prospects of German boxing are now on the best imaginable course of further development."

*Not everyone agreed: Pegler said that Celler's plan was to "shame the Nazis by lying down and rolling in the same gutter with them." Nazi discrimination against Jewish athletes would surely pass over, he predicted, "and the victims will be no worse for it."

well and even understood the dialect favored by fast-talking New York
newspapermen, at least most of the time; whenever anyone asked him
something sensitive, he liked to play dumb, requesting that the question
be repeated more slowly, or asking Jacobs to recast it for him in some
combination of Yiddish and German. Then he wouldn't answer it anyway. "He dodges embarrassing questions even more adroitly than he
dodges punches," the *Sun* reporter wrote. But this time the newspapermen who greeted him were a bit more insistent, especially on the state of
Germany's Jews. Jacobs had warned him of this in advance, radioing him
instructions aboard the *Bremen* to disparage the reports of Nazi anti-
Semitism. This Schmeling promptly did, even though the roster of Jews
in his life was long. Most of his friends in the ateliers, salons, and cabarets
of Berlin had been Jewish. A Jew named Paul Damski may have discovered him, had promoted many of his fights, and had purchased in his own
name a country house for Schmeling, no doubt to save the Uhlan some
money. Since Schmeling had come to New York, Nat Fleischer, Harry
Sperber, and Jacobs himself had all assisted him. Moreover, the Hitler
regime was still young, and Schmeling—a former world champion and
Germany's most famous athlete, as well as someone who made his living
abroad—presumably was freer to speak his mind than just about any German citizen. But when asked about what Hitler was up to, Schmeling had
little to offer but praise.

"What do you think of conditions in Germany?" one reporter asked.

"What conditions?"

"The political situation."

"I don't know anything about politics," Schmeling replied. "Why
don't you ask Dr. Luther?" He was referring to Germany's new ambassador to the United States, who had been on the same voyage. When
pressed, Schmeling answered in essence that he'd seen nothing, but that
what he'd seen was good. "I haff never seen Yermany so quiet," he told the
reporters. "Yermany has never been unify as it is now under Hitler." True,
there'd been that one-day boycott of Jewish businesses, but the Jews had
brought that upon themselves with their anti-Nazi protests and propaganda in places like New York, and he'd seen no one actually physically
molested. So confident was he that the dire reports from Germany had
been exaggerated that he proposed taking Jacobs—"my friend Joe"—over
as a test: Yussel, he predicted cheerily, would find himself "the most popular person in Germany." Just to show how he felt about the Jews, Schmeling said he had accepted an invitation to attend Passover services at

Jacobs's synagogue. No one asked Schmeling about the purge of Jews from German boxing, and he did not bring it up himself. "I tell you this — Germany is improving," Schmeling continued. "More people are going to work. Employers seem to have more confidence. Conditions are brighter. My people are much more hopeful." Besides, he added, "prices on the Boerse [sic] are going up." Schmeling lied to the reporters that he had not met Hitler. He also urged his interlocutors not to be "silly" about the man. "Were I to meet Baer in Germany instead of here, Hitler most assuredly would occupy a ringside seat," he said.

One could hardly fault Schmeling for failing to understand the full significance of what was happening; most Jews didn't, either. Schmeling himself later insisted that he'd simply not been paying any attention, caught up as he was in his own career. But that day on the Brooklyn pier, he had done more than protect his interests or betray his ignorance. He'd participated in a cover-up — becoming, as a result, a propagandist for the Nazi regime. The next morning, a headline in a small Pennsylvania daily encapsulated his message better than any New York newspaper: MAX SCHMELING SAYS GERMANY IS NOT CRUEL TO JEWISH FOLKS.

Afterward, the Warsaw Yiddish paper *Moment* said Schmeling had proved himself "100 percent Hitlerist" with his answers. The German press agreed, congratulating Schmeling on his fine performance. "Schmeling pulled himself through the affair brilliantly, admired all around for the quick-wittedness with which he met the questions," *Box-Sport* reported. Schmeling wrote many years later that following his interrogation, he went off to see his New York friends, many of them Jews. "When I told them about the reception at the Reich's chancellory, they kidded me and asked what Hitler had said when I told him that I would be boxing a Jewish Max Baer," he recalled. "'Wouldn't that be forbidden in the new Reich as a form of athletic "race crime"?' We just laughed."

One more reliable contemporary press report had him going back to the Commodore Hotel, where he was staying, and then out by himself for a show. He was last spotted that night at the Majestic Theater, where Jimmy Durante was appearing. He was rolling in the aisles.

CHAPTER 2

A Regime's Embrace

ADOLF HITLER TURNED FORTY-FOUR on April 20, 1933, and among the many greetings he received were messages from the Deutscher Reichsverband für Amateurboxen. They assured him they stood ready at all times to assist him in his great work and to "stand in defense, with clenched fist, against all enemies." At the national championships a week later, each of the winners received a silver-framed, autographed picture of Hitler. There was a speech from a Nazi functionary, reiterating Hitler's devotion to boxing. Then came the singing of "Deutschland über Alles" and the "Horst Wessel Song." The boxers greeted the crowd with the Hitler salute. They also telegrammed the Führer, thanking him again and promising "to follow in his path with iron decisiveness and unswerving trust." What had formerly been a sporting event had turned into a Nazi pageant.

Everywhere, the Nazification of German boxing was intensifying. In the upcoming competition with Italy, German boxers would sport new uniforms, with black swastikas on the left leg of their white trunks; among the sponsors of a boxing tournament staged by the German police were the two principal Nazi party newspapers: the *Angriff* and the *Völkischer Beobachter*. Just about the only remnant of the old-style German boxing was Schmeling, now poised to start a tour that would take him to several northeastern American cities and a couple more in Canada before the Baer fight in June.

The man watching, and judging, Schmeling most closely was Dan Parker of the *New York Mirror*. It was an unlikely role for both Parker, a Catholic New Englander, and the *Mirror*, a Hearst tabloid whose proprietor, according to his critics, was vaguely sympathetic to Hitler. Parker served his readers zealously and colorfully. Unlike most sportswriters, he did not buy the Schmeling line that politics and sports were automatically and perpetually distinct, and more than anyone else, he took on the vexing task of figuring out just who Schmeling was, how he was behaving, and what the best way was to deal fairly with him.

"The movement to make Max Schmeling suffer for Halitosis Hitler's oppressive policies against Jews in Germany is gaining terrific momentum," Parker reported a week after Schmeling arrived. He then yielded to Morris Mendelsohn, chairman of the "Nazi Boycott Committee" of the Jewish War Veterans. Schmeling's insistence that all was well with the Jews in Germany, Mendelsohn wrote, merely emphasized that "none is so blind as they who won't see." "We think, however, his eyesight will not fail Mr. Schmeling when he notes the empty seats in all of his scheduled encounters here in America," Mendelsohn warned. "Why should we send Schmeling back to Germany with a bag of gold to throw into Hitler's lap? Let us send him back with a ringing message that America will not countenance the persecution of helpless minorities in this advanced age."

Two days later, Parker heard from Heinz Reichmann, the American correspondent for the Ullstein papers, the Jewish-owned German publications which, the Nazis had previously charged, Schmeling had used as his mouthpiece. Reichmann, who had joined Harry Sperber in broadcasting Schmeling's fights back to Germany, defended Schmeling, who, he said, was "no more of a Jew-hater than Rabbi Wise," referring to Stephen Wise, then one of America's most prominent Jews. Reichmann said he didn't know any Germans with so many Jewish friends as Schmeling: nine out of ten, by his estimation. Ernst Lubitsch and Max Reinhardt, notable figures in German entertainment, would burst out laughing if they heard that busybodies were portraying Schmeling as an anti-Semite, he declared. It was a stirring defense, one that could hardly have helped Schmeling back home. Reichmann, like all Jewish reporters, was soon out of a job, and his Jewish publisher was soon out of business.

Parker's column also provided a forum on Joe Jacobs. Jacobs's rabbi declared that by boycotting Schmeling, the Jews were descending to the Nazis' level. And though he'd parted bitterly from Jacobs (after smashing a plaster bust of Schmeling over his head), Jacobs's former business partner, an Irish Catholic named Bill McCarney, now touted Yussel's credentials as a Jew. (Jacobs was not one of those High Holy Day–only types, he wrote; traveling in Europe, the first thing Jacobs always did was find a synagogue in which to say kaddish for his father.) Parker acknowledged the awkward position in which Schmeling now found himself. He "has to return to Germany some time and doesn't want to find a room in the hoosegow awaiting him," he wrote. "All he can do is point to the fact that his record has always been clean and that his long association with Jacobs proves that he doesn't go in for Jew-baiting or hate."

In mid-April 1933, Schmeling and Jacobs set out on their tour. Some five thousand people came to see Schmeling in Pittsburgh. "I'll try to make [Max Baer] think you're to blame for all that trouble over in your country," Jack Dempsey joked to Schmeling before an audience there. "That will be all right," Schmeling replied. "I never care what they say." He even made light of his predicament. "Shall I give them a political talk?" he quipped to Joe Jacobs before going on a local radio station. Although Jewish boxing fans were urged to stay away, four thousand people greeted Schmeling in Montreal. One local cartoonist gave him a Hitler mustache, but he was also feted at a Jewish nightclub there. A special train ferried fans to see Schmeling in Bangor, Maine. But an appearance before the German club at the state university was hastily canceled—ostensibly because Schmeling had to train, but more likely to avoid a ruckus.

Schmeling and Jacobs were in Maine when word of the ban on Jews in German boxing dribbled belatedly into the American press. Schmeling had no comment, but Jacobs did. "We simply ignore it," he said. A German boxing official hastily explained that Schmeling was free to keep Jacobs, but only for bouts outside Germany. "Well, that's awfully nice of him, telling Schmeling what he can do in the United States," Jacobs snapped. "Max and I, we don't have nothin' to do with them guys." Few columnists ever commented on the Jewish ban. One of them was Fleischer, who called Hitler's actions "malicious, vitriolic, and imbecilic." But Fleischer still had faith in Schmeling. "Will he throw aside the man who made him a world champion, Joe Jacobs, American Hebrew, to abide by the German edict?" he asked. "I venture to predict that he will tell the Federation officials to take a trip to Hades, where they belong."

Whatever Schmeling elected to do, New York's Jewish boxing fans now had to decide whether to boycott the fight against Baer. It was difficult to take anything involving the wacky and undisciplined Baer very seriously; certainly, Baer himself rarely did. This was, after all, a man who, when he first came to New York, had banged his head against a radiator to prove his durability. When a boxer named Frankie Campbell died after he was done with him, Baer became afraid of his own strength; that fear, plus his own sunny nature, left him erratic for the rest of his career. Baer could have been the greatest of them all, Benny Leonard, the legendary Jewish lightweight, once said, had he only been able to concentrate. He'd start his fights seriously, only to spot a friend in the crowd; "at that moment," said Leonard, he'd stop being a fighter and become "a friend, or a lover, or something. He'd wave, and the other guy would hit him while he was doing it." "I've got a million-dollar body and a ten-cent brain," admitted Baer, who once sold more than 100 percent of himself because, he explained, he thought he had 1,000 percent to parcel out. Baer was confused about his purported Jewishness, too, a matter with considerable commercial consequences in New York. He said that his father was Jewish, though reports that the old man raised pigs in California did not bolster his case. Many years later, the trainer Ray Arcel claimed that having seen Baer in the shower, he could definitively say Baer was no Jew at all. What Baer was, in fact, was *strategically* Jewish.

In America, Jews were all over boxing, not just as fighters and fans but as everything in between: promoters, trainers, managers, referees, propagandists, equipment manufacturers, suppliers, chroniclers. No major ethnic group in American history ever so dominated an important sport. The phenomenon is largely forgotten, in part because it was only scantily analyzed at the time. For Gentile writers, the topic might have been too sensitive; for Jewish ones, the problem may have been embarrassment. The various strains of American Jewish culture at the time—elite German Jewry; secular, socialist eastern European Yiddishists; the religiously observant—all disdained the sport. They deemed it coarse, uncouth, inappropriate—"*goyishe nakhes,*" the kind of foolishness Christians enjoyed.

Few of the great Jewish boxers were heavyweights—another reason people questioned Baer's Jewish credentials—but at one time or another, Jews dominated all of the lighter categories. Surely the most storied Jewish fighter was Leonard, who sat atop his division from 1917 to 1925, who parlayed his deftness, lethal punch, and good looks into enormous fame and popularity. One Jewish newspaper said he was far more famous than Einstein, and maybe more important. In 1923, in a match with another Jew, Lew Tendler, in the newly opened Yankee Stadium, he fought in front of nearly seventy thousand people. Small wonder, then, that Tex Rickard once said he'd pay all the money in the world for a great Jewish heavyweight. Apparently as a publicity stunt, someone had floated rumors prior to the first Schmeling-Sharkey fight that Schmeling himself was

Jewish, and that he had relatives on the Lower East Side with whom he ate gefilte fish every Friday night. Schmeling politely brushed the stories aside, while stressing that if he really were Jewish, he'd not be ashamed of it. Of course, he'd be unlikely to reiterate that now.

For the Jewish boxers themselves, fighting may have been strictly an economic proposition, a brutal but lucrative alternative to the sweatshops. But for their fans, its appeal was more tribal, and primeval. It was a way to assert their status as bona fide Americans, to express ethnic pride, settle ethnic scores, refute ethnic stereotypes; after all, no one ever cast the Irish and Italians as victims and bookworms, cowards and runts. Every Jewish kid ever set upon by street toughs lived vicariously through his Jewish ring heroes, and the heroes encouraged this, often wearing Stars of David on their trunks. After Arabs murdered sixty-seven Jews in Palestine in 1929, five Jewish fighters took on five non-Jews at a Madison Square Garden benefit; the "Hebrews" scored a clean sweep in front of sixteen thousand feverish fans. Many of them came from the Garment Center, either rank-and-file workers in the needle trades or executives who passed around fight tickets to their customers. But Jews of every background and economic stratum went to the fights. If the garment workers were fans, so too was Bernard Gimbel, whose family store sold what those workers made. What drew Jews to boxing was more than chauvinism, though. Perhaps it was also part of relishing America after their cloistered lives in Europe, or the Jewish love of going out, whether to vaudeville or to Broadway or to the Yiddish theater of Second Avenue.

So pronounced was Jewish hegemony over boxing that some attributed the eclipse into which the sport had fallen by the early 1930s less to the Depression than to the paucity of good Jewish fighters. The exception was Barney Ross, a scrappy lightweight from Chicago. ("Hey, Barney," Ross's trainer asked him before one of his big fights in New York, "if Hitler dropped a bomb on this place, how many of our tribe would he kill off?") The grim news from Germany only intensified the pride Jews already took in their fighters, especially when they were taking on Germans. So while some Jewish boxers in Germany were fleeing for their lives, Gentile boxers in America were pretending to be Jews. Baer did even more, turning himself into a modern, if uncircumsized, Maccabee. "Every punch in the eye I give Schmeling is one for Adolf Hitler," he declared.

Several writers saw through Baer's ruse, though it was hard to get very worked up over it. One newspaperman said Baer was "reported to have become a Jew by press agent edict rather than by Bar Mitzvah." "Baer was only a 50 per cent Hebrew when he set out for New York," Parker wrote. "He became a 100 per cent when he arrived in Gotham and were it not for the fact that the Atlantic seaboard intervened, he might have kept right on traveling until he was at least 350 per cent Yiddle." "Hitler is more of a Jew than is Baer," Fleischer claimed. But his image as a Jew persisted, in both New York and Berlin, infusing the Schmeling-Baer bout with a significance it would not normally have had. Boycotting it was wrong, some argued, because with people like Baer and Joe Jacobs involved, American Jews would suffer a lot more than Hitler ever would. German papers opined that Baer's Jewish talk, along with his anti-Nazi saber rattling, was simply *reklame*, the kind of shameless huckstering for which Americans, and Jews in particular, were so noted. The virulently anti-Semitic *Der Stürmer* took Schmeling to task for fighting a non-Aryan, calling it a "racial and cultural disgrace."

As the fight approached, Schmeling continued to talk up the "New Germany," but selectively—for instance, to German-language publications few ordinary New Yorkers read. "Abroad, one can have no concept of how Germany looks today," he told the *New Yorker Staats-Zeitung.* "A renewal of the Reich is under way which can only be in the best interest of Germany." Otherwise, he made few waves. His German compatriot Walter Neusel had not only kept his Jewish manager but had briefly gone into exile, something Schmeling was not about to do. Neusel had also provided that a part of the gate from a forthcoming fight in London be devoted to a Jewish relief fund; Schmeling was not about to do that, either.

Four days before the fight, at a dinner given by the Jewish War Veterans, Congressman Celler renewed calls for a boycott. "Schmeling is a friend of Hitler," he said. But the protests fizzled. Fight backers worried that Baer's non-Semitism was actually driving away more Jewish fight fans than was Hitler's anti-Semitism. Baer's manager begged Jewish fans to ignore the doubts cast on Baer's ethnic credentials and go watch "a genuine half-Jewish boy fight a 100 percent German." Ticket sales in Yorkville, the German community on New York's Upper East Side, were said to be making up for any losses in the Jewish community. The *Staats-Zeitung* warned that given "the growing antipathy against everything German" in New York, Schmeling would have a hard time landing another fight there were he to lose. Meanwhile, the fight would not be aired in Germany. Sperber and Reichmann, after all, were Jews; shortly before the fight the Nazis decreed that henceforth only Aryan broadcasters would do.

(Sperber promptly wired Goebbels to "Leck' mich am Arsch"—to lick his ass—a message the non-German-speaking Western Union operator dutifully took down and transmitted.)

Sixty thousand people, many getting in at the Depression-era price of a dollar a seat, attended the fight, at least fifteen thousand more than would watch Sharkey lose the heavyweight title to Primo Carnera three weeks later. Millions more were updated by bulletins on NBC. Schmeling was the heavy favorite, but no one knew he was under the weather (or at least he later said he was), and that the heat—the night was stifling even without the powerful lights over the ring—made things worse. Baer, who for the first time was wearing the Star of David on his trunks, started out the fight furiously, while Schmeling was leaden. In the tenth round Baer put an end to things. "A punch all the boxing instructors decry as the sucker's wallop, suddenly arched through atmosphere made milky by tobacco smoke and resin dust," wrote Pegler, and Schmeling was down and out. "That wasn't a defeat, that was a disaster," Machon said afterward in the dressing room. Meantime, Baer was looking at his puffed-up nose in the mirror. "They thought I was a Hebe and now I look like one," he said.

Politics permeated the postfight analysis. The Nazis would probably claim Schmeling had been done in by international Jewry, the *Times* editorialized. In the American Jewish press, there was hope that the outcome presaged better days. With Schmeling's loss, one commentator speculated, maybe those two "gas bags," Hitler and Goebbels, would now harness their energies more usefully. "Let Hitler stop gassing and go to work," he declared. One of New York's Yiddish dailies, *Der Tog*, acknowledged its embarrassment over even caring about a prizefight. Before Hitler came to power, "who would have been interested if [Schmeling] is a German or a Tatar—and whether the boxer who beat him, Max Baer, is a Jew or a Turk?" it asked. But the Hitler crowd had changed all that, it pointed out, and so for the Jews, now facing a peril unlike any other, Baer's feat had come to symbolize Jewry's struggle against the Nazis.

Schmeling vowed to keep fighting until he became champion again, but Gallico thought his pal was washed up. So did many in Germany. "Schmeling's dream of regaining the world's championship is over," the 12 *Uhr-Blatt* declared. Other publications claimed Schmeling had been done in by a life of celebrity, wealth, and luxury. "A man who travels only first-class, sleeps under down covers, and eats the food of millionaires will, after a short while, no longer possess the constitution necessary to grapple with the 'roughnecks' of the American rings," said the *Völkischer Beobachter*. Not surprisingly, the Nazi papers blamed the debacle on Jacobs—for giving Schmeling poor counsel, for letting him remain idle for too long, for having him train in excessively hot Pompton Lakes, New Jersey, rather than in a climate more congenial to a German, for steering him toward Baer rather than to an easier rubber match with Sharkey.

Perhaps because the boxing writers thought they were bidding him farewell, Schmeling got a rousing ovation at a lunch Jack Dempsey threw for him at Gallagher's Steak House five days after the fight. *Ring* magazine even wrote a requiem for the Schmeling-Jacobs partnership. But when Schmeling returned to Hamburg on June 23, he insisted he would not retire. In any case, his relationship with Hitler was intact, possibly even enhanced by a new empathy, as a meeting Schmeling had subsequently with the Führer revealed. "He encouraged me, and told me that he, too, had suffered setbacks," Schmeling later recalled.

The German reaction to Schmeling's loss was overshadowed by something more dramatic: news of his engagement to an actress named Anny Ondra. Ondra, born in Poland to Czech parents, had won a bit of fame abroad: Alfred Hitchcock had given her a bit part in one of his early films, *The Manxman*, then a starring role in his first talkie, *Blackmail*. Blond and perky, she was better known in Germany as a comedienne; "the female Chaplin," one newspaper called her. The pair put out several contradictory versions of their courtship; most stressed Schmeling's infatuated diffidence and Ondra's initial reluctance, usually attributed to her distaste for boxing. Some said they'd been introduced by the film director Karl Lamac; all neglected to mention that she'd been married to Lamac at the time. In the most credible version, Schmeling's friend, the Jewish boxing promoter Paul Damski, played intermediary. The two were married in July 1933, as dozens of photographers hovered nearby. Hitler sent the newlyweds a Japanese maple. Ring lore had it that marriage was very bad for a boxer, and that it took some time to get over it; in any case, Schmeling had no fights that fall. Instead, he and Jacobs went to Rome in October to see Carnera defend his title against Paolino Uzcudun. From the ring, Schmeling gave the Hitler salute to Mussolini, then to the audience, while Jacobs sat with Josef Kirmeier, a Nazi official doubling as a sportswriter. "Yussel Jacobs will be ostracized when he gets back to Lindy's," Parker predicted.

The European trip marked Jacobs's debut as Nazi Germany's most improbable propagandist. When he left New York, the odds among boxing writers there were five to one that he would not dare set foot in Germany, and initially, Jacobs later recalled, he'd been reluctant to do so. But Schmeling had assured him that all this talk of Nazi anti-Semitism was a lot of hooey, and, as it turned out, Schmeling had been absolutely right. "I got to Berlin and when I entered the Bristol they treated me like a king," Jacobs told the press when he returned. "I was treated everywhere with courtesy and consideration." From what he observed, Jews were at all the cafés and restaurants; Jewish businesses were prospering; Jews still supervised various things at the Bristol; the Jewish owner of his favorite cabaret was still packing them in. Nowhere, Jacobs said, had he been embarrassed or humiliated, nor had he been afraid to tour the nightclubs by himself, now that Schmeling was a married man. "All any Nazi ever had to do was to take one look at me to know my name wasn't Murphy," he explained, "but I got along all right. Had a grand time in fact, and even closed up a couple of spots. . . . I suppose there have been tense times in Germany for the Jews, but I saw no evidence of it."

One of Fleischer's German sources speculated that the Nazis would not let Schmeling appear in the States again unless he severed his tie with Jacobs, and that he even risked losing his German property. But any hints of official unhappiness with Schmeling were quashed in late December, when, shortly before he was to leave for another trip to America, Schmeling and Ondra were invited for a "farewell tea" with Hitler in the Reich's chancellory. "The chancellor took a lively interest in Schmeling's plans," said one report. Schmeling, in turn, glowed with enthusiasm when describing the encounter, telling an American correspondent that he had been "deeply stirred by Hitler's personality." Schmeling also discussed the meeting with the sports editor of the *Angriff*, Herbert Obscherningkat. As he described it, Schmeling's audience with Hitler was an eye-opening experience for someone who had strayed too far from his homeland over the past few years and had therefore underestimated its new Führer, but who now saw the error of his ways. "Years ago, in America, [Schmeling] perhaps couldn't understand why thousands of German national comrades were so given over to their Führer and fought for him," wrote Obscherningkat, who himself would soon be described as the "führer" of the newly Nazified Berlin sports press. "He sees more clearly now that behind him stands Adolf Hitler and, with him, the German people." "It was an experience, it was the most wonderful hour of my life!" Schmeling told him. Schmeling would soon return to America, Obscherningkat went on, but now, he would no longer be out only for himself, "but also for his nation, to which he now feels more bound than ever before." And it was true that while so many of their friends and colleagues fled, Schmeling and Ondra sank their roots deeper into Germany. Exile is always a trauma, of course, but their livelihoods were uniquely mobile; Schmeling essentially made his living in the United States, while, with Hollywood filling up with émigrés, Ondra clearly could have found work there. But one more thing separated Schmeling from his departing friends: his life in Nazi Germany was actually getting better. Principles aside, there was no reason to leave.

Schmeling's next scheduled fight, a bout in February 1934 against a Jewish boxer named Kingfish Levinsky in Chicago, had been called off the previous month, ostensibly because, according to the local boxing promoter, Hitler either objected to Schmeling fighting or to his being managed by a Jew. The Kingfish, another of the vaguely (and sometimes deliberately) ridiculous figures who populated prizefighting, had waxed indignant. "Say, wasn't there a lot of Jewish boys in the German army and wasn't there quite a few Jewish fellows who wrote some of those big thick books for the Germans and gave them the big high brow tone?" he asked. Levinsky even offered to fight Schmeling for nothing. Jacobs, too, was indignant. "Hitler may not want Schmeling to fight a Jew," he said, "but Hitler isn't Schmeling's manager and he isn't dictator of the boxing business." "Herr Hitler does not care who Max fights," he added, sounding, oddly, like the Führer's official spokesman. "He does not have the time or inclination to bother in such things." In Berlin, Schmeling called reports of the Führer's interference "absurd." "Herr Hitler advised against any break with my manager, Joe Jacobs, who is Jewish," he said. "So why should he object to Levinsky?" ("It was evident," the reporter noted, that Anny Ondra was "quite in accord" with her husband's "admiration of the chancellor." "Herr Hitler is charming," she said. "He complimented my films in the nicest way imaginable.") The more Jews he fought, "the better Hitler will like it," Schmeling told the *Chicago Tribune*'s Sigrid Schultz. Jacobs quickly signed up Schmeling to fight a promising young New Jersey heavyweight named Steve Hamas (pronounced HAY-mess), in Philadelphia on February 13. The *12 Uhr-Blatt* accused Jacobs of making the match because he was broke; it dismissed Hamas as a second-rater unworthy of Schmeling. But the *Völkischer Beobachter* warned Schmeling not to underestimate Hamas, a former star athlete at Penn State. "He is a football player, and what American football is, we know from the list of the dead this sport is blamed for every year," it stated.

Defying the odds, Hamas bloodied up an overconfident Schmeling and won a twelve-round decision. Once again there were the instant obituaries for Schmeling, but this time, they were especially harsh. "The Schmeling we saw last night would have been a set-up for any fast moving heavyweight," wrote Ike Gellis of the *New York Evening Post*. "His timing gone, his style a memory—really, it was pathetic." Even the loyal Gallico, who had shouted advice to Schmeling throughout a fight he was ostensibly covering, conceded his man was through. And in America, that appeared to be the case; if Schmeling were to make a comeback now, it would have to be in Europe, something for which the Nazis had been pushing anyway. Even on his home turf, however, Schmeling's prospects appeared bleak. "Yesterday Max Schmeling was crossed off the list of leading heavyweights in the world," pronounced the *12 Uhr-Blatt*. Again, it blamed the Jew Jacobs; meeting him, it said, had been "Schmeling's great misfortune." *Der Deutsche*, the paper of the Nazis' pseudo–labor union, expressed schadenfreude over Schmeling's loss. Schmeling had turned his back on German boxing when he'd first gone to America, it said, leaving behind the "international Jewish swamp" that it had become, and hadn't returned home to help revive the sport once the Nazis had deloused it. The *Angriff*, though, praised Schmeling's fighting spirit. When he landed at Bremerhaven, only two press people showed up to greet him. Before the Nazis came to power, *Box-Sport* lamented how Germany always lost boxers like Schmeling to America. Now, Germany had him back.

He returned to a country transformed. His friends from the Weimar days, with whom he'd spent time at the Roxy-Bar, had disappeared, to exile, concentration camps, or suicide. The same was true of Ondra's associates in the film industry, so many of whom were Jews. But boxing was more entrenched, and important, than ever. In early 1934, it had become compulsory for all boys from the ninth grade up, and younger boys were encouraged to learn it, too. And if boxing had come to permeate German life, German life (as defined by the Nazis) had continued to permeate boxing. *Box-Sport* now ventured into eugenics, lamenting the deterioration, physical and mental, of German stock, and complaining of a society encumbered by the weak and the sick. It urged the end of all state-financed medical support and aid for the "inferior"—that is, the blind, the retarded, the mentally unstable, and other incurables. Though he would normally have praised the growth of boxing anywhere, Fleischer castigated the "Mad Monkey of Germany" and his "outrageous, lunatic government." But Fleischer distanced Schmeling from all that:

"Herr Hitler, the Jew Hater, can take a few lessons in true red-blooded sportsmanship" from Schmeling, he wrote.

Schmeling's climb back got off to a bad start. In April 1934, after another meeting with Hitler—this one lasting at least four hours—he left for Spain to fight Paolino Uzcudun on May 13. He'd beaten Uzcudun five years earlier, but this time he could only manage a draw, even though neutral observers had Schmeling winning overwhelmingly. But Schmeling was still Germany's best boxer, its most promising hope in the international arena, and he remained in Hitler's good graces; shortly after returning to Germany, he was invited to see the Führer again. When, a bit later, he was charged with a currency violation, Schmeling asked for and received yet another audience with Hitler, who fixed things for his friend.

The next stop on Schmeling's comeback trail was in Hamburg, for a fight on August 29 against Walter Neusel, who by now had returned from his brief exile. More than just a contest between Germany's two top heavyweights, this would be a celebration of the new Germany and an audition for what Germany really coveted: a heavyweight title fight. The setting would be rudimentary: a dirt track normally used for motorcycle races. But what the event lacked in elegance it would make up for in enormousness and efficiency. The *Völkischer Beobachter* bestowed upon the spectacle what was, in its eyes, the ultimate accolade: "American."

In one sense, though, the Nazis were determined to differentiate themselves from the Yankees. Sports was serious business in the new Germany, and the Nazi sports commissar, Hans von Tschammer und Osten, believed German writers weren't according it due solemnity. Or, to put it another way, they were covering it with the usual propaganda and trivia, hero worshipping and hyperbole, that American sportswriters favored. This was undignified and useless, and had to change. "Sensationalism and star worship are not befitting the National Socialist Man!" the *Angriff* exhorted. Coverage of athletes should not include "how they cleared their throats and how they spat, what they ate, the manner in which they deigned to go walking, what kind of family life they led, all . . . treated in epic breadth such that a sports report became nothing more than a primitive piece of gossip." The *Völkischer Beobachter* urged that all talk of matchmakers, managers, promoters, and camps be eliminated; coverage should focus on the athletes themselves, "who through their honorable striving and struggle are in reality the carriers of the movement."

The new "stadium"—really just some seats in the open air—was completed just before the fight, and was lavishly praised in the cheerleading German press. It spouted off the statistics: with 51,000 seats and standing

room for 60,000 more it was an awe-inspiring sight, unlike anything else
in Europe, with parking for 20,000 cars and 20,000 bicycles. One could
even make long-distance calls from special ringside phones. Some 29,000
visitors were expected for the fight; at least 21 special trains were due from
all over Germany, 5 from Berlin alone, carrying 7,000 Berliners belonging to Kraft durch Freude ("Strength through Joy"), the official recre-
ational association of Nazi Germany's sole "labor union." The fight would
be a great populist celebration, with plenty of cheap seats for the working
class; scalpers were to be arrested. The entire undertaking was suffused
with an upstart's insecurity and boosterism. A cartoon in a Hamburg
newspaper showed two skyscrapers, one with MADISON SQ. GARDEN on
its marquee, the other with HAMBURGER PUNCHING. The promoter of
the Hamburg fight, Walter "Wero" Rothenburg, was shown pasting a
"Schmeling-Neusel" poster on the front of the second, as an envious
Uncle Sam watched from the balcony of "Madison Square Garden."
"Now you're speechless!" Rothenburg tells his counterpart. "We build our
'skyscrapers' by ourselves now!"*

To secure such a fight, and fighter—that is, to have enticed the great
Schmeling to fight on his native soil—was deemed an important tribute
to the new order, "eloquent testimony to the success of National Socialist
leadership," declared the *Völkischer Beobachter*, which also moved to
build up Schmeling by denigrating his Jewish biographer. "A man
capable of arousing so much true Jewish hate must certainly have character!" it said. Schmeling never disowned that sentiment, nor anything else
the Nazis said about him. And this was easily understood, because most of
what they now said was positive, even heroic: he was being recast into a
Nazi hero—"a model of professionalism, sporting decency, and fairness,"
as the *Völkischer Beobachter* put it. But the Nazi newspaper also gave
Schmeling some tactical advice, urging him not to fight Neusel in his typical plodding, methodical fashion. Many people who were not traditional
fans were digging deeply into their pockets to attend the fight, it explained,
and it would be disastrous if their first encounter with boxing, newly
exalted in Nazi culture, was a dull fight. In other words, it was Schmeling's patriotic duty to change his style.

Remarkably, over 100,000 people attended, the largest fight crowd in
Germany or Europe before or since, and a number that outstripped all

*Rothenburg remained in boxing in Nazi Germany only by proving that he was the
product of his mother's extramarital affair with a "German-blooded pub owner," and was
not her Jewish husband's biological son.

American boxing crowds except those for the two Dempsey-Tunney bouts. The *Angriff* proclaimed "a frenzy of boxing enthusiasm, the likes of which one never imagined was possible for us." In so supercharged a setting, it would have been anticlimactic if Schmeling, too, had not been reborn, and in the ninth round he scored a technical knockout. His comeback had begun. As Schmeling left the ring, fans chanted his name. The *Berliner Zeitung am Mittag* devoted more of its front page to the fight the next day than to Hitler's speech in the Saarland.

Both boxers had Jewish managers (Neusel's was Paul Damski), and neither could work in his man's corner that night. But while Damski, who had once done business in Germany, had been banned from the country, Jacobs was at least let in, again suggesting the special treatment he enjoyed. Fearing the Nazis would subject him to the kind of terror he'd once suffered at the hands of the Klan, Jacobs had reportedly agonized over whether to go. But he was not about to pass up the chance to bask in Schmeling's glory, no matter the humiliation or risk. And besides, the free-spending Jacobs always welcomed the chance to escape from his creditors, even—it seemed—if it meant going to Nazi Germany. Not since the days of Dempsey, he wrote upon returning to New York, had he seen such excitement over boxing: riding with Schmeling through the teeming streets of Hamburg afterward, Jacobs said that every window in their car was smashed by the adoring crowds. He also marveled at German orderliness. "I expected Max to win decisively, but I didn't expect 100,000 people to respect authority to the point where they needed no official to keep them in their proper seats," he wrote. (The crowd's docility was all the more noteworthy because the seats were rock hard, and many offered only an obscured view of the action.)

Once more, Jacobs insisted he'd been treated well in Germany. So extravagant was his praise, in fact, that it even prompted the German press to belatedly acknowledge he'd been there. In his memoirs, Schmeling wrote that he stood publicly by Jacobs and that when the Hotel Bristol in Berlin refused to give Yussel a room, he threatened to go public with its bad behavior. (Why that would have alarmed the hotel, given official attitudes toward the Jews, is unclear.) Whatever induced Schmeling to keep Jacobs on impressed people like Kurt Tucholsky, the anti-Nazi writer who was to commit suicide in Swedish exile a year later; he described Schmeling's treatment of Jacobs as "very decent indeed." But Tucholsky probably did not know that Jacobs no longer represented Schmeling in Germany and collected nothing from his fights there.

That the Neusel fight had come off so beautifully was, to the Nazi press, proof positive that Germany now counted, in boxing and beyond. But if the Germans had pulled off something of American proportions, they had done so without all that American vulgarity or sensationalism; while the American fight mob was a mob, the German one was a community of patriots. Schmeling basked in the adulation; a week later he was in Nuremberg for the annual Nazi Party congress, and he was greeted warmly wherever he appeared. While never mouthing explicitly Nazi rhetoric, he participated in other rituals: as newsreel cameras filmed the scene, Schmeling, along with Ondra, Leni Riefenstahl, and others, collected funds for one of the Nazis' favorite charities, the Winterhilfswerk, or Winter Relief Fund. So close did Hitler become to Ondra that his mistress, Eva Braun, apparently grew jealous; once, according to Braun's diary, the Führer kept her waiting three hours outside a hotel while taking Ondra flowers and inviting her to supper.

Once again, Schmeling was a contender. But he'd have to fight Steve Hamas, and maybe Carnera a second time for another shot at Baer, who'd beaten Carnera for the crown a couple of months earlier. (In Dresden, the German-Jewish diarist Victor Klemperer had expressed satisfaction with that result, noting how the Nazi press had previously disparaged Baer, whom they considered Jewish, and given him little chance of beating the Italian.) That, Parker wrote, was a rematch to savor. "Every member of the Goldfarb, Epstein, Rosenbaum and Levy families would cancel all pressing engagements to watch Max Baer pin a Swastika on the eye of Hitler's envoys," he wrote. In the meantime, New York and Germany vied for the right to host Schmeling's rematch with Hamas. Given German currency restrictions, no big fight against a foreigner could ever be staged in the Reich without approval from Hitler or some other high official. But with Nazi Germany intent upon becoming a boxing powerhouse, this proved no problem. By the end of 1934, the deal was struck. The fight would be held indoors the following March; Hamas would collect $25,000, to be deposited beforehand in a Parisian bank. The fervor with which the Nazis had gone after the fight was something the Americans simply could not match. The head of Madison Square Garden complained that he could not fight a promoter who was backed up by a state government. But a bigger loser was Joe Jacobs, who was spotted nearly swallowing his cigar when he learned the news; Schmeling had told him he was too busy making a movie to fight again so soon, let alone in a place where Jacobs would not earn a red cent. *Box-Sport* saw the deal as yet another stinging rebuke to the Americans. They just could not concede that "God's own country"—it used the English phrase—had lost so much influence in world boxing. "The Götterdämmerung has started," another German paper crowed. Having landed one fight, Germany was ready to bid for another: a championship defense by Baer, for which it would put up $300,000. Hitler "wants to have good fights and great champions in Germany," one German fight promoter explained. "Besides, Baer is a Jew. It would be one way of showing the world that a Jew can have fair play and a real welcome in Germany." Baer's manager had already written to Hitler, asking him if he'd approve such a match.

So Germany finally had itself a big international fight. But where would it be held? Germany's largest indoor arena, in Frankfurt, held only fifteen thousand people. So the Nazis resolved to build, or adapt, something especially for the occasion, something commensurate with the match's importance to the Reich. They fastened on refurbishing a former timber warehouse in Hamburg, one that could be used afterward for mass political rallies. The building, to be called the Hanseatenhalle, would seat 25,240, making it—how could it be anything but?—the largest indoor facility in the world. It would have to be ready almost instantaneously, presenting a challenge to German will, industry, and efficiency. Soon a thousand workers were on the job, day and night, determined to prove to the world that Nazi Germany was up to the task. One day, Schmeling himself stopped by to drive in a few ceremonial rivets.

Once again, fight frenzy enveloped the country. By early March 1935, so many people were descending on Schmeling's training camp in Sachsenwald that the police had to be summoned periodically to maintain order. Young people, including the Hitler Youth and their female counterpart, the Bund deutscher Mädel, were everywhere. When Schmeling sparred indoors, people hung from the rafters; outside, uniformed young men and women shouted, "We want to see Max Schmeling!" in much the way they chanted "We want to see our Führer!" in Obersalzberg. Genuine Schmeling autographs were available, but only to those making donations to the Winterhilfswerk. Not since the heyday of the French champion Georges Carpentier in the 1920s was Europe so worked up over a fight, wrote William L. Shirer, who was covering the story for an American wire service.

The Nazis were pleased with Schmeling, and said so. "We would hardly know our youth, who in schools all over Germany swing their boxing gloves according to the will of the Führer, if a majority of them weren't inspired by the silent desire to become a Schmeling," the *Angriff* wrote. The paper predicted that Schmeling would win, and that seemed like a safe guess; shocking his hosts, Hamas drank beer and smoked cigarettes during training, and went to the opera and the theater. Then, a week before the fight he tore a ligament in his left arm. Normally he would have sought a postponement, but with $25,000 on the line he couldn't afford to. Schmeling, on the other hand, was motivated as never before. He could take a punch, Gallico wrote, but not the humiliation Hamas had inflicted on him in Philadelphia. He would be more dangerous than ever before.

Against all odds, the Hanseatenhalle was ready in time, though only after a fashion: it remained unheated, and fans were urged to bring blankets and overshoes. Once again, cars and extra trains from all over Germany converged on Hamburg. For wealthier fight fans, Deutsche Lufthansa offered a special round-trip flight from Berlin to Hamburg. Shirer reported that after requests from "television enthusiasts" in London, New York, Paris, and Rome, the Germans had decided to put "parts of the fight on the air in pictures and sound." He went on to say that Schmeling, whom he described as Germany's sole "non-political hero," was disappointed that Hitler was not coming to the fight; the Führer, it seemed, had a cold. To the great offense of the Germans, who thought of themselves as consummate sportsmen, Hamas insisted that one of the ring judges be an American. The job went to Sparrow Robertson, the veteran sportswriter and boulevardier of the Paris *Herald Tribune*. Wearing his reportorial hat, Robertson described Jacobs arriving at Le Havre with "a bodyguard of four very husky-appearing fellows," then making an incongruous appearance at an official dinner in Hamburg on the eve of the fight. Jacobs again went unmentioned in the German press, though one paper noted the presence at that dinner of "some of the people whom we as National Socialists easily could have done without."

March 10, 1935, was a beautiful, sunny Sunday in Hamburg, and the hall filled quickly—with fans from England, France, Denmark, Sweden, Norway, Holland, and Poland as well as from all over Germany—once the doors were opened. The Nazi government ordered seventy tickets for the fight. Goebbels, Heinrich Himmler, and the interior minister, Wilhelm Frick, had planned to attend, but for reasons that were never made clear, canceled at the last moment. Various other dignitaries and officials were on hand, though, including some of Germany's top film and stage stars, like Emil Jannings. Sausage vendors in chef's garb hawked their victuals. Every surface was festooned with swastikas, as were lapels and what one starry-eyed British reporter called the "gay" armlets of the storm troopers. Over the loudspeaker, people were urged to take their seats—or, to be more precise, their spots on the crowded wooden benches. Inside and outside the building were thousands of uniformed men—fifteen thousand, someone said, though to Trevor Wignall of the London *Daily Express* the number seemed higher, and all quite unnecessary. "Any barked order finds the German of today very ready to obey," he wrote. "The attendance may not have been wholly hand-picked, but it was so definitely and blusteringly Nazi that it could easily have served as the background and chorus for one of Hitler's screaming speeches."

Jacobs, naturally, was barred from Schmeling's corner. One report placed him in a neutral corner, another sitting way back in the crowd, while Jacobs himself said he sat in the press seats. He was chewing his cigar, because that's all he could do with it: smoking had been banned in the hall when it looked as if the Führer, who was notoriously opposed to tobacco, might come. Various officials took the ring microphone to give the usual hosannas to Hitler. The eyes of the sports world were on Hamburg, said Erich Rüdiger, the new head of the German boxing federation; at long last, German boxing was assuming its rightful place in the world. "*Sieg Heil!*" he shouted three times. In each instance the throng responded mightily, all but rattling the windows in the giant shed. A kind of Nazi tide washed over even the wary Wignall. "Nearest the ring are gaunt-faced, fit-as-a-fiddle Storm Troopers," he wrote. "It is a marvelous spectacle now. The best-disciplined attendance the world has ever known are ready to give their countryman, Schmeling, the reception of his life." Schmeling then climbed into the ring and gave the Nazi salute. "What happens now is not a mere welcome," Wignall continued. "It is a hope, a prayer, a heartfelt command from the nation. I hear sighs from women such as are usually heard in cathedrals, and muttered comments from men who in the years ago were associated with battle grounds." Hamas, meantime, received only polite applause.

Once the fight began Schmeling's fists quickly found their range; Hamas's arm injury and lax training left him defenseless. Returning to his corner at the end of the fourth round, Schmeling told Machon that Hamas had had it; his only fear now was hurting him. The man doing the German play-by-play, Arno Hellmis of the *Völkischer Beobachter*, could not contain his enthusiasm: Schmeling was "like a tiger," "merciless," "controlled," and "imperturbably calm," he told the German radio audience. Three times in the sixth round, Hamas went down for a nine count. By the end of the seventh, he was barely standing, and the crowd was calling for a halt. But the referee, a Belgian, was hamstrung by his instructions: believing that the world would pounce on any sign of unfairness, fearing that such perceptions could jeopardize the forthcoming Berlin Olympics, the Germans had decreed that the fight must end unequivocally, with absolutely no room for argument. That meant a knockout. Between the seventh and eighth rounds, the referee begged Hamas's seconds to quit, but they refused.

Thus, what began as a rout became a slaughter. Even hardened fight fans were sickened by the grisly spectacle. By the eighth round, Hamas actually looked near death. Hellmis later said that Schmeling was merciful, throwing body punches rather than yet more blows to Hamas's head. Others insisted Schmeling kept tattooing Hamas with his right, laughing as he did. By the ninth round, the rigid discipline inside the Hanseatenhalle had broken down: even some of the storm troopers were begging the referee to intercede. Finally he called the fight. A deafening roar filled the hall. There was a frenzy in the ring; photographers climbed through the ropes, and the storm troopers threw them out. But perhaps because they didn't know who he was, or because he was standing at Schmeling's side, they left Jacobs alone, whom Schmeling had lifted up into the ring.

Eyewitness accounts of what ensued vary, though perhaps they were merely successive snapshots in a great and swiftly flowing drama. According to the *Angriff,* the celebration swelled "into a hurricane," with the loudspeaker unintelligible even with the volume turned all the way up. Wignall, on the other hand, was struck by a "silence that could almost be felt." As Hamas's seconds dragged him to his corner, the crowd froze, as if waiting for some command or signal telling them what to do. Then, Wignall recalled, something thin and fairylike, "the most beautiful tenor voice I thought I had ever heard," sounded in the distance, breaking up the stillness. It was a recording of Lauritz Melchior, singing the "Prize Song" from Wagner's *Die Meistersinger von Nürnberg.* Wignall asked Arthur Bülow, Schmeling's deposed manager, who was seated at his side, why it was playing now. Bülow looked around, making sure that no storm troopers were nearby. "Hitler's favorite," he whispered.

An official from the German boxing federation draped a laurel wreath with Germany's colors around Schmeling's neck, and the fading strains of Wagner were overtaken by "Deutschland über Alles," starting somewhere in the back rows, picking up ferocity as it rolled forward. Only two times had *Box-Sport*'s editor ever heard the German anthem arise spontaneously at a boxing event; each time, Schmeling had provided the spark. As the words wafted across the cavernous hall, Schmeling and those around him stiffened. Up went Schmeling's arm, his hand still encased in his bloodied glove, and he began to sing along. Twenty-five thousand onlookers also raised their arms. Even the barely conscious Hamas, his left cheek puffed up like some grotesque Zephyr, managed to extend his arm. Jacobs was momentarily at a loss. But everyone else was saluting, he thought, and he was in plain sight; what else was he to do? So up went his right arm, too, though with a cigar nestled between his fingers. The photographers captured the scene: Schmeling's arm was stiff and resolute, while Jacobs's was more limp, as if halfheartedly hailing a cab. If he lived to be one hundred years old, Wignall later wrote, he would never forget the scene in the Hanseatenhalle that day: "German men with their eyes tight closed and singing their hearts out," he wrote. "German women with their hands to their breasts as though at devotion. Thousands of men in uniform, stiff as ramrods, but with their right palms upraised. . . . This was the soul of a nation breathing out its aspirations. 'Germany over all.'" Not even in August 1914, he went on, had they sung that song so fervently. "A strident voice, that must have belonged to a one-time sergeant-major, bellowed something in German," he went on. "Instantly 25,000 men and women echoed the command. '*Sieg heil!*' It swept the oblong building as a wind sweeps a street. '*Sieg heil!*' Never have I believed such a chorus possible." Up went the arms, along with thirteen more jubilant chants— Germany's statement to the world "that it is not only free again, but ready to march at a signal." It was only a boxing match, but unfolding before Wignall was, to him, the future of a continent: Germany was shouting itself into another war. "I have had all I want of war," Wignall wrote once he'd returned to England. "Never again do I want to climb into a uniform. But if the screaming and cheering continue in Germany I may have to, and so may you."

The crowd then moved on to the "Horst Wessel Song," sung, as one foreign observer put it, "in all crudeness" by everyone there. Some of those nearest the ring, who'd witnessed the butchery most closely, stood in silence, put off by what they considered the poor sportsmanship. "They knew that Hamas, for all his poor showing, had given the hysterical crowd a demonstration of that courage about which Nazi leaders continually are talking," wrote Albion Ross of *The New York Times*. Schmeling, too, Ross sensed, was offended, and had sneaked out of the ring before all the raised arms had descended. And that was somehow fitting, because the celebrations, in the hall, then in the streets, then all night in the bars and breweries—"locals with sausages covered in mustard in one hand, and mugs of beer in the other climbed tables, singing old songs, celebrating in their way the victory of their compatriot," a reporter for a French paper wrote—were less for him than for his country. "Germany has outstripped the seemingly undefeatable America," *Box-Sport* later declared. But with its extraordinary pageantry, the Schmeling-Hamas fight had proved that the two entities, boxer and country, had become virtually interchangeable. Dogged, written off, disrespected, determined to confound the critics and establish supremacy, Schmeling, and Germany itself, had come roaring back. Soon he would stand astride the world, and his country would, too.

Untouched except for a small red mark on one eyelid, Schmeling returned to his hotel. The first person to congratulate his wife, he told reporters, had been Hitler, who had been listening at Berchtesgaden. "That's a real fine thing for a politician to do," he said. Schmeling got his own telegram from Hitler, which left him beaming. There was more to come in the morning papers. "The superiority of the ex–world champion is difficult to describe," the *Angriff* enthused. "One doesn't know what one should praise more, his strategic achievement, his unforgettable fighting morale, or his left, which we have never seen so perfect before in German rings." The Americans would have loved to see Schmeling lose, the *8 Uhr-Blatt* declared, but they'd underestimated him, and all Germans, for that matter. They didn't fully grasp German tenacity and endurance, German energy, German vigor and discipline.

Everyone began looking forward. "Now we get Baer," Schmeling yelled jubilantly after the fight, embracing Joe Jacobs as he did. Schmeling could not be denied a fight with Baer now, notwithstanding the intrigues and profiteering so popular with the Yankees, the *8 Uhr-Blatt* predicted. One official in Berlin said that the city would be the ideal site for such a fight. All this required some fancy ideological footwork. "Among the amusing sidelights of Germany today is the denial that Baer is a Jew," Wignall wrote. It was hard to square this euphoria with the Nazis' previous antipathy toward professional athletics. But the *Angriff* now maintained that even a professional contest had value: two fighters at so lofty a level were "altars to manliness," prime recruiters for the worthiest and most important sport. For this reason Hamas was propped up in defeat as assiduously as Schmeling was in victory. All talk that he was "second-rate" suddenly ceased. That was scant solace for Hamas himself, who suffered from a host of infirmities following the fight: a spinal injury, numbness in his leg, slurred speech, double vision. Wignall, who visited him five days later, said he'd never felt sorrier for anyone; it looked as if Hamas would never lift his fists again. And he never did, at least for another prizefight. His career was over.

Schmeling had no such problems, and made his way back to Obersalzberg for another meeting with Hitler. Pictures soon appeared of the Führer there reading a newspaper account of the fight, with a smiling Schmeling peering over his shoulder. In all likelihood, whatever newspaper the two men were reading did not include a photograph of Jacobs giving the Nazi salute. But C. W. Gilfert of the *Fränkische Tageszeitung* had seen the photo, and to him it meant that the process of cleansing German boxing of its Jews remained infuriatingly, inexcusably incomplete; Schmeling would be well advised, he said, to make sure his stables were *judenrein*. According to Schmeling's memoirs, the picture also brought him a dressing-down from the German sports commissar, Hans von Tschammer und Osten, along with demands from both him and Goebbels that he fire Jacobs.

Jacobs was now getting it from every direction. The day he returned to America, the infamous picture appeared in several New York newspapers. "When Schmeling Won . . . And Yussel 'Heiled,'" blared the *Daily News*. All over town, Jacobs found himself ridiculed and excoriated. One paper noted that when he got off the boat, he was wearing a brown suit, shirt, shoes, and socks—"just to carry out the Nazi motif." "In the Broadway delicatessens and nighteries where Playboy Jacobs is a familiar figure the waiters were conspiring to put Mickey Finns in his herring," wrote Jack Miley in the *Daily News*. "In the sports world, it is being considered a big joke, but in every Jew's heart it calls forth disgust," said the Yiddish *Morgnzhurnal*. Jacobs swatted off his critics. As he saw it, he'd had no choice in the matter. "What the 'ell would you do?" he asked one reporter. "When a band plays the 'Star-Spangled Banner' you stand up and take your hat off. And you expect everyone else to." "When in Rome, eat pasta fazoole," he told another reporter. To anyone challenging his religious credentials, he insisted he was "500 percent Jewish" and that he wore *tsitsis*, the fringed undergarments of the Orthodox. He did have his defenders. "What did these birds expect Yussel to do—stand up in Germany and sing the 'Internationale'?" wrote a *News* reader from the Bronx. Gallico considered it much ado about very little: to him the gesture was no more than what children do when they want to leave the room. People had better get used to this saluting business anyway, he said; there'd be plenty of it at the Berlin Olympics. The Jewish athletes who would be participating—and who would be "well and courteously treated" while there, he predicted—might do some of it themselves.

The boxing press quickly handicapped a Schmeling-Baer rematch. Damon Runyon thought Schmeling would be clobbered, and wondered why he'd do it; perhaps Hitler or Ondra was leaning on him, but more likely Schmeling just wanted the dough. But Grantland Rice had studied the fight pictures from Hamburg, and to him Schmeling looked as if "he were going to punch his way right off the printed page." Politics promised to make the fight a windfall for its promoters. "A hard-hitting 'Nordic' meets Max Baer, a tall young Jew who laughs while he fights," wrote Arthur Brisbane. "The meeting will settle nothing. Racial supremacy does not depend on the fist. But in New York City it ought to draw a crowd gigantic." Gallico saw another attraction to the fight: pitting a German against a Jew in the United States on the eve of the Olympics would guarantee fairness for American athletes in Berlin. Not that it would be necessary; Nazi Jew bashing, he believed, had run its course. "As always occurs when religion is used as a political tool, the mob goes too far, and the dangerous conflagration ignited by the politicians gets out of hand and threatens to become a holocaust from which none escape," he wrote. But Germany was now done with anti-Semitic hysteria; it had run its course, he asserted, and all good Germans regretted what had occurred. In any case, his friend Max had no use for such things. "Schmeling does not represent German officialdom and German politics, but German sport and warm-hearted German people," he wrote. "He has been faithful and loyal to his Jewish manager, and no one has been able to make him change. It might be very helpful if petty politicians and agitators on both sides of the water would move out of the way and give the better instincts that lie in every race and every human being a chance."

Others saw Schmeling's relationship with Jacobs very differently. They predicted Schmeling would never fight again in the States because, with extra taxes and Jacobs's commission to worry about, it would be too expensive for him. There were reports that Schmeling had dropped Jacobs altogether. "Schmeling Gives Yussel the Ozone," the *Mirror* claimed. To Schmeling, Parker wrote, "managers are only the means to the end, to be ruthlessly brushed aside when they have served their purpose to him. . . . Now that Jacobs has outlived his usefulness, Schmeling is making him walk the plank, too." Years later, Schmeling said he never considered breaking with Jacobs. "I really need Joe Jacobs," he said he told Hitler. "I owe all my success in America to him. Mr. Jacobs is competent, he is respectable and correct. And beyond that, you can't get anywhere in New York without a local manager. Besides, loyalty is a German virtue." He said Hitler made an angry gesture, then dismissed him. "Hitler's message had been clear, and I understood its meaning," he said.

The story is implausible, and not only because Schmeling had said at the time that Hitler actually wanted him to keep Jacobs, or because, whatever else he was, Joe Jacobs was hardly "respectable" and "correct." Having embraced Schmeling as enthusiastically and as publicly as the Nazis had, Jacobs and all, it is unlikely they would be pressuring him to drop Jacobs now. Whether implicitly or explicitly, unilaterally or jointly, Hitler and Schmeling had surely long since settled on Jacobs's proper status: he was simply the cost of doing business in New York. Without him, Schmeling would have been sunk. For a regime strapped for cash and legitimacy, eager for triumphs of any kind, ordering Schmeling to fire Jacobs would have been self-defeating. So Schmeling had done the next best thing: he'd emasculated him. And Jacobs took it because Schmeling was his former—and, now, perhaps his future—heavyweight champion.

The Nazis also compromised on Max Baer. Whatever its legitimacy, Baer's Jewishness led to his condemnation in Germany; *The Prizefighter and the Lady*, a romantic comedy in which he'd starred, had been banned there. In the most virulently anti-Semitic circles, another match against him, especially on German soil, would be an abomination. The *Fränkische Tageszeitung* acknowledged the appeal of "the Swastika vs. the Star of David," but wanted the fight to take place outside the Fatherland. Some things, though, trumped even anti-Semitism. The Nazis had already let Schmeling fight Baer once, and, after all, Baer was the champ; for Schmeling to regain the crown, he'd have to take him on. That assumed, of course, that Baer could get past Jimmy Braddock, the journeyman boxer then in the midst of an improbable run at the title. Braddock had been matched with Baer only after Schmeling himself had refused to fight him. "Who *iss* Chim Braddock?" Schmeling had remarked at the time. "I haff neffer heardt of Chim Braddock."

But however he fared against Baer, Braddock was not the up-and-coming boxer whom people on both sides of the Atlantic were starting to notice. As the German press charted Schmeling's resurgence, it also carried its first, sketchy reports about another American boxer making a name for himself. It referred to him variously as "The Negro mixed-breed [*Negermischling*] from Alabama," the "half-black" (*Halbneger*), or "Joe Clay Face." "Within a short period of time his right hand has become highly respected by all leading heavyweights," *Box-Sport* reported matter-of-factly in February 1935. It was true. And Joe Louis was only getting started.

CHAPTER 3

A Star Rises in the Midwest

THERE ARE MANY LEGENDS about how Joe Louis Barrow became just Joe Louis. One is that as a boy in Detroit, Louis didn't want his mother to know he was spending the money she'd given him for violin lessons on boxing. Another is that Louis took such a beating in his first amateur bout that he wanted to spare his family any embarrassment. Another credits a ring announcer, who asked Louis his name but introduced him before Louis could get it all out, or his manager, who thought that the "Barrow" made his name too long. Still one more says Louis ran out of space when filling out an application for an amateur boxing show. In Louis's first few years of celebrity, every part of his story was retold, elaborated upon, embellished, or invented. But the facts of his youth are fairly straightforward.

He was born on May 13, 1914, in the Buckalew Mountains of east-central Alabama, five miles from the small town of Lafayette, the seventh of eight children of a sharecropper named Monroe Barrow and his wife, Lillie Reece Barrow. His parents were big people—his father was over six feet tall and weighed nearly two hundred pounds—and Louis arrived big, too: eleven pounds at birth. Shortly thereafter, Louis's father was sent to a state mental institution, where he was thought to have died, and Louis's mother was left to work the farm and raise her family. Before long she married Pat Brooks, a widower with a large brood of his own. The combined families eked out a minimal existence, with the children haphazardly attending primitive schools. Louis did not talk much until he was six, and when he did, he stammered. For youngsters who didn't know any better, it was a gentle and racially benign existence, in the settled way of the segregated South.

When Louis was twelve, his family joined the historic northward migration of blacks. They landed in Detroit, where Louis saw his first trolleys, flushed his first toilet, turned on his first electric lights. But within a few years, as the Depression came and took hold, his stepfather lost his job in one of the car plants. The family went on relief and, sometimes, went hungry. Louis attended school with smaller, younger children with whom he shared little; his speech impediment made him withdraw still more. At fourteen, he went to a vocational school. "This boy should be able to do something with his hands," one of his instructors said. Louis felt the same thing, though not quite in the same way. "All my life my hands felt important to me," he later said. "They felt big, strong, and they seemed to want to do something special." Louis earned spare change—and developed his physique—by delivering ice, hauling sixty-pound blocks up several flights of stairs. Convinced that musical talent ran in the family and that it could earn Joe a living, Lillie Brooks gave him a cheap violin and fifty cents a week for lessons. But the instrument felt funny in those big hands, and in his rough neighborhood it brought him additional ridicule. Athletics came much more naturally. He loved baseball; he was a good hitter and once said he'd have stuck with it had there been more opportunities for blacks. (He ducked football because, as one contemporary writer put it, "the white boys make it too tough on a colored lad.") Instead, he fell into boxing.

In the spring of 1932, when he was eighteen years old, Louis had his first amateur match. His opponent, Johnny Miler, who was to fight for the United States Olympic team later that year, knocked him down seven times. Discouraged, Louis avoided the gym for a time and took a job at Ford's River Rouge plant, pushing truck bodies around on a conveyor belt. But he soon returned to the ring and, having learned to use both of his hands, racked up thirteen straight knockouts. In February 1933 he won the local Golden Gloves tournament as a light heavyweight. "Lewis," the *Detroit Free Press* observed, was a terrific puncher. (Younger children quickly came to idolize Louis; one, Walker Smith, who insisted on carrying his bags, would become Sugar Ray Robinson.) Several losses in amateur matches followed, but in one of them he impressed a Detroit man named John Roxborough. Roxborough, whose line of work was ostensibly real estate, in fact ran Detroit's numbers racket, making him one of the black community's wealthiest and best-connected figures. The "insurance broker" he brought in as his partner on the Louis account, Julian Black, had a similar position, and similar status, in Chicago, though he was known to be a far icier character and Louis never got nearly so close to him. Roxborough bought him clothes and supplies and his first pair of new, professional gloves. Childless, he invited Louis to live with him and his wife. He gave him an allowance, five dollars every Saturday night. And he began instructing him in some of the fundamentals, like how to wash his ears, comb his hair, and hold a fork.*

In February 1934 Louis again captured the Detroit Golden Gloves. The next month, before twenty thousand fans in Chicago, what one paper called "the Detroit colored lad with the frozen face" won the national Golden Gloves in the 175-pound class. In the course of this tournament, Louis made two incongruous but crucial allies: the *Chicago Tribune*, pillar of conservative, midwestern white America, which sponsored the competition; and the *Chicago Defender*, one of the oldest and most influential of the weekly newspapers that covered, and helped sustain, America's separate and completely unequal black community. With paternal, almost proprietary pride, *Tribune* writers documented Louis's every step up the ladder. Arch Ward, the veteran *Tribune* sports columnist who had recently created baseball's All-Star Game, sent Louis travel money so he could participate in one tournament. In its own way, the *Defender* later said, the *Tribune* did more to recognize black athletes than did the NAACP. The *Defender* printed what was probably the first newspaper picture of Louis, and by April 1934 it was touting him as the greatest amateur fighter anywhere. The following week in St. Louis, Louis became the AAU light heavyweight champion. It was the first time mixed bouts had ever been held in that city, whose ballparks were still segregated. By mid-1934, Louis wanted to turn professional. He was tired of working for Ford, and was having trouble finding anyone willing to fight him for nothing. Louis's handlers, who were to collect half his earnings, then took him to see a trainer in Chicago named Jack Blackburn. Blackburn, then in his early fifties, had been one of the toughest, smartest, and wiliest fighters of his

---

*Mentioning the unsavory backgrounds of Louis's backers was generally taboo in both the white and the "race" press. The *New York Sun*, for instance, called Roxborough a "clever Negro lawyer" and depicted him as elegant, discreet, and literate, adjectives the mainstream press rarely used to describe blacks. Occasionally, usually with a wink, there were hints of their real livelihoods. "Neither Roxborough nor Black are benefactors of the type ordinarily associated with U.S. racial-uplift campaigns," was how *Life* magazine once put it. But Louis had no qualms about their line of work. "I figured this way: the fight game is a tough game," he once explained. "They knew their way around. They could protect me from racket guys because they knew the angles."

generation, and one of the best black boxers ever. A compact man, he'd fought hundreds of bouts, often against much bigger men, and usually won. Not all of Blackburn's fights had been in the ring. One earned him a manslaughter conviction, for which he spent several years in prison. Another left him with a large knife scar across his left cheek. Hard living and heavy drinking, along with severe arthritis, had slowed him down, though he still took on promising young boxers. But when Roxborough told him he'd found a potential champion, Blackburn was skeptical—not because of Louis himself, but because of his race.

From the sport's earliest days, there had always been great black boxers. By the beginning of the twentieth century, blacks dominated several weight categories and threatened in others, enough to raise alarms in Jim Crow America. "The coloreds are on average better natural boxers than the average whites because they have a much sharper eye while fighting and recognize very quickly every danger as well as the strong sides of the pale face," Tom O'Rourke, a boxing veteran who had managed several black fighters, once wrote. "They are faster and more agile, and they have good legs and twice as hard a head and body and finally, their endurance and fighting spirit is generally better and greater than ours."

For a time boxing's most precious jewel, the heavyweight championship, was safe. But that changed once Jack Johnson came along. Johnson, a black man from Galveston, Texas, had to go abroad to win the crown, beating Tommy Burns in Australia in 1908. His second American title defense—on July 4, 1910, in Reno, against James Jeffries, the former champion who'd been lured out of retirement as the "Great White Hope"—had been to blacks a triumph second only to Emancipation, but had led to race riots and lynchings throughout the country that left dozens dead. Johnson's behavior in and out of the ring—taunting his opponents, gloating over his victories, fraternizing with and marrying white women of low reputation—made an incendiary situation worse, scandalizing white and black America alike. Prosecuted on a trumped-up morals charge, "Lil' Arthur," as Johnson was also known, fled to Europe for a time, and ultimately lost his title to Jess Willard in a much-disputed fight in Havana in 1915. Eventually Johnson returned to America and served a brief term in prison. But his shadow lingered. Tex Rickard, who promoted the Willard fight and later took over boxing promotions at Madison Square Garden, vowed there would never be another black heavyweight champion. Even had he not, no one had much of an appetite for one.

Nearly twenty years after Johnson's reign, America remained traumatized by it. Rickard had kept his promise: whether or not Dempsey had been tempted to fight the black contender Harry Wills in the 1920s, Rickard wouldn't let him. Their prospects limited, many of the most talented black fighters came to sorry ends. Sam Langford, the so-called Boston Tar Baby, ended his days legally blind and living on welfare. Kid Chocolate, a Cuban-born featherweight, squandered his fortune. Battling Siki, the onetime light heavyweight champion, died after being shot twice in the back. Joe Gans, a lightweight and the first native-born American black to win a title, died of tuberculosis before he was forty. "A colored fighter never knows how old he is, and nobody cares," he once said.

In the early 1930s, with American life almost entirely segregated, lynchings still relatively commonplace, and blacks mired in perpetual poverty made even worse by the Depression, the prospects of most black athletes remained dim. "When the colored brother is capable in sports . . . he is usually too capable for his own good," Paul Gallico wrote. "When we needed him for the track team or the boxing squad, for football or to take part in the Olympic Games, he is a full-fledged citizen, our dearly beloved equal, and a true American. At other times he remains just plain nigger, and we'd rather he weren't around." In professional boxing, where fame and riches abounded, the situation was surely the cruelest. The black boxer, Gallico went on, "is generally a magnificent physical specimen, powerful, wiry, hard, and not nearly so sensible to pain as his white brother. He has a thick, hard skull, and good hands. He is crafty and tricky and, contrary to public opinion, as game as the white man when the cards are not stacked against him." But that was the problem— they almost always were. "The Negro is regarded as pure cattle to be exploited, swindled, and burgled for their own profits and never, if possible, for his," Gallico wrote. "He is after all only a nigger, and so the ordinary rules of conduct applied to white fighters, which are in themselves none too sweet, don't go." Even the praise they occasionally got was disparaging. "The reason they fight so well is that their somewhat primitive brains and their muscles act with one impulse," one sportswriter observed.

Blacks saw things the same way, only from closer up. "Negro fighters are used merely to build up 'white hopes,'" E. B. Rea wrote in the *Norfolk Journal and Guide*, another leading black weekly, in 1934. "Their activities are confined to fake and fraudulent bouts through unscrupulous managers and promoters who are more eager to replenish their inflated purses than to make Negro champions." Things would change, wrote another black columnist, only when white promoters thought some outlandish black fighter could lift lagging attendance. "We've got to wait until somebody can produce a half-clown and half-gorilla to arouse the interest of our pale face brothers," he wrote.

Blackburn, of course, knew all of this firsthand. "Take him away," he said in one of many versions of his first encounter with Louis and his managers. "A colored boxer who can fight and won't lie down can't get any fights." "You were born with two strikes on you," Blackburn is said to have told Louis. "That's why I don't fool with colored boys! They're too hard to sell since Jack Johnson went and acted like he did. I can make more sugar training white fighters, even if they're only half as good." But Blackburn conceded one exception to this otherwise ironclad law: America loved a great puncher, regardless of his race. As Louis— "just a funny-looking boy with high-water trousers and too much arms for the sleeves of his coat"— sat listening, Blackburn laid down his catechism. For a black man to have any chance at all, he said, he had to be "very good outside the ring and very bad inside." "You've got to be a killer, otherwise I'm getting too old to waste any time on you," he told Louis. "I ain't goner waste any of your time," Louis promised him. Blackburn remained dubious, but took on Louis anyway. It was, after all, a job. Louis and Blackburn quickly grew close. "Chappie," they called each other.

Blackburn soon discovered that Louis hit hard; as for the rest, he'd have to be rebuilt from the ground up. Louis needed to learn how to plant his feet for the best balance, how to weave and block, how to shuffle in and out of range, how to spot openings, how to punch with his whole body, how to aim those punches and how to put them together. Blackburn taught him how to hit without hurting his hands, and the virtues of short, snappy punches. He taught him how to be free and easy in the ring, how to stay fresh for later rounds. He taught him defense, and how to hit without leaving himself open. He taught him how to feint. The goal, he drilled into him, was always a knockout: people didn't pay to see dancers or clinchers, and blacks rarely won decisions. "Let your fists be your referee," he said. One of his concerns was that Louis was "too easygoing— too nice a fella" to succeed; Louis "didn't have any blood in his eye." Once Louis had a man on the ropes, he instructed, he must not get cute or sentimental. "You can't show no pity in this game," he said. "When you get a man in distress, toss every punch in the book into him. Finish him right off." On another occasion, he put it a bit differently. "You just gotta throw away your heart when you pull on those gloves, or the other fella'll knock it outa you," he said. In the end, Blackburn said, "Joe Louis ain't no natural killer. He's a manufactured killer."

Blackburn got his new student into a regular routine: Louis arose at six each morning, ran twice around Washington Park on Chicago's South Side, went back to bed, and then got back up for breakfast and a day of training. Blackburn began to develop a feel—and even, quite literally, a taste—for Louis: at one point in his daily sessions, he would lick Louis's shoulder, and if it was salty enough, he'd know he'd had enough for the day. At night, the two of them occasionally watched movies, but mostly they sat around and talked boxing. Blackburn weaned Louis off the few vices he had, like sweets, particularly ice cream, at least while training. He did not flatter Louis, but convinced him that with enough time and seasoning, he could beat anyone. And in time, Blackburn came to believe that himself.

As Blackburn labored to make Louis unbeatable, Roxborough and Black worked to make him unimpeachable. They devised an elaborate code of conduct, most of which came naturally to him anyway. Louis would be the antithesis of everything Jack Johnson had been. He would always be soft-spoken, understated, and polite, no matter what he accomplished. He would not preen or gloat or strut in the ring. If he needed his teeth capped, it would not be done in gold, as Johnson had done. He would always conduct himself with dignity and not, as Louis once put it, like one of those "fool nigger dolls" with wide grins and thick lips. When it came to women, he would stick to his own kind, and platonically at that, at least for now. He would never fraternize with white women, let alone be photographed with them. He would not drive fast cars, especially red ones. Anyone wishing to hold Louis back would get no help from Louis himself. The press would be saturated with stories of Louis's boyish goodness, his love for his mother, his mother's love for him, his devotion to scripture, his abstemiousness and frugality.

When you stripped away all the layers of mythology and idealization, it was hard to say very much about the Louis who remained. He was dignified and decent, uneducated and inarticulate, though with an odd knack for reducing things to pithy truisms. For all of his violence in the ring, he was largely passive, affectless, even dull outside of it. He was not oblivious to the gargantuan impact he had on others, but like just about everything else, he took it all in stride; the hopes that people placed on his shoulders, enough to crush normal people, appeared to impose no particular burden on him. He had few deep feelings of his own, but he had an ability to generate intense passions in others. He was the perfect vehicle for everyone else's dreams; he could be, and was, whatever someone wanted him to be.

A trainload of Detroit fans went to Chicago to watch Louis in his first professional fight, against Jack Kracken at the Bacon Casino on July 4, 1934. In the first round, Louis sent Kracken down for a nine count, then knocked him clear out of the ring. The referee quickly called the fight, for which Louis earned $59, and predicted that Louis would one day be champ. "If he isn't the hardest punching heavyweight of all time—you can have Dempsey, too—I'll eat your typewriter," a veteran Chicago boxing man wrote Joe Williams of the *New York Telegram*. Louis won his first mention in another mainstay of the black press, the *Pittsburgh Courier*. Shortly thereafter, he made his debut as well in *Ring*, in the agate type at the back of the magazine.

In September, in what he later called one of his toughest fights, he beat Adolph Wiater in Chicago. In October, before a sold-out crowd at Chicago's Arcadia Gardens, Louis knocked down Art Sykes so hard that his head bounced off the canvas. Louis knocked out Stanley Poreda—and knocked Poreda out of the ring—in the first round on November 14; the timekeeper couldn't start the count until removing Poreda from his lap. Later in November 1934, as Max Baer looked on, Louis faced Charley Massera, who'd beaten Steve Hamas. It was Louis's first "big" fight, held in the Chicago Coliseum rather than in a neighborhood club, and matchmakers and scouts from all over the country came to see him. It was also the first mixed bout at the coliseum since 1929, when a panic, perhaps racially inspired, left one fan dead and several others injured. In the third round Louis landed two crushing rights, the second of which left Massera "hung like a sack of wheat" over the middle rope. It was the first time Louis had seemed brutal—perhaps, the *Chicago Defender* theorized, because he knew that the champ was watching. Also watching was Nat Fleischer. Just as he had championed a foreigner, Schmeling, he now championed a black man, imagining Louis as a future titleholder. The only question was whether he'd be given that chance. Times had changed, Fleischer stressed; race prejudice, while still pronounced in some places, had ebbed in others. He conceded that much depended on Baer, who was said to have promised his mother that he would never fight a black man. But this was the same man who had also said he would fight the Twentieth Century Limited if there were enough money in it.

In any case, forces beyond Baer would likely decide the matter. Boxing was in trouble. Madison Square Garden had lost money in 1933 and 1934. The gate for the Sharkey-Carnera title fight was $200,000, less than one-tenth what Dempsey and Tunney had drawn in Chicago only seven years earlier. The sport was desperately short of cash and charisma, and Louis promised to fill both voids. "*The Ring* welcomes Louis among America's fighting men," Fleischer wrote. "Regardless of color, boxing needs good talent and in the Detroiter it has the type of gladiator for whom the sport has been looking."

And if Louis promised to bring white fans back to the stadiums and arenas, he would also bring out blacks, many of them for the first time. For all of its enduring, crushing problems, in the years since Jack Johnson black America had become more urbanized, concentrated, cohesive, and assertive. Millions had moved north, from farms to cities, and a whole black subculture had developed. Black businessmen—some legitimate, some running numbers and other rackets—had appeared on the scene, and a small black plutocracy had sprung up. Black culture had blossomed; Harlem had had its Renaissance. Blacks developed greater political power, electing some of their own representatives. The Brotherhood of Sleeping Car Porters won recognition. The NAACP had grown more established, and now had indigenous leadership; it led a campaign against lynching, and filed the first cases against segregated schools. Mass movements had grown around black nationalist leaders like Marcus Garvey. While baseball remained white, the Negro Leagues had appeared. The black press, led by newspapers such as the *Defender* in Chicago, the *Courier* in Pittsburgh, the *Baltimore Afro-American*, the *Philadelphia Tribune*, and the *Norfolk Journal and Guide*, had become more vital and outspoken. The growth of black political and economic power and self-confidence was slow but profound. Though it would have to dig deeply into its pockets to do so, black America was ready to celebrate something, to splurge, to strut, to hope. It only needed an excuse. And now he'd come along.

Louis was next matched, on December 14, with a California boxer named Lee Ramage. Ramage had never been knocked out, and he, too, had defeated Hamas. Gamblers, who thought Louis's managers were putting him in over his head to earn some money for themselves, made Ramage a two-to-one favorite. "If Louis stops the clever Californian he will throw the first ten heavyweight contenders into a panic," the *Chicago American* reported. The *Tribune* disagreed: Louis "already has most of the contenders for the championship shaking in their boots," it said. Louis started the fight slowly, and by the seventh round the crowd had grown impatient for what the *Tribune*'s French Lane called "the jaw-crashing, sleep-producing blow that is being talked about all over America." Ram-

age was Louis's best opponent yet, and Blackburn had told him beforehand to take his time, to learn as much as he could until he gave him the
word. Insiders knew that when Blackburn slapped Louis on the rear end,
it was his signal to "wrap it up" or "go to town." In the eighth, Louis sent
Ramage down twice for a nine count, then down again for good. "Who's
going to stop this new 'black peril' among the heavyweights?" Lane asked.
"Maybe Maxie Baer. Remember, I say maybe." For the first time, Louis
broke into *Ring's* top ten heavyweights, the ninth-ranked contender for
the title.

It may have been while Louis trained for Ramage that a friend came
by with a beautiful nineteen-year-old black girl named Marva Trotter. (Or
Louis may have met her at a party at a South Side hotel. Or he may have
gotten her name from Al Monroe of the *Defender*—the saga of Louis's
courtship had many variants.) Marva, born in the black town of Boley,
Oklahoma, and raised in Chicago, was a high school graduate who as-
pired to dress designing but who was then studying stenography in one of
the few schools that accepted blacks. Julian Black's lawyer was dating one
of her sisters. By any measure, it was a mismatch: Marva was the daughter
of a minister, well spoken and charming, while Louis remained raw. But
to Louis's handlers, that only made her more appealing. They were, of
course, eager to wall him off from white women—to avoid the whole Jack
Johnson situation. But black women were becoming a problem, too, at
least according to *Collyer's Eye*, a sports tip sheet out of Chicago. In July
1935 it cited reports "seeping out of the 'black belt'" that "hotcha gals" in
Detroit had already started in on Louis, with one jealous type tossing a
brick through his car window. "Louis's handlers . . . realize fully that
wine, woman [*sic*] and song have been the most powerful enemy of recent
near-champion negro fighters and understand the temptation con-
fronting their charge," it reported. So Marva and Louis were paired off. "It
wasn't arranged in the European sense of an arranged marriage or the
Oriental sense, but they threw them together," Louis's longtime lawyer,
Truman Gibson, later recalled. "Julian [Black] wanted a control over Joe,
and this was one element of control." At the time, Marva was taking dictation at a tooth powder company. But in black America, she would soon
become a fairy princess, the Jackie Kennedy or Princess Diana of her day.
Officially, none of this was happening. When a *Tribune* reporter asked
Louis whether there was "a little girl back in Detroit waiting to become
Mrs. Heavyweight Champion," Roxborough interceded to insist that
Louis hadn't yet shown much interest in girls. But the specifics mattered

less than the fact that to the mighty *Chicago Tribune,* one of America's most influential newspapers, "Mrs. Louis," whoever she might be, would also be "Mrs. Heavyweight Champion."

The *Tribune* regularly burnished Louis's friendly, wholesome, un-threatening image, often by offering Roxborough a platform. He informed readers, for instance, that Louis didn't smoke or drink, that his money was being saved for him, and that when he left the ring he would, as he said, engage in some respectable business among his own people. But Louis was in a peculiar position. He had to be good enough to prove himself, but not so good as to scare everybody off. In one sense, the better he got, the worse his prospects became. "A pretty good-looking young heavy," one old-timer said of Louis in June 1934. "Too bad he's a black boy, otherwise he might get somewhere in a couple of years."

With vicarious pleasure and pride, the black press touted Louis and served up details from his life. It described, in the manner of a satisfied mother, how prodigiously Louis ate—a crisp fried chicken reportedly failed to last one round in his hands—and his purchasing power, relating how he bought himself five pairs of custom-made shoes at a pop. It beamed over his black management. "Colored people usually reason that unless the head of something is white, it cannot succeed," the *Philadelphia Tribune* observed. "If Joe does nothing except dispel that old fogey idea, he will have rendered a great service." Meantime, a white sportswriter named Gene Kessler struck a deal with Louis to ghostwrite stories under his byline. Soon there would be a flood of stories by "Joe Louis," written in a mishmash of voices, sometimes excessively colloquial, sometimes incongruously erudite ("I noticed he couldn't flick that arm with the same alacrity"). The first mention of Louis in a New York newspaper may have come on December 4, 1934. HEAVYWEIGHTS DUCKING JOE LOUIS, the *New York Post* announced.

That month brought the usual Christmas-gift lists and New Year's predictions. Ed Harris of the *Philadelphia Tribune* wished Louis "a voodoo to hoodoo the heavies that are going to draw the color line." To get a crack at Baer, wrote Al Monroe, Louis had to beat Levinsky and Hamas—but not too convincingly, or "he will find the color line facing his every move up the ladder." But Chester Washington of the *Pittsburgh Courier* disagreed. "Hard rights and lefts, coupled with real economic need for a man's services, will help land a k.o. blow squarely on the chin of Old Man Prejudice," he predicted. Louis resumed his ascent only four days into 1935, besting Patsy Perroni before nearly sixteen thousand people in his hometown. Louis earned $4,000 for the night, enough to make a down payment on the house he was buying for his mother.

Three months before Schmeling and Hamas were to square off in Hamburg, Baer listed the two of them, along with Carnera, as the top contenders for his crown. Louis looked good, he said, but still wasn't sufficiently seasoned; he could knock him out in a jiffy. Instead, he offered Louis five dollars a round to become one of his sparring partners. Baer's flip-flops on whether he'd honor the color line left black writers dizzy and discouraged. Ed Harris marveled at how the color line worked: "The ease with which such an abstract idea becomes a concrete object is enough to raise the envy of any engineer," he wrote. He doubted that Louis and Baer would square off anytime soon; if Baer waited long enough, after all, Louis could burn himself out. In what might have been a matter of wishful thinking, the British, custodians of a restive empire populated largely by people of color, painted a bleak picture of Louis's prospects. "Jack Johnson put the kibosh on the Black Race for good and all," *Boxing* opined in March 1935. "Another coloured man will never hold the heavyweight title so long as the U.S.A. have any say in the matter." But to Fleischer, Louis was simply too good to keep down. Besides, it just wouldn't be right. "When the color line is used as a subterfuge in this country, there can be no difference between such a stand against the Negro race than there is against the Jews by Hitler," he wrote. One fighter who would not duck Louis was Schmeling. Anytime Louis was ready, said Joe Jacobs, Schmeling would be ready for him.

Now that they were talking about Louis constantly, sportswriters, white and black alike, labored to find the right nickname for him. Many candidates emerged: Dark Destroyer, Tan Tornado, Sepia Slugger, Sepia Sniper, Somnolent Senegambian, African Avenger, Ethiopian Exploder, Bible Belter, Kruel Kolored Klouter (or KKK), Walloping Wolverine, Ebony Enervator, Ebony Eliminator, Sable Slugger, Sable Socker, Brown Blaster, Detroit Dynamiter, Detroit Demolisher, Dark Dempsey, Bronze Buddha, Beige Bonbon, Larruping Leopard, Purple Plague, Deadpanned Dusky David from Detroit, Alabama Assassin, Michigan Mauler, Mocha Manhandler, Cream-Colored Cremator, Almond-Colored Annihilator, Saffron Shellacker, Sepia Sandman of Slaughterland, Tan Tarzan of Thump. But it was a Detroit boxing promoter named Scotty Monteith who won the prize. "The kid can't miss," he said. "He's a bomber. Come to think of it, that boy is a real brown bomber." The name stuck.

In February 1935 Louis made his first trip to California, for a rematch against Lee Ramage. He was greeted by a motorcycle escort, as well as by representatives of the governor of the state and the mayor of Los Angeles. This time, Louis didn't have so much to learn from Ramage, and it was all over in two rounds. The West Coast, too, had now been dazzled. "One of these days several thousand Los Angeles residents will say of Joe Louis, 'I saw him when he was on the way up,'" the *Los Angeles Examiner* wrote afterward. "Women—California women from domestic service and filmland's honor roll—women who are inveterate fight fans—women who yip and howl for blood like a pack of coyotes—women who put their babies to bed early to attend the fight—business women who gave the excuse at sorority meetings or choir practice—women doctors who left O.B. cases to God and the wet nurse—all came and gasped at the apparent tenderness and innocence of Louis's expression," the Associated Negro Press reported. The trip also marked Louis's first exposure to Hollywood; Mae West, Bing Crosby, and Clark Gable were among those who attended the fight. "It should please the fearful modern Vardamans and Tillmans [referring to two notoriously racist southern senators] below the Mason-Dixon line to know that Joe kept the same dead-pan to the bewitching smiles and interested looks of the Nordic girlies who surrounded him on visits to the studios as he keeps when facing an opponent in the ring," the *Chicago Defender* reported. Since the fight was filmed, it afforded many black fans their first glimpse of Louis. "The Colored Comet of Clout Marching Toward the Heavyweight Crown!" declared an ad in the *Norfolk Journal and Guide*.

Louis then set out for San Francisco, where he was to take on Donald "Reds" Barry, a man who claimed to specialize in beating black fighters. In Oakland, a bus carrying a black band led a twenty-five-car welcoming procession, and five hundred fans had to be turned away from the gym where he worked out. Two days before Schmeling knocked out Hamas in Hamburg, Louis knocked out Barry in three brutal rounds. (It would have been two, but Louis had promised a local sportswriter to end it in the third.) The real import of the fight came afterward. Looking to establish a beachhead in big-time boxing, Mike Jacobs of the newly launched Twentieth Century Sporting Club in New York called Louis's dressing room, dangling a fight against Primo Carnera. At long last, Louis was poised for his New York debut. Joe Louis and Mike Jacobs were about to change the business of boxing.

Madison Square Garden, which had controlled boxing in New York since the days of Tex Rickard in the 1920s, had already been angling for Louis. In December 1934 it offered him a fight with James J. Braddock. The money was unlike anything Louis had seen—$10,000, plus 30 percent of the net receipts—but, at least according to fight lore, it would come with asterisks, which Jimmy Johnston, who ran boxing at the Garden, spelled out for Roxborough over the phone. "Well, you understand he's a nigger, and he can't win every time he goes in the ring," Johnston told him. "So am I," replied Roxborough. And he hung up. "He's ready for New York, but New York ain't ready for him," Blackburn later remarked. Given the Garden's monopoly on top matches, that would normally have sealed Louis's fate. But the Garden grew tired of subsidizing Mrs. William Randolph Hearst's pet charity, the "Milk Fund for Babies," which had always skimmed off a percentage of the gate, and wanted to change the arrangement. The Hearst organization promptly decided to promote its own fights, and put Mike Jacobs in charge.

Jacobs—no relation to Joe—had always been selling something. As a boy, it was newspapers and sandwiches around Tammany Hall. Then it was peanuts on the tourist boats plying New York Harbor, as well as weak tea for seasickness. Then it was choice tickets—for baseball, football, the fights, wrestling, Broadway shows, opera. For Jacobs had a great gift: he always knew just how much people would pay. The cash Jacobs amassed helped bankroll the new Madison Square Garden, which opened on Eighth Avenue and Fiftieth Street in November 1925. It was a small step for him to start promoting shows himself.

You could easily confuse "Uncle Mike" and Joe Jacobs, particularly if you weren't Jewish or from New York. Both were in boxing, both grew up poor, both were street-smart and thick-skinned, both were colorful, both wrestled perpetually with their "store teeth." (No article about Mike Jacobs was complete without a reference to them: to the rattling sounds they made, to his irritability whenever they didn't fit right, to the number of pairs he went through.) But unlike Joe, Mike, sixteen years Joe's senior, was gruff, profane, unsentimental, humorless, and cheap. Everyone liked Joe Jacobs, even those who knew he was a scoundrel; every man who walked into Mike Jacobs's office a gentleman, someone once said, walked out calling him names. And Mike, unlike Joe, didn't give a damn about boxing or boxers. For him, the real sport lay in staging a show, outwitting the other guy, putting fannies in seats. People paid so much for his tickets that he rarely set one aside for himself. Jacobs backed few losers, trusted no one, took nothing for granted, stiffed friends and colleagues as well as enemies, attended to the smallest details himself. Fight nights he could often be seen patrolling the stadium, or even hawking tickets.

With Rickard dead, Jacobs was the logical man for Hearst to call. With three powerful figures from the Hearst sports pages—Damon Runyon, Ed

Frayne, and Bill Farnsworth—he formed the Twentieth Century Sporting Club and began looking for boxers. "Overnight, Jacobs will become the most powerful sports promoter in America," Fleischer predicted in May 1935. And Fleischer hadn't factored Joe Louis into the equation. Jacobs told Louis and his team that if they went with him, Louis could make a lot of money without ever having to do anything crooked; to a sport on life-support, he was perfect as is. Had there been any journalistic entity less likely to champion a black boxer than the reactionary *Chicago Tribune*, it would have been the racist Hearst papers. But with Louis promising a fortune in promotion and circulation, prejudice, or at least some of it, could be put aside. Before long, Mike Jacobs controlled boxing in New York, and the New York sportswriters had dubbed his world, "the pugilist-infested stretch" of Forty-ninth Street between Broadway and Eighth Avenue, "Jacobs Beach." And Mike Jacobs effectively controlled Joe Louis, too, even though promoters were not supposed to, collecting half the profits from Louis's fights and reducing his ostensible managers, Roxborough and Black, to figureheads and factotums. "It seems that their duties in the management of Louis are to open the mail that comes to the office, take care of the requests for autographed pictures of Louis, and such other arduous duties, which can be capably filled by a secretary earning a salary of $25.00 weekly," one iconoclastic boxing publication observed.

When Louis stepped off the train from California at Michigan Central Station in Detroit on March 13, 1935, he had the aura of history about him. Five days later, Jacobs announced that Louis had signed for three fights in New York, beginning with Carnera in June. If Louis won all of them, he hoped, he could fight for the championship in September. Jacobs wanted the press to see his new acquisition, but wasn't ready to bring him to New York just yet. So in late March he took twenty New York boxing writers aboard a luxury Pullman car to Detroit to watch Louis face a bruiser named Natie Brown. Other writers arrived from Chicago, Cleveland, Washington, Philadelphia, and Boston. "New York is eager to see him go, and if he has what it takes, he probably will make more money than any Negro who ever tried on a boxing glove," the *Detroit Times* reported. All Detroit pitched in for its favorite son; a local judge handling a legal dispute against Louis and his managers postponed a hearing until after the fight. "I don't want him to have anything on his mind except the other fellow," the judge explained.

Brown was a spoiler: he was hard to hit and harder still to knock down. In fact, the latter had never happened. But within seventy-three seconds of the opening bell, Brown was on the floor. The crowd rose in anticipation of an early finish, but he would not give Louis another clean shot, forcing him to settle for a decision. The Hearst writers could not contain their enthusiasm. "The greatest young heavyweight since the California days of the Manassa Mauler [Dempsey]," Ed Frayne, Jacobs's partner, wrote in the *New York American*. But the other papers were more measured, praising Louis's power but noting his inexperience, his inability to penetrate a tough defense, and his robotic movements. Fleischer urged all heavyweight contenders to take on Louis early, before he got better than he already was. But Bill McCormick of *The Washington Post* said he was good for everyone. "Every time he sweeps an opponent off his feet," he wrote, Louis "helps put boxing back on its feet."

The next day, Louis made the final payment on his mother's new house. No facet of Louis's image was more commented upon than that of the dutiful son, and nothing so contributed to that image as the eight-room home, costing $9,500, at 2100 McDougal Street in the Black Bottom section of Detroit. But while the house was ample, it was not ostentatious, and that was deliberate, too. "Listen, Son," his mother declared in the first of several series of "as told to" stories to appear in American newspapers, "we don't want any great big house away from the people we always lived with. We want a comfortable house, but not a great big showoff house."

Louis was now national news, and stories about him and his family began appearing in glossy magazines. Perhaps the best that can be said about these portraits is that they were well intentioned. In *Collier's*, Quentin Reynolds depicted Lillie Brooks as a kind of Hattie McDaniel, forever singin', cookin', and lovin'ly scoldin' her good-for-nothin' son for carin' about nothin' but eatin', sleepin', and fightin'. Biblical references appeared in these stories as often as did talk of fatback and collard greens. The black press, in turn, faithfully tabulated all the nice things the white press said. The *Defender* toted up the number of newspapers in Texas, Mississippi, Alabama, Florida, and Georgia in which pictures of Louis had appeared, for blacks rarely were shown in their pages. SOLID SOUTH DECIDES JOE LOUIS MUST BE SOMEBODY, it proclaimed. Even the daily papers "along the Unterden Linden Strasse [*sic*] in Berlin," it went on, were asking for Louis photographs.

When Louis met Roy Lazer in Chicago two weeks after the Brown fight, five thousand fans had to be turned away. The fight lasted three rounds, and Louis pocketed $12,000. Never had he seen a check with so many digits; one story had him sitting up all night on the train back to

Detroit, staring at it. Baer had once more been at ringside, and had drawn a laugh by looking anxiously at Louis, then breaking into a trot, as if fleeing the ring. When it was all over, he grinned smugly, though as he gazed into the future, some wondered if his smile was sincere. Between April 22 and May 7, Louis squeezed in easy fights in Dayton, Ohio; Flint, Michigan; Peoria, Illinois; and Kalamazoo, Michigan. More than two thousand people showed up in Dayton for a glimpse of him, and that was all they got; the fight lasted one minute and fifteen seconds. The local boxing writer asked Louis what he would do if Baer knocked him down. "I'd get up," he replied.

On May 13, 1935, on the eve of his first trip to New York, Joe Louis turned twenty-one. One of his sisters gave him a razor for his birthday, though he had not yet begun to shave. Louis spent that afternoon taking neighborhood children for rides in his car. At a local ballroom that night, three thousand people came to see him off and wish him well. Detroit's mayor, Frank Couzens, gave him a set of golf clubs and a letter of introduction to Mayor Fiorello La Guardia of New York. Before Louis departed, a black minister sidled up to him. "All the while you're in training and while you're in the ring, I'll be prayin' for you," he said. "My whole congregation will be prayin' for you."

"And," he whispered, "we'll be bettin' on you, too."

CHAPTER 4

New York Falls in Love

A CARTOON IN THE *NEW YORK POST* on May 16, 1935, neatly captured the mood when Joe Louis made his long-awaited entrance into the big city. It showed a giant Louis standing astride the skyscrapers of midtown Manhattan, the words "18 Kayos in 24 Pro Fights" on his trunks, knocking off the tops of the Empire State and Chrysler buildings with his mighty left. It was titled "Big Brown Bomber Hits Town."

Louis was poised to dominate boxing, but few New Yorkers had seen him throw a punch, or heard him say a word. He was a complete stranger to New York, which only added to his mystique. So when he stepped off the Wolverine and onto the concrete at Grand Central Terminal, the metropolis was ready to embrace him. It had, in fact, been waiting for someone like him for a long time.

"Travelers threading their way through Grand Central early yesterday morning had to carry their own baggage," Caswell Adams wrote in the *Herald Tribune*. "The porters were too busy to bother about making any money. They were gazing at Joe Louis, their idol." Actually, they did more than look—they picked him up and carried him across the threshold. In Harlem, Louis's arrival seemed more like a homecoming than a maiden voyage. The upcoming fight against Carnera was causing more excitement there than anything since the halcyon days of Jack Johnson, declared the *New York Age*, which predicted that many a relief check would end up buying milk for Mrs. Hearst's babies. Sure, the world's championship was up for grabs two weeks before Louis was to fight, with Baer defending his title against Braddock, but as one black reporter put it, the Louis-Carnera battle overshadowed that "like the Empire State Building looms over a Harlem housetop."

Louis was some eyeful that day at Grand Central, resplendent in a gray overcoat, white gloves, tan plaid suit, tan shirt, green tie, gray hat, and creamy tan shoes. Soon, he faced his first New York news conference. Would he take Carnera? Yes. How quickly? Won't take no time. Got a girl? I just hit town. But his reception at the train station was minuscule compared to the luncheon later that day at Mike Jacobs's office on West Forty-ninth Street. Jacobs could have sold a thousand tickets for that show; policemen had to be summoned to clear the traffic. Later, at the Renaissance Grill in Harlem, detectives accompanying Louis had their hands full keeping folks away from him; people clamoring for a pencil he'd dropped nearly caused a riot. Soon, they could see him at the Harlem Opera House, where the "New Knockout Sensation" was booked for a weeklong engagement. Louis's show, which played to capacity crowds, consisted of a two-round sparring match, skipping rope, and punching the bag.

Louis appeared on Al Jolson's radio program and was Jack Dempsey's guest at Madison Square Garden. He met Mayor La Guardia. Then he gave his first real exhibition, at the Pioneer Gym on West Forty-fourth Street. Unable to afford the one-dollar admission, many fans from Harlem hung around outside; shortly before things got under way the price was halved, precipitating a stampede. A host of boxing old-timers showed up, including Tom O'Rourke, the fight manager who went back to bare-knuckle days. Louis impressed them all with his footwork, counterpunching, and speed. "I've seen punches thrown this afternoon that I haven't seen for years," one veteran said. Louis and Blackburn also went to see Arthur Brisbane, the Hearst columnist and editor of the *New York Mirror*, who took an interest in boxing and racial matters. Brisbane wished Louis well, but reminded him that as a black fighter, he had two strikes against him. "We're gonna have a lot of fun with that third strike," Blackburn told Louis afterward.

Writers studying Louis were sizing up more than his punches. They saw him as a kind of specimen. Some, who bemoaned how the scrappy street urchins who had once dominated boxing had been replaced by synthetic types bred in gymnasiums and settlement houses, saw him as a throwback, a fighter who really liked to fight, even though he still hadn't hit anyone as hard as he could. "I ain't ever had to yet," he explained. To others, he harkened back to a far more distant era. The *Evening Journal* called him "a throwback to the primeval savage." The *Sun* scrutinized his face: "There never was such a dead pan. The eyes never light, not even when he smiles. That smile, too, is queer — just the drawing of the lips into a thin line. Never a change of thought, nor an impulse is reflected in those tawny orbs. Dead eyes; dead from freezing."

Jack Johnson's big fights had invariably been in remote places like Reno, Nevada, and Havana; not one had been in New York. The Louis-Carnera "mill" (to use one of Fleischer's favorite words) would be the first noteworthy mixed bout in the city in nearly a decade. But the *Herald Tribune* predicted there'd be none of the racial hysteria that had stalked Johnson. Louis wasn't addicted to any of Johnson's "gaudy extravagances," it noted, and the sporting fraternity no longer attached such importance to a prizefight. Besides, Carnera was hardly a hero to most serious fight fans. In fact, for most of his career, he was an object of ridicule and disgust. "This unfortunate pituitary case," Gallico called him. "Freak" was the word most often used to describe the six-foot-seven-inch, 260-pound Italian, who'd been rescued from a circus. Many of his fights were presumed to be fixed, with Carnera getting only a negligible piece of the profits. Carnera was pathetic, but he was also courageous — "game," to use the preferred term of the day. As long as he was champion, he'd been the darling of the Italian Fascists, the closest thing Mussolini had to a Schmeling. In fact, Schmeling was really Hitler's Carnera, for the Fascists had embraced professional boxing before the Nazis had, having boasted in 1933 that a "Blackshirt" had become heavyweight champion.

To Harlem, if to few other American locales in 1935, Mussolini seemed a far more immediate enemy than Hitler. His dagger was aimed at Ethiopia, one of the few African nations actually run by blacks and a source of enormous religious, historical, and political pride among African Americans. In his nationally syndicated column, which appeared locally in the *New York World-Telegram*, Westbrook Pegler warned of pitting an Italian against a black man in a part of New York in which blacks and Italians lived in such close proximity, calling it "the stupidest move in the history of a dumb, rapscallion industry"; only a few weeks earlier, he noted, Harlem had seen riots in which three people died. Making things more combustible, Carnera was controlled by an Italian mob and Louis was, at least ostensibly, controlled by a black mob. Dan Parker thought such warnings preposterous, but the fears resonated; *Variety* reported that with "the race angle intruding," no film of the fight would be made, supposedly on orders from Washington. (Bootleg copies were in fact produced, and circulated widely.)

Pegler's fears infuriated the head of the NAACP, Walter White. White had been monitoring Louis closely and admiringly, viewing him as a rare black success story and as someone who could help break down racial barriers; he'd been assured that Louis's brass were "strong race people" who wanted to build up the black community and would not tolerate mistreatment or segregation. Several prior mixed bouts had been held without any problems, White pointed out to the *World-Telegram*, including fights between blacks and Jews at the Polo Grounds, near the border of Harlem and the Jewish Bronx. "One wonders where Pegler has been keeping himself," he wrote. The black press was also livid, charging that if race riots did ensue, people like Pegler would be to blame. Klansmen and professional southerners still fighting the Civil War were invariably behind such disturbances, said the *New York Age*; why would the black man start anything, when he knew the odds were always stacked against him? Already, Louis's success appeared to have emboldened the black press. The *Age* complained that while Hearst's *Evening Journal* routinely and offensively quoted Louis and his sparring partners in Negro dialect, it turned Carnera's mangled diction into polished English.

Louis set up his training camp in Pompton Lakes, New Jersey, thirty miles northwest of Manhattan. The site was a health spa, complete with a colonial house dating back to George Washington, run by one Dr. Joseph Bier. A potential black invasion of a largely white small town had initially generated some local opposition. But Bier ignored the complaints, and the town quickly reconciled itself to a windfall. Ever attentive to white sensibilities, Louis staged a four-round exhibition to buy the town an ambulance. "I'd be a mean sucker if I didn't get behind that movement, in a town as nice as this," he told the local paper. He also met members of the press, "who could see there was nothing of the show-off, comedy coon here," wrote his first biographer, Edward Van Every of the *Sun*. Blackburn, meantime, hunted for giant sparring partners, just to get Louis in the habit of looking and punching up. One fled the camp after only a very short stint. "Mistah, I'se leavin' while I kin still count ten," he said. Harlem's fight fans arrived in high spirits and fancy duds. Some just wanted to see, and worship, Louis himself. "What a spectacle," a woman wrote in the *New York Age*. "A healthy dark beige youth, lovely to look at. Not a blemish on his saffron-hued skin." The Louis seen by white and black reporters often seemed like two different characters.

Louis had his skeptics, who said he had yet to face anyone worthy. "Can he take it?" was the question they invariably asked. No critic was as insistent as Jack Johnson. To him, Louis was a slow, plodding counterpuncher; he didn't stand correctly, threw his punches off-balance, couldn't shoot a straight right. Blackburn had not taught Louis the fundamentals, Johnson said; Louis would not get by Carnera, and if he did, Baer would beat him in a few rounds. Of course, Johnson came to the topic with baggage; it could not have been pleasant to see himself derided constantly as Louis's tarnished foil. And Louis was challenging two of Johnson's most impressive credentials: the greatest black heavyweight ever, and the only black heavyweight champion. In addition, there was bad blood between Johnson and Blackburn. (The explanations for it varied: Blackburn, who fought or sparred with Johnson several times, was said to have humiliated him in the ring once before some of his girlfriends, or bloodied his nose once in a Philadelphia gym. Or Johnson had refused to run a benefit for Blackburn when he got out of prison. More recently, Johnson had supposedly tried to muscle Blackburn aside and train Louis himself. And Blackburn had grown increasingly willing to compare the two, and to say that Louis would have whipped him, sure.) Black America remained proud of Johnson and, to some degree, still admired him for thumbing his nose at the white establishment. But its goodwill waned once he took on Louis. Black commentators reminded their readers how Johnson's misbehavior had set back black causes, and accused him of disloyalty, treachery, and jealousy. "Louis may not be as perfect a fighter as Johnson was and may never be," wrote one. "But . . . Louis is making amends for the mistakes which Johnson made and is breaking down the barriers raised largely because of Johnson. . . . In the wake of Jack Johnson, our fighters lost all hope. In the wake of Joe Louis, our fighters seen [sic] another era."

Two weeks before Louis fought Carnera, Baer was to defend his crown against Braddock in Long Island City. The twenty-nine-year-old Braddock was a tough, resilient journeyman who'd won and lost with a broken rib, a broken shoulder, a torn ligament, and an empty stomach. Once, too poor to reset a broken hand that was mending improperly, he rebroke it over someone else's skull. The father of three young children, he'd quit boxing for a time and had been working as a longshoreman when his career was resuscitated with an unexpected victory over a veteran boxer named Corn Griffin. Braddock was soon back on relief. But then he won several important fights and became the top contender for Baer's title. His story perfectly suited Depression America, and his longtime manager, Joe Gould, milked it shamelessly: *Relief to Royalty* was the title of Braddock's authorized biography. Baer thought the match a joke, but Braddock, a ten-to-one underdog, won a decision. The "Cinderella Man," Damon Runyon dubbed him, and the name stuck. The fight itself was a dreary affair. "Did you ever see a worse heavyweight championship fight?" one expert at ringside asked another when it was over. "Did you ever see a worse heavy-weight champion?" the second man countered. Asked later how long Braddock would hold the title, Baer replied, "Until he fights somebody else." Louis, who was sitting near ringside, started yawning in the third round, took a nap between the fifth and ninth rounds, and watched the end with a broad grin. "Do you mean those are the two best fighters in the world?" he asked Roxborough. "Shucks, I could lick 'em both in the same ring."

Now Schmeling and the German promoters would no longer have to worry about fighting, or hosting, a "Jew." But the black press quickly conjured up intricate racial explanations for why Baer might have thrown the fight, and why the outcome was bad for black America. The case wasn't hard to make: Braddock was controlled by Madison Square Garden, which had been hostile to blacks. Worse, he held the title by a thread, and would be unlikely to risk it anytime soon, especially to someone so certain to take it away. Black skeptics predicted that the Garden would want Braddock to fight Schmeling or Baer again first, and not for at least a year. This way, Louis could beat both Carnera and Baer and still not get a shot at the championship until perhaps 1937. Then there was Hitler, who might not let Schmeling meet Louis. But before his fans could ponder their grievances, Louis had to get by Carnera. Some thought that a short puncher like Louis would have a hard time reaching Carnera—that was why Schmeling had consistently refused to fight him. "Next Tuesday night the most historic event in Negro boxing takes place," wrote Ed Harris of the *Philadelphia Tribune*. White writers, too, recognized the enormous stakes. Should Louis win impressively, Joe Williams wrote, "he will have definitely qualified as the foremost American challenger, and the pure Nordics will have to take him and like him."

In what was to become a tradition before every Joe Louis fight there, black fans from most major cities east of the Mississippi made their way to New York. By one estimate, three thousand people were coming from Detroit, many in a multicar caravan, with the flimsiest ones leaving first so that more sturdy vehicles could pick up anyone stranded en route. "See the Next World's Heavyweight Champion Whip Carnera," declared an ad in the black-owned *Detroit Tribune*, offering a package that included a train ticket, a fight ticket, and beer. One Detroiter even came by bicycle, setting a new cross-country record in the process. Harlem's hotels quickly filled, and auxiliary housing, like the banquet room at the 135th Street YMCA, was hastily arranged. Harlem's nightclubs—Small's Paradise, the

Cotton Club, the 1-0-1 Club, Brittwood, Club Ubangi—reported "skyrocketing grosses"; white fancies from Fifth and Park avenues who'd steered clear of Harlem after the recent riots had returned. A millinery shop on Seventh Avenue sold out all its straw hats. People trawled for bets, though there was little Carnera money; Louis was the favorite, seven to five. Were Louis to lose, the *Baltimore Afro-American* wrote, Harlem would be eating hot dogs for weeks. Pictures of Louis adorned "every ham-hock, fish-fry, and liquor joint" in Harlem. Anyone who had seen Louis fight or visited his camp was treated like an oracle. The *New York Age* and *Chicago Defender* planned fight extras. White interest was equally intense. The *Mirror* said Louis had as many white fans as Carnera did. Special trains would come from Chicago, Detroit, Pittsburgh, Philadelphia, St. Louis, Indianapolis, Boston, Buffalo, Toledo, New Haven, and Cleveland. On the eve of the fight, Mike Jacobs kept his ticket offices open until midnight. Fearing race riots, a Newark paper urged that the fight be canceled. The New York Police Department assigned 1,300 officers to the fight, including emergency squads with hand grenades and tear gas.

Twenty-five New York policemen on motorcycles met Louis when he crossed into Manhattan on the morning of the bout. He came with a fatherly admonition from Governor Frank Fitzgerald of Michigan, who clearly had Jack Johnson on his mind. "Your race . . . has been misrepresented by others who thought they had reached the heights," he said. "You may soon have on your strong hands the job of representative-at-large of your people. Do that job well, Joe. Michigan will be proud of you." On the radio, Fleischer predicted that Louis would win in seven rounds, but Joe Williams was among the skeptics. Go over the list of Louis's victims, he said, and "you come across a lot of guys named Elmer." Jack Johnson, too, had stuck to his guns: Carnera was bigger, stronger, and had a longer reach and more experience. "I don't want him to beat him, but that's the way it looks to me," he said. To some degree, feelings fell along regional lines: New York was filled with doubting Thomases; not so Chicago and Detroit, where people had seen firsthand what Louis could do.

The crowd of sixty-four thousand at Yankee Stadium on the night of June 25 was nearly twice as large as the house for the Baer-Braddock fight had been, and the fourth-largest ever for a boxing match there, helping to produce the second largest gate ever for a nontitle bout, exceeded only by the Dempsey-Sharkey fight eight years earlier. Along with the cream of New York—"and a great deal of the skimmed milk"—were an estimated fifteen thousand blacks, dispelling the canard that they did not come to sporting events. Most sat in the bleachers, though Mike Jacobs took pains to keep too many of them from concentrating in too small a spot. Far from menacing anyone, the black fans were filled with high spirits and expectations. Whites with ringside seats came fashionably late. Among those spotted that night were Mayor La Guardia, Irving Berlin, Darryl Zanuck, Loretta Young, J. Edgar Hoover, and Babe Ruth. (Eleanor Roosevelt bought three tickets, but gave them away.) A thin, lanky young man, coatless and hatless, came down the aisle, looking forlornly for an usher; it was Howard Hughes. There were also representatives of the black bourgeoisie: Walter White of the NAACP, the Rev. Adam Clayton Powell, Jr., Duke Ellington, Ralph Bunche.

As the sun set, the outlines of hundreds of people clustered atop buildings overlooking Yankee Stadium could be seen. For a few fleeting moments, passengers on the Lexington Avenue subway pulling into the 161st Street station got a glimpse of the field, and inevitably some fight fan would yank the emergency cord to prolong the stay. There were more than four hundred press reservations, exceeding any fight since the second Dempsey-Tunney contest eight years earlier. For the first time, at least one reporter from a black weekly—Al Monroe of the *Chicago Defender*—got to sit with Runyon, Gallico, Walter Winchell, and other press luminaries. Even before he'd thrown his first official punch in New York, then, Joe Louis had already knocked down a barrier.

At around 9:55, Louis entered the ring. The vast crowd rose as one, greeting him with a roar. Louis himself was impassive, "as if he were waiting for a street car," someone wrote. His demeanor was in complete contrast to Jack Johnson's—proving, Heywood Broun maintained, the fatuousness of all racial generalizations. Louis paid little heed when Carnera climbed through the ropes, or when Braddock, Baer, Dempsey, and Tunney followed and took their bows. But when a black man in a tan suit entered, his bald head gleaming like a bowling ball (to one observer), Louis stared intently at him. It was Jack Johnson, who may have gotten a bigger ovation than anyone, and who heartily shook the hand to which his torch might soon be passed.

Louis's debut was not the only one on the program that night. A short man in evening clothes named Harry Balogh was making his first appearance as ring announcer at a top heavyweight fight, and in a fashion that would quickly turn him, along with his stentorian diction, neologisms, and malapropisms, into another of boxing's great characters, as integral a part of the local ring ritual as the timekeepers and the cut men.

Balogh, too, was mindful that history was being made at Yankee Stadium tonight.

"Ladies and gentlemen, before proceeding with this most important heavyweight contest," he bellowed with exaggerated elocution and thespian formality, "I wish to take this opportunity of calling upon you in the name of American sportsmanship—a spirit so fine that it has made you, the American sporting public, world famous. I therefore ask that the thought in your mind and the feeling in your heart be that, regardless of race, creed, or color, may the better man emerge victorious! Thank you." Some thought his oration long-winded and unnecessary, but one black paper said it "did more good than the army of blue coats, plainclothesmen, and 'G' men saturating the place." In any case, it met with wild applause. Balogh then got around to introducing the fighters. "Oh, my goodness," a woman in the crowd declared. "Louis looks like a little boy beside him."

But when the bell rang, Louis suddenly matured, or, as Frank Graham wrote, was "transformed into a sleek and tawny animal." Blackburn had instructed him to work first on Carnera's belly; the Italian's hands would then drop, and Louis could go for his head. He'd also told Louis to go slowly—to study the big guy for a round, hitting him once or twice just for luck. But Louis quickly tore a hole in Carnera's upper lip, giving the Italian a grotesque, horrific look—"a red smile that didn't make sense," as one sportswriter put it. Carnera was too slow and stolid to defend himself. The carnage spilled over into the second and third rounds. Before the fourth, Blackburn told Louis to "ready that guy for the big splash," and by the end of the fifth, he was patting Louis's behind. "You have this boy right where you want him, so let's get it over with," he said. "You just drop old Betsy on that fellow's chin, and we will start the parade for home."

Louis went after Carnera mercilessly. A right cross sent him to the canvas for the first time, and quickly, there was a second time, and then a third. By now, blood was streaming from the Italian's mouth, and cries of "Stop it!" rose throughout the stadium. As Louis reached back for his knockout blow, the writers reached for their metaphors. He measured Carnera as a tailor measured a bolt of wool, or as a tree surgeon surveyed a doomed oak. Gallico likened it all to a bullfight, with Carnera "heavy, menacing, brutish, dumb," playing the bull, and Louis playing "every part, the cap man, the baderillos, the picador, and finally the matador." It was terrible. It was also thrilling.

Finally, at two minutes and thirty-two seconds in the sixth round, the referee, Arthur Donovan, ended the bloodletting. The crowd rose to its feet, exhilarated by what it had just seen, which was just what many in it had come to see. Louis went to his corner, still expressionless, as his seconds slapped his shoulders. He stayed that way until his arm was held aloft, when he offered the photographers a fleeting and unpersuasive smile. He left the ring without a mark on his face, and $60,000 richer. He spotted the Detroit sportswriter to whom he'd made a promise to knock out Carnera in the fifth, and apologized. Jack Johnson entered excitedly. "Boy!" he cried as he grabbed Louis's hand. "You're the greatest fighter in the last twenty-five years. You're going to be another Lil' Arthur." "Say, Jack, that Joe Louis is a second Jack Dempsey, isn't he?" someone asked Dempsey himself. "Why not a first Joe Louis?" Dempsey replied.

Without radio, keeping fans abreast of things took ingenuity. The *Defender* set up an elaborate relay system: Al Monroe described the action to a telegrapher, who transmitted his account to Western Union in Chicago, which called it into the *Defender's* offices, where it was read to the crowd of ten thousand people amassed outside, then to another gathering at a local theater, then to a third assembly in Evanston, Illinois. In the meantime, the copy flowed into the *Defender's* Linotype machines. Within twenty minutes of the knockout, newsboys were hawking copies of a special fight edition on the streets of Chicago's South Side. It marked only the second extra in the *Defender's* history; the first had been for the death of Booker T. Washington. In Detroit, there were public readings of the telegraph wire. (Hearts stopped until people realized that Louis had feinted rather than fainted.) The *Detroit News* reported "impromptu insanity" of "gargantuan proportions" on the city's streets. "Bootblacks blacked brown shoes and browned black ones. Nothing mattered," the *Detroit Times* wrote. A black policeman said he'd seen nothing like it since Johnson had beaten Jeffries twenty-five years earlier, but that this crowd was bigger and better-natured. "They're happier over Louis," he said. "They like him better."

Someone calculated that more lines of type were set and more pictures published about the fight than for any other sporting event in a decade. Older sportswriters saw in Louis skills existing only in distant, gauzy memory; younger ones had seen the sort of boxing they had only heard about. Now they, too, would have stories to pass on. Louis had won no title, but that was a mere formality; all he needed was a chance. "The ring has a new marvel and the boxing writers are a bit shamefaced because they had referred to him merely as sensational, spectacular, and phenomenal," Parker wrote. The fight had come off without a hitch or a hint of racial discord. "As orderly an assemblage as ever gathered for a snooty tennis match," Louis Sobol of the *Evening Journal* called it. Some thought that whites had cheered Louis even more loudly than the blacks. The black press could say "I told you so"—and did. Sam Lacy of the *Washington Tribune* described whites and blacks leaving Yankee Stadium "all but arm-in-arm." If so many black Christians had shown up at a white church, he surmised, there would have been a riot, leading him to conclude that sports fans emulated Jesus more faithfully than churchgoers did.

It was, someone wrote, Harlem's "first chance in ten years to let out a loud yell." So jammed were the streets that a bus ride from 125th Street to 155th Street took an hour. Revelers flush with winnings lindy-hopped along Seventh Avenue, while one old woman walked up and down clapping her hands and singing "Go Down, Moses." The few trees became roosts for young boys and girls. On St. Nicholas Avenue and 150th Street, a drunk proclaimed, "Look-a-here, folks, you is now on Joe Louis Avenue!" Vendors shouted, "Eat Joe Louis peanuts and get strong!" People struggled to no avail to name some precedent—Jack Johnson's entry into New York after knocking out Jeffries in 1910, or the celebrations of Marcus Garvey, or the religious revivals of Father Divine—to which to compare the joy on the streets. It was Harlem's biggest moment since it had become the capital of the Negro world, the *Pittsburgh Courier* declared.

To great fanfare a few months earlier, Dempsey had opened a new restaurant on the fringes of Jacobs Beach, across from Madison Square Garden, a masculine, "gaudily meatish" place that came to embody the glamour of professional boxing. Now Dempsey offered to pay Louis to come by after the fight. Instead, Louis agreed to appear at the Savoy Ballroom at 140th Street and Lenox Avenue, where Chick Webb and Fletcher Henderson were supplying the music. Twenty thousand people showed up, jamming the blocks from 139th to 147th streets. The crowd ultimately stormed the entrance, sending glass flying. One menaced white reporter from Chicago asked a policeman whether to flee. "You are as safe as at 42nd and Broadway," the officer replied. "There will be no trouble tonight. These people are too happy."

Following the fight, Louis first returned to his temporary quarters on West 153rd Street, wanting only to sleep. "I'm tired of this handshakin' business anyway," he said. Roxborough also wanted to stay put, fearing that Louis's fans would tear him apart. Only around three a.m. did they go out, after the police had determined that the crowds were manageable. As Louis entered the heart of Harlem, "all the noise that had preceded his advent became as a mere rattle of dried peas in a gourd." Wearing a cinnamon-colored suit and a green necktie, he was soon in the spotlight at the Savoy. He stood silently, unsmilingly, as if the crowd were looking at someone else. Handed a portable microphone, he held it for a moment, then gave it back, forcing a columnist for the *Amsterdam News*, Romeo Dougherty, to pinch-hit for him. "Joe Louis is a fighter, not a talker," Dougherty said. "But he wants to thank you for this reception. He wants to tell you he'll try to bring you the world's heavyweight title." And then Louis left—without uttering a single word. At a press conference the following afternoon, he hardly said more, offering only what John Lardner called "a sort of lame-duck, Mexican currency smile."

A black professor at Atlanta University expressed fears that Mussolini would regard Louis's victory as an insult to the Italian flag and use it as an excuse to annihilate Ethiopia. To the white press, though, its significance was more anthropological. "The American Negro is a natural athlete," the *New York Sun* wrote. "The generations of toil in the cotton fields have not obliterated the strength and grace of the African native." To the *Mirror*, Louis's background actually diminished his achievement. "In Africa there are tens of thousands of powerful, young savages, that with a little teaching, could annihilate Mr. Joe Louis," it said.

Louis was now the champion-in-waiting. Everyone was talking about him. When Damon Runyon interviewed Alf Landon about politics, the soon-to-be Republican presidential nominee interviewed Damon Runyon about Joe Louis. Some of boxing's more thoughtful observers began working to assure that nothing be thrown in his path. Louis, wrote Richards Vidmer of the *Herald Tribune*, was the answer to boxing's prayers, someone who would electrify, cleanse, and elevate a sleepy, soiled sport. To compare him with Jack Johnson, he said, was "like comparing Lou Gehrig with Al Capone."

But along with sympathetic portrayals, the starker stereotypes persisted. To the Hearst reporters, Louis was a kind of King Kong—an exotic creature, temporarily domesticated, available for public inspection. "You see him awake in bed," went one description. "He lies there without moving. Photographers surround him, but he doesn't even glance at them. Here you get a keener glimpse of the man—a tanned-skin throw-back to the creature of primitive swamps who gloried in battle and blood. . . . He never says a word. He is like a wild thing tethered by civilization—a wild

thing that somehow doesn't belong to civilization." Even "friendly" stories
could be painful. Louis was simply "a healthy Negro boy with the usual
streak of laziness," one writer said.

Louis's mother attended the fight, and afterward dished up a whole
new set of biblical allusions, this time focusing on all the Delilahs and
Jezebels in Harlem who were out to sap Joe's strength. But for all the self-
abasement, she also tried to shame America into treating her son properly.
She knew he'd get his title shot, she said; white folks had always done right
by her, because she'd always done right by them. And she'd taught Joe to
do the same.

Boxing's color line, unlike baseball's, had never been officially en-
forced. The sport was not so organized; it had no Kenesaw Mountain Landis to preserve its prejudices. Rarely was the subject discussed in concrete
terms, and even more rarely was it defended. The British press, perhaps
less intent upon appearing enlightened, confronted things more explicitly. To *Boxing*, the raucous celebrations following the Carnera fight fore-
shadowed what might happen should a black man ever capture the
crown. The *Sunday Pictorial* offered a Solomonic solution: a separate
"colored champion of the world."

In the United States, *Collyer's Eye* claimed it had learned from a
"highly authoritative source" that a title shot for Louis had been ruled out
at "a secret New York conclave," both because he was black and, more
critically, because his black management had refused "to cut in the fixers
and politicians." That the tip sheet, flying in the face of all evidence, regularly decried Louis as the ruination of boxing should have made anything
it said suspect. But given the sport's dicey tradition and America's racism,
the idea of such a decree, a "Protocol of the Elders of Fistiana," was not so
far-fetched, and the report prompted Walter White of the NAACP to
voice his concerns to both the New York State Athletic Commission and
New York governor Herbert Lehman; Roxborough and Black assured
White that no such fix was in. Respected newsmen like Bill Cunningham
of the *Boston Post* confronted the issue head on. "Louis deserves the right
to go as far as he can," he wrote. "If he's stopped, here's hoping that it happens cleanly in battle and not in the dingy offices of a lot of avaricious
buzzards." In the end, two mighty sins, prejudice and greed, had to square
off before Louis and Braddock ever could, and this was even more of a
mismatch than Louis and Carnera. The *Chicago Tribune* had it about
right: Louis was supplying "vitamins C, A, S and H" to an undernour-
ished sport. To Braddock, money would surely trump all other considera-

tions, and neither Baer nor Schmeling was exactly indifferent to it either. "Max isn't interested in the title," Joe Jacobs said of his client. "It's money he wants and he can get more—much more—for fighting Louis than Braddock. Why, the bout will draw more than $750,000, and we'd be suckers not to fight for that kind of a gate."

The *Daily Worker*, which had begun covering sports largely to champion Louis, somehow saw racists and capitalists alike conspiring to block the black man. "If the *Daily Worker* really wanted to help an oppressed race, it might have warned Negroes not to be swept off their feet by the result of a prizefight," countered the *Amsterdam News*. Other black papers agreed that the achievements of a W. E. B. DuBois or a victory in the Scottsboro case or a federal antilynching law mattered much more than any boxing match, and that for blacks to go overboard on Louis suited the white man just fine. But to more of them, there was nothing hyperbolic about the hoopla. "Each victory of Louis will be in effect as good as electing a Congressman," Dan Burley wrote in the Associated Negro Press. And if Louis got a title shot, it would be like getting "a colored vice-president." In the *Baltimore Afro-American*, Ralph Matthews puzzled over white caprice—that while one section of the country lynched a black man for sassing whites, in another section they would cheer him on.

Suddenly, everyone wanted to give Louis advice. Bill Corum of the *New York Evening Journal* offered the cautionary tale of Kid Chocolate, the Afro-Cuban featherweight who'd been the King of Lenox Avenue until succumbing to loud clothes, bottles of gin, "hot cha brown-skin girls," and "the heat of the Harlem moon." "If [Louis] lets things inside of bottles STAY INSIDE OF BOTTLES, and for his business affairs secures the protection of an intelligent, honest lawyer instead of some racketeer, he may not die poor after a few years of leaning against a Harlem bar telling how great he used to be," observed Arthur Brisbane, who predicted that it would take "two or three good fairy godmothers from the upper reaches of the magic Nile to take him safely through what lies ahead of him." Black columnists warned of a different danger. "The white world of sports and the world at large will not deny or envy you any fortune, however large, if you spend it upon a Negro woman," one cautioned. "But if you would lavish it upon some low-caste white woman the white world will rise in wrath and so would the Negro world."

One of black boxing's greatest figures, Sam Langford, was by then nearly blind, but as he walked along Lenox Avenue the day after the

Carnera fight, even he could feel something in the air. "Harlem's got some money today," he laughed. Louis left for Atlantic City. Though the trip was ostensibly secret, five thousand fans awaited him there. They stormed the store where he was buying shoes, forcing him to try on a pair in his car. That night, one thousand young boys staged a tin-can torch-light parade in his honor. Then he left for Detroit, thwarting plans to throw a triumphant welcome for him by sneaking into town.

THE MORNING AFTER LOUIS STOPPED CARNERA, Schmeling and Machon sat down for breakfast at Schmeling's training camp near Berlin. In two weeks he would fight Paolino Uzcudun. But as Schmeling read about the New York fight in the newspaper, he lost his appetite. At some point he would have to confront this Louis. So would Nazi Germany.

In German athletics as in Germany generally, blacks had always been scarce, more objects of curiosity than of disparagement or discrimination. Their very novelty had often made them, quite literally, a form of public entertainment—as actors, circus performers, athletes. Before Hitler gained power, *Box-Sport* wrote about black boxers only rarely and benignly. But the Nazis had always been contemptuous of blacks, in and out of athletics. In *Mein Kampf*, Hitler had dismissed the civil rights movement as part of a Jewish conspiracy. In his first public speech in Berlin in 1928, he lamented that German culture and music had been "negrified." To him, the Negro and the Jew were in cahoots to destroy Aryan values.

Such sentiments spilled over into sports. In November 1930, the *Angriff* bemoaned how the black American boxer George Godfrey had been booked for fights in Paris and London. At least the Americans, "out of a healthy spirit," had rejected the black man, it said. The approving reference to Jim Crow America was not unusual. "In every Negro, even in one of the kindest disposition, is the latent brute and primitive man who can be tamed neither by centuries of slavery nor by an external varnish of civilization," the *Nationalsozialistische Monatshefte* declared. The Nazi press had kind words for lynching, for *The Birth of a Nation*, for the Ku Klux Klan. To Hitler and his followers, the wrong side had won the Civil War; *Gone With the Wind* was to become one of the Führer's favorite movies. When the Nazis pushed for separate compartments for Jews on German trains, they cited the American South as precedent.

After the Nazis assumed power, racial purity became national policy. Blacks lost their jobs. Africans from former German colonies had their identity papers taken away and replaced with "alien" passports. "Negroes don't have anything to grin about in National Socialist Germany," was how a Nazi teacher reprimanded a schoolboy named Hans Massaquoi, the son of an African man and a German woman. Jazz—called "jungle music" or "Niggerjazz"—was banned. Underlying the contempt was the usual empirical data and "scientific" theory that led to the sterilization of the five hundred to seven hundred offspring of the French-African troops who occupied Germany after World War I and their German mothers— the so-called Rhineland Bastards. As a German paper put it, one mustn't let their cuteness now deter the important task of keeping German blood pure.

Obsessed with racial matters as they were, the Nazis paid close attention to race relations in the United States, and two themes dominated commentary on it. The first, sparked no doubt by feelings of inferiority and competitiveness, ridiculed how, in what they disdainfully called "the world's freest country," blacks were discriminated against in every conceivable manner, no matter if the white man were a sewer worker and the black man the heavyweight champion of the world. What rankled the Nazis wasn't the unfairness, however, but the hypocrisy: how America sanctimoniously lectured the rest of the world about tolerance, when it was so deeply discriminatory itself.

Indeed, the second theme was praise for raw, unvarnished American racial prejudice, however it was expressed. Nazi Germany and the United States were really brothers under the skin, this theory went, with Germany steadfastly upholding doctrines that America secretly shared but from which subversives—invariably Jews and Communists—had led it astray. America should just come clean and embrace its racist tendencies, the Nazis urged, for given the natural inferiority of blacks, these tendencies were biologically ordained and historically just. "This law is not inhumane," a 1933 report from a German correspondent in the United States explained. "It's a necessity for America, because otherwise the American race would become a mixed race. The Negro here will always remain a second-class human being. He might be allowed to serve the white man, but he'll never be allowed to become a real American." This principle, rather than coarse stereotyping, provided the lens through which the Nazi press initially viewed Joe Louis. It acknowledged his talent—*Box-Sport* called him "uniquely and colossally dangerous"—and even credited him with a certain dignity; while blacks were ecstatic when Louis won, it noted, Louis himself remained cool and reserved. But Louis—Nazi journals routinely referred to him as the "*Lehmgesicht*," meaning "clay face" or "loam face"—should certainly never be champion and would become so only if America sacrificed its racial principles for its own ego, just as it had by allowing blacks onto its Olympic team in 1932.

Box-Sport quickly bought into the new racial order. In a November 1933 article about the "ever-grinning and sneering" Jack Johnson, it called the black man "a cross between a clown and a beast." Boxing had even more reason to exclude blacks, it said; their physical advantages made every fight unfair. The black man "senses every danger with the primeval instinct of a wild animal," the article stated. "In his movements he is lithe and sure, like a panther. He is wildly uncontrolled on the attack and tremendously hard against blows to the skull, in fact, he is only really vulnerable in one place: on the shin bone (In America every boy knows that a nigger can only be felled by a sharp, downward kick against the shin bone)." Unsurprisingly, after January 1933 fewer black boxers found their way into German rings. The experience of a black wrestler named Jim Wango in Nuremberg in early 1935 may help explain why.*

But Nazi ideology did not capture all the nuances in German racial thinking, nor did it stifle the more innocuous, almost affectionate feelings many Germans had for blacks. W. E. B. DuBois spent five months in Germany in 1936 and later wrote that he was treated with the kind of courtesy and consideration he had never received in America; his greatest indignity there was having people stare at him. Other American black visitors returned from Nazi Germany even more enthusiastic. One noted that blacks were still welcomed at German universities. "Other things being equal, I had rather live in the Rhineland than in Florida or Alabama," one wrote. On the other hand, when Paul Robeson passed through Berlin in 1934, he felt menaced by uniformed men "with hatred in their eyes." Marian Anderson was discouraged from performing there, while the saxophonist Coleman Hawkins was banned outright.

Before any racial matters had to be finally decided, Schmeling faced his encounter with Uzcudun on July 7. It would be Schmeling's first fight

---

*Wango was a typical black athlete of that time and place, playing the savage for laughs. But audiences loved him, and he became the prime attraction during a tournament there. According to the rabidly Nazi *Westdeutscher Beobachter*, however, some spectators objected to watching a black man, whose slippery skin gave him an unfair advantage, humiliating white opponents. Worse, German women were cheering him on. Julius Streicher, the local Nazi leader and editor of the Jew-hating *Stürmer*, called a halt to this degraded spectacle and banished Wango. The Nazi papers said no more about him, but according to the French magazine *Journal*, he left Nuremberg for Berlin, where he died suddenly and mysteriously.

in Berlin in seven years, and there were reports that Hitler would be there, the first time he would see Schmeling box. Schmeling had to dazzle to show he could still draw crowds in the States. "The Americans again have all the trump cards," the *Völkischer Beobachter* lamented, pointing to a popular world champion and a challenger who, though he had black skin, packed a knockout punch in both hands.

The Führer, alas, was not among the thirty-five thousand fans who showed up for the fight, a disappointing gate for what turned out to be a disappointing bout. Uzcudun went into his usual shell, giving his opponent few clean shots at him, and Schmeling remained his frustratingly plodding self. He won a decision after what William L. Shirer called "twelve slow and thrill-less rounds."* Still, Schmeling remained in demand in the United States. Mike Jacobs wanted him to fight Louis in September, and Madison Square Garden wanted him to fight Baer around the same time. Both sides thought they had deals. Somewhere in the middle was Joe Jacobs. He favored Louis because it would be far more lucrative; he'd gone to the Uzcudun fight to convince Schmeling to take him on. Jacobs also needed Schmeling to renew his contract with him, which was about to expire.

But the boxing press doubted whether Schmeling was listening to Jacobs, or if he'd re-up with him. There were reports that Schmeling wouldn't even see Jacobs while he was in Europe, and that Yussel had had to cable someone in the United States for enough cash to get home. "One word from Joe," Bill Corum quipped, "and Max does as he pleases." Here was Germany trying to drive its Jews out, Dan Parker noted, and two Jews named Jacobs were begging a German Aryan to come to America to collect a pile of dough to take back to Hitler.

---

*The fight turned out to be more important politically than athletically. The political commissar of Berlin, Julius Lippert, who'd been the fight's sponsor, had promised Schmeling he'd be paid in full notwithstanding the meager turnout. When he balked, Schmeling sued Lippert personally, rather than in his official capacity. The city and Lippert settled quickly, but when they had trouble coming up with the funds, Schmeling threatened to impound Lippert's property. Members of the Berlin city council were furious. One, Karl Protze, called Schmeling a "jüdische Börsenjobber" (a Jewish stock market gambler)—placing his own greed above the common good—as well as a coward, for taking on an underling when he'd have never challenged, say, Goebbels. Another called Schmeling's behavior "very close to treason," and suggested he'd profit from four weeks in a concentration camp. Noting Schmeling's good relations with Hitler, Goebbels, and Göring, Protze then said it was crucial they be informed about Schmeling's "Jewish behavior."

"Schmeling! Schmeling! Who's got Max Schmeling?" *The New York Times* asked on July 16. The money lay with Louis, but since the Garden controlled Braddock, a title shot ran through Baer. Ultimately, Schmeling made demands seemingly designed to kill any chance of either fight, and suspicions grew that he was not going to come to the United States that fall, because of his fear of taxes, or of having to pay Joe Jacobs what he owed him, or of Louis, or of incurring Nazi wrath for taking on a black man. For the Nazis had grown hostile toward a Louis fight and toward Louis himself. Why, they asked, should Schmeling take on a "clay face" who should never be given a title shot, particularly since the *"Negermischling"* was still too green and untested to face someone of Schmeling's stature? The argument infuriated Fleischer. Schmeling "never saw the day when he was good enough to justify all the fuss that has been made over him recently," he wrote. Soon, all parties got fed up with Schmeling. "I am convinced he's been giving us all the old run around, including me, who put him in the championship," Joe Jacobs complained. "He talks like he was Dempsey and this is 1929," said the matchmaker at Madison Square Garden. "Who in hell does he think he is anyway?" asked Mike Jacobs. He quickly signed up Louis to fight Baer in September. In one stroke, he'd deprived Schmeling of two possible adversaries.

The German assault on Louis now intensified. For Schmeling, after his recent triumphs, to have to fight a comparative rube like Louis, said *Box-Sport*, would be a "national humiliation." With the help of a photograph, it then dissected the racial makeup of this *Mischling*, all to prove, apparently, that he wasn't even a pure version of an inferior being, but some watered-down, mongrelized imitation. "They always say that he is black," it wrote. "But when one looks at this photo, there is not much of Negro blackness left over. . . . There is much of the 'white' element in him, which one very often finds with mixed-breeds in the States." The paper explained that race-conscious Americans could always identify light-skinned blacks by their hair, their fingernails—they always retained a "bluish shadowing"— and their odor: "For that one doesn't need to have an especially sensitive nose." An artist in *Der Kicker* depicted Louis as a generic, cartoonish black man, and his followers as dancing African savages, holding a placard that declared HAIL JOE LOUIS OUR PROPHET. Still, most ordinary Germans seemed to feel about Louis the way most Americans did: they liked him.

Before taking on Baer in September, Louis had a warm-up bout against Kingfish Levinsky, the man whom Schmeling was to have fought the year before. Levinsky, born Harry Krakow, was in some ways a Jewish

Carnera, a giant clown with "the body of a caribou and the guileless mind of a child." In Chicago, though, where the fight was to take place, he was a hometown favorite; "the glorified fish peddler of Maxwell Street," he was called. By now, Louis was practically a Chicagoan, too, so an internecine struggle loomed. Special trains brought in fight fans, mostly black, from throughout the Midwest; ten dollars bought you not just round-trip train fare from Kansas City but a ticket to the Negro League's East-West Game. The fight, set for August 7, was Chicago's biggest since the Dempsey-Tunney "long count" contest of 1927. Few expected anything lengthy about this one, though. Louis had an extra incentive to get it over with fast: his managers pledged that if he ended it in a round, they would all go on the wagon. The wager was aimed primarily at Blackburn, who had been drinking heavily.

The weigh-in was a chilly affair. Someone asked Levinsky the name of the black cocker spaniel he'd brought with him. "Joe Louis," he replied with a grin. "Boy, I bet that dawg sure has a lot of dynamite in him," an unamused Louis remarked. Nearly 40,000 people were inside Comiskey Park, with another 100,000 people, mostly black, milling outside and 50,000 more outside the Savoy Ballroom, where Louis had trained, and where he was expected to appear afterward. In popular mythology, Mike Jacobs, worried that Levinsky might flee, started the fight an hour early. Though this was not so, Levinsky's face, wrote Runyon, was the color of someone "at the rail of ocean liners in a heavy storm" as he entered the ring. Louis threw one of his trademark short punches, a left hook to the jaw. In seconds he had Levinsky down, then again, again, and again. With a single punch, a man at ringside later insisted, Louis had given the Kingfish two black eyes. "Don't let him hit me again, Mister!" Levinsky begged the referee, who quickly stopped the fight. The time: 141 seconds. Louis had won his bet; Blackburn would become a teetotaler, at least temporarily.

Perhaps because of that, Louis showed some uncharacteristic emotion afterward, dancing and laughing his way to his corner. When word came over the public-address system that fight films would be shown the next day, the crowd began hooting. "I must have been in a transom," Levinsky said in the locker room. One local paper called the celebrations "the gayest jubilee Chicago's Negroes have ever enjoyed." (In New Orleans, a white policeman who'd bet on Levinsky told a young black celebrant to desist, and when he wouldn't, broke his teeth with a billy club. "You can kill me but Joe Louis is the king of all," the man shouted before being thrown in jail.) As for Louis himself, he telephoned his mother, then looked on indifferently as some black beauty queens were paraded before him at the Savoy Ballroom. His common sense, wrote William Pickens of the Associated Negro Press, was a greater force for good than his skill. "His personality is more impressive than a thousand sermons, for he will be felt where no sermons will ever be heard," he said. Still, the path would not be easy. In Washington, D.C., a sportscaster called Louis a "nigger," prompting numerous complaints.

Immediately after the fight, Mike Jacobs corralled representatives of Louis and Baer in a hotel room, barricaded the door, and hammered out a contract. The fight was set for September 24, and given the lure of the two principals, it promised a crowd unprecedented in New York boxing or New York sports, for that matter. Would Braddock dodge Louis if Louis beat Baer? "Dodge him?" Braddock's manager, Joe Gould, asked. "Say, listen, I'll follow him around just to make sure nothing happens to him." "I don't care who's in the other corner," Braddock said. "I just like a guy who can draw the dough."

And that he seemed to have.

CHAPTER 5

Champion in Waiting

THE IMPROVED BENEVOLENT AND PROTECTIVE ORDER OF Elks of the World, aka the Negro Elks, had two honored guests when it convened in Washington in late August 1935: the two most famous black athletes in the world. Jesse Owens, then a student at Ohio State University, was the more accomplished; on a single afternoon two months earlier, he had set three world records in track. To Shirley Povich, then a young sportswriter for *The Washington Post*, he was also the more impressive; smart, nimble-witted, and personable, he was the "epitome of Negro progress." But walking around Washington's black neighborhood with the two men, Povich was amazed by what he saw. People might have recognized Owens's face, but track and field meant little to them, and most didn't know his name. "The gasps, the ah's and the oh's" were for Joe Louis alone. Even Owens stood in awe of him, behaving like "some flunky who knew his place."

Louis had arrived in town on August 26, his car escorted by a lone black policeman on a motorcycle. The officer was clearly from Maryland, one paper explained, because Washington had no black motorcycle officers. Louis's host was a local black doctor, whose house was quickly surrounded by mobs of people hoping to catch a glimpse of the contender; among them were many black cooks and maids, some still wearing their aprons. One had simply walked off her job and over to Louis's temporary quarters when her employer refused to let her "get a peek at Joe" during dinnertime.

Louis had a full schedule of activities in the capital. A tour of Washington's "Little Harlem" was marred only by the behavior of the tap dancer Bill "Bojangles" Robinson, whose shuffle and jive threatened to undermine Louis's manicured image of seriousness and dignity. There was a press conference at Howard University, then an "all-colored boxing show" at Griffith Stadium, for which one of the largest fight crowds in Washington's history paid anywhere from 80 cents to $2.20 to see Louis. "Just to see him," one reporter wrote incredulously. "He didn't fight, he didn't referee, he didn't work as a second, he didn't tap dance, he didn't sing, he didn't, to come to the point, do anything." Introduced as "the forthcoming champion of the world," Louis was once more speechless. "How you, Mr. President?" he asked Franklin D. Roosevelt later at the White House, smiling as he shook the president's hand. "Joe, you certainly are a fine looking young man," Roosevelt told him. (The real question, the *Amsterdam News* boasted, was "whether it was Joe Louis who greeted the President of the United States or the President of the United States who greeted Joe Louis.")* "Impossible," one German newspaper called their encounter; it only underlined anew how Germany would have to uphold the honor of the white race by itself.

By August 1935, Louis was receiving more than a thousand letters a week. (One letter, from New York, was addressed simply to "The Punch Without the Smile.") One pillar of Louis's reputation was that he never pitched items, like liquor and tobacco, that he didn't use himself. But his name started appearing in the black weeklies alongside other products. There was Esso, the only gasoline used in his training camp, "smooth and full of punch." And Murray's Superior Hair Pomade, thanks to which Carnera hadn't even mussed up Louis's coiffure. And Fletcher's Castoria, which neatly linked motherhood, upward mobility, and regularity. The black papers became Louis's public bankbooks, offering regular accountings of his wealth. After the Levinsky fight, his earnings stood at $120,000; of that, $40,000 had gone to his managers, another $20,000 to taxes, $7,200 to buy himself a Lincoln, and $2,800 for his mother's Buick. Some saw the Lincoln, which looked like something Rudolph Valentino might have driven, as the first step down the pugilist's familiar path to profligacy. But this still left Louis with a tidy sum; no one, he boasted, would ever be holding any benefits for *him*. Louis's mother even repaid the $269 she had collected on relief seven years earlier. All this money made Louis an alluring target. Churches needed new roofs, women needed their teeth fixed,

---

*One Louis legend has it that after asking to feel Louis's arm, Roosevelt told him, "Joe, we need muscles like yours to beat Germany." The story, unreported at the time and misreported when it made its debut—their encounter was placed in 1938, not 1935—may well be apocryphal; it's dubious whether Roosevelt would have considered Germany so certain a foe at that point, let alone said so publicly.

farmers needed new trucks, children needed boxing equipment. Some requests came in heartbreaking, handwritten scrawls, like one from a widow in Meridian, Mississippi, penned on the back of a brown paper bag. "Send me some money so that I won't be put out of house and home," she pleaded. After a black inmate from Oklahoma asked for, and received, ten dollars from Louis, every black prisoner in the penitentiary sent his own request.

Many letters offered Louis advice, some free and some costly, like the man demanding $1,000 for the secret to beating Baer. Louis was inundated with rabbits' feet and other amulets. There were love letters, too, from the enraptured and the opportunistic. "You really is my kind of man," went one. "I don't like no weakling and a man like you should have a woman like me." A seventy-eight-year-old woman sent Louis two dollars for him to bet on himself. Louis inspired numerous poems, many appearing as letters to the editor. And following the Carnera fight, there appeared what may well have been the first Joe Louis song, Joe Pullam's "Joe Louis Is the Man." It praised his modesty, his dress, and his kindness to his mother, and said he was "bound to be the next champion of the world." Memphis Minnie's "He's in the Ring (Doin' the Same Old Thing)," recorded nine days later, related how she'd "chanced" all her money that Louis's latest opponent wouldn't last a round:

> *I wouldn't even pay my house rent*
> *I wouldn't buy me nothin' to eat*
> *Joe Louis said "Take a chance with me,*
> *I'm gonna put you up on your feet!"*
> *He's in the ring (he's still fightin'!)*
> *Doin' the same old thing!*

Eventually, there would be dozens of songs, exponentially more than for any American sports figure before or since. A composer and musician named Claude Austin went a step further, writing an operetta on Louis's life. Paul Robeson was reportedly to be cast in the lead.

The *Amsterdam News* formed a Joe Louis Boys Club to train youngsters in the manly art as well as in clean living and thinking. An advertisement in the *Chicago Defender* called a new book on Louis "a worth while [*sic*] addition to the library of every home." Parents, Ralph Matthews wrote in the *Baltimore Afro-American*, had found Louis a more effective deterrent than the hairbrush and a greater inspiration than George Washington. Even little white kids were calling themselves "Joe Louis";

"When white children want to be called by a Negro's name, that is news," wrote Gordon Hancock in the *Norfolk Journal and Guide*. Some white intellectuals, like Carl Van Vechten, the semiofficial photographer of the Harlem Renaissance, were also excited. "Aren't the papers wonderful about Joe Louis, and isn't Joe Louis wonderful?" he wrote to the black writer James Weldon Johnson. "Hitler and Mussolini have done their part to make Americans fairer to Negroes, quite a big part, too!"

For all the scrutiny of Louis's life, nothing had surfaced yet about Marva Trotter, the young Chicago stenographer. But speculation about his love life was rife in the black press, and understandably so, for it had great implications for everyone. "The last thing I wanted Joe and Jesse [Owens] to do was fall in love," stated the *Pittsburgh Courier*'s "Talk O' Town" column in July. "It will take the power out of their punch . . . it will rob them of the physical prowess that has set an entire nation wild. . . . Joe, you have got to be the champ . . . then go Mormon, I don't care." Any athlete who marries is "usually no good for a year," the *Afro-American* warned. But if Louis had to have a girl, the *Amsterdam News* pleaded, let it be a black one. There was, one letter writer pointed out, no shortage of attractive candidates, especially in Harlem, "where our beauticians are prepared to use every beauty appliance necessary." In mid-August the *Defender* announced that Louis and Marva were engaged. Louis denied it, but he called Marva every night from his training camp, squeezing into a phone booth with a pocketful of change, sweating so profusely that it got his trainers worried. But soon Louis proposed to her over the phone, and she was "not overlong making up her mind." There would be no more pictures of her taking dictation; "Miss Trotter, who had been employed in the office of a Chicago dentist, has resigned that position," the *Defender* solemnly announced. Marva soon sported a three-carat diamond—"so massive and sparkling that any Queen would want it"—and was buying herself a gigantic wardrobe and furniture for the couple's new apartment. If, as some suspected, Roxborough and Black had engineered the whole thing, they had selected well. "Marva is an old-fashioned girl, sweet, clean, modest, pretty," the *Afro-American* wrote. "She has intelligence, poise, common sense. She has personality and is a pleasant, friendly type who makes friends because she is cheerful and kindly." Most important, she was black.

Louis and Marva discussed their engagement in the *Chicago Tribune*. "Sure, she can cook southern fried chicken," Louis told the paper. "Yes, and she can broil steak, too, with French fried potatoes." (The black press was more candid, admitting that Marva had never prepared an entire meal.) Louis said they'd marry within a few days of the Baer fight; Roxborough said it might happen later that very night. Baer claimed to be happy over the turn of events. "Louis' mind will be on the girl friend when he is in there against me," he said. "And when you're fighting anyone, especially me, you have to think of boxing all the time." A poll in the *Pittsburgh Courier* revealed that of fifteen people in Detroit "representing all walks of life," eleven opposed Louis's marriage to Marva—or to anyone else, for that matter. "If this girl really loves Joe she won't be so selfish as to hinder his career," a female cashier declared. As Memphis Minnie had sung, Louis's fans had a stake in him. "I reckon he knows what he's a-doing, at least I hope so 'cause we have put our life's savings on his fight with Baer," said Rufus Peterson, a laborer. (In fact, marriage was to make little difference to Louis; he strayed almost from the very beginning. "He'd go for coffee and come back three days later," his longtime lawyer, Truman Gibson, later recalled.) *Box-Sport* ran Marva's picture, along with the usual racial analysis. "She is a mixed-blood [*ein Mischblut*], just like Joe Louis," it explained.

Louis had hoped to train for the Baer fight at the Sulphur Springs Hotel in Saratoga Springs, New York, where Dempsey and Tunney, among others, had once readied themselves, but the hotel was not interested in a black man's business. Louis, the black press reported, had been stopped dead in his tracks by Jim Crow, white. So he landed back at Pompton Lakes. He tried to run a disciplined camp, closing the bar because drinkers "become pestiferous and interfere no little with my daily routines," the *Chicago Defender* had him saying. But visitors still came. One Sunday, there were four thousand of them, three-quarters from Harlem. Three black teenagers took ten days to bicycle 750 miles from Detroit. After Louis declined to speak to some two hundred Baptist clergymen gathered in New York, the clergymen came down to see him. "If they can learn to put as many punches into their sermons as Joe Louis did in one round of the Levinsky fight, their congregations will be benefited immensely," the *Afro-American* declared. Also stopping by were Walter White, Charles Hamilton Houston, and Roy Wilkins of the NAACP. "Joe Louis impressed me as a quiet, well-mannered boy who wants to be let alone because he has work to do," Wilkins wrote afterward. When Louis wasn't punching, he was reportedly studying history, math, geography, the New Testament, the life of Booker T. Washington, the Italo-African conflict, and etiquette.

Whites who studied Louis continued to offer conflicting images of nobility and animalism. Not since Othello, *Esquire* observed, had there been a black warrior with half his quiet power. "He lives like an animal, untouched by externals," Gallico wrote. "Is he all instinct, all animal? Or have a hundred million years left a fold upon his brain?" Were a prizefight purely a matter of physicality, Gallico maintained, Louis would prevail. But Gallico was going with Baer, because Baer was more of a human being, with a human being's impulse to win.

Others agreed in their own way that Louis was an entity apart. "The Ring Robot," Edward Van Every of the *Sun* dubbed him, " . . . a thing of gears and pistons in human guise that has been brought to the shop for oiling and tuning up." There was bafflement and resentment that Louis did not conform to type. "He can fight, sure," one white fan complained. "But I like a colored fighter to have something more than that. I like those wild, happy-go-lucky, easy-come-easy-go kind of fighters. This Louis, he's just a dumb, cold guy. . . . He don't give you no kick." Black writers countered that Louis was perfectly sociable with *them*. "Among ofays, who seem to bewilder him, he is strangely shy," not the "laughing, mischievous boy" blacks saw, Roi Ottley wrote in the *Amsterdam News*. But even they complained sometimes of getting only nods and grunts; to one, six words from Louis marked a new personal high. Once, Louis walked out as Ralph Matthews of the *Baltimore Afro-American* asked him something, leaving the newsman alone with a statue. "The statue was a social sort of fellow by comparison," Matthews wrote.

Baer, meantime, trained in Speculator, New York, a small lakeside hamlet in the Adirondacks that Tunney had made famous in the 1920s. The idea was to drag him as far away from the bright lights of Broadway as possible. But the strategy backfired: in the sticks, it turned out, there was little for Baer to do but think of Louis. Bucking Baer up, at least publicly, was Jack Dempsey, who had joined his entourage. Louis, Dempsey said, had only knocked out boxers with "paper chins." It took four years to develop a first-class fighter, and Louis still hadn't put in his time.

New York had had its share of big fights. Dempsey's bout against Luis Angel Firpo in the Polo Grounds in 1923, immortalized by the painter George Bellows, had drawn eighty-two thousand people; the first Schmeling-Sharkey fight drew nearly that. But these were either before the stock market had crashed or before it had fully sunk in. Now, weeks before Louis and Baer were to square off, long lines formed outside Mike Jacobs's ticket offices. A cable came from a ship at sea, ordering six ringside seats. Jacobs set aside one thousand press seats, the most ever. There was talk of the first million-dollar gate in eight years. "Joe Louis: Will This Black Moses Lead the Fight Business Back into Its Promised Land?" *For-*

tune magazine asked. A meeting of the Buffalo school board had to be postponed because most of its members were going to New York. A notice went up in the offices of the Sleeping Car Porters: "All those who, because of their grandmothers' illness or death or for any other important reason, require vacation, are asked to make this known at least three days before the Baer-Louis fight."

On September 20 the "bride-elect" arrived in Harlem, along with five pieces of matching luggage stuffed with fifty new dresses, two silver fox furs, twenty-five nightgowns, five negligees, and various accessories. Chicago's largest department stores and the smartest shops had vied for Marva's business, and everyone, including people close to Roxborough and Black, had urged her to patronize places like Marshall Field's or I. Magnin. But instead the "winsome lass" had taken her trade to Mae's Dress Shoppe, owned and run by blacks, thereby setting what one black newspaper called "an example of fidelity to racial business institutions . . . which could bring shame to the cheeks of most of our racial leaders and saviors, to say nothing of their wives." Marva installed herself in the first-floor apartment of a friend at 381 Edgecomb Avenue, the building where Duke Ellington lived, in the Sugar Hill section of Harlem. Word was that she would not see her husband-to-be until after the fight.

Harlem was more alive than ever. "New York was the delta, and towns, cities and the hinterlands like rivers flowing into a great sea were filtering their human cargo into its fold," Billy Rowe wrote in the *Pittsburgh Courier*. Sure, some unbrotherly price gouging was going on, he admitted, but "Joe Louis only happens along once in a century." "The entire colored population of greater New York and New Jersey, from page-boys, bell-hops, and boot-blacks to the colored money baron, from the colored chambermaid to the Creole diva, they are all already saving their dollars in order to witness the battle of the century, which will be repeated if Louis wins and Max Schmeling steps up," *Box-Sport* reported. "Race consciousness, class differences, until now un-crossable boundaries and unwritten laws have all crumbled under the fists of this knock-out specialist. We hope that the 'white blood' and the spirit of the white race, despite all mixing, will prove to be the stronger and more vital." But even Goebbels's *Angriff* caught some of the excitement. The recent crisis in professional boxing was likely to get "a first-class funeral tonight," it said on the eve of the fight.

By that point, choice seats were going for $200 or more. Restaurants and nightclubs had trouble changing all the hundred-dollar bills that out-of-towners had brought with them. "I haven't seen bills like that since

1928," one recipient claimed. "Maybe the Depression is over." Hotel rooms were so scarce that people were parking near the stadium and sleeping in their cars. For two days straight, the New York Central Railroad broke records for incoming traffic. "Up to just a few months ago, no one believed the fistic game would ever again see the wild excitement and the terrific receipts of the fat days of the mid-twenties, when everybody had money," Runyon wrote. "Then suddenly, out of the West came stalking a brown-skinned, sad-eyed, serious boy just turning his majority, with a strange genius for this strangest of sports . . . and lo! the roar of the fight crowd again echoed over the land." Underlying the fervor was race. To Gallico, there was "something Roman" about throwing a Jew and a black man in the ring together.

Louis was the favorite, but as the fight approached, the odds fell a bit. Rumors persisted that Baer had thrown the Braddock fight. Some thought insiders had decreed that a black man had gone far enough. And skeptics like O. B. Keeler of the *Atlanta Journal* still insisted Louis had beaten only "an array of palookas of purest ray serene." Then the odds rose again, to two and a half to one, amid reports that Baer had hurt his hand. Roxborough and Black demanded that a guard be posted around Baer to assure he did not receive any injections. Fleischer subsequently disclosed that Baer had in fact received a shot of "cocaine" shortly before entering the ring.*

For the weigh-in, five thousand people gathered outside the boxing commission's offices in lower Manhattan, and mounted police had to disperse them to let Louis—who'd alighted from Duke Ellington's car—get through. Pulling an old prizefighter's dodge, Baer kept Louis waiting for an hour, just to rile him up. But Louis looked at the funnies—they didn't make him smile, either—and took a nap. When Baer finally did arrive, wearing what a British reporter called "the loudest suit even Broadway had seen for years," he was grinning. The doctors examined Louis. "If my heart ain't just right, doctor, it's because I ain't et yet," he told one of them. "You could fight twice," one of the doctors replied. Baer, too, got a clean bill of health, bum hand and all. But Baer seemed tense, and one writer who had called for Louis in eight rounds promptly shaved three off his prediction.

The odds stabilized at eight to five. It was one of the biggest betting fights in history; Bill Robinson placed $10,000 on Louis, then had Shirley

---

*Many years later, Red Smith wrote that the injection froze up Baer's entire forearm moments before the fight began.

Temple rub some well-cooked salt into his hand for luck. At a Bowery flophouse, one man hocked his shoes for fifty cents to bet on Louis. In Brooklyn, a white woman and a black woman bet their respective relief checks. In Livermore, California, the farming and cattle town twenty miles east of Oakland where Baer grew up, residents wagered $12,000 on their favorite son. "To hell with the foreman," one worker on relief told another as they waited in line for cheap seats. "We'll tell him we were sick." An elderly black cleaning woman who made three dollars a week said she had been saving for two months to buy herself a seat in the bleachers.

After the weigh-in, Louis went for a walk along the Harlem River, then to the sixth floor of 381 Edgecomb Avenue, upstairs from where Marva was staying, for a nap. Around seven, he got up, showered, put on a double-breasted suit, and went down to Marva's quarters on the first floor. Two and a half hours remained before the fight—plenty of time, it turned out, to get married.

All day long, Louis and his handlers had denied there would be any wedding. But Marva told her fiancé she wanted to watch the fight as Mrs. Joe Louis. Blackburn believed the prospect of coming home to his bride would inspire Louis to work quickly. Around seven-thirty, a marriage license, with the names left blank, arrived from the city clerk's office. Louis was joined by Marva, who'd negotiated her way between floors by a rear fire escape. She was wearing a white velvet gown with "real ermine" at the neck, along with white shoes and a corsage of gardenias and lilies of the valley. Officiating was the bride's brother, a minister from Iowa. Two of Marva's sisters attended her. Roxborough, Black, Blackburn, Mike Jacobs, and a few others were the guests. The service started at a quarter to eight, and was quickly over. After kissing the bride Louis begged off; he had a date, he explained, with a fellow named Max Baer. A few minutes past eight, someone stepped outside to tell the waiting throng the history that had just been made. People screamed with delight. A police emergency squad cleared the crowd, and at 8:10 Louis, wearing an olive green hat and topcoat, got into a car bound for Yankee Stadium. Half an hour later, as the first telegrams began to arrive, Marva followed her husband.

At the stadium, the demand for tickets could not be stanched "any more than you could take a broom and dam Niagara." A Long Island horseman paid $400 apiece for a block of ringside seats. A cabdriver watched four passengers pay $2,000 for seats, then hand him a two-dollar bill for a $1.90 fare. From dinnertime on, the subways were jammed. It was a festive crowd, though there were complaints that no blacks were on the undercard, and picketers from the Non-Sectarian Anti-Nazi League protested American participation in the 1936 Berlin Olympics. Officially, the paid attendance was 83,462, an all-time record for a sporting event in New York, excluding horse racing. With free tickets, press passes, and employees, the turnstile count exceeded 90,000. And with police, firemen, inspectors, attendants, and gate-crashers thrown in, there were more than 95,000 there that memorable night. Even the dugouts were filled. Another 25,000 people stood outside, following the action by taxicab radios and roars. Including the sale of radio and movie rights, the gate squeezed past the hallowed million-dollar mark—the first time that had ever happened in a fight in which Jack Dempsey wasn't on the card, and these were scarce Depression dollars at that. Louis would get $217,337, Baer $181,114. Some 35,000 of the fans were black, and they came early, more eager to share in the occasion than to impress anyone with late entries. By seven o'clock "the outer fringes of the stadium looked like Addis Ababa."

Around the ring, which sat as usual on the outfield side of second base, were Governor Lehman, Mayor La Guardia, one of Franklin D. Roosevelt's sons, Bert Lahr, Al Jolson, George Burns and Gracie Allen, Condé Nast, Edward G. Robinson, Cary Grant, Irving Berlin, James Cagney, and George Raft. Cab Calloway and Duke Ellington were also on hand. So were the white actors who played Amos and Andy, who, for the first time, were missing a broadcast. Jack Johnson was there, as was Carnera. Marva, dressed in green with a shoulder corsage of white gardenias, a fur collar, and a felt hat, sat in the twenty-fifth row. Millions listened as Edwin C. Hill, a voice familiar from newsreels, described what he called "the most amazing spectacle of modern times." For all of the dignitaries on hand, what most impressed him was the large number of women—a throwback, he speculated, to prehistoric days. Everywhere, Hill went on, people were more interested in whether the "Jungle Man" would best the "Jester" than in the threat of war in Europe.

Baer panicked as he was summoned to the ring. Call off the fight! he declared in his dressing room: he was having chest pains, or a heart attack, or something. An incredulous Dempsey practically had to drag him into the ring. To Braddock, Baer looked like someone going to the electric chair. Louis sat impassively as Joe Humphreys, the longtime ring announcer who'd come of age before microphones got good, emerged from retirement to shout out one final set of introductions. He called Louis "the new sensational, pugilistic product" who, "although colored . . . stands out in the same class as with Jack Johnson and Sam Langford—the idol of his people."

For the play-by-play, Hill yielded the radio microphone to Clem McCarthy, who was making his debut in a boxing match. NBC executives had been unhappy over prior fight broadcasts, and had held auditions for replacements, with aspirants going into gyms and barking out their calls. McCarthy, an experienced horse-racing announcer, had opted instead to read a script he'd written. At a time when so much of radio was scripted, it won the day. He sat on his typewriter so that his chin was level with the ring. Another mike was installed near the arc lights to pick up the punches and the din.

Shortly before the fight, the "Inquiring Reporter" of the *Norfolk Journal and Guide* asked for predictions. "I dreamed about the fight not long ago and Louis was hitting Max Baer so fast the man who was broadcasting could only say 'Louis, Louis, Louis,'" one man replied. And that's pretty much how it was. Baer groped, punched wildly, and looked so lost that Louis thought he was throwing the fight. Meanwhile, the Bomber picked Baer apart. Within moments, the outcome was clear. In the second round, Baer kept missing, while Louis landed a series of powerful punches. Baer's face, Hill said, was "a bloody wreck." In the third, Baer went down for the first time, and then the second time, in his career. A black man near ringside jumped to his feet. "Kill him, Joe! Kill him!" he shouted. "Please don't do that," someone in Louis's corner turned around and told him. "We don't want that sort of thing. It will do the boy harm." Dempsey put his hands over his face. "Over against the ropes, and there was a hard smash to the head, and Baer is down!" McCarthy shouted. At eight he was back up. He was down again when the bell saved him at three.

By the fourth round, even "the Negro who came here all the way from Alabama to sit on the back row in the far away centerfield bleachers" knew the end was near. Louis kept stabbing Baer with his left, and when that didn't work, he cut through with a right. By one count, he missed only two punches all night. Finally, a blow sounding like a firecracker exploding under a can struck home and Baer tumbled. "Through it all, the fleeting action of a second, a low rumble had started, the distant thunder of the gallery gods heralding a storm," wrote Arch Ward of the *Chicago Tribune*. "It came on, outstripping any electrical eruption for speed, swelling into a wild roar as tier after tier of maddened humans caught it up until it broke in all its fury over the gleaming square. . . .

Eighty-five thousand persons, gone suddenly mad with excitement, were desperately yelling encouragement to the sinking Baer or shouting cheer to the attacking Louis, all individuality lost in one hoarse, guttural rumble, as the shrill barks of many field pieces far off may be mistaken for the tremendous belching of one giant gun. It was bedlam, nothing less."

Sure he had scored the winner, Louis retreated to his corner without even turning around to look. In fact, Baer was up on his knee at four. He could hear the count, but his legs were numb. "There were so many Joe Louises in front of me it looked like all Harlem had jumped into the ring," he said afterward. Donovan counted him out. Never had he seen anyone take so many murderous punches; one more, he feared, and Louis might have broken Baer's neck. Years later Louis said he was never better than he was that night. That a man so ferocious had married only moments before was simply unfathomable to some. "I wonder if his new bride's heart beat a little with fear that this terrible thing was hers," Gallico wrote. It didn't. Marva had come to Yankee Stadium in a limousine; now, along with four girlfriends, she giddily returned to Harlem in a streetcar, happily springing for the nickel fare.

Baer, bleeding so profusely that he looked to one reporter like an Apache in war paint, was jeered as he left the ring. When he got to his dressing room, he demanded a cigarette and a beer. "I guess I could have got up again but what was the use?" he asked. "He had me licked." The press was merciless; Ed Sullivan and Ernest Hemingway called him a coward. But Baer didn't care. "When I get executed, people are going to pay more than $25 for a seat to watch it," he said. He signed autographs "Max Baer—Palooka."

"That's a great fighter, the greatest I ever saw, I guess," Dempsey said of Louis as he climbed out of the ring. As for Louis himself, he said he'd faced tougher opponents in the Golden Gloves. "If you folks is all through, I'd kinda like to go home," he told the reporters after a decent interval. "I'm a married man now, you know." A crowd at 381 Edgecomb Avenue awaited Louis's return, and it took six policemen to get him on the elevator. Around one in the morning, the *Chicago Defender* later reported, Louis and Marva went out to the Cotton Club; they returned around two-thirty, then went to bed. Around four they were awakened by a sound below their window. A tin-can band was serenading them.

Inside the stadium, under police surveillance, blacks had been subdued, but outside afterward, a few of them executed handstands and then sprinted away, as if rushing the news back to Harlem. Of course, Harlem already knew; some 200,000 people were quickly on its streets. The Savoy

Ballroom had to close its doors, while at the Ubangi, the Cotton Club, Small's Paradise, Big Apple, Pirate, and Horseshoe Bar, there wasn't even standing room. "Why attempt to describe it?" the *Amsterdam News* wrote of the scene. "You probably were in it." Never had there been anything like it, nor could there have been; when Johnson knocked out Jeffries in 1910, Harlem had been too small and too scared to celebrate.

Downtown, the hot spots were jammed. At "21," tables were set up in the foyer for the first time. At the Stork Club, Sherman Billingsley turned away seven hundred people. "Forget repeal. Forget Prohibition. Not since the old days, before Prohibition, has there been such a night on Broadway," said the headwaiter at the French Casino.

Not a single call had come in to the Detroit Fire Department during the fight, and only three came in to the police, one asking who'd won. Cars cruised up and down the streets in Paradise Valley, the center of black Detroit. "With one hand on the horn button and the other waving out the window, each driver let the world know Joe Louis had won," a local paper reported. In Memphis, "Joe Louis has driven the blues away from Beale Street," and outside town "many a cotton picker was sluggish and red-eyed in the field today." In Portsmouth, Virginia, streets in the black neighborhood became "noisy canyons of romping humanity."

Richard Wright described the forces Louis unleashed on Chicago's South Side:

> They seeped out of doorways, oozed from alleys, trickled out of tenements, and flowed down the street: a fluid mass of joy. . . . Four centuries of oppression, of frustrated hopes, of black bitterness, felt even in the bones of the bewildered young, were rising to the surface. Yes, unconsciously, they had imputed to the brawny image of Joe Louis all the balked dreams of revenge, all the secretly visualized moments of retaliation, AND HE HAD WON! Good Gawd Almighty! Yes, by Jesus, it could be done! Didn't Joe do it? . . . Joe was the concentrated essence of black triumph over white. And it came so seldom, so seldom. And what could be sweeter than long nourished hate vicariously gratified? From the symbol of Joe's strength they took strength, and in that moment all fear, all obstacles were wiped out, drowned.

In other places, joy transmogrified into anger. In Baltimore, revelers threw cabbages, old shoes, bricks, and tin cans at cars driven by whites. An unsuspecting white farmer carrying a truckload of tomatoes through a black neighborhood unwittingly furnished the protesters with an entire arsenal, which they threw at policemen. Cincinnati experienced two days of violence. In Utica, New York, an interracial street brawl tied up traffic.

To those who followed the sport, the face of boxing had changed, but would not change again for a while. "Some young fellow now playing marbles or spinning a top" would be the first person to beat Louis, Grantland Rice predicted. Ernest Hemingway called Louis "too good to be true, and absolutely true." He wrote, "We who have seen him now, light on his feet, smooth moving as a leopard, a young man with an old man's science, the most beautiful fighting machine that I have ever seen, may live to see him fat, slow, old and bald taking a beating from a younger man. But I would like to hazard a prediction that whoever beats Joe Louis in an honest fight in the next fifteen years will have to get up off the floor to do it."

Fleischer praised Louis so effusively and incessantly that *Ring* readers accused him of disloyalty to his race. "Warning: To my friend Max Schmeling—Stay in Germany," wrote Gallico. "Have no truck with this man. He will do something to you from which you will never fully recover. You haven't a chance. . . . And besides, Der Fuehrer wouldn't like the pictures."

The next morning, as reporters and photographers recorded the scene, the newlyweds went out for a stroll. "Mr. Louis, what makes you happier, to beat Baer or to be married to this charming lady?" someone shouted. "I think to be married," he replied. Who would he rather fight, Braddock or Schmeling? Braddock, he replied: "Much easier, and the championship, too." "Mrs. Louis, what did you think of your husband?" "I thought he was grand," Mrs. Louis replied. Praise rained down on Louis all day, but his expression never changed—not even when Mike Jacobs handed him a check for $217,337.93. Three evenings later, people standing near the corner of 138th Street and Seventh Avenue happened upon an impromptu, serendipitous show: Jack Johnson was reenacting the fight.

Only Schmeling and Braddock now stood between Louis and the title, and neither seemed very formidable. (To Sharkey, in fact, Louis's most formidable obstacle was Louis himself. "Joe will be the kingpin as long as he keeps his head about him," he said. But the money could wreak havoc: "The first thing he knows he'll find training distasteful. He'll loaf for a month or two and then, when a big bout is announced, say two months hence—he'll keep putting off the starting time for the daily workouts. By that time training will be an awful grind—after that anything can happen.") There was renewed talk of finding a "white hope"; the man who'd discovered Carnera was said to have found a giant somewhere in China. Even to southerners, Louis appeared unstoppable, and that was mostly fine, for Louis had originally been one of them.

To black America, Louis crystallized racial progress, and promised more. The *Courier* saw black champions in golf, tennis, and swimming. A *Defender* reader dared some major league baseball team to sign Satchel Paige. Louis had bridged the racial gap more dramatically than all individuals and organizations combined, wrote Sam Lacy of the *Washington Tribune*. "In deepest Mississippi as well as in highest Harlem, colored and white people listened at their radio loudspeakers without gnashing their teeth or cutting each other's throats," noted *The Crisis*. If blacks could only stand together as they stood behind Louis, one black commentator predicted, someone "could go down to Washington and say, 'Mr. President, the Scottsboro boys must be freed. Lynching must be stopped.' And both would be done in a month." Among South African blacks, the reaction was jubilant, if more understated. "All sportsmen, more especially the Coloured races of the world, are very proud of him," stated *Bantu World*, which put a picture of Louis on its front page. (Among Louis's South African fans was the young Nelson Mandela, four years the Bomber's junior, and a boxer himself.) The Japanese papers offered blow-by-blow descriptions of the fight. In Paris, Josephine Baker was thrilled over Louis's victory, which she'd predicted.

But Louis could accelerate things only so much. Enforcement of the interstate ban on fight films enacted during Jack Johnson's day had been lax—but only, it turned out, when two white men shared the card: Virginia's state censorship board had already banned films of the second Louis-Ramage fight, and now films of the Louis-Baer fight were prohibited, too, on the grounds that they "might tend to arouse racial animosity." Brisbane, the Hearst columnist, thought Louis nothing special: send Jack Blackburn to Somaliland and give him "a promising young savage of 17 or 18," and you'd have yourself a champion. But for the next decade, he warned, only another black man had a prayer against Louis, and since fights between blacks were box-office poison, a separate "colored championship" might be necessary. Louis's managers would in fact not match him up with another black fighter, fearing that such a fight would not draw.

It was a voice from the outside—the music critic of the *New York Post*, Samuel Chotzinoff—who best captured what Louis's victory did and didn't mean. Louis was "sweet recompense for a degrading past and a hopeless future," he wrote. "Booker T. Washington and Duke Ellington are all right in their way, but they do not represent Might." With Louis charging toward the championship, he went on, "it will be easier to bear the usual number of lynchings in the year. If you are riding by compulsion in a Jim Crow car it is something to know that Joe Louis is ready and willing to take all comers."

Ten days before the Louis-Baer fight, the Nazis had held their annual party congress at Nuremberg, and Schmeling had met with some Nazi leaders there. Though he'd clearly had nothing to do with it, it was at that gathering that the Nazis had unveiled the infamous Nuremberg Laws, which defined, expansively, who was a Jew, then stripped of German citizenship all those who fit the criteria. Marriage and sexual relations between Germans and Jews were also barred. Within a few weeks, the same restrictions were placed on "Gypsies, Negroes, and their bastards." But wherever Louis and Baer would have fit in the new Germany, their fight was followed closely, for in their fortunes lay Schmeling's, too.

The *Angriff* conceded that Louis had revitalized boxing, creating great moneymaking opportunities for Schmeling. Baer, it noted, had said after the fight that Schmeling could give Louis a hard time, and maybe even beat him. The *8 Uhr-Blatt* doubted whether the Americans would offer Schmeling a shot; they preferred an American, even a black American, to "a purebred white European" as champion. The journal of the Reich Association of the German Press took umbrage that coverage of "Negroid-Jewish matters" had crowded out information about German athletics from the country's newspapers. "In America, once so full of racial pride, a Negro is fighting a Jew!" exclaimed the *Fränkische Tageszeitung.* "It's a disgrace if you can't come up with any other contenders for the title of world champion."

The night after the fight, Rudy Vallee interviewed Joe Louis's mother on the *Fleischmann's Yeast Hour* radio program, and asked whether she worried about her son in the ring. "Just a little," she replied. "I don't want him to get hurt. You know, Joe is very delicate." Hearing a black mother talk endearingly about her son was another of the ways in which Louis was touching mainstream America as no black man ever had. Walter White marveled at it all. "Isn't it superb the way the press and public have reacted to Joe's smashing victory?" he wrote Roxborough and Black. The task of bringing Louis along had been "loaded with T.N.T.," he went on; "only your skilled handling has achieved the impossible—promoting racial good will and respect for the Negro through a Negro's defeating white men."

As for Louis himself, he wanted nothing more than to get back to the Midwest to watch the Tigers and the Cubs in the World Series. He arrived in Detroit on Sunday, September 29. Word leaked out that he planned to attend services at the Calvary Baptist Church; two hours beforehand, 2,500 people awaited him inside, with another 5,000 outdoors. As if to warm up the crowd, the preacher proclaimed that Louis had done more than anyone since Lincoln to uplift the race and extolled him for neither smoking nor for letting any red-hot liquor pass down his throat. Finally Louis and his bride pulled up, in a black limousine with red wheels, then walked through the cheering throng to greet Louis's mother on the steps of the church. The preacher announced that Louis would speak on "The Ideal Son and a Devoted Mother." Louis stepped up to the pulpit, his hands trembling. Once again, he said nothing, fleeing to the comforts of the communal lunchroom instead. "The assembly whistled and stamped approval for just his smile," the *Afro-American* reported. Before departing, Louis put $100 in the collection plate. Three members of his entourage each put in an additional $5. The total raised that day was $118.34.

The next day, Louis took the train to Chicago, where he and Marva installed themselves in a third-floor apartment in the Rosenwald Houses on Forty-sixth Street and South Michigan, a common address for the black elite. An *Afro-American* reporter found them listed as "Mr. and Mrs. James McDonald" and revealed that their "unusually attractive bedroom" had twin beds. Louis met with the mayor of Chicago, Edward Kelly, and officially ruled the city for ten minutes. A black pastor urged local congregations not to compete for Joe and Marva Louis too aggressively. "You busy businessmen, who crowd everything into your heart and life but Christ and His church, 'Go to the Brown Bomber' and be wise," another minister sermonized.

Joe Louis busts—"in fighting pose"—were being sold for one dollar. Babies named for Louis abounded. Joe Louis Wise, born in Georgia during the Baer fight, was even white. "We only hope that he will be as clean a sportsman as the man for whom he was named," his proud parents wrote. Marva had only enhanced the interest. When their appearance at the annual Wilberforce-Tuskegee football game at Soldier Field in Chicago was announced at halftime, a thousand people "streaked pell-mell across the field," gathered below their second-row seats, and stared. The state of their marriage was always newsworthy, as were constant rumors that they were, as Walter Winchell liked to say, "blessed-eventing." Marva's every comment, activity, garment, purchase, and ailment was followed, analyzed, and assessed. Soon she, too, was getting lots of mail, from black women urging her to watch over her husband as conscientiously as his mother did, or asking her for discarded clothes or handkerchiefs or money, or requesting that she be godmother to their children. They admired her thrift and her extravagance alike. She could do no wrong.

"She's nice to look at, and what's better, she doesn't seem to mind working," the "Feminine Viewpoint" column in the *Journal and Guide* observed. "In addition, she acts genuinely honest and her disposition seems to be O.K. She didn't mind riding home from the fight on a street car, but on the other hand, she made no bones about ordering twenty dresses at one clip, or picking expensive furniture with 18-carat gold knobs for the drawers. It just happened to be what she wanted and she got it without apologizing. And that's grand!" "Marva is sweet . . . that is the appropriate description of her soft beauty and her child-like simplicity," said the *Courier*. Some readers choked on all the adulation. "Instead of beautiful headlines of interest commenting on some of the good deeds done by some of our leading educators," a *Defender* reader griped, "the front page of the 'World's Greatest Weekly'" was "graced, adorned and magnified with the picture of a woman who hasn't done anything to help bring her people out of chaos, or help in any way to develop manhood or womanhood into a 'downtrodden' race." But most would have thought that curmudgeonly.

Black intellectuals began taking an interest in Louis. Eslanda Robeson, the wife of Paul, interviewed Louis for three hours for a book she hoped to write on prominent black Americans. "I found him charming, and very very simple and natural," she wrote to Carl Van Vechten, who was to take photographs for the book. "He only goes clam when you take him out of his field. He's as sweet as he can be, and crazy about the RACE. So, all you have to do to go great with him, is put him at his ease." Writing to the publisher Alfred A. Knopf, Van Vechten predicted in November 1935 that Louis, along with Paul Robeson, Ethel Waters, Bill Robinson, Josephine Baker, Gershwin's *Porgy and Bess,* and the Italian invasion of Ethiopia would keep blacks very much in the news that winter.

White reporters began making pilgrimages to Louis's birthplace, and wading into his gene pool. They heard of his paternal grandfather, a well digger who was "just about the toughest darky we ever had in these parts." And of Louis's mother, who as a girl could pick more cotton than most men. And of Louis's father, "big and strong as an ox." (Not everyone was sure he'd really died, but neither the family nor the press bothered to check.) The stories traced Louis's ancestors back to a white slave owner named James Barrow and a Cherokee chief named Charles Hunkerfoot. Some of the Barrows "could easily pass for Indian braves and princesses," one visitor wrote, while others were "as fair as any Anglo-Saxon." "None of them is dark-skinned like the average southern Negro, though many are the typically freaky-looking zambos," one article explained. Their light skin was said to be a source of pride to the family and resentment from others. One of Louis's black forebears was supposedly a former slave who entertained Union soldiers by wrestling with a baboon. One writer steeped in Louis's bloodlines pronounced that his "coolness and cunning" were Indian, his "quick wit and shrewdness" white, and his "brute strength and endurance" black.

LOUIS, SCHMELING, AND BRADDOCK were in play; the only question was who would fight whom when. "If Schmeling wants gold he can get it fighting Louis," Mike Jacobs said. "If he wants glory, he can fight Braddock. Anyway, Louis can lick both of them." In late September the Ford Motor Company offered to build a 100,000-seat stadium at the Michigan Fairgrounds for a Louis-Schmeling fight. But Schmeling appeared in no rush to fight anyone, perhaps because the money wasn't right or his contract with Joe Jacobs was due to expire in December. Louis, on the other hand, would not remain idle. Mike Jacobs arranged three quick indoor fights: against Paolino Uzcudun in early December, followed by the Cuban heavyweight Isidoro Gastanaga in Havana on New Year's Day and Charlie Retzlaff in Chicago two weeks later. None figured to be too taxing. Louis's frantic pace swelled black hearts; in five months, he'd have fought more than Dempsey and Tunney had in all their time as champions.

With characteristic diligence, Schmeling began studying Louis, but it was not easy; film of the Louis-Baer fight had been banned in Germany. The Nazis' favorite boxing writer, Arno Hellmis of the *Völkischer Beobachter*, had to watch it in Basel, Switzerland, while *Box-Sport* sent a man to Katowice, Poland. This was odd, because to the Nazi press at least, the proscribed footage proved Louis was overrated. *Box-Sport*'s correspondent described him as "an ambitious, determined fighter of mediocre technical ability, if also of undeniably large talent," who'd beaten "a boxing corpse," a "living punching bag." There was no way he was a world champion, especially against the Schmeling of the second Hamas fight. According to " —— s." (presumably Hellmis) in the *Angriff*, when the fight film ended, everyone in the theater looked puzzled; Louis was not the "*Überboxer*" they'd expected. Though his punches were "lightning-fast" and "incredibly hard," he was a neophyte. "Max Schmeling, to the front!" he proclaimed. "You are just the right man to give this little Negro . . . a couple of rounds of boxing lessons."

Hellmis further described this overrated "loamface," this "masterpiece of bluffing," in the *Völkischer Beobachter*. Louis possessed the black man's proverbial tough skull, he said, but he had beaten only has-beens; he was "custom-made for Schmeling." Perhaps, as Schmeling later insisted, the Führer had misgivings about the German champion taking on a black man. But at this stage, at least, the two leading Nazi papers were actually urging such a fight. So was *Box-Sport*. "This Negro is no champion; the film has taught that with cruel clarity," it stated. "Massa Louis from Detroit, the day you meet a true, class boxer for the first time in your young life—we're waiting for that day."

Wherever he managed to watch the film, Schmeling was first struck by how nervous Baer had been and how poorly he had done. More important, he spotted a flaw in Louis's technique: he dropped his left arm after jabbing, leaving himself open for a right cross. Amazed that no one had spotted this before, wanting to make sure it was true, Schmeling stayed for a second showing. It was just as Benny Leonard liked to say: To win, you gotta make another man do what you want him to do. And Louis was already doing it on his own. He could beat this Louis, Schmeling felt; he just had to get to him fast, before anyone else saw what he'd seen. So in early December 1935, Schmeling again boarded the *Bremen* for New York. His objective was to sign to fight either Louis or Braddock, to watch Louis fight Uzcudun, and to resolve Joe Jacobs's status. The Nazis gave him an additional mission: to allay lingering American fears that the Berlin Olympics in the summer of 1936 would discriminate against blacks and Jews, and thereby to beat back the campaign in the States to boycott the Games. An assistant to the Reich sports minister asked Schmeling to "exert a positive influence on the right people," while the president of the German Olympic Committee gave him a letter to carry to his American counterpart, Avery Brundage.

It was Schmeling's first trip to New York in eighteen months. Professionally, his stock had soared from the dark days of 1934. Having won his last three fights, *Box-Sport* maintained, he had become America's "white hope," its "knight in shining armor, the bulwark against the black danger," and he was returning to the United States almost by popular demand. "They are not exactly altruistic, these people on the other side of the ocean, and they would hardly come back to Max Schmeling if they had another white boxer in their own country" on whom they could lean, it concluded. But for Germans in general the climate in New York had deteriorated. In late July, La Guardia had triggered a major diplomatic row when, responding to discrimination against American Jews in Germany, he refused to license a German-born masseur in New York. That La Guardia's mother was at least part Jewish only further stoked the resulting rage of the German press. The *Angriff* denounced "New York's Jewish Mayor" and his "wire pullers"—the German term, *Drahtzieher*, was one the Nazis invariably used to describe Jews—and called New York "world metropolis of Jewry." A few days later, with the *Bremen* about to depart for Europe, some 1,500 protesters staged an anti-Nazi rally at the pier; some managed to take down the swastika from the ship's bow and hurl it into the Hudson River. The episodes sparked large pro-Nazi rallies in Yorkville, including two in one night, attracting six thousand people, many in Nazi-style uniforms. In September, a New York judge freed five of the six men arrested in the *Bremen* mêlée, equating their protest with the Boston Tea Party. Then, only two weeks before Schmeling arrived, ten thousand people marched against American participation in the Olympics.

Even if Schmeling deserved a title shot, Parker wrote, giving him one would insult the Garden's many Jewish patrons. The *Daily News* characterized Schmeling's welcome as "ten degrees colder than the weather"; with his excessive demands for his next fight and the political situation, it said, his popularity had waned almost to nothing. Meeting with the boxing press, Schmeling seemed surprised at, and even offended by, suggestions that he was dropping Joe Jacobs, who, he insisted, could manage him as long as he liked. Once more, he steered clear of all Jewish talk, but said it would be "a joke" if America opted out of the Olympics. "I'd like to fight this Bomber," he also said. "I think my style would bother him." His only fear, he added, was that someone might hit Louis with a lucky punch before he could get at him, thereby ruining a million-dollar gate. "A million and a half," Jacobs interjected. "The first time I get him alone," Gallico wrote of his friend Schmeling, "I must find out what Der Fuehrer would think, and say, if the No. 1 Nazi pugilist were subjected to public indignities at the hands of our famous Untermensch from the canebrakes of Alabama."

Schmeling faithfully discharged his mission to the Olympic commit-tee. According to Schmeling's memoirs, Brundage came up to his room in the Commodore Hotel—the same venue where the AAU was debating a resolution to boycott the Games—to receive the letter he carried from the German Olympic Committee, and asked for assurances that black and Jewish athletes would be treated fairly in Berlin, which Schmeling promptly made. It is unlikely that Brundage, a Hitler sympathizer and leader of the isolationist America First movement who was determined to see Americans participate in the Berlin Olympics, pressed Schmeling too hard on anything. In any case, because the committee rejected a boycott by only two and a half votes, Schmeling's input may well have been deci-sive. "In retrospect, it was incredibly naïve of me to guarantee things that were completely beyond my control," Schmeling later wrote.

Louis faced four challenges in his fight with Uzcudun, which was set for December 13. The first, pronouncing his name, was something he never managed to do; he settled for "Upside Down." The second was reaching him with a punch. Baer, Levinsky, Carnera, Schmeling—all had fought Uzcudun, but none had knocked him down, largely because they could not penetrate his turtlelike defense. The third was beating him more quickly and decisively than Schmeling had in his three tries. The fourth lay in disproving the canard that marriage ruined a fighter.*

Schmeling came to Pompton Lakes on December 8, and sat near ring-side as Louis sparred. Again, he was not impressed. "See how he stands in front, and open," he told Gallico. "A quick right hand and you haff got him. . . . He leaves so many openings. . . . See, now he looks even ama-teurish. . . . Yah, I sink I haff a good chance with him. I do not know if I can win, but I am not scared." Gallico was struck by Schmeling's calm. "I can report faithfully that he did not change color, blanch, or head for the exits," he wrote. To others, too, he denigrated Louis. JOE LOUIS LOOKS LIKE JOE PALOOKA IN (PUBLIC) OPINION OF SCHMELING, the *Herald Tribune* pro-claimed. Gallico, whose long relationship with Schmeling gave him freer rein to bring up sore subjects, asked him whether Hitler would allow him to fight Louis. Schmeling laughed; the Führer, he said, had more serious things to think about. Politics had not infused sports to such an extent, he insisted, and besides, Germany needed hard currency.

On December 9, Schmeling signed a new two-year contract with Joe Jacobs. During that time, he might get a crack at the crown, but it

---

*Louis and Marva agreed to live apart three weeks before all his fights, which was rea-sonable enough until Louis suggested fighting once a month. "But Joe, that would hardly be fair to your wife," Roxborough told him. "We'll get along," Louis replied.

wouldn't happen right away; Braddock wasn't interested. A champion had to cash in when he could, Braddock explained, and Schmeling wasn't worth much, certainly not as much as Louis. He and Joe Gould had just come back from a western swing, Braddock said, and "all we heard was Louis." Besides, they remembered Schmeling's reaction when they'd tried to get him to fight Braddock. "Well, we're asking now, 'Who is Schmeling?'" Gould said. "What right has he to come over here and demand a championship bout?" The New York boxing commission felt the same way, decreeing that Schmeling could not fight Braddock without facing Louis first. So on December 10, Schmeling signed to fight Louis in June 1936. For his part, Louis agreed that once his three pending fights were behind him, he would not fight again until then. The next day, Mike Jacobs signed up Louis for another five years, locking him in through 1940. Louis had boasted periodically about retiring once he'd won the title and made his million, but Uncle Mike was not about to let that happen. "I've got him sewed up like a sweater," he said.

On the night of December 13, 1935, boxing's good old days, which Louis had already brought back to the summertime fights in New York's stadiums, returned indoors to Madison Square Garden. Limousines disgorged men in high hats and women in furs who joined the masses at the turnstiles. The crowd of 19,945 was the Garden's largest in six years. It was all a tribute to Louis's incandescence, for as the dearth of betting indicated, everyone knew who would win. So many celebrities were on hand that night that, as the *Herald Tribune* put it, it was easier to list who *wasn't* there—like Hitler, Stalin, and the Dionne quintuplets. Schmeling got some boos when introduced, but they were mostly drowned out by cheers. When Louis's turn came, Harry Balogh left out his usual plea for tolerance; "through as gentlemanly conduct as ever shown by any fighter," one writer theorized, Louis had already "earned the respect and well wishes of every boxing customer in the country." Louis looked youthful, clean-cut, innocent; Uzcudun was unshaven, hairy-chested, ferocious. He crossed himself while awaiting the bell. God must have been looking the other way.

There was little action in the first three rounds, as the Basque covered up in his usual fashion and Louis probed for openings. Louis repeatedly jabbed with his left, affording Schmeling ample opportunity to study it. Louis had to get past his opponent's elbows but couldn't be careless: Why break a hand in a penny-ante bout when a bonanza beckoned? By the third round, some fans began to jeer. But it was just a waiting game; sooner or later Uzcudun would grow overconfident or impatient or sloppy, and open himself up, at least for an instant, and Louis would make his move. Everyone knew it was coming. The only question was when, and how devastating it would be. The tension was unbearable. Two minutes and thirty-two seconds into the fourth round, it happened. Louis saw his opening, and shot his right at Paolino's jaw.

It was one of those rare times when a fight was won on a single extraordinary punch—a punch, Gallico wrote, that "hurt everyone sitting within 15 rows of the ring." Damon Runyon called it "the swiftest and most explosive" he had ever seen; the referee, Arthur Donovan, called it the hardest. Louis himself said he was scared stiff when it landed—he had never hit anyone like that. Paolino, a tooth suddenly peeking through his hemorrhaging cheek, fell like someone who had been shot, landing on the canvas—for the first time in his career—with a resounding thud. In the Garden, there was a vast, dim roar, as though, as one eyewitness heard it, someone had dropped piles of lumber from a great height.

At the count of eight, Uzcudun pulled himself up, struck a fighting pose, and motioned for Louis to continue. Louis complied, throwing a few more punches before the fight was called. "I no queet!" Uzcudun screamed as he was dragged away. In his dressing room afterward, Louis was asked whether Uzcudun had dropped his hands before the fateful blow. "He dropped his chin," he replied. Louis was more interested in whether he'd hurt his opponent. "I don't want to kill anybody in this business," he later said. After half an hour under a cold shower, Uzcudun finally took a few steps on his own. Then he fell flat on his face.

Reporters who thought they had already expended all of their superlatives now reached for reinforcements. By any standard, the fight was a mismatch. But like many others, Richards Vidmer of the *Herald Tribune* felt he had just witnessed something transcendent.

> No mere words are adequate to paint the perfection of Joe Louis's performance. When Caruso sang, when Pavlowa danced, when Kreisler plays his violin, there is no contest either.
>
> The skill that Louis possesses is something which never could be acquired. A fighter could be schooled for years and never obtain the rhythm of his reflexes, the speed of his hands or the timing of his blows. It is something natural, and I don't believe a white man ever would be born with such physical syncopation, for there is something of the jungle in the way Louis fights; something smooth and silent and swift; something as decisive as death. . . . Joe Louis

stands alone in the heavyweight world. . . . Yet the farther he goes, the cleaner he sweeps the field, the greater will be the crowds that clamor to see him fight. Those who have heard Paderewski play only want to hear him again; those who have seen the masterpieces of Rodin never quite quench their thirst for the beauty of his work; those who have read Shakespeare constantly reread his words and phrases. And Joe Louis is a master in his own line who has brought a real meaning to the science of boxing. They will want to see him fight again and again.

This, I agree, is high praise and dangerous prediction, but it is my honest reaction and my sincere belief after the greatest performance of pugilism I ever viewed.

One dissenter was James J. Braddock. Louis, he said to himself, was a sucker for a right hand; every time he jabbed he leaned way over and stuck his kisser out there, just begging to be socked. Schmeling felt the same way. He had studied Louis intently, just as he had set out to do. And the newspapermen studied Schmeling studying Louis. An Associated Press photographer trained his camera on Schmeling, recording his reactions over a series of four pictures: "Grins at Start"; "Let's see what happens"; "Say, that guy can hit"; "M-mm—He's gonna be tough." One reporter thought he saw Schmeling suck in his breath and jerk when Louis's fateful punch hit home. But whatever people were reading into his reactions, Schmeling himself was not just unperturbed, but pleased.

Later, the myth developed that in a blinding epiphany that night, Schmeling had cracked Louis's code. "I zee zomezings," he supposedly said. In fact, both in watching the Baer fight on film and in studying Louis at Pompton Lakes, he had seen those same somethings before. Schmeling, Machon, and Joe Jacobs made their way out of the Garden, pushed through the crowd along Eighth Avenue to Forty-ninth Street, then crossed Broadway heading east. No one said anything until Schmeling suddenly blurted out, "I vill tell you something, Choe. I vill knock him oud." Then, Jacobs later related, Schmeling drew both of them into the darkened front of a tailor's shop and, as the fight crowd hurried by obliviously, showed them the moves he would use to do it. Schmeling explained as much to Gallico, who remained skeptical. "If Schmeling is as smart as I think he is, he will go back to Germany, write a polite note to Mr. Mike Jacobs advising him that he has changed his mind and that he will not fight Mr. Louis," he wrote. Uzcudun, who had now fought them both, thought Louis would kill the German. Even the perpetually pessimistic Al Monroe of the *Defender* now predicted that Louis would be champion within a year.

Jack Dempsey agreed, announcing a global search for a new "white hope." He said he was willing to spend $100,000 to find him, bring him to New York, and teach him how to fight. The French newspaper *Paris Soir* announced plans for a European search, too. *Box-Sport* saluted Dempsey's campaign, calling it the "best indication that the race problem in the United States is still alive." But it quite naturally irritated the black press, which had never forgiven Dempsey for dodging black boxers, along with the U.S. Army, during the Great War. "When did this 'palooka' appoint himself the defender of boxing, and incidentally, when did the United States come to mean so much to Dempsey, who was nowhere to be found when Americans fought in France in 1918?" the *Courier* asked. But Dempsey saw a need; Braddock had no chance against Louis, he believed, and Schmeling even less.

"Do you know how long Max Schmeling will last with Joe?" Dempsey asked. "I'll tell you now—less than one round!" But as Schmeling prepared to leave New York, his suitcase full of Louis films, he radiated confidence. "I have discovered that Louis can be hit by a right hand," he said. "I will beat him. Wait until June. You see." His trip to New York, he declared, "was what you would call a good investment."

CHAPTER 6

The Condemned Man

O N DECEMBER 21, 1935, a rumor swept the country that Joe Louis was dead. This was nothing new; at least ten times over the past few months there had been similar reports. Some had him killed in a car accident, others at the hands of mobsters or a murderous woman with a knife. By five-thirty that afternoon, the switchboard at *The New York Times* had received more than one thousand calls; the total count eventually topped the 1,267 logged on the day Will Rogers really did die.

"Sho' 'nuff if I'm dead, I'se a mighty lively corpse," Louis told one reporter. As 1936 began he was not yet officially champion, but he was de facto champion in nearly all important respects: earnings, attention, ability, aura. *Ring* magazine even ranked him number one, ahead of Braddock. While Louis had earned $400,000 in 1935, was talking about making his "first million" by 1937, and was traveling in his own luxury Pullman, Braddock was making one-night stands in tank towns, taking in a measly $1,000 a week, and extending his tenure by steering clear of Louis. Braddock was content to let Louis build himself up, thereby guaranteeing himself an even more glorious payday. Blackburn had an apt rejoinder about rumors that he and Louis had split. "Do you think I'm crazy, quitting a gold mine?" he asked.

And that's what Louis had become, for all of boxing, as Fleischer loved pointing out. Gymnasiums were crackling with activity. Newspapers were once more filled with boxing stories; writers who had wandered off to cover baseball, hockey, or tennis were back. People were again debating who were the best fighters of old and comparing them to Louis. Old-timers were attempting comebacks. And everyone was spending money. "Boxers, managers, promoters, manufacturers of shoes, boxing trunks, and shirts, gloves, bandages, liniments, leather goods that go to make up the head guards, nose guards and protectors, punching bags and other paraphernalia used in training and in active ring combat and even Uncle Sam and the various states where the bouts are staged, are all benefiting by the new life set into motion by one fighter," Fleischer wrote. Even *Ring* itself had picked up nearly eleven thousand new subscribers. Nothing in Fleischer's thirty years in the business could compare to what he was witnessing now. "One man—Joe Louis—has done more for boxing than have any ten dozen men since Jack Dempsey was in his prime," he wrote.

The search for a "white hope" was another part of this renaissance. "Tall men, skinny men, fat men, roly-poly men—men of all sizes and shapes—are being hauled from their work—whatever it might be, to 'save' the day for the white race," Fleischer observed. Of course, the object was not just to hold the black man back, but to cash in on his allure. Whether or not Louis won the title, wrote Fleischer, "he is so big a drawing card that any white boy who shows ring ability is certain to draw more money with Louis than the average fighter can obtain through an entire career." Even Jack Johnson had gotten into the act, spending six days in Boston courting a promising white boxer. "It's a commercial affair with me," Johnson explained. "There's big money for the man who can develop a white fighter to cope with Louis and I'm out to find such a man."

After the Baer fight, Johnson had resumed his usual role of irritant and critic. He insisted that even at his advanced age, he could still go three rounds with Louis without getting touched. He thought Louis would beat Schmeling, but not Braddock; leaving nothing to chance, he offered to help Braddock give Louis "a worse whipping than Mrs. Barrow ever gave him." Black commentators were predictably infuriated with "Lil' Arthur." "Benedict Arnold" and "'Uncle Tom' Johnson" were some of the names bandied about for him. "A jimsonweed in the nostrils of those who once cheered him," one black sportswriter called Johnson.

"Johnson down in his heart doesn't believe half the things he is saying about Joe, but he is a demon publicity hound and knows that most any remark about Joe will land him on the sports pages," Lewis Dial wrote in the *New York Age*. But Gordon Hancock of the *Norfolk Journal and Guide* praised Johnson for helping blacks surmount blind group loyalty. Blacks, he maintained, should be able to say what they want or root for whomever they wish without being accused of treason. Johnson himself insisted he was only speaking his mind. "Say, I like Joe," he said. "He's done wonders and I wish him all the luck in the world. But what's the use of kidding ourselves into declaring that Joe is the greatest ring warrior of modern times?" The black press continued to view the "white hope" campaign with amused contempt. And for all those whites wanting to knock off the incumbent Joe Louis, there were blacks vying to be the next one. Of the seventeen thousand boxers trying out for places on the American Olympic boxing team, six thousand were black. Louis also remained an object of intense interest and curiosity elsewhere. When the *Pittsburgh Courier* questioned Haile Selassie in Addis Ababa in March 1936, Selassie questioned the *Courier* about Louis.

Louis was to have fought three times before the Schmeling bout in June, but his schedule turned out to be far less hectic. His fight against Isidoro Gastanaga in Havana in late December was abruptly canceled after six machine-gun-toting Cubans greeted Mike Jacobs as he began an inspection tour. There were fears that if the fight went forward, someone might be kidnapped. Louis did fight Charley Retzlaff in Chicago on January 17, 1936—for all of eighty-five seconds. So between mid-December 1935 and June 1936 Louis spent less than two minutes in the ring, at least when it counted. It was by far Louis's longest layoff, and was, presumably, just what Joe Jacobs had wanted. Readers eager to keep abreast of Louis, then, had to settle for news of him outside the ring.

In December, Louis gave "Joe Louis banks"—with 50 cents in each— to 150 black schoolchildren in Detroit. In January, he placed an order for twenty-five new suits with Billy Taub, the New York tailor who had dressed every heavyweight champion since Corbett. Woolworth and Kresge were selling Louis figurines. There was talk of Louis backing a black baseball team in Detroit or Chicago. And in planning the group's annual meeting in Baltimore that June, Walter White warned that "the N.A.A.C.P. would blow up in despair" if the Louis-Schmeling fight were held in Chicago, making it either too expensive or too much of a conflict to attend. In February, Paul Gallico, frustrated at American ineptitude during the Winter Olympics in Garmisch-Partenkirchen, Germany, wired an unusual cry for help. "For heavens sake, send over Joe Louis," he pleaded. Meantime, the bandleader Jimmie Lunceford handed out autographed pictures of Louis to the first fifty girls attending a performance in Wheeling, West Virginia, and rumors that Marva was expecting swept Chicago. In March, Louis was elected a director of the Victory Mutual Life Insurance Company, a black-owned firm in Chicago, and the *Courier* announced a symposium on "What I Think About Joe Louis and His Future Fights." A jury in Chicago took all of twenty-five minutes to acquit Jack Blackburn of criminal charges arising from a gun battle in which a stray bullet killed an elderly man. "With the Brown Bomber present as a character witness, testimony proved needless," the *Amsterdam News* reported, though some walking-around money may have helped. In April, a group in Nashville hinted that if Louis visited there, mixed bouts would be allowed. In Pittsburgh, his reception was rivaled by only— maybe—"Caesar's triumphant entry into Rome." In May, Fleischer reported that the stash of Louis photographs and handkerchiefs he'd brought with him was quickly exhausted by worshipful fans in Jamaica, Panama, Trinidad, and elsewhere. In June, Mrs. Viola Place of Englewood, New Jersey, had twin boys, and named them Joe and Louis.*

As the Schmeling fight approached, some observers continued to see secret cabals and grand conspiracies against Louis. One intimated that Roosevelt, fearing that a black champion might offend southern voters, would delay a title bout until after the election in November. The *Daily Worker* cited a "report" that England, France, and Holland, all countries with third-world colonies, had sent "secret suggestions" to Washington that a Louis championship was unacceptable. Meanwhile, Mike Jacobs weighed bids from various cities for the fight. For him, the issue was the impact of a Jewish boycott, and whether it justified moving the contest out of New York. Fleischer supported such a boycott; by this point, *Ring* had been banned in Germany. But Jacobs concluded that Louis's star power, plus the likelihood that he would crush Schmeling, would more than offset any boycott. The fight stayed put.

*One of the stock stories about Louis from this period is apocryphal—that a young black man on death row in North Carolina cried out, "Save me, Joe Louis! Save me, Joe Louis!" as he was asphyxiated. "Not God, not government, not charitably-minded white men, but a Negro who was the world's most expert fighter, in this last extremity, was the last hope," Martin Luther King, Jr., later wrote about the episode. In fact, nineteen-year-old Allen Foster, the first man to die in the state's new gas chamber in January 1936, said no such thing, nor had the the room been miked, as King had claimed. Instead, chained down in the frigid room, wearing only a pair of boxing shorts and speaking through glass that forced eyewitnesses to read his lips, Foster apparently told of sparring with Louis as a boy in Birmingham, clenching and moving his fists to demonstrate. Twice prior to the execution, he'd told reporters the same thing. But there is no record of young Louis ever having been in Birmingham, let alone fighting anyone there, and even Foster's mother conceded that her son was "half-crazy." The embroidered version may date from a story in the *Daily Worker* a month later, and it probably took hold because it seemed so plausible. "I'm in death row, and I got only six more weeks to go," stated a letter Louis did receive from a black inmate in a southern penitentiary in the summer of 1935. "Your picture hanging on the wall will make me feel better as I wait for the electric chair."

In Germany, where the Olympics would soon take place and appearances temporarily mattered, the Nazis had suspended their withering rhetoric about Louis. *Box-Sport* said that Louis had become a "darling of the Americans" not just because of his talent, but because he had remained a child within: "kind-hearted, honest, and without falsity." It presented him as a religious man and a fair fighter, whose only vices were "fine suits and a splendid car." Louis wasn't subhuman, said *Box-Sport*, just shallow, caring only about money; unlike Dempsey or Tunney, he had "no understanding for the honor and dignity of being the world champion." The 12 *Uhr-Blatt* conceded that Louis was "surely no unintelligent fellow" and cited his good manners, particularly compared to his boorish brethren. Of course, he had his reasons: "Were Louis arrogant and impudent, the Americans would not tolerate him at the spot he's occupying right now." *Box-Sport* actually paid Louis an extraordinary tribute, admitting him into the honorable fraternity of anti-Semites. The only fighter he ever really hated was Kingfish Levinsky, it said approvingly, since "one cannot think of any man more unpleasant, arrogant and repugnant than the Jewish kingfish from Chicago." (There was nothing to the charge.)

A myth was to arise and persist that Nazi Germany saw Schmeling as a sure loser, ignoring him as he set off for the suicide mission he'd so foolishly undertaken. Schmeling fostered this idea, later describing how Hitler "seemed disturbed and somewhat angry" that he would place German honor on the line against a black man, especially one so likely to beat him. In fact, the Germans clearly thought they had a winner. While blacks had greater endurance, were "predestined" to fight with their fists, and had eyes that were not so easily read, their moral weakness opened the door for whites, *Box-Sport* said. "A better fighting morale can move mountains," it declared. Far from discouraging people from attending the fight, the North German Lloyd Line reduced rates on two of its premier liners, the *Bremen* and the *Europa*. The cruises were announced in Goebbels's *Angriff*. Whatever ambivalence the Nazis felt about the fight was for professional athletes generally. "This great commercial enterprise can very well be fought without us," declared the *Reichssportblatt*, the official publication of the Berlin Olympics. But this viewpoint was clearly losing ground.

Early in the year, the German sports ministry declared that nonpolitical sportsmen were "unthinkable" in the new Germany. Henceforth, all athletes had to be trained as fighters for Nazism and tested for their "political reliability"; no athlete was complete without mastering the details of Hitler's career, along with Nazi principles and racial theories. But Schmeling was either exempted from all this or satisfied some broader construction of the new rules. He did not join the Nazi Party, though he had high-ranking Nazi friends like Hans Hinkel, Hitler's overseer of Jewish culture, whose ties to the Führer went back to the Beer Hall Putsch of 1923. He gave the Nazi salute when circumstances warranted, appeared at Nazi events, and made the occasional pro-Nazi statement, as in late March 1936 when he, the conductor Wilhelm Furtwängler, and other German celebrities urged Germans to vote for Hitler in a "referendum" on his leadership. "In my heart I view this day as a collective expression of the deepest trust in the Führer," he said.*

Schmeling never said any more than he had to to stay in the Nazis' good graces. He did not spout Nazi rhetoric or wrap himself in the swastika. It will never be clear whether this was a matter of conviction or calculation, or even whether the decision was his or someone else's. But for all concerned, things worked out quite nicely. Whenever the Nazis asked him to pitch in, he obliged. Never did they ask him to do anything that would unduly foul his American nest, which produced great capital for both Schmeling and the regime. To one anti-Nazi German émigré paper in New York, it was Schmeling's earning power that most interested the Nazis; any country that barred its citizens from taking more than four dollars' worth of currency beyond its borders was seriously strapped for cash. "Max Schmeling will remain Hitler's hero . . . willing to take a beating from a Negro [and] managed by a Jew, to bring his bankrupt fatherland money in the hour of peril," it said. Schmeling conceded as much to an American reporter. "I expect to bring home a couple of hundred thousand dollars," he said. "I guess Dr. [Hjalmar] Schacht [the minister of finance] won't mind that."

Schmeling never indulged in Nazi racist rhetoric or "anthropology" regarding Louis, though sometimes his views reflected popular prejudices of the time. "You see, Louis didn't make the mistake other colored boxers made," he told one German interviewer. "He never tried to gain access to the circles of white society. For me there exists no racial dividing line in sports and no one has mentioned the matter to me over here."

---

*Not everyone went along: the commander of the dirigibles *Graf Zeppelin* and *Hindenburg* refused to participate, whereupon his name disappeared from the German papers. Whether the Nazis would have, or could have, imposed a similar ban on the country's most famous boxer is unclear; Schmeling never put them to the test.

"Schmeling is the most famous and best loved athlete in modern German history and the Reich wishes him well," Guido von Mengden, press chief of the Nazi sporting organization, said before his departure. "Naturally, we hope Schmeling wins, but if he loses, the nation will not go into mourning." Schmeling heard no defeatism from Goebbels, whom he and Ondra visited shortly before Schmeling's departure. "The Schmelings are quite open, and tell about their lives and doings," the propaganda minister wrote in his diary, in the first of many such favorable references to the couple. "He is traveling to America to fight Joe Louis. Best wishes!" Noting the article in the *Reichssportblatt*, *The New York Times* called Schmeling's sendoff "shabby," feeding what became the hoary myth that his government had disowned him. "Race-conscious Germany cannot forgive Max for fighting a Negro and letting himself be paid therefor," it claimed. In fact, Schmeling kept his departure plans private and left in the middle of the night to avoid any fuss; the glad-handing and backslapping could come when he returned victorious. Even Ondra, who had the flu, didn't see her husband off. But to those who did, Schmeling hardly seemed beleaguered or ostracized. "If the mood at Schmeling's departure is an omen for his return, then at the beginning of July there will be a giant reception appropriate for a great victor," wrote the editor of *Box-Sport*, Erwin Thoma. "Seldom have we seen Schmeling before a big fight in as good a mood as this time. An aura of confidence literally radiated from him."

As for fighting a black man, the Nazis were making precisely the kind of compromise they repeatedly made in other spheres—for instance, tempering anti-Jewish agitation whenever it threatened German interests. As Schmeling saw it, even if Louis landed a big one on his chin, he would be taking it for the Fatherland. "It has been confirmed to me many times that my mere participation in this bout already promotes the German cause abroad," he told the 12 *Uhr-Blatt* shortly before his departure. The paper agreed, suggesting Schmeling had little choice but to take the fight to help assure Yankee participation in the Berlin Olympics. None of this coverage would have appeared, just as Jacobs would not still have represented Schmeling, had Hitler not wanted it to happen.

On April 21 the *Bremen* again arrived in New York, a swastika now hanging routinely from its mast. Fifty reporters, cartoonists, and cameramen sailed out from the Battery and boarded the ship, then accompanied Schmeling as it headed north to the West Forty-sixth Street pier. Photographers recorded scenes unlikely to appear in any German newspaper, like a smiling Schmeling with his arms around the two Jacobses. Then, for two hours, reporters yet again questioned Schmeling, who was sun-burned from the passage and a bit above fighting weight, even though he'd run twelve miles a day on deck. He repeated what he'd said about Louis—that he was amateurish and a sucker for a good right. "I guarantee you, if Louis makes the same mistakes with me that he did with Baer, I shall knock him out!" he said. Someone asked whether Hitler had seen him off. "Why should he?" Schmeling replied. "He's a politician and I am a sportsman."

As the swarm headed to the promenade deck, some reporters lingered below with Max Machon and the Münchner beer. He disputed those reports that the Germans opposed the fight. "Against it?" he exclaimed. "That is all they talk about. They do not even talk about the Olympics. All they talk about is Schmeling and Louis." Millions would be listening over the radio, he predicted, not just in Germany but throughout Europe. Meantime, Mike Jacobs repeatedly tried to welcome Schmeling for the newsreel cameras, only to keep flubbing his lines. Schmeling and the reporters continued their conversation at the Commodore Hotel, which Schmeling was once more making his New York base. "I'll tell you what: you'll lick this guy and lick him good," Joe Jacobs cried out at one point. "What do you think would have happened to this Louis if you hadn't soft-ened Paolino up like a wet doughnut?" Schmeling told reporters that even at $400 per head for the trip, nearly two thousand Germans were coming to see the action. His chores for Mike Jacobs finally discharged, Schmeling went to see a film about another legendary impresario: *The Great Ziegfeld*. A couple of days later, Ed Sullivan spotted Gene Tunney at the Stork Club and Schmeling at Leon and Eddie's, and surmised that Tunney had to be the happier of the two. "How much enjoyment can Schme-ling get out of night clubs, when he knows that on June 18 he walks the last mile of resin through the little green door of pugilism to face the thunder-bolts of Massa Joe Louis?" he asked.

With that surely in mind, Schmeling skipped a planned detour to the Kentucky Derby and went right into training. His camp would be at the Napanoch Country Club, a small, remote resort in the Catskills about a hundred miles north of New York. Schmeling had preferred Speculator, the Adirondack hamlet where Baer had trained for Louis, but Mike Jacobs wanted him closer; that way, reporters would be more likely to speak with him, and to suggest he could actually win. Joe Jacobs, who selected the place, figured that having Schmeling stay in a Jewish-owned resort might mollify Jewish fight fans. Though it was prohibitively far from corned beef sandwiches and chorus girls, Jacobs pretended to like the sylvan setting. "This is the life," he declared as a fire crackled behind him. "The country is the joint for me."

Schmeling arrived in Napanoch on April 30, and formally opened his camp a week later. It was 1,400 feet above sea level and he enjoyed the cool nights. His living quarters were higher still. He had dinner with the local district attorney and threw out the first pitch at a local baseball game, all to ingratiate himself with the community. An electrician set up a radio wire, through which half-hour reports on Schmeling's activities would be broadcast to New York on Tuesday, Thursday, and Friday nights. (There'd be reports from Louis's camp on Monday, Wednesday, Saturday, and Sunday.) Also on hand was Arno Hellmis. That Nazi Germany's most important sportswriter was on the story (even though he'd had to pay his own way there) was another sign that it was by no means being buried.

Just as Schmeling settled into one upstate New York hamlet, Louis set out for another: Lafayetteville, forty-four miles to the northeast. On the day Louis decamped, Schmeling was on the radio, describing how he'd win. "I know a way, but I better not tell it," he told the interviewer. "Who knows but what he might be listening in?" In fact Louis was, not that he learned much. "I couldn't understand him most of the time," he said afterward. "He talks kinda funny, like a foreigner, I guess. Well, he is a foreigner, sure enough."

There was no boxing in Lafayetteville, only jogging and chopping hardwood. After about a week there, Louis headed for his real training camp, in Lakewood, New Jersey. A resort town near the shore sixty miles south of New York, Lakewood had been a part of boxing history before; Jim Corbett had trained there, as had Schmeling. Roxborough liked its dry climate and thought its pure air, scented with pine and salt, would guarantee Louis some sleep (though why that should ever have been a concern with Louis wasn't clear). Roxborough also liked the cachet: the Rockefellers and the Goulds had places nearby. LAKEWOOD, THE TRAIN-ING CAMP OF JOE LOUIS, THE NEXT HEAVYWEIGHT CHAMPION OF THE WORLD, the signs strung over the highways leading into town soon proclaimed. For the next five weeks, the main thoroughfare of what had always been a lily-white resort was transformed into what the local paper called "a vest pocket edition of Lenox Avenue."

The center of it all was the Stanley Hotel, the rambling caravansary where Louis would train. The hotel's owner, one Harry Cohen, hoped to make Louis's training a long-term industry, and cut down a grove of pines to build an outdoor stadium for three thousand people. There was also to be a bandstand and a nightly floor show, but only after Louis had left the premises. For Louis and his team, Cohen found a furnished mansion two blocks away belonging to a Jewish man wanting to contribute to the cause; according to one black paper, the man was "not only a great admirer of the Brown Bomber, but wants to see Joe give Schmeling, the Nazi man, a good trouncing."

When a columnist from nearby Asbury Park returned from Lakewood on May 12, he carried "visions of Barnum and Bailey and Ringling Brothers combined circuses floating before his eyes." "Gaily colored strips of bunting and screaming banners bearing the name of Joe Louis in letters which reach out and knock you on the noggin fly from every gable of the rambling hotel," he wrote. In the lobby, near a chair that was hot-wired to give unsuspecting visitors a jolt, was a nearly lifesize portrait of Louis draped with American flags and boxing gloves, bearing the legend "Our Next Champion." Outside was a huge tent with a "40-foot chromium refreshment bar." "It may be that Mr. Cohen has decided to get Joe's mind off a little thing like a fight, and enable him to enjoy the lighter side of life," the columnist wrote.

On May 13, Mike Jacobs threw a breakfast for the boxing writers at Lindy's, then formed an eight-car caravan to the camp. It was Louis's birthday, and Braddock was also on hand; in honor of his visit, the hotel had thoughtfully removed the sign in the lobby proclaiming Louis the champion-in-waiting. Louis, who'd fought Carnera at 196 and Baer at about 200, planned to fight Schmeling at 204. But he had come to town weighing 214, and he hit 216 that day even before getting to the cake. In every sense, as he turned twenty-two years old, Joe Louis had a lot to lose. He greeted the governor of New Jersey, Harold Hoffman, and horsed around with Braddock, who found himself in the bizarre posture of a champion challenging a challenger. "What's the matter with you, fella, are you trying to duck me?" Braddock asked theatrically. "As soon as I smack down this Schmeling, I'm your man," Louis replied. (No matter how one rendered his words, everyone agreed on how Louis actually pronounced "Schmeling": "Smellin'," he called him.)

Louis also received his personal copy of Edward Van Every's new biography of him. Louis hagiography had become a staple of the "race press," but here was something truly unprecedented: sainthood conferred by a white reporter from one of New York's most staid newspapers, the *Sun*. The book had a lyrical, almost biblical tone, describing Louis as a "Black Moses" in its very first line, and calling his story "something in the nature of a miracle." The rest of the press now dissected Louis as never before, and not always so reverentially. "You notice his mouth first," wrote Jimmy Cannon in the *New York American*. "It is a red capital O. It is a soft doughnut stuck on his moon-face, and it does not go with his narrow and shifty eyes." W. W. Edgar of the *Detroit Free Press*, who had followed him from the outset, explained that Louis could read a bit, but could write only his name. Once, a fan asked for an inscription to "my friend," and Louis could not spell the second word. The Hearst papers were the harshest, calling him "Mike Jacobs' pet pickaninny" and rendering his remarks in the most primitive dialect. In "Joe Louis Takes His June Exams," a Hearst cartoonist showed a schoolmaster labeled "Old Man Experience" questioning man-child Louis as his classmates—Schmeling, Dempsey, and John L. Sullivan, among others—sat at their desks. "Joseph, make me up a sentence with the word 'defeat' in it," he asks. "Sho!" Louis replies. "I pops 'em on de chin an' dey drags 'em out by de feet!!"*

But others sensed a growing maturity and confidence in Louis. "In his native, untrained way he is an interesting, amusing talker," said Joe Williams. Southern reporters also described him sympathetically, albeit in the idiom of their day. "These are good colored folks," wrote a columnist from Charlotte. "Money and fame hasn't changed them. They are satisfied to be among their own people, and I can give them no higher recommendation." Sometimes Louis wasn't allowed to show his smarts. When a reporter for a Communist youth magazine asked him his views of the Scottsboro case, Roxborough pulled the writer aside. "Don't think Joe isn't intelligent," he said. "He feels these things keenly. But he's a prizefighter right now. He's got to think of the nation as a whole; and he can't afford to alienate anybody."

In a fifteen-part series, Damon Runyon meticulously deconstructed Louis's boxing technique. Louis was not the greatest puncher ever, he wrote, but probably the greatest ever with both hands. He had "perfect coordination of mind and muscle," an uncanny sense for what opponents

---

*As Wilfrid Smith of the *Chicago Tribune* later pointed out, one's view of Louis came to depend partly on what paper one read, and what stylebook it followed. In one paper, he might sound like the old, ungrammatical South. "Ah ain't afraid of Smellin'. When Ah gets ready this time, Ah'm goin' to punch him right in de mouf and see how he likes that," he might say. But in another, the same thing would come out as "I am not afraid of Max Schmeling. It is true he whipped me two years ago, but this time the German will not face an inexperienced youngster. I will wait for my chance and then I will shoot my right to his chin. There will be another ending to this fight."

were about to do, plus a knack for hiding what he was about to do himself. He was incredibly accurate. His physique was perfect for punching: long arms like whiplashes and muscles so "silky" that he looked lackadaisical until he started to fight, when his arms became "snaky" and his legs like steel springs. He had disproportionately big hands, and his wrists and fore-arms were enormously powerful. He had perfect balance; hitting from his heels, he quadrupled his punching power. And he had a textbook temperament: cold, methodical, unflappable, unhurried. Runyon found only a couple of dissenters. One, eighty-four-year-old Tom O'Rourke, said John L. Sullivan would have beaten Louis with a straight right.

Louis began his workouts. Sparring partners earned $25 per round, though Mushky Jackson, the Mike Jacobs factotum running the opera-tion, considered paying them by the minute to keep them on their feet. Louis went through them fast; among those who'd quickly had enough was future heavyweight champion Jersey Joe Walcott. A band supplied the music at ringside. Louis entered the ring to trumpet fanfares. After some brutal exchanges the sounds of "I'm Sorry I Made You Cry" or "Let's Call It a Day" filled the air. As the sparring went on, spectators main-tained a steady dialogue with Louis, sometimes shouting so robustly that the announcer had to ask them to stop.

As the crowds grew—four thousand people showed up one Sunday, paying $1.10 a head—the actual business of boxing became almost secondary. Everywhere, street merchants hawked Joe Louis pins, Joe Louis rings, Joe Louis charms, Joe Louis medallions, Joe Louis keys, Joe Louis statues, Joe Louis flashlights, Joe Louis pictures, Joe Louis pen-nants. "An enterprising salesman could catch Joe Louis perspiration in cologne bottles and peddle it at two bucks an ounce," Ralph Matthews joked. The hordes, overwhelmingly black, came from Atlantic City, As-bury Park, and, mostly, Harlem, and temporarily transformed a Jim Crow town. "Park Avenue has its Newport, but now Harlem has its Lake-wood," the *Courier* announced. Black reporters arrived in droves; so eager was the man from the *Houston Informer* to get there that he was arrested for speeding near the camp. "The whole atmosphere here is a revela-tion," wrote Roi Ottley of the *Amsterdam News*. "Residents and trades-men have the glad hand out when Negroes approach.... Some cynic reminded me that to be in New Jersey is the same as being in Georgia ... but at the moment this feeling has been completely dispelled. Money is a persuasive talker.... And Joe is bringing hoards of it to this village."

The transformation was especially notable at the previously all-white Stanley Hotel. "Now the place is as genuinely democratic and impartial to everyone as heaven is expected to be when (and if) we ever get there," the *Norfolk Journal and Guide* said. But the changes only went so far. While white reporters slept and entertained themselves upstairs, their black counterparts were relegated to the basement, and were barred from sitting on the front porch or in the lobby. "The only thing they give the Race freely [at the hotel] is bills and they come large and fast," complained Al Monroe, who, with the backing of the *Defender*'s publisher, refused the second-class accommodations.

Marva's arrival on May 16 only enhanced the glamour. "As she walks the streets, women and men, alike, stop to watch her glide by," the *Amsterdam News* wrote in wonder. "Murmurs of admiration follow in her wake." Society columns in the black press offered regular updates on her wardrobe and her marriage. The lovebirds' every public moment together was monitored, though not everyone was pleased about her presence. "With her around all Louis wanted to do was to indulge in mumbling sweet nothings," said the *Richmond Planet*. His great passion in Lakewood wasn't boxing or his marriage, though, but golf. Watching Tony Manero win the U.S. Open at nearby Baltusrol had inspired him, and after a dozen rounds he was shooting in the low nineties. He played the game so often that the local country club awarded him a trophy. When his managers hid his car keys to keep him from escaping to Yankee Stadium for a ball game, he slipped off and played eighteen holes of golf instead. After breakfast one morning, he sneaked out to shoot another round, forcing his frantic management to have to go find, and then fetch, him.

Before long the adulation, frivolity, and warm weather started getting to Louis. His timing was off; his punches were anemic; he appeared lethargic and indifferent. Stupid, lifeless, and "exhibitionistically frivolous," Jimmy Cannon wrote. Physically and mentally, Louis had grown fat. "Hunger is the fighter's friend," Cannon explained. "Success and plenty are his enemies. Instead of the relentless kid fighting for his life, Joe is now a guy fighting for more money in the bank, another car, another suit, another day in the sun over Lakewood." "His admirers say not to worry," wrote Runyon. "They say he must be in the pink because he's Joe Louis, and that, anyway, no matter how he looks or what he does he is bound to flatten Max Schmeling." Maybe Schmeling didn't know Louis was ordained to knock him out, Runyon mused. But in the world of professional boxing, where everything was hyped and newspapers doubled as boxing promoters, who knew what or whom to believe? Louis could deliberately be dogging it to build up the gate. Having made the "grave error of looking too dangerous" one day, the *Daily News* observed, Louis "caught the ticket-selling spirit" by letting himself be pummeled the next. Despite reports that he had "housemaid's knee, leaping dandruff and hurry-up halitosis," Louis was actually "sharper than a Bowie knife," the *News*'s Jack Miley claimed.

For his publicity operations, Mike Jacobs employed six former sports-writers, well versed in all of the angles. One of his veteran flacks, Jersey Jones, had been assigned to Pompton Lakes, and complained about the suicide mission he'd been given. "I've got to make Louis look bad," he griped. "Get that! I've got to make him look bad so the public will think Schmeling's got a chance against him. The greatest young heavyweight of all time, and my job is to sell him to the public as a bum!" To the *Daily Worker*, the jeremiads were just "plain ordinary anti-Negro propaganda." *Collyer's Eye* saw the news from Lakewood as an attempt to juggle the odds. Bundles of black money, including from gamblers in Detroit and Philadelphia, were being placed on Schmeling, it said; by betting on the German and then throwing the fight, Louis and his backers could make themselves a lot more money, although it conceded there were problems with that thesis, unique in its customarily sordid world: "Throughout his brief professional career, Louis has always refused to do business, even carry an opponent." Besides, it said, it would "seem like insanity" to throw the title when it was within reach. Some black sportswriters rushed to the Bomber's defense—insisting, as one put it, that Louis's timing remained "as accurate and as rhythmical as a Beethoven sonata." "If you've got the stuff, lay it on Joe and lay it on heavy," another urged.

Publicly, Louis's camp wasn't worried. "Its attitude seems to be that at his worst, Shufflin' Joe still is a far better fighter than Max Schmeling at his best," a reporter from Newark wrote. Now that Louis had a reputation, Blackburn told the press, there was no need for him to flatten everyone in training. Louis's handlers started talking of breaking Dempsey's record for brevity: nineteen seconds, against Fred Fulton in 1918. Schmeling's claims about discovering a weakness in Louis's technique was foolishness, they said. Louis himself appeared utterly unconcerned. Taking on Schmeling, one black columnist said, was for Louis "the same as if he were a janitor who had agreed to scrub some floors for a price." The Louis team was already thinking about Braddock—in 1937, when he'd have a clean financial slate and the tax bite would be much smaller than in a year in which he'd already fought one lucrative bout. "We don't have to rush him," said Julian Black. "He's going to be good for a mighty long time."

Privately, though, there was some concern; Jersey Jones's facetious comments turned out to be not so far off the mark. "Chappie, what's wrong with your fighter?" the trainer Ray Arcel, who was in camp one day, asked Blackburn. "He's on his honeymoon, and she's here with him," Blackburn grumbled. Two weeks before the fight, Marva was finally banished to Harlem. The press criticism now got to Louis. He started bearing down before he was ready, losing weight in the blistering heat that he was then unable to put back on. Walter White sensed none of this when he visited Lakewood, but the signs were there; he tried to talk boxing with Louis, but all Louis wanted to discuss was baseball. "Gosh, how worried he is about Schmeling!" White mockingly wrote Roxborough afterward.*

Schmeling's mission at Napanoch was to get the legs that had failed him so badly in the Baer fight back into peak condition, so that he could move quickly. And he had to build up his endurance so he could outlast Louis. This meant lots of running; Machon later estimated that the two of them ran more than six hundred miles around the hilly terrain. He also had to take lots of jabs, so that when the time came he could get close enough to Louis to penetrate his flawed defense. He brought much of his food with him, including German sausage, German cheese, German bread, and even German mineral water; American water, he believed, helped account for his American losses. Just about his only indulgence was movies, which he would see in nearby Ellenville. Schmeling wasn't out to dazzle anyone; only twice did he throw his right with full force. Though his crowds didn't rival Louis's, Schmeling also had his following; the *New Yorker Staats-Zeitung* printed detailed directions to the place by car or train.

While others were busy writing him off, Schmeling had his program all mapped out. He would beat Louis, go back home on one of German's zeppelins, then return a few weeks later to begin training for the title fight with Braddock. That would mean missing part of the Berlin Olympics, but that's how it would have to be. Already, he'd arranged to leave his equipment in Napanoch. In early June, Schmeling told *Liberty*

---

*White wasn't thinking only about boxing, either. He hoped to launch what was to become the famous legal arm of the civil rights revolution, the NAACP Legal Defense and Educational Fund, and had asked Louis to donate the seed money "when you have gotten the [Schmeling] fight out of the way." It was the first of several such appeals, all of which fell on deaf ears; the very thing that made Louis successful enough to interest the NAACP—his appeal to the American mainstream—made the NAACP too radioactive for him to embrace. Whatever Louis gave to it, he did discreetly; the public knew only about the five dollars he donated to a fund for the Scottsboro Boys. When it came to civil rights, his example would have to suffice, and that wasn't always perfect. Apart from being faulted for refusing to take on black fighters, he was accused of snootiness for staying in white hotels in New York and Philadelphia.

magazine he'd win, and how. "A good right hand will beat Louis," he
wrote. "I feel certain that when he shoots his left I can cross my right over
it and score." His victory would come sometime after the third round, he
said, and would be by knockout. Eventually, he grew tired of discussing
Louis's technique. "Why don't you ask Louis what he plans to do?" he
retorted. "That don't do any good," quipped Joe Jacobs. "Louis only
grunts or yawns or goes to sleep." Schmeling laughed heartily.

On June 4, Mike Jacobs came by Napanoch with a contract binding
Schmeling to fight Braddock if he beat Louis. Jacobs was merely covering
all contingencies, but Schmeling and Joe Jacobs saw portents in it. "So!"
Schmeling declared. "I see you give me a chance to win, after all." To the
Angriff, it meant that Schmeling was the favorite. That's certainly how
Schmeling felt. "If confidence were music, Schmeling would be the
whole Philharmonic," wrote Jack Miley of the *Daily News*. Some nonetheless detected the ravages of time in the nearly thirty-one-year-old Schmeling. To Anthony Marenghi of the *Newark Star Eagle*, "fistic senility"
hung over him; he'd become "an old third baseman stumbling in for a
bunt." Al Monroe thought Schmeling wouldn't last two rounds. "Today
he seems so vitally alive," Richards Vidmer observed in mid-June. "What
will he seem a week from today when his fine, strong, bronzed body has
been bruised and battered and covered with vicious welts where the lightning of a Dark Angel has struck?"

Joe Jacobs managed the press and, like Jersey Jones in Lakewood, he
did not have an easy time of it. The "Reich sports idol" and his "spectacularly non-Aryan" manager, as *The New Yorker* described them, remained
the oddest couple in sports. Their relationship had so deteriorated that
when the *Mirror* described Jacobs as Schmeling's manager, it put quota-
tion marks around the term. Max Machon was really in charge, and got a
larger commission than Jacobs did—a reported 18 percent, rather than
15⅓. Schmeling had all but stopped talking to Jacobs except in public, and
then just for the sake of appearances. Jacobs did not live in Schmeling's
cottage, as Machon did; he had to call before going there.*

But Jacobs nonetheless served Schmeling tirelessly, ingeniously, vol-
ubly. He planted stories compulsively, informing the world that Schmeling's sparring partners were being fed steak, the better to withstand all
those ferocious punches. He would hide the newspapers from Schmeling,

*Schmeling later said he'd isolated Jacobs only because his "constant upbeat chatter
made me nervous" and because he "often came home at night singing or making a
racket."

so that he'd be spared all the dire prophesies. And he denigrated Louis at every opportunity. "I'm telling you something: That Louis has lost it," he declared. "He's going the way of all flesh, get me? He's got plenty of money, and he's tired of the grind. Why, he's even cut out his road work to play golf every morning. Get a load of that, will ya? Golf!" Louis fought dirty, Jacobs said, throwing sneak punches that referees were afraid to call because of his "so-called greatness." Louis was overrated, overconfident, and overpadded, wearing far more gauze and tape on his fists than the regulations allowed. "Them guys have been making a plaster cast of Louis's mitts," he shrieked to the boxing commissioners. The boxing commissioners responded, limiting Louis's bandages.

Jacobs kept at it because he still got a cut of Schmeling's earnings, however diminished. But more, it was a kind of addiction. "It was he who made Schmeling a champion," Joe Williams wrote. "Perhaps he still has a sculptor's enthusiasm for his masterpiece." A few years later, Williams described this stage of their relationship more brutally. "By now [Jacobs] knew he was dealing with a Grade A rat," he wrote, "but in some indescribable, mystic manner he was able to ignore completely this part of the fighter. All he could see was the champ he had made." Jacobs added a veteran boxing man called Doc Casey to the team because he believed he brought Schmeling good luck; Casey had refereed some of Louis's early bouts and had previously worked in Schmeling's corner. Another ring veteran, Tom O'Rourke, stopped by the camp. He had spotted the same flaw in Louis that Schmeling had, and urged Schmeling to cross with a right to Louis's chin whenever Louis dropped his left hand. That, he told Schmeling, is what John L. Sullivan would have done.

In early June the German consul in New York, Hans Borchers, stopped by Napanoch, and was asked whether Schmeling's prestige in Nazi Germany would suffer were he to lose or if there was official unhappiness with him over his decision to fight a black man. He belittled both ideas. Borchers was a career diplomat, though, and it was unclear whether he spoke for the regime. The sportswriters covering Schmeling rarely broached politics. But near the end of camp, he was asked about a possible war between Germany and England or France. "Dere will be no war, not in dis generation," he replied. "The German people do not wish it. Over here the Americans did not have any war. Yah, I know, maybe one hundred thousand dead. But in Germany it was millions dead and more wounded. A big shell costs $3,000. It iss better to spend that for homes. Do you think Germany would have voted 99 percent for Hitler if it wass to be for war?" To *Champion of Youth,* the Communist magazine, Schmeling distanced himself from Nazi racial attitudes. He grew upset when asked about statements in the German press that blacks were more cowardly than whites. "In sport, the Negro and white man are just the same," he said. "The best man wins." More than that, though, he would not say. "Schmeling evidenced great reluctance to answer our questions on the Nazi regime," the reporter wrote. "We asked him if he felt it was true that the German race is superior to all others from a cultural and physical viewpoint. He seemed not to understand."

The most political element in Schmeling's camp was Hellmis, who by now had become all but Schmeling's official Nazi chronicler. A balding, ruddy-faced, and portly thirty-five-year-old veteran of World War I, Hellmis was a Nazi Party member in good standing, having joined around the time the Jews were eliminated from the German boxing community. He approached his work with patriotic fervor; his American counterparts quickly came to regard him with wariness and revulsion. "A sweaty hog of a man," Jimmy Cannon called him. One night at the Stork Club in New York City, a German reporter in his cups told an American journalist that Hellmis was monitoring everyone, Schmeling included, making sure no one strayed from the party line. The next morning, the German reporter begged the American not to print what he'd said; he feared he'd be killed.

In the pages of the *Völkischer Beobachter* and the *Angriff*, Hellmis reassured Germany about Schmeling. "He knows very well that it's not going to be a stroll, yet he believes he can defeat the Negro because he wants to bring the world champion title back to Germany," he later wrote. "The unanimous opinion of all of America, the sneering of the press, the doubts of his fellow countrymen, of his own training partners—nothing can jar his belief in himself!" He described what he viewed as the vulgar American-style publicity—"*Reklame*"—surrounding the fight. Hellmis conceded that having whipped up press interest to a degree unfathomable to Germans, Mike Jacobs was "a very smart boy." Hellmis saw the matchup in starkly racial terms: Schmeling would have the loyalty of all whites at Yankee Stadium. While Schmeling felt the tight security around him unnecessary, it made perfect sense to Hellmis: "Some woolly head of a Negro" could always pour something into Max's coffee. But such pejorative racial references were rare. With the Olympics looming, the German propaganda ministry, which by now had begun issuing written orders to the German press, instructed editors that racial questions were "absolutely not to be broached" in fight coverage. Neither Louis nor Schmeling was to be depicted as a representative of his race, not even if Schmeling won.

Crowds continued to descend on Lakewood. After four thousand people showed up on June 7, Harry Cohen vowed to enlarge the arena for the final weekend. That Friday, Lucky Millander and his band jumped into the ring and played as a grinning Louis shadowboxed to the beat. The next day, Louis applauded enthusiastically as Ethel Waters sang "Stormy Weather" just for him. Louis predicted a knockout, but would not say when. "Well, it won't go fifteen rounds," he finally offered. "Maybe half that." And despite the disquieting reports, 90 percent of black America believed the fight would end in the first round. Jack Johnson called for Louis in six, though, according to *Collyer's Eye*, he also had "a nice piece of dough riding on Schmeling," and he told *Ring* that at least two dozen fighters over the past forty-five years could have beaten Louis. Schmeling saw the article, and reviewed it closely with Machon.

On the eve of the fight, black America was positively giddy. Even before the first punch it had won, simply because so much of white America—even in the South—was pulling for a black man. A newsman from Atlanta sized up the situation. "As between Schmeling the German and Joe Louis, the colored boy, southerners generally will quietly pull for Joe," he wrote. To Ed Harris of the *Philadelphia Tribune*, the way in which whites were lining up behind Louis was little short of miraculous. "In the face of this one waits for the pyramids to crumble, the Statue of Liberty to truck around its base, the Empire State Building to start singing 'Sidewalks of New York,'" he wrote. "Anything can happen now. . . . Brothers, the battle is over. . . . Soon you will be able to travel all over the Southland, marry women of other colors if you so desire, go any place and do anything."

Reporters vied with one another to capture just how bleak Schmeling's prospects were. As much chance as a silk shirt in a Chinese laundry, someone wrote, or of an ice cube in a smelting furnace. Schmeling was likened to Bruno Hauptmann, the convicted Lindbergh kidnapper who two months earlier had gone to the electric chair. Dan Parker urged Schmeling to practice his farewell wave to the crowd—a difficult maneuver, he conceded, for someone who usually used his right arm to heil Hitler. "One can only ask ourselves with what sauce, sorry . . . in which round will Max Schmeling be eaten," said Robert Perrier in the French sports newspaper *L'Auto*, writing from Lakewood. If he were the German, he wrote, he would spend the day before the fight practicing his fall. "You have to know how to fall down in a ring, once that fatal punch lands," he explained. "There is the pure and simple dive; there is, if you are looking for something luxurious, the angel jump; and finally, steeped in artistry, the gracious fall, like Pavlova's swan. Max should study in depth the art of falling beautifully in front of the most prestigious boxer of all time. Poor Anny Ondra, so beautiful, so beautiful, how your pretty eyes will weep." Why would fans lay down scarce Depression dollars for something so nasty, brutish, and short? Because, the *Sun* theorized, "a killing is still the best show on earth." Some out-of-towners thought the fight frenzy a phenomenon peculiar to New York, which Elmer Ferguson of the *Montreal Herald* called the "City of Suckers." "It is a city of hero-worshipping hicks," he wrote. "It goes head over heels for strange things."

All of boxing's brightest lights—Dempsey, Tunney, Baer, Braddock—lined up behind Louis. It would end before five, Dempsey said, and when it did, Joe Louis would be "greater than me or anybody else the game has ever had." Betting was light; no one wanted Schmeling. "They won't even bet he has black hair," one bookie said. The only action was on the round of the knockout. The *Mirror* promised good seats to the fifty people submitting the most clever coda to the following ditty:

> *What's going to happen to Schmeling*
> *In the Joe Louis bout is hard telling*
> *Can YOU name the round*
> *When Max hits the ground?*
>
> _____ .

A few brave souls did pick Schmeling—some because of Louis's overconfidence, some because of the German's eerie self-assurance, some because, as George M. Cohan once said, "There is nothing so uncertain as a dead sure thing." Fred Kirsch, a German boxing promoter who'd brought Schmeling to the United States with Arthur Bülow, said Schmeling would go down as the "man who came back." George Raft and Marlene Dietrich also favored Schmeling. Some writers chose Schmeling, or at least wanted to. "Everyone knows Louis is going to win!" Willie Ratner's editor at the *Newark Evening News* huffed when he read Ratner's daring prediction. "What they want to know is how many rounds it will go! Rewrite it!" Gallico had been to the Winter Olympics in Germany, where he'd seen the dreadful but unstoppable power of "Nazi Aryan Pride." "For Schmeling, a personal friend of Hitler and Goebbels, a quick knockout at the hands of the Negro would have made them look ridiculous," he wrote. "Germans do not like to be made to look ridiculous." Gallico called for Schmeling to knock out Louis around the tenth or twelfth round. His editors dumped the story in the trash.

Everyone was going with Louis, but some confessed to misgivings. Grantland Rice thought Louis was due for a bad fight. To Hy Hurwitz of *The Boston Globe*, Louis was "too sure of himself for his own good." "This guy Schmeling is no chump," said Clark Gable. Some blacks also equivocated. Louis's recent marriage, Schmeling's scientific nature, odds long enough to lure unsavory elements into the mix, a distrust of auspicious things: all blended into what the *Norfolk Journal and Guide* called "an undercurrent of distant fear." Blackburn privately confessed to some of the same qualms. "The trouble with Joe is that you newspapermen have made him think he can just walk out and punch any one over and that Schmeling is the softest pushover of the lot," he said. "Joe's likely to get hit on the chin with one of them Schmeling rights and what with his legs not being what they should be and his being only a two-year fighter—well, lots can happen that's not so good."

"It is not our place to predict a defeat for our countryman, even if he were fighting a completely lost battle," *Box-Sport* pronounced. "The concept of national sports representation is too important and noble." Having said that, it noted that odds of ten to one for Louis weren't unreasonable. Schmeling was past his prime and not good enough for Louis, the *Westdeutscher Beobachter* noted. Schmeling's estranged manager, Arthur Bülow, made grim predictions to a couple of German papers. Louis, he said, was "fresher, younger, stronger, tougher, and more professionally ambitious" than Schmeling, who'd grown rusty and lost much of his power. "Most likely he'll manage to simply run Max over," he said, though he quickly added, "I'd be happy if things turn out differently."

Though his initial projections had come down, Uncle Mike was still saying that the gate couldn't miss a million dollars. The Hearst papers reported long lines outside the ticket offices. Thousands of World War I veterans were said to be buying seats with their newly arrived bonuses; Jacobs talked of installing ten thousand more of them. In fact, Jacobs had headaches. He'd set the top ticket at $40, the highest ever for a nontitle fight and the first time since the Depression that anyone asked more than $25. At the New York Stock Exchange, $40 seats were said to be selling for $20; the *World-Telegram* reported that around the scalpers' offices there hadn't been such wholesale unloading since the troopships returned from France after World War I. "Possibly the town has come to the conclusion that, since Louis shapes up as invincible, it will be a lot more fun to stay at home, criticize the radio announcer, razz the fighters and try to stop the ladies from talking," wrote Art Lea Mond in the *Morning Telegraph*.

The Jewish boycott was another problem. It was a shadowy thing, scarcely mentioned in a largely unsympathetic New York press. The paper most likely to cover it, the *Mirror,* said little on the topic, though Dan Parker called talk of it "tripe." Jewish fans would attend in droves, he wrote, just to see "one of Herr Hitler's representatives treated like some of their kinsmen are in Herr's land." One had to read papers from the hinterlands to learn that letters were circulating, primarily in the largely Jewish garment industry, urging fans to stay home. "Why let a German take home our money?" one of them declared. "Listen to Louis knock out Schmeling on the radio." "The boss told me if we wanted to help make money for this Nazi fighter we'd have to do it out of our own pockets," a garment district employee said to an Indianapolis newspaper. "The biggest fight of all is now going on in the mind of every Jew in New York," the London *Daily Herald* reported; every one of them had to weigh whether or not to go.

"It's the silliest thing I ever heard," Joe Jacobs predictably griped from Napanoch. "Schmeling is training at a Jewish resort. Most of those who come in contact with him up here are Jews and he's never been treated better in his life." In fact, New York's Jews were characteristically fragmented on the issue. Three of the city's Yiddish daily newspapers—the *Morgn-zhurnal, Der Tog,* and the *Forverts*—asked for credentials for the fight. A rabbi from Brooklyn pledged to be at ringside with the minister of a black Baptist church to cheer Louis on—and there would be thousands of others like him.

But most blacks remained too busy with their own grievances and too ambivalent about the Jews to make common cause with them, or to let politics stand in the way of an extravaganza. Some resented being asked to show so much solicitude toward another group in another country. "While condemning Hitler . . . let us remember that there is nothing that he is now doing to the Jews that has not been done by the United States on a longer, vaster and more brutal scale to its black citizens," the *Amsterdam News* had written the year before. It figured that the fifteen thousand extra blacks attending the fight would make up for the fifteen thousand Jews who stayed away.

The black weeklies mobilized. The *Amsterdam News* planned to hold the presses until after it was over. The *Courier* weighed the relative importance of two big stories—Louis vs. Schmeling and the Democratic National Convention in Philadelphia the following week—and deployed its troops accordingly: eight reporters to the fight, three to the Democrats. Harlem's better hotels were mostly filled, the pawnshops had been cleared of field glasses, the liquor stores had upped their stock, the larger restaurants had added waiters. According to one purveyor, on fight day Harlem ordered ten thousand chickens. Woolworth's had stocked up on Louis photographs and books, and a legless man dragged himself up and down 125th Street selling postcards announcing the round in which Louis would win. At the Apollo Theater, beautiful dancers donned boxing gloves for a fight routine. Pictures of Louis peered out of every store window.

Marva remained in Harlem. She had spoken with her husband nightly, and had no fears about the outcome, only about the potential cost. "Joe is so handsome," she said. "I know he'll win like he always does, but I get nervous for fear something will happen to his face . . . like cauli-flower ears or a twisted nose." Signs went up around Detroit promising that Louis would wire home his best wishes after the fight. Harlem would also have its customary revelries. "Stage parties, banquets and dances EVERYWHERE," the *Philadelphia Tribune* predicted. Louis agreed to be the guest of honor at a Negro League baseball game in Newark the night after the fight. A movie theater in Buffalo announced plans to show films of the fight alongside Dempsey's battles with Luis Angel Firpo, Georges Carpentier, and Gene Tunney, so that people could finally decide which fighter was the greatest.

A cartoon in the *Amsterdam News*, titled "When and If Joe Louis Loses," captured how comically dependent black America, and Harlem in particular, was on Louis. In it were scenes of grown men jumping off a pier, pimps on Lenox Avenue dressed only in barrels, a stream of moving vans leaving Sugar Hill, and a crowd outside of Goldberg's pawnshop. "Sorry, pops, but the line starts around the corner—an' then, you have to have references to even get on the line," a cop tells one customer.

A week earlier, the paper had struck a rare cautionary note. "The white world has long believed that a Negro is not able to carry success grace-fully," it stated. "If Joe Louis should come out of this fight a loser, the white writers will pounce on him with venom and tear him to shreds." It did not say how the black world would feel under the same circumstances. But to Murray Robinson of the *Newark Star Eagle*, the danger was less of Louis losing than of losing the chance to see Louis at his peak. Awash in money, with few good men to battle, and from a race not known for longevity in the ring, Louis, he predicted, was bound soon to go into decline.

Now was the time, he said, to see Joe Louis at his greatest—which was "just about the greatest heavyweight you've ever seen."

CHAPTER 7

Victor and Vanquished

THE SKIES, someone said, were weeping for Max Schmeling.

The rain had begun on the night of June 17, and by the morning of the day of the fight, June 18, it had turned into a downpour. The papers were filled with fight news; the prize for the shortest, bluntest lead paragraph went to the *Newark Evening News:* "What round?" Whatever the weather, the weigh-in would be held as scheduled at the Hippodrome, the Victorian-era hall on the corner of Sixth Avenue and Forty-third Street that Mike Jacobs had recently annexed to his growing empire. At the *World-Telegram*, the pressmen had already set LOUIS WINS BY KNOCKOUT in boxcar type. But the odds were that everyone would have to spin their wheels another day before anything actually happened.

Louis and his retinue drove the nine miles from Lakewood to Point Pleasant, New Jersey, where they boarded a private club car attached to the 9:10 train to New York. Clusters of fans greeted them as they headed north, but after struggling for fifteen minutes with "I Can't Give You Anything but Love" on his harmonica, Louis fell asleep and had to be awakened at Pennsylvania Station. Police created a wedge through the crowd, and he made his way to the Hippodrome. He arrived half an hour early, went into Jimmy Durante's dressing room, played what he said was "Gloomy Sunday," then fell back to sleep on the couch.

It was raining in Napanoch, too. "Bad day, eh? I think we have no fight tonight," Schmeling said. When they set out for New York, Joe Jacobs rode with the state troopers in the lead car, with Schmeling following behind. It was a harrowing and interminable drive, with the rain making it nearly impossible to see anything on the narrow, winding mountain roads. For much of the ride Schmeling read a German magazine, speaking only as his car approached the George Washington Bridge. Again, he said it looked as if there'd be no fight that night. Wearing a gray suit and a maroon tie, his right eye puffed and discolored from training, he joined Louis around twelve-thirty. The Hippodrome had recently hosted a circus attraction called "Jumbo," and the smell of elephants, camels, and kangaroos still permeated the place.

The two fighters shook hands coming out of their dressing rooms, then ignored each other until they were inside the arena, when the reporters hurled questions at them. Schmeling again said he had a plan for the fight; Louis displayed a complete lack of concern for the hullabaloo around him. "You gentlemen know each other, I think," the head of the boxing commission, General John J. Phelan, told the two. Louis, wearing black trunks with a red border, was examined first, while Schmeling, in purple and blue trunks, watched. Then they traded places. Louis plucked his face nervously. He then picked up a newspaper, lips moving as he read about the Tigers. "Now on the scales: Joe Louis!" a functionary announced. A deputy commissioner fiddled with the weights. "Louis, 198!" he declaimed. There was stunned silence: no one had figured it would be so low, four or five pounds lighter than what Blackburn had forecast. Then Schmeling got up. "Schmeling, 192!" Predictably, it was right on target. Phelan called the two men together and warned them about proper conduct—not to kick each other, for instance, or to use foul language. Louis said nothing. "Thank you, General," Schmeling remarked. "Good luck this evening, Joe!" he told Louis. Then the bulbs started popping.

Watching it all, Hellmis thought that Louis appeared flustered. Others saw the same thing; Louis seemed afraid to look at Schmeling—the photographers had to coax him into doing it—and welcomed the chance to look away. "As the condemned man and the executioner stood side by side," wrote Vidmer, "a stranger might have thought that it was Louis, not Schmeling, who was going to his doom." Schmeling smiled and spoke quietly to his attendants; Louis stood and glowered at his feet. One of the medical examiners, Dr. Vincent Nardiello, was struck by how relaxed Louis was—too relaxed, even half asleep. Louis's blood pressure, 130 over 32, was "too normal, too perfect," while Schmeling's, 144 over 84, was much more appropriate; the German was "excited, eager, ready." Nardiello looked at James Dawson, the boxing writer for *The New York Times*, and Louis Beck, the boxing commission's chief inspector, as they stared at Louis. They were like two moonstruck kids.

Mike Jacobs then pulled the curtains, revealing an enormous catered spread. Louis grabbed some chicken, which Blackburn made him put back. The men then returned to their dressing rooms and inspected their gloves. When Louis approved of his, an official wrote "Lewis" on them. "That ain't no way to spell my name," Louis said. "Here, give me them gloves." He then drew a circle with three dots inside and a line beneath. "See, that's me." Joe Jacobs then took the gloves and put his own initials in them.

Louis liked to golf in the rain, and thought that maybe boxing in it might be fun, too. "How's about it, Uncle Mike?" he asked Jacobs. "Let's have it anyway. Or does you care 'bout folks coming?" Jacobs then bade the fighters good-bye. "Go to bed now and don't get run over by a truck," he said. A well-drenched crowd stood along Sixth Avenue as the men emerged. Schmeling went back to the Commodore Hotel. Louis repaired to the Hotel Alamac, on Broadway and Seventy-first Street. Like Tex Rickard before him, Jacobs always consulted the *Farmers' Almanac* before picking a fight date, and this time it had let him down. After calling the weather bureau one last time, he postponed the proceedings until the next night: Friday, June 19. There was no sadness in his voice; the veterans were still cashing their bonus checks. If it rained again on Friday, the fight would be held Saturday afternoon, forcing Louis and Schmeling to go up against Carl Hubbell of the Giants and one of the Dean brothers from St. Louis at the Polo Grounds. To Mike Jacobs, that was an easy call. "You can see them guys all summer long and for the next ten years," he said. Unless it was "raining pitchforks," there would be no more delays: Jacobs could feel enthusiasm for the fight waning and didn't want a "dead fish on his hands." Harlem that night was filled with over-anxious fans, waterlogged Louis posters, and counterfeit tickets for cheap seats; J. Edgar Hoover was already on the case.

Joe Jacobs said the postponement was catastrophic for Louis. "He worried off four pounds," he said. "Give 'em another twenty-four hours and he'll be a flyweight." The pause would also help Schmeling recover from his nerve-racking drive from Napanoch. But everywhere else, there were the predictable wisecracks about the condemned man getting a brief reprieve. One came from Morton Moss of the *New York Post*:

> *The stay the heavens gave him*
> *Expires tonight at ten;*
> *Now nothing more can save him—*
> *Unless it rains again!*

But Schmeling had a hearty lunch, read another German magazine, and went for a walk—unrecognized, under his hat. Then he saw a Jack Oakie movie, went for another walk, played some cards, and went to bed. Louis passed the afternoon in Harlem, had dinner, spent a half-hour with Marva, and went back to the Alamac.

The weather was still unsettled on Friday. The papers contained one novelty: Bill Farnsworth, Jr., of the *Evening Journal* was now picking Schmeling. "Max will weather Louis' early assault and come on in the final rounds to win the decision," he wrote. But Farnsworth's sportswriter father was his boss as well as Mike Jacobs's business partner, and people assumed the young man was simply doing as he'd been told, just to spice things up. A rumor circulated that a Jewish boy had slashed Schmeling's arm. The boxing promoter Walter Rothenburg, a friend of Schmeling's, reportedly telegraphed him from Germany: *"Heute sieg swelft runde"* [*sic*]: "Today twelfth round." Louis got up early, had breakfast, walked three miles in Central Park, then came back and slept. That afternoon, W. W. Edgar of the *Detroit Free Press* found him cocky, bored, already looking beyond the fight and beyond fighting. His conversation was "all golf, stances and grips and hooks and slices," a perplexed Edgar wrote.

As evening approached, people again converged on the stadium. The bleacher fans arrived earliest, bringing umbrellas to fend off any new rain and newspapers to soak up the old. With the weather still threatening, holders of costlier seats tarried even longer than usual; the preliminaries, beginning around eight, played to a largely empty house. Ushers wearing tropical hats—color-coded to match tickets—escorted fans to their seats. The wind shifted and the weather stabilized. People leafed through the programs Mike Jacobs had put together—which featured a glowing profile of Mike Jacobs.

The paid attendance was 39,878. Joe Jacobs didn't buy it—"That was the biggest 39,000 I ever saw," he complained—and he was right: with thousands plunking down a few dollars at the last minute and told to sit wherever they liked, the stadium was more filled than that. But to anyone who'd seen Louis fight Baer nine months earlier, the contrast was startling. Empty seats "yawned in the darkness like divots on a fairway," Vidmer wrote. Mike Jacobs attributed it less to wariness over Louis's expected easy victory than to Jews who had indeed opted to stay home, shaving a third or more off what turned out to be a $547,000 gate. According to one black paper, Jewish firms had bought large consignments of tickets from Jacobs to sell to their employees, then dumped thousands of unsold tickets on Uncle Mike the day of the fight. At least one black newspaper was impressed. "Unlike the American Negro, Jews do not believe in licking the hand that smites them nor in feeding the mouths of those who seek to crush them body and soul," the *Richmond Planet* declared admiringly.

Clem McCarthy had scored points for his work at the Louis-Baer fight, and nearly six of ten American radios were now tuned in to hear him again. That meant sixty million Americans—more than twice as many people as would hear the keynoters at the political conventions that summer, and five times the audience when King Edward VIII abdicated the throne six months later. Once again, Edwin C. Hill supplied the color. He served up all the usual clichés about the vast darkness of the stadium, the twinkling of all those thousands of cigarettes, the diversity of the crowd, all presumably written out before he had actually seen any of it.

In Radio City, one hundred fight fans would get to see the fight on "television." But it was two older generations of technologies, the radio and the newswire, that would now bind and spellbind the nation. In Culpeper, Virginia, the fight was broadcast from a bandstand in front of the courthouse. Thousands gathered in front of the home offices of the *Buffalo Evening News*, the *Columbus (Georgia) Enquirer*, the *Laurel (Mississippi) Call*. The fight would be reconstructed, blow by blow, on an "illuminated bulletin board" outside the *Boston Post*. The nightcap of a doubleheader between Newark and Syracuse "was just something for the fans to look at while listening to the broadcast." Fans gathered in New London, Connecticut, for the Harvard-Yale regatta the next day assembled around a radio in the lobby of the Mohegan Hotel. In Chicago, all Balaban and Katz movie theaters promised fight results. An Indiana man parked outside the Polk Street station in Chicago to listen, and soon two hundred people had massed around his car. The Red Sox listened on the train from Chicago to St. Louis, crouched around a small portable radio in the dining car, with Moe Berg relaying to his teammates whatever he managed to hear. The game between the Dodgers and the Cubs at Ebbets Field that afternoon had been called off, giving the Chicagoans ample time to get to Yankee Stadium. Loudspeakers were set up on the corner of Eighty-sixth Street and Lexington Avenue, as well as outside Rockefeller Center.

The fight would be broadcast overseas in English, Spanish, and German. Harry at the New York Bar in Paris announced he would give out the results. The play-by-play would start at four a.m. in Johannesburg; anyone able to understand the fast-talking American commentators would know the outcome before the *Rand Daily Mail's* fight extra hit the streets. The bout would go on at three in the morning in Germany, broadcast from stations in Berlin, Breslau, Hamburg, Cologne, Königsberg, Leipzig, Frankfurt, Stuttgart, Munich, and Saarbrucken. Some thirty million Germans were expected to tune in, many on the "People's Receivers," or *Volksempfänger* (known more colloquially as "*Goebbels-Schnauzen*"— "Goebbels Snouts"), the Nazis had popularized. Many listened in their homes, others—as in Klein Luckow, Schmeling's birthplace—in bars allowed to remain open beyond their normal curfews. In some instances, the broadcast was played over loudspeakers, notwithstanding the ungodly hour. Having already directed that his radio be in perfect order, Hitler listened in his private railroad car en route to Munich.

Anny Ondra had remained in Germany. Perhaps to calm her nerves, she'd spent the previous two days in the country, picking strawberries. Now, rather than listen at home, as she'd told one Berlin newspaper she would do (and as she later told one American newspaper she had done), she went to the home of Joseph and Magda Goebbels in Berlin's posh Schwanenwerder section. This was not so unusual; since Schmeling had gone to the United States to prepare for the Louis fight, she'd seen Goebbels at least four times. "Chatted and laughed with her," he'd written after one such visit. "She is so wonderfully naïve." They'd had ample time to enjoy one another's company; Ondra had also been there the previous night, before the fight had been canceled. "We're anxious the entire evening," Goebbels wrote. "Little Anny Ondra is hysterical. . . . We tell stories, laugh, and cheer up Anny. She's delightful." A photographer was on hand to record the hosts and their guest as they listened intently together alongside the giant radio.

The Deutscher Rundfunk had advertised a "Night of the Boxers," with fight-related programming starting two hours before the opening bell. Anyone tuning in heard a hodgepodge of poems, announcements, music (some taken from the theatrical films Schmeling and Ondra had made), and jokes, along with an occasional interview. "We will broadcast the Louis-Schmeling fight from Yankee Stadium today at dawn," someone would holler every fifteen minutes. "It is every German's obligation to stay up tonight. Max will fight overseas with a Negro for the hegemony of the white race!" Many fans skipped the preliminaries and set their alarms for around the time Hellmis would come on from New York. A paper in Stuttgart reported "a true symphony of rattling alarm clocks" around three. During summers, people listened to radios with their windows open; the Viennese police were besieged with complaints from those unfortunates who were trying to sleep.

At around a quarter to eight New York time, Joe Jacobs fetched Schmeling at his hotel. "Good luck, Max!" the desk clerk shouted as they left. They made their way to the stadium, and into the dressing room. Just before Schmeling was summoned to the ring, Tom O'Rourke stopped by. "I know you can win, Max," the old man told him. "You just have to be careful, and above all, use your head." Then he keeled over and fell to the floor. In one of several similar versions of what followed, Schmeling took one look at his prostrate friend. "*Tot,*" he muttered—German for "dead"—and then, "cold as ice," he headed for the ring. Along the way, what he felt wasn't grief or fear or superstition but excitement: finally, he was about to learn if he'd sized up Louis correctly.

At ringside, Braddock, the incumbent but oddly inconsequential champion, sat next to J. Edgar Hoover. Fannie Brice sat with the sportswriters. In the third row, a gum-chewing Mayor La Guardia offered to write the *Herald Tribune* man's story in exchange for his front-row seat. James A. Farley, the former boxing commissioner and now the Democratic Party chairman, was there. So was his Republican counterpart. So were David Sarnoff, Eddie Rickenbacker, Bernard Baruch, Irving Berlin, George Burns and Gracie Allen, George Raft, Al Jolson, Jack Benny, George Jessel, Joseph Pulitzer II, Toots Shor, Sherman Billingsley, Nelson Rockefeller, Rudy Vallee, Condé Nast, Thomas Dewey, Babe Ruth, Mel Ott, Carl Hubbell, Alfred Gwynne Vanderbilt, Sonny Whitney, George D. Widener, Colonel Theodore Roosevelt (Teddy's son), and Jimmy Roosevelt (Franklin's son). Just about the only black at ringside was Bill Robinson, wearing a plaid-on-plaid combination. Somewhere in the cheaper seats was Langston Hughes. A reporter from Macon, Georgia, looked overhead; an airplane circled in the sky, announcing in flashing red lights that fight films would be in theaters the next day. Maybe in New York, he mused; where he came from, a film of a black man fighting a white could never be shown.

The prefight frenzy had driven Marva to bed. But now she, along with two of her girlfriends, entered the stadium. She was wearing a red and gray outfit trimmed with a large, square, bloodred suede hat, red gloves, and red shoes. A loud cheer erupted as she smiled obligingly for fifty photographers. She then took her place in the fifth row, flanked by Mrs. Julian Black and Carl Van Vechten, the photographer. Marva expressed her disappointment that she wasn't facing her husband's corner. "I want to

Max Schmeling in 1927, a hero in Weimar Germany to fans and aesthetes alike.

The savior of boxing: Joe Louis on the eve of his New York debut, spring 1935.

For more than a decade, Schmeling
was a constant presence on elegant
ocean liners arriving in New York.

Schmeling (second from right) at his
country house in Bad Saarow, Germany,
in the early 1930s. When lightning set the
place ablaze, he took special care to rescue
the bust of Hitler inside.

One key to Schmeling's popularity in
the United States was his striking
resemblance to the recently retired
and much-missed Jack Dempsey.
(Schmeling is on the left.)

Schmeling and his manager, Joe "Yussel the Muscle" Jacobs, early in their association, one of the most incongruous and politically fraught in the history of sports.

As Governor Franklin Roosevelt campaigns for the presidency in May 1932, he visits Schmeling, then training in Kingston, New York, for his rematch against Jack Sharkey. Eleanor Roosevelt is to the left of her husband, who spoke to Schmeling in German.

Above: A fund-raiser at Madison Square Garden in 1929 for the embattled Jews of Palestine, in which five Jewish boxers beat five Gentiles before 16,000 fervent fans, attests to the significant Jewish influence in the sport. *Below: The New York Times* took nearly a month to report that Nazi Germany had banned all Jews from every facet of German boxing, then placed the story on the back page of its sports section, beneath a banner headline on something it evidently deemed more important. Most other papers didn't mention the news at all.

FINAL **DAILY MIRROR**

New York, Monday, March 27, 1933

Vol. IX. No. 236   2 cents

BRAVES Rally in 8th to NIP YANKS, 4-3

Story on Page 16

א מעסעדזש צו די אידען אין א קריטישען מאמענט

מענשליכע רעכט פון אידען אין דײטשלאנד, קען מען מיט רער צײט אויס־
וועישען הערען אלס א פראצענטען צו פאראיניקען אונ׳ע׳ע מענשען
און פ׳ ׳צ׳׳ען וואס די צוולװירדען וועלם אלסם מויער.

EDITOR'S NOTE:—The following message in Yiddish
is addressed to the Jewish Citizenry of the Nation.

די פאראמעלונג פון מאסמא אדענוא אים גניפ׳פען נעואונער׳ דיפם־
ועכ׳ער צו לאזען הערען די שטים פון געזועמען פון גים־אידען און וואם

ערקלע׳עדרונג פון בערנא׳ד ב. דויטש. פרעזידענט פון
אמעריקאנער אידישען קאנגרעס

אלע׳ן׳אונגען אין דער פרעסק, וואם זיינען אריבעדגעקענעם און
וואי׳פ אונבער פאריארשטיעע דזול, פאראוגעט ניט ראם שוויעגען פון
דעם גיירעקערשען רימאמלסא, העלקער ראם לידע׳ר אין די פיקלא
רערעקא הקל עד ראם געראאלמוו. גים נעקונע פאר נימען אידישלוען
און הארק וואם וואם בעדרינעם ער קרבנות פון זיין אנאניזדויע
מנא׳א.

די פראמעלטם פאראומעלמו וואס יעם אבנעראסען העוען אין
מעראאן סקוא׳ער נארדען זעם זיינ יוך אטעד זיו א פראמעטסא פאראומ׳נו
אי פאוריסמעלטפען פון מעגליא׳ע׳יטשעריס וואס ראם פאראואנטעסען דעם
היעל פון אידישען אלק אין רער לאנד אין ועמוא אין מעניאלסאוו
פאריסם מעסקר דו א פראומנאט׳ אאם נעפ׳רל פון מעניאליכער אוזשערער
ריימ׳א אין סעלייריענע נעקאעי אין רעם או אלעמען אדוסאלעו
אונ׳ענען. אם אירנוע וואמאמטיאנו אין ואל אלע רער פ׳רט אום ערא
היסר, אם דאס אמפקיא באקריעות פון רעל׳ינ׳ען. בעראדיא אין

איך אפקל׳ער צו אלע אידען אין קרמטקע׳ן וואם זיינען זורפט פעם
ראונ׳גע וואמען. צו מאכען דעם סעניאלס אקווער נארדען די בעסט־
מעראסעע באקריונו אן רער נעט נעשעבע פון זיין ארק.

Captors and

Mrs. Helen Tapley and son Jack holding pails of water, read notice about discontinued water supply.

WATER supply at Clifford Island of New Rochelle N.Y. has been shut off because of non-payment of $70 bill.

Champion Sea Gulls Rout

When Yussel Went Nazi

Outraging Nazis and Jews alike, Yussel the Muscle Jacobs—at right, cigar in hand—joins Schmeling and salutes Hitler after Schmeling knocked out Steve Hamas in Hamburg. The *New York Daily News*, March 22, 1935.

Yiddish-speaking organizers of an anti-Nazi rally in Manhattan in March 1933 knew how to reach their constituency, placing a notice—untranslated—on the front page of the *New York Mirror's* sports section.

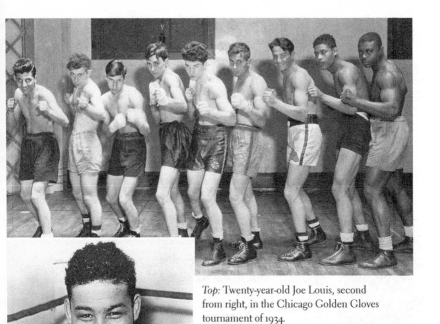

Top: Twenty-year-old Joe Louis, second from right, in the Chicago Golden Gloves tournament of 1934.

Above: The young Louis was normally deadpan, but on occasion he betrayed the sweetness his fans detected in him anyway.

Louis with his trainer, Jack Blackburn. "I ain't goner waste any of your time," Louis promised him.

Louis with his mother, Lillie Barrows Brooks, in June 1935. Profiles of Louis invariably stressed his love for her, along with his clean living and religious faith.

With promoter Mike Jacobs, July 1936. Ignoring any racial barriers, "Uncle Mike" ushered Louis to the championship, while Louis made Jacobs the kingpin of "Jacobs Beach."

With Jesse Owens, August 1935. Around the exalted Louis, wrote Shirley Povich of *The Washington Post*, Owens acted like "some flunky who knew his place."

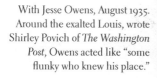

Big Brown Bomber Hits Town ✦ ✦ ✦ by Uhlmann

In May 1935, the *New York Post* conveyed the excitement as the city awaited Louis, who would fight Primo Carnera at Yankee Stadium the following month.

The porters and railroad workers at Grand Central Terminal lifted Louis off his train when he arrived in New York for the first time, in May 1935. Other travelers that morning "had to carry their own baggage," the *New York Herald Tribune* reported.

Joe and his bride, Marva Trotter Louis, stroll triumphantly through an adoring Harlem on September 25, 1935. The previous night, only a couple of hours after marrying Marva, Louis knocked out Max Baer before 95,000 fans at Yankee Stadium.

Top left: Visiting Louis as he trained for Paolino Uzcudun in December 1935, Schmeling checked out Louis's fist, along with the flaw he thought he'd detected in Louis's technique. *Top right*: Louis walking away from Uzcudun, down and out for the first time in his career. Watching Louis box, wrote Richards Vidmer of the *Herald Tribune*, was like hearing Caruso sing or Fritz Kreisler play the violin.

On the eve of the first Louis-Schmeling fight, *Ring* magazine sized up the contestants.

LOUIS·SCHMELING SOUVENIR NUMBER

25 CENTS

JULY

the RING

MAX SCHMELING		JOE LOUIS	
AGE	29 YRS.	AGE	21 YRS.
WEIGHT	192 LBS.	WEIGHT	195 LBS.
HEIGHT	6 FT. 1 IN.	HEIGHT	6 Ft. 1¾ In.
REACH	74 INCHES	REACH	76 INCHES
CHEST (NOR)	40 "	CHEST (NOR)	41 "
CHEST (EXP)	43 "	CHEST (EXP)	44 "
NECK	17 "	NECK	16½ "
BICEPS	13 "	BICEPS	13½ "
FOREARM	10¾ "	FOREARM	12½ "
WRIST	8 "	WRIST	8 "
WAIST	34 "	WAIST	34½ "
THIGH	19½ "	THIGH	20 "
CALF	13½ "	CALF	15 "
ANKLE	9 "	ANKLE	10 "

Clem McCarthy, the NBC announcer. He missed some key punches, but immortalized an epoch.

Nat Fleischer, editor of *Ring*. In an era of intolerance, he championed the underdog, including a foreigner like Schmeling and a black man like Louis.

Arno Hellmis, the Nazi announcer. In victory, he was ecstatic and crystalclear; in defeat, he was inconsolable and almost unintelligible.

Joe and Mike Jacobs flank Schmeling aboard the *Bremen* in April 1936, as Schmeling arrived for the first Louis fight. For the Nazis, such fraternizing with Jews was a *Rassenschande* —a racial scandal—but business was also business.

Louis with black reporters in Lakewood, New Jersey, in the spring of 1936. Coverage of him in the black weeklies was lavish, lively, and loving.

The weigh-in for the first Louis-Schmeling fight, at the Hippodrome, June 18, 1936.

Marva at ringside before the first fight, June 19, 1936.

Louis in his corner just before the knockout, peering into "a world full of pinwheels and skyrockets."

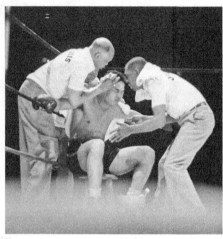

As a Berlin newspaper subsequently documented, Anny Ondra listened to her husband's first fight with Louis at the home of Joseph and Magda Goebbels, as her hosts hovered protectively nearby.

As Arthur Donovan counts
out Louis in the twelfth round,
Schmeling exults. "The condemned
man executed the warden," wrote
Joe Williams of the *New York
World-Telegram*.

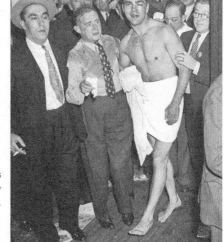

Schmeling, a drenched Joe Jacobs
at his side, walks triumphantly
through his dressing room.

ATLANTA DAILY WORLD

ONLY NEGRO DAILY NEWSPAPER IN THE WORLD

ATLANTA, GA., SUNDAY, JUNE 21, 1936

THE SPECTACLE THAT CHILLED A RACE!

The nation's only black daily newspaper neatly summarized reaction to the Schmeling fight.

JOE PLAYS THE BLUES

Louis allowed no pictures after the fight, when his inflated face was likened to a loaf of bread, a coconut, a cantaloupe, and a watermelon. But a couple of days later, he looked like this.

The *Chicago Defender* saw diabolical manipulations behind Louis's loss.

TRUTH ABOUT LOUIS-MAX FIASCO!

How The Brown Bomber Looked As Victory Went To Another For The First Time

THOUSANDS ATTEND RITES FOR BISHOP WM. DECKER JOHNSON

24 PAGES
IN THIS ISSUE

THE Chicago Defender

WORLD'S GREATEST WEEKLY

NATIONAL EDITION

While much of New York mourned Schmeling's stunning win, spirits were high in German Yorkville, on the city's Upper East Side.

Berliner illustrierte

Nachtausgabe

20. Juni 1936

10 Pf.

Schmeling: „Der glücklichste Tag meines Lebens!"

Gespräch nach dem Triumph über Louis
Weltmeister Braddock über den großen Kampf

Glückwünsche des Führers | Gruß an die Heimat

Das erste Funkbild aus New York

Jubel über die Siegesnachricht aus Amerika

"Schmeling: 'The happiest day of my life'": front page, *Berliner illustrierte Nachtausgabe*, June 20, 1936

About to board the *Hindenburg*, June 23, 1936. On a cake labeled "K.O.," the marshmallow victor stood triumphantly over his prostrate, chocolate-covered foe.

"If they think I'm too old already, I at least have to make use of my 'fatherly authority.'"
Der Kicker, June 23, 1936

see him," she said. Shortly before ten, the two fighters entered the ring. Schmeling, wearing his favorite spotted gray bathrobe over purple trunks, entered jauntily, a slight grin on his face. He was greeted with surprising warmth. With him was Joe Jacobs, startlingly (but only temporarily) without a cigar. An expressionless Louis followed, in his familiar shining dressing gown, blue silk trimmed in red, over black trunks. His brown body glistened under the intense lights, making him appear almost white.

Those attuned to the nuances detected something amiss in Louis's demeanor, a turbulence beneath his customary impassivity. He looked paler, meaner, edgier. Again and again, he rubbed his left glove against his neck. He appeared to be mouthing off to Blackburn. Once again, something about the way Schmeling looked at him seemed to unnerve Louis. His anxiety radiated to some of the blacks sitting in the crowd. "A sort of premonition seemed to hang over Yankee Stadium," one black reporter later recalled. "There was that something that seemed to whisper out of the darkness, 'Louis is not ready.'"

An NBC technician handed a microphone to Hellmis, who had been relegated, in what *Box-Sport* construed as a slap to German honor, to a makeshift nest of chairs and boxes in the twelfth row. He took some deep breaths to gain some composure. Holding the mike in one hand, he corralled Gene Tunney and Jack Dempsey with the other. "I wish good health to all my friends in Germany," Tunney said. "And I also hope that Schmeling will spend the evening in the best of health." German fans might not have liked that last crack had they heard it; but it was hard to make out what anyone was saying amid the roars in the Bronx and all the scratches, crackles, and hisses picked up on the line between Poughkeepsie (site of the General Electric transmitter) and Berlin.

The referee, Arthur Donovan, sprinkled the canvas with powered resin out of a yellow can. As the men put on their gloves, Harry Balogh introduced Dempsey, Tunney, Braddock, and other ring notables. Despite his now-customary plea for tolerance, he failed to introduce the three great black fighters present: Jack Johnson, Sam Langford, and Harry Wills. But that was a slight only blacks noticed. Then he got to the principals: Schmeling, striving to win back the title both for himself and for his Fatherland, and Louis, "one of the greatest heavyweights in the annals of Fistiana." Louis got the bigger hand. "Let us cast aside all prejudism," Balogh declared. "Let us say 'Ring the bell, let 'er go, and may the best man be the winner.'" The crowd roared back, part approvingly, part derisively.

Donovan gave his instructions. To one reporter, Louis seemed "sneeringly confident and patronizingly bored." "He gave Max a fleeting glance, as much as to say, 'You've got your nerve,'" he wrote. Schmeling studied the left side of Louis's face, still boyishly smooth and perfectly intact, which, if he hit it as often and as hard as he hoped to, would quickly be pulverized. Soon, it was that electric moment before the bell. "Nervous conversation popped on all sides like firecrackers," wrote James T. Farrell, who was covering the fight for *The New Republic*. Louis was in his corner, eyes darting; Schmeling sat imperturbably in his. Their seconds gave them last bits of advice. For Schmeling, it was to hit early, to win Louis's respect, and to hit late, too, so that Louis would be too groggy to absorb whatever his seconds told him between rounds. For Louis, it was to take his time, to keep jabbing, to keep Schmeling off balance so that he couldn't land his right. The lights went down everywhere but over the ring. At 10:06, the bell sounded.

Louis came out with "an almost insolent confidence." He began jabbing Schmeling at will, until the German's left eye quickly began to puff and discolor. But Louis was leaving himself open for a right cross, just as Schmeling had expected. Schmeling missed with his first one, but the crowd cheered; it was the first daring punch many of them had ever seen thrown at Louis. In the first clinch, Louis was "filling in"—throwing meaningless punches, often a sign of someone on edge. Sitting at ringside, Tunney thought he saw an old truism emerging: a boxer needed a year to adjust to marriage, and here was Louis, married but nine months. To Hellmis, the cheering was strictly racial: shrill screams from blacks and *Mischlinge*—people of mixed race—whites holding back, soaking in the drama. At the bell, both men returned to their corners confident. "This baby is easier than either Carnera or Baer," Louis told Blackburn. Louis could hit, Schmeling acknowledged. But "he iss going to fall for it."

Beforehand, Louis had bragged that he hadn't felt a single blow in his last fourteen fights. This changed in the second round. Ignoring Blackburn, he came over with a left hook. That created an opening for Schmeling's right, which landed squarely on Louis's chin. Louis was dazed momentarily and fell into a clinch. The punch "sort of deadened everything—bounced off a nerve or somethin'," he later said. "Now your fight is really on!" rasped McCarthy, who was scurrying to get in as many plugs for the sponsor, Buick, as he could; Louis fights, after all, always ended so quickly. Jabbing continuously, Louis won this round, as he had the first. But Schmeling was impressing people. As for Hellmis, who was clearly enthralled by New York, he filled in between rounds describing the sky-line of the "fairy-tale city" before him, which would not have been visible from his seat.

As the third round got under way, Schmeling's left eye was already closing. Though Louis had yet to unload, he was inflicting enormous punishment with left jabs; after one of them, Schmeling turned and spit blood from his split lip. But Hellmis remained optimistic. "Schmeling is delivering a wonderful fight," he said. "Doesn't respect the Negro at all. He is probably the first heavyweight since the rise of Joe Louis who is giv-ing him a manly fight." Some sensed the end was already near. Two black gamblers waved wads of cash, offering twenty to one that Schmeling would soon be knocked out. The German was so bloodied that one box-ing commissioner was shouting to stop the fight. Even Hellmis knew that Schmeling had to do something soon. In fact, Schmeling had gotten through with another right. Many had missed it, but not in Schmeling's corner. "You fetched him a pretty good one," Machon told him after the bell. "I think I knock him out," Schmeling replied. "I have him where I want him."

Schmeling waited for his moment. Suddenly, in the fourth, he got through one hard right, and then another, and then the unimaginable happened. "Schmeling is backing away cautiously," McCarthy croaked, "waiting for some opening that he wants . . . and . . . ahhhhh! Schmeling got over a right hand . . . high, on Louis's jaw that made Louis rock his head! Schmeling has sent Louis down! Joe Louis is down!" Louis, who had not been on the canvas in his entire professional career, was there now. Completely unaccustomed to working the count, he remained down for only two seconds. The mood in Yankee Stadium jolted into an entirely unfamiliar gear; with one punch all of boxing had been upended. Hats and papers came cascading down from the upper decks.

"Louis is struggling! Louis is struggling!" Hellmis exclaimed. "Louis is down. . . . Max knocked him down! Bravo Max! Bravo Max!" Hellmis apologized to his audience: he couldn't hear himself above the din. "The Americans are literally ecstatic!" he declared. "They never saw Joe Louis down." But the same was true in Germany; in a farming hamlet outside Magdeburg, people were jumping for joy as the first tractors pulled out of the village. For Hellmis and everyone else in the stadium it was hard to follow the action, as people stood up, or stood on their chairs, or stood in the aisles. Cries of "Down in front!" sounded plaintively, uselessly. "Joe, honey, get up! *Get up!*" Marva shouted, as people around her yelled, "Kill him, Max! Kill him!" Louis was transformed. He looked like a "young cub who had been roundly cuffed by a grizzly that he thought to be playful." Even Schmeling seemed startled, standing agog rather than rushing in for the kill.

"The gasps that went up in the night sky were the loudest and most incredulous ever heard," Trevor Wignall later wrote. Most shocked of all, he thought, were the boxing commissioners and Mike Jacobs. But the face he remembered was Julian Black's: he was shaking his head, as if "some idiot had played a joke on him." Blackburn stuck a sponge in his mouth. Outside, on the streets of Harlem, a great moan was almost audible. In Yorkville, where people had initially been too pessimistic to get involved, there was jubilation.

Now the fickle loyalties of the fight crowd, and even of some of the reporters, began to shift—not so much because they no longer liked Louis or suddenly preferred Schmeling, but because they knew they could be witnessing one of the greatest upsets in athletic history, and they longed to see the deal done. They exhorted Schmeling to finish Louis off, but Schmeling had his plan, and he would not be rushed to please a crowd. Black fans pleaded with Louis to be Louis again. Maybe it had been a lucky punch, or maybe he had slipped, or maybe he'd now be aroused enough to stop the dillydallying. But the Panglosses were mostly in the cheap seats. Up close, one could see the damage from that single punch. "Those far back . . . cannot see the stupor in Joe's eyes," Damon Runyon wrote. "They don't notice the dull, dead manner in which he lifts his legs across the ring."

Louis staggered to his feet, blinking. When the two fighters came together again, Louis managed a clinch. Twenty seconds later the round mercifully ended. Donovan turned Louis toward his corner; he'd have fallen en route had Blackburn not rushed to his rescue and steered him to his stool. The trainer shoved ammonia under Louis's nose and doused him with ice water. He shouted at Louis, but Louis didn't seem to hear. "Now I got him," Schmeling said matter-of-factly in his corner. Jacobs was jabbering with excitement, but Schmeling listened only to Machon, and Machon stayed cool. "So. *Den Übermensch haben wir jetzt in unserer Tasche. Nun vorsichtig!*" he told him: "So, now we have the superman in our pocket. But be careful!"

"Jack Blackburn, for the first time that I've ever seen him, looks worried," McCarthy told the radio audience, before passing the microphone to Hill, who began cramming in various public service announcements in case the fight came to an abrupt end. Hellmis lamented that Louis had been saved by the bell. As the fifth round began, Louis had to be pushed into the ring. "Schmeling has got all the confidence in the world," McCarthy declared, as the German quickly connected again. "Louis is meeting the hardest right-hand punches that he has ever faced. . . . This is the only punch [Schmeling's] got, but what a punch it is tonight." Louis, by contrast, pawed more than punched, "following Schmeling like a hurt boy," as McCarthy put it. At the end of the round, Schmeling struck Louis with another ferocious blow, worse even than the punch that had decked him before. Donovan said it landed precisely at the bell; Fleischer, three seconds after; Blackburn, ten seconds later. Blackburn was almost furious enough to go after Schmeling himself; now, Louis's head might never clear. But the bell was hard to hear, and Schmeling, surely more than any other fighter, would hardly have risked everything with an illegal punch. Louis's camp never formally complained; even now, they had to be beyond reproach. But they would remember.

In Louis's clouded brain, all of Schmeling's punches were blending into one. "I just remember one pop, a sort of sudden blaze of lights that turned loose in my head, and after that I felt as if I were trying to run through a field and kept running into things and falling over things," he later said. He walked back to his corner, *The Washington Post* reported, "like a man on stilts with his kneecaps bending the wrong way with every other step he took." A new wave of betting swept the stadium, with the smart money suddenly on Schmeling to win. "*Der Übermensch hat ja Gummibeine*," Machon told Schmeling: "The superman has rubber legs." As the sixth round began, Louis was, as McCarthy saw him, "a dazed, tired, bewildered fighter." Schmeling was hitting him almost at will. Louis's famous deadpan had been replaced by a look of pain and surprise. He kept blinking, as if emerging from a bad dream. His jaw swelled, and his eyes kept tearing. "Finally, a blue, the color of lapis lazuli, rimmed his eyes brightly," wrote Bill Cunningham of the *Boston Post*. "He was by this time a strange symphony of unusual colors."

Hellmis, meanwhile, was having a private conversation with a friend, to which twenty or thirty million Germans happened to be listening. "That's right, Max!" he said during the sixth. "Stay away. Keep a good distance and don't get trapped! We have plenty of time. The bout's over fifteen rounds, and we'll catch Herr Louis again soon enough." Then he remembered his audience. "Max Schmeling is now absolutely superior," he said. "There's no one in this stadium who would bet a cent on Louis's victory any longer." Louis soldiered on "with all the boxing instinct of his race," he continued. "The Negro now has a nervous, childish smile on his young face. Doesn't quite know what to do. That's not how he had imagined it. That's no helpless, beaten boxing geezer he's facing there. It's a fighter with heart and energy and in splendid condition. The Black Uhlan from the Rhine is here, and he's showing the Americans that we know how to fight." As the round ended, a black reporter looked over toward Louis's mother. She was on her knees, praying.

Roxborough and the others worked frantically over Louis, cheering him up, sponging his face. At first, it was Louis who had been Clem McCarthy's sleek and powerful Buick, cruising to glory; now Schmeling was in the driver's seat. Louis rallied in the seventh, in part because, at Machon's insistence, Schmeling had resolved to rest a round. Once again, the crowd seemed poised to shift its loyalties. Hellmis suspected that during the break Louis had been given drugs; how else could this completely beaten man storm out now as if nothing had happened? Louis threw the first of several low blows. *"Der wird frech. Nehm's ihm wieder ab,"* Machon told Schmeling afterward: "He's getting fresh. Take the play away from him."

In the eighth, Schmeling was back on his usual, methodical course. A black man sitting in the bleachers couldn't make out much, but this much he could see: Schmeling kept getting through with those rights. With one of them, the crowd rose and cheered so loudly that, once again, Hellmis could not hear what he was saying. He turned to his technician, an American, whose job it was to regulate the crowd noises, only to see that he was standing on his box of instruments, roaring at the top of his voice, "Go on, Maxieboy, kill that nigger, kill him!" Louis threw two more low blows, drawing a warning from Donovan and boos from the crowd. He then placed his hands briefly on Schmeling's shoulders and shook his head, as if to apologize for things beyond his control.

By the start of the ninth round, it was clear that Louis couldn't possibly last the distance. "A ship in a storm without a rudder or a mast—a punching bag hung up beneath the white arc lights for Schmeling to nail," Grantland Rice wrote. Dempsey wondered what Schmeling was waiting for. The blacks in the crowd seemed dazed. The tenth round began a bit late; Louis was fumbling with his mouthpiece. He fouled again, then threw a right so lame that it made the normally sporting Schmeling—by now with nose red, left eye completely shut, lips swollen and rimmed with blood—laugh a grotesque laugh. Louis had become "a little heap of misery," Hellmis told Germany. Donovan considered calling the fight;

Schmeling couldn't seem to put Louis away, even though he was winding up like a pitcher. Then Louis hit low again. Schmeling now concluded the fouls were no accident; Louis himself was honest and clean, he thought, but Louis also did what he was told. In fact, while in a clinch near Louis's corner, he thought he heard Blackburn tell Louis to foul him. With boxers no longer disqualified for low blows—thanks to Schmeling's "victory" over Sharkey, violators could only lose the round—such tactics were Louis's only hope. Once, the German would have been happy to win on points; now he knew he had to knock Louis out.

So the fusillade began. Blackburn watched his creation, his livelihood, the closest thing he had to a son, disintegrate before his eyes. Whenever Louis was hit, Blackburn winced. Schmeling hit Louis with three consecutive rights. Louis fell on top of him, and Donovan had to pull him off. Schmeling then forced Louis onto the ropes and crushed him with another right to the chin. Donovan was about to stop the fight. But Louis's arms had dropped and Schmeling had the clean shot he wanted. Already, Rice wrote, Louis had taken more punches in twelve rounds than Corbett, Fitzsimmons, Jeffries, Johnson, and Tunney had absorbed in their entire careers. And now there was one more. It sent Louis sprawling into the ropes, then down to his knees, "like a tired child at bed-time prayer," as Hype Igoe of the *New York Evening Journal* put it. A reporter dictating his story to the telegraph operator shouted, "And Louis is down again and this time it looks as if he will not get up." Louis stayed there until the count of four, his hand on the middle rope. Then he lost his grip and toppled over, his face buried in the canvas. Donovan rushed Schmeling off to a neutral corner and picked up the count, raising his arm up and down with each successive digit. Louis looked to Blackburn. "Up, Chappie! Up, boy! Steady!" the old trainer shouted at him. Louis lifted his head a bit and shook it. It was, he later said, as if a train had run over Blackburn's voice, thinning it out so he'd sounded like a ghost. And the numbers Donovan shouted reached him as if through water. At nine, Louis's body convulsed. In another second it was over. More than forty thousand people had to make sure they weren't dreaming.

Even with his rapid-fire horse-racing cadences, McCarthy could not keep up, and his oddly evenhanded commentary left the impression that Louis remained much more in contention than he really was. So when the end came, millions of listeners were more shocked than they should have been. "Louis is down! Louis is down!" McCarthy shouted. "Hanging to the ropes, hanging badly! He's a very tired fighter! He is blinking his eyes, shaking his head! The count is . . . the fight is over! The fight is over and Schmeling is the winner! Louis is completely out!" As Harlemites listened to their radios, "there was a miserable, frightened look on their faces, an incredulous stare into space." In Columbus, Georgia, cheers had gone up every time Schmeling hit Louis, and "a terrific burst of acclaim" erupted when Louis was counted out. In his Chicago café, Dempsey's old manager, Jack Kearns, who'd won himself $30,000 by taking Schmeling at six to one, bought champagne for the house. And play could now resume at that minor league game in Newark, where distracted fielders had let so many fly balls drop in for hits that the umpire had finally called time so that the players could give the fight their undivided attention.

As McCarthy's raspy message raced across America, Hellmis's words, ebbing and flowing, thickening and thinning, descended upon Germany and much of the rest of Europe. "Schmeling is now fighting like he never fought before!" he said as the twelfth round heated up. "He's literally thrashing the soul out of the Negro. The Negro steps back . . . shaking . . . can't go on. There, he's down! Schmeling has knocked him down! He doesn't come back up. He can't come back up. He's shaking his head. He knows he's finished. *Aus* [Out]! *Aus! Aus! Aus! Aus! Aus! Aus!* . . . Max Schmeling has won the greatest triumph of his entire glorious boxing career! He has badly knocked out Joe Louis, Loamface Joe Louis!"

All over the stadium, fans were on their feet. "For a fraction of a moment, the crowd seemed unable to cheer," one reporter wrote. "Then a hysterical bellow broke out." It was for the winner, but it was also, in a way, for themselves. "Sixty thousand people stood in glorious tribute to the man who had come back," wrote Vidmer. "They stood shouting at the spectacle they never had hoped or expected to witness, thanking their good fortune for having come." But the cheering was, like so much of the world around them, segregated, racially and even religiously. It was, wrote Roi Ottley of the *Amsterdam News*, "the white gentile section" that was cheering hysterically: the Jews were taking Louis's loss as badly as the blacks were. And blacks took it in much the way Wendell Smith of the *Pittsburgh Courier* described:

> You, yourself are still trembling and shaken from the excitement.
> The stunning knockdowns, the staggering, helpless man with the
> brown body trying for 11 long rounds. You have seen a man down
> limp and useless, his eyes glassy and swollen. You have seen the rich
> blood of your idol flowing from his nose, mouth and cuts about the
> face. The inevitable, it happens to all fighters, is now before you,

but you refuse to believe it. It is a dream, a terrorizing nightmare, that you keep fighting off but find that it is impossible. The dream is too real. The roar of 70,000 people [*sic*], the photographers, the "ticky-tick" of the typewriter and that beaten brown body before you . . . is the proof! On this night, June 19, 1936, in Yankee Stadium, you have seen the greatest fistic upset the world has ever known. You have seen the perfect fighting machine, Joe Louis, beaten by a grim, determined German. . . . You will never forget the things you have seen. Never, as long as you live . . . will you forget.

"There lay Joe Louis in an abject heap . . . ," wrote Davis Walsh of the Hearst wire service, "his cold agate of an eye grown surprisingly softened and docile and a little piteous, like that of a brown setter which has been beaten beyond all natural dignity. . . . He did not glance up and, I think, would have done so unwillingly. Up there, as a matter of fact, was the white master, Max Schmeling, who would beat him down again if he mustered the will to rise."

At ringside, Louis's mother wore a look of disbelief. Marva hid her face in her hands and said, "He's hurt. He's hurt bad." One report had her fainting when Louis went down, another fleeing. "Her face streaming with tears, her hair straggling, her little red shoes dirty and torn," a reporter sitting with her wrote, Louis's bride "dashed up the aisle like a wild animal. Gone was her make-up and pride: all she wanted to do was to comfort Joe in his hour of defeat." Schmeling helped Black, Blackburn, and the others lift Louis up and carry him back to his corner. In the meantime, Joe Jacobs and Doc Casey had jumped ecstatically into the ring to embrace Schmeling, who was leaping up and down himself. Jacobs's suspenders had popped and his pants began to fall; he was jumping, stuffing his shirt back into his trousers, kissing Schmeling, and throwing his hands up in the air all at once. Schmeling darted toward the ropes, reached into the crowd for "a blocky young man in a chocolate-brown suit," and dragged him into the ring. It was James J. Braddock. Braddock, too, was a loser that night—surely there'd be no lucrative title defense against Louis now—but he was a good sport and celebrated with Schmeling.

Schmeling had "beaten his way back over the rough trail from Hasbeenville," Runyon wrote, and now, tens of thousands cheered him on. For him, and for Adolf Hitler, too, it was a total triumph—technical, physical, psychological. It was just as the Nazis had said—discipline, dedication, intelligence, courage, and will had prevailed over brute strength—and it was almost frightening. "We never saw a gamer fighter,"

Joe Williams later wrote of Schmeling. "He was so game that he scared us. He was so game we looked at him . . . as a deadly, sinister, unhealthy thing." Balogh lifted Schmeling's arm and, his voice reverberating throughout the stadium, declared him the winner. Schmeling turned to the newspapermen in the press rows. "I guess I fooled you guys," he shouted. He also waved to Hellmis, which to Hellmis meant he was greeting all Germany. Schmeling, Hellmis told his audience, had disproved one of boxing's most venerable adages: "They never come back." He apologized again to his audience: His voice had faded from having had to yell over the crowd. "Please don't hold that against me," he pleaded. "It was just too exciting to deliver a quiet, perfect radio report." Schmeling was standing in the ring, giving what Hellmis, if no one else, saw as the Hitler salute. "And you can hear what's going on," he said. "They're cheering. He's the man of the day. . . . Here stands the greatest heavyweight of all times."

McCarthy corralled Schmeling to his microphone. "Congratulations, Max. Congratulations, my boy," McCarthy shouted. "This is the happiest day of my life!" Schmeling breathlessly replied, his head clear enough to switch to English, and to graciousness. "And I think I fought the toughest fellow I ever met. And I still think Joe Louis is a very, very great prospect." McCarthy asked Schmeling how early he thought he'd won. "Well, I had a hunch in the fourth round," Schmeling said. McCarthy then asked the same thing of Joe Jacobs. "From the beginning!" Jacobs snapped. "Never thought he was going to lose!"

Louis, his robe over his shoulder, sat despondently in his corner for several minutes, peering into "a world full of pinwheels and skyrockets," while Schmeling made his way to the dressing room. Louis had entered the ring young and virile and invincible, and now, barely an hour later, he had become "a grotesque Stepin' Fetchit type of a tired Negro." "Wrapped in his garish red and blue ring robe, his head completely [covered] in a huge bath towel, he was led stumblingly down the steps and to at least temporary oblivion," wrote Bill Cunningham in the *Boston Post*. He collapsed while walking across the field, and had to be carried on a cop's back the rest of the way. "There goes one of them supermen," Braddock muttered. "Put this in your hat, pal: All fighters are born free and equal. And if one of them *looks* better, remember that a couple of good right-hand chops to the whiskers will soon bring him back to the rest of the field." Yet Louis could claim one small victory. They had always said he couldn't "take it." Now, he had — "in vast and amazing plenitude."

The crowds filed out of the stadium. One departing spectator told a young black boy outside that Louis had lost. "Don't fool me, Mister," the boy replied. "Our Joe can't lose." "They wouldn't believe their eyes," Marvel Cooke of the *Amsterdam News* wrote of the black fans at Yankee Stadium. "There was something terrible—something fascinating, too, in watching a great idol fall to the ground and break up in little pieces." A defeat was just what Louis needed, she overheard one man say; now he'd know his weaknesses when he went for the championship. "We agreed with all he said," she remarked, "but somehow we were thinking of Hitler celebrating Maxie's victory in Germany, and that burned us up." For many black children, that night marked the first time they had ever seen their parents cry.

Their emotions high and their deadlines tight, reporters at ringside struggled to capture how the universe had just been realigned. "Some day the sphinx will talk, the pyramids will crumble, the oceans will stand still," Joe Williams wrote. "Something loosely akin to that was recorded . . . under a frowning sky at the Yankee Stadium last night. And so today you will read that the greatest upset in ring history took place, that the impossible happened, that the condemned man electrocuted the warden." To Grantland Rice, the atom had just been taken apart. Then there was Robert Perrier of *L'Auto*, who'd counseled Schmeling to practice all those different dives. "Had I found God himself shaving in my bathroom, or if I were to walk down Fifth Avenue and find the Eiffel Tower in place of the Empire State Building, I think I would be less surprised than at witnessing what I did last night at the Yankee Stadium," he wrote.

Listening to the fight was such torture for Anny Ondra that she often left the room, gauging her husband's fortunes from periodic peeks at the Goebbelses' faces. Once the direction of the contest became clear, though, a photographer captured her—smiling, with fists clenched—as she sat by the radio and listened, with her friends Joseph and Magda hovering protectively at her side. "For your wonderful victory, which we have experienced tonight on the radio, my most heartfelt congratulations," Goebbels quickly cabled Schmeling. "I know that you have fought for Germany. Your victory is a German victory. We are proud of you. With best wishes and Heil Hitler." "In the twelfth round, Schmeling knocks out the Negro," he wrote afterward in his diary. "Wonderful. A dramatic, exciting fight. . . . The White man over the Black man, and the White man was a German. His wife is magnificent. The whole family delights in joy. Don't get to bed until 5 a.m. I'm very happy." A crowd gathered outside Goebbels's home, where Ondra spent what little remained of the night. Her husband telephoned her there after the fight. Hitler contacted her, too. "For the wonderful victory of your husband, our greatest German boxer, I must congratulate you with all my heart," wrote the Führer, who also sent her flowers. Goebbels ordered that for those who hadn't managed to stay up to hear it live—or who, like him, wanted to hear it all over again—the fight would be rebroadcast throughout Germany at seven the next night.

In the meantime, all of Germany celebrated. The straitlaced German newspapers offered only meager descriptions, but a Frenchman in Berlin who'd listened to the fight in a bar on the Kurfürstendamm described the scene as it unfolded. "What joy, what deliriousness," he wrote. "Everyone is talking about this victory that many had not even dared to hope for. The working class, the late-night workers, the police, the housekeepers are all happy about Max's success. And here come the street vendors running at full speed shouting 'Special edition! Colossal! Colossal!'" The excitement spilled over into the next day. "All of Berlin is joyful," he wrote then. "On the bus, in the street, at the butcher, the bistro on the street corner, the conversations go on and on." Near the Berlin zoo, he watched someone deck a man who was now claiming to have predicted a Schmeling victory when in fact he'd picked Louis. "The aggressor moved back, as proud as if he were Max himself, and said to his opponent 'that's how Louis stayed on the ground,'" he wrote. "The press has exploded with joy—there is no room left for information or day to day politics. . . . The special editions all sold out quickly this morning; I know a certain street vendor who did a golden business on this magnificent day. . . . Nobody is talking about the Olympic Games and politics anymore. That is all secondary and not very important."

A reporter for one of the Chicago papers was crushed in the mad rush to the dressing rooms and had to be carried away on a stretcher. In Schmeling's quarters, pandemonium bordering on hysteria prevailed. La Guardia, too, nearly got trampled. Joe Jacobs strutted in, his shirt drenched and his cigar cocked "at a million-dollar angle." It was his moment, too: a time to celebrate, and, at least as important, to settle some old scores. "Where's all dem guys? Where's all dem guys?" he shrieked. "Dem name-da-round guys? Dem name-de-punch guys? Dem name-de-minute guys? Youse newspaper guys, youse experts, whad'ya got to say now about my Maxie? He knocked out the superman! You hear? What's that make him? You wouldn't listen to me, would ya? Little Joey, back in the dough! You hear that? Nothing's too good for us now!" In between sentences, he kissed Schmeling wildly. "I'm even with the world! I'm even with the world!" he shouted.

Schmeling, his lips puffed and bleeding, his teeth discolored from blood, his left eye completely closed and his right eye swollen and red, sat on the rubbing table. "I'm so happy. I'm so happy," he said. "I leave here three years ago beaten by Hamas and now I come back and win. It is very good. And he is very good. Good, man. My, how he can take a punch." He explained watching Louis fight Uzcudun, and knowing afterward that he could beat him. "I am a proud man," he said. "I would not have taken this fight if I did not think I, a white man, could beat a colored man." He said he didn't blame the Americans for the odds against him; they'd missed his German fights, and still thought him a loser. Not that the odds were a bad thing for Schmeling; a Chicago paper claimed he made more money betting on himself than he had fighting the fight. Never, Schmeling said, had he been scared. Fighting was a profession, he explained, and any man who was afraid had no business in any profession. Had Dempsey or Corbett or Sullivan been afraid? "When Louis hit me low, he hurt me," he said. "But I made up my mind I would never again win a fight on the floor." Julian Black came in to congratulate Schmeling, and Schmeling thanked him.

"Please tell my countrymen at home that this is the greatest and happiest day of my life," Schmeling told the *Berliner Lokal-Anzeiger*. "At this moment I have to tell Germany, I have to report to the Führer in particular, that the thoughts of all my countrymen were with me in this fight; that the Führer and his faithful people were thinking of me. This thought gave me the strength to succeed in this fight. It gave me the courage and the endurance to win this victory for Germany's colors." He said he looked forward to returning to Germany shortly, and that as happy as he was now, he'd be even happier when he could see Hitler. When Hellmis caught up with Schmeling, he wrote, the winner's first question to him was whether Hitler had been listening. Schmeling greeted his mother and his wife by radio, and then—in a lower voice, as if self-conscious in the crowded dressing room—he appended a "*Heil Hitler*" at the end. When the Deutscher Rundfunk resumed its normal musical programming, around four-thirty in the morning, it played a song called "I'm Dreaming with Open Eyes." Throughout Germany, groggy but euphoric fight fans prepared to go to work. In Magdeburg a "wall of people" waited for extras of the local paper as the first rays of sunlight gleamed off the cathedral.

Schmeling returned to a hotel room filled with noise and drowning in flowers. "We knocked that Brown Bomber right back to where he came from," Joe Jacobs exclaimed. Bellhops kept bringing in and dumping telegrams—at least eight hundred of them. A friend sat on the sofa and ticked off the senders: "Primo Carnera." "Ernst Lubitsch." "Marlene Dietrich." "George Grosz." "Douglas Fairbanks." "Adolf Hitler." "I was the only one in Hollywood who bet on you," wrote Sonja Henie. Another telegram—surely a forgery, but reported as fact—came from the graduating class of Lakewood High School. "We could not stand him, either," it said, referring, presumably, to Lakewood's recent guest. Many of the telegrams came from the South, often with barbed, racist sentiments. Schmeling insisted he wasn't interested in such things. The message said to have pleased him most came from St. Mary's Industrial School in Baltimore, where the young Babe Ruth had lived. But the one telegram he kept atop the pile, the one he read aloud and translated for his audience, was Hitler's.

Part of the time, Schmeling relaxed in the bathtub, his eyes closed. Then he mixed. He turned his back on Joe Williams, who had been among those describing the postponement as a stay of execution. But for the most part, he rejoiced. "Germany—it vas going crazy ven I talked mit my wife on the telephone after der fight," he said, turning his head and peering through his half-closed right eye to see anyone or anything. "She told me everyone vas avake there." Jews and Germans, now forcibly separated by law throughout the Reich, commingled freely that night in Schmeling's suite. "You could understand better what was going on if you spoke both German and Yiddish," the *New York Post* stated. "Nazism seemed pretty remote and academic, for the moment, at least." "Youse guys don't know nothin'," Jacobs exclaimed at one point. "You see this mezuzah?" He reached into his pocket and pulled out the amulet Jews affix to their doorposts to symbolize the sanctity of the home and wear around their necks for good luck. "Why, I had this in my mouth every time I stepped into the ring between rounds." But after the fourth, he explained, he no longer needed it. Only around sunrise did Jacobs drive off the last of the well-wishers, and Schmeling got some sleep. He rose around ten, when the reporters began coming back.

As for Louis, his first postfight memory was being carried to his dressing room and hearing Blackburn say, "Cover up yo' face, Chappie." And that was how he arrived, supported by Blackburn and Black, his head buried in a towel. Marva had rushed there, too. "Is he hurt much?" she cried. "Did it spoil his nose?" Louis was deposited on a rubbing table, massaged, and given smelling salts. A doctor pried open his eyes and took a look. For a time, Louis hid his face in his hands and cried. To one observer, the left side of Louis's face looked as if it had stopped a tractor. But outside a small circle, no one would really know—no photographs were allowed.

Louis was even more monosyllabic than usual, his jaw too swollen to open. He lay motionless as Blackburn cut off his gloves, and the trainer had to lift him off the table to remove his trunks. He asked Blackburn what had happened. "You just got tagged, Chappie, that's all," Blackburn replied. Fifteen or twenty reporters had slipped in before the police barricaded the room, but Louis largely ignored their questions. After a few minutes he was half-carried into a shower. When he emerged, his mind still clouded, he was helped back to his table. "You can't get to him nohow," he muttered. "You can't do it, the way he fights. He fights turned around." He said he remembered nothing after the second round. "Everything was in a fog," he lamented. He asked someone to apologize to Schmeling for the low blows, which were really uppercuts gone awry. "I sure didn't mean to hit him low," he said. "Guess I musta been arm weary. Couldn't make my left hooks behave. Couldn't make nothing behave."

"Say, don't forget that one Max hit after the bell one round," Blackburn said, as he rubbed ice on Louis. "That was a honey, wasn't it, Joe?" "No, I ain't going to retire," Louis said through puffed lips. "I'm gonna come back." "That knockout was the best thing that could have happened to the boy," Roxborough said. "He was beginning to get a little cocky and wouldn't listen to anybody. Maybe he'll listen after this." "Yes, maybe we can tell him sumthin' from now on," Blackburn interjected. "He learned a good lesson."

So the finger-pointing had started, and Roxborough finally acknowledged what others had suspected. "I don't want to resort to alibis, but we had a lot of trouble with Joe during the training for this fight," he said. "It got so bad that he was beginning to tell Blackburn what to do, instead of listening to his trainer. Understand, this is not an excuse for Joe's defeat, but I saw what was coming." Louis, it was now revealed, wouldn't even take minute breaks between rounds in Lakewood, so eager was he to finish up and loaf. He refused to skip rope and punch the bag, claiming that his roadwork and his sparring were enough. Schmeling "did Joe a world of good," Roxborough concluded. "Joe won't be so cocky any more." But if Louis was responsible for his fate, Roxborough gave Joe Jacobs an assist. It was Jacobs, he conceded, who had convinced Mike Jacobs to keep Louis idle until he'd grown rusty. Then, by limiting the bandages Louis could use, he'd stripped Louis's hands of the necessary protection. Louis had ended up with two sprained thumbs, which had kept him from putting Schmeling away. "Joe Jacobs outsmarted us," Roxborough conceded.

Mike Jacobs tried to make the best of the turn of events. "This fight will make him a great fighter," he said. "Best thing in the world for him." Besides, the heavyweight division had now been cracked wide open, with innumerable new commercial possibilities. Uncle Mike scribbled pairs of names on the back of an envelope. "Louis vs. Schmeling would draw a million and a half in a return bout," he said. "There's Braddock vs. Schmeling . . . Schmeling vs. Baer . . . Baer vs. Braddock . . . Baer vs. Louis . . . Braddock vs. Louis . . . plenty of angles now." Soon, he left Louis's dressing room for Schmeling's. Louis's adoring mob now amounted to four concerned people: Roxborough, Black, Blackburn, and Marva. Outside his dressing room, a small black boy in a jockey's hat stood and wept.

They dressed Louis in a gray suit and white sports shirt and put a red-banded straw hat, suitable for shielding him from the curious and the gloating, on his aching, outsize head. He asked someone to tie his shoes. "You mark my words," Blackburn said as he helped Louis on with his coat. "Chappie will come back from this defeat to be greater than ever." He was asked if he'd ever expected to see Louis nailed. "Fighting's a nailing business and I always carried an ammonia bottle with four whiffs in it," he replied. Marva grabbed her husband and, with a cordon of police protecting them, they walked arm in arm to a car.

Louis went back to his hotel. "Joe, your head looks like a watermelon," one of his sisters told him. Marva appeared briefly at what was to have been a victory party. "Poor thing, he is sleeping," she said stoically. "He is suffering." Then, shortly before midnight a big car pulled up in front of 805 St. Nicholas Avenue, where Marva was staying, and where a crowd of five hundred people—some sympathetic, others blaming her for the debacle—awaited her. Cheers and jeers followed her as she went inside. "She covered her face with her handkerchief as if to defend herself from the hostile crowd, who an hour before were raising hosannas to her husband," wrote Roi Ottley in the *Amsterdam News*. "She tried in vain to hide the tears that streamed down her face." Marvin Smith, the photographer who, with his twin brother, Morgan, chronicled Harlem, took no pictures of Marva that night, or of anything else documenting Harlem's desolation; only whites, he later said, photographed Harlem when it was sad.

Around New York, reactions varied. One theatergoer came out of a Broadway show and heard someone singing "Schmeling made the chocolate drop," and it was chilling to her, the kind of gloating she'd heard in Germany a few years earlier. At Jack Dempsey's and Mickey Walker's, "every man you met had a five or six-to-one wager on the German," someone wrote, "but not many of them were treating the house." Gene Tunney strolled into "21" and was instantly besieged for explanations. "Nothing can take the place of experience," he pronounced. "Max smashed that nigger!" a bartender yelled at the New York hotel where Willie "the Lion" Smith was playing piano. Smith got up, jumped over the bar, and brandished his cane like a baseball bat until the man apologized. New York's clubs were crowded, but something was off. Louis's loss had cost the high rollers dearly, one waiter whispered, and the tabs had shrunk proportionately.

Up and down East Eighty-sixth Street in Yorkville, people marched arm in arm, singing and shouting. Business boomed in Café Hindenburg, the Vaterland, and Jaegers, with buxom fräuleins and waiters in Bavarian outfits carrying overflowing steins through the crowds. A mob fell upon a news dealer selling extras of a local paper: MAX SCHLÄGT JOE LOUIS IN DER 12 RUNDE K.O., the headline screamed. Street fights erupted as people who'd bet on Schmeling demanded payment. Two charwomen who'd collected their two-dollar winnings in pennies scattered them like confetti into the air and onto the street.

Returning from Yankee Stadium, Schmeling's party passed through Harlem as quickly as it could. It was no place to be when Louis lost, especially for the man who had beaten him. Those who hadn't crawled miserably into their beds or drunk themselves into a stupor poured out into the streets, for company or consolation or simply by force of habit. "Big black, brown and yellow feet tread in funeral time on the swarming pavements of Harlem," wrote one observer. Residents "just strolled along . . . trying to walk it off. . . . Everybody walking here, there, and anywhere . . . getting nowhere." Around anyone attempting to explain what had just happened, crowds gathered. At the corner of Seventh Avenue and 140th Street, a seven-year-old girl holding an old family cake pan suitable for banging out a victory tattoo stood and cried. A block south, three women who'd bet a month's salary on Louis were, one black reporter noted, "weeping desperately and wearing the most pitifully forlorn expressions I have ever seen." Langston Hughes walked down Seventh Avenue and saw grown men weeping like children and women sitting on the curb, their heads in their hands.

On every block were four or five patrolmen, with a mounted policeman on each corner. Originally, they'd been sent to control the expected merrymaking; now they were guarding against violence and vandalism, and they couldn't get to it all. Much of the mayhem was directed against whites who, whether out of bad luck or foolish voyeurism, found themselves in Harlem. Thirty blacks knocked down and kicked a fifty-year-old white WPA worker who'd come uptown for a union meeting. At Amsterdam Avenue and 116th Street, black youths threw stones at whites driving back from the stadium. At 155th Street and Bradhurst Avenue, the windows of buses returning from the fight were smashed. Blacks set upon blacks, too—for denigrating Louis or for betting on Schmeling, or for boasting about those bets, or for trying to collect on them too quickly, before tempers had cooled. "Joe didn't land a single good punch," a man declared, and was shot. Wilmer Cooper walked into a bar and charged that Schmeling had reneged on a deal, designed to prolong the fight films, to start battling in earnest only after the fourth round. First Cooper was stabbed, then a blow to his head with an auto jack fractured his skull. All night long, doctors in Harlem hospitals were busy sewing people back together.* One white man who'd unwisely decided to walk home from the fight closed his eyes, pretended he was blind, and, walking stick in hand, "tap-tap-tapped his way" out of Harlem and into safety. Jack Johnson could say "I told you so," and did; in forty years his jaw hadn't taken as much punishment as Louis's had in a single night, he declared upon showing up at the Renaissance Grill with his white wife. He was literally run out of the joint.

When Walter White and his wife returned from Yankee Stadium, their young son was sobbing "as though his heart would break." And barely three hours after the fight, Harlem resembled a cemetery. Lenox Avenue was deserted. "Not even the worst days of the Depression could achieve such blanket sadness," wrote Walter Wendall of the *Boston Chronicle*. "The musician who usually thumps the piano with such abandon that the diners sway back and forth as they eat, goes thru his numbers mechanically. The diners sit and look at each other. Few speak. Words are futile. Finally a young couple venture on to the dance floor with forced gaiety, but their feet are leaden, and they give up the attempt. They return

*To some British reporters, the violence in Harlem only proved the wisdom of the color line. "Schmeling has done boxing a service," wrote Geoffrey Simpson of the *Daily Mail*. "He has post-dated to the distant future the prospect of a coloured heavyweight ruling the ring." Given the "outrageous" scenes in Harlem, *Boxing* agreed. No sport, it said, "should be made the means of national uprising and revolt."

to their table in a dark corner in silence. All is depressing in this gay spot. Even the waiters speak in hushed tones. Harlem is sad, very sad tonight."

The next morning, long lines formed outside Manning's Pawn Shop even before it opened. People who'd bet on Louis stayed home for weeks for fear of being dunned. A man fined five dollars for scalping got a break by pleading how much he'd lost on Louis. Two days after the fight, cars with southern license plates were still cruising Harlem's streets; all had been wagered on the fight, and had been lost. The former owner of a Lincoln Zephyr explained that he'd taken twelve hours to drive north, and expected to take twelve months to scratch up the funds to get back to Alabama.

Harlem's anguish played out on a smaller scale in black neighborhoods everywhere. In Buffalo, "there was a deathly silence," a local reporter wrote. "Not even a blizzard this hot June night, not even another earthquake, nothing could have produced such a shock." In St. Louis, a thirty-four-year-old black man criticized Louis and got his skull fractured for it. A New Orleans man said to no one in particular, "That Louis let me down. I bet money on him and he let me down." "I'll let you down, white man!" replied an eavesdropper, who stabbed the man, then fled. In Detroit, women wept in front of Lillie Barrow's house. Louis's stepfather, who'd suffered what turned out to be a fatal stroke just before the fight, was not told the outcome. In Coldwater, Michigan, a seventeen-year-old boy murdered his foster father after an argument over the fight.

On Chicago's South Side, bars and restaurants expecting to cash in on another Louis victory closed up before midnight. In Cincinnati, Lena Horne, performing with Noble Sissle's band, was nearly hysterical by the final rounds, and some of the musicians were crying. To her, Louis had suddenly become "just another Negro getting beaten by a white man." The owners of a black nightclub in Kansas City angrily tore down the bunting decorating the place. GLOOM ENGULFING THE CITY'S HARLEM, ran a headline in Louisville, Kentucky. A young boxer named Walker Smith, soon to be Sugar Ray Robinson, despaired briefly of the sport and pawned his equipment. Black communities in other countries shared in the sadness. "The blow came all the harder to the Coloured people who had visions of another Negro champion of the world," a newspaper for South African blacks stated.

Conversely, it was a joyous night for many whites. Cheers halted business in the House of Representatives for several minutes: members who had slipped out to listen to the fight "surged back onto the floor in a rousing demonstration," and the presiding officer rapped vainly for order. There was similar chaos in the Senate. "The people know now that they have legislators whose souls are so shriveled and corroded by Negrophobia that they prefer seeing a white foreigner take honor, title and money away from America than see one of their own citizens regain them if he is a Negro," a North Carolina man wrote. As Democrats gathered to renominate Franklin D. Roosevelt in Philadelphia, concerns arose that his ostensibly hapless Republican rival, Governor Alf Landon of Kansas, could turn out to be a "political Max Schmeling."

Father Charles Coughlin, the right-wing radio priest from Royal Oak, Michigan, whose program had been preempted by the fight, called the spectacle "a one hour's wonder, appealing to all lovers of honest, virile sport." In white Detroit, horns blasted, paper floated out from windows, and people "paraded in bedlamic pilgrimages up and down the main streets." Macon, Georgia, "resembled midnight of New Year's Eve." As the fight ended in New York, a white woman named Loula Wiley gave birth on a houseboat in rural Louisiana, and her husband proclaimed that the boy would be named "Max the Great." (When his wife objected, he settled for Max Berlin Wiley.) Playing before a white crowd in Texas, Cab Calloway gave the bad news to his musicians. While his men moaned, their audience cheered. South African whites celebrated, too—at least once they'd figured out what McCarthy and Hill had actually said.* Their excitement, *Box-Sport* explained, stemmed from "the limitless aversion of the colonial English, and especially the Boers, to all black skins."

"What the race lost in money was as dust to diamonds compared with the loss suffered in hope," wrote Enoc P. Waters, Jr., in the *Defender*. A race that had been "brow-beaten, kicked about, ignored and segregated" had recently fixed its eyes on a "glorious hallowed trinity": Joe Louis, Jesse Owens, and Haile Selassie. But the Italians had banished Selassie, and now Louis, too, was gone. "It is a mighty difficult job," Waters concluded, "for 12,000,000 persons to balance themselves on a stool which now has but one leg." "An idol," wrote a columnist in the *New York Post*, "representing everything that was good and kind and wholesome and sportsmanlike; an idol that meant pride and self-respect and an incentive to honor and religion—an idol fell last night, and the crashing was so com-

---

*The two, a reporter for the *Rand Daily Mail* complained, "talked at a rate at which only American broadcast commentators can talk, and in Johannesburg it sounded just as if an auction sale were being held in the ring. . . . No amount of dial manipulation could make the description intelligible."

plete, so dreadful and so totally unexpected that it broke the hearts of the Negroes of the world." From that point, as Mabe Kountze of the *Boston Guardian* later put it, "the Negro race went around for months singing songs in a minor key." The shadow of Louis's loss lay "draped like a vulture's wings" over all of black America.

Black weeklies that had predicted whites would pounce on Louis were he to lose were quickly vindicated. "From a conquering fistic idol Joe Louis was transferred today into a beaten, pitifully dejected colored boy who craved nothing but seclusion from the world which had heaped glory on his kinky head and piled gold at his feet," wrote Lester Avery of the United Press. Louis's "jungle cunning" was no match for Schmeling's much superior intelligence, Grantland Rice wrote. To William McG. Keefe of the *New Orleans Times-Picayune*, boxing's "reign of terror" was over: "The big bad wolf has been chased from the door." "Joe Louis is just a legend today," observed John Carmichael of the *Chicago Daily News*. "You couldn't scare the kids away from the jam pantry with his name."

Never had so many "experts" been so wrong, and the boxing press ate prodigious helpings of crow. An annoyed Dan Parker dubbed June 20, 1936, "I-Told-You-So Day." In the southern press, Louis's loss unleashed a torrent of pent-up resentment. O. B. Keeler of the *Atlanta Journal* sent out gloating telegrams—collect—to twenty-two writers who'd praised the "Pet Pickaninny" most effusively. "Who the hell ever had the right to nominate this fairly good, flat-footed Senegambian boxer as a superman?" he asked irately. "Louis did what all the negro prize fighters before him have done. He quit," the *Memphis Commercial Appeal* said. The black press, meanwhile, described the ugly vein of American racism that the fight had exposed. The *Defender* detailed the ensuing hate mail, filled with terms like "nigger," "darkie," "coon," and "Sambo." The *Richmond Planet* complained about Schmeling's fan mail, most of which came from the South, "that hinterland of barbarism which wallows in the filth of ignorance, bestiality, prejudice and wanton depravity," dominated "by hillbillies, ignoramises [*sic*], slant eyes tobacco and snuff spitting morons, self-styled aristocrats and egotists who are too cowardly to attack except in packs like wolves."

The day after the fight, while Louis remained in seclusion, Schmeling basked. He stayed in bed until noon and then, hiding his shiners behind a pair of brown sunglasses, gave interviews at the hotel. Louis would be a good fighter once he learned a bit more, he said, but had shown him a fresh flaw that would make him even easier the next time. He weighed various commercial offers—endorsing a soft drink, taking an interest in a fruit farm—and said he had turned down $152,000 for ten weeks of vaudeville appearances. "Americans are interested in money. Not me," he said. In fact, Schmeling's agent had booked him—in the event he won—for a week in Atlantic City for $7,500, followed by appearances in Montreal, Toronto, and Baltimore. But Schmeling received a call from someone— never specified—in Germany, and the road show was scotched. He was to have gone home by ship, but to Hitler and his associates—who had perfected the art of dramatic arrivals by air—so pedestrian a passage would now never do. Schmeling was directed instead to return on the dirigible *Hindenburg*, which was leaving the United States in three days. The flight was fully booked, but one of the officers was either relinquishing his berth for the *Heimat* or had been bumped. Machon would return by boat, accompanied by the cars, which, in what some saw as an effort by the promoter to sever Schmeling's already rocky relationship with Joe Jacobs and cement his own ties to the German, Mike Jacobs had given them: a Cord for Schmeling, a Chevrolet for his trainer.

Schmeling saw a fringe benefit to his victory. "Maybe the people in Germany look on me as Max Schmeling and not Mr. Anny Ondra," he joked. In fact, he had little to worry about. The day after the fight, the *Angriff* effectively made Schmeling a metaphor for the new, resurgent Germany. When "the victorious German boxer raised his arm for the Hitler salute, 80,000 went head over heels in enthusiasm," it said. "Loud cries for Germany were heard, and all prejudices collapsed." Goebbels and his colleagues now had other favors to bestow on him. First, the propaganda minister banned all statements by Schmeling's former manager, Arthur Bülow, from the German press; it seemed Bülow had offended German dignity by doubting Schmeling's chances. "I will liberate Schmeling from his mean adversary. He'll be happy about that," Goebbels told his diary. Two days later, Hitler pardoned Schmeling on a tax violation. As Westbrook Pegler later put it, Hitler had suddenly discovered "that the swarthy brunet with the narrow black eyes and high cheek bones was a true, blond Aryan."

"Germany, the land of the fastest race cars, the land of the safest airships—this Germany now also has the 'Greatest Heavyweight Boxer of All Time,'" a newspaper in Dresden boasted. A paper in Regensburg linked Schmeling's win to other signs of German revival, like the autobahn. (But a merchant in Karlsruhe discovered the comparisons could only go so far. "An achievement like that of Max Schmeling has by no means anything to do with the quality of a mattress," the local newspaper remonstrated.)

Cartoonists gloated, often with primitive renditions of Louis as a generic, primitive-looking black man. One showed him with a meat cleaver in his hand, strutting along with Schmeling on a leash. "My sacrificial lamb," he states. In the next panel, Schmeling is stuffing Louis into his mouth. "What the Negro thought . . . and our 'Maxe' did," the caption declared. Several papers pushed to bring Schmeling's forthcoming title bout against Braddock to Berlin. Schmeling himself threw cold water on the idea, candidly confirming everything Nazi diehards had always said about professional athletes (and belying his own insistence that filthy lucre really didn't matter to him). "You know, the money is in this country," he told the *New York Post* before leaving for Germany. "Here is where I made my money. Here is where I will make more if I win the championship."

Even before Schmeling arrived back home, there were official celebrations of his victory. One was a mammoth pageant marking the summer solstice, held on a mountain overlooking Nuremberg. There, Julius Streicher, editor of the violently racist *Der Stürmer*, analyzed the fight for 200,000 people, including 20,000 uniformed Hitler Youth and Unity Mitford, the notorious British Nazi, and declared that Schmeling was part of "a New Germany . . . a Germany that has faith in itself again." The magazine of the SS, *Das Schwarze Korps*, said that Schmeling's fists had defeated the enemies of Nazism and "saved the reputation of the white race." Hitler's friends in Fascist Italy agreed. Schmeling, one Roman paper opined, had "confirmed the supremacy of a race that could not be undone by brute force." England, France, and North America could not thank Schmeling enough, stated another German magazine, *Der Weltkampf*, for he had checked black arrogance. "The Negro is of a slave nature, but woe unto us if this slave nature is unbridled, for then arrogance and cruelty show themselves in the most bestial way," it declared.

Though the Nazi press had built up Schmeling's previous adversaries to make his triumphs that much more magnificent, extolling a Negro proved too much to bear. One newspaper claimed that Louis "made a one-sided and primitive impression." Another charged that his low blows were deliberate. Schmeling had not just knocked out Louis, a *Box-Sport* editor suggested, but dispensed with him once and for all. "Beaten is not the right word for the terrible catastrophe that has befallen the Negro," it stated. "The myth of Joe Louis is smashed, smashed for all times." Thankfully, the *8 Uhr-Blatt* wrote, the moral inferiority of black boxers gave whites a fighting chance to overcome any physical disadvantages. Hellmis agreed. "When an acquaintance said, 'The mind is just better,' he hit the nail on the head!" he wrote. Sure, Louis took Schmeling's punches with inhuman toughness. "But what a man of 'genuine' courage would have done—once again, with fierce determination, to risk everything and try to turn the match around—one waited for that in vain," Hellmis wrote.

The day after the fight, during a press luncheon at the Forrest Hotel, Schmeling donned a chef's hat for the photographers and ate turkey with élan. At one point Braddock came by, and took Schmeling's right fist in his hand. "Take good care of that, Max, until September," he said. "You will need it." "Dot's a good idea, Jim," Schmeling replied. "I take care and expect I will use it." Julian Black also stopped in, and was asked about Louis. "Joe's all right," he answered. "He's on the train now for Detroit." The legendary black boxer Harry Wills, who'd also congratulated Schmeling, expressed faith in Louis's future. "I don't think Louis is through," he said. "Sure, he took an awful licking, but I was proud of that boy as he lay on that canvas. He showed his heart was right. And when a man's heart is right, he can win. Didn't Mistah Schmeling prove that las' night?"

The *Daily News* described how Schmeling, "beaming like a school kid on the first day of a Summer vacation," "twitching" and "trembling" with excitement, watched films of the fight in a darkened Broadway movie house. Three sounds, always in the same sequence, filled the theater: the ominous thud of a Schmeling right; then the awestruck "ooooph" of the audience; then Schmeling's husky, throaty laugh. "Dot is good, dot is good," he would roar. Then he would slap Joe Jacobs on the back.

"Should clean up," *Variety* predicted about the fight films, which, in a rare lapse of judgment, Mike Jacobs had sold for a mere $27,000. Theaters hyped them—"The End of the Reign of Terror of the 'Brown Bomber,'" the *Oshkosh Northwestern* advertised; "The Fight So Thrilling It Caused the Death of Twelve People," claimed the *Times Recorder* of Zanesville, Ohio, alluding to all those who'd had heart attacks during the broadcast— but it was hardly necessary. In San Francisco, police were called in to handle the nearly 100,000 people who passed through one theater; in Chicago, three cinemas in the Loop showed it simultaneously. Everywhere, North and South, people who once cheered Louis jeered him now, laughing or applauding whenever Schmeling landed a punch or Louis faltered. "All this turning of coats to be on the winning side, all this mirth and high spirits in the face of a man's ambition and body being broken under spotlights—this is callous, knavish . . . somehow obscene," wrote Otis Ferguson in *The New Republic*. "Daddy, I could kill those people who laughed when Joe was knocked down," Walter White's son said sobbingly after watching the film in New York. If Louis really had it,

White replied consolingly, he'd come back greater than ever. "*If* he's got it?" the boy replied. "He *has* got it!"

The Associated Negro Press complained that while films of Louis victories had been banned in the South, films of his loss to Schmeling were shown. In Memphis, however, the film was prohibited. In Virginia, the hairsplitting state censorship board found a way to allow the Louis-Schmeling films to be shown, but let stand its ban on the Louis-Baer fight. "If it were not for the deep tragedy beneath, it would be great fun being a Negro in America," Arthur Davis wrote of Richmond's peculiar solution in the *Norfolk Journal and Guide.* "One could really enjoy oneself watching the delightfully inconsistent and foolishly paradoxical situations which grow out of the kind of segregated living we have in this land." "Foolish, foolish Southerners!" he concluded. "When will . . . you ever lift the crushing weight of the Negro idea from your mind?" The inconsistency soon proved too much for a local white judge, who ruled that both films could be shown. The *Richmond Times-Dispatch* approved, noting that since Virginia's theaters were segregated anyway, the threat of violence was minimal. Indeed, in those southern communities where the Louis-Schmeling films could be seen, blacks and whites watched from entirely separate worlds— separate theaters, or separate portions of theaters, or at separate times of the day. In Dallas, the Rialto Theater offered three special showings—each at 11:30 p.m.—for blacks. The local black paper predicted that despite the late hour, all 1,300 seats would be sold for each show.

The fight was on everyone's lips. When British reporters besieged Felix Frankfurter, then a key Roosevelt adviser, for his comments on the Republican platform, he feinted. "Was not that a surprise about the way Schmeling beat Louis?" he asked. Frank Nugent of *The New York Times*—who rechristened Louis the "Brown Bouncer"—pitied any movie unlucky enough to appear with the fight film. "Herr Schmeling's was . . . the most devastating right we've observed in a theater, more compelling even than the right to live, the right to love and the other rights which the film industry has defended at one time or another," he wrote. A British reporter fed up with Yankee contempt for European boxers thought America had gotten a well-earned comeuppance. "If a German, with the best of his fighting years behind him, can beat a young coloured boy who had the whole of the United States hypnotized, then the fist-swinging business here cannot be all that is claimed for it," he wrote.

The press kept Schmeling company in his hotel suite on June 23 as he packed for Germany. If he beat Braddock in September, he pledged, he'd defend his title the following June against anyone, Louis included. He was still wearing his sunglasses, removing them only to go over his receipts and to get a shave. Schmeling left New York late in the afternoon, ate steamed clams and lobster at Mike Jacobs's house in Red Bank, New Jersey, then headed for the Naval Air Station in Lakehurst, where the dirigible was docked. There, a thousand people had gathered in the pouring rain to see what one local reporter called "two marvels of the Twentieth Century": the world's largest airship, and the man who had just knocked out Joe Louis. And of the two, Schmeling proved the greater attraction. A mob of photographers, plus many of his fifty-six fellow passengers, took his picture, sunglasses and all. He was presented with a cake shaped like a boxing ring, in which a marshmallow fighter stood erect over his prostrate, chocolate-covered opponent. "I just want to touch him! I just want to touch him!" a young woman shouted as she lunged toward him.

Schmeling pushed his way through the crowd and boarded a bus that ferried him to the enormous aircraft, moored half a mile away. As he stood on the gangplank, the last hand he shook was Mike Jacobs's. "Get Braddock ready!" Schmeling told him. Having paid his American taxes and settled some old debts, he was leaving with only $12,000. He still faced German taxes, the money the boycotters had warned would land in Hitler's coffers: another $40,000, by one estimate. Yet the balance sheet didn't include the most precious item in his luggage: a film of the fight, for which Schmeling had bought the German rights, and for a song. Some speculated it would make as much as $800,000, with Schmeling pocketing a quarter of that.

The zeppelin, a swastika on its tail, lifted up and out of Lakehurst at 11:25 p.m., fighting its way skyward through the raindrops. It quickly flew over Lakewood, over the Stanley Hotel, over some of the golf courses Louis had so loved. Within an hour it was over the Statue of Liberty. It moved uptown along the Hudson, its searchlights trained on the skyscrapers below. It floated over the Garment center, over the Hippodrome, over the pier where he'd disembarked, over Madison Square Garden and Jack Dempsey's and Jacobs Beach. Before reaching Yankee Stadium, as the Upper West Side blended into Harlem, it took a sharp right, grazing the tip of Central Park, then disappeared into the clouds as it headed northeast toward the Atlantic. Its journey to Germany would take fifty hours, enough time for Max Schmeling to imagine many things. But no one could have conjured up the stupendous reception awaiting him there.

CHAPTER 8

Climbing Back

To SCHMELING, riding aboard the *Hindenburg* was as thrilling as beating Louis. He couldn't sleep, so busy was he staring out the window. When the dirigible passed over Doorn, the residence of the former kaiser, Wilhelm II, it dipped several times, and Schmeling could see him waving his hat. Around four on the afternoon of June 26, it flew over Cologne. And when it approached Frankfurt, five fighter planes formed an escort. Below were ten thousand people, many of whom had waited for hours in the heat, humidity, and tumult as vendors sold Max Schmeling Almonds and Anny Ondra Fruit Drops. Among those in the crowd were Schmeling's mother and wife, who had arrived that morning from Berlin on a plane Goebbels had supplied—Ondra's first flight ever.

Around ten minutes past five, the giant silver-gray zeppelin floated silently into view over Frankfurt. Someone stood at the cockpit window and waved. It had to be Max! After doing a "lap of honor" around the city, the dirigible landed. Schmeling, fittingly, was let out first, before the zeppelin was even moved to its hangar, where the mere mortals would disembark. "It seemed as if a hurricane were let loose," one paper reported. "The crowd waved, rejoiced, and cried out their congratulations to him from afar and wanted to rush to him." A band of Brown Shirts played, but the music was drowned out by the exuberant fans. Schmeling greeted his wife and his mother. He and Ondra received flowers galore, including an enormous bouquet of carnations from a blond girl representing the Bund deutscher Mädel. Another bouquet came from the City of Frankfurt, presented to "the greatest spokesman for Germany."

There were speeches from Nazi and municipal officials, which were broadcast throughout the country. Schmeling, too, said a few words.

Then, as the crowd surged toward him, chanting his name, and hundreds reached out to shake his hand, he walked arm in arm with his mother and his wife to the parking lot. There, they hopped into an open car and headed through the teeming streets to the old city hall, where tens of thousands more had gathered, and where throngs surrounded his limousine. Three small girls brought him additional bouquets before he went inside to inscribe his name into the "Golden Book of the City of Frankfurt." Outside, people chanted "We want to see our Schmeling! Where is Max?" He then went out to the balcony to greet them, and gave them a Hitler salute. "Frankfurt couldn't have been more excited had Goethe come down from Mount Olympus," a French newspaper reported.

Then it was back to the airport, and the next leg of his triumphant tour: Berlin. En route, as Hitler's personal photographer, Heinrich Hoffman, recorded the scene, Schmeling recounted his recent exploits to his admirers. He also talked to two of Nazi Germany's most important sports editors, Herbert Obscherningkat of the *12 Uhr-Blatt* and Heinz Siska of the *Angriff*. Shortly after the fight, Walter Winchell had expressed the hope that Schmeling would bring a positive message about America back to Germany. "Even those of us who bet against Schmeling admire his courage and realize that the best man won," Winchell told his radio audience. "And some of us hope that when he arrives in Germany Thursday by way of the Zep that he will tell them all of the great sportsmanship displayed by Americans, who love a fair fight." Instead, with a candor and venom he had rarely revealed in the United States, Schmeling unloaded on the American press.* They had made him seem contemptible, like a criminal, he complained, referring to the comparisons to the Lindbergh kidnapper. All the talk of Louis's superiority hurt the gate, he went on; whites didn't want to see one of their own "clobbered by a mulatto." But the Americans were pleased by the outcome, he said; Louis's success had made blacks brazen, leading them to ambush and throw rocks at cars, and his loss had subdued them. He described the enthusiastic letters he'd received from the South, and criticized the "loudmouthed manner" of Americans who considered a Louis victory inevitable. By putting uppity American blacks in their place, Siska wrote, Schmeling had bestowed a

---

*So did a newspaper in Munich, which ran a cartoon showing three reporters, fat and with large noses, standing beside a ring, with a prostrate black man inside. "Schmeling Knocks Out Jewish Horror Press," it was titled.

great gift on unappreciative white America. "And [Schmeling] says that he alone would never have had the power, had he not known how much support he had in his homeland," Siska continued. "He was allowed to speak with the Führer and his ministers, and from that moment on his will to victory was without limit."

Streetcar service to Berlin's Tempelhof Airport was increased to accommodate the anticipated crowds. Many people were already in place by two in the afternoon, even though Schmeling wasn't due before nine. Between musical selections, an announcer updated Schmeling's progress above the Reich: Frankfurt, then Erfurt, Dessau, Beelitz. Hundreds of people streamed across the field when Schmeling finally landed. Greeting him were an honor guard of two hundred amateur boxers in blue tights, along with state secretary Walter Funk; someone representing sports minister Tschammer und Osten; one of Hitler's adjutants; and other assorted Nazi functionaries. Luft Hansa had brought a special "lighting car" with huge spotlights so that people could see more clearly what was unfolding. Schmeling and Ondra were presented with a long cake, plus free passes to the Olympics. There were more speeches and several thunderous *"Heil!"*s. A ladder truck, normally used to board planes, was brought out so that everyone could see the happy couple, and Schmeling was lifted and carried off the field.

When he reached his home, he discovered a triumphal arch outside, reading "Welcome, Max." Storm Troopers (the *Sturm Abteilung*, or SA) had decorated the house with a swastika and a Reich eagle, and had hung a banner containing a poem:

> *Lieber Max, sei Willkommen,*
> *Louis haste Mass genommen.*
> *Glücklich biste wieder da,*
> *Heil und Sieg Dir, die SA*

> *Dear Max, welcome home,*
> *You really gave Louis a thrashing.*
> *Happily, you're back again,*
> *Hail and victory to you, the SA*

Inside, the house looked like a flower store and gift shop, stacked with everything from marzipan boxing gloves to letters from children. Ondra had had to buy extra laundry baskets to accommodate all of the communiqués. Schmeling dined with Goebbels that night. The next afternoon, accompanied by his mother and his wife, he met with Hitler in the Reich's chancellory. In formal fashion, Hitler thanked Schmeling on behalf of the German people and, over cake, pressed for details about the fight. He lamented that he could not see the film, and when he was told that it was in customs, he arranged to have it fetched. When it arrived, they sat down and watched: Hitler "gave a running commentary and every time I landed a punch he slapped his thigh with delight," Schmeling later wrote. "Goebbels, listen—this isn't going to be used as part of the *Wochenschau* [weekly newsreel]!" Hitler decreed. "This film is going to be shown as a main feature. Throughout the entire Reich!" "Dramatic and thrilling," Goebbels wrote in his diary. "The last round is quite wonderful. He really knocks out the Negro." The gloves Schmeling wore in the Louis fight would soon hang at the Roxy-Bar, Schmeling's favorite hangout in Berlin, alongside the pair he'd used against Young Stribling in 1931 and Jack Sharkey the following year. (The right glove in the newest pair was softer because of the great workout it had endured.)

Four days after his return, Schmeling's festive homecoming was rudely interrupted when lightning struck the thatched roof of his country home in Bad-Saarow, forcing the Schmelings to flee outside. The fire spread quickly, and Schmeling went back in to salvage whatever he could. Most of his boxing mementos were lost, but, as the German papers duly noted, Schmeling managed to save a bust of Hitler given him by the Führer himself. Schmeling told one reporter that it was the first object he retrieved. (In a postwar interview Schmeling dismissed the bust as "the most worthless kitsch" and insisted it had been saved mistakenly by the son of the sculptor who'd made it.) Out of sadness for the Schmelings, Goebbels canceled a garden party scheduled for that day.

Schmeling's victory had broadened the potential market for the fight films. In countries where, as the *Los Angeles Times* put it, "a white man must not be beaten"—India, Australia, much of colonial Africa—"the pictures would have been barred instantly" had Louis won. Now they could be shown there. Of course by far the biggest newly opened market was Germany itself. But what Germans would view was not the straight, unadulterated footage shown elsewhere, including in Vienna, where local Nazis disrupted screenings with cries of "Heil Hitler!" "Heil Germany!" and "Heil Schmeling!" Instead, they would view it as Goebbels wanted them to, cut and pasted and repackaged. *Max Schmelings Sieg—ein deutscher Sieg*, it was to be called. "Max Schmeling's Victory: A German Victory."

In early July, ads for the film began appearing in mass-circulation newspapers and magazines. "A Film That Concerns All Germans," read one. A record number of prints were produced, and theater owners were promised a historic document as well as one of the biggest hits ever to hit the screens. Striking yellow posters for it popped up all over Berlin. The hype proved quite unnecessary; demand was enormous, and besides, with clips omitted from the weekly newsreels, it was the only way to see the fight. The premiere was set for Dresden on July 8. The next day it would open at forty-seven theaters in Berlin alone, and soon it would play throughout Germany.

The film began with a cultural oddity, as various Jewish names — Mike Jacobs among them — appeared in the credits. Nor was there any way to hide Joe Jacobs. (To assure themselves that there were no more Jews involved than was strictly necessary, the Nazis made Hellmis prove that he and his wife were pure Aryans before letting him narrate. This Hellmis did with birth and baptismal certificates dating back to his great-grandparents.) The earliest scenes were from Louis's training camp. Elevating Louis, at least as a boxer, would make his fall all the more dramatic, and this the film set out to do. "Long before the fight he was in excellent form," Hellmis declared. "In the last year alone he clobbered the world's five best in a few rounds." Then the scene switched to Napanoch, and a shot of Schmeling exercising. "In every one of his movements there speaks a concentrated energy," said Hellmis, "a will that shall be heard in the following weeks." Hellmis himself then appeared, at his microphone, and Germans could see the man so many had merely heard: roundish, fair-haired, utterly serious. "Max Schmeling's fight against Joe Louis became the most difficult of his long, successful career," he declared. "His victory was more than merely the success of a German athlete. It became a German victory." Really, he suggested, it was a victory for whites worldwide, who greeted the outcome "with genuine joy and admiration."

"Everything, but everything, spoke for [Louis]: his unusual, racially-conditioned gift for boxing, his youth, his unheard-of punching power, and his super-human toughness," Hellmis went on. "He [Max] alone never lost courage. He believed in his ability and his power. And when, finally, in the twelfth round the opponent lay annihilated on the canvas, then Schmeling won the warm and honest sympathy of the Americans. This German had accomplished what no one believed possible! The most dramatic fight in the history of the sport of boxing, which you will now see, is . . . a wonderful document attesting to the ability of a will as hard as Krupp steel to accomplish everything."

Then came the fight, beginning with Louis's stumbling entrance into the ring. From Schmeling's first blow, Hellmis said, Louis could tell that this was no ordinary adversary. This man was tough, and needed to be, for the black man was incredibly strong, incredibly dangerous. "Fighting is rough in American rings," Hellmis explained. "The rules aren't as strict as in Europe. Holding is allowed, as are punches to the kidney." By the fourth round, Schmeling's strategy—taking all those left jabs in order to get over his right—had emerged. Schmeling fired one at "the wooly head of the Negro." "There, a smash! And again! He's wobbling, he's wobbling, he's wobbling! The page has turned!" The moment was repeated in slow motion. Louis was down. Already, Schmeling was master of the ring.

Not surprisingly, the film made no mention of Schmeling's late punch after the fifth round. The demoralized Louis began fouling Schmeling, and Schmeling retaliated with a mighty punch. "That was for the low blow, Joe!" Hellmis exclaimed. By the twelfth, the incredibly tough "nature boy from Alabama" was tottering, staggering, completely shattered. Then, in slow motion, came his final, fateful low blow. "A boxer has to be able to control his punches," Hellmis scolded. "That won't turn out well, Joe Louis! You'll pay for that!" The masses in Yankee Stadium stood on their seats as Schmeling put Louis away. "Max! More, more, more still! More Max! The right! Once again! There he lies! Out! Out! Out! Out! Out!" The film ended with Balogh's announcement and the German national anthem.

Schmelings Sieg was a crude effort, with none of the gorgeous images or production values of more sophisticated Nazi productions like Leni Riefenstahl's. But it swept the country, giving Germans everywhere a chance to celebrate all over again. In Dresden, every show in two theaters sold out, in part because Schmeling himself appeared at each. At the dénouement, the local newspaper related, audience members clapped and screamed "as if they hadn't known about the outcome of the fight before"; when Schmeling appeared, the "applause wouldn't end." "Maxe! Maxe! Maxe!" the crowd outside, using the familiar form of "Max," chanted whenever Schmeling emerged. Late into the night, mobs lingered outside Schmeling's hotel, hoping for a glimpse of him. One fan made it into Schmeling's bathroom.

The night after the Dresden premiere, the crowds outside the Titania-Palast in Berlin were "downright life-threatening." Searchlights shot up into the sky; admittance was by invitation only, and but for the Führer, the panjandrums of the Reich were all there: Göring, Goebbels, Hess. When Schmeling entered, Ondra on his arm, he nearly brought down

the house. "Hollywood scarcely could have outdone the scene," Gayle
Talbot of the Associated Press was to recall. Bellowing and raving on the
soundtrack "like an off-key calliope," he wrote, Hellmis worked the audience into a terrific lather—so much so, in fact, that it was hard to hear
him over the din. "By the time the knockout finally came some of the
more excitable Nazi youths were trying to get at Louis personally." The
lights then went up and a smiling Schmeling appeared on the stage.
The audience stood and screamed for five minutes. Schmeling took
numerous curtain calls, and the police had to escort him to his car. He
and Ondra then dined with Hans Hinkel, Goebbels's protégé in the Nazi
propaganda ministry. With the film opening all over town the next day,
one German paper theorized that Schmeling's punches would soon leave
all of Berlin "joy-groggy."

In fact, all Germany would soon be just that. A 1,200-seat cinema in
Bremen sold out for the local premiere, and two additional theaters were
soon showing it. In Leipzig, "the audience was literally shivering out of
excitement." Its run in Bochum was extended after it broke an all-time
attendance record. In Regensburg the audience applauded during the
film, something Germans rarely did. Breslau, Danzig, Karlsruhe, Chem-
nitz, Halle, Ludwigshafen, Erfurt, Saarbrücken, Augsburg, Stettin, Gör-
litz: everywhere, the reports were the same. More than three million
Germans saw *Schmelings Sieg* in its first four weeks. It was still playing in
Berlin in late July, when the Americans arrived for the Olympics. By one
account, Schmeling had paid only $20,000 for the German rights to the
film but within two years had earned $165,000 from it.*

Schmeling's popularity at home had reached unimaginable heights.
Göring invited him to go hunting. Relations with Hitler remained cordial; when Gallico went to Schmeling's house in Berlin to interview his
old friend for a story about the Louis fight for the *Saturday Evening Post*,
he noticed that a large inscribed photograph of the Führer dominated
one room, while the remnants of the mammoth floral arrangement—
"decorated with red, swastika-ed ribbons"—that Hitler had sent Ondra
after the fight were nearby. "It must have taken three men to lift it," Gallico wrote. And Schmeling wrote the introduction to a book called

---

**Schmelings Sieg was confined to Germany, but unadulterated fight films showed to
large audiences elsewhere. "An atmosphere of tension spread, infecting everyone present,"
Box-Sport reported from Basel. "Every landed punch was met with an 'ouch,' an 'ooh,' or
an 'ah.' And at the end, such applause and rejoicing broke out as have probably never
greeted an image projected on the screen." In Paris, the films were "the biggest box office
attraction of the season." Among those viewing it in London was George Bernard Shaw.

Deutscher Faustkämpf nicht prizefight: Boxen als Rassenproblem [German Fistfight not Prizefight: Boxing as Race Problem]. In it the author, Ludwig Haymann, posited that Schmeling's style—scientific, precise, sophisticated—perfectly exemplified the German temperament. The book was a racist and anti-Semitic tract, stating that Louis had grasped for the heavyweight crown with a disdainful sneer and that Jews, drawn to boxing not by its sporting element but by pure greed, had degraded German concepts of heroism and idealism. Schmeling praised Hitler's appreciation of boxing and wished Haymann's book the success he said it deserved.

Schmeling later maintained that, politically speaking at least, all was not well for him at this time. A few days after his return to Germany, he said he had been offered a "dagger of honor" and the title of "Honorary Commander of the SA," and as someone who disdained politics, he hadn't known what to do. He said he called Hitler's personal photographer, Heinrich Hoffman, and begged off. But anyone in the Nazi hierarchy surely would have realized that allying Schmeling so explicitly with Hitler was professionally counterproductive, even suicidal, abroad; surely it was the work of an unsophisticated, overzealous underling. In any case, by July 1936 it's hard to see how such a gesture even mattered. Whatever his official status, Schmeling was thoroughly enmeshed with the Nazis, and he was perceived as such on both sides of the Atlantic. That he retained a Jewish manager in the United States may or may not have been an irritant in Berlin, but it was clearly tolerated by those who mattered. Hitler was so proud of Schmeling, Walter Winchell wisecracked, that he was thinking of naming a concentration camp after Joe Jacobs. Only with Goebbels had relations soured; it seemed he'd been in a theater the same night as Schmeling once and had been irked afterward when Schmeling, and not he, had been besieged for autographs.

Schmeling was never the man his most intemperate critics claimed. He was never "Nazi Max," the man who had supposedly worn a storm trooper uniform during the early days of the regime, whose picture in a brown shirt had been widely displayed in Germany. Nor does anything support the hearty canard—the details of which vary—that Schmeling or Machon carried Nazi flags or uniforms with them when they came to the United States. But Schmeling's dogged insistence that he was a sportsman rather than a politician made him more useful to the Nazis, not less. It allowed him to do business with Jews in New York, then hobnob with Nazis in Berlin and Berchtesgaden. The Nazis had Schmeling precisely where they wanted him, and while Schmeling always kept his own counsel, he was, to all appearances, content to be there. He had the best of both worlds: he was making enormous amounts of money, was poised to regain the heavyweight crown, and had the approbation of his people and his government. There is no evidence, in anything he said or did at the time, to suggest that he ever agonized over anything. Every athletic hero encountered parasitic "champion chasers," wrote Pegler, but Schmeling was the first "to discover among the cooties in the seams of his shirt a ruler of a world power." "The spectacle of the front-running chancellor chasing after a winner, whom he had previously disavowed, and yelling 'Atta boy, champ, I was with you all the time,' is the cheapest display of ki-yi sportsmanship in all the history of sports," Pegler went on—as pathetic as making a model Aryan out of someone who once told Pegler he could well be part Mongolian.

The hostility American Jews felt toward Schmeling before the fight only intensified upon seeing the Nazis embrace him afterward. "When he went back to Germany and tossed himself (figuratively speaking) on Hitler's manly (?) chest he was through over here," wrote Doc Daugherty of the *Daily Worker*.* Giant photographs of Schmeling and Anny Ondra hobnobbing with Hitler popped up throughout New York's garment district. "It would seem that Schmeling made a mistake in posing for the picture men," Davis Walsh wrote. "It coupled him with Hitler's regime, formally and for the first time." In early July, the *Angriff* declared that only his fellow blacks wanted to see Louis fight Schmeling again; for everyone else, a Braddock-Schmeling fight for the title was all that mattered. In reality, a rematch against Louis was the only Schmeling fight many American boxing fans, especially in New York, would now pay to see.

ON SUNDAY, JUNE 21, two days after the fight, a group of newsmen stood outside Michigan Central Station in Detroit awaiting the train carrying Joe Louis back from New York. "One nice thing about Joe," a photographer there said. "He'll always give a guy a fair break on a shot." That meant that he would always alight from the same car, so they could prefocus their Speed Graphics at the standard twelve feet.

But this time a different Joe Louis emerged—"hiding behind everything except a set of false whiskers"—and at a different spot, for the train had slowed down to let him jump off early. Though the day was sunny, he wore a gray topcoat with a turned-up collar that covered much of his face;

---

*In the *Worker*'s short-staffed sports section, Daugherty was one of the many pseudonyms of the sportswriter Charley Dexter, whose original name was Lou Levinson.

a straw hat and big blue sunglasses obscured the rest. When he spotted the photographers, he turned away and began running across the tracks. They scrambled in pursuit, trying to salvage a "steal shot"—the kind of picture one usually took of someone entering a jail. One of Louis's handlers threatened to destroy their cameras and waved his hat in front of their lenses. Louis dived into a cab, and for a split second one could see why he'd suddenly grown so shy: the left side of his face was far too big.

Louis had made himself scarce in New York before leaving. His only appearance was at Mike Jacobs's office, where he said he had no plans to watch the fight films. "I saw the fight," he explained. Louis canceled his appearance at the Negro League game in Newark, passing up a plaque calling him "the most outstanding athlete in the country." Instead, he got himself a drawing room on the Red Arrow, leaving—fleeing, was more like it—New York at five in the afternoon. Less than twenty hours after the knockout, he was heading home to Detroit, and to his mother. The fashion in which Louis slithered out of town could not have been more different from his triumphant arrival but five weeks earlier. "No angels sang as he sat there in the locked compartment, no trumpets lashed the air with shrill effrontery," one sportswriter observed. "Trumpets are not for idols with the cracked clay still sticking to their feet." The *Detroit Tribune*, the local black weekly, welcomed Louis home with an open letter. "Detroit and its people still believe in you," stated the message, which was signed by, among others, a congressman and a former governor of Michigan. "We believe your greatest victories are yet to come." For the next couple of days, Louis remained secluded in Roxborough's apartment. It was there, presumably, that he read a letter from Walter White, urging him to keep a stiff upper lip amid the abuse and second-guessing. "What happened last Friday night does not in the slightest change the attitude of some of us toward you," White wrote. "The next time you fight Schmeling or anyone else I venture to predict that they will never be able to hit you with rights, or lefts either for that matter." "I wanted him to know that not all of us were like the rats who desert a sinking ship," the NAACP leader explained to Roxborough and Black. White himself confessed four days after the fight that his entire family remained "literally ill over the beating Joe took."

Someone suggested that the Democrats gathering in Philadelphia pass a resolution extending the sympathy of the convention to Mr. and Mrs. Joe Louis of Chicago. Actually, condolences to all of black America would have been more apt.

Some black commentators were calm and philosophical about Louis's loss. "Joe is human and is just a kid yet," a black paper in South Carolina said. Others were practical: now that everyone wanted a crack at Louis, he'd make more money. Some were actually grateful to white America for sparing bruised black feelings more than they'd expected. But all this begged a bigger question: What in heaven's name had happened to Joe?

Few black fans believed that the outcome was as simple as the best man winning; there had to be some other explanation. The Trinidadian calypso duet "Louis-Schmeling Fight" by the Lion and Atilla with Gerald Clark and His Caribbean Serenaders, one of a mounting number of Louis songs, captured the prevailing suspicion.

The Lion sings:

> *The fight between Schmeling and Joe Louis [Lou-ee]*
> *Is an epoch in boxing history.*
> *The critics said the Bomber lost the fight that night*
> *Because he couldn't stop Maxie's smashing right*
> *Though his disappointment he has now faced,*
> *He has been defeated but not disgraced.*

To which Atilla replies:

> *I do appreciate your song,*
> *But on the night of the fight, well, something was wrong,*
> *It wasn't the same Bomber that we saw*
> *Smashing Baer and Carnera on the floor.*
> *I wouldn't say it was dope or conspiracy,*
> *But the whole thing looked extremely funny to me.*

There were some sober, traditional explanations for Louis's collapse. One was that he'd grown cocky and incorrigible, just as Roxborough and Black had belatedly conceded. Or he'd succumbed to a "maelstrom of flattery" from so-called friends. Or the city of Detroit was to blame, for its wild parties, close to which Louis's Lincoln could invariably be found at all hours of the night. Or Lakewood was responsible; its salt air, its heat, its friendly people, and its "Coney Island trimmings" had fatally weakened Louis. The black nationalist Marcus Garvey blamed Louis's selfishness and narrow-mindedness: while Schmeling felt responsible for all of Germany, to Louis it was all about himself and how much money he would make. "We wish Joe well, but we hope he has learnt a lesson from the fight, that when a white man enters the ring in a premium bout with a black man, he realizes that he has in his hands the destiny of the white race," Garvey wrote.

For many, Marva was the prime culprit. Within hours of the knockout, her life "would not have been worth two cents in the Avenue," the New York correspondent for one black paper reported. "Too much Mrs.," a black actor suggested. A colleague agreed. "He should have married sooner," he said. "He would have had more time to recover." Marva had driven a wedge between him and Blackburn. Or Louis had seen too much of her, and too recently and too intimately, maybe even spilling his seed with her the night before the fight. While Schmeling's wife was safely out of the way in Germany, Louis's was in Harlem, tempting the natural appetites of a youthful groom at the very moment when he needed his entire reservoir of physical and mental energy. Or, conversely, Louis had argued bitterly with Marva after finding a letter from one of her old suitors. Or Marva should have stuck around Lakewood longer, keeping her husband from attending wild parties on the New Jersey shore or hanging out with all the pretty visitors. One black newspaper saw Marva as a tragic figure, set upon by her husband's entourage, fans, and jealous women alike. Polls taken after Jesse Owens's spectacular showing in Berlin six weeks after Louis's debacle revealed that while Louis remained the more popular of the two, Jesse's wife out-pointed Marva.

Some of the second-guessers charged that Louis slept too much. Some said Louis simply had an off day. After all, didn't Babe Ruth sometimes spend an afternoon popping out to the infield? Some saw the hand of God, either beneficent (He was saving Louis for bigger things) or vengeful (He was offended by Louis's quasi-religious status). But by one estimate, only one black in a thousand considered the fight legitimate; the rest saw something darker. Convinced it was fixed, many refused to pay off their bets. In dispute was only how the conspiracy was carried out, by whom, and how high up it went. Louis hadn't been Louis at all, but a double. Or he'd been given the evil eye by a "professional jinxer." Or he'd been a pawn in an anti-Semitic plot to bankrupt the many Jews who'd bet on him. Or Schmeling had double-crossed him on that purported deal to prolong the fight films. Or Blackburn had to pay off his debt to the underworld figure who'd helped him beat his murder rap. But in intensity, popularity, variety, and ingenuity, rumors that Louis had been "doped" dwarfed all the others.

To those inclined to believe it, the evidence was everywhere: that Louis had come into the ring late; that his hair had been disheveled; that he'd had a funny stare in his eyes; that he'd blinked so often; that he'd seemed agitated; that his color had been terrible; that he had suddenly and inexplicably forgotten how to box. How Louis had been administered the dope was more problematic—whether by injection, or on trick bandages, or in his food or water, or on his mouthpiece or the towels with which he'd been rubbed down. Maybe some "slickster" had dropped a "deadening pill" into Louis's broth. Or Schmeling had put chloroform on his gloves, making Louis sleepy when they passed under his nose, or had had a "daze producing chemical" smuggled in from Germany, or had put something extra, like an iron bolt or lead, into his gloves. In Danville, Illinois, a young Bobby Short heard one of his mother's friends, a maid in a local department store, speculate that someone had put dope in Louis's orange juice, or his milk, or his oatmeal. Some blamed lax security at Louis's hotel, and asked why he'd stayed on the Upper West Side rather than in more friendly and reliable Harlem. Gamblers could have been behind everything; anyone betting heavily on Schmeling, after all, had made himself a small fortune. The Nazis, too, could have been responsible, or Joe Jacobs, clever as he was. Or maybe it was Mike Jacobs, for Louis was actually a bigger draw as a threat to the crown than as champion. Most theories shared one feature: Louis himself was blameless. For him to be complicit was more than even the most deranged conspiracy-monger could contemplate.

Within hours of the knockout, rumors spread that Louis was seriously ill or dead. Once again, switchboards were flooded. There were reports that seventeen doctors were trying to stop the blood from hemorrhaging in Louis's head; that Blackburn was in jail; that a doctor had confessed to fashioning some potion that had sapped Louis's strength, and had subsequently committed suicide. Street-corner agitators accused the white media of suppressing the truth. Coverage in the black press was intense, with the nation's two most powerful black papers on opposite sides of the issue: while the *Pittsburgh Courier* became the house organ of the Louis camp, insisting nothing untoward had happened, the *Chicago Defender* fanned the flames, accusing Louis's team of an overconfidence and arrogance that allowed people already out to exploit or hurt Louis to pull off their nefarious deeds.

To refute all suspicions, the *Courier*'s city editor retraced Louis's movements for the thirty-one and a half hours between the weigh-in and the opening bell, meticulously reconstructing Louis's naps, meals, and walks, along with what he insisted was his short and entirely platonic interlude with Marva. On the eve of the fight, he had Louis back in his hotel room by eight p.m. and in bed by nine-thirty, with a bodyguard alongside him in a twin bed, two state troopers in the next room, Blackburn and a third officer in another, and two more poised outside their door. Louis's food was "specially prepared by a friend," and he drank only "specially prepared bottled spring water" from Lakewood, even in the ring; so tightly corked had it been, in fact, that someone had to get a can opener from the dressing room. (Blackburn had a quicker rejoinder to all such talk. "What kind of dope was used that required twelve rounds before it's effective?" he asked.) Louis himself tried to lay the rumors to rest. "There was nothing wrong in my fight with Schmeling but his right hand," he wired the *Kansas City Call*, which reprinted the telegram on its front page. "Mr. Schmeling is a fine gentleman and a clean sportsman and I don't like to hear my people takin' credit away from him by sayin' I was doped," he told reporters. Such statements, while clearly sugarcoating Louis's feelings about Schmeling, impressed Ed Sullivan. "The town is gabbing about Joe Louis. . . . Not so much about the lacing he took from Schmeling, but rather about the Detroit youngster's refusal to cook up any phony alibis," he wrote.

White writers generally ridiculed the rumors, which, they hastened to point out, arose after every controversial fight. Only *Collyer's Eye*—whose jaundiced view of boxing was under ordinary circumstances probably closer to the mark than the see-no-evil stance of the mainstream press— suspected something sinister. "The mere fact that those back of the 'Black Bomber' are known mobsters and racketeers . . . who also control the picture rights . . . gave some credence or insistence to the hunt for the gentleman of color concealed in the metaphorical woodpile," it said. Some black commentators quickly tired of the whole topic. "One thing I'm not going to write about is Joe Louis," the Rev. Adam Clayton Powell, Jr., declared in the *Amsterdam News* a few days after the fight. "In my office there is an unwritten and unposted sign calling upon all who enter to refrain from discussing last Friday's debacle. The sooner it is forgotten, the better for all of us." Gradually, the focus turned from what had befallen Louis to how he would pick himself up and whether the loss would rob him of his confidence and ferocity or would, instead, give him the only things—wisdom, seasoning, humility—he didn't have already.

Jack Dempsey was among those who believed that Louis had become irreparably damaged goods. "Joe Louis will be licked by every bum in the country," he said. "The Negro is all right in his place, but the prize ring is no place for him," he said in Greensboro, North Carolina. Braddock, too, wrote Louis off. "Young or old, two hundred right hands on the kisser does something bad to you," he said. Many felt that Louis now had the "Indian Sign"—a kind of hex or voodoo—on him. But others predicted he would be back, and how. "We think he will become a far greater fighter than ever, now that he has had his lessons, but he needed that," said Damon Runyon. "He needed it to get him back to the schoolroom and his teachers."

In the black community, there were some signs of disillusionment. Plans to star Louis in a motion picture to be shown in black theaters were dropped. "Negroes are now defiling the name of Louis and even accusing him of 'selling out,'" the *Atlanta Daily World* reported. Roi Ottley wrote of a new expression on the streets—"Don't be a Joe Louis"—and claimed the black public was deserting him for Jesse Owens. But votes of confidence were far more common. "I have nothing but pity and sympathy for Joe's next rival," wrote Ed Harris of the *Philadelphia Tribune*. "He's going to get the hell beat out of him." "Joe Louis is not through! My boy, Joe, will come through with flying colors," Louis Armstrong declared. "Joe Louis We Are with You," the makers of Murray's Superior Hairdressing Pomade declared in advertisements in the black press. There were open letters to Louis, along with a new batch of encouraging poems. But perhaps the greatest expression of loyalty to Louis was disdain for Jack Johnson. Introduced before twenty-five thousand fans at a Negro League doubleheader in the Polo Grounds that fall, "the thunder of boos that followed must have rattled the very graves of Johnson's ancestors," wrote Roi Ottley in the *Amsterdam News*. "Jack Johnson played Joe Louis cheaply—and Harlem played him cheaply."

The day after the fight, Mike Jacobs announced that Louis would return to New York in August, against an opponent still to be determined. Some, Schmeling among them, thought this too quick; Louis should take six months off after such a beating. But Louis's handlers didn't want him to have too much time to brood. When Louis came back to New York only two weeks after the fight, he was already in good cheer. "Guess I got a bit swell-headed, before and during the fight with Schmeling," he said. "The swelling's gone down considerable now."

But Louis's magnetism was undiminished. With the press of fans along West Forty-ninth Street he had difficulty entering Mike Jacobs's office. Even the boatload of black athletes heading for Olympic glory in Berlin did not dim Louis's luster. They were mostly college kids, after all, difficult for the black masses to embrace. And they were in track and field, a sport that held little appeal in black America, at least next to boxing. "A carload of Jesse Owenses, Ralph Metcalfes, Cornelius Johnsons and others could not attract as much attention as Joe Louis's chauffeur," the *Afro-American* observed. Two weeks later, Jacobs announced Louis's next opponent: Jack Sharkey. Sharkey, who had lost the heavyweight crown three years earlier, was one of those fighters attempting a comeback to cash in on the renewed popularity Louis had brought to boxing. But he'd been only modestly successful, making him the perfect rival for a man on the rebound. Louis needed a knockout or his star would set.

But Louis's next bout was no longer the biggest fight in the offing anymore. In late July, Madison Square Garden and Mike Jacobs agreed to team up for a Braddock-Schmeling showdown in September. It was a historic agreement, ending the Garden's seventeen-year-long monopoly on heavyweight championship fights. With a boycott of Schmeling looming, though, Jacobs chose not to be involved, yielding his control for half the profits.

Under normal circumstances, staging a championship fight on Yom Kippur, the holiest day of the Jewish calendar, would be suicidal. That the Garden would have even considered that possibility for the Braddock-Schmeling bout confirmed the feeling that with Schmeling involved, the Jews would stay away anyway. Braddock's manager, Joe Gould, nixed the proposed date (his Jewish mother objected, he explained), and the fight was moved to September 24. With Germany consumed by the Olympics, no one there was giving boxing much thought, but the *Völkischer Beobachter* took note. "After a long, difficult, and unprecedentedly successful resurgence," it said, Schmeling would soon "attempt to regain for Germany the world championship lost years ago because of an unjust decision against Jack Sharkey."

A small crowd was only one of the problems Schmeling faced. In late July the boxing commission revoked Joe Jacobs's license, for his repeated failure to produce his contract with Schmeling. The speculation was either that no such contract existed, or that it gave Jacobs such a pittance that he was too embarrassed to make it public. Managers generally got one-third of a boxer's winnings, but according to one report, Jacobs collected half that, and only because Mike Jacobs had leaned on Schmeling. Yussel's problem wasn't his religion, it was said, but that he was dealing with someone whose credo was "Pfennig über Alles." "Max Schmeling's business conferences these days are 100 per cent Aryan," wrote Dan

Parker. During one meeting with Mike Jacobs, Parker claimed, Schmeling literally pushed Yussel away and ordered him to wait outside.

Schmeling planned to begin training in Napanoch in early August.
Until then, he remained in Germany, enjoying his fame. On July 29 he
visited the Olympic Village, where he was stormed by athletes, coaches,
and officials. A dozen soldiers rescued him from his admirers "only with
the greatest difficulty," reported *Box-Sport*. At one point, he rushed over to
Jesse Owens and grasped his hands. "I've heard lots about you!" he said.
(Schmeling must have been shocked to learn that Owens had bet on him
in the Louis fight.) Owens and his black teammates grew incensed at how
the Nazis paraded Schmeling around that day; it was another reminder of
how Louis's shadow hung over all the black Olympians. "Inwardly, many
of us were trying to atone for Joe's loss," he later said. Even when Owens
won the 100-meter dash, Schmeling remained the center of attention;
groups of Hitler Youth hounded him for autographs, forcing him to jump
over a hedge and flee to the parking lot. The dean of British boxing writers, Trevor Wignall of the *Daily Express*, spotted Schmeling in one of the
"exalted pews," inaccessible to the press. "In rank and importance he did
not seem to be much below Hitler and Goering," he wrote.* But before
long Schmeling was again aboard the *Hindenburg*, this time heading
toward America. Ondra would soon follow, and after the fight the two
planned to go to Hollywood—he as the new heavyweight champion, she
as the film star America was about to discover. The day after he arrived,
Schmeling visited Louis in Pompton Lakes, where he was training for the
Sharkey fight. It was their first encounter since the knockout. "How you,
Max?" Louis greeted him. "How was the zeppelin thing?"

Louis's latest camp was as much reform school as training headquar-
ters. Gone were the crowds, the jazz bands, the hawkers, the hangers-on.
So was the golf. The signs outside read NO TRESPASSING rather than JOE

---

*With the Olympics safely secured, there was no more need for public-relations
niceties on racial matters. The *Angriff* was soon praising lynching as "popular justice to
expiate racial disgrace" and an element in "the healthy racial defenses of the largest state
of Teutonic origin." Another paper printed a photograph of Jesse Owens and Bill Robinson dancing. "The white audience is cheering, but none of them would share a table with
these niggers," it said. But here, too, the attitude of ordinary Germans was more benign.
Covering the black Olympians for the *Amsterdam News*, William C. Chase described
Germans of all ages staring at them. "The people expected to see us eat with our fingers
instead of silverware," he wrote. Some Germans knew only four English words: "Jesse,"
"Owens," "Joe," and "Louis." "I met a number of Germans who admire Louis," wrote
Chase, "and think he is the greatest fighter of all times." At one point Louis was receiving a
dozen fan letters a day from Germany.

LOUIS BOXES TODAY. "A tractable Joe Louis has replaced the spoiled child of Lakewood," the *Courier* reported. "Jack Blackburn again has the upper hand and Louis is his willing pupil. The hero worshippers can't tell him how good he is, but Jack can and does tell him how 'lousy' he is." Roxborough was satisfied. "Now you are watching the real Joe Louis, the Joe Louis he was before Lakewood," he said. Or, as Blackburn put it, "Chappie heah got believin' all you newspapah boys say 'bout him—that he ain't human. . . . Mr. Schmeling learned him something." Even Louis's sleep had been restricted: no more than ten hours a day. Under the new regime there was nothing for Joe to do but talk about the upcoming fight, eat, spar, jab the bags, skip rope, and do roadwork and calisthenics. Louis's handlers now kept his toothbrush, hairbrush, and towels under lock and key.

Sparring partners were to give it all they had, or be fired. But reports quickly surfaced that Louis wasn't throwing his right with the same abandon, that his punches lacked their old sting and pep, that his sparring partners were tagging him, that he was sulking. "He has tried to cram ten years of boxing lessons into ten days of intensive training," one reporter wrote. John Kieran of *The New York Times* thought Louis's stupidity was now his greatest asset; since he didn't "go in for thinking on an extensive scale," he wouldn't dwell on what Schmeling had done to him. Louis was a three-to-one favorite, but blacks remained apprehensive. There was very little betting on him, and ticket sales were modest. In the racially stark thinking of the time, Sharkey was thought to have a strange power over black fighters; he'd beaten Harry Wills, whom Jack Dempsey had ducked. Jack Johnson, for one, was going with Sharkey: "After they are through teaching him how to avoid a right he will be a sucker for something else," he said. The fight generated little buzz. To Jimmy Powers of the *Daily News*, the principals were "a washed up old man and an overballyhooed colored boy."

As the Louis-Sharkey fight approached, the Braddock-Schmeling fight receded. On August 12 Braddock, who was already in training, notified the commission that he'd hurt himself. The diagnosis varied: arthritis in various places; an injured pinkie (or left arm); a growth between two of his fingers. Whatever it was, it required surgery, or at least delay. Coming from the indestructible "Cinderella Man," it all seemed dubious; everyone assumed Braddock was trying to get out of the fight, angling for a more lucrative match with Louis, and hadn't known he was hurt until Joe Gould told him so. So on the afternoon of August 18, the New York boxing commission had two orders of business. At noon, Louis and Sharkey weighed in at the Hippodrome for their fight that night. Then, at the State Building downtown, seven doctors inspected Braddock's hand, and promptly divided over whether he needed surgery. A "burlesque," the *News* called the proceedings.

Yankee Stadium that night reflected Louis's sharply diminished stature. Fewer than thirty thousand people showed up, a third of what Louis and Baer had drawn less than a year earlier. Black fans were conspicuously absent, as was Marva. When Schmeling, who was there to watch, stepped into the ring, he received pleasant applause, if only a perfunctory greeting from Louis. Balogh's introduction had been stripped of superlatives; now Louis was simply Sharkey's "very capable opponent." But Louis still had faith in himself. When Roxborough warned him that he'd be asking Henry Ford for his old job back if he lost, Louis told him not to worry—the fight wouldn't go three rounds.

"Schmeling was the luckiest man in the world," Blackburn said shortly before the bell. "You'll see." "And everyone saw," Vidmer wrote in the *Herald Tribune*. "They saw [Louis] look like the brown bomber again and not a man who was pawing about helplessly, hopelessly in a fog. . . . They saw Joe Louis leave no doubts as he pounded away with sledge-hammer hooks when there was time and lightning thrusts when there was only a brief opening. And they saw him keep diligently at work until he had completed his job." Sharkey was down twice in the second round. In the third, a right sent him over the lower rope. He was up at eight, when a right and a left to the jaw put him away for good. "Joe's mad at Schmeling, but Sharkey paid for it," Blackburn said afterward. The few black fans on hand let out "one long sustained guttural chant of victory," one that reflected both their renewed hope in Louis and, perhaps, their shame over ever having doubted him. To Al Monroe, it wasn't the old Louis, but the real one; for whatever reason, "they" were letting Louis be Louis again. "Youth must be served," Sharkey said afterward. "Louis will find that out. He'll be thirty-four some day." He predicted that Louis would easily beat Schmeling the next time around. Louis couldn't wait. "I want Max Schmeling next," he kept saying. As for Schmeling, he said Louis was "alright," but that Sharkey had fought a "stupid" fight. Louis had made some new mistakes he hadn't noticed before, Schmeling added. "I could beat him every time I fought him."

Harlem was magically transformed. "Not fifteen minutes before," wrote Ralph Matthews of the *Baltimore Afro-American*, "Harlem was as quiet as a convent at twilight. . . . Harlem was an apprehensive mother at the bedside of a dying child; Harlem was a huddled family in a cellar retreat waiting for an air attack by a squadron of bombing planes. Harlem was meek, trembling, and silent, and then — Joe knocked Sharkey out and Harlem became a seething inferno of uncontrolled joy." Calls went out again for another crop of white hopes.*

On August 21, the boxing commission officially postponed the Braddock-Schmeling fight until June 1937. That would give Braddock's hand, or whatever ailed him, plenty of time to heal. "I hope the twenty-one doctors can keep him alive until next summer," Schmeling said sourly. Parker thought Schmeling wouldn't get a chance even then. "By next June, some convenient excuse for sidetracking him will have been found and, if Louis stands up, he will get the shot," he predicted. Mike Jacobs offered Schmeling $300,000 to fight Louis again before that. It was, he said, the fight the public, black and white, wanted. But Schmeling wasn't buying. What he most wanted — "dreadfully and gnawingly," Gallico wrote — was to be the first man ever to regain the crown. He'd fight Louis again, but only for twice what Jacobs was offering.

A day before a triumphant Jesse Owens returned from Berlin on the *Queen Mary*, Schmeling left angrily for Germany on the *Bremen*. Once more, there were protesters: a number of leftists, dressed in evening wear, had managed to board undetected and had occupied the cabin deck, some chaining themselves to the rail. "A Red Mob in Dinner Jackets," one Berlin newspaper called them. Schmeling steered clear of the scuffling. The German papers blamed the "men in the background" (*Hintermänner*), that is, the Jews, for Schmeling's fate, though Braddock, too, took his lumps. Even the black press felt sorry for Schmeling. Blacks knew all about runarounds, after all. But any pity evaporated two weeks later, when Schmeling's account of the Louis fight, as told to Gallico, appeared

---

*Around this time the *Daily Worker*, which had previously published sports news only on Sundays, launched a daily sports section, which, given its interest in the man, could have been called the "Joe Louis Section." In Communist eyes, professional sports was yet another way for capitalists and their journalistic handmaidens to distract the public from more serious matters. But given the way he was upsetting the established order, the *Worker* argued, Louis was an example of how this bread-and-circuses strategy could backfire, creating a "nice little Frankenstein monster that's going to eventually sock [capitalism] out of existence." Like the Nazis, the American Communists concluded that some professional sports were simply too popular to ignore, and in fact could be turned to their advantage; both groups followed the Sharkey fight and were pleased with the result. To the *Worker*, it meant Louis was back; to the *Angriff*, it proved that Louis was no pushover and, therefore, showed how great Schmeling's victory over him had been.

in the *Saturday Evening Post*. In it he reiterated his charge that Louis had fouled him on orders from his handlers; it was, he said, Louis's only way to win. Louis said the accusation was bunk, and his circle was indignant, too. On September 17, Louis, Roxborough, and Black sued Schmeling, Gallico, and the magazine.

The *Post* called Gallico Schmeling's "best friend among writers," and that was certainly true. For years he had essentially been Schmeling's mouthpiece; when he wasn't writing stories under Schmeling's name, he was advising or defending him or cheering him on. Shortly after he'd arrived in America, Schmeling had even asked Gallico to manage him. When questions arose about Schmeling's politics, intelligence, or character, Gallico always vouched for him. But now, Schmeling insisted he had never told Gallico any of the incriminating things Gallico had him saying. "Maxie stepped out from under again, putting all the blame on his ghost writer with the moth-eaten gag: 'I was misquoted,'" Parker wrote. Louis soon opted not to pursue the lawsuit. As one black paper later said, he "wanted a revenge that money could not buy."

On September 23 Louis brought his comeback to Philadelphia. His opponent, Al Ettore, had beaten Braddock five years earlier, but Louis faced greater peril from an exploding flashbulb at the weigh-in than from anything Ettore threw at him in the five rounds he managed to last. But Ettore was a local white boy, and the scene in Philadelphia offered more evidence of how raw the issue of race remained. "I suppose there were close to 500,000 Ettore fans along the sides after the fight and 499,000 spat into each passing car carrying Negro occupants," one black reporter wrote. On October 9, Louis knocked out Jorge Brescia of Argentina in three rounds in the Hippodrome. A lull followed that fight, during which the *Afro-American* ran an alarming banner headline: JOE LOUIS UNDER KNIFE. (It turned out he had been circumcised.) He recovered quickly enough to stage an exhibition in New Orleans; the 7,200 fans on hand gave him a reception unlike anything the city had seen in years.

As Louis honed his skills, the scheme to bypass Schmeling intensified. As early as September, Damon Runyon reported plans to stage a Braddock-Louis fight in Atlantic City in February, four months before the scheduled Braddock-Schmeling fight. It would be a strange animal: a "no decision" contest, winnable only by knockout, with no title ostensibly at stake, though that of course was not how the world would view it. Dan Parker saw through the fog. "Now, one presumes, the plan is for Joe Louis to meet Braddock, win the title from him . . . and then fight Max Schmeling in a return bout next June, in which his chances of wiping out the one blot on his career will be greatly improved," he wrote. By November, these plans were taking shape. They promised a windfall for Braddock, far more than he'd make fighting Schmeling. Louis would earn far less, but also collect far more: a chance to be de facto champion, and far sooner and easier than many people, particularly blacks, had ever anticipated.

For Schmeling, though, it was a raw deal. "I don't believe it," he sputtered. "It can't be true." The Nazi press once again denounced the *Drahtzieher*, and also went after Louis. Schmeling made plans to travel to the United States to defend his rights. His insistence on representing himself fed yet more rumors that he had finally, and officially, fired Jacobs. Of course, it couldn't have been true, and wasn't. "Schmeling's only defense is Joe Jacobs," wrote Walter Stewart of the *World-Telegram*; keeping him around "does not completely clean the slate in Jewish eyes," he said, "but it helps." When he arrived in New York on December 10, Schmeling insisted the talk of dropping Jacobs was all a misunderstanding. More important than that, though, was stopping the Atlantic City fight. "Such things cannot be!" he protested. "What is the heavyweight championship? Is it a joke? Is it stuff like wrestling?"

Schmeling's pleas for fairness stuck in the craws even of those who agreed with him. "Imagine Promoter Mike Jacobs or Manager Yussel Jacobs going before one of Hitler's crackpot commissions and demanding their rights!" Parker wrote. Besides, Schmeling was a past master at runarounds himself. Even so, on December 12 the New York boxing commission killed the Atlantic City fight, ordering Braddock to fight Schmeling at the Madison Square Garden Bowl in Long Island City on June 3, 1937. Five years after he lost it, then, Schmeling was now a giant step closer to regaining the crown; most people thought he would. "The heavyweight champion of the world a Nazi!" Joe Williams wrote in wonder, and horror.*

The commission's action was predictably assailed in some quarters. The boxing authorities had "goose-stepped with Schmeling," the *Amsterdam News* complained; the *Daily Worker* said the "superannuated

---

*Perhaps the commission had suddenly sided with Schmeling simply as a matter of fairness. Or maybe Schmeling had discovered, or rediscovered, a friend. A few weeks earlier in London, at the Walter Neusel–Ben Foord fight, he had run into James A. Farley, the former New York boxing commissioner. Farley, now chairman of the Democratic Party, postmaster general, and close friend of Franklin D. Roosevelt, had tangled with Schmeling years earlier, but had grown to like him. According to the *Völkischer Beobachter*, Farley had pledged to help him with his difficulties in New York. It would not be the last time.

geezers" were doing everything they could to deny Louis a title shot. The Nazis now labored to move the Braddock-Schmeling fight to Berlin. The maneuver came with Schmeling's connivance, earning him more charges of disloyalty and treachery, but it also came to naught. In Nazi eyes Schmeling's mission to New York was already a great victory: it was a rebuff to the *Weltjudentum*—world Jewry—which had tried to deny him his rights. But Schmeling could not get too complacent. Two Jews, Mike Jacobs and Joe Gould, still had several months to figure out how to yank him out of—and get Louis into—the heavyweight championship picture.

Louis's final fight of 1936 took place on December 14, against Eddie Simms in Cleveland. This time, the action lasted all of twenty-six seconds. "I'm sorry it had to be like that," Louis told Simms afterward. "But you know how it is—either me or you." As short as it was, it earned the notice of the NAACP. "What a superb job Joe, Jack and you have done on the matter of a right hand," Walter White wrote Roxborough. "If our friend, Schmeling, read this story of the superb defenses against a right which Joe now has I am sure he would have no great enthusiasm about coming back to America to fight Joe."

It also caught the eye of another of Louis's tireless champions, the *Daily Worker*. By sending the strongest possible signal that Louis was indeed back, it declared, the Simms fight "knocked one more nail in the coffin" of a Schmeling-Braddock bout. But any move to sideline the German only postponed the inevitable. "Whether you like Hitler or the Nazis or Germans or spinach," Grantland Rice wrote, "the fact remains there can be no recognized heavyweight champion of the world who hasn't beaten Schmeling."

CHAPTER 9

A German Commodity

IT WAS, SOMEONE LATER SAID, "an unprecedented event in the annals of Detroit night life." On the evening of December 31, 1936, Joe Louis, dressed in white tie and tails, presided over the official opening of the Brown Bomber's Chicken Shack. Louis had sunk $10,000 into the place, not so much as an investment as to provide his pals with a place to hang out. While hundreds watched enviously from outside, Detroit's black elite, dressed in formal wear and fur wraps (some of which Louis himself supplied), toasted the new establishment, the new year, and their newly rehabilitated host. The chicken ran out—and so, too, did Louis, to join his mother in church, as he did every New Year's Eve.

The new year opened with the boxing world in a fix. Braddock was the champion, but no one gave him much of a chance to beat either Louis or Schmeling. The only questions were who would beat him first, whether racial or international politics would help make that choice, and whether the two challengers would fight each other again before it happened. Fleischer saw an epochal era in the offing, one in which black boxers would surge forward. Mike Jacobs agreed that it would be a big year for Louis; he talked of having him fight once a month, enough to make him the first boxer ever to earn a million dollars before he won the title, which Jacobs had scheduled for September. Louis promised to be, as Jacobs put it, "the greatest money-making athlete the world has ever seen."

Al Monroe of the *Defender* remained convinced that Louis would not get a shot in 1937, or at any other time: since Louis was too honest to cut them in on the deal, the "Nordic" boxing powers had decided that a title shot wasn't worth the dangers. In an article titled "Joe Louis Should Never Be Champion" in *The Commentator*, a popular radio announcer,

John B. Kennedy, urged that for the sake of domestic harmony and the "tranquil progress" of Louis's own people, the color line should be maintained. Walter White promptly countered that America had come "a long, long way" from the Jack Johnson era, and that Louis was no Johnson. He urged the magazine to publish something called "Joe Louis *Should* Be Champion," offering, to no avail, to write it himself. The *Daily Worker* was even angrier, claiming that the article was permeated with "the stench of the old slave market" and consisted of "underhanded lynch incitement masking itself as 'friendly advice' to the Negro people."

Shortly before Louis's next scheduled fight, against Bob Pastor on January 29, Bob Considine encountered Mike Jacobs nibbling with his store teeth on a pencil stub while jotting down some big numbers on the back of a bill. Uncle Mike was totaling up the take from Louis's fights since Schmeling beat him. "That bust on the chin Max gave Louis is going to be worth two million dollars before Joe gets back the reputation he had before the Schmeling fight," Jacobs said. "And the funny part of it all, he's still got another crack at Schmeling waiting for him, and you can just guess how high that one would go. All things considered, it was a great break for Joe." And for the fight game, too, he added.

While Louis was fighting his way back, Pastor, a graduate of New York University, was fighting his way backward: for ten rounds that night at Madison Square Garden, he followed his manager's advice not to stand still. The result was one of the most infuriating bouts in history. Pastor, Parker wrote, had beaten "all records for retreating since Napoleon set the standard at Moscow." But simply for having lasted, it was a moral victory for him, and a setback for Louis, even though he got the decision. For the first time, he heard catcalls. The criticism only intensified in the papers, which said Louis was too bewildered or too dumb to adjust to Pastor's dodge. Maybe, Fleischer admitted, Jack Johnson had been right about Louis after all. But black sportswriters charged that had Pastor been fighting a white man, the referee would have tossed him out of the ring. "The legend of 'American sportsmanship' proved to be just a myth as they applauded the rank cowardice of the white man," Roi Ottley wrote.

In Kansas City three weeks later, Louis had a rematch with Natie Brown, the fighter he'd beaten two years earlier, before all those sportswriters in Detroit. This time, too, it was a historic event: local officials had authorized mixed bouts only six months earlier. Fans, black and white and from all walks of life, greeted Louis when he arrived. "Thank God! I've seen him at last," one bent old man murmured afterward. One section of ringside seats, along with part of the balcony, was set aside for blacks. The anticlimactic fight lasted four rounds. Traveling in the Pullman car Alf Landon had used late in his presidential campaign, Louis then embarked on a monthlong barnstorming tour through Nebraska, Iowa, Colorado, Oklahoma, Texas, and California. In Wichita, plans called for Louis's car to stop at some undisclosed location just short of town, to keep fans from descending upon it. In Houston, admiring blacks lined the tracks for blocks as the train pulled in. At the local arena, the 2,500 ringside seats were reserved for whites; blacks, who made up more than half the crowd, were confined to the bleachers and had to use a special entrance. The tour ended in California, where Louis insisted he'd learned his lesson well. "They say I can't take a punch to the jaw," he said. "Well, I'm not supposed to take one." By one estimate, in three weeks of barnstorming Louis had played before 150,000 people.

Jack Johnson continued to haunt, and taunt, Louis. Bill Corum caught up with him one day at Hubert's Museum and Flea Circus on Forty-second Street, west of Broadway, where he had become part of the freak show, selling memories "at a penny a throw." "What about Joe Louis?" he was asked. "Just another fighter," replied Johnson, who was to keep a photograph of the 1936 fight—it showed Louis approaching Schmeling with a left, leaving his chin conspicuously exposed to the German's cocked right—conveniently within reach. On those frequent occasions when fight arguments arose, John Lardner wrote, "the brown wizard of Galveston reaches for the photograph and shows you why Joe Louis will never be a Jack Johnson." "People claim I'm jealous, but that picture tells different," Johnson told him. "I ain't jealous. I just state facts." Even at age fifty-two, Johnson told another writer, he'd have bet "a hundred dollars to five" he could have cornered Pastor within three rounds. Johnson paid a high price for his opinions: in Harlem once, he stood in the center of the ring for five minutes as a jeering crowd refused to let him speak. Half of Louis's mail was about Johnson, mostly admonitions from elderly southern blacks not to follow his bad example. For three consecutive months, the *Defender* asked readers which of the two boxers was greater with prizes promised for the pithiest answers. Among nearly forty thousand voters, Louis won by better than five to one. "His clean living and high-minded morals were perhaps his greatest asset," the paper explained.

SHORTLY AFTER HITLER CAME TO POWER in 1933, someone who signed his name "Patriotic American" wrote a letter to the Non-Sectarian

Anti-Nazi League, an ad hoc group set up to boycott German goods in the hopes of strangling the Nazi regime. He urged a campaign against the Schmeling-Baer fight. "Think: practically all of the money Mr. Schmelling [*sic*] will earn he will take back to Germany—HIS VATERLAND—to help continue [Hitler's] barbaric abominations," the man wrote. The suggestion had been ignored; the letter had been filed under "Cranks." But four years had passed. The lot of German Jews had grown increasingly desperate, and Schmeling seemed about to recapture the heavyweight crown. "Patriotic American" was about to be vindicated.

In late December 1936, the league decided to add Schmeling to its list of verboten German goods. This boycott, unlike the one surrounding the Louis fight, would not be a surreptitious campaign of chain letters between Jewish clothing manufacturers, but open and conspicuous, complete with advertisements, circulars, and pickets. It would also be far more broadly based. The league had consciously kept the word "Jewish" out of its name, and along with a Jew like David Stern (owner of the *New York Post*) and quasi Jews like Mayor La Guardia, its directors included prominent Gentiles such as the editor and publisher Oswald Garrison Villard and the Methodist bishop of New York.

On January 8, Davis Walsh of the Hearst wire service broke the news of a boycott that would "make all others seem pale and pointless by contrast." All events at the Hippodrome and Madison Square Garden would henceforth be shunned, he wrote, until the Schmeling-Braddock fight was called off. Hitler was preparing for war, a league official explained; depriving him of money and raw materials was the only way to stop him. He predicted that a victorious Schmeling would become head of "Hitler's Youth Movement" and that "another surge of hysteria of nationalism" would ensue. If the fight were moved elsewhere in America, so, too, would the protests; the Jewish War Veterans, which had chapters everywhere and had previously opposed Schmeling's fights against Baer and Hamas, would see to that. On January 9, the league asked the state boxing commission to withdraw its support for the fight. Its protest, it stressed, was not against Schmeling himself, but the government "which he willingly or unwillingly represents." Asked why the group had not boycotted Schmeling when he fought Louis, a league organizer admitted that its leaders thought Louis would win, and that the chance to humiliate Hitler was worth enriching him a bit.

The boycott generated a storm of criticism from writers and fans alike. They called the move immature and silly and said it betrayed the same intolerance the protesters were trying to combat. Anyone unhappy about the fight could stay home, the *Herald Tribune* editorialized. Some of the reactions were more crude. "Why should Americans boycott the Schmeling-Braddock fight because the Jews insist on hounding Germany?" Puzzled Gentile Fighter wrote to the *Daily News*. "Does every prize fight have to be kosher?" "God help the Jews in Germany if the proposed Schmeling-Braddock boycott forces cancellation of the bout," a Brooklyn man warned in another letter to the paper. "The suffering the German Jews have already endured will be as nothing compared with the attacks, both financial and physical, to which they will be subjected if Schmeling is cheated of his hard-earned shot at the title. I suggest that the boycott committee arrange to evacuate all Jews now in Germany if it insists on going ahead with the boycott." A group of German businessmen based in New York's Upper East Side predicted that the "almost stupid beyond belief boycott" would "ultimately produce an overwhelming wave of Anti-Semitism in this country." "Must we allow these most loathsome and despicable of all human forms (the Jews) to dictate to us americans [*sic*] what they allow us to do in our sports and privat [*sic*] business in our own country?" asked another letter, to the head of Madison Square Garden. "That is the result of freedom and equal rights that we give to these vermins."

Bill Cunningham of the *Boston Post* sympathized with Schmeling's plea to keep sports and politics distinct, but noted that Germany itself had crossed that line most flagrantly, and that Schmeling was doing his share. Dempsey's wins over the Argentine Firpo or the Frenchman Carpentier had never been billed as an American victory over inferior races, nor had any president sent flowers to the wife of an American boxer when her husband knocked out a foreigner, nor invited that boxer to the White House. Schmeling "is forced to be a Nazi if he doesn't want to rot in jail," he wrote. But if anyone had to be sacrificed to make a larger political point, a wealthy prizefighter from Nazi Germany was probably a suitable target.

The Anti-Nazi League, headed by the prominent lawyer Samuel Untermyer, was a Potemkin village of a protest group, with little of the clout attributed to it, perhaps by those inclined out of either solidarity or paranoia to exaggerate Jewish power. For all the demonizing he endured in the German press, Untermyer actually opposed the fight boycott originally, warning that it could make the league "one of the most hated organizations that was ever brought into existence." But the movement quickly assumed an air of inexorability. Chicago, Detroit, Cleveland, Westchester County, and New Jersey were also said to be on board. "Schmeling might just as well remain in Germany," wrote a columnist in New Orleans; any

American city staging one of his fights would be deemed pro-Nazi. Also supporting the campaign were Jeremiah T. Mahoney, who led the unsuccessful attempt to withdraw the American team from the Berlin Olympics, and the American League Against War and Fascism, which urged Schmeling to donate three-quarters of his take to German exiles in America.

Jewish fans could make or break any big-time bout. Tex Rickard once said that Jews spent $250,000 on each of Jack Dempsey's fights, while Mike Jacobs claimed they'd put down $300,000 apiece for Louis's fights against Carnera and Baer. "Even without the aid of any other organizations the Jews of New York could make the Braddock-Schmeling fight a financial flop," a sportswriter from Minneapolis said. The Yiddish *Forverts* declared it a Jewish duty to support the boycott. While some Jews were still loath to classify "easy-going Max" as a Nazi, one had to consider his "continued voluntary residence in Hitlerland," the *Jewish Examiner* editorialized. Schmeling "has as much chance of earning another American dollar as his boss Hitler has of owning a delicatessen store on Delancey Street," it predicted. But typically, the Jewish community did not speak with one voice on the subject. The *Jewish Advocate* in Boston said its beef was with the Nazis, not with Schmeling. "People tell stories about Schmeling 'Heiling Hitler,'" it noted. "What of it? The boxer was merely responding to greetings in the way that is now unfortunately accepted in his country." Boycotting Schmeling, it said, was "just as nonsensical as refusing to eat cheese because the Germans also eat it, or refusing hospital facilities to people with German measles."

But the two most important Jews in the equation—Mike Jacobs and Braddock's manager, Joe Gould—all but embraced the campaign, quickly meeting with its organizers and exaggerating how effective it would be. The boycott that had robbed him of $400,000 at the Schmeling-Louis fight had been mild by comparison, Jacobs said; this one would be the father of them all. Schmeling, he conceded, had always been very friendly with Jews. But business was business, and Jacobs saw a chance to jettison a star-crossed fight for something far more lucrative. As for Gould, he "leaped at the excuse like a speckled trout coming out of a stream," wrote Richards Vidmer. A Braddock-Schmeling fight wouldn't "draw flies," Gould insisted. He asked fifteen sportswriters to guess the gate for such a contest; their estimates ranged from a paltry $250,000 to a pathetic $100,000, a tenth of what Gould thought a Braddock-Louis fight would draw. "I want to be fair to Schmeling," he said, "but I got to take care of Jim."

For Jacobs and Gould, then, the boycott was a godsend, letting them put an altruistic gloss over a pure money grab. Jacobs, wrote one critic, was hiding behind some "anti-Nazi front men." "There is a powerful aroma of larceny about this boycott business, a strong scent of lilies-of-hokum," John Lardner wrote; to Braddock and Gould, the only question was "whether to fight Joe Louis for a stack of dough or Max Schmeling for coffee money." And once Louis had beaten Braddock, Jacobs would have his real prize: a second, boycott-proof Louis-Schmeling fight. But even those who opposed the boycott made it clear that they had little concern for Schmeling. "We don't owe the Horst Wessel muzzler anything," wrote Jack Miley in the *News*. Shunning Schmeling, Joe Williams chimed in, was "akin to boycotting smallpox." For all the labels it stuck on him—"Hitler's boyfriend," "Storm Trooper Moxie," "Hitler's emissary to America"—even the *Daily Worker* conceded that Schmeling was no anti-Semite. "He never was the kind of guy who sneaks up behind you and knifes you until Hitler got him," it said. His sin, instead, was simply betting on the wrong horse. "He should have known on which side of the Atlantic his bread is buttered," it wrote. "He didn't read the American newspapers except on the sports pages. The result is that he has fallen for the Hitler hooey. And he is going to pay for it."

The campaign only stoked Nazi claims of Jewish power and deviousness. SCHMELING HECKLED IN UNBELIEVABLE WAY BY USA JEWS, the *Angriff* shouted. Surely, urged the *Berliner illustrierte Nachtausgabe*, "racially conscious Americans" would not let "the Jewish Marxist gang" in New York cheat them out of a championship fight. The German news agency, Deutsches Nachrichtenbüro, insisted the bout could succeed even without Jews; hadn't sixty-five thousand people attended the Louis-Schmeling fight, despite boycott calls in the synagogues? The indignation of real Americans upset over Jewish meddling might actually increase attendance, it speculated. Caught between two anti-Semitic stereotypes—of Jews as either manipulators or hucksters—the *Angriff* couldn't decide whether the boycott was designed to kill the fight or to publicize it. It predicted that Americans would not be impressed by posters appearing throughout New York declaring IF YOU LOVE YOUR CHILDREN, BOYCOTT THE FIGHT! "Schmeling hasn't kidnapped any children, nor has he imprisoned any women," it said. "Schmeling is an upright German and an honest, fair sportsman—certainly a fact that Untermyer regrets." The *Tageblatt* appealed to the "traditions of fairness and chivalrous treatment of competitors which are common to all Anglo-Saxon nations." The German-American Bund deluged Madison Square Garden with letters stating that "100 per cent Americans" wanted the fight to go forward.

That Schmeling's titular manager was Jewish only complicated things.

When boycott organizers tried meeting with "the Hitler-Heiling Joe Jacobs," he stood them up. On January 18, Jacobs announced that Schmeling would soon return to New York, but would start training only after taking a twenty-two-city tour. The itinerary included Philadelphia, Chicago, and Detroit, but concentrated on the South. "Schmeling is a hero down in the South for knocking out that Louis guy, and we intend to cash in on it," explained Jacobs, who had apparently overcome any lingering fears of returning there. BOYCOTT BROKEN! SCHMELING'S EXHIBITION BOUTS IN THE USA BEGIN ON MARCH 1, the *Völkischer Beobachter* proclaimed. The Nazi press, which rarely acknowledged Jacobs's existence, now cited him as the authority for the proposition that the boycott was doomed. The *Reichssportblatt* soon advertised trips to New York for the Braddock-Schmeling fight. But the Germans and Jacobs were unduly optimistic. Opponents of the fight now targeted the tour, too. The commander of the Jewish War Veterans asked posts in the cities on Schmeling's itinerary to become involved, and urged blacks to pitch in.

Blacks and Jews had been on opposite sides of the boycott of the Berlin Olympics. For blacks the Games promised to be—and became—a moment of glory. Besides, there was an element of payback. "The Jews don't help us so why should we help them?" one Berlin-bound black athlete asked. Now, though, with Schmeling catering to crackers and threatening to abscond with a prize that a black man stood to win, things changed. No fight should be a windfall for the "Negro-Jew-Catholic-hating Nazis," the *Amsterdam News* editorialized. Roy Wilkins urged blacks to support the boycott; no one who knew persecution himself, he wrote, could remain indifferent to the plight of German Jews. But Wilkins complained that many of those same Jews who'd bankrolled the campaign against the Olympics hadn't given five dollars to combat race prejudice. In fact, he faulted the Jews for being AWOL on civil rights generally. While Jewish radicals, like the staffers on the *Daily Worker*, were among the most fervent civil rights champions, most blacks encountered Jews only as landlords and businesspeople, relationships that bred far more resentment than camaraderie. "Maybe they have some Negro servant of whom they are fond and they let it go at that, or maybe they give the Negro porter or elevator boy ten dollars at Christmas and call it square with their consciences," Wilkins wrote. "Let us do all we can to see that no disciple of Hitler and fascism reaps any benefit here in America. At the same time, let us hope our Jewish friends will not have too short memories when next we appeal for aid."

Boycott organizers tried repeatedly to enlist the NAACP, but Walter White balked. The group opposed Hitlerism, he said, but felt the movement had been hijacked by "certain individuals in the boxing game"—presumably Jacobs and Gould—"for selfish and ulterior motives." He worried that the group's opposition to Schmeling's sputtering southern tour could, oddly, help revive it. Then there was the matter of fairness: Schmeling *had* been promised a title shot. "I do not think that we should be demanding fair play and then join in denying it to others, even if we dislike and disapprove of those others," he concluded. Besides, overzealous publicity men had turned the boycott into a joke: only fourteen people showed up for a much-touted luncheon the Anti-Nazi League threw for sportswriters at Jack Dempsey's restaurant on February 16—some, undoubtedly, just for the free lunch.

By late January the papers were writing obituaries for the Braddock-Schmeling bout. Rather than fight Schmeling in Long Island City on June 3, they speculated, Braddock would fight Louis in Chicago a week or two later. Authorities in Illinois had already gone into action, and by February 19 it was official: Braddock would take on Louis for the world heavyweight championship at Comiskey Park on June 22. The champion would collect 50 percent of the gate, Louis the challenger's take of 17½ percent. The Cinderella Man, who'd once sworn eternal fealty to the Garden for taking him off the breadline, had changed his mind. Mike Jacobs would run the show as a silent partner, with a local man acting as his "promotional stooge." That way, Jacobs hoped, he would be spared the full wrath of the New York boxing authorities. Madison Square Garden vowed to sue, but the Hearst papers lined up, unsurprisingly, behind the switch. "Why should Jim, who was on relief for years, who hasn't made a real dollar since winning the title, who has a bunch of youngsters he wants to educate, who has a wife that he wants to build a home for, take $75,000 to fight Schmeling instead of $700,000 for facing Louis?" asked Bill Farnsworth of the *Evening Journal*.

Box-Sport could not believe what was happening: "a clique that has nothing to do with sports" had shafted someone "just because he is a son of the new German Reich and supports the Fatherland abroad, inside and outside the ring." It was "simply inconceivable" that a valid contract could be so utterly ignored. But Schmeling and the Nazis had already begun their countermove. In late January, Schmeling asked Hitler to salvage the fight by luring Braddock to Germany. Despite stringent German currency regulations, by February 1 a proposal was in the works offering Braddock

$250,000 to take on Schmeling in Berlin's Olympic Stadium. "It is understood that Chancellor Hitler has already voiced his general approval of such a match," an internal memo from the American embassy in Berlin to the State Department declared.

Within the Nazi apparat, the proposal generated a kind of euphoria. "This fight will be the greatest sporting event of the year 1937," Hermann Esser, a friend of Hitler's who was president of the German tourist committee, gushed to the Reich's chancellory. "The significance of the event for propaganda cannot be overestimated. . . . The entire world will say that a country that can finance and carry out such a huge sporting event must possess entrepreneurial spirit and can't be at the end of its financial powers." With a capacity of 130,000, the Olympic Stadium was the greatest space ever for such an event, and with only the snooty Bayreuth festival to offer otherwise, Germany needed a summer tourist attraction. As for foreign currency, the income from visas alone would cover two-thirds of the $300,000 Braddock was by now demanding. Then there was all the money travelers would bring with them, along with the home-court advantage the fight would confer on Schmeling. "As a fighter in his hometown, and probably in the presence of the Führer, Schmeling will offer a first-rate performance and thus carry the victory," Esser predicted.

Since Schmeling would win, Esser went on, the fight would inevitably lead to a rematch with Louis that would earn more money for the Reich, even though that battle would surely be in the United States. The Führer "placed the greatest value on the [Braddock-Schmeling] fight taking place on German soil," Esser concluded. Goebbels expressed concern about scrounging up enough hard currency; Germany had just embarked upon an ambitious four-year plan for economic self-sufficiency, supervised by Hermann Göring, a key part of which consisted of curbing imports, and thereby stanching the outflow of capital. (Even the head of German boxing had to apply for permission to take the equivalent of ten pounds sterling out of the country.) Rubber, fuel, textiles: Germany itself could produce all of them, or at least ersatz versions of them; but one thing it would have to import was champion boxers, and for them, Goebbels realized, it would have to pay dearly. "This still needs to be discussed with Göring," he wrote in his diary. But Schmeling met with a representative of the Deutsche Reichsbank and the sports ministry, and the Reich office of foreign currency ultimately found enough money to make a credible offer to Braddock. When Schmeling arrived in the United States for his exhibition tour, he would carry the proposal with him.

As Schmeling's southern tour encountered difficulties and delays, so, too, did the date of his departure from Germany. Finally, on February 24 he boarded the *Berengaria*, the German-built steamer given to the British as reparation for the *Lusitania*. It was a sop to public relations: the *Berengaria* would not be flying the swastika—surely an inopportune image for someone fighting an anti-Nazi boycott—as it entered New York Harbor. A large crowd of boxing officials, newspapermen, and fans saw Schmeling off. He arrived in New York on March 2, six days before his tour was scheduled to start. The boycott, he remarked, made him laugh. "You know, they do me an honor, in fact they compliment me," he remarked. "If they thought Braddock could beat me in two or three rounds there wouldn't be a boycott movement." He issued appeals to Braddock and to American good sportsmanship, but pledged to fight a "ghost battle" with Braddock if the champion didn't show up.

But with anti-Nazi feelings in New York intensifying almost by the hour, the fight seemed doomed. The day after Schmeling arrived, Mayor La Guardia told an audience of Jewish women that a pavilion at the upcoming New York World's Fair dedicated to religious freedom should include a "chamber of horrors" on Nazi Germany, featuring an exhibit on the "brown-shirted fanatic who is now menacing the peace of the world." The speech prompted another venomous attack on La Guardia in the Nazi press, in which he was denounced as a "shameless Jew lout," "New York's chief gangster," and "a dwarf with a grotesque belly, a knave with a screechy voice, a master blackmailer, a nose completely Semitic—a truly magnificent specimen of his race." New York, meantime, was labeled the most "un-American city in the country," a place known to other, real Americans as "Jews-York." "No less than three million members of this race of criminals live on the banks of the Hudson," the *Fränkische Tageszeitung* declared. "They dwell both in stinking outer boroughs, great examples with black coats and temple locks, as well as in the bank palaces of Wall Street and in the great millionaires' quarters where they surround themselves with their stolen luxury, 'representing' New York's High Society." Pro-Hitler groups met in Yorkville, and the German-American Bund called La Guardia "a product of the lower east-side of New York . . . where the boys grow up in an environment of garbage cans and fishy odors." Meanwhile, in what was probably the worst verbal peacetime attack against it ever, the Nazi press depicted the United States as a place of crime, violence, and Jewish-inspired strikes—like Germany before Hitler rescued it. In contrast to what the *Angriff* called a land of "real culture"—

of Goethe, Kant, and Beethoven—America was a cesspool of heartlessness, corruption, and philistinism. At its decadent core were not just Jews but blacks, subhumans who were nonetheless entitled to better than the poverty and lynch mobs to which a pious and hypocritical America subjected them. In reaction to all this, Jewish groups announced plans to hold a mass meeting against Nazism at Madison Square Garden on March 15.

In so overheated an environment, how could Max Schmeling possibly ply his trade? His tour foundered; two of the first stops, in Newark and Philadelphia, were canceled. And with the Jewish War Veterans mobilizing—"All posts are requested not to diminish vigilance, but watch newspapers and stand by prepared for instant action"—the whole exhibition schedule appeared doomed. So, too, did his fight against Braddock, unless Braddock could be enticed to Berlin. Schmeling's opening offer—Nazi Germany's, really—was $250,000, free of German taxes, to be deposited in a bank outside Germany, plus film and radio rights worth another $150,000, plus the right to help pick a referee, plus an American judge. Mike Jacobs and Madison Square Garden would be bought off for another $50,000. Schmeling also agreed to post a $25,000 bond, guaranteeing that if he won the title, he would defend it in the United States in September, against Joe Louis or anyone else. For cash-strapped Germany it was an astonishing gesture, another sign of how central the business of boxing and the heavyweight crown had become to the Nazi psyche. So as not to jinx anything, the propaganda ministry issued instructions to the German press to soft-pedal anti-Semitism for a time, "since in American boxing the Jews play a great role." The *Daily Worker* called it "the most boot-licking contract ever advanced for a title match." But Braddock was in the catbird seat, and he wanted still more. On March 21, the Nazis upped the offer to $350,000. The black press feared that Braddock was running out on Louis. But Joe Gould balked, and the Berlin fight fell through, as did Schmeling's tour. On March 23, Schmeling returned to Germany empty-handed. The propaganda ministry instructed the Nazi press to say no more about a title bout in Berlin.

Legend has it that Gould pulled out because of what happened when someone from Goebbels's office asked him to state his demands. He listed them—$400,000 in cash in a London bank, all expenses paid, an American referee—and all were readily agreed to. "What else?" the Nazi official asked. "We want equal rights for the Jews," was Gould's response. And the German hung up. But this was presumably just Gould boasting to

Leonard Lyons of the *Post*. The truth was surely that Gould, who once said he'd stage a fight in the Sahara if the money was right, was simply ransoming the title to the highest bidder, and in this auction, Mike Jacobs outbid Adolf Hitler. Gould, imprisoned during World War II for profiteering, had few scruples. He knew Jacobs knew that if Braddock lost to Schmeling, Germany could sit on the heavyweight crown for the best years of Louis's career, whatever assurances to the contrary Schmeling now offered. So he and Jacobs struck an extraordinary deal: Braddock would fight Louis all right, but only if Gould and Braddock collected 20 percent of the net profits from all heavyweight title fights Jacobs promoted over the next decade. For Jacobs it was costly indeed; it also attested to Louis's astronomical value. (Ultimately, the secret arrangement became known; twice, Gould took Jacobs to court to enforce it.) So Louis had his title fight— almost. With Hitler now out of the way, only Madison Square Garden, and the federal courts, could stop it.

The Garden had steered clear of New York State's courts, evidently convinced that anything involving Schmeling would not get a fair hearing there. It went first to Miami— "Joe Louis is colored and it was easier to get an injunction against him down there," Gould theorized—and ultimately landed in federal court in Newark, where Gould's best defense was that the boycott threatened to ruin the proposed fight. Not only were three out of every four fans at title fights Jews, Gould asserted, they sat in the most expensive seats. To prove it, Gould's legal team canvassed the garment district, collecting signatures on prefabricated affidavits from executives at places such as Blessed Event Dresses and Maywine Frocks. All confirmed how they usually bought chunks of tickets but wouldn't if Schmeling were on the card. The Garden countered that anti-Nazi sentiments were nothing new. And if they were so serious, how could the Louis-Schmeling fight have produced a $550,000 gate? For every Jew who spurned the contest, it predicted, an extra Irishman or German American would go. That the matter would end up in court disgusted a sports press still pretending that "the sports pages are for sports" and that lawyers should never be in the mix. But some felt the Garden was simply trying to preserve its authority; it, too, knew that a Braddock-Schmeling fight was a dog, and half hoped it wouldn't have to stage it.

America's growing hostility made Schmeling an even greater hero at home, if that was possible. On April 15, a few days after boxing was made a mandatory part of physical education for all German boys thirteen and older— "The Führer doesn't want soft mamma's boys but real men," the head of German boxing, Franz Metzner, explained—Schmeling refereed a boxing benefit at the Sportpalast in Berlin. The affair was sponsored jointly by the local government and Kraft durch Freude, the social club the Nazis organized for German workers, and benefited the Winterhilfs-werk. Before six thousand cheering fans, Schmeling was made "German Champion in All Classes," a newly devised title he would hold until retirement. For Schmeling and the regime, all bygones were bygones; "the wonderful style of his victory over Louis has left behind anything in the past that might have been divisive," one paper reported. "Max Schme-ling has long deserved such a distinction, after having to make his way through a swamp of undeserved insults in earlier years," Metzner told the crowd. "They never understood that this Max Schmeling wasn't fighting for himself alone; rather he was also a pioneer for his Fatherland outside the borders of the homeland." There were "storms of applause" when Schmeling collected his award.

A few days earlier, Schmeling had talked with Goebbels about his troubles getting Braddock into the ring. "Braddock is a coward, and con-tinually searching for new excuses," Goebbels wrote afterward in his diary. "I advise Schmeling to publicly challenge him in an open letter, which must be very carefully formulated. That should work." But Braddock was unapologetic. "I'm not going to sacrifice my family just to please some fighter who never in his ring career has done anything to please anybody but himself," he said. Most Americans sympathized with that; despite its well-established loyalty to Louis, even the *Daily Worker* liked Braddock, "a longshoreman who proudly carries a union card" and "a really swell guy" who'd refused "to scab on the fans' anti-Nazi boycott." Only the black papers were unimpressed; Louis, they pointed out, was Braddock's meal ticket. "Braddock looks upon Louis as his chance to cash in at least a half million smackers before being overtaken by age and defeat," the Asso-ciated Negro Press said.

In April 1937 heavyweight championship boxing became a three-ring circus. The world's three top heavyweights all began training, but only two of them would actually square off. Braddock was in Grand Beach, Michigan. His camp was a characteristically down-to-earth, casual opera-tion, with the titleholder eating and sleeping with his sparring partners and dispensing with bodyguards. "If the heavyweight champion can't pro-tect himself he must not be much of a champion," Gould mused. Louis was in Kenosha, Wisconsin, where he was welcomed after the local homeowners' association in nearby Lake Geneva, composed mostly of wealthy Chicagoans with summer homes, objected to his training there. "The ugly monster of race prejudice . . . has come out in the open against

Joe Louis and his handlers," one black weekly reported. And Schmeling was in Speculator, New York, the picturesque town in the northern Adirondacks where Tunney had trained and Baer had communed with the trees before losing to Louis.

In the wee hours of April 27, a delegation from the German boxing federation saw an unusually chipper Schmeling off into what *Box-Sport* called his "journey into the unknown." By the morning of May 3 he was once more back in New York, but only after he'd dodged a hydrogen-filled bullet.* The next day, with what some thought were tears in his eyes, Schmeling pleaded with the commission to protect his fight with Braddock. It did nothing. The action then shifted to the United States District Court, where, nine days later, Judge Guy Fake ruled that Braddock was free to fight Louis. Unless an appeals court reversed, or the commission intervened, the fight in Chicago was on. In Germany honor always came first, a disgusted *Box-Sport* declared, but Mammon controlled American boxing. And cowardice. "I've told you again and again, don't box against Schmeling," Braddock's manager scolded him in a cartoon appearing in a Berlin newspaper. "A broken word hurts a lot less than a broken jaw!"

As Schmeling prepared for a fight that would almost surely never come to pass, the American press disparaged him mercilessly. Underlying the ridicule was disdain for Schmeling's stereotypical German punctiliousness. He was training for "the shadow-boxing championship of the universe," the *Mirror* said. When the *Herald Tribune*'s Caswell Adams visited Schmeling in Speculator, he found him reading German studies of American society. "Evidently Max is trying to fathom these people who have ditched him," Adams wrote. With almost comical dutifulness, Schmeling stuck to his regimen. He never drank coffee while training, for instance, but one morning there was nothing else to drink, and his host urged him to make an exception; what difference would it make? Schmeling demurred. "If I make excuses this time maybe I make them again another time," he explained.

The charade played out. Hellmis arrived to broadcast the fight that would not be held. Ticket sales exceeded all expectations, Parker wrote: someone actually bought one. In fact, by June 1 fifty-four tickets

*Schmeling had originally planned to travel to America via the *Hindenburg*, arriving on May 7. But at Joe Jacobs's insistence—Jacobs wanted him in New York when the boxing commission met on May 4—he had departed earlier by boat. The dirigible, minus Schmeling, blew up as it arrived in New Jersey; thirty-six of the ninety-seven passengers and crew died. Among the dead was the heir to Schmeling's ticket.

had been sold—"a fair indication of just how many curio collectors there are in this city." (They got a bonus: Schmeling's name was misspelled.) The Garden announced the undercard for the evening, which featured real-life heavyweights like Tony Galento and Jersey Joe Walcott. Meantime, lawyers for the Garden argued their appeal before a panel of three federal judges in Philadelphia. Braddock, a "mediocre boxer" the Garden had lifted off the breadline, was morally obliged to keep his word, one of them argued.

As fight day in New York approached, the hilarity only grew. There were imaginary interviews with Schmeling's spectral opponent; the *Daily Worker* ran a head shot—a blank square—of "Kid Ghost." Reporters talked of writing their stories in invisible ink, and filing them by Ouija board. A deaf-mute would do the play-by-play, for a broadcast going "ghost to ghost." There were predictions, including one that Schmeling wouldn't lay a glove on his adversary. "If the sports injustice weren't so great, and if Max Schmeling, who really has entirely earned his shot at the crown, weren't affected, one could laugh at these authentically American methods," *Box-Sport* observed bitterly. "A cabaret is nothing compared to them." Hitler and Goebbels followed events closely. "With the Führer this afternoon," Goebbels wrote in his diary on May 27. "Question if we, ourselves, in the event that Braddock chickens out, should declare Schmeling world champion. I say yes to it. The Americans are the most corrupt people on earth."

Schmeling followed his traditional prefight routine. On June 1 he broke camp, drove to New York, and checked in to the Commodore. On the eve of the fight, he gave a radio interview to Hellmis. "This fight for the fight has maybe been harder than the fight for the world championship itself," he told the German audience. "You, Max Schmeling, we wish that you'll keep calm in this struggle," Hellmis replied. "That justice will prevail, we already know. And also that the name of the uncrowned champion of the world still is Max Schmeling!" Schmeling thanked him, and sent his best wishes to his fans back home. "If I have to wait three years, eventually I'll bring the world heavyweight championship back to Germany!" he pledged. The taping complete, Schmeling followed another of his prefight rituals: going to the movies. This time it was *Kid Galahad*, with Edward G. Robinson as a pugnacious fight manager modeled, some said, after Joe Jacobs.

At ten o'clock on the night of June 3, when the bell had been scheduled to sound, Schmeling would be "the most popular man in America,"

Hellmis wrote in the *Völkischer Beobachter*. He added that "those representing Schmeling's interests in America"—he couldn't bring himself to
say "Joe Jacobs"—hoped that when the boxing commissioners met earlier
in the day, they would strip Braddock of his title and forbid Louis to fight
him. He concluded with a rant about American prejudice against Nazi
Germany, ridiculing press reports suggesting "bodies of shot Jews [lying]
in heaps in the tunnels of the Berlin subway" and castigating America's
self-image as "the freest country in the world." (Hellmis, who had already
lionized Schmeling in newspapers and magazines, on radio, and in film,
would soon add a book to the canon. Titled *Max Schmeling: The Story of
a Fighter*, it opened as Hellmis's ship headed homeward after the Louis
fight, when Hellmis realized he was destined to compose "a singular song
of praise" to the victor. It seemed to matter little that his victory was over
"a block of wood of a primitive negro, who can't even read or write, with
the exception of his name, and who when he hears the word 'Lincoln,'
associates with it a beautifully varnished, shiny chrome automobile.")

By the day of the fight, the appeals court still had not ruled. "The
greatest injustice in the history of sports," the 12 *Uhr-Blatt* called Schmeling's fate. It was already a day of high drama: that morning in France, the
Duke of Windsor was marrying the woman he loved. His timing had originally irked Joe Jacobs—"We set our date last winter and here [he] comes
along and grabs it for his wedding. It ain't right. It'll kill our publicity"—
but now Edward and Mrs. Simpson could have the day to themselves.
New York had a spectacle of its own: "the most titanic farce ever connected with boxing." Schmeling, characteristically, showed up for the
weigh-in, at the State Building in lower Manhattan, five minutes early,
and his superb condition impressed the examining physician. Fighters in
the preliminary bouts also got weighed. "This here business is sorta nutty,
ain't it?" one of them remarked. It was raining; someone quipped that the
bad weather could affect the gate.

Everyone then proceeded to a fifth-floor auditorium, where the boxing
commission pronounced sentence on Braddock and Gould. Each was
fined $1,000, and Braddock was suspended in New York until he fought
Schmeling. That meant, of course, that he could still fight Louis in three
weeks' time, and after that, who would care whether he was suspended? It
was, wrote Frank Graham in the *Sun*, "the consummation of as complete
a rooking as any one ever received in sport." Schmeling stormed back to
his hotel, leaving Jacobs—Parker called him Schmeling's "phantom
manager"—and Machon to speak for him. When the press caught up

with him, they saw something they had never seen before: the quintessential control freak out of control. "Bitterness is strictly a new act with
Schmeling," Davis Walsh wrote. "Heretofore, he has been evasive, ur-
bane, uninformative and slightly patronizing." "Who cares about being
suspended in New York?" Schmeling thundered. "Dempsey was suspended. I was suspended before. Is that a punishment for a world champion who chickens out? What is the decision—noddings! They make a
joke of the title. The championship, it is a joke. And your commission is a
bigger joke. I cannot help it that I beat your Joe Louis. Louis will be your
champion June 23, and I knocked Louis out. Can you figure that?" On a
desk nearby was a newspaper picture of Braddock taking a shower, cap-
tioned "Chubby Champion." Schmeling grabbed it, crumpled it up,
threw it on the floor, and kicked it. "That's your champion," he growled.
"For two years he has not fought. Bah." Schmeling paused. "It's all my
fault," he finally said. "That's what I get for knocking out Joe Louis."

Mike Jacobs quickly tried to mollify Schmeling by promising him a
bout against the winner of the Chicago fight, and Louis offered the same
thing. But Schmeling would not commit himself to anything. That afternoon he was to be interviewed by NBC. The session, for which he was to
receive $1,500, had been entirely scripted; Joe Jacobs and Nat Fleischer,
both of whom were also incensed by what the commission had done,
wrote a text for Schmeling that was essentially a toned-down version of
his tantrum that afternoon. But NBC refused to let him read it over the
air. The network prepared a more anodyne script, which Schmeling
spurned.

On the night of June 3, newspapers were swamped with phone calls
from people thinking a fight was really taking place. Dutifully, mockingly,
a few intrepid reporters ventured into the rain and across the Queensboro
Bridge to the Garden Bowl, just to describe the nothingness there. As one
made his way, he heard shouting, applause, and music in the distance,
but it was only a WPA circus in the next lot. "The sense of justice in every
civilized man will rise up against this comedy," the *Völkischer Beobachter*
declared. One Berlin newspaper blamed New York's Jewish governor,
Herbert Lehman, for the whole fiasco, claiming he'd bought off the boxing commission. A cartoon in the *8 Uhr-Blatt* of Nuremberg showed
Braddock cowering in an outhouse, his gloves hanging forlornly on the
door. "Severe diarrhea?" one man standing nearby asks. "No, Mister,"
another replies. "He's just scared of Schmeling!"

Schmeling would not be among those watching Louis and Braddock in Chicago. Instead, he boarded the *Europa* for Germany on June 5 in what Grantland Rice called "the Mt. Everest of all dudgeons." "Schmeling being given the run-around by Braddock," Goebbels wrote in his diary. "The pig is too cowardly to take to the ring. Really American!" The German press was prohibited from pondering a Louis-Schmeling rematch because it would diminish the fury the Nazis hoped to stoke. The press "must continue to write in the sharpest manner about these American sports methods," Goebbels instructed. Madison Square Garden did pick up one vote from the United States Court of Appeals; Braddock had been "seduced from the path of contract duty by sordid money making promoters," one judge wrote. But he was overruled by the other two, and it was all academic anyway; the ruling came five days after Schmeling had left for Europe, with a strategic stop in London en route.

Months earlier, a Berlin paper had suggested that having been shafted by the Americans, Schmeling could fight a European like Tommy Farr, a Welshman, for the *real* world championship. A few days after the phantom fight, the führer of German boxing, Franz Metzner, informed one of Hitler's aides that he was going to London to take in the fight between Walter Neusel and Farr—the favorite—on June 15, and that while there, he would begin arranging for what he oxymoronically called a "world championship of the old world," pitting Farr against Schmeling. Joachim von Ribbentrop, then the German ambassador to Britain, was already on the case, and said the English had shown "the greatest interest" in the idea. Metzner told a currency official that Hitler had asked him to organize such a fight "as a counterweight against the American methods of deception."

Farr won the bout, with Schmeling watching alongside Ribbentrop. Already buoyed by his reception in Britain—"The incredible enthusiasm with which the fair Englishmen received him has washed away all the anger about New York's boxing swindlers," one German paper reported— he now had the Nazis' top boxing official trying to arrange for him an alternative championship. In fact, the Nazis were already portraying him as the de facto world champion, the true world champion, the "moral" world champion, and when he returned to Berlin he was greeted accordingly. A week later, Metzner wrote to officials of the International Boxing Union, the British Boxing Board of Control, and their counterparts in Belgium, Spain, and Italy, urging them to break "the arrogant monopoly" of American boxing. By the end of June, Metzner reported to Tschammer und Osten that the BBBC had fallen in behind the scheme and that the IBU would soon follow suit. "The European front of unity against American gangsterism was able to be established," he exulted.

Schmeling had already cabled Joe Jacobs, who was in Chicago for the other championship fight, and declared that he was done with America. Jacobs was asked if he thought Schmeling was serious. "You can bet all the tea in China he is," replied Jacobs, who saw his meal ticket floating away before his very eyes. "When he makes up his mind on something it stays made up."

CHAPTER 10

Banishing Jack Johnson's Ghost

SHORTLY BEFORE THE LOUIS-BRADDOCK FIGHT, perhaps as he was about to board the train for Chicago, Grantland Rice talked to a redcap at Grand Central Terminal. "Joe Louis was a great fighter when he was tearing three chickens apart," the man told him. "But now, he's eating chicken en casserole, and I'm afraid he won't do much. I'm afraid Joe's gone soft." Rice agreed. Strictly as a physical matter, Louis should win in five rounds, he believed. But mentally and psychologically Louis wasn't even close to Braddock, and Braddock was no Aristotle. "The Schmeling fight almost wrecked Louis," Rice warned. "When anyone throws a right now, Louis begins to duck before the punch starts."

As the comic opera of the phantom fight played out in New York, Louis and Braddock quietly trained. Braddock was as he always had been: shopworn but scrappy, rusty but determined. The more interesting issue was which Louis would be on hand—the wunderkind or the busted phenom. The question hung over his camp in Kenosha like the smoke from the nearby car plants. The newsreels showed mobs of happy white children clustered around him. In twelve years of school, Roy Wilkins observed, those same youngsters would never learn a good thing about Negroes, but Joe Louis was real to them—a "living argument against the hypocrisy, meanness, and hatred of the color line in America." Thousands of Chicago blacks hopped on special trains to watch Louis practice. One, a paraplegic who had not left his hospital in three years, arrived by ambulance and watched his hero while propped up on a stretcher.

Louis insisted he would not make the same mistakes he had made a year earlier, and that even if he did, Braddock was no Schmeling; it took Schmeling sixty swings to knock him out, he said, and Braddock was only half as strong. Already, Louis and his handlers were anticipating Schmeling. Louis said he wanted to fight him in the fall, and then quit; by then he'd be earning $10,000 annually from his properties, and that would be enough. He'd already rented the camp at Pompton Lakes, and after two weeks off, he planned to train for Schmeling for the rest of the summer.

But once again, the reports from Louis's camp weren't good. He looked lethargic. He was no longer hungry—a trap, some sportswriters believed, which black fighters were particularly prone to fall into—and had gone soft and flabby. He had too much to learn and too little time to learn it, or had learned too much and had too little time to unlearn it. The Louis of old would have no trouble with Braddock, but the Louis of Kenosha was "just a cheap and sleazy road company of the original production," Jack Miley wrote in the *Daily News*. His handlers had tried instilling fanciness into an instinctive fighter, and had ruined him; nobody, said Miley, "will ever be able to pound anything through his kinky skull." Louis, *Collyer's Eye* gloated, was "going the way of nearly all negro gladiators": "Money and food have the best of him." It still picked him to win, discounting rumors that the fight was "in the bag" for Braddock. "The group of Nigger mobsters controlling the Brown Bomber was strong enough to turn thumbs down on all requests to 'do business,'" it reported. So worried was Mike Jacobs that he dispatched Harry Lenny, a savvy retired white lightweight who'd once fought Blackburn, to check Louis out. The black press once more saw the horror stories as a racist plot, and was more concerned over rumors that the Louises' marriage was foundering. "This is Joe's first romance and if it is on the rocks it is also Joe's first heartbreak, and brother, you can fight better with a broken hand than with a broken heart," warned Lewis Dial of the *Amsterdam News*.

Once again, many dismissed the gloomy dispatches as Mike Jacobs's usual manipulations; Braddock was too old and had absorbed too many punches to put up much resistance. "I can think of a million things wrong with Louis," observed Jimmy Powers. "He is green. He is slow-witted. He stands like a dope when he is nailed. He has absolutely no defense against a right cross. He has had a lot of easy fights. . . . He can't feint, jab, block or in-fight for sour apples. A dancer, a cutie, can slap him silly." He picked Louis anyway. So did most of the experts: eighty-six out of one hundred, according to one poll. The oddsmakers favored him twelve to five, the first time since 1892 that a challenger—at least one who hadn't previously been champion—was favored over an incumbent. "Youth, speed, strength, reflexes, punishing power—with all the advantages Louis carries into action he ought to be ashamed of himself if the fight goes beyond the sixth or seventh round, because it will be the final proof that he is lacking in both smartness and courage," Rice maintained. Neither man impressed Jack Dempsey—"One guy is getting old and hasn't been in the ring for a long time. And the other guy doesn't know much and goes off his nut when you hit him in the head"—but he picked Braddock, especially if the fight lasted more than a few rounds. Braddock wasn't discouraged, for he'd been a ten-to-one underdog against Baer; odds of three to one against him, he joked, ought to make him a sure thing.

With all that preceded the match, it was easy to forget that something many had vowed would never happen again was about to: a black man stood to become heavyweight champion. Pegler once more called it insanity to stage a mixed bout in a black neighborhood; Miley warned that if Braddock won, the riots that followed the Johnson-Jeffries fight would seem like "mild contusions and abrasions" by comparison. The NAACP braced itself for a Louis win. Should that happen, Walter White advised black newspaper editors, "there should be a minimum of exultation shown." He urged his organization to mobilize ministers, social workers, and others so that a Louis victory "might be taken in its stride and not made the occasion for serious clashes." A black weekly in Nashville felt compelled to remind readers of all the whites who had befriended Louis throughout his career. "Louis will be the last colored man to get a crack at the title if you guys start painting the town," the *Baltimore Afro-American* warned. "Race pride is one thing and hooliganism is quite another," another black writer admonished. The *Houston Informer* cautioned blacks to remain calm and modest even when whites praised Louis. "A white man can say a lot more about the defeat of a white man in the presence of other white people than a Negro can, and get away with it," it explained. "The saner ones of our group can help a lot by pouring cold water on the over-enthusiasm of loud-mouthed-street-corner talkers by changing the subject or distracting the listener. Quietly work for suppression of bragging in the presence of white people."

This was Chicago's first big fight since Tunney beat Dempsey there a decade earlier. Things had calmed down since those days when Al Capone still reigned and everyone seemed to pack heat. But Chicago was still Chicago. On the town with Damon Runyon, Trevor Wignall observed that everyone seemed to be named "Red," "Lefty," "Good Time Charley," or "One-Eye," and cabdrivers routinely asked fares whether they wanted additional "entertainment." The lobby of the Morrison Hotel became a temporary isthmus off Jacobs Beach. It was from there that New York sportswriters could cast their jaundiced eyes on America's second city, and describe what a hick burg it really was—a place of poor service, bored shopgirls, and conniving taxi drivers, in which even the most pretentious bars served lemon soda in their mixed drinks and ginger ale in their gin rickeys. "Chicago is one of those places good for one big splash about once in every five years," was how one veteran New York sportswriter put it.

Ticket sales lagged a bit, because of either the turmoil surrounding the fight or the high price of seats. Or maybe in Chicago people were accustomed to getting their mayhem for free. "Why pay $27.50," one New York sportswriter asked, "when you can see a massacre for nothing any time the coppers fire on the pickets? Or any time the mobsters decide to settle a territorial dispute?" Scalpers reported little business. "They ain't educated out here," one New York dealer complained.

But black America wasn't jaded. By one estimate, blacks bought three of every ten tickets, leading one writer to rechristen the fight site "Black and White Sox Park." More than five thousand blacks were due in from Detroit on three special trains. Another large contingent came from Harlem, "and among all of these you find not only the notables, but Shoeshine Sams, hoboes, and others whose exchequer is very limited," one black journalist wrote. Three hundred people boarded a train from Memphis. From Kansas City there was a $21 special. From Houston the "Joe Louis Special," sponsored by the local black weekly, cost $35, but that included round-trip fare, fight tickets, a night's lodging, a meal, "a good time en route"—and precious peace of mind.* Whites could also come, in a separate whites-only car.

Some blacks still suspected the fight was fixed, that "Washington" had decided America was not yet ready for another black champion or that fight bigwigs, fearing the heavyweight division would shrivel up if Louis won, had made sure he wouldn't. Black fans hounded Mike Jacobs for assurances that things would be legitimate. Adding to the unease was the nagging sense that Louis wasn't Louis anymore. When he visited Harlem, Ted Poston of the *New York Post*—the first black reporter hired by a mainstream New York newspaper—was struck by how many people had stuck around. Anxiety or poverty had kept some of them home; others had had

---

*"At every fight where Negroes flood in, there are hundreds who can't get lodging and have to walk the streets," the paper warned. Others stayed in clip joints and got "completely robbed." It promised to take care of everyone who signed up.

their fill of trains when they'd left the South. Not that people weren't following the fight: as it approached, one store owner said he'd fixed more radios in the past two days than in the previous three months.

Five hundred fight writers from all over the world converged on Chicago, though one place went conspicuously unrepresented. "Germany isn't interested," the *Herald Tribune* reported. "The outcome of the fight between Braddock and Louis should not be covered excessively," the German press instructions declared. Only short reports would be tolerated, the newspapers were told, and should focus on how it was more of a financial than an athletic affair. Only Americans, said *Box-Sport*, considered this a real title bout; the shadow that Schmeling would cast over the proceedings, it said, would be darker than Louis's skin. As for Louis, he was "a primitive man, a boxing machine without the sparks of divine intellect."

More than two thousand people showed up for the weigh-in at the Auditorium Theater. Joe Gould tried giving Louis the evil eye, and when that failed, took another tack. "Gee, Joe, you sure are light for this fight," he said. "Only 197½. You must be doin' a lot of worryin'." "You claim Schmeling sneaked the punch that knocked you out, don't you, Joe?" he went on. "Well, don't worry about that tonight. We'll fight you clean. Jimmy's right was never better. We won't have to sneak with it. We know you don't take it so well on that side, but we won't club you the way Schmeling did. Jimmy's a puncher, not a clubber. The first clean shot he gets, it will be over. We won't have to mess you up the way Schmeling did." On and on he went; Louis even smiled.

Whatever the hoopla, there was disappointment in the air. Not long ago, Louis had seemed destined to take the title by storm; now, he stood to win it almost by default. Even his friends at the *Chicago Tribune* had fallen out of love with him. "There is no legend of world domination or invincibility about either of tonight's contestants," Arch Ward wrote. The letdown was visible at the box office: at noon the day before the fight, 40,500 tickets remained unsold. But the police were taking no chances. Officially, they would station a thousand men in the stadium and another two thousand nearby, but rumor had it there'd be more. By one account, one-sixth of the entire Chicago police force would be working, augmented by a regiment of state troopers "armed to the molars." Firemen laid hoses to douse potential rioters.

At dusk, people began making their way to Comiskey Park, passing vendors hawking fried chicken, pennants, jars of gin, and Louis photographs. The ring, shipped from New York, was the same one in which Schmeling had knocked out Louis. Sitting closest to it was the usual Hollywood contingent: this time, Clark Gable, Bette Davis, Edward G. Robinson, Bing Crosby, Mae West, Carole Lombard, and George Raft. Where Al Capone and his cronies had congregated a decade earlier, J. Edgar Hoover now sat. Kenesaw Mountain Landis, the commissioner who had kept baseball lily white, and Branch Rickey, the man who was to integrate it, were on hand. So were Joe Tinker and Johnny Evers, two-thirds of the famous double-play combination for the Chicago Cubs. Also at ringside was much of boxing's storied past. The last heavyweight title combatants here, Dempsey and Tunney, now sat next to each other. Nearby was Jess Willard, who'd beaten Jack Johnson twenty-two years earlier in Havana in the last "mixed" heavyweight title bout. He shook hands with Dempsey, who'd mauled him in Toledo, Ohio, four years later, in what became the gold standard of heavyweight ferocity. (As they posed, someone yelled that it was the longest Willard had ever stayed upright with Dempsey.) Jim Jeffries, the former champ whom Jack Johnson had beaten in 1910, was also present. Only Johnson was nowhere to be seen. Perhaps, the black papers speculated, he feared being dunned—or jeered. The choicest seats were "completely alabastered"; the black celebrities who did show up—Bill Robinson, Fletcher Henderson, Chick Webb, Ella Fitzgerald—sat farther back. Louis had asked his mother and Marva not to come. (Marva would listen on the radio with the society editor of the *Chicago Defender* and the wife of a "widely known mortician." Louis's mother stayed home.)

A preternaturally calm Louis, surrounded by policemen, made his way toward the ring—"a sheepish-faced boy in a long bathrobe, his eyes on the ground, his lips those of the old-fashioned shuffling 'coon,' not those at all of the alert, educated modern Negro," one Chicago reporter said of him. Braddock followed. Louis wore his usual blue silk bathrobe; Braddock's was bright green, with a shamrock. Around his neck was a Catholic medal. The Chicago ring announcer introduced the celebrities, with none of Harry Balogh's brio. Louis got more boos than cheers. Before the first punch was thrown, history had been made: at twenty-three years old, he was the youngest challenger in heavyweight history. The fighters had been specifically instructed to head for the farthest corner in the event of a knockdown; Chicago wanted no reenactment of the "Long Count." "Chappie, this is it," Blackburn whispered to Louis shortly before the bell sounded. "You come home a champ tonight." Meantime, life stopped in black neighborhoods everywhere. "Every man, woman and child with normal emotions dedicated the night to prizefighting, put aside every other consideration, and crammed their heads as close to the nearest radio loudspeaker as possible," the *Norfolk Journal and Guide* said. Once more they would hear Clem McCarthy sharing the microphone with Edwin C. Hill.

The fight started at an astonishing clip, with Braddock taking charge. He was thirty-two years old, and figured to run out of steam first; he had to win fast. The two traded punches furiously, and with a right uppercut to the chin, Braddock knocked Louis down, becoming only the second person—after Schmeling—to do so during Louis's professional career. The crowd was electrified, though Louis popped up before the referee could start a count. Quickly, he had Braddock's left eye bleeding. Braddock had never been counted out before, nor, he insisted, had he ever felt any real pain in the ring, but Louis's first left hook made him feel sick. In the second round things slowed down. In the third, fourth, and fifth the fight wasn't settling in so much as it was evolving: Louis was becoming more precise, while Braddock was faltering.

In the sixth, the assault intensified. Braddock's knees wobbled and the fight appeared to be almost over. Once the bell had sounded, through his damaged eyes, Braddock saw Gould reach for a towel. "You throw that towel in there and I'll never speak to you again. Never," Braddock told the man who had managed him, through good times and lean, since 1926. Gould held on to the towel. But in the seventh, his legs wide apart, his arms leaden, his right eye swollen, his left eye ready to shut, Braddock continued to wilt. "Braddock fought a more relentless foe than Joe Louis last night," the *Chicago Tribune* wrote. "He fought an enemy no boxer has beaten. He fought age." In the eighth, Louis readied himself for the kill. "Get your hands up, Jimmy! Get your hands up, Jimmy!" Gould shouted. Braddock tried to obey, but he couldn't get them high enough. McCarthy ticked off the punches: a left to Louis's body, a hard left to Braddock's head, then another under the ear. "And there Braddock came up with a right uppercut that missed, Louis has backed out of the way in time," he said. "Now Braddock is in the center of the ring. . . . And Louis gave him . . . and Braddock is down!"

McCarthy, characteristically, never caught up to the fateful punch, but it was a right hook to the jaw, one of the hardest, most visible, and most audible ever; never, someone later said, had a punch sounded so loud. Even in the slow motion of the fight films, Braddock's head twisted quickly. Louis's blow knocked every bit of moisture off it, encasing it momentarily "in a halo of gleaming particles." "Braddock went over stiffly—like something wooden and unreal," Considine wrote. It was only the third time the Cinderella Man had been down, and now he lay flat on his face, blood running onto the canvas. "The count is two!" McCarthy chanted. "Three! Four! Five! Six! Seven! Eight! Nine! Ten! A new world's champion! Joe Louis is the new world's champion!" And a new kind of world's champion, too, one whom blacks and whites could share. Louis had come back—not to the Louis of myth, perhaps, maybe just to what he had always been.

Braddock remained on the canvas—as cold as a frozen haddock, Runyon wrote. "Get up, Jim!" some yelled, but not even a muscle twitched. Four men carried him to his corner, the blood from his eyes and mouth dripping onto his shoes, leaving behind a red trail a foot long. It took him several minutes to come to. Louis blinked and grinned slightly when, to an oddly equivocal reception—borne, perhaps, of sympathy for the fallen white man—his hand was raised. McCarthy and his microphone quickly caught up with the new champ. "Joe!" he exclaimed. "A great fight!" "Oh, it was a great fight, a very good fight," Louis replied gently, sweetly. "When did you think you had him beat?" McCarthy asked. "When I took the match," Louis replied. He sounded happier than he let himself look; even now, he would not let down his guard.

But in his dressing room, all was joy. "Chappie! Chappie!" Louis shouted at Blackburn. "Let's cut the title in two and celebrate!" Blackburn kissed the glove Louis had worn on his right hand. "Ol' glove, you shoa had dynamite in you tonight," he said. "I guess them years jes' crept up on him," Louis said of his foe. "Nice to be young, ain't it?" Asked how it felt to be champion, he replied, "It don't feel no different." Nor, he said, would he ever let it. He pledged to be "the fightingest champion there ever was." "Just give me one more shot at that Schmeling . . . just one more!" he added. On the other side of an improvised partition, Braddock was too drained to talk. He would require stitches over his left eye and on his right cheek. More than one thousand people wired him their condolences, among them James Cagney, Lionel Barrymore, J. Edgar Hoover, and Lou and Eleanor Gehrig. Braddock had even taken a beating financially, making far less than he could have gotten (tax-free) in Berlin. But the secret agreement with Mike Jacobs would sweeten the pot for a decade to come. When Braddock did start talking, he said he wanted another shot at Louis. "I guess the poor guy hasn't come to yet," Dempsey's old manager, Jack Kearns, was heard to say.

That night, wild celebrations once again convulsed black America.

The most glorious, unsurprisingly, were in Chicago. "Swirling, careening, madly dashing from house to house . . . yelling, crying, laughing,
boasting, gloating, exulting . . . slapping backs, jumping out of the way of
wildly-driven cars . . . whites and blacks hugging . . . the entire world, this
cosmic center of the world tonight, turned topsy-turvy, this is the South-
side [sic] of Chicago," the *Courier* reported. Someone had had the fore-
sight to prepare thousands of placards declaring simply I TOLD YOU SO.
They nicely captured the faith, exultation, defiance, and sense of vindica-
tion the celebrants felt. "They threw that party down on 35th street last
night—the one they've been 22 years getting ready for," was how the
Chicago Tribune saw it. "Pickaninnies who should have been in bed
paraded the streets in dishpan bands. Old folks who hadn't stayed up so
late in years went shouting up and down the streets." There were bonfires
in the boulevards; people rode in cabs and trolleys and on the L for free.
Rumors that Louis would show up at the Eighth Regiment Armory, where
Roy Eldridge and Benny Goodman were playing, caused hundreds to
line the streets outside. Thousands also gathered in front of Louis's apartment, to which he returned shortly after the fight. Before long, the new
champion and his wife went out on the balcony and waved to the throng.
Someone shouted for a souvenir, and Louis, having nothing else handy,
threw down his straw hat, which was quickly torn to shreds. Twenty more
times that night, Louis went out and took curtain calls.

   In Detroit, the large crowd that had listened to the fight over a loudspeaker outside the home of Louis's mother demanded, and got, a cameo
from her. She was relieved it was over, she told reporters, because she
didn't really like fights. Then she paused for a moment. "His right really
was pretty good, wasn't it?" she asked. In Harlem, celebrants materialized
out of nowhere. "One moment there wasn't nobody," one amazed officer
remarked. "Next minute there was a million." A crowd marched down
Seventh Avenue, waving Ethiopian flags and chanting, "We want Schmeling!" "We want the Nazi man!" There was a racial edginess to the celebration that hadn't been apparent after other Louis victories. "How do you
like that, white man?" people shouted at passersby. "One thousand
policemen fingered clubs menacingly in an obvious attempt to cow the
Negro people and stifle their enthusiasm," the *Daily Worker* reported. It
counted fifty-eight cops on the corner of Lenox Avenue and 135th Street
alone. Louis "kayoed the same barrier of discrimination that corrals talented young Negro university graduates into post offices as clerks, that
bars Negro workmen from the skilled jobs in industry, that segregates the

Negro people in slums," the *Worker* stated a few days later. "That was behind the joy in Harlem. . . . The Negro people are going to smack Jim Crow right on the button like Louis hit Braddock."

In "darktown Baltimore" it was like "Christmas Eve in darkest Africa," Alistair Cooke later wrote. Russell Baker heard "a tumult of joyous celebration" coming from the same neighborhood, while Baltimore's whites reacted with "the silence of the tomb." In Americus, Georgia, 136 blacks who'd gathered at Dopey Joe's, a rickety, riverside juke joint and dance hall, jumped for joy. Down went the building, and the celebrants with it, into the creek. Blacks in Lansing, Michigan, went "wildly happy with the greatest celebration of race pride our generation had ever known," recalled one of them, who would later be known as Malcolm X. Only Jack Johnson dissented. "I guess the better man won," he said sourly. Schmeling, he added, could still knock out Louis "seven days a week."

"The cynical philosopher will shake his head at such goings on," the *Norfolk Journal and Guide* said of the festivities. "After all, this celebration was occasioned not by an exhibition of something beautiful like love but by commercialized physical strife, primitive carnage, bloody fighting. But the philosopher is invited to take a running broad jump into the nearest lake by fight fans. For Mr. and Mrs. Colored America, the triumph of Joe Louis in Chicago was something more than just another fight victory for the hero of most Americans, white or black. That win epitomized a struggle for recognition, for achievement against almost impregnable odds of prejudice, injustice, discrimination, disadvantages." To the *California Eagle*, Louis had advanced "into the brightest limelight that can shine upon the head of any public figure except the President."

Louis's victory gave the black press a chance to reflect upon how far race relations had come, and how far they still had to go. "If this same Joe Louis . . . had remained in his native Alabama, no southern governor would have ever known he lived," a black weekly in Oklahoma City said. The *Washington Tribune* lamented that in the nation's capital, the Louis-Braddock fight would have been illegal. Floyd Calvin of the *New York Age* took Walter White to task for having urged black editors to calm down their readers. "That letter should have been sent to white editors, and not colored," he wrote. "The colored people can't do anything but express their joy. It's the white folks who can and do raise sand when they take a notion, win or lose." Louis's victory emboldened his fans. When one radio announcer called him something sounding like a "flat-footed nigger," sixty-four people called to complain. The *Afro-American* saw implications for colonial Africa. "England trembles every time a black man shows prowess against whites, for England rules by sheer psychology," it stated. "Any incident which might send cowed natives in Africa on the war path might become a bloody incident in British history."

The *Courier* noted that whites and blacks listened to the fight together, then discussed it afterward, without any trouble. But in the very same issue, the paper reported that Miami's chief of police had banned films of the fight, citing laws against "Negro entertainment in a theater for white persons" and prohibiting a black man from baring "any part of his body above the knees or below the chest before white people." There were racial disturbances in Durham, North Carolina, New Orleans, and probably many other places that went unrecorded. The black newspaper in Durham chastised some local blacks for their "utter lack of restraint" following the fight. "An inferiority complex, born in the days of slavery, inevitably arouses, among the untutored, a fierce exultation in the triumph of a race representative," it explained. "Driven by jealousy and the 'Can't Take It' mood," the *Louisiana Weekly* reported, whites in two New Orleans neighborhoods set upon black passersby and trolley passengers. There was also violence between young black and white women at a reform school in Washington, D.C. A newspaper in Columbus, Georgia, urged that mixed bouts, still criminal throughout the South, be banned everywhere for fomenting race hatred.

The *Daily Worker*, which had agitated tirelessly against baseball's color line, got fresh inspiration from Louis's victory. The black press made the same point, on strictly economic grounds. Even in bad times boxing was booming, thanks to black boxers and fans; baseball could be, too, but "there are none so blind as those who will not see." The white South accepted the new black champion, though with some misgivings. The *Birmingham News* saluted his "quiet, inoffensive personality," but noted that "Joe Louis won't duplicate his feat of knocking out Jim Braddock on Birmingham theater screens"; the local federal prosecutor threatened to indict anyone showing fight films. Such films were shown in Nashville at three theaters, two black and one white. That was a far cry from the Louis-Schmeling films, which appeared at numerous white theaters. Fleischer contended that even where fight films were shown, the bloodiest footage was omitted to prevent race riots.

Louis's relatives in Alabama walked four miles into the black community of "Powder Town" to listen around two radios belonging to one of Louis's aunts. Afterward, a thousand people danced in the streets. Two days later, Louis's family had something else to celebrate: Louis's father, Monroe Barrow, long assumed dead, miraculously resurfaced at the Searcy State Hospital for the Negro Insane in Mount Vernon, Alabama. Within a few days, a reporter from Chicago ventured there, and described "an old, sad-eyed, gray-pated Negro" poring over pictures of the Braddock fight. "My little Joe the heavyweight champion of the world?" the old man said. "I can hardly believe it. Say, it must be all of twenty years or more since I last saw my Joe. He was a husky baby, all right. And now he's the greatest fighter in the world. Well, well, well." Again, he grabbed the pictures and studied them more closely. "He looks more like his mother, I think," he added. "But here, doesn't he look something like me, too? Gee, I'd like to see him now." The superintendent of the hospital promptly asked Louis for money; to those who could afford it, the institution charged $30 a month. Louis pledged that once he confirmed the man's identity he'd be happy to oblige.

The *Montgomery Advertiser* promptly followed up, and did a bit of math. Monroe Barrow, who suffered from "dementia praecox of the recurring type"—schizophrenia—had been institutionalized since 1912, but Joe Louis had been born in 1914. The hospital's records explained the discrepancy: "In his earlier manhood," the paper revealed, Monroe Barrow "demonstrated an annoying propensity for escaping. Nostalgia invariably led him back to home and family. One such unauthorized leave lasted two years; ladies and gentlemen, the heavyweight champion of the world—Joe Louis." A writer in the *Norfolk Journal and Guide* saw in Barrow's sudden emergence an effort by embittered whites to pull Louis off his pedestal, and faulted the black press for playing along. But he praised Louis for embracing the old man rather than running away from him. In fact, Monroe Barrow died within a year and a half, and Louis apparently never met him.

The day after the fight, Mike Jacobs suggested that Louis would defend his title four times a year. "If he rests too long, he gets fat and lazy," he explained. That prospect excited some black fans and offended others, who sensed a double standard at work. "If white champions can loaf two or three years without risking loss of the title, why should Joe Louis defend his title more than twice a year?" the *Courier* asked. And then there was the question of whom he would fight. Despite all the "white hope" campaigns, there was really only one white hope: Schmeling. Everyone agreed that a Louis-Schmeling rematch would be, as Davis Walsh put it, "as natural as young love." And Schmeling wasn't getting any younger; in

September he'd be thirty-two years old. Using Fleischer as his emissary, Jacobs tried to entice Schmeling into a fight that fall. The boxing commission also weighed in. But Schmeling was still steaming, or holding out for more money. He "merely wanted Rockefeller Center, 51 percent of Andy Mellon's fortune, and a first mortgage on the Ford plant," one black paper wisecracked.

In fact, Schmeling, and the Nazis, had different plans. Following Goebbels's instructions, the German press wrote little about the fight.* One paper ran a large head shot of Louis. "That's What America's Boxing World Champion Looks Like," it said. "The Yankees, greedy for money, let the sport go down the drain," it explained. The 12 *Uhr-Blatt* devoted almost its entire front page to boxing, but Louis wasn't the headliner; the continent was. "Europe Steps In," it announced. "Louis the Victor—But Schmeling World Champion!" "June 22 will remain the darkest day in the long history of American boxing," it declared, a day when gangsters and world Jewry had crowned a heavyweight champion. Schmeling, who had now been elevated to "the greatest boxer the world has ever known," would meet not Louis but Tommy Farr for the real world championship.

Whether in German eyes the fight would be for an open title or would be Schmeling's first title defense was never entirely clear; in any case, it would be a "historic event." "We will box in September in one of London's great open-air arenas!" Schmeling excitedly told the *Angriff*, for the largest purse in British history. The British, too, had signed on; everywhere except New York, the *Daily Mail* reported, the Schmeling-Farr match would be seen as a title fight. For the Nazis and for Schmeling, their plan was meant to strike a blow for honor and idealism. The *Angriff* said that Germany had had enough of American crookedness, and would now have its own world championship, one recognized by everyone placing sports above dollars. Having helped engineer the Schmeling-Farr title fight, the Nazi regime placed considerable resources behind it. Hitler met with Schmeling on June 29, and told him that German fans should be encouraged to attend, even though that would again mean easing

---

*Box-Sport's foreign stringers were predictably unimpressed with footage of it, which Germans once again could not see for themselves. "One leaves the theater a little ashamed that something like that is called 'sport,'" its man in Basel reported. In Katowitz, only Louis's glass chin was deemed newsworthy. In Argentina, only blacks went to watch. Schmeling himself had to go to Switzerland to study the films. "I see no improvement in Louis," he said afterward.

German currency regulations. "The Schmeling fight against the Englishman, Farr, should be presented as a 'world championship fight,'" Goebbels instructed the German press. "Coverage not only in sports section!" By government fiat, then, sports had become too important for the sports pages. Now it was officially impossible for Schmeling to be "just a sportsman."

The maneuvers in Berlin and London quite naturally met with scorn in New York. The *Daily Worker* called the proposed fight "the sour-grapes edition" of the heavyweight championship. Pegler again expressed amazement over how enmeshed with boxing the Nazis had become. "The Reich is the first state in the world so hard up for honors as to regard the title as a valuable national asset," he wrote. But the Germans were about to get a real lesson in Realpolitik. First, the New York boxing commission ruled that as long as he offered to fight Schmeling first, Louis was in fact champion. Then Mike Jacobs set about to scuttle the "European championship." He briefly considered having Louis fight in London immediately before the Schmeling-Farr contest simply to steal its thunder. But it was easier just to steal Farr. Which he promptly did, by doubling what the Germans had offered him.

Goebbels now had to make a hasty, humiliating about-face. "Nothing should be carried about the reports in the English press that the boxer, Farr, doesn't want to appear against Schmeling," he told the German media. Farr now got the Braddock treatment in German newspapers; he, too, was a coward and a money-grubber. German publications could acknowledge the Louis-Farr fight, but only buried deep inside; to play it any more prominently than that "would amount to a lack of self-respect." "One beaten by Schmeling against one who chickened out of a fight against Schmeling—a 'fine' fight for the title!" one Berlin paper complained.

The Louis-Farr fight was set for August 30. Jacobs kept it in New York, despite his puzzling complaint that Harlem's fans did not come through for Louis at the box office. As Jacobs saw it, delaying the Schmeling rematch only helped; the public could savor the fight longer, the boycott fervor might subside, and Schmeling would be even older and less likely to win. "Promoter Jacobs' plans call for stalling Max until next Summer when he'll be so rusty all the erl in Oklahoma won't enable him to get in shape for Louis," Parker surmised. "The longer they postpone the fight, the better it'll be for Schmeling," Joe Jacobs countered. "Two years from now, Louis won't be a fighter at all. He'll be through."

Louis did appear to be wearying. Blackburn claimed he was still three years from his prime, but Louis himself said he wanted to quit once he'd beaten Schmeling, and go back to school. One visitor to Pompton Lakes, where Louis was training for Farr, understood why. As Louis tried to read a newspaper, scores of people "with mouths wide open and eyes pop-eyed" stared at him "with an intensity worthy of the most fanatical Nazis." "Can you blame the man for wanting a little peace and freedom?" the reporter asked. The time had finally come to determine when Schmeling and Louis would get back into a ring together, which made Schmeling's departure for New York on August 11 front-page news in Germany. By now, Schmeling's frequent transatlantic crossings had become a joke; he was threatening "the back and forth record now jointly held by Larch-mont Doakes, motorman of the Times Square shuttle, and Hemingway Forsythe, jai-alai champion of Bronxville," a paper for German émigrés in New York joked. "In Germany they call me the champion," Schmeling told reporters upon his arrival. "Dot is not so—only morally. Louis is the champion. He won the title from Braddock. Now I want my chance." He said he'd seen the fight pictures, and "if poor old Chim can knock down Louis, I can. I don't think he has improved, this Louis." When someone suggested that he might not get his shot until June, Schmeling "laughed with all the cheery good humor of a spoon tinkling in a medicine glass," wrote Bob Considine. But the passage of time did not scare him. "Not having the championship keeps me young," Schmeling insisted.

A few days later Schmeling visited Louis in Pompton Lakes. The two performed for the photographers, first around a pool table, then with Schmeling quite literally whispering nothings in Louis's ear. One black paper detected "a clear dislike" between them. Schmeling never took his eyes off Louis in the ring, and afterward he was beaming, ostensibly because he'd picked up yet another flaw. Someone asked Schmeling if Farr had a prayer against the Bomber. "Everybody has a chance," Schmeling replied. "Even Shirley Temple." On August 26, Schmeling had another contentious encounter with the boxing commissioners. Then he feasted on movies as rain forced a four-day postponement of the Farr fight. When Louis and Farr finally squared off in Yankee Stadium, the police presence was sparse; Louis had made interracial fights routine. To Consi-dine, the applause for Schmeling was clear evidence that the boxing public "would tolerate no further gypping of the German." "If that sponta-neous demonstration for Maxie is the off-shoot of a 'boycott,' then I wish someone would boycott me," Parker wrote.

The fight was dull, at least for Louis's fans. Louis bloodied the Welshman but could not put him away, partly because he'd hurt his hand early on. Spoiled and fickle, the mob once more turned on Louis. When the decision for him was announced, boos resounded throughout the stadium. While five thousand men and women in Farr's hometown lit a bonfire for his moral victory, Harlem was bewildered and gloomy. "He iss not more the same Louis," said Schmeling. His greatest fear, he said, was that someone else would get a shot at Louis's title before he did. Braddock said he'd have beaten Louis that night, too. So, too, did Baer. The press pummeled Louis far worse than Farr did. "Joe Louis lost everything but his heavyweight title last night at the Yankee Stadium," the *Herald Tribune* reported. "His footwork is atrocious; his headwork, nil," Jimmy Powers wrote in the *Daily News*. When Louis and Schmeling met up again, *Ring* predicted, the German would win in five rounds. Even Louis's greatest backers despaired. With a punch that "would hardly knock over a pillar of thread spools," Farr had made Louis "look dumb, timid and futile," wrote Parker. "Never a mental giant, Joe was the personification of stupidity in this fight. He couldn't think his way out of a subway turnstile. Schmeling would have slaughtered him." Maybe it was time to reassess Louis altogether. "The Alabama-born darky was rushed to the front at a time when the field was unbelievably bad," wrote Harry Grayson in the *World-Telegram*. "Through the medium of a string of stumblebums he was built up as a Dark Destroyer."*

Following its marching orders, the Nazi press downplayed the fight. "Bomber Without Bombs" was how the *Reichssportblatt* summarized it. AND THEY CALL THAT A WORLD CHAMPIONSHIP! read a Hamburg headline. The comparatively low attendance, thirty-five thousand, was a triumph of a different sort, proof that Americans hadn't been hoodwinked by a bogus title bout. The *Daily Worker* was more sympathetic. Criticizing Louis's performance, it said, could only be compared to faulting Babe Ruth for hitting merely a single, two doubles, and a triple. The *Defender*'s Al Monroe was also steadfast. "Instead of the milling, man-eating panther of old, the champion was a steady, plodding fighting machine," he wrote. "He was a boxer with a purpose and not a killer seeking blood." Some marveled at Louis's fair-weather fans. "If he knocks his man out in a jiffy,

---

*Grayson's use of "darky" brought a complaint from Walter White. "We note that you at no time have referred to Bob Pastor as 'Kike' or 'Sheeny'; to Jim Braddock as a 'Mick'; to Lou Ambers as a 'wop,'" he wrote the paper.

they call his opponent a set-up," Fleischer complained. "If he fails to score a knockdown, he is dubbed a phoney [sic] and when the fans find his opponent on his feet at the end of the bout . . . then 'bum' is the title given him."

Black writers saw jealousy and frustration in the criticism: Louis had annoyed white reporters who preferred short fights and long evenings at the nightspots, the *Defender* claimed. Feeding black anger was what many considered Clem McCarthy's biased play-by-play, which left some thinking Farr either had won or should have. "It would be better for the fight game, racial and international understanding, if Clem never broadcast another fight," the *Amsterdam News* griped. Both NBC and Mike Jacobs got numerous complaints, the network for bias, the promoter for rigging the fight. "You done me half a million dollars' damage! I'm getting these squawks by the basketful!" Jacobs shouted at McCarthy when he ventured into the Hippodrome. The promoter threatened to end fight broadcasts if such a thing ever happened again.

But most commentators, black and white alike, agreed on one thing: Louis had, of all things, turned dull. "Too much teaching" had spoiled him, one black paper lamented; he should unload everything drilled into him in the past year and go back to his old self. By scrutinizing him too closely and correcting mistakes before they were made, Louis's trainers "had taken the glamour away from the colored boy," wrote French Lane of the *Chicago Tribune*. Lane described how, during a recent visit to a local racetrack, Louis had been all but invisible. "It was a perfect spot for a celebrity to strut his stuff," he wrote. "Imagine Gable, Ruth or Dempsey in a similar situation." Unless a showman like Billy Rose were soon added to Louis's bloated entourage of lawyers, doctors, schoolteachers, and etiquette instructors, Lane warned, people wouldn't know "whether he is Joe Louis or Rufus Rastus Johnson Brown." Louis would soon replenish his pizzazz a bit; in October he would head for Hollywood to star in a semi-autobiographical film called *Spirit of Youth*. But it would feature an all-black cast and have only limited distribution. And it wouldn't improve his fighting.

The day after the Farr bout, the Anti-Nazi League announced a boycott of all future Schmeling fights. But it all looked moot, at least for a while. Doctors diagnosed some badly bruised muscles and tendons around Louis's knuckles, and prescribed two to six months of rest. To some, it was the same old dodge as Braddock's arthritic pinkie. "Champions often come up with broken bones which require months to heal when they are confronted with professional and economic problems," noted Pegler, who pointed to the tax advantages of delaying the fight until 1938. Besides, he asked, why would "such a mediocre fighter" be in a hurry to get back in the ring? The 12 *Uhr-Blatt* called it "bad stage management" and "disgraceful theater." Mike Jacobs said he'd given up on a Louis-Schmeling rematch anyway, and would hold an elimination tournament to decide Louis's next opponent. That angered Parker. Schmeling was an unsympathetic ingrate, he wrote, but basic American fair play demanded no more runarounds. In the end, though, both Jacobs and Schmeling had too much to gain from a Louis-Schmeling rematch to put it off much longer. On September 3, as hordes of reporters awaited word at the Hippodrome, the players finally struck a deal. The fight would be in June 1938. Schmeling would get 20 percent of the gate, Louis 40 percent. It would probably be held in New York, but if a boycott pushed it elsewhere, Jacobs could live with it, given all the alternatives. "They'll be in a line, from here to San Francisco," he predicted. Throughout the negotiations between Uncle Mike and Schmeling, Joe Jacobs was literally left outside. "You could see them breaking Joe's heart," another fight manager later recalled.

Louis was pleased at the news. "That's the best thing I've ever heard you say yet!" he told Mike Jacobs. Schmeling, who left immediately for Germany, also expressed satisfaction. "I do not think I will get what you call the run-around any more," he said. The deal had been closed, *Box-Sport* maintained, thanks to Schmeling's magnanimity; by accepting the lower percentage, he'd "placed the sport above the money." Only Hellmis expressed bitterness. Unscrupulous American promoters, he complained, had made Schmeling endure nine Atlantic crossings to get what he deserved. Even now, he warned, one should have no illusions about what had just been signed; the Americans would break this contract, too, if "any other opponent for the glorious 'world champion'" could be found.

Having stalled Schmeling for so long, Mike Jacobs and his people might now think him too old to win, Hellmis went on. "In this regard, the gentlemen are fooling themselves. When the bell rings next year in New York, I wouldn't want to be stuck in the skin of Joe Louis from Detroit, not even for a million."

CHAPTER 11

The Rematch Becomes Reality

THE INTRIGUE AND THE POLITICKING were finally over. For both men, there was little to do now but wait, stay in shape, offend no one. For Louis, this was relatively straightforward; there would be a period to heal, a few safe fights, and some harmless activities to keep him in the public eye. He toured with his softball team, for instance, though even this could be hazardous, and not just while playing first base; in Philadelphia that September, frenzied fans practically overran him.

Politically, Europe was inching toward war. Civil war was already raging in Spain, where Hitler and Mussolini were helping the fascists of Francisco Franco overthrow the Spanish Republic. The noose was tightening around Germany's Jews, as the Nazis, bent at this point on merely driving them out of the country, progressively deprived them of their rights and livelihoods. Of all this, Louis could remain blithely ignorant. His very success was enough of a political statement, and he rarely strayed beyond that. He campaigned briefly for Franklin Roosevelt once, but neglected to mention his name and forgot the place where he was delighted to be.

For Schmeling, the situation was much more complicated. Even routine tune-ups in New York would bring out protesters. Placating Hitler, Goebbels, Mike Jacobs, and the American public simultaneously was not easy. His every move—including his visit on September 12 to the annual Nazi Party congress in Nuremberg—would be noted in the American press. Two weeks later, in top hat and morning coat, he was present when Hitler greeted Mussolini in Munich. Knowing of Il Duce's appreciation for beautiful women, Leni Riefenstahl arranged to have four hundred German actresses on hand for him. But Schmeling threw off her calculations; a "bevy of the comeliest stars" gathered around him instead. Not long afterward, the capo of German boxing, Franz Metzner, urged the authorities to reward Schmeling's loyalty by granting his request for a tax break. "Schmeling has suffered extraordinary financial losses," he noted, pointing to his repeated trips to the United States, because he had "always stood up for his Germanness and the Third Reich, and has never made even the slightest negative remark about Germany"; had he done so, "he would no doubt have come into countless fights and [a great deal of] money in America." Whether or not he got that break, Schmeling was able to buy a large estate—"as big as Central Park," Machon said—in the Pomeranian town of Ponickel, ninety miles northeast of Berlin. It was adjacent to a nature preserve, where he could hunt eleven months of the year. Schmeling later said that he'd have left Germany had the Nazis not effectively held Anny Ondra hostage, refusing to let her travel with him. Whether or not that was true, investing in so substantial a property suggests he was only digging in.

In October, he began casting about for someone to box. "To find an opponent for Schmeling is not especially easy," the *Angriff* said. "In the entire world there is hardly a man who would have a chance." Unlike lighter fighters, Hellmis wrote reassuringly, heavyweights seemed to improve with age; Schmeling would most likely win back the title in 1938, at the age of thirty-three. Schmeling elected to fight the South African Ben Foord in Germany in January; Mike Jacobs spread before him and Joe Jacobs a smorgasbord of five American possibilities to take on in New York before that. Yussel's choice was a young Minnesotan named Harry Thomas, whom the Nazi press instantly attempted to elevate beyond cannon fodder. News of the fight appeared on front pages throughout Germany. The Nazis were less happy when *Ring* placed Louis atop Schmeling in its annual ratings. The *12 Uhr-Blatt* suggested that Germany produce rankings of its own.

In early November, Schmeling again left Berlin for Bremerhaven and New York, this time for a genuine, guaranteed fight. Eighteen months had passed since he'd last been in a ring, and he needed work badly. With this in mind, he insisted that the Thomas fight, set for December 13, be fifteen rounds rather than ten or twelve. *Box-Sport* described how he was received "with open arms and with joy" in New York, speculating that it reflected renewed affection for Schmeling and disillusionment with Louis. Mike Jacobs, it said, knew that Schmeling was his greatest draw. As for Joe Jacobs, who needed him? "Has Schmeling not proven through his business negotiations here that he, himself, is the best manager he's ever had?" *Box-Sport* asked.

Of course, the reception wasn't quite so rosy. Four days after Schmeling arrived, the Anti-Nazi League announced that picketers would march outside the Hippodrome and Madison Square Garden for the next four weeks, urging fans to steer clear of the Thomas fight. One of their signs contained a grotesque caricature of Hitler, whose arms and legs jerked wildly when you yanked a string. The boycott, which Jacobs had so handily turned to his own advantage earlier in the year, was now a real problem for him, and in a letter to Samuel Untermyer he pleaded for fairness. The Thomas bout, he explained, was really only training for the Louis fight—Schmeling would earn just $30,000 from it—and by matching Louis with Schmeling, he was merely meeting public demand. Besides, Schmeling had led a clean and exemplary life, and it would be unsporting to deny him a title shot because of his nationality. Untermyer wasn't persuaded. "The League is not willing to feed the treasury of the German Government—even to a minor extent," he replied.

His patience worn thin by picketers on the sidewalk beneath his window, Jacobs threatened to move the Louis-Schmeling fight to Philadelphia or Chicago, or sell it to the Germans for $750,000. Meantime, tickets for the Thomas fight, at least in the better seats, were selling slowly. As Schmeling contended with hostility in New York, he also faced a civil war in his own camp. Joe Jacobs and Max Machon had always been an odd couple, and their rivalry had only intensified as Schmeling marginalized Jacobs and Machon's influence grew. Now, some German Americans whispered to Machon that Thomas was not quite the pushover Jacobs said he was. With Schmeling paying Jacobs a pittance and Thomas managed by one of Joe's friends, Jacobs's loyalties were suddenly questionable. Here, then, was another Jewish conspiracy, and Schmeling believed it. "They do not want me to have easy fights," he told Jimmy Cannon. "Joe Jacobs and Mike Jacobs do not want me to get ready. They do not want me to knock out Joe Louis again. This is what I think." Machon insisted that Joe Jacobs had been relieved of all of his duties, even at the training camp.

Cannon later caught up with Jacobs, while he was getting a midnight shave from a Broadway barber. Sure, he admitted, he and Machon had been "wrangling endlessly" for control of Schmeling, but this talk of a plot was a joke. "Why should I be angling to have a meal ticket punched?" he asked. "Tell that Machon he's daffy. Listen, I'm the boss of that camp.

I'm running it. I always ran it. I'm still Schmeling's manager. Machon is just the trainer. He does what I tell him. Joe Jacobs is the boss." The rift was serious enough for Mike Jacobs to pay a visit to Schmeling's camp. In fact, were Thomas all that good, more people would have heard of him. Drew Middleton of the Associated Press called him "the willing whetstone for Max Schmeling's dulled ring weapons." Still, whatever Schmeling was doing to Joe Jacobs, Joe Jacobs stood by Schmeling. "I haven't the slightest doubt that, even if Schmeling had him chucked in a concentration camp in the morning, he would continue to talk of him in the awed tones of a schoolboy discussing Babe Ruth," Parker wrote.

On December 12, Louis arrived from Chicago to take in the fight. Had he ventured over to the Hippodrome, he'd have seen the picketers with their placards, accusing Schmeling of helping to bankroll Hitler's wars. Hellmis saw them, and was amused; they were peddling the same old smears. "The passersby smile, if they look at all," he wrote.* Hellmis enthused about Schmeling's high standing with the New York boxing writers, even those of a "particular racial character" for whom "the word 'German' works like a red flag in front of a Spanish bull." He speculated, foolishly, that Mike Jacobs actually hoped Thomas would win, even though it would ruin his million-dollar rematch. Uncharacteristically, he gave Jacobs a chance to defend himself. "We're all fighting for [Schmeling] and his rights," Jacobs declared. "Write that back home, too, after you spent all last summer writing that we're all gangsters."

On the night of December 13, three men and a woman marched in the frigid air along Eighth Avenue as boxing fans filed into the Garden. SCHMELING IS A GERMAN COMMODITY—DO NOT BUY! read their placards, which the woman supplemented with chants: "Don't send money to the mad dog of Europe!" "Schmeling is an agent of Hitler!" Passersby made fun of her, while a policeman nearby smiled indulgently. When Mike Jacobs alighted from a taxi, the protesters immediately surrounded him and shouted, "Jacobs would sell out his own mother!" Inside, by one estimate, German Americans composed 60 percent of the turnout of eighteen thousand. Mike Jacobs looked over the crowd contentedly. "Well, I hope them boycotters don't feel hurt," he said. When Schmeling entered the ring, the crowd greeted him tumultuously. When Braddock was introduced, they jeered. And when Louis was announced—"the champion

---

*In Nuremberg, Julius Streicher took the picketing more seriously: to retaliate, he declared a boycott of local Jewish shops.

who fears no man," Harry Balogh called him—"the crowd almost tore his ear off with a torrent of boos," Joe Williams wrote, though Louis swayed some of his detractors when he shook Schmeling's hand. Schmeling himself got "one of those old Dempsey ovations" when introduced.

Listening to it all, throughout Germany, were those stalwarts who had again managed to stay up, this time until four a.m. As usual, Schmeling's chums gathered at the Roxy-Bar, Hitler's personal photographer, Heinrich Hoffman, among them. Each put up a bottle of champagne, with the person predicting the outcome most accurately collecting the lot. No one picked Schmeling to lose, or even just to win on points. For several rounds Schmeling simply shook off the cobwebs. Then he went to work, knocking down Thomas six times. In the eighth round Thomas was poised to fall yet again when Arthur Donovan called the fight. "Max's rooters rattled the windows with their 'heils,'" the *Daily News* reported. Joe Jacobs vaulted to the nearest microphone. "Schmeling desoives all the credit in the woild, 'specially since he's been out of the ring such a long length of time," he said. For a fighter his age, Trevor Wignall wrote, Schmeling was absolutely remarkable, almost a freak. Coming after Louis's dismal showing against Farr, the match convinced many that they'd watched the next heavyweight champion.

In his dressing room, Schmeling said he felt the long layoff in his bones. That, plus all those Atlantic crossings, had taken their toll; though he believed he could face Louis as he was, he wanted two more tune-ups, a desire that greatly displeased Mike Jacobs. "My nerves are shot," Jacobs complained. "Why doesn't he hide himself until June?" As Jacobs spoke, the German ambassador to Washington, Hans Heinrich Dieckhoff, and the German consul in New York, Hans Borchers, entered. Dieckhoff seized Schmeling's hand, still wrapped with gauze. "Max, you were wonderful!" he exclaimed. They spoke German a bit and then he left, with the ambassador's aide giving a Nazi salute on his way out. The now-customary telegrams from Göring and Goebbels were joined this time by one from Rudolf Hess. Göring conferred on Schmeling the right to hunt a moose, a privilege reserved for VIPs. When Schmeling called Ondra to report his victory, he learned that Hitler had called her first.

Only two years earlier in the same spot, people had watched Schmeling watching Louis for the first time, and thought they saw him blanch. This time, everyone watched Louis watching Schmeling for the first time, at least as a spectator, and thought they saw him squirm and wince. "Emotionally, Louis probably took as much punishment last night as Mr.

Thomas," Joe Williams wrote. Actually, Roxborough, Black, Blackburn, and Louis saw nothing special or terribly alarming. Black said that Schmeling "looked terrible," and that if Louis couldn't knock him out in two rounds "he ought to go back and work for Mr. Ford." Louis, his interest in the fight "contained in a prodigious yawn," agreed; if he couldn't whip him, he said, he never wanted "to see another pair of gloves." Schmeling would encounter a different Louis come June, he said, someone who wouldn't "go messin' roun' in no fog for twelve rounds."

The postmortems were as much about politics as pugilism. Of enormous symbolic concern to all involved was the size of the crowd—the place was sold out—and of the gate: "Some of my friends informed me quite a few Jewish persons were in the crowd and I want to acknowledge my gratitude for their sportsmanship," Schmeling said afterward. As Parker pointed out, there was something bizarre about Jews protesting a fight promoted by a Jew between two boxers with Jewish managers. Any anti-Nazi cause that had lost him was clearly doomed. No longer, he wrote, could Mike Jacobs hide behind the threat of a boycott to protect his hegemony over the heavyweights.

The German coverage was routinely ecstatic. The newspapers were filled with reports of Schmeling's proficiency and Thomas's bravery. "Max Schmeling's popularity, particularly with the Brown Shirts, now knows no bounds," *The New York Times* reported from Berlin. Schmeling was ageless, crowed the *Angriff*, impressing even the Americans; on this evening at least, "he would have knocked out any other heavyweight in the world." But more noteworthy than Schmeling's performance was the blow dealt to the boycotters. "Schmeling Also KO'd the USA Jews," the *8 Uhr-Blatt* proclaimed. "The Agitation Against Schmeling from the Synagogues Has Collapsed." A cartoon on its front page showed one of Schmeling's punches sending Thomas missile-like into the gut of a corpulent, scraggly tycoon labeled "Samuel Untermyer & Co." A similar cartoon was more prophetic, showing an Untermyer-like figure wearing a Star of David on his jacket. The *Völkischer Beobachter* called the fight a great victory for German-American friendship. The calumnies heaped upon Schmeling weren't American at all, but the work of alien, un-American influences, "the circle of Jewish boycott agitators, polluting the entire world." Real Germans and real Americans had so much in common; it was such a shame the Jews in each place had to muck things up.

Boycott organizers tried to put the best face on the situation. They said Jacobs had sold many tickets at reduced prices, and only after pro-Nazi groups had all but ordered their members to go. The fight had actually netted considerably less than what Jacobs had predicted. As for the rousing ovation Schmeling received, it came from "an audience of appreciative storm troopers." Schmeling ended up with only $25,000 for the fight; once Uncle Sam and Uncle Mike were through with him, he would have precious little to show for his labors, and Hitler even less. If it were any consolation to the league, Jacobs himself wasn't satisfied; he hadn't recognized many of the faces at ringside, meaning that the usual Jews weren't there. Again he threatened to move the Louis-Schmeling bout out of New York, and even talked to Schmeling about transplanting it to Berlin. "I'll get rid of all those headaches," he groused. Indeed, like Joe Gould before him, he even contracted a brief case of missionary zeal, informing Schmeling that Germany could have the fight if Hitler stopped discriminating against Jews and Catholics.

Schmeling hastily left for Germany to be home for Christmas. Before departing, he thanked the Americans for their good sportsmanship. Some of those seeing him off raised their arms and shouted "Heil!" as he boarded the ship. But Schmeling kept his hands in his pockets and looked straight ahead as he walked up the gangplank. Thousands cheered him in Bremerhaven, and friends, reporters, and boxing officials, Metzner among them, greeted him when he reached Berlin. Tschammer und Osten saluted Schmeling's victory "not only over a strong opponent but also over the hatred and slander of the eternal enemies of the German nature and of the athletic spirit." A band of storm troopers serenaded Schmeling outside his home and staged a torchlight parade, which Schmeling watched through his window.

His ever more exalted status, and his usefulness to the regime, was apparent from the latest work in the Hellmis oeuvre: a long series on his life in *H.J.: Das Kampfblatt der Hitler-Jugend*, the magazine of the Hitler Youth. In twelve installments over nearly three months, Hellmis retraced Schmeling's career and portrayed him as a regular, hardworking guy, loved and respected by all. This included all Americans—except for the American press, which was riddled with Jews. Torment at Jewish hands was nothing new for Schmeling, Hellmis maintained; "a small clique of sleazy Jewish agitators" had turned Germany against Schmeling in 1930, when he'd won the heavyweight championship. "The great boxer never learned to kiss up to the newspaper Jews," he wrote. "Disgusted by their phony phrases, he had treated them coldly." It marked one of the few times that the German press portrayed Schmeling himself as anti-

Semitic. There's no evidence that this was ever the case; what was significant was the extra degree to which the regime was now casting Schmeling in its image, and its confidence that Schmeling himself would offer no objection. Hellmis told his young readers that among Schmeling's greatest treasures was a photograph of the Führer, inscribed, "To Our German World Champion in Boxing in True Admiration, Adolf Hitler." Schmeling carried it with him at all times, Hellmis said.

"JOE LOUIS HADN'T HUNG UP his 'sock' for Santa Claus," Chester Washington of the *Courier* wrote in his column for Christmas 1937. "He was saving it for Maxie Schmeling next June." Washington's colleague Wendell Smith asked Santa to give Louis something with which he could protect his jaw. The fight was still more than six months off, but the anticipation had begun. Sitting around the Chicken Shack in Detroit, Washington sensed that Louis was angry: his crown still had an asterisk attached. And Louis still considered the German a bad sport for deliberately hitting him after the bell. "I'll show him the next time," he said. That was his only New Year's resolution for 1938.

Various cities were maneuvering to inherit the rematch if Mike Jacobs abandoned New York. Chicago's pitch was spearheaded by one Max Epstein, whose very name would presumably help defeat any boycott. Philadelphia, Cleveland, and Detroit also made bids; a remodeled Briggs Stadium, where the Tigers played baseball, could hold ninety thousand fans. While Schmeling fought himself back into shape, Louis rested his weary hands and found that his marriage had become fodder in the bitter rivalry between two of New York's premier gossip columnists, Walter Winchell and Ed Sullivan. Winchell said that the Louises were "definitely apart"; Sullivan said "a Harlem night club chorine" was responsible. A black weekly reported that the woman in question was a "sepia songstress" at the Plantation Club; another had Louis and Marva planning to break up after the Schmeling fight, with Marva walking off with $200,000 to $250,000. "Wherever she goes, she is the object of all eyes," a friend of Marva complained. "The clothes she wears are torn to pieces by idle tongues which can find nothing else to talk about."

From the beginning, Louis did not seem to feel unduly bound by his wedding vows. But before long, there were very public rebuttals. "Despite all of the upsetting rumors that have caused me so much embarrassment and worry, I will continue to trust the man I married September 24, 1935,"

Marva declared on the front page of the *Courier*. Louis, in turn, called Marva "the sweetest little wife a man ever had" and pledged that after beating Schmeling he would take her to Paris, where she would study dressmaking. Black America would do well to stop all this gossiping, the *Defender* warned; it could cause Louis to quit—win, lose, or draw—after the Schmeling fight. His fans, the paper said, had "meddled and meddled and meddled until they have driven both Joe and his wife to seek a place far away from the multitude, many of which seek to crucify both of them." But the threat was undercut by something Louis said on the very same page. "Will defend my title as long as I keep it and the public demands me to," he announced. "Ten years if necessary." So the couple remained intact, at least for now. Marva even took on a new role, as the *Defender*'s fashion columnist.

Louis, meantime, bowed on the screen when *Spirit of Youth* opened in black movie theaters. He followed the premieres up the eastern seaboard, appearing before thousands of feverish fans in Washington, Baltimore, Philadelphia, and New York. Many couldn't get seats or, even if they did, were too busy staring at the live Louis in the audience to watch the filmed Louis on the screen. That may have been just as well, for the critics, white and black, were not kind about the film, which, with its tale of a young fighter falling for a nightclub actress, breaking training, and giving lip to his managers, sounded too much like 1936 and reportedly had Mike Jacobs squirming in his seat. Louis was a great fighter and a good guy, but as a screen lover he was "a dud, with a capital D," the *Afro-American* declared. But an *Afro* columnist thought most wives would like Louis anyway. "His awkwardness will remind them of their husband and they will feel perfectly at ease," he wrote.

Louis inched his way back into boxing. On January 19 he stopped by Pompton Lakes, where Braddock was training for Tommy Farr. While dozens crowded around Louis, another visitor that day, Joe DiMaggio, was virtually ignored. A week later, Louis himself was training at Pompton Lakes, for a fight on February 23 against a Connecticut heavyweight named Nathan Mann. It was there, remarkably, that Louis watched the films of the Schmeling fight for the first time. A visiting newspaperman had brought it, and after a bit of hesitation, Blackburn consented to let Louis see it. So they pulled the shades, hung a sheet, and relived that fateful night of a year and a half earlier. Louis had not thrown his first three lefts before Blackburn muttered about Louis dropping his arm after every punch and then keeping it in his pocket. They watched the blow in the second that sent Louis spiraling. "I don' 'member nothin' from that punch," Louis said. "Next thing I know I'm on my way to the dressing room and Chappie heah is saying, 'Cover up yo' face.'"

As Louis prepared for Mann, Schmeling readied himself for a bout with Ben Foord, the onetime heavyweight champion of the British Empire, in Hamburg on January 30. For Germany it would be a double celebration: it was Schmeling's first fight on native soil in nearly three years, and the fifth anniversary of the Nazi seizure of power. Schmeling's resurgence, and Germany's, could be marked on the same bill. Goebbels felt it necessary to order the German press to play the anniversary celebration more prominently. An elaborate program had been planned: first would come the marching music, and then, at Goebbels's specific direction, Hitler's speech to the Reichstag. The fight would start as soon as the Führer finished. The Reichstag session was canceled, however; though it was not made public right away, two key generals were purged that day as Hitler consolidated his control over the German army. Instead, the audience had to settle for Metzner, who offered the usual paeans to the Führer. Both Schmeling and Foord were escorted to the ring by a phalanx of SS commandos; each gave the Hitler salute after climbing through the ropes. For half an hour, the crowd dutifully stood up and sat down through all the speeches, chants, and anthems. So swept up in the fervor was one British reporter that he, too, rose, gave the Nazi salute, and sang along. But it was Schmeling's turn to disappoint his fans: though he was clearly superior, he couldn't knock Foord out, settling instead for a decision. Derisive whistles filled the hall. Schmeling removed the laurels placed around his neck and gave them to Foord. The same SS men, resplendent in their black uniforms, then escorted Schmeling out of the ring.

Schmeling professed to be pleased, but others felt let down, partly because Hellmis's call had led people to think that a knockout was near. "One had expected more," Goebbels wrote in his diary. Hitler, too, derived scant satisfaction from Schmeling's victory. "He tirades a lot against America and its scum," Goebbels wrote. "He goes on about America's miserable treatment of Schmeling." Watching the films afterward, though, Goebbels reassessed Schmeling's performance: "Thrilling and dramatic. A truly manly fight," he wrote. With postproduction work done in a "real American" fashion, films of the fight, titled *A Great Victor—A Brave Opponent*, were soon showing all over the Reich. Still, the regime realized it had to maintain a certain distance from Schmeling. Sometime around Christmas 1937, a man had come to Schmeling's apartment in

Berlin to offer him honorary membership in the Brown Shirts. Schmeling ducked the visitor, but afterward told his friend Hans Hinkel, Goebbels's deputy in the propaganda ministry, that if he were to join any Nazi group, it would be the SS. In February, Hinkel asked Heinrich Himmler for his thoughts. Himmler's staff concluded quite correctly that it was a terrible idea, citing German interests abroad, and instructed Hinkel to back off.

Louis was even less impressed than Goebbels had initially been. Baer had knocked out Foord, he noted, and look at what *he* had done to Baer! Old age, he theorized, had finally caught up with Schmeling. "I'm kinda sorry today's fight happened," he said. "Because now, when I belt out Mr. Schmeling in June, people'll say I just licked an old man who couldn't even stop Foord. But I'll get considerable pleasure from knockin' him out anyway." *Ring* marveled that Foord, ranked only thirty-sixth in the world, had lasted so long. "Tab this—Louis over Schmeling, by a knockout when and if," it said. Fearing that Schmeling would embarrass or injure himself, Mike Jacobs ordered him to take on no more warm-up bouts. But Schmeling, who seemed to take pleasure in tweaking Jacobs and ignoring his directives, signed to meet an American heavyweight, Steve Dudas, for a last tune-up on April 16.

Jacobs now went public, sort of, with the offer he'd made Schmeling the previous December: a rematch with Louis in Berlin, but only if Hitler stopped picking on Jews and Catholics. He admitted that it sounded like public relations but insisted he was sincere. Before weighing bids from other cities, he wanted to hear from Berlin. "I only hope that Hitler takes me up on this," he said. "It would really please me." The proposition was fine with Louis, as long as a million dollars, free of German taxes, were deposited in a New York bank beforehand (a personal check from Hitler, payable to Roxborough and Black, would do). Of course, the whole idea was ludicrous. As much as Hitler and Goebbels wanted a heavyweight championship fight in Germany, they wanted the Jews out far more. The anti-Jewish campaign accelerated when Hitler annexed Austria on March 13; in the second half of March alone, seventy-nine Austrian Jews committed suicide. When Hitler staged a "referendum" to ratify the Anschluss, though, Schmeling, along with other German celebrities, lent his support. For him and all friends of boxing, he said in an advertisement in the 12 *Uhr-Blatt*, voting "yes" was a way to thank the Führer for his support of the sport. "Under his leadership, German boxing has earned worldwide recognition," he wrote. "He's interested in everything that happens inside the ropes. So can there be any question at all for us athletes about whether we stand behind him and support him when he needs us?" German newspapers ran photographs of Schmeling and other prominent athletes happily casting their ballots.

Perhaps because a second Louis-Schmeling fight seemed too good to be true, no one quite trusted it to happen. Germans feared that "sportsworld gangsterism" or "World Jewry" would do it in. Some American commentators, meantime, thought Schmeling had deliberately looked bad against Foord to keep Louis from fleeing. There were rumors that, in a further effort to sidetrack Schmeling, Louis would purposely lose to Mann, fight the German as a nontitleholder, then win back the crown. Then there was the question of war in Europe.

Mann hailed from nearby New Haven, and his partisans packed the Garden for the fight on February 23. They cheered him so loudly that Balogh could scarcely complete his introduction, and they booed Louis heartily. "It won't be long tonight," Roxborough told Blackburn. "Joe doesn't like that." Blackburn, in fact, hoped to catch an early train to Chicago, and asked Louis to work fast. Louis knocked Mann out in three rounds—the first time he jabbed Mann in the nose, Donovan, who sensed that Louis was more fired up, as well as more skilled, than he'd previously seen him, heard it crack—and Blackburn made his train. Much would one day be said about how the white press regularly, and degradingly, likened Louis to an animal. But the black weeklies did, too; one described Louis that night as "a snarling, fighting man of the jungle." Bob Considine wrote something in the same vein. Some day, he prophesied, fans would consider the late Joe Louis's victory over one Nathan Mann in February 1938 only a minor event. They would not realize that on that historic night Louis finally let himself be himself. "Sitting there on his dinky little stool . . . his kinky head dropped half-way to his knees, puzzled and hurt by wintry boos that greeted the announcement of his name, the long dormant tiger in Joseph Louis twitched and awakened," he wrote. "The citizens who booed him before the fight the other night will boo him no more," he predicted. "And when Time, which lends glamour to an athlete, goes to work on Louis, our sons will call him 'the greatest fighter who ever lived.'"

Louis had one more chance to sharpen up, against Harry Thomas in Chicago on April 1. The fight was an opportunity for head-to-head comparisons; Schmeling had dispatched the same man in eight rounds only four months earlier. Wary of a Levinsky-like rout, only 10,468 people attended; the meager turnout probably killed any chances Chicago ever had to stage the Louis-Schmeling rematch. One of those watching was

Joe Jacobs. Convinced that Mike Jacobs was still looking for a way out of a second fight, he wanted to be there should Louis come up with any funny stuff—like a claim that he'd fractured his hand. By the middle of the third round, Thomas was so dazed that even before the bell sounded he walked to his corner and sat down, while his manager vaulted into the ring. That, Louis's seconds argued, should have ended the fight then and there. But Thomas stood up and the referee let the fight go on; the fans, he believed, were entitled to a knockout. Louis quickly obliged, in the fifth round. He was asked later what took him so long. "I guess it was too cold," he replied. "Wasn't there a hockey game in the building last night?" Thomas said afterward that Louis hit harder and from more angles than Schmeling; he'd bet his purse that Louis would knock Schmeling out.

Like Foord, Steve Dudas was a setup for Schmeling. "Although it takes long residence in a city to be accepted as one of its own, Steve Dudas, less than a month in Hamburg, will be a Hamburger tonight—when Max Schmeling is done with him," Parker wrote. He fell in six rounds; the only mark on Schmeling's face was one he'd given himself shaving. Schmeling had fulfilled his mission: another poor showing, Hellmis explained, would have given American boxing officials an excuse to put him off yet again. (Of course, in the Nazis' paranoid worldview, Schmeling couldn't be too scary, either—that might give Louis second thoughts.) Schmeling's performance pleased Goebbels. "He really is a brave lad," he wrote after listening to the fight. The next day, Schmeling met Hitler yet again. The film of the fight was soon showing in 160 theaters around the Reich, including sixty in Berlin, but at his forty-ninth birthday party on April 20, Hitler got a personalized screening, with Schmeling narrating. That film was dwarfed, of course, by the premiere of Riefenstahl's film on the Berlin Olympics, which Schmeling and Ondra—along with Hitler, Goebbels, Himmler, Ribbentrop, and Streicher—also attended. A Berlin newspaper now advertised a travel package to the Louis fight (it went for 990 marks, about the price of one of the new Volkswagens soon to roll off the assembly line near Hannover). So did the *Reichssportblatt*. "Schmeling is expecting you!" it declared. If the fight weren't enough, the tour included stops in Atlantic City and Niagara Falls.

The more political conditions deteriorated in Europe, the more fragile the second Louis-Schmeling fight became. Mike Jacobs wanted Schmeling to set sail early, so that he'd be safely ensconced in New York should war break out. One German reporter heard the two Jacobses talking on a transatlantic call, with Mike urging Joe that when he left Germany he should bring Schmeling with him. All the talk of war was "crazy," insisted Yussel; Berlin was more peaceful and quiet than New York. Mike decreed that if Schmeling couldn't come over, Baer would fight Louis in his place. Mike also made inspection tours of Detroit and Chicago; Philadelphia, too, had bid for the fight. The two biggest sports events of 1938—the Louis-Schmeling fight and the race between Seabiscuit and War Admiral—were "as homeless as Orphan Annie," Considine wrote. But on April 26 Jacobs announced that the fight was staying put: he said he felt an obligation to the city of New York. "His main and valid 'obligations' are his convictions that the fight will draw 80,000 people and more than $1,000,000 when held in the Yankee Stadium," one magazine commented. Here, after all, was a fight that needed no ballyhoo; the front pages offered enough. "Boxing's oldest gate gag is trotting out a 'man you love to hate,'" one reporter wrote. "In Schmeling the promoter has one such ready made." "For every customer who stays away to keep from enriching Schmeling there'll be ten who will go to see his block knocked off," Braddock said. Harlem fans were pleased to have the fight in New York, but not in Yankee Stadium. Simply being back in the place, they feared, would traumatize Louis.

Once Jacobs opted for New York, the Anti-Nazi League announced another boycott, though this time with a caveat: it would be dropped if Schmeling agreed to turn over his purse to a fund for refugees from Nazi Germany. The group gave him until May 2 to decide; after that, the picketing would start. But even boycott stalwarts now seemed halfhearted, almost apologetic. A tidal wave of interest, much of it among people who felt about the Nazis just as they did, threatened to sink the movement. Reporters canvassed the garment district and Jacobs Beach to gauge the boycott's prospects. A furrier called Schmeling "a Nazi tool" and said he might have to miss his first title fight in twenty years, but another man said he wanted to see Louis knock Schmeling out. The *Brooklyn Eagle* found a bare majority favoring the boycott. The *World-Telegram* surveyed around the Hippodrome. Boycotting Schmeling was unfair, the consensus ran, and besides, the fight was too good to miss. "Unless Schmeling shows himself an active Nazi propagandist I will patronize him, just as I would a German actor or actress with real talent," one man said.*

In late April, Joe Jacobs returned from Germany. Reports that all German Jews would soon be forced to liquidate their property had thrown

---

*For all those who thought Schmeling was in Hitler's pocket, there were others convinced that if he lost to Louis he faced disgrace or even the hoosegow. After all, one German athlete who'd spoken out against Hitler, the tennis star Baron Gottfried von Cramm, had

them into another panic, but Jacobs presented his usual benign view of things. "Most of the trouble with the Jews over there is caused by the Jews in this country," he declared. The synagogues were still open, he noted; he'd been to one three times in a single day. *Box-Sport*, which rarely acknowledged Jacobs, now made an exception, noting his positive impressions of Germany. But among some American Jews, Jacobs was denounced as never before. "Jacobs said he did not see any concentration camps, but admitted he did not look for them," I. Q. Gross wrote in *The Nation*. "He did not see non-Aryan business men being stripped of all their earning power or Jewish professional men forced to wash the streets on their hands and knees. He wasn't looking for that type of Nazi entertainment. The ears of Yussel, the son of an orthodox Jew, were deaf to any mention of the hundreds of his co-religionists who had committed suicide in the new Great Germany or been reported dead from unknown causes." The Jewish War Veterans were more pointed. "It is unfortunate that such as he must be classed as a Jew," its magazine stated. "Every race has a minority of black sheep, so let's just ignore him."

Mike Jacobs had ordered Schmeling to be in New York by May 12, and Schmeling arranged to arrive several days before that. On May 2, tanned, healthy, and in good spirits, he met with the press in Berlin. Hellmis, the *Angriff* announced, would accompany him to the United States; this time, it seemed, he wouldn't be paying his own way. German newspapers offered free trips to New York to the winners of fight-related contests. The Anti-Nazi League introduced a set of brochures designed to help people "Out-Talk the Nazi Spellbinders." "Weaken Hitler by Boycotting the Louis-Schmeling Fight!" stated the flyers, which claimed that a "cheering squad" of a thousand storm troopers would attend the fight, threatening to make it "the largest Nazi ego-builder of 1938." "No ticket sale, no fight. No fight, no 'Nazi Supremacy' ballyhoo," they stated. Inside were photographs of Schmeling, along with his wife and his mother, smiling with Hitler. "'I never went in for politics'—Max Schmeling," read the caption.

League officials devised tactics to advance the cause, like having "six attractive women" leafleting in front of Madison Square Garden, the Century Club, and the New York Athletic Club. By May 6, ten women

---

already been arrested, his homosexuality providing the Nazis with a convenient pretext. Some American athletes, like Don Budge and Joe DiMaggio, criticized the arrest of Cramm, runner-up at Wimbledon in 1935, 1936, and 1937, but Schmeling defended it. "It's too bad, but there was nothing else for the police to do," he said.

were in front of the Hippodrome and Mike Jacobs's ticket offices on West Forty-ninth Street. One of Jacobs's minions watched the picketers from a window upstairs. "Those folks are crazy," he said. "Joe Louis will knock Schmeling as flat as a German pancake, and what will Herr Hitler do then, poor thing? His shining knight in Nazi armor chopped into mincemeat by a Negro! That's something these anti-Nazis are overlooking." To Mike Jacobs, too, such campaigns made no sense, given how they only inflamed Nazi anti-Semitism. "Every time these boycotts get under way over here those guys over there take it out on the Jews, who can't protect themselves at any time," he said.

The protest generated little sympathy in the New York newspapers. Once again, the *Herald Tribune* called it "silly." "Herr Schmeling may be a Nazi. He probably is," wrote John Kieran in the *Times*. "But over here Schmeling is just a prizefighter when in the ring and a quiet, inoffensive foreigner outside the ropes." Reader reaction to that piece was strong enough, however, for Kieran to hand over his space one day to a Jewish dissenter, who argued that Americans should not patronize a representative of a repressive regime whose earnings subsidized the whips used to humiliate Jews. Kieran stuck to his guns. "A representative of a government?" he wrote. "Come, come, good people! If Shufflin' Joe Louis fought in London, would he be a representative of the government of the United States? To link a prizefighter with a political program, or to view a prizefighter as the official standard-bearer of a race, a creed or a nation still seems to this observer to verge on the fantastic." *Times* readers backed Kieran with gusto. Maybe, one wrote, the Yankees should sell Joe DiMaggio to protest Italy's invasion of Ethiopia, or boycott Lou Gehrig because his forbears were German.

On May 9, Schmeling's ship steamed into New York Harbor. Near the Statue of Liberty it took on the usual boatful of writers and photographers. The newsreel men set up on the main deck. Schmeling first closeted himself with the Jacobses; then, over the traditional German beer and sandwiches, he took questions in his suite. Immaculate in a single-breasted worsted suit, with only a few stray gray hairs on the back of his head, he told the reporters he felt good; he'd now fought three times in the last six months. Asked whether he'd knock out Louis again, Schmeling replied, "I didn't make this trip for fun." "How is it already, the gate?" he asked at one point, before adding that the money didn't really matter. Joe Jacobs — hovering around Schmeling "like a blue mountain in a Maxfield Parrish painting," as Parker put it — then swung into action, seeking to tamp down any notion that Schmeling was in line for some top Nazi post overseeing German youth were he to win. "This is—how you say?—'noose' to me," Schmeling said. The press conference over, the entourage headed up to the sun deck so that the cameras could capture what Hellmis called the "most photographed head in the world of sports."*

At customs, Schmeling faced the usual interrogation, half official, half playful. As Hellmis heard it, an official joked that it was forbidden to punch any honorable citizens of the United States, but concluded, "Here's your stamp, my good young man. Go now and knock that nigger out, good and clean, understood?" An American reporter, by contrast, heard the official ask Schmeling why he needed a visa for three months, since the fight was barely a month away. "You won't need six weeks to recuperate," the official said, before giving Schmeling two months instead. As several hundred admirers awaited him, Schmeling walked down the gangplank and hopped into a cab. A photographer from one of the black papers ran breathlessly alongside the car, begging for a picture, and Schmeling ordered the driver to stop. "You see, he's a Negro," he explained. The press then followed Schmeling to the Essex House, where he again held court. "Louis may not even know it himself, but he'll always be afraid of me, down deep inside," he said. Louis had now had two years to ponder the last fight, Schmeling explained, and they had taken their toll. "That is the psychological aftermath," he said. "This is especially so in a man of Joe's race."

Many years later, Schmeling wrote that as the ship pulled into New York that day, people screamed abuse and carried signs calling him "an Aryan Show Horse" and representative of the "master race"; the police, he recalled, had been forced to escort him through an angry mob and take him via the backstreets to his hotel, where more picketers awaited him. On Broadway or Fifth Avenue, he went on, people taunted him with upraised arms, and he received "thousands" of hate letters. "In small groups I would try to explain—to no avail—that I would hardly have Joe Jacobs as my manager if I were a Nazi," he was to write. But writing at the time, *Box-Sport* described a very different reception, one that was "completely heartfelt and friendly." "The general public opinion is for Schme-

---

*A "Tijuana Bible"—one of the small, pornographic booklets popular during the era—offered a more fanciful view of Schmeling's trip to New York, and his arrival there. It depicted some rich hussy seducing "Max Smellin" aboard the *Bremen*; during passionate—and very graphic—lovemaking, "Smellin" throws out his back, and by the time he lands in the United States, he is hobbling around on crutches. "Maxie vot der hell iss. . . . ?" a flabbergasted friend exclaims upon seeing the incapacitated German. "Ach!" "Smellin" replies. "I tell you I vass fowled by a sea gull!"

ling," it wrote. That wasn't true either, of course. At the same time, none of the Americans following Schmeling that day reported anything approaching the hostility he later described. But there were picketers outside Schmeling's hotel, and though Hellmis insisted that they didn't rattle Schmeling, they left Hellmis himself indignant. "The contents of the flyers are too stupid to describe in detail," he wrote.

Three days after Schmeling's arrival, at eight in the morning, a thousand people greeted Louis when the Commodore Vanderbilt pulled in to Grand Central. He sported a wisp of a starter mustache, a green sports coat, a green sweater, and fawn-colored pants. He seemed poised and nonchalant, a far cry from the shy young man who had stepped off the train in the same spot only three years earlier. At 209 pounds, he was 9 pounds above his optimal weight. "All I have to do will be to cut down on my ice cream," he said. This time, he'd left his golf clubs at home. Someone mentioned Schmeling's claim that Louis couldn't shake off his fear of him. "When I get in the ring with S'mellin' I'll shake it off onto him," he replied. Louis would not pick a round, but insisted the fight would end fast. "You can bet all de money you got the fight ain'ta gonna last as long as the other," he said. "Either me or him will drop early. They ain't gonna be no decision. All the judges can stay home that night."

Later that day, Louis and Schmeling made their way downtown for a "signing ceremony" at the boxing commission. Shortly after Schmeling entered Louis walked over to him. "Hah'ya, Max," he said. Schmeling seemed taken aback, but quickly recovered. "How are you, Joe?" he replied. "You look goot! How you feel, goot?" Louis took a step back, and lowered his eyes. "Fine. I feel fine. You look good, too." The two then sat down to sign something. "Joe, we want two words from you," one of the cameramen asked. "Hel-lo," Louis replied. Then the two men shook hands, exchanged platitudes, and shook hands again. "Louis handed him what must have felt like a large damp herring which Max seized, squeezed, and shook it hard enough to set up a movement in Joe's chubby cheeks," wrote Considine. Louis just gazed at the door, his expression unchanging. Once the cameras stopped rolling, the two fighters separated, in such a way, Considine wrote, "as you would if a friendly-looking fellow came up, began shaking your hand and said 'I'm Joe Doakes—the leper.' "

Hellmis saw it as a pleasant affair, in which Schmeling was greeted with loud cheers. He continued to insist that Schmeling was more popular than ever in the United States, received warmly wherever he went. (The only discordant note came when the boxing commission, citing the latest of Joe Jacobs's infractions—apparently letting another of his fighters, "Two Ton" Tony Galento, be photographed with a beer mug in one hand and a cigar in the other—said it would not renew his licenses as a manager or second. This meant that, once again, he would not be in Schmeling's corner the night of the fight. If this had happened in Germany, Jacobs shrieked, people would have cried anti-Semitism!) For Hellmis, these were busy days indeed: he was now writing simultaneously for the *Angriff,* the *Völkischer Beobachter,* the *Reichssportblatt,* the *8 Uhr-Blatt, Box-Sport,* and other publications, typing frantically in order to get his dispatches to the *Bremen* before it set sail. At first blush, his role as a one-man cheering squad reflected how amateurish, at least at this stage, the publicity machine of mighty Nazi Germany could be; alternatively, it illustrated how little attention the German press generally gave to sports. All this writing required Hellmis to recycle some information, like the fact that Schmeling carried that autographed picture of Hitler wherever he went. This trip, it turned out, was no exception. "His eyes shine in proud delight when he has a chance to show it to a friend," Hellmis wrote.

After the "signing," the fighters went their separate ways. Louis headed north to Lafayetteville, the village he'd gone to before the first Schmeling fight, to work out and split logs until his friend Henry Armstrong, training to fight Barney Ross for the welterweight title (one of three that Armstrong, the second most famous black fighter of his day, once held simultaneously) on May 31, cleared out of Pompton Lakes. Schmeling hopped aboard the Upstate Special, the train bound north for Speculator. When he stepped off in Amsterdam, an old factory town an hour southwest of his training camp, five thousand people awaited him.

The political pressure finally got to Mike Jacobs, who announced via a letter to President Roosevelt that he would donate 10 percent of his net profits from the fight to European refugees. Apart from the antilynching button he had once bought at a Louis camp, people were hard pressed to cite any previous philanthropy from him. The actual donation would be small change, probably around $7,500, but to the boycotters it was a blow, promising to deprive them of whatever breeze remained in their sails. "A master stroke of diplomatic strategy," the *World-Telegram* called Jacobs's maneuver. The German press was ordered to ignore the gesture, which Goebbels assailed in his diary. "Jews are once again trying to sabotage the Schmeling fight by giving the surplus . . . to German emigrants," he wrote on May 18. "They want to prevent him from fighting at all. But the Führer determines that Schmeling is to fight."

CHAPTER 12

Pompton Lakes and Speculator

JOE LOUIS WAS AT THE GARDEN BOWL in Long Island City on May 31, three weeks short of his date with Schmeling, when Henry Armstrong fought Barney Ross for the welterweight crown. Twenty-six thousand people showed up, a disappointing crowd, but the explanation was simple: even a fight pitting the dazzlingly fast Armstrong against the Jewish Ross in New York was overshadowed by Louis and Schmeling. "The world heavyweight championship is making all other events kaputt," Hellmis wrote.

Louis was not just a spectator that night, but a student. Armstrong's trainer, Eddie Mead, told Roxborough, Black, and Blackburn that it was silly to have Louis box—that is, rely on tactics and finesse—when he was the greatest puncher in the game, and fighting an old man to boot. They should let him go out and slug away from the opening bell, just as Armstrong, a master of perpetual motion, always did. So this is what Louis was studying, just as he had at Armstrong's training camp. One reporter speculated that Louis's brain trust was contemplating how such a "tornadic" start would affect the cool, calculating German.

"Last time Chappie f'ot jus' the' way Schmelin' wanted him to," Blackburn said after Armstrong won. "This time, it'll be different. Chappie's going to learn from Armstrong. He's going to set a fast pace right from the start, work inside Schmelin's defense and batter away at his body. Schmelin' ain't goin' to stan' up long under that pace and that poundin'. He'll start cavin' in after three or fo' roun's, then Chappie'll git down to real business and finish him." Not everyone was so sure. Fans debated whether Louis needed to change his style to beat Schmeling, whether he had the intelligence to understand what that change should be, and, even if he did, whether he remained too haunted by the last fight to pull it off.

Once again word went out, largely through the black press, that the routine in Pompton Lakes was all business. Louis studied hard, seldom left camp, played no golf, went to bed early. Marva kept a safe distance, as she had all year; the *Afro-American* calculated that out of 173 elapsed days in 1938, the Louises had been together "only about sixty-six" of them. One reporter saw flashy white women turned away from the camp; Louis, someone said, was harder to get to than the president of the United States. No one was taking any chances on anything. Amid fears that he would injure a finger, Louis was even forbidden to catch a baseball.

There were huge crowds at Pompton Lakes—including, one day, a staggering nine thousand people, probably the biggest gathering ever to see any boxer work out anywhere. People gazed upon Louis from trees, fences, roofs, and cars. Many wore their fanciest duds: "men in sports clothes, linen suits and flannel trousers along with women wearing the latest styles in shoes, dresses and hats of every imaginable description," the *Richmond Afro-American Planet* related. A Chicago reporter saw "jeweled octoroons from the Cotton Club on Broadway, sport-togged, white-spectacled young blades from Harlem, conservative mulatto business-men, all rolling up in sedans or touring cars—and one group of laughing showgirls in a taxicab that had brought them the forty miles from 42nd Street and Broadway." For black America, it was not just a fashion show but a reunion, featuring frequent encounters with old friends. Even when Louis had the day off, people came by just to stare at him. The mob included lots of children. "There's wire netting round the four sides of the ring," one British reporter wrote, "and behind this scores of kink-haired negro boys flatten their pancake noses like monkeys behind bars at the Zoo."

There were distinguished visitors, including Braddock, whose jaw still ached from the Louis fight, as well as Dempsey, Tunney, and Richard Wright. Again, reports about Louis's form and attitude were mixed. His sparring mates said they pitied anyone who had to fight him for real. His defense was said to have improved, even though his staffers made a point not to talk about Schmeling and what had happened the last time. The object, according to Louis's new deputy trainer, a white man named Manny Seamon, was to treat this like any other fight, and Schmeling like "just another fighter he was going to stop when he got around to it."

But there were plenty of skeptics. To one, Louis was training "with all the savage vigor of a great-grandmother knitting woolen wristlets." To another, he was getting hit by punches "that started in Albany." To a third, sparring partners who couldn't "hit hard enough to dent a cake frosting" were hitting Louis hard enough to bend him over. BROWN BOMBER LOOKS LIKE TAN TARGET, the *New York Post* claimed. After one such pummeling, fans were so derisive that the ring announcer asked them to keep their thoughts to themselves. If there were the usual conflicting reports about Louis, there were also conflicting reports about the conflicting reports. Louis was trying to bamboozle Schmeling, or Schmeling was trying to fool Louis, or Mike Jacobs was trying to fool everyone. The evaluations often fell, like so many things, along racial lines. White reporters described how ineffectual or lethargic Louis looked; black reporters said he simply no longer saw a need to dazzle.

Louis was a good-natured fellow, and it was hard to find too many Americans who didn't like him, or didn't want him to win. But the issue of his intelligence still cropped up often, especially when facing someone as shrewd and scientific as Schmeling. And on that score, the press continued to be unkind. Many thought Louis incurably stupid, and felt no inhibitions saying so in various ways: "Louis has never been accused of being erudite" (the *Herald Tribune*). "Schmeling will make no mistake in strategy. Louis doesn't know what the word means" (the *World-Telegram*). "They tried Shufflin' Joe at class work out here and gave it up as a failure" (the *Times*). "Experimentation to him is just a word, and a powerful long one" (the *Mirror*). "There can be no question regarding Schmeling's mental advantage. Joe is not very bright" (the *Los Angeles Times*). Bill Corum asked Louis about the psychology of the fight, and claimed to have gotten this answer: "I don't know that Cy what-you-calls-him, so why should I be worrying 'bout him?" "They are saying Joe Louis had begun to think, now," James Dawson of *The New York Times* told O. B. Keeler of the *Atlanta Journal*. "That is the worst thing Joe Louis could begin to do." Keeler concurred. "Joe Louis is not constructed for thinking," he wrote. "He is designed for action unhampered by any mental process that does not spring from the instantaneous reaction of the motor centers of the animal mind." Louis was clearly in better shape physically than he was for the last fight, Grantland Rice observed, but "I don't think he has changed a lick on the other side—call it mental or psychological or whatever," he wrote. "On this side, I don't think Louis could ever change—not in a thousand years. He just doesn't work that way." To Rice, the title of Hemingway's latest novel, *To Have and Have Not*, summed up Louis to a T: he had everything on the physical side, and had not on the mental.

There were more animal comparisons. Give Schmeling six pounds of peanuts, someone wrote, and he would spend hours coaxing a chipmunk to eat them out of his hand; give them to Louis, and he would eat them himself, then take a nap. The most egregious of these came from Austen Lake of the *Boston Sunday Advertiser,* who compared dinner at Pompton Lakes to "feeding time at the zoo." "Joe's ears waggled while he chewed," he wrote. "His lips made moist, smacking noises and his eyes, as impersonal as twin cough drops, roved the company with the chill and scrutiny of a house cat." While Blackburn, "the simian-faced Negro with a knife scar along one cheek," offered fight talk, Louis "made guttural grunts which filtered through his food in thick blurbs, and focused the full beam of his attention to chewing."

Occasionally there'd be a backhanded compliment. Hugh Bradley of the *Post* said Louis had "vastly improved mentally." Parker insisted that his mental deficiencies were irrelevant. "In Joe's trade a well-delivered clout on the chin makes up for quite a few points in the Intelligence Quotient Department," he wrote. Almost everyone agreed that if he tried outsmarting Schmeling, he'd lose; his best strategy lay in reverting to his former primitive self. The plan at Pompton Lakes, Considine wrote, could be reduced to four words: "Keep Joe from thinking." This inability to work out a plan and stick to it was something all blacks shared, Bill Corum stated. But like Duke Ellington, Cab Calloway, Bill Robinson, and Ethel Waters, Corum continued, Louis had "that remarkable sense of rhythm, timing, instinctive pace," and in the ring, that made him formidable indeed. Of course, there were others who argued that Louis wasn't an animal at all but a marionette whom Blackburn controlled, or a robot, more machine than human.

There were exceptions. Richard Wright said after talking to Louis that while he was uneducated, he was an amazing guy with a full sense of what he represented to other blacks. Another defender was the writer Maxwell Bodenheim, who complained in the *Daily Worker* about the "chauvinism and backwardness" of the mainstream sports press. "A prize-fighter is not supposed to be an intellectual giant and Louis possesses an average amount of intelligence and is a man who has fought his way through poverty, discrimination and the lack of education inflicted upon him by our economic system," Bodenheim wrote. While sportswriters threw "verbal bouquets" at "the Nazi challenger," he charged, they went "miles out of their way to heave rotten fruit at the Negro heavyweight champion, a clean, normal, honest lad."

Many assumed Schmeling still had the "Indian sign" on Louis. Even Louis's sympathetic biographer conceded the possibility: Freud would ask whether Schmeling had "inflicted an inferiority complex" on the Bomber, he wrote. There was, of course, a racial tinge to all of this: no one ever asked Schmeling whether Hamas had the "Indian sign" on him before Schmeling crushed him in their rematch. As for Louis, he brushed it all aside. How, he quite sensibly asked, could he never forget something he couldn't even remember?

Some southern writers thought Louis could not escape his blackness. "Joe Louis never will admit it, but when he gets into the ring and looks down at the German's right fist, he's going to be a scared nigger," one columnist wrote. A student sportswriter at the University of Texas pondered what a local black man had told him: that a nigger was a fighting fool until you knocked him down, and after that he was worthless. "The psychology is true . . . for the Southern Negro who is used to being downtrodden, but it is not true of the Northern Negro," he observed. So, where would one situate a black man born in Alabama but raised in Detroit? Even for many southerners, though, national, regional, and personal loyalties mattered more than race. "Joe Louis is as much an American as the whitest American who ever lived," a columnist in Richmond wrote. "For the first time in the history of the old South a colored boy has become the fair-haired child of the masses," observed a reporter for the *Daily News*. A few Georgians remembered Joe Jacobs from his run-in with the Ku Klux Klan, and resented Schmeling's treatment of him. Schmeling had been "immensely popular" in the "corn pone area" after his 1936 win, the *News* man observed, but clearly that was no longer true, undoubtedly because of his ties to the Nazis. Walter White again wrote to Lowell Thomas, editor of the magazine that had said Louis should never be champion, this time to remind him how wrong it had been. "The public, even in the deep South, has accepted Joe Louis as champion and not only without bitterness but with tremendous enthusiasm," wrote White, who said he'd polled newspapermen on the topic throughout a recent southern swing. "I probably sound like a professional Pollyanna but I do believe that at least in the field of prizefighting we have inched forward a bit."

Preparing Louis for Schmeling became a joint effort. Noting that Louis didn't retain things very long, Armstrong gave him a refresher course on rushing in and swinging. Even Dempsey, who'd liked Schmeling and written off Louis (and all black boxers) after the 1936 fight, pitched in, almost as if it were his patriotic duty. He paid a clandestine visit to Pompton Lakes, telling Louis how to roll away from punches more easily. He then left the camp, only to order his driver back. "You fight him the way you did the last time and the way you boxed today and you got to get licked again!" he scolded Louis after rejoining him. He then removed his coat. "Move into me!" he'd scolded. "Come on! Move! Bend! Get your tail down! Don't wait! Start punching!" Louis must have thought he was nuts, Dempsey said, but he didn't give a damn; he was just trying to help him. And maybe he had.

Gene Tunney also hovered around the camps, but his role was more ambiguous. As the *Mirror* reported breathlessly, Tunney had visited Louis in Lafayetteville, also unsolicited and in great secrecy. Together, they watched films of the Schmeling fight, with Tunney pointing out Louis's mistakes and Schmeling's flaws. Then he, too, rolled up his sleeves and talked technique, all to help keep the heavyweight crown in the United States. Black newspapers were floored by this revelation, given Tunney's past hostility to black fighters; only a few months earlier, Tunney had praised Schmeling for "the greatest right hand I ever saw," and predicted he could "whip Louis tomorrow." "One of the most liberal and genuine American gestures in the history of boxing," the *Courier* called his tutorial. Tunney promptly wired Schmeling, calling the story "ridiculous" and insisting on his neutrality. Schmeling, for one, believed him. "Gene, he not only never fought a Negro fighter, he never had one for a sparring partner," he explained.

Tunney, boxing's house intellectual ever since he had once been caught reading Shakespeare, analyzed the matchup in *Connecticut Nutmeg*, the weekly magazine he had just launched with Heywood Broun and others. To him, the fight pitted Louis's natural gifts against Schmeling's experience and "spiritual fortification." Like Gallico and some British writers, Tunney appeared to get a kind of thrill from the new German ardor. "To Schmeling this is not merely another fight for which he will be well paid," he wrote. "It is a sacred cause and he feels he is the standard bearer of 65 million Germans, a nation of determined people who have inaugurated a new worldwide racial movement. He is their hero, their Hermes who will herald to the world the Nazi supremacy." Louis was superior mechanically, Tunney conceded, but Schmeling, well, he had something greater: a quasi-religious spark. Hellmis endorsed Tunney's sentiments enthusiastically; because of its independence, he said, Tunney's publication "did not have to dance to the tune of Jewish big interests." Up in Speculator, Schmeling's handlers professed to be

A joyous crowd welcomes Schmeling at Berlin's Tempelhof Airport, June 26, 1936.

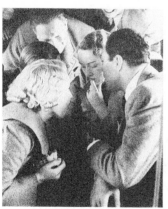

Hitler's personal photographer, Heinrich Hoffmann, caught Schmeling and his awestruck claque en route to Berlin, June 26, 1936. Schmeling's wife, Anny Ondra, is at left.

Hitler meets with Schmeling's mother (at left), Ondra, and Schmeling at the Reich's chancellory, June 27, 1936.

Left: The documentary
Goebbels ordered up
of the first Louis-Schmeling
fight, *Schmeling's Victory:
A German Victory*, gave millions of Germans another
chance to celebrate.

Right: Champion of Youth,
February 1937. As his relations
with the Nazi regime deepened
and he seemed increasingly
likely to regain the heavyweight
crown, Schmeling became ever
more demonized, particularly
in the radical press.

Athletes greet Schmeling at the 1936 Berlin Olympics. "In
rank and importance he did not seem to be much below
Hitler and Göring," a British journalist wrote.

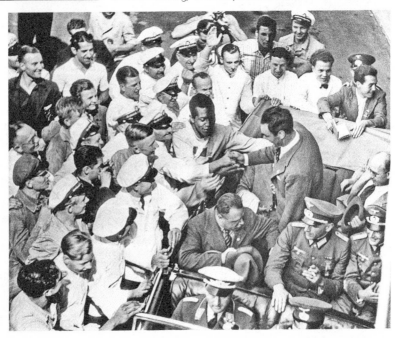

The anti-Nazi boycott in January 1937 created a great opportunity for Jim Braddock's manager, Joe Gould, to extricate his fighter from the contract to fight Schmeling and take on a far more lucrative fight with Louis, as Willard Mullin of the *New York World-Telegram* suggested.

With comic dutifulness, Schmeling trained for a fight that would clearly never happen.

Louis and his entourage—including Blackburn (to Louis's right) and Louis's co-managers, Julian Black, (to his left), and John Roxborough (behind Blackburn)—celebrate after Louis knocked out Braddock, June 22, 1937.

JOE LOUIS WORLD'S CHAMP

Joe Gets Up Off the Floor to Win Before 65,000 Spectators—$100,000 His

The *Baltimore Afro-American* announces the news.

Jimmy Braddock, eleven stitches in his lips and eye, files out after losing the title.

Above: Shortly after Louis won the crown, his father, Monroe Barrow, surfaced. Long thought dead, he was a patient at the Searcy State Hospital for the Negro Insane in Alabama.

Ring recognized what Louis repeatedly said: he wouldn't really be champion until he'd beaten Schmeling.

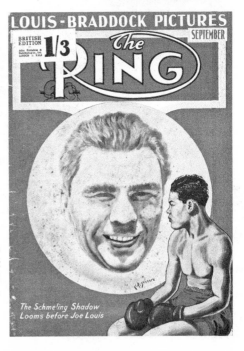

LOUIS-BRADDOCK PICTURES

SEPTEMBER

BRITISH EDITION 1/3

The RING

The Schmeling Shadow Looms before Joe Louis

Forty thousand readers tackled the all-important question the *Chicago Defender* posed in early 1937.

Protestors outside the Hippodrome urge fans to boycott Schmeling's fight against Harry Thomas, December 1937.

The yellow star makes an early appearance: Schmeling reaches over Harry Thomas, whom he has just knocked out, to punch Samuel Untermyer of the Non-Sectarian Anti-Nazi League on his outsized Jewish nose after the League's boycott of the fight sputtered. *8 Uhr-Blatt* (Nuremberg), December 31, 1937

Reichssportblatt

48799·269
Deutsche
gaben
dem
Führer
ihr „Ja"!

Though he always insisted he was a sportsman rather than a politician, Schmeling loaned his name and image to pet Nazi causes. Here, along with 48,799,268 other Germans, he votes to ratify the annexation of Austria, April 1938.

Schmeling and Joe Jacobs arrive at Newark Airport from Speculator, New York, site of his training camp for the second Louis fight, June 21, 1938. To Schmeling, flying was not only faster; it was an act of insubordination, a declaration of independence.

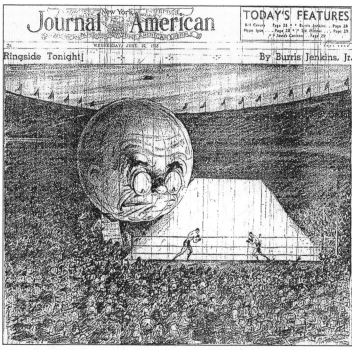

The world watches as the rematch looms: Burris Jenkins, *New York Journal-American*, June 22, 1938.

The Communists leafleted outside Yankee Stadium, but they were too keen on watching Louis smash Schmeling to support a boycott.

The program for the second Louis-Schmeling fight.

Walking to the weigh-in for the rematch, Madison Square Garden, June 22, 1938

J. Edgar Hoover and
Walter Winchell, fight night,
at Yankee Stadium.

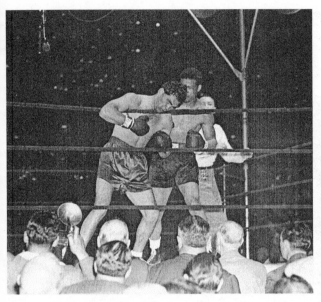

Louis pummels Schmeling
along the ropes. A cry—"half human,
half animal"—filled the night air.

Schmeling goes down
for the first time.

As the cornermen mobilized and Louis—
his night's work done 124 seconds after
it had begun—begins to walk off, Donovan
cradles the vanquished Schmeling.

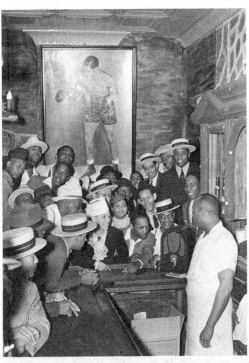

In Harlem, residents gathered once more around the radio. Silence reigned.

A Harlem street scene after the second fight. "Take a dozen Harlem Christmases, a score of New Year's Eves, a bushel of July 4ths and maybe—yes, maybe—you get a faint glimpse of the idea."

Schmeling quickly retracted any claim that Louis had beaten him unfairly and later blamed others for raising it. But one newspaper recorded the truth for posterity.

Louis reads all about his victory.

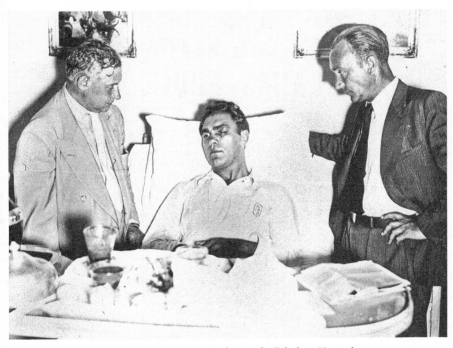

Schmeling, flanked by Joe Jacobs and Max Machon, at the Polyclinic Hospital following the second fight. Louis never came by.

"It's over."
8 Uhr-Blatt
(Nuremberg),
June 23, 1938

New Masses, July 5, 1938

Louis celebrates his victory over Schmeling with two more of his victims, Jimmy Braddock (left) and Tommy Farr, at Braddock's bar near Madison Square Garden, June 23, 1938.

"The Nazi fistic hero Max Schmeling is returning to Germany
with such a pathetic face." Drawing by William Gropper in
Freiheit, June 23, 1938.

The reunions of the two old antagonists were well documented.
Here, they bond over some of Schmeling's Coca-Cola.

pleased by all the advice Louis was getting; it was certain to confuse him as much as Schmeling's right had done. Machon asked one reporter to do him a favor: when he reached Pompton Lakes, please encourage Louis to come rushing in like Henry Armstrong; "he would be awkward as a school girl on her first pair of ice skates," he said.

White commentators suggested Louis was too simpleminded to bring any passions of his own to the fight. But black writers knew better. They knew Louis hated Schmeling, less for his politics than for accusing Louis of fouling him intentionally, and for that late hit after the fifth round. He'd also learned that that punch had been cut from the German fight film, and that Hellmis had roused German audiences against him. "His burning desire for revenge is so deeply imbued within his heart that I believe it will overshadow any other emotion that Joe might have," Chester Washington wrote. As if that were not enough, Blackburn went to work on Louis. Hating an adversary was good strategy, he knew, but with the sweet-natured Louis, this was not easy. So he outdid himself by heaping scorn on the Nazis and telling Louis what Hitler thought of blacks. "I don't like Schmeling because his people don't like my people," Louis told one writer. "The old drowsiness is gone and in its place has come an alert anger," Jimmy Cannon reported.

Louis watched films of his first fight with Schmeling again and again. And he astonished everyone with a prediction: two rounds. "I know how to fight Max, now," he explained. "I won't waste any time going to work. Of course, if he dogs it a while, it will take me at least four or five rounds. If he fights, it won't go three." To Cannon, he cut it down to one. The predictions astonished fight writers. "Sheer youthful exuberance and should be disregarded," the *World-Telegram* counseled. Blacks, too, squirmed at such hubris. One called Louis "a fit subject for the psychiatric ward, releasing smart talk like that in the face of so grave a crisis." But Louis had told Blackburn the same thing. "My rheumatics will give me the miseries, climbin' up that mountain every round," Blackburn had complained before the fight. "Don't you worry about that mountain climbing," Louis replied. "You'll only have to climb it twice." Louis's fervor impressed the bookies, who lengthened the odds favoring him from eight to five to better than two to one. "They've finally got that boy mad," one handicapper observed. "That's the one thing he needed."

Hellmis stopped by Pompton Lakes, and his impressions of Louis remained the same: light, elegant, incredibly powerful, quite sympathetic, honest, sincere, compliant, dumb. "All of his work leaves the impression of a nature boy who doesn't quite understand why he should do [this or] that, but who has learned from past experience that he will receive many lovely dollars for doing so," he wrote. Since everyone associated the heavyweight championship with a good mind, Hellmis felt Louis was most unworthy of the crown. While his "racial brothers" (*Rassengenossen*) still idolized him, Louis's drawing power was nil, Hellmis told Germany; the enormous interest in the fight stemmed from Schmeling. Even in tranquil times, Hellmis would have been delusional, but in fact, tensions were growing: at a birthday rally for Hitler in Yorkville on April 20, uniformed American Nazis beat back Jewish War Veterans with blackjacks, belts, and chairs. A few weeks later, two thousand people in Yorkville heard the German consul praise Hitler, then watched Leni Riefenstahl's *Triumph of the Will*. Shortly thereafter, six leaders of the German-American Bund on Long Island were arrested for spying.

Perhaps because of the tempests around him, Schmeling came to appreciate Speculator all the more. He liked its coolness and low humidity, along with its tranquillity and remoteness: 250 miles from New York, 60 miles from the closest train station. The view from his cottage, of the mountains looming beyond a crystalline alpine lake, reminded him of his estate in Pomerania. Only Mike Jacobs was unhappy with the arrangement: it was too far from New York and from the New York reporters who would publicize the fight. To Hellmis, training in such a spot was more important to Schmeling "than the dollar assets of Herr Mike Jacobs, who obviously showed little concern last year for Maxie's dollar worries as he booted him out of the world championship."

Schmeling quickly fell into his usual routine. First came a few days of running and walking. Then came the sparring matches, in an outdoor ring, with Joe Jacobs introducing the various opponents. They were generally inferior to Louis's sparring partners, but the thrifty Schmeling wasn't paying them as much; Max had nothing to learn from them anyway, Hellmis maintained. Between rounds Schmeling posed for the cameras. Afterward, he punched the bag, shadowboxed, skipped rope, and performed tricks; one sure crowd-pleaser was a precision punch that knocked the ash off the cigar in Jacobs's mouth. One Sunday, five thousand people showed up. On another occasion, the mayors of Syracuse, Utica, Albany, and Rochester came by. Mike Jacobs was there to announce that the two men would fight yet again if the forthcoming bout went the distance.

The overarching question at Speculator was whether Schmeling had slipped in the last two years, and if so, by how much. Rice thought Schmeling was "as close to perfection as imperfect humanity can hope to reach"; he could be whipped, he wrote, but only by someone far better than Louis had been two years earlier. Braddock thought Schmeling had indeed faded, and would never be able to move against a younger fighter like Louis in the way he needed to. To Hellmis, of course, Schmeling was mounting the latest in a series of apexes.

Surely the most conspicuous—and courageous—visitors in Schmeling's camp were the representatives of the black weeklies. Al Monroe of the *Defender* spent five days there, tripling as a reporter, spy, and cheerleader for Louis. Schmeling was in fine shape, he wrote, but Louis should not fall for fish stories that he had suddenly sprouted some new punches. "He is planning to right-cross you out of the title, Joe," Monroe advised. "Go out there and knock his block off, Joe, and the fight is yours. That is your only chance." St. Clair Bourne of the *Amsterdam News* saw some slight sagging in Schmeling's face and "the merest shadow of embonpoint"—that is, fat—around his waist. One of Bourne's colleagues, Bill Chase, spotted varicose veins. "We were the center of attraction at this Nazi-sympathetic community," observed Chase, who'd already covered the Berlin Olympics. "Of course, at this stage of the game, we're all pretty used to people of the opposite race staring at us when we get out of the bounds of Harlem, so that didn't bother us in the least." But all was amicable as they posed for pictures with Schmeling. "It was too bad that such a personable and swell guy as this had to be a Nazi," Chase wrote.

Schmeling rarely confronted racial issues head-on, and when he did, he was usually conciliatory. But in early June he spoke with unusual bluntness to one reporter. "The black dynasty of pugilism must come to an end," he told the *Chicago American*. He was doing his part in the heavyweight division, he said; whites in other divisions should follow suit. No one in the mainstream press picked up on Schmeling's comments; the white papers hid Schmeling's racism, one irate black columnist wrote, because its racial ideas and Hitler's were the same. (He urged that Schmeling be deported.) Schmeling's politics also came up during the visit with the *Chicago Times.* "Make no mistake, Max Schmeling is Fuehrer Hitler's greatest booster," the reporter later wrote. "Ve haff no strikes in Germany," Schmeling told him. "Most everybody has job. Times are goot. Ve have only one union. Ve haff only one party. Everybody agreeable. Everybody happy." "Both he and Machon sincerely believe Hitler is Germany's man of destiny," the reporter noted. (In a bit of revisionism, Schmeling told the same reporter that Anny Ondra had listened to the first Louis fight in Detroit rather than at Goebbels's side.)

When the *Hamburg* left Cuxhaven for New York in early June, it was crowded with Schmeling fans, a "floating sports hotel." But officially, the Nazis were hedging their bets. "Only the sporting side of the contest is to be taken into account," the propaganda ministry instructed the press on June 10. "The odds can be noted, but not in the headlines." In other words, with Louis the favorite, the symbolic importance of the fight should not be stressed. In a front-page editorial, the *Frankfurter Volksblatt* ridiculed the tendency to view sporting events as "preludes and omens" for political struggles, claiming that only New York Jews and "Haarlem Negroes" went for such balderdash. But it was a little late to back off Schmeling. Craving athletic glory, international respect, and validation of its culture of merciless machismo, Nazi Germany had fallen in love with Max, and that love had blinded it to the vagaries of the ring.

Schmeling and Machon insisted that anti-Nazi feeling in the United States had abated and that they felt completely at home there. But reporters found Speculator far more regimented, paranoid, and Nazified than Schmeling's camp at Napanoch had been. Going there from free and easy Pompton Lakes, Parker wrote, was "like stepping from this enlightened republic into one of the totalitarian states." "The flavor of Nazi Germany permeates Schmeling's camp," Parker continued. "One expects to see brown shirted soldiers popping out from behind every telegraph pole with a 'Heil Hitler!' challenge." Schmeling's house, he went on, was an island of Nazi Germany, encircled by barbed wire and state troopers. And Schmeling himself was encircled by Germans: Machon, Hellmis, and other reporters, friends like Heinz Ditgens, owner of the Roxy-Bar in Berlin, and Willi Lehmann, a Berlin restaurateur who was always quick to stress that he—unlike his namesake the governor of New York—wasn't Jewish. The topics, too, were German; one visitor recalled Schmeling and his guests spending an hour poring over photographs of Hitler's glorious new autobahn. Hellmis in particular discomfited some American reporters, who quickly concluded that he wasn't reporting only to his editors. "Nasty Adolph's oaf-ficial observer," one called him. Not only New York journalists attuned to Jewish sensibilities picked up something chilling in the air. One southern reporter talked of "the spirit of Horst Wessel in trunks and boxing gloves" permeating the place. "The diabolically patient manner of preparing for this fight makes strong men shudder," he wrote. "No wonder the Germans came back after the World War and built a new nation out of the debris."

As one Hungarian paper, *Est*, noted, everyone in Schmeling's circle around Speculator met the requirements of the Nuremberg Laws except one.

That one, of course, was Joe Jacobs, and he was an outcast. "Little wonder," Parker wrote, "that he dashes back to kosher New York at every opportunity." Jacobs was not allowed to stay in the large house with Schmeling, Machon, and his German cronies, and he cut a pathetic figure around the camp, reduced to asking reporters what Schmeling was telling them. His suspension made him even more expendable, especially since it appeared Schmeling hadn't strained himself to get him reinstated. "He made Max what he is today and is treated like a necessary pariah by the ingrate," wrote a *Times* reader.

Jacobs still insisted, though, that Schmeling treated him right. Depriving Schmeling of his wise counsel, he said, was part of a plot to deny Schmeling a fair shot at the title. Once again, Jacobs found little sympathy in his own community. The *Forverts* acknowledged Schmeling's ingratitude, comparing Jacobs to the hapless stepfather who'd paid for his stepson's wedding, only to learn that more important relatives would walk the boy to the chuppah. But it wasted no pity on him. "Jews will not forget that he did business with one of Hitler's favorites during a time when not a day goes by without articles in the newspapers that tell about the suffering, about the terrible troubles and insults that Jews are going through in Hitler's Germany," it declared. Nor, to the *Forverts*, was Mike Jacobs much better, whatever he had pledged to the refugees; both were worms that could not be washed clean. Undeterred, Joe Jacobs touted Schmeling with his usual indefatigability. After ostentatiously making sure that no one else was listening, he offered an Atlanta columnist "the absolute low-down" on the fight; it was, he said, the least he could do after those good Georgians had rescued him from the Klan. "Max will knock Joe out in the ninth round, positively, and you can take that from me absolutely guaranteed," he whispered. "I say the ninth round. Why? Because I like to give myself a chance for a slight mistake. I think it might come sooner, but you know Max. He never rushes things. You can quote me further as saying that Max will knock him out with a left hook. Yes, sir, a left hook."

The state trooper guarding Schmeling's house had more trouble with drunken American reporters than with anti-Nazi saboteurs. But Hellmis was vigilant nonetheless. Schmeling had blamed the heat for his loss to Max Baer five years earlier. But Hellmis had other notions, and, apparently, duties. "In Germany, we still believe there were other reasons why Max Baer whipped Schmeling than the punches he received in the ring," he told one reporter, suggesting that someone had tampered with Schmeling's food. "There will be no chances for anything to happen this time." No one—not even Machon—would be allowed in Schmeling's kitchen; the trusted chef from Germany bought and prepared all the fare.

The old debate over Schmeling's character raged anew. On one side were those who considered him dignified and decent, courageous and gentlemanly, while others demonized him as Hitler's pet. "This fellow isn't a sportsman," wrote Lester Rodney of the *Daily Worker*, which was, predictably, harder on Schmeling than was any other paper. "He is an outspoken representative of the perverted, bestial nationalism and race hatred fanned by the oppressors of the real German people to hide their bloody war against all progressive humanity." The American Communist press speculated that if Schmeling lost, perhaps some sexual crime of his would be discovered, as had happened to von Cramm, or that Hitler would decide that excessive exposure to weak democracies had sapped him of his Teutonic strength. Either way, a concentration camp was the best he could expect.*

As conditions for Jews and other victims of Nazi persecution worsened, some reporters grew impatient with Schmeling's gripes about past American mistreatment. "Look, Max, you're a nice guy and we all like you a lot and admire the way you keep in shape, etc., but let's not have any more of this complaining about how you're being jobbed," wrote a Boston columnist. "Because it could be a lot worse. You might have been born a Jew in Germany and then, no doubt, you'd have been glad to be one of us." In a letter sent to Speculator, a Brooklyn prosecutor asked Schmeling whether he supported the extermination of Jewish life in Germany. There was no way to keep politics out of the prefight publicity. "If this dirty nigger Joe Louis dares to beat our Max Schmeling, we'll kill him," some Bundists told the *Amsterdam News*. (The Bund denied the accusation, calling it "an old Jewish trick to put our organization on the spot.") Two days before the fight, a federal grand jury in New York indicted eighteen Germans on espionage charges.

Some thought Schmeling seemed more burdened than before. The last time he fought Louis, expectations were low and he had nothing to lose, while now he was the uncrowned champion and a national idol. Others found him more cocksure than ever, "under orders to speak arro-

---

*The Nazi press laughed off such speculation. A paper in Hamburg joked that were Schmeling to lose, he would have to report to the Gestapo daily and recite a Christian prayer of repentance 207 times. Then he would be thrown in the meat grinder, with his remains fed to the fishes. But if he won, Berlin would erect a monument for him along Unter den Linden, and Hamburg would be renamed "Schmeling."

gantly and to carry on the tradition of his home government that victories can be won by sweeping assertions of determination and power," wrote Heywood Broun. Schmeling avoided discussing Louis. "He's willing to gab about food, wild life, ornithology, architecture, golf, sculpture, books, but mention of Louis or the fight is pretty much taboo," one reporter noted. Told of Louis's vow to win in two, Schmeling feigned indifference. "He made his prediction. Let him have his fun," he said. "It used to be that Louis's opponents did all the talking before a fight, and he just did like this," he continued, putting on a glum, pouting face. Nor was he concerned that everyone, the referee and promoter included, wanted him to lose. All he needed was his right hand, and no one could deprive him of that.

By Saturday, June 18, the rematch was only five days away. Detroiters held a going-away party for Dorothy Darby, a black aviatrix—perhaps the only black woman in the world with a pilot's license—bound for Pompton Lakes. Her cargo included a petition of support for Louis with 100,000 signatures attached, along with letters from the governor of Michigan, the mayor of Detroit, and Louis's mother. "May the best man win, for you are the best," she'd written. Louis reportedly tucked it into his shirt pocket and read it again and again. That same Saturday, four thousand fans crammed into Pompton Lakes. Many got in for nothing, after ripping their suits on the barbed-wire fence installed after freeloaders stormed the place the week before. On Sunday, hundreds had to be chased off the roof of the indoor gymnasium for fear it would collapse. The spectacle, with celebrity guests and smaller fry from Lenox Avenue tenements "attired in regalia that made Hollywood look positively dowdy and the clubhouse lawn at Santa Anita seem drab and colorless . . . could happen nowhere else in America and might not happen again," one southern reporter wrote. His afternoon's labors done, Louis, along with his bodyguard and Blackburn, left the camp for a while, hoping the crowd would disperse. But when they returned a few hours later, a thousand people still awaited him.

While he proved a bigger draw than ever, Louis's boxing was still confounding. On Saturday, he was completely unimpressive. After counting half a dozen clean shots to Louis's jaw, Bill Cunningham of the *Boston Post* called him "as wide open as Boston Common." But on Sunday, Louis dazzled everyone. This time, his people promised, there would be no pussyfooting around for the newsreels. "You can bet all the marijuana in Harlem he won't be klieg-conscious," the *Brooklyn Eagle* wrote. "His title is on the line. And it's worth more than movie money." Louis was adamant that the referee not stop the fight; he'd shown he could take a licking, and he wanted to see if Schmeling could, too. Louis was so sharp on Sunday that Blackburn gave him Monday off. That morning, while three hundred laborers began assembling the ring and placing thousands of seats on the Yankee Stadium infield, Louis did only a bit of roadwork. In Speculator, enormous crowds watched Schmeling wrap things up. In *Liberty* magazine, Schmeling now predicted another deliberate, methodical fight. "I think in our first round we will feel each other out," he wrote. After that, nothing much would happen right away; he would just wait for Louis to make his usual mistakes, then shoot over a right hand and beat him.

Betting was sporadic, and a bit hesitant. "Harlemites who daily risk 600 to 1 odds on the numbers were skeptical about supporting Louis at 9 to 5," wrote Ted Poston in the *Post*.

An astrologer noted that Schmeling had beaten Louis the last time just as Pluto was setting, and Pluto was now due to set again between 9:24 and 9:32 p.m. Eastern time. Jack ("Wrong Again") Tulloch of the *Alexandria (Virginia) Gazette*, who always picked losers, opted for Louis, leading Lem Houston of the *Fredericksburg Free Lance-Star* to go with Schmeling. "Everything I could beg, borrow, and beg again has been bet on the Brown Bomber," a Harlemite named John McClain told the *Amsterdam News*. "I'm therefore picking round one for the end of Herr Moxie." But a Harlem social worker named Guildford Crawford reluctantly disagreed. "I think Schmeling is going to win," he said. "You can't beat the Germans. They win in everything." A couple on West 111th Street argued passionately about the outcome; she heaved a glass pitcher at him, then a pot of boiling water, and was held on $500 bond. At Small's Paradise, 138 people participated in an "Honest Opinion Poll" tacked on the wall. Twelve of them picked Schmeling, but their bravery had its limits: they referred to themselves as, among other things, "Uncle Don," "Dimples," "Popeye," and "Shirley Temple." In Birmingham, Alabama, Mr. O. Kay—listed as "Kay, O.," picked Schmeling. A Kansas City police captain who'd guessed every heavyweight winner since 1892 went for Schmeling. So, too, on a radio station in Memphis, did a Welch's Grape Juice executive. "I think he will whip the nigger again," he said. Blacks whose churches used the drink during communion promptly announced they would boycott the company.

A numbers man from Detroit bet $25,000 that Louis would win before the eighth. Louis boosters in Harlem posted placards inviting Schmeling fans to make bets, or went to Yorkville to find them. (They might have found some action in Berlin, where the betting for Schmeling was two to

one, and Louis money, understandably, was scarce.) Franklin D. Roosevelt, Jr., had $20 riding on Schmeling. Doris Duke placed a very small
part of her fortune on Louis. Toots Shor put $5,000 on him. One fight vet-
eran insisted that politics, and sentiment, had warped the wagering: half
the experts favored Schmeling, he said, but Jews had lengthened the odds
by refusing to bet on him. In a pool at his local saloon, Joseph Mitchell of
the *World-Telegram* bought three chances at fifty cents apiece; all turned
out to be for Schmeling. But he refused to bet on him, and traded one of
them, Schmeling in the eleventh round, for Louis in the first. Mike Gold
of the *Daily Worker* had wanted to bet on Louis, but in his circle, no one
would take Schmeling. So he bet a dollar that when Schmeling did lose,
he would cry "Foul!" "A young Christian Science lady, who wants to hold
beautiful thoughts about even the meanest of God's creatures, took the
other side of the bet," he wrote.

The last time they'd squared off, Louis in one round seemed like a
good bet. "Come early and don't drop your program," one paper had
advised in 1936. But despite Louis's grand pronouncements, bookmakers
were betting ten to one against a first-round victory now. In an office pool
in Charlotte, North Carolina, a man who drew Louis in the first tossed his
ticket disgustedly on the floor. A Memphis man offered to bet his restaurant on Louis, against $3,500 for Schmeling. Marva put up $15, picking
her husband in the fourth. In a daily feature called "Joe or Max? Max or
Joe?" the *World-Telegram* asked celebrities for their picks. On the Yankees, Tommy Heinrich, Frank Crosetti, and Joe DiMaggio picked Louis,
while Lou Gehrig and Red Rolfe chose Schmeling. George Halas of the
Chicago Bears picked Louis, who, next to Bronco Nagurski, he said, "hits
harder than any man alive." Dizzy Dean and Henny Youngman picked
Louis. So did Edgar Bergen, but Charlie McCarthy picked Schmeling.
Robert Taylor picked Schmeling, but Amos and Andy picked Louis.
When Babe Ruth picked Schmeling, the odds against the German fell.
That the Bambino was making his debut coaching first base for the Brooklyn Dodgers would normally have dominated the sports pages, but not
now. "Now, let's see," wrote Lester Rodney of the *Daily Worker* the day
before the fight. "Babe Ruth and — oh, hell, tomorrow's the night and
that's all there is in sports until it's over."

In a technological breakthrough, NBC tracked down eight former
heavyweight champions and put them on the air simultaneously two
nights before the fight. Jim Jeffries in Los Angeles, Jack Johnson in New
York, Jess Willard in Lawrence, Kansas, and Jack Dempsey in Philadelphia all picked Schmeling (though at other times and to other reporters

Dempsey either picked Louis or hinted at a draw); Tommy Burns in Seattle, Jack Sharkey in Boston, and Max Baer in New York picked Louis. In Stamford, Connecticut, Gene Tunney remained on the fence, though leaning slightly toward Louis. The two champions the network couldn't corral, Jimmy Braddock and Primo Carnera, each picked Louis in an early round.

Jimmy Powers of the *Daily News* pushed to have Joe Jacobs reinstated because, he wrote, Louis already enjoyed all of the advantages: a friendly referee (the man who'd officiated at most of Louis's fights in New York, Arthur Donovan, would likely work this one, too); friendly boxing commissioners; a promoter who had every reason to be friendly because he effectively owned him; and a friendly gallery. "Because there has been a revolting pandering to racial prejudice, poor Max has been blamed for all Hitler atrocities from Vienna to Cologne," Powers wrote. "The crowd definitely will be biased." (*Collyer's Eye* took the conspiracy one step further. While Schmeling had spurned $50,000 to take a dive, it claimed, "it is understood the 'proper arrangements'" had been made for Louis to win. "The cards are stacked against Schmeling," it added two weeks later. "Jacobs and his Mob, who won't stop at anything to retain their hold on the heavyweight championship, can be expected to resort to various means in order to be assured that Schmeling will not be returned the winner. Jacobs again may beat Schmeling for the world's heavyweight championship.") Though Powers's colleagues were far more divided than they'd been the last time around, a majority of them still backed Louis. Two of Louis's greatest champions, Dan Parker and Lester Rodney of the *Daily Worker*, foresaw the shortest fight: Louis in three. Others, convinced Louis had slipped, predicted he would eke out a decision. Some picking Schmeling did so with reservations; a single mistake, wrote one, and the German would be "as stiff and cold as a stalactite." Others, who thought the deck was stacked for Louis, thought Schmeling needed a knockout, and Bill Cunningham of the *Boston Post* thought that's what he'd get. "Herr Hitler has our title," he predicted glumly.

Al Monroe picked Louis in nine—or sooner, if he abandoned bobbing and weaving and reverted to "the Joe Louis of old." Walter White had Louis in seven. Louis would normally win in five, wrote Mabe Kountze in the *Boston Chronicle*, but the fix against him was in; Schmeling would win, thereby setting the stage for another natural: Schmeling against Baer, German against (supposed) Jew, for the title. Only one reporter at the *Daily Worker* picked Schmeling, and only because he felt that given what awaited any loser in Nazi Germany, he was essentially fighting for his life. "There are a few things of which we may be reasonably certain," wrote Wilbur Wood of the *Sun*.

> That Schmeling will be jabbed early and often; that Louis will be tagged at least once by Schmeling's right to the jaw; that Arthur Donovan will referee; that Louis will be the betting choice, probably at 11 to 5 ringside; that Announcer Harry Balogh will introduce the fighters with only a few million words; that Joe Jacobs will have the longest cigar in the Stadium; that photographers jumping up to take pictures will block others' views of the ring as soon as something happens that all wish to see; that Louis will not tear out of his corner swinging with both hands at the opening bell.

"The fight may not go more than six," wrote Jack Troy of the *Atlanta Constitution*. "But I think you could safely bet your shirt that it won't, as Louis says, end in one."

Box-Sport polled seventeen German experts; all picked Schmeling (while acknowledging that because he was really taking on an entire country, he could never win on points, and would have to knock Louis out). The *Angriff* offered 200 marks to the first person to pick the winner and the round. Four German correspondents in New York differed only on when Schmeling would win. A cartoon in the sports magazine *Der Kicker* showed a large-lipped Louis in bed, dreaming of victory. "Joe Louis has a big mouth once again . . . which was stuffed by Maxen's iron fist before," it stated (using a variation of Schmeling's nickname), suggesting Louis faced a second helping of humiliation. A leading Roman newspaper forecast that Louis would keep his pledge to come out swinging. "On this point we can agree with the presumptuous Negro: that he will combat like a beast, with sheer, brute, savage force," *Il Popolo d'Italia* declared. "And for this reason also we desire Max Schmeling's triumph, because boxing, a combat sport, must also represent the fusion of force with intelligence." But that was a hope, not a prediction.

On the morning of June 22 in Germany, fight stories had to vie with reports of Goebbels's speech the previous day to 120,000 fanatical followers in Berlin's Olympic Stadium, in which he pledged to drive the Jews out of the capital. In many cities, Schmeling got higher billing, sometimes even crowding the propaganda minister off the front page. "150 Million Will Listen to the Schmeling-Louis Bout Tonight," the *Berliner Zeitung am Mittag* proclaimed. A photograph of a smiling Schmeling ran next to the newspaper's logo. "We'll keep our fingers crossed, Maxe!" ran the caption. If millions of hearts were beating for Maxe tonight, the 8 *Uhr-Abendblatt* declared, it was out of gratitude for his service to the Fatherland. Schmeling was "full of confidence without bragging like the Negro," proclaimed the *Fränkische Tageszeitung* of Nuremberg, which boasted that already "America's boycott Jews" had been knocked out.

Schmeling spoke periodically to Germany while training, either in print or on the air, promising not to disappoint the *Heimat* and thanking it for its loyalty. "To feel that the homeland is standing behind me will make me twice as strong," he said in one interview. "W.G." — probably the boxing promoter Walter Gratenau — shared with readers in Hamburg the telegram Schmeling had sent him. "Have correct fighting weight and feel like I'm in top shape STOP," it read. "Will box Louis as opportunities arise without fixed plan STOP Didn't notice anything of a Jewish boycott or hostile mood against me in America STOP Blacks and Jews are against me STOP All others have a fair attitude STOP No incidents in the training camp STOP American press by and large stayed neutral STOP Believe the referees will be correct STOP If the temperature tomorrow is like today I'll be fine STOP Don't think Joe Louis is stronger in this fight than in the last STOP." The *Berliner Volkszeitung* reminded readers to set their alarms; maybe, it said, everyone could go back to sleep after a few minutes.

As vital as boxing was in Nazi culture, as important as Schmeling had become to the German psyche, as much as Germany coveted the heavyweight crown, some activities couldn't cease; persecuting the Jews mattered even more. Even as the fight loomed, teams of Nazi marauders fanned out through Berlin, beating Jewish shop owners, smashing their windows, defacing storefronts. Every third store along the Kurfürstendamm had "*Jude*" painted on it. Outside a jewelry store, a Western reporter heard the "screams of terror" of a Jewish man set upon by "one of the Jew-hating gangs." "The crowd closed in, and the screams were shortly changed to moans," he wrote. "In Jewish homes there is a fresh pang of anxiety whenever the bell rings, or there is a screeching of brakes outside the house and the sound of heavy footsteps." The reports found their way into New York's papers, intercepting readers en route to the sports pages. One reporter called Germany's Jews "a doomed people," and noted that a prominent Nazi had already called for their extermination.

This didn't make things easy for the two Jacobses. "Mr. Joe Jacobs must think that of all times the Hitlerites could have chosen for their exhibition of barbarism the present is the worst, when he is trying to get an indulgent public opinion for his prize fighter," the *Chicago Tribune* wrote. But Hitler didn't have to choose between pogroms and prizefights; he could have both. The American public either had grown inured to events in Germany, or saw the fight as a way to strike back, or had grown tired of protests, as even the league conceded. "New York City has been overrun by men and women pickets for more than a year, each one flaunting pasteboard banners, shouting messages against this, that or the other thing," it stated. "The medium has become commonplace, has lost its zip. It receives as much public attention as a bridal party in Niagara Falls."

The New York press barely mentioned the protests, and usually only to belittle them. "For humanity's sake, heed the cries of torture of those cursed with Hitler's terror and stress the Schmeling boycott," an activist wired Joe Williams. "If you boycott Schmeling don't you boycott Louis at the same time?" Williams replied. "And what has Louis ever done to anybody?" "We have kept Schmeling waiting long enough," stated a letter to *The New York Times*. "He is probably too old now to defeat Louis again, anyhow. But now that he is finally getting his great chance, let's give Schmeling, the sportsman, fair play and forget Schmeling, the commodity." Jews remained divided on the topic, sometimes embarrassingly so. *The American Israelite* reported that an officer of the Anti-Nazi League had bought a block of tickets for the fight.

Someone handed a British reporter a boycott flyer. It stated, inaccurately, that "a quarter of every dollar" spent on tickets ended up with Hitler and reminded people, accurately, that none of Schmeling's take went to refugees. "The first knock-out in next week's big fight has been landed: the boycotters have taken it," he observed. "The intensity of the boycott will not stop thousands of Jews and all Harlem from going to the fight, but they will go with the fervent hope of seeing Louis cut Schmeling to ribbons." Berlin newspapers were as pleased with brisk ticket sales as Mike Jacobs was. "The alleged anti-German attitude of the New York audience, once used to justify the cancellation of the Schmeling-Braddock bout, could not have been refuted more convincingly," a reporter wrote.

The Broadway columnists had ignored the boycott. Though staunchly anti-Nazi, Walter Winchell had praised Schmeling and taken him and Joe Jacobs on a tour of local hot spots. The publisher of the *Post* was on the league's board, yet his paper, I. Q. Gross charged in *The Nation*, had "ballyhooed the fight like it has never ballyhooed any other fight in history." Gross pleaded with league leaders to be more aggressive. The group boasted that Mike Jacobs was well short of the million-dollar gate he envisioned; Schmeling would bring home far less bacon than Goebbels had expected. "The League expresses the profound hope, inasmuch as the fight is to be held, that it will result in a knockout wallop to the Nazi yowl of Aryan supremacy," it declared. In other words, the fight was going forward anyway, so pull for Louis. Picketers were outside Yankee Stadium the day before the bout, carrying BOYCOTT THE FIGHT banners. But no one picketed the Hippodrome, where tickets were actually being sold, and most fans bought them by mail anyway.

In a radio interview from Pompton Lakes, Nat Fleischer predicted a paid attendance of 74,982 and a gate of $1,062,000. Scalpers were selling $30 tickets for $100 to $110; ringside seats were fetching $200. A reporter from New Orleans detected last-minute demand among conformist New Yorkers afraid to miss something big. A Virginia paper sneered at how, in a country racked by Depression, seventy thousand fools could drop $1 million on something so inconsequential. "As long as people are boobs enough to pay a fortune to a couple of prizefighters to perform for their entertainment, the pugilists can't be blamed for taking the money," it added.

Finally, the time came for the fighters to break camp and head for New York. Louis's trip was uneventful. Schmeling's was not.

On the afternoon of June 21, some thirty hours before the fight, Schmeling was scheduled to board a train in Amsterdam, New York, that would reach Grand Central around ten that night. For a week, though, rumors abounded that he would come by air. On his Sunday night radio program, Walter Winchell made it official: "Max Schmeling will fly to New York on the day of the fight!" he announced breathlessly. "Dick Merrill will handle the stick!" Merrill was a legendary aviator, the first ever to fly round-trip across the Atlantic, holder of several speed records, rescuer of Antarctic explorers. The year before, Franklin Roosevelt had invited him to the White House, and Eddie Rickenbacker called him the best commercial pilot in the United States. But Mike Jacobs wasn't impressed. To him flying was still too dangerous, and was, like horseback riding or baseball playing, on his list of proscribed activities. Jacobs went further, calling a local company that rented planes to make sure no aircraft was available. But Schmeling, and Merrill, could not be stopped. For Schmeling flying was simultaneously a way to save time, have a great adventure, show his sangfroid on the eve of the biggest moment in his life, tweak Jacobs, intimidate Louis, and protect his own well-being: he and his people believed Jacobs wanted him rattled by a long and rickety train ride.

Jacobs's phone call scuttled Merrill's original, spectacular plan to rent an amphibious craft and land it on the lake outside Schmeling's cottage. Instead, Merrill obtained a plane from Eastern Air Lines, which he flew to Schenectady on Tuesday afternoon. He then drove to Speculator, where he dined with Schmeling and some of his friends. By seven-thirty the group—which included Joe Jacobs, Machon, two state troopers, and a pair of reporters—was at the airport in Schenectady. Schmeling boarded fast, taking time only to wave to the two hundred or so people who had somehow caught wind of what was afoot. Within ten minutes, the hour-long flight to Newark had begun. Once the plane leveled off at four thousand feet Schmeling took the controls, where he remained until they were over the George Washington Bridge. He appeared almost boyishly gleeful over evading Jacobs's strictures. But the German was "Sphinx-like" as he emerged from the plane, leaving all the talking to Yussel. He would not even say where Schmeling was spending the night, though it was one of his usual haunts: the Essex House, on Central Park South.

The staff there had readied the place, installing an air conditioner to protect Schmeling from New York's blistering summertime heat. His chef was already on the job, in a secure kitchen. A reporter in Berlin reached Schmeling by phone just as he arrived in the lobby. "Next time we'll speak, you'll be world champion," the reporter said. "Hopefully," Schmeling replied with a laugh. "Things should work out fine." Around nine, Erwin Thoma and two other German journalists went to Schmeling's suite, on the thirty-sixth floor. Greeting them in an anteroom were three detectives, armed to the teeth. Thoma was struck by how suspiciously the policemen eyed even the maid who came to make up Schmeling's out-size bed. More detectives were in the lobby; Schmeling was protected like a jewel. "We find this all a little strange, exaggerated," Thoma later wrote. "At home a guard of detectives would be ridiculous. But here in the United States, the country where kidnapping, along medieval lines, is still known as a form of blackmail, this caution is entirely appropriate." Even stranger to him was the mood in Schmeling's room: something "serious and depressed" hung in the air. For two hours, all attempts at sociability failed. "I don't know what's wrong up there," Thoma told his colleagues after they'd left. "Schmeling is so quiet, like I've never seen him before. Is something worrying him?" The night was oppressive, at least for Germans, one of those New York summer evenings when even the walls seemed to sweat. "We sink into the asphalt and the skyscrapers disappear in the fog," wrote Curt Riess, the German-Jewish émigré covering the fight for *Paris Soir*. "Everyone is drained of their energy." Thoma worried that going from the cool breezes of Speculator to the "city of wash-house air and the smell of gasoline" could weaken an athlete, cut his force of will in half.

A fan had approached Schmeling in Speculator once, saying he'd come 1,500 miles to see him. "You've traveled 1,500 miles to see me but I've traveled 60,000 miles to get a close-up of Louis," Schmeling replied. And it was true: for Schmeling and for those who followed him, the fight marked the end of a long, long trail. Six years had passed since Schmeling had lost the title, and a year had gone by since he'd been robbed of his chance to regain it. He had overcome all the setbacks, obstacles, disappointments, and harassment, but he still faced every athlete's greatest adversary: time. For most boxers, thirty was the fatal divide, when legs, judgment, reflexes, and stamina began to wane. Though Schmeling was now pushing thirty-three, Thoma thought him still as young, ambitious, self-confident, and strong as a twenty-five-year-old. Louis, at twenty-four, enjoyed youth and all the physical advantages of his race, Thoma acknowledged, but with it came the black man's weaknesses: indifference, melancholy, a spirit easily broken and impossible to repair. Hurt a black man only once, Thoma believed, and "something somehow turns off in his brain and in his heart."

Throwing caution to the wind, the *Angriff* now apotheosized Schmeling into a modern Germanic hero: "In him, too, the wanderlust of the typical German has always been alive." Always, he had been "called by the far-away, like all those who feel a drop of the blood of the conqueror in their veins." Schmeling personified everything positive: "He is life affirming, he is the embodiment of optimism, and when others doubt, then Max becomes calm for a few moments, stands up, and then says with his deep voice, 'Even that we can do!'" A newspaper in Königsberg fit Schmeling specifically into Nazi ideology. "National-Socialist Germany, the sports people, is imbued with this: that man can be not only in top form for a few years, but perform at a high and respectable level over a long period of time if only the will is hard enough," it wrote.

For "Germany's best-known radio announcer," as the *8 Uhr-Blatt* called Hellmis, it was also a climactic moment: his faith was about to receive its sternest test. A visitor to any German kiosk found Hellmis expounding on Schmeling wherever he turned, and in none of those venues did he ever waver. His conclusion was inescapable: logically speaking, Schmeling simply could not lose. "Nothing but a dumb accident, which in boxing must certainly always be taken into account, justifies pessimism," he wrote. Schmeling would need six rounds or so to thwart "the primitive nature-boy." Most American sportswriters would have agreed with him, he said, if denigrating Schmeling was not just a matter of professional self-preservation—they had, after all, to placate their Jewish bosses—but one of self-enrichment, too; by raising the odds against Schmeling, they'd collect more betting on him.

Thirty thousand people had entered the *Angriff*'s pool. Readers picked Schmeling by one hundred to one. Of the 6,000 who participated in a similar contest in Nuremberg, only 150 brave souls went with Louis; the ratio was about the same in Hamburg.* The *Angriff* offered snippets from twelve entrants, all picking Maxe, all parroting the Nazi party line. "I'm just afraid that Schmeling will still lose a sure victory through some kind of treacherous incident," one wrote. "Schmeling will do it, even though Louis probably hopes to be able to bring about the opposite through low blows," stated another. "A Negro can and never will summon the ambition Schmeling has," said a third.

As the fighters made their way to the city, so did thousands of fans; three-quarters of them, Jacobs estimated, came from out of town. "Not a train pulled to a stop in Grand Central or Pennsylvania Station without pouring out fight customers," wrote Henry McLemore of the United Press. "Not a bus jerked to a halt in the city's dozens of terminals without unloading more of the same. Not an airplane taxied to a halt at Newark airport without a fight fan included in its cargo." Never, in fact, had so many fans arrived by air. Others came by boat, be they one-day excursions from Boston (round-trip fare: $6.75) or transatlantic voyages. Tommy Farr came via the *Queen Mary*, and spotted a crowd around another celebrity passenger as they disembarked. It was Joseph P. Kennedy. "Who's he gonna fight?" Farr asked. Trains teeming with Louis fans came from Detroit, Chicago, and Washington. A "Louis Victory Special" pulled in from Philadelphia. A caravan of two hundred cars arrived from Pittsburgh; a similar procession came from New Orleans. Relief officials in Cleveland and Chicago were reportedly checking whether anyone on their rolls had headed to New York. A hundred blacks came from Atlanta, infuriating a minister there. "I can count on the fingers of one hand the Negroes who are really able, without sacrifice to their families or themselves, to take this long and expensive trip," he groused. But his complaint, like the boycotters', was futile.

The density and pace of New York changed. Jack Dempsey's anticipated an additional $10,000 a night in business. With so many people in town, attendance at Aqueduct Racetrack was of "holiday proportions." A Broadway movie theater did a brisk business showing films of the first fight. "As jittery as a bridegroom fumbling for a wedding ring," was how *The Washington Post* described the city. But the neighborhood that was

---

*It was a far cry from Warsaw, where an estimated eight thousand people placed bets, with most wagering their zlotys on Louis.

most transformed was Harlem. Its hotels, penthouses, guesthouses, flop-houses, and crash pads filled up, as did its bars and restaurants. The Hotel Theresa put beds in its lobby to deal with the overflow. "Not even General Washington in his Revolutionary War rambling had as many headquar-ters as do the Joe Louis fans," the Associated Negro Press wrote. The rich flaunted their money—the *Amsterdam News* reported more Packards and other fancy cars on Harlem's streets than on the assembly lines of Detroit—while the poor scraped together what little money they had. One reporter spotted a black woman purchasing two $11.50 seats. "From her bag, she drew an old blanket-sized $20 bill that must have been under a rug since Dewey steamed into Manila Bay," he wrote. A store on 125th Street had marked radios down to $50 for the occasion, with many buyers paying for them in installments. "Of course, after the fight, there will be a rush to reclaim these machines from delinquent customers, but they shall have heard the fight," one black weekly reported. The neighborhood went about its business with a mix of eagerness and apprehension. Most of the visiting Germans stayed on their ships. But in a bow to Schmeling, the Casino movie theater on East Eighty-sixth Street featured *Gross-reinemachen*, a comedy starring Anny Ondra.

Uncertainty over the fight was ubiquitous. "It is a grab in the dark, a guess thrown to the winds, a groping in the fogs of chance—no matter what anyone may tell you," Grantland Rice wrote. Another sportswriter spent the day before the bout on Jacobs Beach, schmoozing with man-agers and seconds, trainers and reporters, fighters and hangers-on—the greatest concentration of fight experts on the planet, at least until the next night in Yankee Stadium. And from all those conversations, he reached only one conclusion. "This," he wrote, "is the fight nobody knows any-thing about."

CHAPTER 13

The Fight

ARLY IN THE AFTERNOON OF JUNE 22 — fight day—five thousand people stood on the south side of West Forty-ninth Street and Eighth Avenue. Someone with an eye for drama and publicity had wisely decided to move the weigh-in from the dingy, claustrophobic downtown offices of the boxing commission to something more spacious and splashy: the center of the arena at Madison Square Garden. Five hundred policemen held back the teeming crowd as it awaited the two principals.

Schmeling had spent a fitful night, disturbed by the traffic around his hotel, and slept until eleven. A mass of people cheered as he left the Essex House and made his way south a few blocks to the Garden, in a car driven by Joe Jacobs's detective brother. The perpetually punctual German arrived thirteen minutes early, at 12:47 p.m. He was very much unshaven, and wore a dark suit. He clasped his hands above his head as the crowd shouted its approval. When he stepped inside, someone handed him an envelope. As strange as it seemed—why there, rather than at his hotel? and who was the courier?—it was a cablegram from Adolf Hitler. "To the next world's champion, Max Schmeling," it said. "Wishing you every success."

Louis arrived twenty-five minutes later, in a shiny blue limousine, followed, in what some saw as an ill omen, by a long black hearse. So many people clogged the thoroughfare that the car had to slow to a crawl as it approached. The Louis that emerged was a "Creole fashion plate," wearing a gray plaid suit with pocket square, soft hat, open-collared shirt, foulard, and sunglasses. He, too, received a boisterous ovation. Mike Jacobs, wearing a straw skimmer, escorted him inside. Three doctors examined the fighters in their respective dressing rooms. One of them pronounced Louis to be in much better shape than for the last Schmeling fight; never, he said, had he examined a more perfect athlete. The two boxers met coming out of their quarters and shook hands. A grinning Schmeling was the first to say hello, and Louis—irritable because the weigh-in had been postponed an hour, thereby upsetting his sleep cycle—mumbled a reply. Then they walked together to the ceremony, clad incongruously in suit coats and trunks. Louis, the area beneath his left eye slightly swollen from sparring, wore gray suede oxfords, Schmeling a pair of bedroom slippers. The head of the boxing commission, General John J. Phelan, greeted the two of them and joked that because they presumably knew one another already, there was no need for introductions. A courtly Schmeling asked Louis how he was, and held out his hand. Louis said hello.

Ignoring the old boxing shibboleth that it brought bad luck, Schmeling had shaved. Stripped naked, he stood on the scales, grinning and winking at the press. He came in at 193, a bit lighter than he'd expected, but a pound heavier than for the first Louis fight. When Louis's turn came, he balked. "I ain't going to take my pants off," he declared. "Make 'em turn those things off," he added, pointing to the cameras. After a three-minute huddle, Roxborough announced that if the cameras were shut off and the lights lowered, Louis would drop his trunks. He weighed 198¾. The Bomber was "as emotionless as the corner of a house." The two fighters mugged for the photographers, with Louis offering Schmeling a limp handshake and Schmeling holding his right fist a quarter inch from Louis's jaw. James Dawson of *The New York Times* thought that Schmeling looked intimidated. Chester Washington, one of ten *Courier* reporters covering the fight, reminded Louis of the New Year's resolution he'd made to him. "I know, and I'm gonna finish this one in a hurry," Louis replied. He had heard about the Führer's telegram, and said he would make Hitler sorry he had ever sent it.

The boxing commission barred the Chicago-made gloves Louis preferred, whose protruding thumbs, Schmeling charged, could have poked him in the eye. It was a victory for Joe Jacobs, who had seen them to be, as someone joked, "not only a menace to his fighter, but also a violation of the Constitution, a reversal of the Dred Scott decision, an insult to the American flag, and an abuse of the pure food and drugs act." Schmeling and his entourage quietly repaired to the Concourse Plaza Hotel in the Bronx, four blocks from Yankee Stadium. It was a way to shake the press, avoid the long drive from Manhattan later on, and take an afternoon walk in the fresh air. Louis went to Duke Ellington's apartment, where neither Blackburn's jokes nor someone tickling his feet could make him laugh. For a couple of days he'd been surly, barely talking to people, grunting out monosyllables. "We'd better let the champ rest," Blackburn said. "He's in a bad mood." "I'm goin' out and fight three rounds as fast as I can go," Louis told Blackburn. "If Schmeling is still on his feet after that you'd better come get me." Blackburn himself was satisfied. "I did all I could," he said. "He's as good as hands can make him."

The weather was iffy. When Mike Jacobs belatedly consulted his *Farmers' Almanac*, he saw that June 22 would be "very disappointing." At his request, around noon a United Airlines meteorologist went up twelve thousand feet and forecast an occasional shower or light mist between six and midnight. Around three o'clock there was indeed a light shower uptown, but barring a downpour, Jacobs decreed, the fight would go on. Both fighters were to report to the stadium by eight, two hours before the scheduled start. Harlem's streets were jammed. People were wearing their holiday best, and waving red pennants proclaiming JOE LOUIS, WORLD'S CHAMPION. "We were in the land of Louis and his countrymen already were celebrating," a reporter from Richmond, Virginia, wrote. When Louis's car stalled in traffic, it was immediately swamped. It arrived at Yankee Stadium half an hour late, and was again engulfed. In the meantime, out-of-town fans kept streaming into Manhattan and up to the Bronx. Holding fight tickets but stuck in Albany until midafternoon, Roy Wilkins of the NAACP begged the conductor to "step on it," and his train reached Harlem three minutes early. "That good enough for you?" the conductor asked him with a wink. Coming in from Baltimore, Lula Jones Garrett, who was covering Marva for the *Afro-American*, needed no directions from Pennsylvania Station. "The crowd simply carried you through the gates, up the Eighth Avenue exit, into the sub[way] and into the Stadium," she wrote. By evening the threat of rain had waned, and the air had cleared. Some 1,700 policemen joined Jacobs's private army of 1,000, including 675 ushers and 75 ticket takers. Uncle Mike's mobile ticket offices circled the ballpark, picking off buyers otherwise headed for the scalpers. (Perhaps he'd put them in his newly created rows 9a, 12a, and 15a.) The place was ringed by flags; the swastika was not among them.

Members of the Anti-Nazi League, having failed to convince fight-goers to shun one particular German product, reiterated calls to boycott all the rest. Meantime, the Communists handed out flyers:

Usually a sports event is not a matter of "politics." Far from us to make it so.

But Hitler, and his anti-Semitic, anti-Negro, anti-fair-play pugilist, Schmeling, make this fight a matter of "politics."

Last time, Hitler played up Schmeling's victory as an "aryan triumph." Americans remember, also, Hitler's personal insults to American athletes in the Olympics.

Schmeling has been a willing tool of Hitler's propaganda, and has many unsportsmanlike, un-American statements to his discredit.

So if it's "politics," let's tear the mask off!

SCHMELING STANDS FOR NAZISM —

NAZISM MEANS Spy-rings against our Country, pogroms against Jews, Catholics and Protestants. Nazism means bombing and slaughter of innocent Catholic women and children. NAZISM means BARBARISM.

SO WE AMERICANS ALL PULL WITH OUR JOE LOUIS, WIN OR LOSE!

LONG LIVE GOOD, CLEAN AMERICAN SPORTSMANSHIP!

The last line on the flyer provided one more reminder of why the boycott had failed. "READ CRACKERJACK FIGHT NEWS IN TOMORROW'S DAILY WORKER," it read. People just cared too much. In fact, anyone carrying that day's *Worker* into the stadium could have read lots about the fight. "I'd like to see Joe Louis blast Schmeling all over the ring tonight, knock the false bluster and braggodocio [*sic*] right out of Hitler's pal much the same as the people of Germany will eventually knock out Hitler," Lester Rodney had written. "If that sounds like wild overemphasis on a fight between just two men, that's due only to Schmeling and his Nazi cohorts. They've stuck a little swastika right out there on Schmeling's chin tonight for the greatest hitter of ring history to knock into the thirtieth row along with the wildly screaming Nazi headlines."

Inside the stadium were hundreds of vendors, all white, and in white uniforms, who had arrived several hours earlier for their assignments, hawking candy, soda, and programs. At a quarter apiece, the programs contained the life stories of the two fighters, along with another profile of Mike Jacobs, a compilation of record gates — this fight instantly took sixth place on the all-time list — and, on the back cover, Joe DiMaggio pushing

Camels. (They aided his digestion, he said.) The fans "seemed electrically charged as they went through the turnstiles," an eyewitness later
recalled. Then they found their seats, settling in with the contented sighs
of those arriving at the center of the universe in good shape and in plenty
of time. The celebrities again came fashionably late, taxing reporters who
needed to cram a few names into boldface for the early editions. Popping
flashbulbs heralded their arrivals.

General Phelan entered with James Farley and ordered Larry
MacPhail, president of the Brooklyn Dodgers, to move down to make
room. Frank Hague, the dictator of Jersey City, and Mayor Edward Kelly
of Chicago took their places in the "press rows," along with other high-
muck-a-mucks and plutocrats. Some were Mike Jacobs's "personal" customers, who paid as much as $500 for the privilege. Alongside them, one
by one, were the greatest sportswriters of their generation: Damon Runyon, Grantland Rice, Frank Graham, Bill Corum, Dan Parker, Murray
Lewin, Bob Considine, James Dawson, Richards Vidmer, Joe Williams,
Jimmy Powers, Jack Miley, Al Buck, Bill Cunningham, Arch Ward,
Anthony Marenghi. Though they didn't have the choice seats, and few
whites would ever know any of their names, the cream of black journal-
ism was there, too: Ed Harris, Al Monroe, Ralph Matthews, and Chester
Washington, among others.

Swells from the Brook and the Links clubs, along with the patrons of
chic restaurants like "21" and the Colony, arrived en masse; twenty or
thirty people from the River Club, all dressed to the nines, came up by
boat via the East River, docking not far from the stadium. "A Gatsby sort
of atmosphere," a participant later called it. The evening was cool, with a
pleasant breeze, just chilly enough for women to wear a light wrap over
their summer finery. The air was filled with the scent of the gardenias that
many of the women wore. A group of Germans came in together and
occupied a block of seats. At ringside, Tallulah Bankhead and her husband sat in front of four Schmeling fans. Mrs. Evalyn Walsh McLean,
wearing the Hope diamond, filed in, escorted by the *Herald Tribune*'s
society columnist, Lucius Beebe. La Guardia was one of the latecomers.
J. Edgar Hoover was there, along with his confidant Clyde Tolson. So was
Thomas E. Dewey, Manhattan's crime-busting prosecutor. On the other
end of the social spectrum were the people watching from the rooftops
beyond center field. Here, too, space was in short supply, by order of the
building department, which was concerned with collapses: admission was
by rent receipt only, and the police were checking. Atop 831 Gerard

Avenue, someone had placed planks between two chairs so that the small fry could peer down into the stadium.

Black fans were again among the first to take their seats, primarily in the bleachers, bringing with them chicken wings, pork chops, and ham sandwiches. Others, the upper crust of a downtrodden people, appeared closer in, and in the same outfits they'd worn to Pompton Lakes. A German paper described the "rich Harlem Negroes and their gem-laden [*juwelenbehangen*] wives." Cab Calloway and Bill Robinson were present. So were the Mills Brothers and the Nicholas Brothers, Louis and Henry Armstrong, Ethel Waters, and Jimmy Rushing. Duke Ellington had postponed hernia surgery just to come. Jack Johnson sported a derby, a blue serge suit, and a cane. Four of Louis's siblings came. So did Walter White; he might have been the head of the most important civil rights organization in the country, but he could manage no better than a seat in the upper deck. But at what other function in American society—or American history, for that matter—could Mrs. John Roxborough and Mrs. Julian Black sit just behind Mr. Vincent Astor and his party? "A sea of faces," the *Afro-American* society correspondent wrote wondrously. "Black faces, brown faces, ivory faces, white faces: a sea of folk. Richly dressed, shabbily frocked, 98-cent dresses, furs worth a king's ransom; the elite, the hoi polloi."

At 8:25 the ring lights went on. Twelve minutes later, the first preliminary bout began. There wouldn't be time for them all; some would be shunted to after the main event. Mike Jacobs walked around, asking the men in the press rows to take off their hats (the words "no ladies admitted" were stamped on all press tickets). A hundred Western Union wires, seven more than at the second Dempsey-Tunney fight, had been installed. But wires could bear only so much traffic. All night long, foreign correspondents in Warsaw found the international phone lines busy; Louis and Schmeling had them all tied up.

A German reporter watched his American counterparts, sleeves rolled up, cigarettes stuck in the corners of their mouths, talking into telephones or pecking away at their typewriters. The stadium, he wrote, lay "in an unreal gray haze," looking like "the open, greedy jaws of an antediluvian beast." Everything seemed surreal to him, poised somewhere between day and night; tobacco smoke, viscous and heavy, shrouded the giant bowl like fog over a deep ravine. Accustomed to the Teutonic orderliness of the Sportpalast and the Hanseatenhalle, the American-style tumult impressed him. "It is a chaos of voices, an indescribable excitement, a rushing, a chasing, screaming and raving like in a mental asylum," he wrote later. "The people here behave completely differently than at home. They pull out their hair, they roar ceaselessly, they change their bets after every round (sometimes in the middle of the fight), and they rave in such a manner that after a fight they're at least as exhausted as the two boxers in the ring."

The fight appeared sold out, but in fact, paid attendance was only 66,277; even with the freeloaders, employees, and policemen factored in, another 25,000 people could have squeezed into the stadium that night. But most of those who had stayed away, along with sixty million other Americans, were by their radios, awaiting Clem McCarthy. Assisting him this time was Ed Thorgersen, the sports commentator for Fox Movietone News. Listening to them, *Radio Guide* predicted, would be the largest radio audience in the history of sports, which probably meant the largest radio audience in history. Apart from Hellmis's German play-by-play, the fight was also being broadcast in Spanish and Portuguese, so much of South America would be listening. Around ten, an NBC announcer thanked Lucky Strike cigarettes for relinquishing the slot normally filled by *Kay Kyser's Kollege of Musical Knowledge*. Then, as if to build the momentousness, a second voice came on, greeting listeners on the "NBC coast-to-coast network, Canada and Honolulu." "And now," it continued, "light, curtain, the ringside, Yankee Stadium and Ed Thorgersen!" After a few seconds, Thorgersen came on. There was no time for small talk. "Good evening, ladies and gentlemen, the two principals in the greatest bout in a generation are in the ring," was all he said.

In Indianapolis, bar owners along Indiana Avenue had moved their radios out to the sidewalk. On the east side of Los Angeles, blacks gathered up and down Central Avenue. W. E. B. DuBois sat listening with a group of professor friends in Atlanta. Eleanor Roosevelt also listened, almost in self-defense; for days now, all she'd heard about was "the fight." When Jersey Joe Walcott looked out his window in Camden, New Jersey, the streets were deserted. In Chicago, Studs Terkel and his friends stopped rehearsing *Waiting for Lefty*, hopped into a car parked in front of the theater, and turned on the radio. Woody Guthrie wandered through the central plaza in Santa Fe, where he "listened in at car doors, trucks, stores, hotels, the hot buildings of sun baked mud, to the Indians, Mexicans, farm and ranch hands, to the artists, cowpokes, tourists on all of their radios." "Let's not have speaking now," the governor of Virginia told a convention of undertakers. "Let's have a radio." Campaigning for governor of Ohio, John W. Bricker had the good sense to time his talk to the Republicans in Coshocton to end before the opening bell. In Kingston, Jamaica, fight fans too poor to own radios were invited to listen outside the Biltmore House, and to enjoy curried goat afterward. The high school band in Kaukauna, Wisconsin, postponed its summer concert a night. An ill-timed thunderstorm in nearby Neenah made radio reception treacherous. The field hands on Earl Carter's peanut farm in Plains, Georgia, listened on his porch along with Carter's eldest son, thirteen-year-old Jimmy.

In a roadhouse near Lake Mashpee on Cape Cod, black Portuguese cranberry pickers prepared to cheer for Louis. The boys at the Broad Channel Baths near Rockaway, New York, left their lindy-hopping girlfriends and, sixteen-ounce beer bottles in hand, went to the parking lot to listen. In the Bronx, fourteen-year-old Arthur Donovan, Jr., sat down by the radio with a bag of peanuts. In Philadelphia, Angelo Dundee, sixteen, went to listen at the local firehouse, while in Detroit, Eddie Futch, destined, like Dundee, to become one of boxing's most famous trainers, listened in a locked office at the Brewster Center, where the young Louis had once trained. In Lafayette, Alabama, members of Louis's extended family gathered in a black restaurant. In the Searcy State Hospital for the Negro Insane, Louis's father listened in bed. In his hand was an autographed picture inscribed, "To my father, Monroe Barrow, from his son, Joe Louis Barrow?" Marva listened on St. Nicholas Avenue in Harlem, in the apartment of a family friend, a steward for the Pennsylvania Railroad. She fiddled with the dial, just "to show she was absolutely composed."

Anyone scheduling something opposite the fight obviously had to make some accommodations. In Charleston, South Carolina, the Palmetto Theater pledged to interrupt *Joy of Living*, starring Irene Dunne and Douglas Fairbanks, Jr., for as long as the fight lasted. Wrestling fans in Mobile, Alabama—whites in the 40- and 60-cent seats, blacks in the 25-cent ones—were also promised a blow-by-blow account. A black church in Chicago revamped its schedule so that all who ordinarily prayed on Wednesdays "could come and root for Joe." At a "championship ball" for blacks in Brooklyn, there would be dancing until three, with a short time-out while, as the *New York Age* put it, Louis "knock[ed] Der Moxie loose from his dental work." In Manhattan, the Muzak Corporation made plans to pipe in the broadcast to hotels and restaurants serving thirty thousand people on an ordinary night. Throughout crowded apartment blocks radios blared, and with windows open, the broadcast bounced around courtyards and reverberated along empty streets.

Gold and diamond miners listened in the jungles of British Guiana. Jurors at a murder trial in Port-of-Spain, Trinidad, had a radio installed where they deliberated. South Africans hoped atmospheric turbulence wouldn't make Clem McCarthy even less intelligible than he normally was to non-Americans; those who couldn't understand him would have to wait for the fight extra the *Rand Daily Mail* planned to publish. Harry, who presided over the New York Bar in Paris, promised patrons he would tune in. "The world will hold you responsible for failure to spot announcers equipped to give sensational account of this epoch making event no kidding," an anxious Mexican official wired NBC. The fight was not to be broadcast in Italy, the *Chicago Daily News* reported, perhaps because Mussolini feared embarrassment "should a Negro defeat a Fascist." And sitting by their *Volksemfänger*, Germans again awaited Hellmis. A special fight broadcast had begun two hours earlier, at one a.m. Berlin time, featuring some commentary, a statement from Metzner, a reading from Hellmis's book on Schmeling, and two live bands. A reporter for a Yiddish paper in Warsaw was among those listening. "There was no doubt whatsoever that victory was on their side," he later wrote; at stake was "the absolute survival and honor of the nation." Like the other Jews of Warsaw, he was pulling for the "Schvartser Bombardier." Hitler was reportedly listening at his Bavarian retreat.

Several movie theaters in Berlin planned to play the radio broadcast. In Karlsruhe, a boxing exhibition would carry on until the fight began. The mandatory closing hour for pubs had once more been moved from 3 a.m. to 5:45 a.m., though the anticipation had begun long before then. At around midnight, a reporter for the *Angriff* motored around Berlin. "Behind the windows in almost every apartment, the lights were burning," he wrote. "In the west, in the south, in the north; on the Kurfüstendamm, in Friedenau, in Potsdamer Strasse, and around Alex [Alexanderplatz]. We turned on the radio in the car. For the time being, music. Up above, behind the windows, they are just as impatient as us." He called to wake up a number of people, but they were all up already, and indignant: "'No time. Listening to the broadcast. Call after the fight.' Click. Hung up!" Though the owner and many regulars were in New York, seats at Schmeling's table in the Roxy-Bar on Rankeplatz remained at a premium. Sitting there were, among others, Goebbels's deputy, Hans Hinkel, and the man who directed *Schmelings Sieg*, Hans Zerlett, along with athletes, actors, and journalists. The only Schmeling on the premises was a cardboard cutout; earlier that evening it had toppled over. Anny Ondra planned to spend this fight night at home, and would spare herself another nerve-racking broadcast. What worried her most, she told the *Angriff*, was "the murderous American heat," in which a black man was in his element. Her maid was to listen for her, and give her the results in the morning. At a small bar in the western part of Berlin—and at hundreds like it—a man ordered perhaps his sixth cup of coffee as zero hour approached. At Berlin's Hildesheimer Yeshiva, members of what would turn out to be Germany's last crop of rabbinical students, hiding from both the authorities and their rabbi, sat by a crystal set someone had built just for the fight, preparing to pull for Louis. Yet many Jews around them pulled for Schmeling. They still thought of themselves as Germans first.

Shortly before three in the morning, the sound of military music came over German radio. Then Hellmis's first words from New York crackled through. "*Hallo Berlin.* . . . *Hallo Deutschland.* . . . *Hallo Deutschland. Hier ist das Yankee Stadium in New York,*" he began. "The moment has finally come," he went on. "This isn't a stadium anymore. . . . This is an overflowing, feverish melting pot full of passions let loose, and if one should throw a match I am sure the whole stadium with all its people will be blown up into the air with one single explosion. . . . A fever rages in the veins of all these people." In fact, the fans had quickly tired of the preliminaries, and were shouting for the main event. Once Al Bray and Abe Simon finished poking each other in the ring, the crowd roared with delight and rose to stretch, as if readying itself for the serious business at hand. Two boys selling sodas spotted a pair of empty seats at ringside and abandoned all thoughts of work.

Before most bouts, Louis shadowboxed for five or ten minutes in his dressing room; this time he did so for forty minutes, hoping to enter the ring revved up. Blackburn put a terry-cloth robe on him, then on top of that the familiar one of blue and red silk, with "Joe Louis" stitched on the back, so that Louis would retain as much of that heat as possible. Roxborough, who smoked and chewed his way through numerous cigars during most fights, had come well stocked tonight. "You'll need only one," Louis assured him, "and you won't have time to light it well. That Schmeling is going to think he's in there with a tiger tonight." Mike Jacobs stopped by Louis's dressing room; reports of what he said there differ. In one version, he recounted a promise he'd made to the anti-Nazi protesters: that they'd be pleased with the outcome. "Don't make a sucker out of me," he then told Louis. "Give this guy the beating of his life—but quick." In another version, he called Schmeling "a Nazi son-of-a-bitch" and added, "Murder that bum and don't make an asshole out of me."

Louis made his way to the ring, "prancing and dancing as a Man O' War at the bit." He was the first to enter, at two minutes to ten, preceded by handlers in white sweaters, encircled by bodyguards and policemen. His reception was rather tame, perhaps because so many of his fans were so remote. "Did you hear the applause when the world champion appeared?" Hellmis gloated. Louis sequestered himself in his corner, the closest to third base, flexing his arms, rubbing his feet into the resin. With him, as usual, were Blackburn, Roxborough, and Black; joining them were Henry Armstrong's manager, Eddie Mead, along with trainers Larry Amadee and Manny Seamon. To Hellmis, Mead's presence showed how insecure Louis felt. But two years earlier, Louis had entered the ring languidly, nonchalantly, indifferently. Now, drenched from his exercising, he radiated a tense, febrile energy.

Then it was Schmeling's turn. Years later, he compared his walk through Yankee Stadium's infield that night—out of the dugout, down the baseline toward home plate, then straight over the pitcher's mound toward the ring—to running a gantlet; though twenty-five policemen escorted him, he wrote, he was pelted by cigarette butts, ashtrays, banana peels, and paper cups, and pulled a towel over his head for protection. All of this weighed heavily on him once he got into the ring, he was to claim, and upset his concentration. But in fact Schmeling would have had to walk through only the most expensive seats; anyone inclined to heave something would have been too far away. Certainly no reporter present that night saw anything of the kind, nor any such hostility when he stepped into the ring. "No challenger in memory of the oldest scribes was ever given such a welcome," one veteran fight writer reported. "Everyone is shouting and applauding," Hellmis declared. They were, one Berlin newspaper explained, the cheers of every white in the stadium. Schmeling looked positively cheerful when he climbed between the ropes; Bill Cunningham of the *Boston Post* described him as "the picture of suavity, condescension and confidence" as he acknowledged the ovation. He bowed gallantly to the four corners of the crowd, then went over to Louis, whose back was toward him, nearly hitting the hanging microphone along the way. He tapped him on the shoulder playfully, then tapped him again. Louis finally turned—"expressionless, unmoved," Hellmis told the radio audience—and briefly shook Schmeling's outstretched hand, before quickly turning back away. "Max sits in his corner, unusually serious and composed after he first greeted the masses with his smile," Hellmis observed. Schmeling stared ahead, he said, "darkly, decidedly, energetically."

Harry Balogh took his place in the center of the ring and began his introductions. He called for Tony Galento, then Sharkey, then Dempsey, then Braddock and Tunney and Tommy Farr. And then, "last but far from least," the man who was to meet the winner, Max Baer. Baer received loud cheers, Bronx and otherwise. "Do you hear the booing?" Hellmis asked his listeners. "The public does not want him."* Though both Jack Johnson and John Henry Lewis, the light-heavyweight champion, who was black, were at ringside, neither was introduced; again, only the black press seemed to notice. Louis danced, flexed his arms, punched the Bronx night. Normally, his face was round, soft, babyish, emotionless. But now, it seemed older and more taut—taut with rage.

Representatives of the opposing camps—Blackburn for Louis, Doc Casey for Schmeling—looked on as the gloves were placed on the two fighters. This allowed Hellmis to remind his listeners how Louis had pressed unsuccessfully for gloves with larger thumbs, the better to gouge out Schmeling's eyes. Hellmis explained that Schmeling's American manager—unnamed, as usual—had been disqualified; Jacobs had been placed in a front-row seat behind a neutral corner, presumably to keep him out of kibitzing range. The bell rang twice, and Balogh announced the ring officials, including, once more as referee, Arthur Donovan. Then, in his portentous, stentorian bellow, as if he did not fully trust the microphone, sprinkling ellipses liberally between his hyperenunciated words, he got to the principals. "This is the featured attraction, fifteen rounds, for the world's heavyweight championship," Balogh began. "Weighing 193, wearing purple trunks, outstanding contender for heavyweight honors, the former heavyweight titleholder, Max . . . Schmeling." He got the German pronunciation right: "Mox Schmayling." The German arose from his stool, gathered his bathrobe, walked forward a few steps, put his gloved right hand over his chest, and bowed in courtly European fashion to two sides of Yankee Stadium. The crowd roared. Predictions that Schmeling would get "the biggest Bronx cheer in the history of the Bronx cheering section" didn't materialize. Eyewitnesses—white and black, German and American—were struck instead by how warmly he was received. Schmeling smiled at what was clearly an unequaled and, in fact, rather surprising display of American sportsmanship.

---

*Two people sitting directly behind Hellmis later claimed he'd lifted his microphone to pick up the catcalls for Baer, and then said, "Listen to this booing. You will see from this that the Jews are no more popular here than they are in Germany." The two eavesdroppers relayed what they said they'd heard to Herbert Bayard Swope, the editor and author, who passed it along to NBC chief David Sarnoff, who asked that an English transcript of the broadcast be prepared. It contained no such statement.

The bell sounded two more times, sternly summoning the house back to order. "Weighing 198 and three-quarters, wearing black trunks, the famous Detroit Brown Bomber, world's heavyweight champion, Joe Louis." Louis arose, skipped out a few steps, then turned around. There were lots of cheers, but mixed in were some boos—some undoubtedly racial, some just the usual raspberries for the favorite, some from Schmeling boosters, some for Louis's recent, disappointing performances. The crowd, one embittered black reporter wrote afterward, "saw fit to give Schmeling, a Nazi, a greater hand than it did an American-born world champion." Balogh then pointed to Donovan, who tugged at his trousers, made his way to the center of the ring, and readied himself for another ring ritual, one that now reverberated throughout the stadium and over the air. Louis, Black, and Blackburn huddled around him on one side, Schmeling, Machon, and Casey on the other. As they assembled, Thorgersen handed the microphone to McCarthy, who, unlike Hellmis, had no time for pleasantries, or even a greeting. "Aaaaaaaaand, boxing fans, Arthur Donovan has the two principals in the ring," he growled. "I want you to listen to their instructions. Arthur Donovan speaking to the two fighters, with their seconds surrounding them."

"Now how do you men feel? All right? Fine," Donovan said quickly, mechanistically, without waiting for any response. "Now I want to impress upon you men now, of the terrific responsibility that you have in this ring tonight." He talked about how the fans in the stadium, plus the untold multitudes sitting by their radios, expected one of the greatest fights ever. "Now let us not disappoint them," he said. He warned them about low blows, then turned to the seconds. "Now at no time now in this contest do I want anybody in this ring, outside of the minute rest," he said, pointing his finger for emphasis. "The first man that even sticks his head through those ropes, something drastic is going to happen." Schmeling looked directly at Louis; Louis did not look back. Blackburn removed Louis's blue robe, only to reveal the white robe underneath. Hellmis thought it a fashion statement rather than a reflection on Louis's state of readiness. "Oh, how pompously Joe Louis is dressed up," he told his audience. "First a white woolen dressing gown and over it a blue-silken robe." "Now, let's go," Donovan concluded, "and may the best man win."

"The old slogan of boxing, 'May the best man win,' and she's about to start, with this Yankee Stadium packed to the doors! There isn't an empty seat!" McCarthy croaked, even though it wasn't quite true. As the ring microphone was elevated and the two men retreated to their corners, a reporter near ringside heard a contented sigh. It came from Mike Jacobs, who was, for the moment at least, at rest. The skies had cleared, his house was nearly full, his two fighters were healthy and at hand. His show could now get under way, and the tensions that had, as one British reporter said, "wrinkled his forehead like a washboard" could begin to flow out of him. For a few seconds, the only noises came from the crowd. "Unchain them!" someone shouted. "Kill that Nazi, Joe! Kill him!" another voice rang out. In the distant seats, fans struggled simply to see. "It seemed that each man and woman was straining forward to peer at a colorful puppet show," Richard Wright later wrote. Louis continued to dance about. He "had the look of a murderer in his eye," one eyewitness later recalled. "He didn't lick his lips or do anything." To Ernest Hemingway, Louis seemed "nervous and jumpy as a doped race horse." "They've got that guy hopped up," someone remarked. Schmeling stood still, taking last-minute instructions from Machon. Hellmis reminded his listeners that Louis expected to win in two rounds. But to Schmeling that was just talk, he explained; after the beating he'd taken the last time, surely Louis would be careful, get a sense of things, wait a few rounds before trying anything drastic. "They're ready with the bell just about to ring," McCarthy said. And ring it did, at precisely the moment McCarthy uttered the word, at 10:08 p.m. To the radio audience, it sounded loud and clear and true; to the boxers themselves, it was still not quite right. "And there we are," McCarthy declared. "The gong!" said Hellmis. "The fight for the world heavyweight championship is on."

For one brief, immeasurable interval nothing happened, except an ineffable surge of mass anticipation. Baseball had its innings; football, hockey, soccer, and basketball their clocks. All of them had teams, and all lasted a couple of hours, come what may. Here, two men were about to square off, in something that could end at any moment. There was no sitting back. "This is the million-dollar thrill of sports," one reporter explained. "This is a second pregnant with drama and suspense, and no matter how often it occurs you never forget the strange shivers that sweep over you. This is The Big Fight." And after two years of anticipation, this was the biggest big fight of them all.

Throughout the stadium, people leaned forward. "One hundred and sixty thousand knees became uncontrollable," one man wrote. To one apprehensive Louis fan, Schmeling suddenly looked too fierce and powerful for anyone to handle by himself, and the man felt like jumping out of his seat, springing into the ring, and lending his hero a hand. As the action was about to begin, wrote a reporter for the *Philadelphia Tribune*, "a silence, like the calm of Heaven, prevailed over Harlem." And not only there, but all over America, and especially black America. "Fourteen million brown men, women and children cussed and prayed in 14 million ways for Joe to come through," wrote Frank Marshall Davis. "Probably never before in American history were so many black voices silent."

Schmeling walked out of his corner matter-of-factly, like a businessman going to an appointment. Louis, who normally came out slowly, shuffling, feinting, jabbing, all but bounded out now, as if eager to complete something he relished, meeting Schmeling three-quarters of the way across the ring. The two had feinted for only seven seconds before Louis hit, and hurt, Schmeling with a left jab, then threw two more that snapped the German's head back. Then came a left hook to the body. The two then fell into a clinch. Already, Donovan could see that Louis was keeping up his left after jabbing; he seemed to have learned the only thing he had still needed to know. Louis's chastened fans assumed nothing. "Look out, Joe!" they shouted. "Watch out, Joe!"

Barely twenty seconds had passed—Machon was not even fully down the steps—when there came a deafening roar. In a flash, Louis had Schmeling against the ropes, connecting with a series of devastating blows to the head and body, so fast that the human eye, let alone the voice, could not keep up. "And Louis hooks a left to Max's head quickly!" McCarthy exclaimed. "And shoots over a hard right to Max's head! Louis, a left to Max's jaw! A right to his head! Louis with the old one-two! The first the left and then the right! He's landed more blows in this one round than he landed in any five rounds of the other fight!" Donovan had never seen anything like it: after that first left to the head, Schmeling's face seemed to swell out of proportion and turn a faint bluish green. Then came the first right. It was so hard that Schmeling's head seemed to spin, then "bobbed up and down like a Halloween apple in a tub." The contest was not yet thirty seconds old.

Hellmis had to admit it: Louis had started quickly, and Schmeling had all he could handle just covering himself. But he emphasized the positive: Schmeling had neutralized Louis by clinching, then breaking loose with splendid footwork. And he had gotten in a punch to the jaw through Louis's lowered guard, but Louis had been backing away when it landed. Some Germans stood up and applauded the punch. So, too, did some white Americans. "These folks at once sensed another victory—not for the Germans but for the white race," a black reporter noted bitterly. Louis hesitated, but only for a second. Had he remained traumatized by the last fight, were the "Indian sign" still on him, even that single palsied punch might have triggered something. Instead, he stepped forward relentlessly, and kept at the German. It was just as Blackburn always said: if you get hit, hit the other fellow before he can hit you again.

Schmeling's face was already marked when, nearly a minute into the fight, Louis chased him back toward the ropes once more. They fell into another clinch. Coming out of it, Louis hit Schmeling again. Then he hit the German with two more straight lefts to the face and a right to the temple before they clinched once more. Louis stalked Schmeling, searching for an opening. Back to the ropes, he missed a roundhouse left. Then he delivered a right uppercut, a left, and a devastating right to Schmeling's suddenly defenseless face. Schmeling staggered backward. As he twisted along the ropes to avoid the blows to the head, Louis, his gloves a brownish blur, landed a series of body punches—to the side, to the stomach, and then to the left kidney. "The Negro swung, hooked, swung and hooked at him as though he were the big bag," Hemingway wrote. Even in the press box, where partisan cheering was forbidden, there were cries of excitement, astonishment, horror. Schmeling grimaced, letting out a high-pitched cry that echoed throughout the stadium. Some heard "Oh! Oh!" To others, it was *"Genug! Genug!"*—Enough! Enough! "I thought in my mind, 'How's that, Mr. Super-race?'" Louis later said. "I was glad he was hurt. That's what I wanted." Many, Louis among them, thought the scream had come not from Schmeling but from a woman at ringside. "Did you hear that?" Hype Igoe of the *Journal-American* asked the man at his side. "Did I hear it?" he replied. "I felt the punch!" So terrifying was the sound—"half human, half animal"—that some fans reached instinctively for their hats, as if Louis was about to come for them, too. Donovan had never heard anything like it, and it frightened even him. But to others it was welcome indeed. "Sweetest music I ever heard in my life," Blackburn said afterward. "Sounded like a stuck pig."

Immobilized by the body blow, Schmeling then absorbed five colossal punches to his face. Framing his target with his left glove, Louis concluded the fusillade with two mighty rights. Schmeling sank, his knees collapsing halfway to the canvas. "Schmeling is going down!" McCarthy shrieked. "But he's held to his feet, held to the ropes, looked to his corner in helplessness!" A minute and a half had passed. "Hitler's wilted pet looked like a soft piece of molasses candy left out in the sun," Richard Wright wrote. "He drooped over the ropes, his eyes glassy, his chin nestling in a strand of rope, his face blank and senseless and his widely-

heralded powerful right arm hanging ironically useless." Hellmis, meanwhile, sounded "like a spinning wheel." Never had he had to describe
Schmeling in trouble, and he wasn't sure what to do; it was, a Jewish
listener in Warsaw wrote, as if Hellmis himself was absorbing Louis's
blows. He, too, had lost his bearings, and he now devoted himself more to
rescuing his beloved Maxe than to describing what had befallen him,
lapsing into importuning incoherence. "Max is backed up against the
ropes . . . to the right, Max. . . . Now Louis throws another one, misses . . .
moves to the side. . . . Bang! Maxe! Go back! *Um Himmels willen!* [For
heaven's sake!], Maxe! Maxe! Joe Louis! Stop him! Hold on, Maxe! Hold
yourself! The rope! Max Schmeling stands at the rope, holds himself.
Max is on his knee. Gets up again, stands . . ." Hellmis's cries, a listener in
Prague wrote, were "like the shrieking of a mother watching her son die."
It was, as the 12 *Uhr-Blatt* of Berlin wrote afterward, the sound of utter
despair, of shock. It was an SOS. Hellmis was making the unimaginable
unintelligible; Germans simply could not fathom what they were hearing.
"*Unmöglich!*" they cried. "Impossible!"

Donovan rushed over to the two men. Though Schmeling technically
remained on his feet, only the ropes were keeping him aloft, and to the
referee, it was a knockdown; for one thing, he feared that another of
Louis's blows at that moment might kill Schmeling. Donovan shooed
Louis away and, his arms raised, began a count. But he'd only reached
one when Schmeling righted himself. Donovan gestured for the fight to
continue, and Schmeling moved forward tentatively. Puzzled momentarily by what the referee had done, Louis, expressionless as always, resumed
his work. He stung Schmeling with another vicious right that sent him
sprawling, then rolling over. The knockdown timekeeper fumbled for his
mallet. This time Schmeling was up at four. Two years earlier Schmeling
had pooh-poohed Louis for failing to take a count: a sure sign of his inexperience, he sniffed. Now, in his own befuddled state, he had done precisely the same thing. From that alone Donovan knew Schmeling
couldn't last much longer.

"Louis attacks again!" Hellmis shrieked. "*Aber das ist doch Wahnsinn!*
[Why, that is madness!]" "And Schmeling . . . is . . . down! Schmeling is
down!" McCarthy exclaimed. "The count is four. It's . . ." While Hellmis
managed to say little, McCarthy tried capturing it all, but even with a
rapid-fire delivery honed at hundreds of racetracks, he could not keep up;
no horse had ever done so much so fast. It was the crowd's muffled, dense,
thunderous roars, and not what McCarthy blurted out a millisecond later,

that told the story. "With each blow you imagined Louis saying: 'So I fouled you, eh?' . . . Boom! . . . 'So you gave me a beating I'll never forget, eh?' . . . Boom!" Joe Williams wrote. Black America could now exhale. "Laughter roared through the land like mighty Niagara breaking through a cardboard dike," Frank Marshall Davis wrote. So startling was what was unfolding at the stadium that not everyone knew how to react. To Richard Wright, it was all "so stunning that even cheering was out of place."

"Joe Louis is in his corner," said Hellmis. "*Steh auf, Maxe! Maxe!* [Get up, Max! Max!]" . . . No, he is down for good. . . . No, he gets up!" And Schmeling was up again, but only for an instant. Another powerful combination again sent him to his knees. "A red drool dribbled from his lips and formed a crimson beard of bubbles on his chin," wrote Austen Lake of the *Boston Evening American*. Again, Schmeling was up too quickly, this time at one. Donovan wiped the resin off Schmeling's gloves with his shirt before jumping out of Louis's way. "Joe Louis throws himself again at him," a horrified Hellmis declared. McCarthy, meantime, was rattling off the punches. "Right and left to the head! A left to the jaw! A right to the head! And Donovan is watching carefully! Louis measures him. Right to the body! A left hook to the jaw! And Schmeling is down!" For the third time, Schmeling was on the canvas, this time on his side, trying desperately to get back up.

Louis's final right to the face, the *Herald Tribune*'s Caswell Adams wrote, seemed "to smash it like a baseball bat would an apple." Louis was Louis again, "abandoning all science and newfangled lessons, fighting as he must have done it in the Alabama canebrakes, as men have fought since men have borne hatred toward one another." Even some of the reporters were shouting, "Stop it!" Machon, his face "a pale study in vicarious suffering," then sprang into action. As the two men fought in the ring, another fight had been under way: twice already, Machon had tried to throw in the towel, and twice, Doc Casey had stopped him. Now he could no longer be restrained. He took his towel—lifted from the Concourse Plaza Hotel that afternoon—and threw it into the ring. It floated down "like a seagull" and almost landed on Donovan. "*Das Handtuch!* [The towel!]" Hellmis shouted. "*Max Schmeling ist geschlagen! Max Schmeling ist geschlagen!* [Max Schmeling is beaten! Max Schmeling is beaten!]" "Schmeling was no longer a man," Gallico later wrote. "He was a broken, glass-eyed, silly, blubbering thing."

Technically, boxing's classic gesture of surrender was no longer recognized in New York State, and Donovan grabbed the towel, crumpled it up, and threw it contemptuously toward the green, velvet-covered ropes. It landed on the middle strand, where it hung limply, much the way Schmeling himself had hung only a few seconds before. Then, as Schmeling, on his hands and knees, tried once again to stand up, Machon dashed into the ring. That did have legal standing: it was against the rules, just as Donovan had reminded everyone beforehand. The referee shoved Machon aside, but it was all quite pointless. He counted to five, then declared the fight over. McCarthy struggled to disentangle what had happened, and began a count of his own. "The count is five," he cried. And there it stayed for several seconds, before he resumed. "Five! Six! Seven! Eight! The men are in the ring! The fight is over, on a technical knockout! Max Schmeling is beaten in one round!" There was another fleeting, timeless interval, this one born of incomprehension rather than anticipation. Handlers and policemen clambered through the ropes. McCarthy fobbed off the microphone on Thorgersen and climbed into the ring as well. "Joe Louis is practically smothered by seconds, handlers, photographers, policemen, and about fifty others who've crowded into the spotlighted square," Thorgersen said. "You have a feeling as you see Joe sitting there now for the first time he believes himself to be the undisputed world heavyweight champ. And the beating he handed Schmeling tonight in that one terrific, frightful round certainly dispels any doubt as to who is the preeminent heavyweight boxer in this world today."

Donovan moved seamlessly from officiating to ministering, cradling Schmeling with his arm and, with the help of Machon, Casey, and one of Louis's seconds, dragging his bloody carcass back to the corner he'd left so confidently only three minutes earlier, kicking up a small cloud of resin along the way. Schmeling was quivering; someone squeezed a sponge over his head, "and the water ran past the corners of his mouth in little pale red streams." As Machon slapped his face, Schmeling came to. What was the matter? he asked. Why were they not fighting? It was all over, Machon told him: He had lost. Meantime, Joe Jacobs climbed through the ropes. "He was—for the first time in his life—speechless," someone wrote.

In the stands there was bedlam. Tallulah Bankhead sprang to her feet and turned to the Schmeling fans behind her. "I told you so, you sons of bitches!" she screamed. Whites were hugging blacks. "The happiest people I saw at this fight were not the Negroes but the Jews," a black writer observed. "In the row in front of me there was a great line of Jews—and they had the best time of all their Jewish lives." Inside 938 St. Nicholas

Avenue, Marva let out a squeal. "Wasn't it swell?" she asked. Champagne was then served, though the abstemious Mrs. Louis had none of it. "My daddy told me that he was fighting this fight not only for me but for his mother and the Race," she later said. Elsewhere, everywhere, people leaped out of their chairs. "Beat the hell out of the damn German bastard!" W. E. B. DuBois, a lifelong Germanophile who rarely swore, shouted gleefully in Atlanta. In Hollywood, Bette Davis jumped up and down; she had won $66 in the Warner Bros. fight pool. Joseph Mitchell of the *World-Telegram*, who stood to collect $16 in his pool, also jumped up, kicking over a cabinet with his precious—and, he learned, fragile—Bessie Smith records. "Everybody danced and sang," Woody Guthrie wrote from Santa Fe. "I watched the people laugh, walk, sing, do all sorts of dances. I heard 'Hooray for Joe Louis!' 'To hell with Max Schmeling' in Indian, Mexican, Spanish, all kinds of white tongues." In an auditorium in Macon, Georgia, Jimmie Lunceford and his band were temporarily, joyously ignored as "dusky maids in evening gowns and gay young bucks in the latest fads . . . danced spontaneous jigs without the music they had paid to hear." Whites watched it all from the balcony.

Eighty miles away, the black field hands who had listened on Earl Carter's radio quietly thanked him for the privilege. "Then," Jimmy Carter was to write, "our visitors walked silently out of the yard, crossed the road and the railroad tracks, entered the tenant house, and closed the door. Then all hell broke loose, and their celebration lasted all night." "It was hard to explain to the wife why I was taking a prizefight so seriously," the American Communist writer Mike Gold later wrote.

> But it was Joe Louis versus Adolf Hitler Day, and I just couldn't think of another thing. And when I jumped up as the knockout came over the radio, and hopped around the room and howled like a curly wolf, I guess she just about gave up on the male sex. She was rooting for Joe, but not this wild way. "After all, it's only a prizefight, and prizefights don't decide anything real." "Baby, dear, it's more than a prizefight; it's another nail in the coffin of fascism, and almost everybody, including the Nazis, feels it deep in their bones."

Balogh fought his way into the center of the ring and announced the time: two minutes and four seconds. It was the second-fastest heavyweight championship fight ever, thirty-six seconds longer than when Tommy Burns beat Jem Roche in 1908, and four-fifths of a second faster than the

1938 Kentucky Derby six weeks earlier. Blackburn "did a fandango" as he slapped Louis on the back. But Louis showed not even a semblance of a smile as Balogh raised his hand. His lips parted only when he removed his mouth protector.

Legend later had it that when Schmeling went down, so, too, did the German broadcast. In fact, the Nazis weren't quite so quick. Throughout German-speaking Europe, Hellmis's dirgelike commentary continued. Now that the action had stopped, he became calmer and a bit more coherent. He had, the Jewish listener in Warsaw observed, regained consciousness more quickly than his hero, and, realizing that at some point he'd have to return home, had begun to rehabilitate himself.

> He is on his knees . . . on the floor. Joe Louis has battered him down in the first round. . . . No, he has not suffered a heavy defeat, he has taken the blows, the towel just in time. . . . Joe Louis has succeeded in his revenge. Schmeling is beaten. Shortly before his goal he broke down. What a meanness of fate. This man who tries so hard, fails within sight of his goal. Joe Louis was terribly strong, he attacked, he threw himself at Schmeling, shattered him into pieces. One moment Max could not get away in time from the ropes and then it was too late, it happened, it was too late. . . .
>
> Max, our hearts are all with you, you have prepared yourself as conscientiously as anyone. . . . It was not meant to be, Max. But you were defeated as an honest fighter . . . you have shown the world what can be done with a strong will and heart and courage.

Hellmis's soliloquy became a Festschrift, with the ambient noise of Louis's exultant fans as its soundtrack; little did these people, the *Rassengenossen* and *Lehmgesichter* and *Mischlinge* and "wire pullers" and "parasites" and "children of Israel" so often vilified in German print and over German airwaves, know that while they saluted their hero that night, they were also—at least in the few remaining seconds before Goebbels's minions finally did pull the plug—taunting Nazi Germany.

Black writers would grope to describe Louis's astonishing power. "Fighting Fury . . . Forked Lightning . . . Blinding Speed . . . DESTRUC- TION . . . JOE LOUIS! They're all the same!" one wrote. "Horror, dynamite, mayhem, destruction, devastation, atonement are some of the choice words chronicled by Mr. Webster that found their true definition in the murderous mittens of the thundering Tan Terror last night," said another. But the Louis with whom McCarthy caught up in the ring, only moments after the knockout, warranted other words: gentle, shy, awkward, laconic, inarticulate, boyish, sweet. "You said it would take you two rounds," McCarthy said breathlessly to him. "You know how long it took you?" "No, I don't, exactly," Louis replied politely. "I imagine about a minute and a half," McCarthy told him. "Well, that's fine." "Joe, which punch, if any, do you think, was the one that started him downhill?" "I think the right hand to the ribs," said Louis. "I saw it going in there, Joe, and she looked terrible," McCarthy replied, before throwing it back to Thorgersen. "I think Clem will agree that this is a scrap to be long remembered," he said. Others had that same sense. "In every land and in myriad tongues they'll tell you for years to come of the blows which laid Schmeling low," wrote Bill Nunn of the *Courier,* which put out one of the several extras published by the black press that night. What turned out to be the most famous description of the fight was written by Bob Considine in the *Mirror.*

> Listen to this, buddy, for it comes from a guy whose palms are still wet, whose throat is still dry, and whose jaw is still agape from the utter shock of watching Joe Louis knock out Max Schmeling. Louis was like this: He was like a big lean copper spring, tightened and re-tightened through weeks of training until he was one package of coiled venom. Schmeling hit that spring. He hit it with a whistling right hand punch in the first minute of the fight—and the spring, tormented with tension, suddenly burst forth with one brazen spang of activity. Hard brown arms, propelling two unerring fists, blurred beneath the hot white candelabra of the bright lights. And Schmeling was in the path of them, a man caught and mangled in the whirling claws of a mad and feverish machine.

Fred Digby of the *New Orleans Item* put it more succinctly. "Mox kept a bold front until the gong sounded," he wrote. "Then he saw zomedings. It was stars." But the prize for the shortest story went to the book editor of the *Charlotte News,* whose piece, headlined BLOW-BY-BLOW STORY OF FIGHT, consisted of one word: "Bang!" As the writers wrote, the photo agencies rushed out their stock. "I told you I sent out the last picture!" one harried editor shouted over the phone. "The one with Schmeling on his ass, that's the last one!" It was the most technical of technical knockouts, declared only because Machon had rushed into the ring; no fighter had ever been more knocked out. "Donovan could have counted off a century and Max could not have regained his feet," the *Times* declared. Though counts varied, one tally had Louis landing forty-one blows, thirty-one of them "serious," fourteen of them to the chin. Schmeling landed but two, and they were cream puffs. "I was in a hurry to get that guy outta there," Louis was to say many years later. "Artie, that was the softest dough you ever made," someone later told Donovan. "You're wrong there, pal," he replied. "A referee lives a lifetime in two minutes like that."

Schmeling made his way across the ring and threw his arm around Louis's shoulders. It was virtually the only glove he'd laid on him all night. "Joe, you are a real champion," he said. "You are a goot fighter." Then he went back to his corner, stood for a moment—and began to cry. "He wept softly at first," the *Daily News* reported. "Then his whole body shook, and the man, who for six years has chased his dream of winning back the world's heavyweight title, buried his face in his soggy gloves and cried his heart's disappointment like a chastened schoolboy." Six rows back, Hellmis had calmed down. "Max Schmeling is sitting in his corner, quite recovered," he announced. " 'Why,' he probably is saying, 'was the towel thrown?' It was better, Max, much better. . . . You were beaten the moment you had the bad luck to catch that one blow, and now it is too late." It was, Hellmis pronounced, the end of a glorious career, one to which only the greats could be compared. And had Schmeling not been denied his title match a year earlier, he'd have regained the crown. Now, it looked like retirement. "But our hearts, Max, are with you," Hellmis continued. And when he got home, he predicted, all that talk that Germany would despise him, would even throw him into prison, would be exposed as the foolishness it always was.

Microphone in hand, McCarthy tried nabbing Schmeling before he left the packed ring. "Max! Max, come over here!" he shouted. "Bring him over! Max! Max! Max Schmeling! Bring him over, officer! Get Max Schmeling! Officer! Get Max Schmeling over here, get him! Bring him over! *Max!*" McCarthy was about to surrender. "They [sic] don't look like I can get him, they're crowding him through the ropes on the far side, he's never even seen us. Max! I'm trying to get him. Officer! Get Max Schmeling, will ya? And I can't get him. He's going out of the ring."

For the gravel-voiced announcer, it was only the latest of his many misses that night. He had missed at least one knockdown. He had missed the kidney punch. He had missed Machon's flying towel. Twice, he'd said mistakenly that the title had just changed hands. The press would pick him apart for his performance. "Reduced to dithering bewilderment," said *Time*. Should stick to the horse racing and stay away from prize fights, urged the *Bronx Home News*. "Some of the noble 72,000 appear to have by now a fair notion of what they saw," a young sportswriter named Red Smith wrote in the *Philadelphia Record*. "In this respect they have a marked advantage over the 72,000,000 who still have no clear idea of what they heard." Even the sponsor called him "a little addled." In fact, McCarthy had produced one of the immortal moments in the history of radio. He hadn't caught every punch, but he had captured the incomparable drama of the moment for an entire generation of Americans, and for posterity, too. With such an audience, one prescient observer speculated, "Mike Jacobs must be spending wakeful nights wondering what kind of a tie-up he can make with the television companies when that invention is as commonplace as the radio today."

The fans made their way to the exits. One encountered a new arrival in a tuxedo, white scarf, and top hat, running wildly into the outgoing traffic. "What round is it?" he asked. "What round is it?" Many black fans lingered; on a night like this, they weren't quite ready to leave. Others were too stunned to move, including some of the Germans. The knot of them who had earlier cheered Schmeling's single, puny punch now sat disconsolate. "*Unser Max!*" someone sitting nearby heard one of them say. "*Die Juden haben ihn vergiftet*": The Jews poisoned him. A German reporter cried over his typewriter.

For all the money they had spent, some fans were unhappy not to have seen more action, or at least not to have seen Schmeling suffer longer. Then there were all those who had missed the climax altogether. There was the fellow who, thinking he could beat the clock, had gone to buy a sandwich. There was Count Basie, who had bent over to pick up his straw hat. There was Roy Wilkins, who had finally reached his seat as the opening bell rang, and who was still draping his coat over it when the end came. (He still considered the fight "the shortest, sweetest minute of the entire Thirties.") There was the man from *Variety* who turned around to greet Damon Runyon and turned back to learn the fight was over. There was the *Courier*'s business manager, who, concerned about soiling his white Palm Beach suit, had been cleaning off his seat. And the man in the mezzanine still fiddling with his opera glasses. And the woman whose purse opened, spilling all of its contents onto the ground. And the fans in adjacent seats arguing over which one of them would sit behind the pillar. And all of those behind all of those who stood up with the opening bell and never sat back down. And those whose seats, thanks to Mike Jacobs's sleight of hand, had not been as advertised. "We might just as well have been in Anny Ondra's chamber in Berlin," complained an irate owner of some "ringside" seats.

Similarly, countless radio listeners tuned in too late or chose the wrong moment to fetch a beer. One man listened aboard a Greyhound bus just as it entered the Holland Tunnel in New Jersey; it was all over when the bus emerged into New York. The tubes in Dizzy Dean's radio took too long to warm up. At a softball game in Coffeyville, Kansas, someone accidentally kicked the radio cord running under the stands out of its socket. The newest graduates of City College were unable to flee commencement ceremonies as quickly as La Guardia had. Because of crossed lines, Spanish speakers in South America heard the Portuguese play-by-play and Portuguese speakers heard the Spanish; things ended too quickly to fix the problem.

But few of those at Yankee Stadium that night felt shortchanged. Purely as a matter of boxing, they had witnessed, or at least been part of, something extraordinary—an exhibition, Grantland Rice conceded, even greater than Dempsey in Toledo. Jim Corbett once said that in the life of every champion there came a night when he had everything; for two minutes and four seconds, Joe Louis might well have been the greatest boxer who ever lived. And to those at the stadium who had missed it, or had seen little more from their cheap seats than two specks in a phosphorescent square, there was still the lifelong privilege of saying that they'd been there. The *Defender* told of a man who, over three years of self-denial, set aside $350 to see the fight in style, buying himself new clothes and a ringside seat, flying to New York, staying in a first-class hotel, finding himself a woman. Though the trip had cost him his job, he had no regrets. "I'm willing to eat crusts of bread until I find another job, because I have pleasant memories to feast upon," he told the paper. "I have lived a dream I've dreamed since I became a man. That's more than most people ever do."

Afterward, Louis remembered how everyone had patted his back as he made his way to the dressing room. When he arrived, forty reporters crammed in with him, while forty more struggled with the police outside to join them, in a fight that was longer and more evenly matched than the one in the ring. The room was stifling and sepulchral, brightened only by flashbulbs. Louis sat on a dressing table in his bare feet, covered by towels. Policemen made it nearly impossible to get close to him; many were collecting his autograph. "Lift up that hand that did it!" a photographer shouted at him. "Ah sho 'nuff a real champion now," Louis was quoted as saying.

"Yeah, yo' sho' are," replied Blackburn, wiping the damp off his brow.

Someone said that Schmeling had already asked for a rubber match.

"What for?" Julian Black shot back. "Didn't he just have his chance and lose? We'll take anybody else. Anybody."

"You must have felt different tonight, Joe, from the other night," one reporter said. "What was it?"

"Ah just felt stronger," Louis said. "Ah was off that other night. Did me lotta good, though." He was calm, matter-of-fact. That must have been someone else altogether in the ring. "He never hurt me," he went on. "That right he threw just barely grazed me. I saw it coming and I rode with it. I've been telling all the folks at my camp for the last few days that I'd do it in one round. They thought I was kidding, but I meant it. I've felt all along that he was meat for me." It was, Louis said, one of his easiest fights. As he said it, he yawned.

So they don't come back, eh, Joe? "I got what folks call revenge—and how." Did he know how many punches he threw? "Ah don't know how many. Ah was throwin' 'em in there a mile a minute. I bet Smellin' couldn't count them, either." When did he know he would knock Schmeling out? The moment he signed the contract. Was it the easiest fight of his career? "Levinsky was pretty easy. This is right with it, though." Had he felt any animosity toward Schmeling? "I was sore at some of the things Schmeling's been saying." But what if they'd been planted? "Well, he didn't deny them, and that's just as bad to me." Would he visit Germany on that European trip he'd been planning? "Now man, you know 'ah ain't got no business in Germany." He said it with a faint smile. Bill Robinson came in and planted a kiss on Louis's forehead. "Why, you old son of a gun!" shouted the mayor of Detroit. "How did you do it?" "I guess I just done it, Mayor," Louis replied. The governor of Michigan, Frank Murphy, told Louis he'd never know how much he'd made his heart thump. "I'm glad I made it short for you, sir," replied Louis, looking, as the *Times* put it, "exactly like a wool-gathering youngster standing in awe of royalty, instead of a young man who had just earned about $400,000 in 124 seconds." A beaming La Guardia, somewhere underneath a ten-gallon hat, grabbed Louis's hand. "Nice work, Joe!" he said. Braddock came in, too. "This is our anniversary tonight," he explained. And it was true: exactly a year had passed since Louis had taken his crown, in what had turned out to be, when it came right down to it, a preliminary event.

The other big winner of the night came by, too. "Nice work, Bomber," said Mike Jacobs. Louis just smiled.

It was left for Julian Black to say, "How's that for our old boy?"

"I knew he would do it," Jacobs replied. But he'd given Louis an assist, given him time to get over the other fight and, as for Schmeling, "giving Father Time time to whet his scythe." Jacobs said he would have another fight for Louis in September, and Louis said that was fine with him; all he wanted was a month's vacation, and then he'd be ready to go back to work. Two years earlier, Black had gone to Schmeling's dressing room to congratulate him. But now no one from Schmeling's camp reciprocated. "Sportsmanship, I suppose," one of Louis's handlers muttered. Half a dozen fans stood by the door of Louis's lair and raised their right arms. "*Heil Louis!*" they shouted in unison. Mounted policemen were needed to control the crowds awaiting Louis outside.

Moments earlier, as he exited the ring, Max Schmeling had managed a wan smile for a photographer. Damon Runyon watched him take his leave, probably for the last time, at least from an American ring. If old age hadn't already killed whatever hope he harbored of yet another comeback, war soon would. "He is a pugilistic old man from the first belt on the chops," Runyon wrote, "and there is only one fate for old men in the ring, when a youngster is on their trail." Joe Williams of the *World-Telegram* was also watching Schmeling. "To put it bluntly, he was a complete flop," he wrote. "No other reputable challenger ever went out so ingloriously, ever looked so pathetically outclassed."

Williams's thoughts then turned to Louis. "They said he'd never forget the first beating he took from Schmeling," he observed. "In view of what happened last night, it might be added that Schmeling will never forget the beating he took from Louis. All right, Adolf, take him away."

CHAPTER 14

Aftermath

A NNY ONDRA HAD KEPT HER VOW. She had not listened to the fight, though she lay wide awake in her room as it unfolded. But Hellmis didn't know that, and having spent most of the night talking to Schmeling, he spent his last few seconds on the air talking to Schmeling's wife—or, as he put it, to "a young blond woman in Berlin," assuring her that her husband was leaving the ring clearheaded, standing tall, and intact, without any serious battle scars. Then someone in Germany decided to end the transmission. "Our broadcast from the Yankee Stadium in New York is finished," Hellmis suddenly declared. For more than two hours, Germans had been sitting in their homes and cafés and *Bierstuben*, and suddenly, it was all over—"*aus*," as the *Angriff* man later wrote, using the very word Hellmis had invoked so memorably two years earlier. "That was the last word in the ether," a listener in Prague wrote. "Germany no longer reported." In fact, there were a few more words. "That was the Schmeling-Louis fight," an announcer in Berlin stated simply, without offering the result. There followed the sounds of the "Horst Wessel Song" and "Deutschland über Alles" and then one more word: "*Heil!*" "That was the last word from the receiver," the Jewish listener in Warsaw noted. "We said, 'Bravo, Louis!' It was our answer to '*Heil!*' And then we turned off the radio."

Now Hellmis, like McCarthy, came in for second-guessing. It was, as *Box-Sport* later put it, "as if someone had suddenly turned the lights off on someone reading." So busy had Hellmis been eulogizing Schmeling, guaranteeing him safe passage home, and comforting his wife, that he had neglected to tell Germany what had actually happened; an entire nation now scratched its head. "Everyone was asking, how was it possible??" *Box-*

Sport complained. "How did Schmeling actually go down? Which punch was it? What was the cause? When and how did Louis hit Schmeling? No one could say. No one had any idea what was going on." Sure, it had been—to use a word not quite yet in vogue—a blitzkrieg, too fast for anyone to describe completely. But instead of offering a recapitulation, the broadcast was over, "and everyone sat bewildered in front of the radio." Anyone tuning in late might have thought his receiver wasn't working. In one neighborhood in Nuremberg, the silence was broken by the sound of someone taking an ax to his radio. In Schweinau, people heard a loud bang, then saw the remains of a radio in the street. Were the two owners upset over having missed the fight? Or over having heard it? Like everything else about that night, it was unclear. After months of conditioning, Germans were utterly unprepared for what had happened, then utterly baffled by it.

"Shaking our heads silently, we disperse," wrote a reporter for the *Angriff* who'd listened in a small restaurant in Berlin. "In the streets, from all the bars and cafés which had tuned in to the fight, came other men who stared soberly into the morning. Only slowly were they able to speak again." The Roxy-Bar was like a tomb. As Louis pummeled Schmeling, "a breathless, half-loud crossfire of weak cries" had gone up in a bar on the Alexanderplatz. Then all grew quiet and completely still. "We looked at each other silently," a newspaperman from Dresden wrote. "No one can find a word. We turn off the radio. Could that really be, Max defeated? No, that can't be. 3:10 and everything is over. We went back to bed, sleeplessly tossing and turning into the morning."

Marked only by a swollen and discolored left eye, Schmeling had made his way out of the ring, unassisted but hardly unscathed. "Go back to Germany!" someone shouted. "You Nazi bum, you never could fight!" Schmeling entered his dressing room a "woebegone and tragic figure," his left hand clutching his side. "Too bad, Max," Braddock told him, patting him on the back. "I know how you feel." But he didn't. Something had happened between Schmeling's final moments in the ring and when he met with the press: the gracious, smiling loser had been supplanted by someone filled with pain and pique. "When he got in his dressing room he found out he had been fouled," someone put it afterward. Standing in a corner of the room, which stank of men and adhesives and unguents, Schmeling now said he'd been done in by an illegal punch. He'd been fouled. From Schmeling it was a familiar refrain, though this time he was on his own; while he was feeling robbed, Joe Jacobs apparently was not.

"Yah, he hit me such a terrible blow on the kidney. I can't think. I can't zee," Schmeling told the reporters, slowly rubbing his left side as he spoke. "Such terrible pain. I can't move. . . . My legs vould not move. They were paralyzed." *"Paralyzed"*: it was the very word he'd used after the first Sharkey fight, eight years earlier. Before that one punch, he insisted, his head had been entirely clear, notwithstanding all the blows he had already taken; after it, he was blinded and immobilized. The Germans knew American rules—a kidney punch was perfectly legal as long as it wasn't thrown while in a clinch—or should have known: Schmeling had complained of one during his first fight with Louis, and Donovan had explained the rule to him then. Hellmis had made that precise point in *Schmelings Sieg*. It didn't matter. "A kidney blow is a foul," Schmeling now maintained. "He didn't mean to hit me with one, I know, but he did and it blinded me. It made me so I can't feel."

Schmeling got little sympathy from the Americans. "Max! Max!" the photographers shouted. "Point at your kidney!" "It wasn't vare, it wasn't," Schmeling remonstrated to Mike Jacobs, who gave him a patronizing pat and walked away muttering a curse. Even within his own camp, Schmeling's charge was disputed; Doc Casey conceded that it was "strictly legal." For succor, Schmeling had to turn to his countrymen. The German ambassador to Washington, Hans Heinrich Dieckhoff, who had blanched as the slaughter unfolded, gave him a long handshake. Then Heinz Ditgens of the Roxy-Bar, an overstuffed man who looked like Hermann Göring, appeared, buried himself in Schmeling's shoulder, and began to cry. "But Max," he said between heaving, violent sobs, "how was dot possible, how was dot possible?" It was not fair, Schmeling assured him, too. The German reporters looked embarrassed, as if not knowing just what to send back to Berlin. Schmeling helped them, though. "What's clear is that his version was very well-received by the German press," wrote Curt Riess of *Paris Soir*. "And what an imagination: they all saw the wound in the kidneys!" Things might have turned out differently, Jacobs said, had he been in Schmeling's corner. Right, one sportswriter mocked: "Jacobs could not have done a more polished job of towel tossing himself." Aside from that, Yussel was oddly, even unprecedentedly, detached—and mute. You "wondered if Louis had hit hard enough to silence both Schmeling and Jacobs," wrote Anthony Marenghi of the *Newark Star-Eagle*.

"What will Hitler think?" one reporter shouted to Schmeling. "Der Führer won't say anything," Schmeling replied. "It's a sport, isn't it?" How would his loss affect his standing in Nazi Germany? "Nothing. Dot's foolish," he replied. He grew indignant when asked if he would fight again. "Yah, I fight again. Why not? I want to fight Louis again. Next time Joe won't slip over a kidney punch like that. If he is a good sportsman he will give me a return bout." Finally, the man with the NBC microphone caught up with Schmeling, and he talked to America. "Well, ladies and gentlemen, I have not much to say," he said. "I'm very sorry but I won't make any excuse but I had such a terrible hit the first hit that I get in the left kidney I was so paralyzed I couldn't even move."

Machon led Schmeling to the shower. The defeated fighter walked with catlike strides, his hand still on his kidney. Waiting outside, Joe Jacobs told a reporter they were going to take Schmeling to the hospital to have him examined. Schmeling reemerged a few moments later and put on his street clothes. Music returned to the American airwaves; a station in Chicago resumed with "You Go to My Head." Louis was still in his dressing room when he learned about Schmeling's charge. "No, sah, dat was no foul," he said. "Ah hit him right in the left kidney and ah really hit him. Ah felt that punch touch home." His managers were incensed, then contemptuous. "That's for German consumption," one of them huffed. Maybe Schmeling's mind remained clouded, Parker wrote; otherwise, he was the poorest loser on record. But the charge would "make good stuff for the home trade when Herr Doktor Goebbels gets his flippers on it." "It must have been a kidney punch to the chin," Bill Corum wrote.

Largely unnoticed and under his own power, Schmeling walked out of the stadium, stooped over, still holding his side and dragging one of his legs, his face set in grim, pathetic lines. He was then taken to the Polyclinic Hospital on Fiftieth Street and Eighth Avenue, across from Madison Square Garden. Schmeling walked into the building and plopped himself into a wheelchair. When he got to his room, he reached his wife in Berlin, then took a call from one of Hitler's adjutants. He asked hospital personnel to turn off his telephone and, after getting some injections for pain, he went to sleep. Around 2:30 a.m. his cabbie called the *Daily News* with the whereabouts of his famous passenger, guaranteeing there would be a mob outside the hospital when Schmeling woke up.

Joe Jacobs's policeman brother, who moonlighted as Schmeling's bodyguard, did his man a great favor that night. Rather than have the driver head due south into Manhattan from the stadium, he directed him to go west toward the Hudson River, then hug it all the way south to the city. In other words, he steered clear of a delirious Harlem. New York's police chief, Lewis Valentine, did come back via Harlem, stopping at the

West 135th Street station long enough to lay out department policy for the occasion. "This is their night," he declared. "Let them be happy." "Too bad it ended so early," one of his officers griped. "That gives them so much more time to celebrate. We'll be on duty here all night." And they were. Harlem, recalled a white woman who had gone to the stadium by boat but returned by car, was "aflame in happiness."

"Had you been in Harlem Wednesday night," the *Courier* reported afterward, "you might have thought another World War had just ended. Joy was simply unconfined." "There never was a Harlem like the Harlem of Wednesday night," Ben Davis, Jr., wrote in the *Daily Worker*. "Take a dozen Harlem Christmases, a score of New Year's Eves, a bushel of July 4ths and maybe—yes, maybe—you get a faint glimpse of the idea." "They wanted to make a noise comparable to the happiness bubbling in their hearts, but they were poor and had nothing," Richard Wright later explained. "So they went to the garbage pails and got tin cans; they went to their kitchens and got tin pots, pans, washboards, wooden boxes, and took possession of the streets." Private cars cruised, streaming banners. THE BLACK RACE IS SUPREME TONIGHT, one said.

By one estimate, 500,000 people crowded Harlem's streets. All traffic on Seventh Avenue between 116th and 145th streets—"their Broadway," Valentine called it—halted, immobilized by pedestrians, snake-dancers, and stranded cars; the "quick tattoo" of blowouts from tires crushing into broken glass sounded like firecrackers in the night air. People hopped on roofs and running boards until everything that moved "looked like clusters of black ripe grapes." A dozen sets of boys carried mock stretchers bearing pseudo-Schmelings; whenever an ambulance passed, people wondered whether the real thing was inside. Soapbox speakers and signs nominated Louis for mayor of Harlem, Congress, president of the United States. "The Lord is a good Man to take care of us this way," one elderly black woman told another. Celebrants had that indescribable feeling of being surrounded by thousands of strangers who felt exactly as they did. "I remember for a while I wasn't mad at any white person," one recalled. Harlem's nightclubs—the Big Apple, Small's Paradise, Brittwood's, the Elks, the Rendezvous, the Horseshoe, Dickie Wells's, the Savoy Ballroom (Dizzy Gillespie was playing there)—were all bulging, fed by rumors that Louis would stop at any or all of them. Stepin Fetchit glided up Seventh Avenue in a long, gleaming Dusenberg.

Everywhere were references to the regime with which Schmeling had been tagged. It was on placards: LOUIS WINS, HITLER WEEPS. It was in a newsboy's chant: "Read about the big fight! Hitler committed suicide!"

And in all the mock Nazi salutes: "Seventh Ave. looked for a while like a weird burlesque of the Wilhelmstrasse in Berlin—staggering, yelling, singing, jumping, dancing, hugging men and women, jutting out their hands to one another," Elliot Arnold wrote in the *World-Telegram*. To the few whites in Harlem that night, and even to some blacks, there was menace in the air. The police rescued eight hysterical white women from a bus enveloped by merrymakers. The Irish cabdriver who ferried a black reporter from the stadium to Harlem pulled his cap down to hide his face and race, but soon people were crawling all over his car and someone kicked in his windshield. A white reporter from Milwaukee described how sixteen blacks hung from his cab until a policeman took out his nightstick to "clear off the excess baggage." Other white reporters huddled in the Theresa Hotel. Ralph Matthews of the *Afro-American* called the frenzy "the type of stuff from which dictatorships are created," adding: "Going around punching everyone in the nose who happens to be of a different race . . . is not a legitimate expression of race pride."

Schmeling was only one of the casualties that night. A South Carolina man who had hitched a ride to the fight went around shouting "Joe Louis! Joe Louis!" Then he dropped dead. A Brooklyn man was hurt when he drove his fist through two windshields. One policeman was knocked off his horse by a flying garbage can cover; a milk bottle hit another, while a third was struck by a large hunk of wood. At 130th Street and Seventh Avenue, police sprayed the crowd with a fire hose. "I bet all of 'em are on relief but Joe Louis," one officer muttered. Sure, cars were careening around the corner of Seventh Avenue and 135th Street, a black paper conceded, but "Joe Louis doesn't knock out Max Schmeling in less than a round every night." A German paper reported "repeated wild shooting like in the jungle," but there was really nothing of the sort. The *Herald Tribune* commended Harlem on its civility.

The celebrations went on for hours. "There wasn't no nighttime then," one participant recalled. Meantime, in midtown, at the Stork Club, Tunney, Hemingway, Franklin D. Roosevelt, Jr., Winchell, and Rice sat around discussing what they'd just seen. Suddenly, Tunney boasted of not just visiting Louis in his camp but helping to devise the winning strategy. Nearby, at Jimmy Braddock's restaurant, Donovan defended the kidney punch. Dempsey would have lasted no longer against Louis than Schmeling had, he later said, and John L. Sullivan not even as long. But Yorkville's streets, the *Post* noted, were "a well of weltschmerzen." "I wonder what they think of Max now in the old country," someone in Café Mozart remarked glumly. "He better not go home right away." Around twenty minutes past midnight, Louis reached the apartment on St. Nicholas Avenue where Marva was staying. She played a game of hide-and-seek with him before she appeared. "I made it as quick as possible, honey," he told her. While many of the others quaffed champagne, Louis contented himself with ginger ale and a quart of ice cream—half vanilla, half chocolate. Then he and Marva went to bed. There, at least, Louis was down for the count.

Outside, things didn't quiet down until noon the following day, and even then, knots of people still gathered to discuss the fight. Or fights: they talked about the 1936 fight, too, more convinced than ever now that Louis had been doped. The *Baltimore Afro-American* suggested facetiously that this time, Schmeling might have been, too. Along Lenox Avenue, young bootblacks offered the "Joe Louis shine": it took only two minutes and four seconds. The next morning Louis slept in, then sent out for the papers. For him it was the dawn of a new day, and a new era. "Joe is on top of the proverbial heap today," one black columnist wrote. "On top of a heap higher than any one he ever occupied before. It amounts to a throne."

The fight, the *Courier* declared, had generated the greatest show of Negro unity America had ever seen. Certainly anyone visiting any black neighborhood in the United States immediately afterward would have seen many of the same things. In Detroit, where black leaders were confident enough to have applied for a parade permit two weeks earlier, twenty thousand people marched thirty blocks into Paradise Valley, chanting, "Joe knocked old Hitler cold." Louis's mother had not listened to the fight, learning the outcome from a newsboy selling extras; by the time she'd returned home, a jubilant mob awaited her. She hadn't been worried, she explained; she knew Joe was going to win because he'd told her so. A reporter turned on her police siren to get through the mob on Chicago's South Side. "Louder! Louder!" a woman screamed at her. "Don' yo'all know Joe Louis won?"

In Philadelphia, "police making an attempt to keep the crowd orderly finally gave up, folded their arms and for once acted like human beings," reported the local black paper. What followed was "an inter-racial sight on South Street that will long be remembered": Negroes and Jews celebrating together, blasting car horns, snake-dancing on the streets. In Baltimore, Russell Baker watched as newly emboldened blacks marched into the previously forbidden white territory of Lombard Street. In Washington, D.C., crowds on U Street looked on as two men carried a huge placard of Schmeling, topped by a dead cat. "Little children rushed by my house shouting 'Joe Louis won!'" the black educator Mary McLeod Bethune wrote. "Grandmothers sitting on the doorsteps smiled and praised the Lord." In Buffalo, even the man whose placard shouted I'M THE SUCKER THAT BET ON SCHMELING had himself a good time. In Indianapolis, "thousands of Negroes and many Jews paraded back and forth along the streets of the Harlem of Indiana." In Kansas City, more than twenty thousand fans gathered along Eighteenth Street. "On the grass on the Paradeway three children lay on their stomachs, legs kicking in the air, shouting in unison, 'Joe Louis! Joe Louis!'—a perfect picture of hero worship." A Milwaukee man was fined a dollar for blowing his horn for two blocks. In Cincinnati, "the mellow voice of a Negro Paul Revere" spread word that Louis had won. In Los Angeles, celebrants along Central Avenue used "plain old cheap" toilet paper instead of more expensive confetti; times, after all, were tough. "Boy, am I glad Joe Louis doesn't fight every night in the week," said a Newark policeman monitoring the wild celebrations there.

Until the police dispersed them, two hundred people paraded through the streets of Chattanooga, proclaiming Louis's victory. In Memphis, a young black man on Beale Street cried out, "To de ring, to de ropes, to de flo!" and crowds took up the chant. Two days later, with neither fanfare nor opposition this time from the local censorship board, fight films opened at local theaters. Blacks in Mobile snake-danced up and down Davis Avenue to the tune of nickel pianos and the beat of wooden paddles pounding fifty-pound cans of lard. In Louis's birthplace, the auditorium of the local black high school hosted a "Joe Louis ball." While his fellow patients were disappointed over the quick finish, Monroe Barrow was pleased. "That's my little Joe," he said as the fight ended. He then asked his doctor how much his son had just earned. At least $300,000, he was told. "That boy must be worth a million dollars now, isn't he?" Barrow asked. "Probably more," the doctor replied. "That's fine," Barrow declared. "If Joe would come for me I'd be glad to go home with him."

In Panama, blacks "began to scream in all directions" once the outcome became clear. The *Defender's* man in Paris arrived in Montmartre an hour after the fight and found "joy-mad Race members kissing everyone who came within their reach." When a group of German-Jewish refugees arrived, they "automatically became part of the wild rejoicing." Some gold miners in British Guiana made plans to send Louis a gold medal studded with diamonds. In Kingston, Jamaica, word of the sensa-

tional outcome threatened to disrupt the speech that Alexander Busta-
mante, a future prime minister, was giving to workers, until he told them
their battle was as great as Joe Louis's. "The gathering thereupon cheered
him anew and he completed his address enjoying undivided attention,"
the local paper reported.

Some celebrations got out of hand. With all the debris scattered
about, it was as if a cyclone had hit black St. Louis. "Throwing garbage,
tin containers, obstructing traffic, jamming the pathways, throwing at
cars containing passengers of der Maxie's hue, and even wrecking an officer of the law on his motorcycle. They called it a Joe Louis celebration,"
said the *Atlanta Daily World* about events there. In Cleveland, two hundred policemen with tear gas tangled with crowds; a fifteen-year-old boy
was shot dead, fourteen streetcars were taken out of service, and looting
was reported. Newark witnessed "hugging and street fighting, kissing and
knifings." Police clubbed demonstrators in Augusta, Georgia. In
Durham, North Carolina, blacks attacked whites driving through their
neighborhoods. And in Charlotte, a black man driving on the wrong side
of the street, his head stuck out of the window as he shouted "Where is
Max Schmeling?" struck a white woman. But some of the worst violence
occurred in Gary, Indiana, where a white woman was killed, and a black
man was subsequently convicted of murdering her.* Police in Roanoke
attacked black celebrants on Henry Street with tear-gas bombs and guns,
seriously injuring several. "Henry Street is the only place where the black
people can go to congregate," a black lawyer complained, and "whenever

---

*Two Gary residents, a white woman named Florence Nehring and Joseph Pitts, a
black barber, had listened to the fight—she at her home, he at his barbershop. Each then
went out to reconnoiter. Whites near one commercial strip began pelting the car carrying
Pitts and two of his friends with tomatoes and eggs. Pitts got frightened, opened the door,
and brandished a revolver, which went off accidentally. After ricocheting off a wall, the
bullet hit Nehring in the abdomen. Hundreds of angry whites then swarmed around Pitts's
car; cries of "Lynch the nigger!" filled the air. A policeman pulled him to safety, but whites
turned over the car with the other men still inside; one rioter tried puncturing the gas tank
with an ice pick and setting the car on fire. Fearing he'd be lynched—the crowd had
swollen to more than two thousand people—authorities took Pitts to a remote jail. "Prizefights between white men and Negroes always supply enough dynamite for an explosion,"
the local newspaper observed. Gary's black weekly apologized to its white neighbors: "We
have, as a whole, tried to so conduct ourselves as to merit the respect of the white people of
Gary, and their attitude toward us has been so exceptional, that we blush with shame at
this lapse of good sense," it stated. Nehring ultimately died and Pitts was convicted of murder and sentenced to life imprisonment; he spent five years in jail before his sentence was
commuted. He later became head of the local branch of the NAACP.

Joe Louis has a fight, the negroes are going to celebrate." Rioting broke out in black Richmond when a white motorist forced his way through the "teeming mass of joyful humanity" on Second Street. In the Arizona State Penitentiary in Florence, a racial free-for-all followed the fight, with white inmates stabbing one black prisoner to death and severely beating another.

Black papers were both defiant and embarrassed by the outbursts, sometimes on the same page. "When colored people are filling streets and having their own celebration in their own community, it is no time for Nazi-minded sympathizers to interfere," the *Afro-American* editorialized. "Anybody who doesn't like to see us have a little innocent fun can stay at home." But an *Afro* columnist blamed more primitive southern blacks, along with West Indians and followers of Marcus Garvey, for the lawlessness. Another black paper sounded a single sad note. "The tragic aspect of the whole affair is that all the people who have died since that fateful night two years ago when Max put Joe to sleep went to their graves believing that maybe Max really was the champion after all," it said.

Early in the afternoon of the day after the fight, 350 schoolchildren, most of them black, crowded outside the building where Louis was staying. "We want Joe!" they chanted. "We want Joe!" Louis was mobbed as he left for the Hippodrome, where he collected his paycheck of $349,288.40. It was his share of a gate which, with $75,000 thrown in for radio and movie rights, eked past the magic million-dollar mark. Schmeling's take was $174,644. Louis reenacted for reporters the now-famous kidney punch, and took another round of questions. Later, at Braddock's restaurant, he said he had knocked Schmeling out so quickly because he was scared — "I remembered my first fight with him" — and gently second-guessed the referee for pulling him off Schmeling when the German was on the ropes. Murray Lewin of the *Mirror*, who had grabbed the towel Machon had thrown into the ring, now cut it into squares and had Louis scribble his name on each piece.*

Louis was not present when the fight film was screened that afternoon. For the writers, the footage promised to clarify a host of issues lost in the blur of events, like the number of knockdowns, the order of the punches, and the points at which Donovan began counts. Given the film's brevity — one trade publication said it would be better sold as a slide — the

---

*The towel reputed to be the one Machon threw, now in the Smithsonian Institution, is almost certainly an impostor.

entire fight would be shown in slow motion, and shown repeatedly from several angles, simply to stretch things out. The twelfth round of the first fight was tacked on for additional padding, as was an interview with Donovan. Still, the film lasted only seventeen minutes. Close inspection confirmed that the shots to the head had crushed Schmeling before the kidney blow was delivered. Tunney felt that for the sake of his soul and his self-respect, Schmeling shouldn't see it at all.

The films were shown widely everywhere in the United States except the South. And while they drew well on opening day, they were a bust after that. The kidney punch didn't look as dramatic as it had actually been, complained *Variety*, nor was Schmeling's injury the hoped-for lure; the film's "feminine draw is nil," it said. Even in black theaters, it did badly. "The one round isn't giving the fans enough action for their money," the *Philadelphia Tribune* reported. But to other blacks, it was something to savor. Vernon Jarrett of the *Chicago Tribune* recalled how his schoolteacher father, whom Jack Johnson had seemingly forever soured on prizefighting, put down his money at a segregated theater in his Tennessee town and then, fighting off his rheumatism, climbed the stairs to the buzzard's roost to bask in the glory. For Patsy Booker, a seventy-eight-year-old black woman in Los Angeles, the film made more of an impression: it was the first motion picture she'd ever seen.

Roughly twenty-four hours after the fight, Louis boarded a Chicago-bound train at Grand Central. A huge crowd saw him and Marva off. "The champ hasn't got a scratch on his perfect body!" the *Amsterdam News* marveled. He was still en route when the boxing writers gathered at Jack Dempsey's restaurant. "I think Louis'll be the champion for at least ten more years and maybe until 1950," Dempsey said. "The guy who'll beat Louis is still playing marbles somewhere." The bout with Schmeling, Roxborough pointed out, was Louis's first as "a full-fledged man." "Great as you may think Joe is, you have not seen him at his peak," he said. "A year, or even two years, from now, and he'll be the best fighter of all time—if only we can find opposition for him." And that was a real problem. There was something almost poignant about Louis's situation. As a matter of money, drama, and sheer artistry, how could he ever top what he had just done? A rematch with Max Baer was on tap, but no one could get very excited about that. Some blacks worried that the competitive vacuum in the heavyweight division left it ripe for manipulation, and urged Louis to retire while he was still pristine. Eleanor Roosevelt, meanwhile, worried about Louis's finances. "We congratulate him," she wrote a few days after the fight, "and hope that he has some wise member of his family who takes his money and puts it away, so that when he no longer has any opponents he will be able to do something else to make life interesting and pleasant."

The Louises were received rapturously in Chicago. Louis met with Mayor Kelly and took over the city for a few minutes. He watched a Negro League doubleheader between the Chicago American Giants and the Birmingham Black Barons, and between games he and Jesse Owens competed in a sixty-yard race. (Owens conveniently tripped and fell down at the start and Louis beat him to the tape.) But plans to take the *Queen Mary* to Europe with the John Roxboroughs and the Julian Blacks were scrubbed, ostensibly for reasons of safety. "The Nazis stacked their political all on the outcome of the fight, and it is now feared that if Joe had gone . . . his life might have been endangered by some Nazi secret agent," the *Amsterdam News* reported.

The day after the fight, John Kieran of the *Times* wrote that when all was said and done, it had signified absolutely nothing. Of course, black commentators saw things very differently. For Frank Marshall Davis of the Associated Negro Press, it was a victory for fourteen million black Americans. "It was as if each had been in that ring himself, as if every man, woman and child of them had dealt destruction with his fists upon the Nordic race of Schmeling and the whole Nazi system he symbolized," he wrote. "It was the triumph of a repressed people against the evil forces of racial oppression and discrimination condensed—by chance—into the shape of Max Schmeling." For many, it hadn't mattered how long the fight lasted, only how decisively, incontrovertibly, and even how brutally it ended. That was why, Lem Graves, Jr., wrote in the *Norfolk Journal and Guide*, few complained afterward of being cheated. The *Philadelphia Independent* claimed that Louis had created more goodwill for American blacks than anything since the Civil War.

If it was possible, Louis-worship reached new heights. A black minister in Mobile wrote that God had strengthened Louis as He had already empowered Samson, David, and Elijah. Even Jack Johnson called Louis's victory "a great fight by a great champion." (But some blacks weren't quite ready to allow "Lil' Arthur" aboard the Louis bandwagon. "He is one of the worst we have and any paper that would even print his death notice should not have our support," one Maryland woman wrote.) There were more Louis poems and songs, including Bill Gaither's "Champ Joe Louis (King of the Gloves)," recorded the day after the bout.

I came all the way from Chicago
To see Joe Louis and Max Schmeling fight
I came all the way from Chicago
To see Joe Louis and Max Schmeling fight.
Schmeling went down like the Titanic
When Joe gave him just one hard right.

Even after Louis's day was done, James M. Reid wrote in the *Defender*, "[H]is spirit will stalk the world—everywhere black men shall dwell, carrying a message of inspiration to youths reminding them of their fine lineage and of one who sought right and justice for a race." But perhaps the greatest encomium came from a headline in the *Pittsburgh Courier*: DUKE ELLINGTON RATED JOE LOUIS OF MUSIC, it declared. It all got to be too much to one black woman. "I have been a reader of the *Afro* for years but I will have to give it up if I keep reading about Joe Louis," she complained to the paper.

The white press featured fewer grand pronouncements, but there were some. Heywood Broun conceded that a fight was just a fight, but prophesized that "even the tiniest hint that the Nazi bark is more than the Nazi bite could possibly loose a train of consequences. . . . And one hundred years from now, some historian may theorize, in a footnote at least, that the decline of Nazi prestige began with a left hook delivered by a former unskilled automobile worker who had never studied the policies of Neville Chamberlain and had no opinion whatsoever in regard to the situation in Czechoslovakia." The world would rejoice "not so much that Schmeling himself was battered to wreckage," wrote Elmer Ferguson of the *Montreal Herald*, "but that the arrogant, bold ideals Schmeling stands for, the ideals of intolerant superiority of birth and blood, the ideals that fire and steel must prevail, the complete indifference to personal rights and liberties, are all rebutted by this quiet young negro who was born the descendant of slaves in a little cabin on a southern cotton plantation."

"With the defeat of the boxing Hitler envoy, the whole Nazi blabber about race becomes the joke of the world," said a German émigré paper in New York. It also ridiculed Schmeling's foul claim. "It doesn't prove any 'moral superiority' of the superman that he now tries to sell the world a new myth of a stab in the back, just as the Nazis did regarding the—for now—last World War," it said. The *Philadelphia Record* marveled not only that a black man was heavyweight champion, but that he was so popular among all Americans. "Grandfather wouldn't have believed that possible," the paper said. "But grandfather may have been wrong about a number of things, including the rate at which America was progressing toward tolerance." Several Americans sent Hitler derisive telegrams after the fight; "Our sympathies on the disgraceful showing Herr Max made tonight," said one.

Of course, though Louis had beaten Schmeling, he still could not beat all the stereotypes. R. M. Hitt, Jr., of the *Charleston News and Courier*, who had predicted Louis would be "a scared nigger" when he saw Schmeling's fists, confessed error. Instead, his Louis was "like a tiger which had been kept in a cage without food for two years while succulent hunks of beef dangled in the air just out of reach"; when the bell rang, "the door to the cage was flung open." Somehow this barbarism coexisted with laziness and indolence. "Joe Louis, the lethargic, chicken-eating young colored boy, reverted to his dreaded role of the 'brown bomber' tonight," was how Lewis Achison of *The Washington Post* began his account of the fight. "It is nothing for us to weep about and seek white hopes," wrote General Hugh Johnson, the head of Franklin Roosevelt's National Recovery Administration. "These black boys are Americans—a whole lot more distinctly so than more recently arrived citizens of say, the Schmeling type. There should be just as much pride in their progress and prowess under our system as in the triumph of any other American. For all their misfortunes and shortcomings they are our people—Negroes, yes, but our Negroes."

Bill Corum said Louis was the greatest fighter he'd ever seen, or expected to see. "Somebody'll beat him," he wrote. "But nobody will ever beat the Louis you saw last night." One of Louis's most persistent critics, Davis Walsh, called the fight "the greatest exhibition of punching that I and Max Schmeling ever saw." "Probably he punches faster and harder than any heavyweight that ever lived," wrote Hemingway. Characteristically, Frank Graham of the *Sun* put it most elegantly. "The ring may have seen a greater fighter than Joe Louis, but it never saw a greater one over a span of little more than two minutes than he was at the Yankee Stadium last night," he wrote. For Schmeling, on the other hand, there was little but contempt, both as a boxer and as a man. "Schmeling was worse than Kingfish Levinsky," Jimmy Powers wrote. "I'm undecided whether Joe put up a great fight or Max an awful one. Probably a little of both." Gene Tunney called Schmeling "just pathetic." That very week, the pitcher Johnny Vander Meer of the Cincinnati Reds had thrown consecutive no-hitters; now, someone cracked, Schmeling had tossed a third. The *Charlotte Observer* theorized that the notoriously anti-Semitic *Der Stürmer* would now claim the Jews had poisoned Schmeling, shone blinding lights into his eyes, and pelted him with kosher food. The *Herald Tribune*'s Caswell Adams predicted that when Schmeling returned to Germany, "he'll find that he had a grandfather named Goldberg."

O. B. Keeler, the Atlanta sportswriter who had denigrated Louis from the outset, was now simply resigned to a black champion; after all, he noted, "our fastest runners are colored boys, and our longest jumpers, and highest leapers." But most southern editorialists were more generous. "The colored people do not win many great victories, and when they do win in a fisticuff in New York or a foot race in Berlin, we don't grudge it to them," the *News and Courier* in Charleston said. "No intelligent person, of whatever color, is likely to claim that this proves Alabama negro stock is superior to Aryan stock, but the situation appeals to the American sense of humor and love of fair play," the *Huntsville (Alabama) Times* said.

The outcome prompted mirth and contempt from various Jewish papers. It was just like World War I, the New York Yiddish daily *Morgn-zhurnal* opined: the Germans were great at delivering punches, but when the Allies fought back they'd "lost all of their courage, lifted their hands high and screamed, 'Kamerad!'" Schmeling had taken the blows, but the Führer had taken it squarely in the "philosophy," said the *Forverts*. "If only Schmeling's collapse can be taken as a portent of the weakness of Nazism as a whole, our troubles are almost over," the *Jewish Times* editorialized.

The Communists, too, rejoiced in Louis's win. If Neville Chamberlain had stood up to Hitler over Austria and the brewing conflict over the Czech Sudetenland the way Louis had to Schmeling, several papers commented, the world would be a safer place. Lester Rodney marveled at the Nazis' idiocy—how on Schmeling's exposed chin "they stuck the whole stupid myth of 'Aryan' supremacy for a member of one of the 'non-Aryan' races to swing at." "The Negro sent the 'pureblooded Aryan' down for the count," declared *Izvestia* in Moscow. In Poland, there was widespread satisfaction over German embarrassment. A newspaper in Lodz recalled how the Nazis had touted Schmeling's win two years earlier as the triumph of intellect over brute strength. If that were really true, it said, Thomas Mann, Bruno Walter, Freud, and Einstein would now be running Germany, and the world wouldn't have to fear another war. Poland's Jews reacted more emotionally. What the fight proved, the principal Polish-language Jewish daily declared, was that Jews must recognize the symbolic value of sports, and stop treating its athletes as stepchildren. "Let's not disrespect good fists, developed muscles and everything that is not intellectual," it said. In the same paper, a Jewish poet named Wladyslaw Szlengel wrote a poem.*

> *Hey Louis! You probably don't know*
> *What your punches mean to us*
> *You, in your anger, punched the Brown Shirts*
> *Straight in their hearts—K.O.*

A Jewish boy in Katowice cut out a photograph of Schmeling at Louis's feet that appeared in a local newspaper and placed it in the mailbox of the German consulate.

The fight was front-page news in Tokyo. In Britain, it got bigger play than the death of the queen's mother. In Johannesburg, fans snapped up the "special fight edition" of the *Rand Daily Mail*. HITLER'S RACISM KNOCKED OUT LIKE LIGHTNING, a paper in Buenos Aires stated.†

"A terrible defeat," Goebbels wrote in his diary the day after the fight. "Our newspapers had reckoned too much on victory. Now the entire nation is depressed. I'll send an encouraging telegram to Schmeling and flowers to Anny Ondra. They could both use that now." Contrary to much that was written later, Schmeling and Ondra remained in good official odor, even if he was understandably less lionized and conspicuous than before. Schmeling could expect a perfectly respectful reception in Germany if he wanted one. Hitler, who had not listened to the fight but had awakened in the middle of the night and asked for the result, was said to be both "extremely depressed" and to have received the news "philosophically." The "triumphal entry through a beflagged Berlin" that had been planned for Schmeling, culminating in a meeting with the Führer, now had to be scuttled, though it was said that Hitler would still see him upon his return.

At eleven on the morning after the fight, the Polyclinic Hospital issued its first bulletin on Schmeling's condition. He had a fracture on the transverse process of the third and fourth lumbar vertebrae, with a hemorrhage

---

*Szlengel, who went on to become the unofficial poet of the Warsaw Ghetto, was killed in the uprising there in April 1943. He was not yet thirty years old.

†But surely the most novel interpretation of the outcome came from W. C. Fields. "It simply bears out what I've always contended," he told Ed Sullivan. "A kidney needs a good alcoholic lining to stand up under wear and tear. Schmeling was the victim of clean living. I dare say that if Louis or any other professional slasher dealt me such a blow that their hands would crumple from the impact. As a result of long and serious drinking, I've developed protective ripples of muscles over my kidneys."

of the lumbar muscles. Schmeling would recover, but would have to spend three weeks in the hospital. Word of the diagnosis spread far more slowly than the inevitable rumors that Schmeling had either died—NBC had to broadcast a bulletin denying it—or been irreparably maimed. Once again, concerned fight fans jammed newspaper and radio switchboards. New York's municipal radio station urged listeners to stop calling the hospital, whose emergency services were threatened by the deluge. The *Times* took more than two thousand calls that afternoon and evening, and newspapers elsewhere reported similar experiences. "It seemed as if everyone in Jacksonville had heard that the German had suffered a fatal injury," the local paper reported. Germany, too, was rife with rumors. "It was impossible even for a minute to put down the telephone receiver," the *Angriff* noted.

Enormous crowds soon gathered outside the hospital. By four-thirty p.m. the day after the fight, the entrance and lobby were so crowded that the police had to be summoned. Inside, immobilized in an upraised bed, Schmeling received a few visitors: Machon, Joe Jacobs, General Phelan of the boxing commission, Hellmis. Schmeling and Machon persisted with the foul charge, but said they would not file a protest. Ondra reassured her husband that Germany had not turned on him, describing the torrent of letters, flowers, and calls she had received. "It's terrible that punches like that are permitted," she told the German press. She made plans to travel to the United States, but canceled them once doctors authorized Schmeling to return via the *Bremen*, which was leaving New York in less than two weeks, provided he remained immobilized during the passage. The *Daily News* managed to sneak a photographer into Schmeling's room and splashed a picture of the pajama-clad patient, looking demoralized and weak, on its front page. Some cynics suspected Schmeling was faking it, either in league with the Nazis or to protect himself from them. 'MAX' INJURY A RUSE TO FOOL HITLER, read a headline in the *Chicago Times*. An unnamed doctor told the *Forverts* that the German could walk out of the hospital if he wanted to. Seeking to set things straight, the Jacobses prevailed upon the hospital to release Schmeling's X-rays, which promptly appeared on the front pages of several newspapers. To those who could read them, they showed that Schmeling's injuries were quite real.

Joe Jacobs lobbied for a third fight, but only halfheartedly. "Max didn't go out of his way to get me in the corner," he admitted. All around, it was a bad time for him. For services rendered to the Reich, Parker wrote, Hitler would now place Jacobs in charge of all concentration camps for Jews. "Disowned by his race because he sold them out for an office boy's job with Schmeling, Jacobs cuts a rather sorry figure today," Parker opined. "His meal ticket gone, Yussel will have to find himself another racket because he has worn out his welcome in the fight game. Maybe, through his pull with Herr Goebbels, he could get a job as a photographer on *Der Angriff*." Writing in the *B'nai B'rith Messenger*, Irv Kupcinet called Jacobs "the sorriest figure in sportdom."

Two days after the fight, Ambassador Dieckhoff checked in on his most famous invalid. Mike Jacobs also visited, though perhaps only because Schmeling owed him $40,000; three times, Schmeling had left the country without paying taxes, and Jacobs had footed the bill. At one point, Machon and Uncle Mike got into a shouting match; Jacobs vowed that if Schmeling ever fought for him again, he would deal with him directly, and not through mouthpieces. "He is his own manager and has been for a long time," he said. Contrary to another hoary myth, Louis was not among those stopping by nor even attempting to do so. "No, I ain't going over to see him," he explained. "I just guess he was just the only man I ever been mad at. Sorry if he's hurt, tha's all. I don't like to hurt nobody." Instead, Louis and his advisers dashed off a note and sent it by messenger to Western Union. "Wishing you good luck and hope you are not seriously hurt," it said. That was enough.

Goebbels's ministry quickly tried to distance itself from the debacle, insisting that it had always counseled caution on all fight coverage. "The newspapers now only have themselves to blame if they've made fools of themselves," it declared. Having gone so far out on a limb, the state-controlled press could hardly pretend the fight hadn't happened, or bury fight-related stories in the back pages. Schmeling himself, meantime, was to remain praiseworthy. "It is entirely clear that Schmeling continues to have our sympathies," the orders stated. On the streets of Berlin, some professed indifference to the outcome. On the Berlin underground, a man was overheard to say he felt bad about Schmeling's ordeal. "Yes, Schmeling may have been almost killed," his friend replied, "but Beethoven's Ninth Symphony still lives on." A South African paper, however, described Berlin as "dumbfounded" by the outcome. Only two papers published their planned fight extras, it said; the rest "were canceled in disgust." A Frankfurt paper offered its own absurd explanation: "The reports from New York were so contradictory that we, in the interest of accurate coverage, decided not to publish a special edition."

Throughout the Reich, conspiracy talk was rife; many believed that Louis had had lead or cement in his gloves. So was racial stereotyping. "*Neger und Elefanten vergessen Prügel nie!*" the saying went: Negroes and elephants never forget a beating! But good sportsmanship was to be the official Nazi party line. All talk of fouls and all denigration of Louis were forbidden; perhaps this was why Schmeling dropped the charge so fast. Schmeling was officially decreed to be the victim of a bad break. And Schmeling, moreover, was not Germany; there was to be no talk about loss of national prestige. The image of Schmeling the tenacious, impeccable sportsman who had shown Germany how to persevere and prevail over all obstacles lived on, at least for now. For many years Schmeling's victories had made the Germans "proud and happy," one paper declared. Now, it said, Germans had to "show we can be fair losers." Newspapers wished him a speedy recovery and promised him a gracious welcome home.

A few German papers gave Louis, or Louis's advisers, some credit. "Schmeling seems not to have reckoned with the tactics of Louis who apparently was brilliantly advised," one wrote. Schmeling, the *Angriff* noted, was simply not up to an attack from someone nine years younger. But despite the officially sanctioned good manners, there was plenty of scapegoating and stereotyping. A few days earlier, the German press said Schmeling couldn't lose; now it insisted he never could have won. Schmeling hadn't lost because Louis was a superman, but because "certain American profiteers"—the Jews, of course—had made him wait for a fight to which he'd been entitled. Under such circumstances, it would have been miraculous if he'd prevailed. In other ways, too, it hadn't been a fair fight; for one thing, Louis wasn't quite human. He "attacked like an animal," with an "animal-like will to annihilate," *Box-Sport* said. The fight hadn't been between two men, but two species; all of Schmeling's evolutionary advantages—craft, experience, intelligence, will—had been nullified by the primitive biological edge of "an uncontrolled half-savage."

Others insisted, notwithstanding Goebbels's edict, that Louis's punches had been dirty and deliberate. "To be beaten by such means is not dishonorable," a Freiburg paper said. "Such an ending fits the image we had of the Negro Joe Louis all along, although we never spoke about it out of a feeling of athletic chivalry toward the American sports community." Last time, Louis had merely tried to stave off the inevitable by fouling; this time, he had succeeded. The paper discouraged talk of a third fight; who could guarantee that Louis would not cheat yet again, putting Schmeling's health at risk? "We gladly leave to the Americans world championships that are won this way," it concluded. On June 24, the propaganda ministry moved to control the story more tightly, and to tamp it down. "It is time to have the subject of Schmeling disappear from the first two pages of the newspapers," it directed. Newspaper editors threw in the towel as quickly as Machon had. Virtually overnight, a story that had dominated the German press for weeks, first excitedly and then either ruefully or indignantly, all but disappeared.

Still, there was some unfinished business. One item was the *Angriff's* pool. Not one of the thirty thousand entrants had called for Louis in the first round, but four intrepid souls had picked him in the second. The pot was divided among twenty people, each of whom received 10 Reichsmarks each. The magazines, with their longer deadlines, also weighed in. Louis was now the honest world's champion, said the *Reichssportblatt*. *Volkssport und Leibeserziehung* claimed that Schmeling had actually been *too* smart, relying excessively on strategy and not enough on instinct. "Two minutes determine the work of five years," Thoma wrote in *Box-Sport*. "There could hardly be a greater tragedy in sports." He pushed for a third fight. And if the Americans wouldn't hold it, he asked, then why not the Germans? "Since here, as is well known, Negroes are not lynched and Jews are not shot, the fight can take place without difficulty," he wrote. He urged against writing Schmeling off: it was just not the Nazi way. "National Socialism is not a creed professing the success of the moment; it is not jingoism," he wrote. "Serious work is rewarded with serious recognition, even at times when success is elusive." The Hitler Youth certainly weren't writing Schmeling off; always, its magazine stated, he would "keep his place in the heart of the youth." That said, the promised second installment of a feature on Schmeling never appeared.

On June 29, Goebbels decreed that "it is now time to stop with the picture reports about Schmeling, his fight, and his private life." The ban would extend to coverage of Schmeling's return to Germany. Hellmis, meantime, remained in New York; Parker suggested he was afraid to return home. Unable to write any more about Schmeling, he turned to New York itself, and why every third boxer there wore the Star of David on his trunks, "even if he looks like a Norwegian sailor." Soon, Hellmis put off to sea. This trip would be very different from his epic journey two years earlier, when he'd felt an almost divine calling to tell Schmeling's story. For all his vigilance about what Schmeling ate and drank, Hellmis had neglected to look out for himself, and shortly before he left, someone slipped him a Mickey Finn; he was sick for two days. Several took credit for the deed, but Joe Jacobs's claim was the most credible. "I got even with that big Nazi bum," he said later.*

---

*In another nearly equally plausible version of the story, it is Machon to whom Jacobs slipped the Mickey Finn.

Schmeling's condition stabilized quickly enough for the hospital to discontinue its daily bulletins. His room was so filled with flowers that extra bouquets were distributed in the wards. But his spirits remained low. His face was still bruised and it hurt whenever he moved, something the nurses had to help him do. "A man who had been run over by a steam roller could not have suffered more," wrote Al Monroe, who visited him a week after the fight. To Monroe and others, Schmeling now insisted that he never intended to claim a foul, but only that the kidney punch was illegal in Europe. As for the other punches, Louis had hit him as hard in the first fight, and he had handled it just fine. "He could have hit me on the head or the stomach, but it had to be *there*," he complained.

The *Bremen* was to set sail around midnight on July 2, a Saturday. Seeking to elude the press, Schmeling arranged to leave the hospital quietly twenty-six hours earlier. He was taken by stretcher to the pier on West Forty-sixth Street, and by the time the press knew anything about it, he had been installed on board, with guards surrounding his stateroom. Few people were sorry to see him leave. He'd be back, Joe Williams predicted, because he had "a lyrical enthusiasm for the American dollar." But he'd never fight Louis again, because Louis could beat him any night of the week. Before leaving, Schmeling had several accounts to settle. He owed money to Jack Dietz, the owner of the 1936 fight film. He also owed Mike Jacobs, Uncle Sam, Madison Square Garden, and Steve Dudas. Dietz and the United States marshall boarded the *Bremen* early Saturday morning to make sure Schmeling paid up. By Parker's calculation, $153,000 of Schmeling's $174,000 take was already spoken for, and that didn't count training expenses, hospital bills, Machon's fees, or Joe Jacobs's cut, however skimpy that might have been.

His business done, Schmeling met with reporters. He was propped up in his bed, dressed in blue pajamas with red piping; his back was fixed tightly with adhesive, his left eye still "in mourning." "I haff moved from one prison to another only this iss a nicer chall, because it iss moving toward home," he said. Again, he said he had no plans to retire: "There is vork to be done. Great vork." Again, he stressed that he'd gotten a bad break. All he wanted was "anozzer chance." The Nazis ordered cautious coverage of his plans. "Since Schmeling's future sporting activities are not yet certain, one is warned against taking up reports about supposedly firm plans and new agreements," the press was told.

A nurse would accompany Schmeling during the crossing, as would Machon. Also on board was a German sports reporter named Carl Otto Haymann, who neatly summed up his experience thus far. "We traveled seven thousand miles for—poof!" he said. Schmeling was again bringing back footage of the fight; Machon, the ship's captain, and four of Schmeling's friends watched it at sea. But confined to his cabin, Schmeling could not, and it was surely just as well. He owned the German rights to this film, too, but its commercial prospects were bleak. "The Nazis will break down no doors trying to get a peek at the movies showing their hero being punched into a protoplasmic mass," wrote Shirley Povich of *The Washington Post*.

Ondra called the ship several times to check up on her husband, and to plead with him to retire. Sitting up in his bed, a phonograph playing swing music in the background, Schmeling told a reporter that he'd radioed officials in Bremerhaven, asking that no reception be held for him. His wishes dovetailed nicely with the regime's: the more low key, the better. The *Bremen* docked in Cherbourg on July 8 and reached Bremerhaven the next day. Among those meeting Schmeling were his wife, his mother, and one of Tschammer und Osten's representatives. Schmeling was not on a stretcher; "that would never have done," he explained. Instead, the two women helped him down the gangplank and toward the boat-train to Berlin, where a special compartment had been readied for him. Schmeling complained of dizziness, probably from having been in bed so long. Asked about the fight, he said he appreciated the fairness of the Yankee Stadium crowd. "A few intimates emitted a heil or two," wrote an American reporter with no knowledge of Schmeling's request. "There is either a tacit verboten on Max in Germany or else a definite order to play down this dark-browed Aryan who lost to a Negro." An equally cheerless welcome greeted Schmeling in Berlin, where just two dozen people—friends, newspapermen, photographers—awaited him at the Zoo station. "That's certainly one thing the Germans of today have to learn: how to be good losers," another American reporter wrote.

Schmeling said he planned to enter a hospital the next day to complete his cure, but beyond that he'd make no statement. Five days later, he checked out of the clinic, telling Thoma that his career was not yet over. To allay reports that Schmeling had killed himself, the propaganda ministry directed German magazines to print pictures of him; in mid-July *Box-Sport* put him and his wife, walking together down a street, on its cover. "Today, Schmeling has more friends in America than before, and Joe Louis hasn't won any new ones since his doubtful victory," the magazine wrote. "Anywhere else, and under any other ring rules, Joe Louis would have been disqualified."

Immediately following the fight, *Box-Sport* said it awaited the fight films with "burning curiosity," presumably to document Louis's perfidy. When Thoma saw them, necessarily while still in New York, he suggested that the fateful kidney punch had been excised by "the all-powerful Mike Jacobs and his friends." There's no evidence this is true. But rather than using the film to prove Schmeling's point, Goebbels barred it outright. "[Schmeling] is brutally beaten," he told his diary after screening the footage. "Can't be shown publicly." Asked why the films were not distributed, the German news agency explained that they had arrived "too late." Reports soon surfaced that the Nazis were showing doctored fight films, with footage from the two fights interspersed. The resulting pastiche supposedly showed Schmeling winning handily (the first fight) until the kidney punch (the second fight). Roxborough complained to the American ambassador in Berlin, Hugh Wilson, whose investigation revealed that no fight films, real or doctored, were being shown in Germany.

With Schmeling out of commission, boxing promoters launched yet another search for a "white hope." "The hunt is on," *Ring* reported in September. "Hundreds of managers and scouts throughout the world are on the lookout. The lumber camps are being combed. The C.C.C. [Civilian Conservation Corps] camps are being scoured. There is a sharp lookout in every gymnasium where boxing is followed for the young man who some day may come up as did Louis and be able to survive the flaying fists of the Bomber." It was a vain wish, Fleischer conceded six months later — "No champion was ever as far removed from the available opposition as this somber socker" — but also an entirely unnecessary one: "Gone are the days of the white hope hysteria when every muscle-bound truck driver, stevedore, laborer or what-have-you was looked upon as a potential savior of an harassed humanity," he wrote. And that was the glory in Louis's story: it offered hope not just to his own people and nation, but to a much larger constituency, too: "In a world tormented by a tidal wave of intolerance," Fleischer said, "the American attitude toward Louis stands out like a beacon of hope on a stormy night."

That may all have been true. But soon, there'd be no need for fighters, at least in the ring, nor would there be much cause for hope of any kind. Not even the mighty Joe Louis could prevent the catastrophe to come.

Epilogue

F OR JOE LOUIS if for almost no one else, the legendary second
Louis-Schmeling fight faded fast. "I thought that would be the happiest moment of my life, the night I knocked out Smellin' and got my
revenge," he noted a few months later. "And when I did, somehow it
didn't seem important any more." For the next few years, he had more
trouble finding decent opponents than beating them. One of his victims
was another of Joe Jacobs's charges, Tony Galento; Jacobs accused Louis
of having had a gadget in his glove the night he'd crushed Schmeling—a
charge he quickly recanted. By September 1939, Jack Blackburn pronounced Louis the greatest heavyweight ever. After that, Mike Jacobs kept
Louis extremely busy; he had eleven fights in 1940 and 1941 alone. His roster of undistinguished rivals was famously dubbed "The Bum-of-the-
Month Club." Only Billy Conn, who had Louis beaten on points in June
1941 until foolishly going for a knockout late in their fight, put Louis to
any kind of test. "It may be impossible for any Negro to be altogether
happy in the U.S. but Louis probably comes as close to this ideal as any
other member of his race," *Life* magazine declared in the spring of 1940.

Even before Pearl Harbor, Louis had signed up for the peacetime
draft, and his patriotic deeds following America's entry into World War II
only broadened and deepened his appeal. In January 1942, he donated all
his winnings from a title defense against Max Baer's younger brother,
Buddy, to the Navy Relief Fund, to be given to the families of fallen
sailors. Louis had "laid a rose on Abraham Lincoln's grave," former New
York mayor Jimmy Walker said afterward. He then enlisted in the still-
segregated army. In March 1942, Private Joe Louis told a New York audience, "We'll win, 'cause we're on God's side," a slogan that made its way

into songs and posters. Then he again put his title on the line for charity, this time against Abe Simon for the Army Relief Fund. Louis's qualms about American racism didn't lessen his patriotic ardor. "There's a lot wrong with our country, but nothin' Hitler could fix," he said. But he would not box before segregated crowds on American military bases, complained to the War Department about the poor treatment of black soldiers, and defended a black private named Jackie Robinson following his altercation with a southern cracker. Footage of Louis in basic training appeared in a government documentary called *The Negro Soldier*. The film also noted that while Louis was serving his country, Schmeling was serving his, as a paratrooper in the Wehrmacht. Once again Louis and Schmeling had squared off, the narrator solemnly declared, "this time in a far greater arena and for much greater stakes."

Schmeling had hoped to resume his boxing career upon recovering from his injuries in the Louis fight. In July 1938, Machon announced that Schmeling would resume his training as soon as his doctors approved. That September, the *Reichssportblatt* reported that Schmeling and Ondra were in Berlin, "as happy and gay as one can be," notwithstanding reports to the contrary abroad. Six weeks after the fight, Schmeling was invited to the Harz Mountain town of Benneckenstein to celebrate the tenth anniversary of the founding of the local chapter of the Nazi Party, and his friend and Goebbels's deputy, Hans Hinkel, accepted his invitation to go with him. That never happened, but no high-ranking Nazi would have ever even considered accompanying anyone who was in official disfavor. That September Schmeling again attended the annual Nazi Party congress in Nuremberg, as he often had, and met with Goebbels as well. Though mentioned far less often in the German papers—as a boxer who wasn't boxing, he was doing little worthy of mention—the Nazi press continued to praise him. The magazine of the Hitler Youth described him as a role model to German boys; *Box-Sport* pronounced him "as popular as ever, because he went down as a fighter." Celebrating Schmeling was different from acknowledging what had happened to him, though; when the *Reichssportblatt* listed the monthly athletic highlights of 1938, the Louis-Schmeling fight was omitted.

Schmeling would not have remained in official favor had the authorities known that on the night of November 9, 1938—Kristallnacht, when the Nazis destroyed Jewish businesses and synagogues throughout Germany and sent thousands of Jewish men to concentration camps—he picked up two Jewish teenagers, sons of an old friend, drove them to his hotel suite in Berlin, and sheltered them there for several days, until the worst excesses subsided. While Schmeling the public figure had always been oblivious of or indifferent to the larger symbolic importance of what he did, Schmeling the private citizen was capable of acts of courage and compassion toward particular individuals, which by their very nature remained unsung. In fact, Schmeling himself never talked about it, or even cited it on his behalf once the war was over. And though it is hard to find other specific examples, his helpfulness to the victims of Nazi persecution is said to have intensified as Hitler's atrocities worsened.

Any official unhappiness with Schmeling stemmed initially from comments attributed to him in the Western press later in 1938, following reports that Goebbels had been roughed up by friends of the husband of Lida Baarova, the Czech actress with whom the propaganda minister was said to be having an affair. It was lucky for Goebbels that he had never tried to play around with Anny, Schmeling was quoted as saying, because he would have broken Goebbels's neck. There were reports that for those remarks Schmeling had been thrown into a concentration camp, but he soon made plans to return to New York, and to attempt to fight Louis again. "I am Joe Louis's master," he declared before sailing from France in January 1939. "I proved it once and I'll prove it again." Guessing precisely why Schmeling was making the trip "provides boxing with its best puzzle since Max Baer sold 108 percent of himself," the *Chicago Tribune* observed; Bob Considine called it "the strangest and perhaps the most sinister trip ever taken by an athlete."

The assumption was that the Nazis wanted him to prove he had not been imprisoned, though if that were really the case, they had no illusions it would work. "The fact that Schmeling is allowed to travel not only domestically but also outside the borders should silence all the lies about his 'disappearance' or 'death,'" the *12 Uhr-Blatt* declared. "Schmeling's trip will surely bear some results, but rabble-rousers and the Jewish criminals will certainly come up with a new lie." Or he had debts to settle with the owners of the 1936 fight films, or he wanted to tend to the money he'd squirreled away, or he wanted to borrow more of it from Mike Jacobs. Schmeling said simply that he wanted to see some friends and a few movies, and take a vacation. "I am not what you say in bad with the government," he declared upon arriving in New York in early February, noting that Hitler had sent him a telegram after the Louis fight. Never, he insisted, had he criticized Goebbels, either publicly or privately. Once again, he didn't want to discuss politics; when a New York paper quoted Schmeling asserting that

Hitler didn't speak for all Germans, he denied ever saying such a thing and demanded a correction. Schmeling was happy to talk boxing, though, and he claimed he could beat Louis in a rubber match. Few took him seriously—"The reporters looked at each other and smiled, but not so Schmeling could see them," one wrote—and fewer still hankered, as Schmeling clearly did, for such a fight. That included Joe Jacobs. Reporters noted that his fierce loyalty to Schmeling had netted him little more than "chicken feed and a million enemies among his own race," and that the German "had done everything except kick the little guy down a flight of stairs to prove that he no longer valued his services." But now Jacobs had a weapon more potent than a Mickey Finn with which to exact his revenge, arranging for Louis to fight a client who respected him and paid him appropriately—Galento—rather than one who did not. Jacobs "considered that he had squared accounts with Max," one reporter observed. "He whooped it up for several days, and the drinks were on him." Schmeling and Jacobs did not see each other on this trip, nor ever again.

In any case, both German boxing officials and Hitler himself opposed a third Louis fight; their examination of the fight film—Nazi officials at least were allowed to see it—proved that Schmeling had been crushed fair and square rather than by some fluky foul. The word from Hitler came to Schmeling in March 1939 via Metzner. Though it was not an official ban, Metzner explained to him, it was "self-evident" that for the organization of German professional boxers, "a wish of the Führer is an order," and he should break off any negotiations. Schmeling was crushed—as much, it seems, by the suggestion that he was "supposedly no longer good enough" to fight Louis as by the dashing of his hopes for a rubber match. "You can imagine that this has affected me in a peculiar way," he wrote Metzner plaintively. When he tried to learn from Hitler's office the basis for the decision, he was assured it was entirely political; Metzner told him the same thing, insisting that Hitler's opposition did not reflect any "lack of trust in your abilities." The white lies told to soothe Schmeling's feelings were yet another indication of his continued high stature. Nazi Germany wasn't angry at Schmeling; it just didn't want another humiliating international loss. Schmeling would have to be content fighting Germans in Germany. He did, and he won, raising hopes for yet another comeback. But when war broke out in September 1939, the thirty-five-year-old Schmeling was soon drafted—punitively, he later insisted, either by Goebbels or by the sports minister, Tschammer und

Osten. He ended up as a paratrooper—assured, he later asserted bitterly, that he'd be used for propaganda purposes and to spur enlistment, and not for combat.

Of course, all of Germany was being mobilized. That included Schmeling's friend Arno Hellmis, who had long since moved from delivering ringside eulogies to the far happier task of reporting smashing German victories in Poland, Belgium, and France. Soon, Hellmis predicted, he would be broadcasting from the Eiffel Tower. But on June 6, 1940, he was killed in an ambush in France. Then, after glowing tributes to him appeared in the Nazi press, he all but vanished from the annals. While Hellmis was surely the most universally known sports broadcaster in German history, and the man who covered the single most epochal moment in German athletics, no German scholar or journalist in the past seventy years has ever written anything about him. He was someone whom everyone would just as soon forget.

It was not Schmeling's only loss that spring: six weeks earlier, Joe Jacobs had died of a heart attack. He was forty-two years old. For a short time afterward, Jacobs Beach moved to the Riverside Memorial Chapel on Manhattan's Upper West Side. "Y'know, he looked so natural lying there that I felt like popping that old cigar in his mouth," Harry Balogh said after paying his respects. Schmeling had to hear the news from the Associated Press reporter in Berlin, for Jacobs's death went unmentioned in Nazi newspapers. "It is too bad, for boxing loses a man who has done a lot for it," Schmeling commented from Berlin. "Joe and I always got along well together." American boxing writers knew better, as had Jacobs himself. "Why, I made Max rich, gave him fame, worked my tonsils raw advertising him and then—well, he was a good fighter, but you can have him," he had said a year earlier. "I don't hold no hard feelin's toward him, though I gotta confess he didn't have the loyalty that makes a real man . . . and a true friend. I like Max personally. But they musta put a poison into him over there." Had Jacobs Beach had its own marquees, they would have dimmed for a minute—perhaps at three in the morning—to honor the fiery manager. The boxing writers mourned him, knowing they would never meet anyone like him again. A woman claiming to be Jacobs's secret wife fought with his family over his meager estate.

In April 1940, only weeks before the Nazis began bombing London and invaded France, Schmeling was still trying to float above politics, still talking to American correspondents in Berlin about fighting Louis again, sending Franklin Roosevelt stamps for his collection. But his career as a

German paratrooper was beginning. The Nazis happily chronicled his progress, and Schmeling, to all appearances, happily played the part. "Max Schmeling, Germany's most popular boxer and former world champion, has enlisted with the paratroopers," a Nazi newsreel from February 1941 declared. Schmeling, the *Angriff* said, was a soldier first, and only then a boxer. "As an athlete, he is a role model for ambitious youth, even more so today than earlier, because now he wears the gray coat [of the Wehrmacht]," it declared. In May 1941 he appeared on the cover of the paratroopers' magazine.

When the Nazis invaded Crete later that month, German radio announced that Schmeling was the first paratrooper on the first plane, and among the first to jump. Quickly, he also became among the first reported fatalities—killed, Western news reports stated, while fleeing his British captors. His death was front-page news everywhere outside Germany. Dempsey eulogized him as "a great fighter and a great fellow" as well as a secret anti-Nazi. But once Schmeling was declared alive—he'd merely been incapacitated, either by aggravating an old boxing injury or by an extreme case of diarrhea—Runyon depicted him as a cheapskate and an ingrate, "not at all the fellow the premature obituaries would have you believe."

While in a German military hospital in Athens, Schmeling gave conflicting accounts of what he had witnessed. To the German press he accused the British of flagrantly violating the rules of war, conduct that had justified harsh German retaliation. They, too, he essentially said, had committed a foul. But to an American correspondent, he insisted the British had not mistreated German soldiers, contrary to what Goebbels had claimed. Goebbels attempted, unsuccessfully, to have him court-martialed. Instead, Schmeling earned an Iron Cross, and a promotion, for his service. But his combat career had ended, and his mind turned back to boxing. Barely three months later he said that as soon as the war was over he would rush to America to "fetch Joe Louis' scalp." He talked of parachuting into Mike Jacobs's office as he had into Crete, though with boxing gloves rather than a machine gun. It sounded like a joke, but according to Pierre Huss, a Hearst correspondent close to Schmeling, it was for real; before Germany had declared war on America, the Nazis had hoped such a gesture would cool off anti-German sentiment and, incidentally, hint at German omnipotence in any air war. Schmeling was for it, too, convinced by Louis's trouble beating Billy Conn that he could take him. That Schmeling was ready to return to New York didn't impress

Uncle Mike. "Right now he wouldn't be any more welcome here than I would be over there," he said.

For the rest of the war, Schmeling, still referred to in the Nazi press as the "German Champion in All Classes," was an emissary with an uncertain, ambiguous portfolio, participating in the German effort but always attempting to maintain a sportsman's aloofness from it. In Germany as well as in occupied Belgium and France, he appeared at *Truppenbetreuungen*, or USO-style gatherings for Nazi troops, usually boxing exhibitions. They were organized by Machon, under the supervision of Hinkel; always, German soldiers greeted him rhapsodically. In Berlin in late 1941, for instance, the crowd clapped rhythmically and chanted "*Maxe! Maxe!*" when he arrived. The same was true in Warsaw in January 1942. While Schmeling was there, Hans Frank, the Nazi governor general of Poland, later hanged at Nuremberg for his war crimes, held a reception for him. The Italian writer Curzio Malaparte claimed to have witnessed Schmeling's encounter with Frank, during which, Malaparte maintained, Schmeling endorsed the nobility of war and witnessed atrocities against the Jews. Malaparte is a notoriously unreliable source, and what he wrote probably never happened. But it is hard to say for sure, in part because Schmeling was never asked about it afterward.

Schmeling was officially discharged from the German army in mid-1943, but on several occasions he was either reported killed in action or captured by the Russians. Given his enormous notoriety, this led to a macabre ritual: whenever such rumors popped up, curious GIs and reporters would go to inspect Schmeling's purported remains. "We are thinking of putting up a sign at the [cemetery] gate saying 'Max Schmeling positively isn't buried here,'" the captain of an American unit charged with registering the German war dead declared in 1944.

In January of that year, Schmeling was back in occupied Paris—again, presumably, to entertain German troops. Simply for being photographed with him, the French boxer Georges Carpentier was later accused of collaboration. In March, Schmeling was in occupied Rome for another boxing exhibition, and, on behalf of Goebbels, who hoped to get him to speak out in favor of the Third Reich, had an audience with Pope Pius XII. Such a high-level mission is hard to square with Schmeling's later claim that Goebbels so loathed him that he could easily have been murdered in the reprisals following the attempt on Hitler's life on July 20, 1944. Clearly, the regime still had its uses for him. So did the Allies, who turned Schmeling into a symbol of the enemy. Even *Liberty* magazine, for which Schmeling had occasionally written, now called him a liar and a coward. "An aroused American, like an aroused Joe Louis, can be a fearful thing to a hated enemy," it declared in 1943. "A lot of other Max Schmelings in Berlin—and their yellow counterparts in Tokyo—are learning what one Max Schmeling learned in a New York ring nearly five years ago." When GI Joe Louis arrived in England, he was asked what he would do if he encountered Schmeling on the battlefield. "I'd kill him . . ." he said, ". . . with a gun."

Oddly, though, Schmeling also maintained that the attempt on the Führer prompted the Nazis to reverse themselves and allow him to visit American prisoners of war in camps throughout Germany and Italy. Schmeling later said he visited the GIs to build up their morale. Others claimed that people in the Resistance had actually asked Schmeling to undertake such missions, to improve camp conditions and arrange clemency for the condemned among them. But to the Germans, too, such visits were useful, promising to pacify or at least distract embittered and potentially mutinous soldiers and, as the Third Reich sank into defeat, to curry favor with the eventual victors. The same was said about Schmeling himself: the visits, the *Daily Worker* charged, marked his "desperate attempt to save his skin from the avenging Allies."

Schmeling's tours apparently began in the spring of 1944 in southern Italy, where he and Ondra journeyed from camp to camp in a shiny black Mercedes. At Cisterna, a camp near Anzio, he told people he was the head of all sports in the prison camps. At Laterina, near Florence, he handed out German cigarettes and pledged to take the winner of a boxing tournament staged for his visit to a beefsteak dinner with him and his wife. Six emaciated soldiers reluctantly agreed to take part; when Schmeling reneged on his promise, a near riot broke out, and the Schmelings hastily fled the camp.*

On Christmas Day 1944, Schmeling, still on crutches, invited some POWs working on a farm to visit his estate, where he served them pretzels and weak beer. Then, in the spring of 1945, as the war neared its end, Schmeling toured American POW camps in Germany—particularly Stalag Luft I, a camp for downed airmen near the Baltic Sea, and Stalag

*According to one eyewitness, the camp commandant introduced Schmeling as a living legend who had "destroyed the nigger Louis" only to lose two years later on a foul. He had served his Fatherland faithfully, the commandant went on, and was now volunteering his services to the Führer when he could have spent his furlough at a spa.

3A in Luckenwalde, thirty miles outside Berlin. At least on some occasions, he was accompanied by high-ranking German officers, like Field Marshall Albert Kesselring, who commanded German forces in Italy. What struck the Americans was how well dressed and well fed he looked, in contrast to their own anemic, ragged state. He was also smiling and cordial, blithely or willfully ignorant of any resentment he generated. He again avoided all politically charged subjects, chatting instead about how the war would soon end and, he hoped, both they and he would be back in the United States. Some soldiers, particularly younger ones who had been captured recently, greeted him like a celebrity, pressed him for autographs, joked and reminisced with him. Once, as a tall, athletic black POW approached one group to whom he was speaking, someone shouted "Here comes Joe!" and Schmeling joined in the laughter. Others were too cold, hungry, or demoralized to pay him much mind. And still more considered him a Nazi, or a Nazi stooge, and turned away contemptuously as he approached. In some instances, higher-ranking American officers ordered their subordinates to steer clear of him rather than fraternize with the enemy. Some prisoners took the photographs of himself that Schmeling sometimes handed out and threw them in the communal troughs, taking special care to place them faceup so that dozens of GIs could urinate on him at once.

In early 1945, as the Red Army approached his home in Pomerania, Schmeling fled west, first to Berlin and then to northern Germany, where British troops arrested him in May. They took him to Hamburg, where he found much of the city in ruins, including his own home and the Hanseatenhalle, destroyed by British planes during an air raid in 1943. (His estate in eastern Prussia was subsequently seized by the Russians.) Schmeling reportedly ingratiated himself with the British by telling them where Ribbentrop, the Nazi foreign minister, was hiding. But he had harsh words for the Americans, supposedly telling one officer that America had never given him a fair break. "He's a Nazi through and through, no better than Hitler, Göring, and the rest," the officer told *The Stars and Stripes*. "I'd like to see him dangling from a rope on Broadway and 42nd Street." To Shirley Povich of *The Washington Post*, that simply didn't sound like Schmeling. "He may, indeed, be no better than the rest of the Nazi scoundrels, but he wouldn't be the brazen one," he wrote. Fred Kirsch, who had come to the United States with Schmeling and Bülow in 1928 and was now a boxing promotor in Washington, agreed. "Schmeling wouldn't act tough after the Americans captured him," he told Povich.

"He was always thinking of Max Schmeling first and he would try to make friends with anybody in a position to help him."

Schmeling promptly tried to strike a deal with the British, in which he and some associates would begin publishing books to reeducate German youth weaned on Nazi values. "As a patriotic German I naturally hoped Germany would win the war but nevertheless realized we had to lose it to get rid of Nazism," he explained. But when word of the negotiations broke, the British quickly backed out. In fact, they jailed Schmeling for three months for attempting to build a home with improperly procured materials. But showing the same doggedness with which he had pursued all his comebacks, Schmeling labored to clear his name and resume his career. For a British de-Nazification court he collected affidavits from various friends and colleagues who testified that he had frequently—and, to their minds, foolishly—criticized the Nazis in their presence, refused to give the Hitler salute, and interceded on behalf of persons the Nazis persecuted. In 1947 he was declared free of Nazi taint. That allowed him to resume his boxing career, and put on exhibitions for GIs in Germany.

Schmeling labored for rehabilitation in the United States, too, through two key surrogates. Anny Ondra stressed to Paul Gallico how her husband had refused to join the Nazi Party, or to give speeches to the Hitler Youth, or to invite Hitler, Goebbels, or Göring to their home.* Machon, too, spoke out, declaring that what had really beaten Schmeling in the second fight was a broken heart. "It was all psychological," said Schmeling's loyal trainer, who spent his last days running a bar in Berlin. "Max actually had an inferiority complex because almost everyone in the United States thought he came to fight for Hitler. Before the fight we received hundreds of threatening letters every day and the newspapers called Max a Nazi. When came the night of the fight, Max was all tied up—petrified."

But Schmeling, whose frequent trips to the United States were once a joke, now could not get back in, partly because sportswriters like John

---

*Schmeling may have distanced himself from Göring, but Göring still stuck by Schmeling. His lawyer at Nuremberg recalled coming to the prison in January 1946 to find Göring arguing animatedly over the Louis-Schmeling fight with one of his American guards. "Göring became very animated, jumped up and practically demonstrated how the blow of the Brown Bomber went into Schmeling's kidneys," he wrote. "He said this was clearly not fair!" The debate proceeded good-naturedly for a while, "and eventually Göring was satisfied when the Americans confirmed for him that Schmeling had been the technically superior and fair fighter while Louis's victory had been brought about mainly by the primeval nature of his race."

Lardner, Dan Parker, and Jimmy Cannon did their best to block him. "The people who used to know and talk with Schmeling over here are prepared to believe that he is not a Nazi now," Lardner wrote in 1946. "In fact, it goes without saying, for Maxie is one of the world's keenest students of trends. Before the war, however, he made no particular secret of his views, and they were such as to make his leader's bosom swell with pride and satisfaction." "Ever since the American Army crossed the Rhine and found Max in a fair state of health and preservation, there has been a campaign in progress to prove that the world has done him wrong," he went on. "It may be so, but bear in mind that if you bought the biggest piece of Max's broken heart you would still need a microscope to see it, and that runs into real money."

Around the same time, Parker reported that Machon had recently contacted Mike Jacobs. Machon related that both he and Schmeling had survived the Nazi terror—"Time out for those who feel nauseated," Parker interjected—but that having lost half his fortune, Schmeling wanted to return to the American ring. "The guy must be hard up when he, a member of the Master Race, appeals thus to a Jewish fight promoter to take him out of hock," Parker wrote. "All those in favor of running a benefit for Maxie, please say 'No,' but loud." In November 1946, Cannon argued that America had no place for Schmeling, even as a tourist. By now Schmeling's every prior accomplishment was viewed through the prism of the war. "With Schmeling, nothing was haphazard, nothing was left to chance any more than he could help it," *Ring* declared in May 1946. "He had the bullhededness and the arrogance of the Nazi, he had the regimented mind, the capacity for taking pains, the one-track line toward his objective." Two years later, Fred Kirsch, hoping to stage a Schmeling bout, asked Secretary of State George Marshall to admit him into the country, but reporters, veterans groups (including some former prisoners of war), and a member of the House Un-American Activities Committee objected. Even the normally amiable Louis weighed in, recounting for *The New York Times* Schmeling's charge that he had fouled him deliberately in their first fight. "That's one more reason why I don't like Max Schmeling," he said in November 1948.

After losing a ten-round decision in Germany in late October 1948, the forty-three-year-old Schmeling hung up his gloves for good. Held in an outdoor arena in the British sector of Berlin in weather so cold that the fighters had to keep covered between rounds, the fight was a grim finale to a glorious career. But by now Schmeling had made enough money to buy himself a farm in Hollenstedt, between Hamburg and Bremen, where he began to raise minks and tobacco. When the new West German state was born in 1949, Schmeling quickly moved into its pantheon. Starved for heroes, the fledgling country wasn't inclined to scrutinize anyone's anti-Nazi credentials too closely; Schmeling's record—particularly his never having joined the party and his apparent loyalty to a Jewish manager—more than sufficed. Assisting him were the close friendships he maintained with three of West Germany's most powerful publishers—Axel Springer, John Jahr, and Franz Burda—who made sure he received an adoring press.

Joe Louis faced a different set of obstacles after the war. For one thing, his old team had broken up. Jack Blackburn died in 1941. John Roxborough went to prison for racketeering. And tired of her husband's long absences and perpetual womanizing, in 1941 Marva had sued for divorce. The two quickly (and very publicly) reconciled and had a daughter, but in March 1945 the marriage ended. (They remarried the following year, only to divorce once and for all three years and another child later.) But Louis's most serious problem was debt. All of the abstemiousness and discipline for which he was once renowned had long since disappeared. A soft touch for flashy new clothes, pretty women, people in need, buddies promising him a good time, investors with dubious schemes, and gamblers, he long lived well beyond even his considerable means, forcing Mike Jacobs to float him funds between fights. "They should have called him 'Can't-Say-No Joe,'" Manny Seamon, who'd taken over for Jack Blackburn, once said. Then there were the taxes he owed on the two charity bouts. By V-E Day, Louis owed Uncle Mike and Uncle Sam more than $100,000 apiece, and was as much as $350,000 in arrears.

Resuming his ring career seemed to promise a way out. His successful rematch against Billy Conn in June 1946 earned him $626,000, nearly twice any previous purse. But his skills were fading, and after two difficult victories over Jersey Joe Walcott, he retired in 1949. His record was unrivaled: winner of sixty of sixty-one professional fights, fifty-one by knockout; a reign of nearly twelve years; twenty-five title defenses. But money woes soon brought him back to the ring, an aging, flabby facsimile of his former self, and he suffered humiliating losses to Ezzard Charles in 1950 and Rocky Marciano in 1951. After that, he quit for keeps. He had earned $4.6 million for his labors but had virtually nothing to show for it, becoming living proof of the paradox John Lardner had noted at the very outset of Louis's career: "The rules of arithmetic do not apply to the fight business," he'd written. "The longer you stay in it, the less you have." Louis received a pittance from the organization that had bought out Mike Jacobs, dabbled in public relations, and peddled Chesterfield cigarettes, "Joe Louis Punch," and "Joe Louis Kentucky straight bourbon." And, for $25,000 plus ten percent of the net receipts, he sold his saga to Hollywood. "The Joe Louis Story," with Louis playing himself in a few scenes (and a young boxer named Coley Wallace in the rest), opened to indulgent reviews in November 1953. Playing Schmeling was Buddy Thorpe, son of the immortal Jim. There were fears that Schmeling might sue over the portrayal—in which, he claimed, he'd been made to look like a gangster. In fact, those scenes were eventually cut, and Schmeling appeared mostly in historic footage. He was also given a share of the profits.

Louis, still living in Chicago, began refereeing wrestling matches. So, too, oddly enough, did Schmeling, who in 1954 had quietly applied for and received a visa to enter the country, for the first time in fifteen years. His tour would begin in Milwaukee, which, with its ample German population, promised him about as hospitable a reception as any place in America. But making money, Schmeling later wrote, was not his main mission. It was to see Louis—and to clear the air. Schmeling flew to Milwaukee, where he was received coolly. Only begrudgingly did the state athletic commission give him a license. Then a disappointingly small crowd showed up for the match; when Schmeling was introduced, the cheers couldn't quite drown out the boos. "I don't believe the people in this country will pay to see Schmeling do anything," said the promoter, who canceled the rest of the tour. "He is stuck with the stigma of Nazism. The public can't forget that." Once again, Schmeling seemed perplexed by the hostility and bemoaned the unfairness of it all; he hadn't fired a single shot in wartime, he pleaded, and had visited all those GIs. "Twenty-five thousand soldiers can tell you that I did not talk about war or politics, but only about sports and America," he said.

His visit with Louis proved more successful. As Schmeling later recalled it, he began by trying to explain that he had never been the Nazi ogre he'd been depicted to be, only to have Louis promptly cut him off. "Max, there is nothing to explain," Louis said. "We are friends. It is all over." The two ended up shooting the breeze at a black nightclub on Chicago's South Side. "It wasn't a bit like old times Sunday when Joe Louis and Max Schmeling got together," a reporter wrote of their sparsely covered reunion. "For one thing, both parties were much too friendly." "We were the victims of bad propaganda," said Schmeling. "There never was any bad feeling on my part." To Louis, such a rendezvous hardly mattered; he'd never lifted a finger to arrange one. But he was a gentle, sunny soul, and was pleased to play along. Those who lived through the second fight knew better. "The years have softened Louis' feelings . . . for he was a vengeful man that night in 1938," recalled Frank Graham.

En route back to Germany, Schmeling stopped off in New York. It made Milwaukee seem cordial. At Jack Dempsey's restaurant, Schmeling tried, without success, to be interviewed and photographed. "Maybe a few decadent democrats remember the pictures of him in his Nazi uniform in Crete," the *New York Post* theorized. A columnist at the paper, Leonard Lyons, expressed outrage that the U.S. government had let in Schmeling while barring John Gielgud, who had just been convicted in London of soliciting a homosexual. "Is it less reprehensible for Schmeling to have fired on Allied troops in wartime than for someone to be found guilty of a sex offense?" he asked. While in New York, Schmeling had a second reunion, with James Farley, the former state boxing commissioner. Farley was now a top Coca-Cola executive, and he offered Schmeling a valuable distributorship in northern Germany. (In this respect, Schmeling had bested his old rival; Coke had never wanted anything to do with Joe Louis, even in his prime.) The job ultimately made Schmeling a multimillionaire and even more of a member of the West German establishment, as well as a philanthropist. But just as important, it burnished his jolly, avuncular image; though some grew annoyed by his tireless pitches, he became a paterfamilias for a sweet, bubbly, and energetic new Germany.

Schmeling had one more appointment before leaving New York, one that was as important to him as his reunions with Louis and Farley. This one, with a reporter present, was in a cemetery in Queens—with Joe Jacobs. "Joe, here is a friend of yours!" the elderly Jewish caretaker said as Schmeling stood by Jacobs's headstone. "It's Max Schmeling! He didn't forget you." That was certainly true, for Schmeling continued to invoke their association often. So it was that even posthumously, Jacobs continued to represent—and to sanitize—him. But Yussel could do only so much. After what Gayle Talbot of the Associated Press called his "crowning rejection"—he was discouraged from visiting the training camps where Rocky Marciano and Ezzard Charles were preparing for their championship fight—Schmeling quietly left the United States. He'd probably never return, Talbot theorized. "The Black Uhlan's return to the scene of his fistic triumphs must have been a disheartening experience, even for a man who never was noted for his delicate sensibilities," wrote

Talbot, who'd been following Schmeling for nearly two decades. "Before he left he fully realized the trip had been a mistake, that he could not roll back the years."

But as well as he knew Schmeling, Talbot underestimated his determination; six years later he was indeed back, and back on the case. In October 1960 the American television program *This Is Your Life* profiled Louis, reuniting him with Roxborough, Black, and Braddock, among others, along with his siblings, children, and third wife, whom he'd wed after a short-lived second marriage a few years earlier. When his turn came, Schmeling bounded onto the stage to embrace Louis, almost knocking over the program's host, Ralph Edwards, in the process. "What about this fellow?" Edwards asked him. A beaming Schmeling surveyed Louis, top to bottom. "Well, Joe Louis is a great friend, and the biggest sportsman, the finest sportsman I ever met," he said. The program was striking for the dignity with which it portrayed Louis, alluding very gently to his tax problems, saying nothing about the most recent and degrading stage of his descent: professional wrestling. By this point, he had also begun taking drugs. "You have lived your life in honor with respect for your fellow man and for God, with great courage and with a great heart," Edwards told him.* But the show was also a milestone for Schmeling: it was his first appearance on American television, and he had been received courteously, uncritically. In the United States as well as in Germany, he was starting to become accepted.

More skeptical observers still spotted a man in denial. "There is an aura of unreality about Max Schmeling," one New York sportswriter wrote during this visit. "Somehow it's a feeling he cultivates, begging belief that there was no Nazi Germany, no war, no blood, nothing but a time when men spent themselves gloriously only in the square arena of boxing." This antipathy resurfaced a year later, when Schmeling arrived in heavily Jewish South Florida for the third Floyd Patterson–Ingemar Johansson heavyweight title fight. "Max Schmeling invaded Miami Beach, which took some courage, although Max, like sixty-seven million other Germans, was never a Nazi," Roger Kahn wrote in the *Herald Tribune*. "As I get the picture, there were never more than five or six Nazis in Germany, but, of course, they worked very hard." At the same time, old antagonists like Joe Williams of the *World-Telegram* had to concede that Schmeling was never the Nazi monster he had portrayed him to be.

---

*Despite his exemplary intentions, twice during the show Edwards called Louis "boy."

Though Louis owed Mike Jacobs a fortune, Jacobs, who had a stroke shortly after the war, never pressed the point. "He's done enough for me," he told associates. But the IRS hounded Louis, and as it did, Louis's problems multiplied. Gradually he slid into mental illness, convinced that the Mafia or other dark forces were out to kill him. In 1970 he was briefly committed. Medication made him functional enough to become a $50,000-a-year greeter at Caesars Palace, paid to shake hands with the thousands who still idolized him. But to a younger generation, black and white, Louis was beyond pathetic: he was irrelevant, a relic, superseded by all those younger, hipper black athletes whose paths he paved. Confident, combative, outlandish Muhammad Ali was now their model of a boxer and a black man. Ali only made things worse, dismissing Louis as an "Uncle Tom."* What Ali did do was save boxing, at least for a time. But when he retired, the sport resumed its long downward slide. Changing tastes, the growing popularity of other sports, the multiplicity of competing titles, the role of television in killing off fight clubs, corruption, and even American prosperity—"There's no more tough guys around, not enough slums," the owner of the New York landmark Stillman's Gym lamented. "The golden age of prizefighting was the age of bad food, bad air, bad sanitation, and no sunlight"—reduced boxing to a secondary sport, making Louis appear even more remote and inconsequential.

After heart surgery in 1977, Louis had a stroke, which left him paralyzed. The following year, Caesars Palace staged a tribute to him. Two thousand people, Schmeling among them, together watched footage of the 1938 fight. Then, as the theme song from *Rocky* blared over the public address system, Frank Sinatra wheeled Louis into the gigantic hall. It was a night in which sentimentality was outdone by Vegas-style vulgarity; people squirmed as Ali recounted how he'd been warned not to wind up "like poor Joe Louis," how Louis was broke because he'd surrounded himself with "white people" and "Jews," and how, while Ali had spoken out on social issues, Louis had remained silent. Then, Howard Cosell droned on so endlessly that Paul Anka never got to sing the special version of "My Way" he'd prepared for Louis. "No one said it out loud," wrote Michael Katz of *The New York Times*, "but this was a farewell testimonial to . . .

---

*Later, they patched things up, and Ali played straight man to another of Louis's famous lines. "Joe, you really think you coulda whipped me?" Ali once asked him. "When I had the title, I went on what they called a bum-of-the-month tour," Louis replied. "You mean I'm a bum?" Ali interjected. "You woulda been on the tour," said Louis.

one of the greatest athletes in history and one of this country's greatest heroes."

That was about right. Louis died of a heart attack on April 12, 1981, at the age of sixty-six. One of those babies named for him, the Rev. Jesse Louis Jackson, gave the eulogy at Arlington National Cemetery; a rabbi, who'd been a boy in Vienna at the time of the second fight, recalled how Louis's victory gave new hope to the city's Jews. "For that alone, Joe Louis deserves to be blessed," he said. Schmeling later claimed to have paid for Louis's private funeral, a point that Louis's lawyer later disputed. But dying afforded only a brief respite to Louis's battered reputation. He slid further into oblivion, commemorated only in down-at-the-heels black Detroit, which named an arena after him and honored him with a statue—in the form of a giant fist—nearby. Only for those who had lived through his glory years did he remain an icon. When Martin Luther King, Jr., was shot, more than one middle-aged African American told a reporter on the streets of Chicago that it was his saddest day since Schmeling had beaten Louis. To mark Nelson Mandela's birthday one year, President Clinton—knowing how much Mandela loved boxing and that he had even listened to a recording of the second Louis-Schmeling fight while in prison—presented him with an unused ticket to that fight.

But as Louis's star faded, Schmeling's grew ever brighter, in part because he became the author of his own story. He wrote three autobiographies, in 1956, 1967, and 1977. Though they became increasingly elaborate, and though eminent historians like Joachim Fest assisted him, all were filled with omissions and inaccuracies. In the longest and most ambitious, *Erinnerungen* ["Reminiscences"], even the date of his own wedding is wrong.* But they stood, and took on increasing credibility, because few Germans were sufficiently skeptical, energetic, or courageous to scrutinize them. And those few got no help from Schmeling; for decades he turned aside all scholarly inquiries, including multiple attempts in the 1970s by the greatest authorities on sports in the Third Reich, Professors Hajo

---

*Schmeling's rendition of the second fight—in seven pages—is typical, and instructive. He wrote that the experts favored Louis "almost unanimously"; that it was only the second fight to produce a million-dollar gate; that Yankee Stadium was sold out; that his reception there had been unremittingly hostile; that Doc Casey had been too scared by the anti-Nazi fervor to be his second that night; that the German ambassador pushed him to charge Louis with a foul (a move he says he personally opposed); that Louis attempted to visit him at the hospital, but that Machon and Jacobs had turned him away; that he did not hear from Hitler after the fight; and that his name "simply disappeared" from the German press afterward. Every one of these claims is untrue.

Bernett and Hans Joachim Teichler. "Mr. Schmeling doesn't answer such questions any longer," they were informed on postcards from his office at Coca-Cola—if they heard back at all. Visitors to Schmeling's estate could not get past the gate; instead, they were shunted off to one of his friends, who plied them with autographed pictures and assured them that interviews were quite impossible. In fact, Schmeling talked from time to time to a few friendly journalists, who could be counted upon never to stray from the same predictable, innocuous, and reverential script. And so it was that long after West German, and then German, culture had come to grips with its behavior during the Third Reich, Schmeling held himself aloof. Asked once if he had any regrets, Schmeling said no: he would do everything again in exactly the same way.

Anny Ondra died in 1987; the Schmelings never had any children. But Schmeling remained vital and vigorous. His extraordinary longevity—in part a tribute to his lifelong physical discipline—only burnished his reputation further. The man who was malleable enough to fit into Weimar Germany and the Third Reich with equal ease now became an exemplar of West Germany, of its economic miracle and its fledgling democracy. He was a constant presence on German television, bestowing awards on young athletes. At one point he was named the German sportsman of the century. His image, one observer later wrote, was that of a squeaky-clean Sunday school boy. Apart from the immunity old age generally confers, Schmeling had outlived anyone who knew any better. His legend grew further when, at a tribute in Las Vegas in 1989, the owner of the Sands Hotel, Henri Lewin, offered a story about Schmeling no one had previously known: Lewin was one of those two Jewish boys Schmeling had sheltered on Kristallnacht. The story quickly became a staple in Schmeling's biography, right behind the Louis fights. From the cartoonlike Nazi he'd been in prewar America, he became a cartoon figure of a different sort: a righteous Gentile. There were even rumors that a tree had been planted for him at Yad Vashem, the Holocaust memorial in Jerusalem.

The story about the Lewin brothers, along with tales of his loyalty to Joe Jacobs, earned a prominent place in the obituaries when—this time, for real—Max Schmeling died, on February 2, 2005, seven months shy of his hundredth birthday. By the time his death was announced, he had already been buried, with only a dozen or so friends present, thus affording him more of the privacy he had always cherished. It did not matter where the tributes appeared, whether in Berlin or London or New York: now, there was only one verdict on Schmeling, and it was almost uniformly positive. "The embodiment of the decent German who wouldn't be co-opted by anyone for anything," wrote the *Frankfurter Allgemeine*. "Our last hero is dead, our only star," declared *Welt am Sonntag*. Such comments prompted a caveat from the left-wing *Die Tageszeitung*, which described Schmeling as "a simple, modest, somewhat naïve and friendly man who wanted to please everyone—and, if it had to be, even the Nazis." The German chancellor, Gerhard Schröder, seemed to acknowledge as much in his own carefully phrased statement. Like nearly everyone else, he saluted Schmeling's athletic proficiency, fairness, and modesty, but he steered altogether clear of politics and said nothing of Schmeling's behavior during the Third Reich.

Though one could scarcely have imagined it at the time, Max Schmeling picked himself off the canvas on the night of June 22, 1938, and lived another sixty-seven years. But no matter how successful or beloved he turned out to be, and no matter how impoverished, enfeebled, or ignored Louis became, Schmeling stuck by him, repeatedly flying halfway around the world to appear with him, greeting him like a lost brother, praising him lavishly. And it all made perfect sense. His triumph over Louis represented the capstone of his career. His loss to Louis spared him greater infamy, and gave him immortality. Louis represented his youth. He also represented his link to America, the nation he had always loved, if only in his own utilitarian way. Most of all, it was Louis who provided Schmeling with what he coveted most: expiation. If *der braune Bomber*, the simple and decent man whom more Americans, black and white, loved more than just about any other man in his generation, harbored no hard feelings toward him, how could anyone else? So of course Max Schmeling honored Joe Louis when he lived, and once Louis died, Schmeling embraced him even more tenaciously, until he, too, passed on. "I didn't only like him," he once said. "I loved him."

ACKNOWLEDGMENTS

I CAN THINK OF few greater favors someone can bestow than nurturing another person's labor of love. And over the past seven years, this book had lots of nurturing, and nurturers.

First, there were those who helped in the research. I especially want to thank Mitch Abramson, Elizabeth Dribben, Ruth Ben-Ghiat, Leslie Friedman, Leah Garchick, Stephanie Goldberg, Rick Hornung, Kenneth Janken, Arnold Kaplan, LeeAnna Keith, Dave Kelly of the Library of Congress, Martin Krauss, William Lin, Ken Maley, Dan Morgenstern of the Institute of Jazz Studies at Rutgers University, Eddy Portnoy, Jonathan Shenfield, Karol Stein, Studs Terkel, Paul Tilzey, Mike Welch, Esther Wilder, and Chris Willis. I'm also indebted to the extraordinary boxing mavens who gave generously of their time, insight, and materials, particularly the incomparable Hank Kaplan, Mike DeLisa, and Mike Silver.

In all of my explorations, the New York Public Library was the mother ship. It is one of mankind's towering achievements. David Smith of the library staff took great interest in my work and helped me more than I can say. Warren Platt also pitched in. Though I've never met them, I'm much indebted to the folks in the Interlibrary Loan program there, particularly Jacqueline Willoughby and Terry Kirchner. The morgue of my alma mater, *The New York Times*, is another inspiring institution, also built up and run by generations of unsung heroes. It is an irreplaceable, and endangered, resource; long may it exist, even in the age of Nexis and ProQuest! I want to thank Jeff Roth and Lou Ferrer there for their gracious and knowledgeable help.

Finding, translating, and analyzing the German materials was a huge undertaking, and I very much appreciate the efforts of Rick Minnich, Bernard Bindzus, Mark Landsman, and Stefan Knerrich. Thanks, too, go to those who read the manuscript at various stages, usually when this was an even more considerable undertaking than it eventually became: Richard Bernstein, Eric Fettmann,

Andrew Margolick, Gertrude Margolick, Joe Margolick, Fred Morton, and Ray Robinson. Their constructive criticism improved the book and spared me from making all sorts of embarrassing mistakes.

Throughout a long period of gestation, I was blessed with the perfect work environment, one that gave me time, flexibility, and security, and I'm deeply grateful to Graydon Carter, Doug Stumpf, and Chris Garrett at *Vanity Fair* for their support—and their patience. My agent, David Black, not only got this project off the ground, but steered it in the right direction: to Alfred A. Knopf. My editor there, Jonathan Segal, was just what I wanted, and needed: discerning, demanding, meticulous. His assistant, Ida Giragossian, was helpful in innumerable ways. Maria Massey tolerated with great grace the infuriating last-minute manipulations of a lapsed newspaperman. Virginia Tan and Melissa Goldstein put together the wonderful pictures. Thanks, too, to Paul Bogaards, Carol Carson, Elizabeth Cochrane, Roméo Enriquez, Kate Norris, Amy Stackhouse, Evan Stone, and Sonny Mehta.

It's always said that newspaper work is ephemeral, but that's not so: the best of it is not lost at all, but merely waiting to be rediscovered and beheld. Reading the journalists who covered boxing, and the world, in the 1930s, and realizing the care they lavished on their work (on tight deadlines and primitive machines, to boot) was a thrilling experience for me. It was also inspiring, a reminder that words matter, and endure. A few of the best white reporters of that era are justly lionized, though most—Dan Parker, Richards Vidmer, Anthony Marenghi, John Lardner, Bill Cunningham, to name just a few—are almost entirely forgotten. At that, their fate has been kinder than that of black contemporaries like Al Monroe, Ed Harris, Roi Ottley, and Ralph Matthews, whose glorious work was almost entirely unread outside Afro-America. That these men and so many like them are unknown, and unsung, is a crime. Thank God for microfilm; someday, someone will do them justice.

I'm grateful to Aline Gittleman for her encouragement and support as this project neared completion. Finally, I want to thank my parents, Moses and Gertrude Margolick. Whatever intelligence and empathy this book contains comes, ultimately, from them. And if, more than forty years ago, my father hadn't brought home a record called "I Can Hear It Now," in which Edward R. Murrow introduced me to Clem McCarthy's call of the second Louis-Schmeling fight, this book never would have happened at all.

David Margolick
New York, July 2005

NOTES

Introduction

5 "Ringside Tonight!": *New York Journal-American*, June 22, 1938.

5 "Wars, involving the fate of nations": *New York Mirror*, June 22, 1938.

6 "On this day": *Angriff*, June 15, 1938.

6 "The Night of the Bright Windows": Ibid., June 24, 1938.

6 "The relative merits": *Daily Worker*, June 22, 1938.

6 "Louis or Schmeling?": *New York Sun*, June 4, 1938.

6 "Louis represents democracy": *Boston Traveler*, June 22, 1938.

7 "Judges and lawyers": *New York Times*, June 22, 1938.

8 "World Series scarcely": United Press International, June 20, 1938.

8 bubbly and alive: *Paris Soir*, June 21, 1938.

8 "If Joe loses": *Amsterdam News*, June 25, 1938.

9 "The first nationally-sponsored heavyweight": *New York Journal-American*, January 15, 1938.

11 "Tonight's the night": *New York Post*, June 22, 1938.

11 "the public loves": *New York American*, May 12, 1936.

11 "Fame and money": Sterling A. Brown, "The Negro in American Culture: Sports," p. 1, in *The Negro in America*, Schomberg Center for Research in Black Culture, New York Public Library (1938–1940).

11 "You can't Jim Crow": Lester Rodney, *Detroit Metro Times*, June 11–25, 1981.

11 "The ring was the only place": *The Autobiography of Malcolm X*, with Alex Haley (New York: Grove Press, 1964), p. 23.

12 "Bronx Bombers": Associated Negro Press, June 24, 1936.

12 "a big, superbly built Negro": *New York Evening Journal*, June 19, 1937.

12 "There is not one iota": *Ring*, May 1938.

12 "Day by day, since their alleged": *New Masses*, July 5, 1938.

13 "in purring limousines": *New York Mirror*, June 23, 1938.

13 "Now let's go": This and all quotations from the American fight broadcasts in this book come from recordings in the collection of the author.

Chapter One: Just Off the Boat

16 "Oh, Max!": *New York Evening Post*, April 15, 1933.

16 "Athletic Club": *New York Daily News*, April 15, 1933.

17 "Hundreds of Jews": *New York Evening Post*, April 5, 1933.

19 "our greatest hope": *Box-Sport*, January 6, 1927.

19 "an insufficient will": Ibid., April 12, 1927.

19 *"Künstler, schenkt mir Eure Gunst"*: Max Schmeling, *Erinnerungen*, revised and amended edition (Frankfurt a.M. and Berlin: Ullstein, 1995), p. 87.

19 "swimming after the dollar": *Box-Sport*, May 22, 1928.

20 "Joe Jacobs gave 'em": *Washington Post*, May 2, 1940.

20 "If all the newspaper copy": *New York Mirror*, June 26, 1936.

21 "It's too darned quiet": *The Boxing News*, June 1936.

21 "my little wife": *New York Mirror*, October 7, 1940.

21 "Why do guys have to sleep at all?" *Ring*, July 1940.

21 "a New York sidewalk boy": *New York World-Telegram*, April 26, 1940.

21 "If you hang me": *New York Sun*, April 26, 1940.

22 "You take the big tree": *New York World-Telegram*, June 8, 1933.

22 "triple pneumonia": *Collier's*, July 1, 1939.

22 "The Black Uhlan of the Rhine": Schmeling, *Erinnerungen*, p. 128. Frank Graham, among others, attributed the nickname to Damon Runyon, *New York Journal-American*, February 6, 1961.

22 "Dempsey! Dempsey!": *Box-Sport*, January 7, 1929.

23 "all Berlin was frantic with joy": *New York Times*, June 29, 1929.

23 "He is quiet, modest": *New York Sun*, June 7, 1930.

23 "an insolence": *New York World-Telegram*, May 29, 1941.

23 "punch harder than": *Forverts*, June 22, 1930.

23 "the fighting son of the Fatherland": *New York Daily News*, June 13, 1930.

23 "the man on whom every American": Ibid.

24 "paralyzed": *New York Times*, June 14, 1930.

24 "Stay down, you idiot!": *Forverts*, April 27, 1940.

24 "a screaming, dancing midge": *Outlook and Independent*, July 2, 1930.

24 "You're the champion, Max!" *New York Mirror*, June 13, 1930.

24 "as though an armored truck": *New York Journal-American*, April 25, 1940.

24 "a severe blow": Associated Press, April 13, 1930.

24 "From the bottom of my heart": *New York Daily News*, June 13, 1930.

25 "If anyone won": *Outlook and Independent*, July 2, 1930.

25 "You know, that *Yacobs*": *New York Daily News*, June 14, 1930.

25 "I'm sure it helped me": *Forverts*, June 22, 1930.

25 "this unpleasant, loud-mouthed": *Angriff*, November 25, 1930.

25 "We're on our way": *Der Abend*, quoted in *New York World*, June 14, 1930.

25 "a concert of boos": Rolf Nürnberg, *Die Geschichte einer Karriere* (Berlin: Grossberliner Druckerei für Presse und Buchverlag, 1932), p. 148.

26 "a disgrace to German": *New York Times*, January 8, 1931.

26 "mean, impertinent, incompetent Jew": *Angriff*, January 8, 1931.

26 "Ruthlessness was the": Nürnberg, *Die Geschichte einer Karriere*, p. 13.

26 "He was robbed": *New York Evening Post*, June 22, 1932; "He was jobbed": *New York American*, June 22, 1932; "We were robbed": *New York Graphic*, June 22, 1932.

26 "The great Sharkey-Schmeling": *New York Daily News*, June 23, 1932.

27 "someone closing a deal": *New York World-Telegram*, June 23, 1932.

27 "German boy of the future": Hajo Bernett, *Nationalsozialistische Leibeserziehung* (Schorndorf bei Stuttgart: Karl Hofmann, 1966), p. 25.

27 "There is no sport that cultivates": Adolf Hitler, *Mein Kampf* (Munich: F. Eher Nachf., 1933), p. 453.

27 "a German revolution of pimps, deserters": Ibid., p. 453.

27 "the high cheek bones of an Indian": *New York Mirror*, December 4, 1937.

28 "incapable of performing even a single knee-bend": *Angriff*, November 6, 1930.

28 "a man from whom even his own kind turn away": Ibid., January 7, 1931.

28 "mean," "impertinent," "incompetent" Jew: Ibid., January 8, 1931.

28 "grubby" Jacobs; "spruced-up numbskull and toady": Ibid., January 7, 1931.

29 "Finally, Finally!": Ibid., April 4, 1933.

29 "Jewish capital or Jewish persons": *Box-Sport*, April 3, 1933.

29 "a defensive action against": *Angriff*, April 4, 1933.

29 "whatever else these blood-suckers call themselves": Ibid.

29 "a clique of corrupt": *Box-Sport*, April 3, 1933.

29 "Jewish big-wigs and corrupt exploiters": Ibid.

30 "giving the cold shoulder": Ibid., April 18, 1933.

30 "If anyone over there": Schmeling, *Erinnerungen*, p. 263.

30n "exaggerated and untruthful": *Boxing*, April 5, 1933.

30 "It would be paradoxical": *L'Auto*, April 2, 1933.

31n "The fact that the new, great leader of the German people": *Box-Sport*, October 24, 1933.

31 "the decrepit medievalism": *New York Mirror*, March 27, 1933.

31 "We all know what would happen": *New York American*, April 14, 1933.

31n "shame the Nazis by lying down": *New York World-Telegram*, April 17, 1933.

31 "Delancey Street dandy": *New York Daily News*, March 22, 1935.

31 "There are many Hebrews here": *Montreal Herald*, April 14, 1933.

32 "He dodges embarrassing questions": *New York Sun*, April 15, 1933.

32 "What conditions?": *New York Evening Post*, April 14, 1933.

32 "I haff never seen Yermany": *New York Daily News*, April 18, 1933.

32 "my friend Joe": *New York World-Telegram*, April 14, 1933.

32 "the most popular person in Germany": *New York Evening Post*, April 14, 1933.

33 "I tell you this—Germany is improving": *New York American*, April 15, 1933.

33 "prices on the Boerse": *New York World-Telegram*, April 14, 1933.

33 not to be "silly" about the man: *New York Evening Post*, April 14, 1933.

33 "Were I to meet Baer in Germany": *New York Mirror*, April 15, 1933.

33 MAX SCHMELING SAYS GERMANY IS NOT CRUEL TO JEWISH FOLKS: The paper is probably the *Plain Speaker* of Hazelton, Pennsylvania.

33 "100 percent Hitlerist": *Moment* (Warsaw), June 11, 1933.

33 "Schmeling pulled himself": *Box-Sport*, May 1, 1933.

33 "When I told them about the reception": Schmeling, *Erinnerungen*, p. 266.

Chapter Two: A Regime's Embrace

34 "stand in defense, with clenched fist": *Box-Sport*, April 25, 1933.

34 "to follow in his path": Ibid., May 1, 1933.

35 "The movement to make Max Schmeling suffer": *New York Mirror*, April 21, 1933.

35 "none is so blind": Ibid., April 25, 1933.

35 "no more of a Jew-hater": Ibid., April 26, 1933.

36 "has to return to Germany some time": Ibid., April 27, 1933.

36 "I'll try to make [Max Baer] think you're to blame": *Pittsburgh Post-Gazette*, April 18, 1933.

36 "Shall I give them a political talk?": *Pittsburgh Press*, April 17, 1933.

36 "We simply ignore it": *New York Times*, April 26, 1933.

36 "Well, that's awfully nice of him": *New York Mirror*, April 26, 1933.

36 "malicious, vitriolic, and imbecilic": *Ring*, June 1933.

37 "at that moment . . . a friend, or a lover, or something": *New York Journal-American*, March 3, 1965.

37 "I've got a million-dollar body": *New York Times*, November 25, 1959.

38 "Hey, Barney": Barney Ross, *No Man Stands Alone: The True Story of Barney Ross* (Philadelphia: Lippincott, 1957), p. 133.

38 "Every punch in the eye": *New York Times*, March 14, 1935.

38 "reported to have become a Jew by press agent": *New York Post*, June 13, 1935.

38 "Baer was only a 50 per cent Hebrew": *New York Mirror*, April 14, 1933.

39 "Hitler is more of a Jew than is Baer": *Ring*, May 1934.

39 "racial and cultural disgrace": *Der Stürmer*, June 1933.

39 "Abroad, one can have no concept": *New Yorker Staats-Zeitung*, May 4, 1933.

39 "Schmeling is a friend of Hitler": *New York Evening Post*, June 5, 1933.

39 "a genuine half-Jewish boy": *New York World-Telegram*, June 5, 1933.

39 "the growing antipathy against everything German": *New Yorker Staats-Zeitung*, June 7, 1933.

40 "Leck' mich am Arsch": Interview, Irwin Rosee; *Washington Post*, October 4, 1942.

40 "A punch all the boxing instructors": *Chicago Tribune*, June 9, 1933.

40 "That wasn't a defeat, that was a disaster": Schmeling, *Erinnerungun*, p. 267.

40 "They thought I was a Hebe": *Variety*, January 13, 1933.

40 "gas bags": *B'nai B'rith Messenger*, June 23, 1933.

40 "who would have been interested if [Schmeling] is a German or a Tatar": *Der Tog*, June 10, 1933.

40 "Schmeling's dream of regaining": 12 *Uhr-Blatt*, June 9, 1933.

40 "A man who travels only first-class": *Völkischer Beobachter*, February 13–14, 1934.

41 "He encouraged me, and told me that he, too, had suffered setbacks": *New York Times*, February 23, 1938.

41 "the female Chaplin": 8 *Uhr-Blatt*, February 11, 1933.

41 "Yussel Jacobs will be ostracized": *New York Mirror*, October 30, 1933.

42 "I got to Berlin and when I entered the Bristol": *New York Times*, November 9, 1933.

42 "All any Nazi ever had to do": *New York World-Telegram*, November 9, 1933.

42 "The chancellor took a lively interest": *Hamburger Fremdenblatt*, December 22, 1933.

42 "deeply stirred by Hitler's personality": *Chicago Tribune*, January 4, 1934.

42 "perhaps couldn't understand why thousands of German national comrades": *Angriff*, January 5, 1934.

43 "Say, wasn't there a lot": *Chicago Tribune*, January 2, 1934.

43 "Hitler may not want Schmeling": *Washington Post*, January 3, 1934.

43 "Herr Hitler does not care who Max fights": *New York American*, January 3, 1934.

43 "absurd": *Lincoln (Nebraska) Star*, January 4, 1934.

43 "the better Hitler will like it": *Chicago Tribune*, January 4, 1934.

43 "He is a football player": *Völkischer Beobachter*, February 13–14, 1934.

44 "The Schmeling we saw last night": *New York Evening Post*, February 14, 1934.

44 "Yesterday Max Schmeling was crossed off the list": 12 *Uhr-Blatt*, February 15, 1934.

44 "international Jewish swamp": *Der Deutsche*, February 17, 1934.

44 end of all state-financed medical support and aid for the "inferior": *Box-Sport*, April 17, 1934.

44 "Mad Monkey of Germany": *Ring*, May 1934.

45 calling the dirt track "American": *Völkischer Beobachter*, July 6, 1934.

45 "Sensationalism and star worship are not befitting the National Socialist Man!": *Angriff*, August 15, 1934.

45 "who through their honorable striving and struggle": *Völkischer Beobachter*, August 16, 1934.

46 MADISON SQ. GARDEN; HAMBURGER PUNCHING: *Hamburger General-Anzeiger*, August 25/26, 1934.

46n "German-blooded pub owner": Völker Kluge, *Max Schmeling: Eine Biographie in 15 Runden* (Berlin: Aufbau-Verlag, 2004), p. 194.

46 "eloquent testimony to the success": *Völkischer Beobachter*, August 23, 1934.

46 "A man capable of arousing so much true Jewish hate": Ibid.

46 "a model of professionalism, sporting decency, and fairness": Ibid., August 26/27, 1934.

47 "a frenzy of boxing enthusiasm": *Angriff*, August 27, 1934.

47 "I expected Max to win decisively": *New York Post*, September 7, 1934.

47 "very decent indeed": Letter, Kurt Tucholsky to Hedwig Muller, in *Briefe aus dem Schweigen 1932–1935* (Reinbek bei Hamburg: Rowohlt, 1977), p. 145.

48 "Every member of the Goldfarb, Epstein": *New York Mirror*, August 18, 1934.

49 "God's own country": *Box-Sport*, February 25, 1935.

49 "The Götterdämmerung has started": *8 Uhr-Blatt*, February 25, 1935.

49 "wants to have good fights and great champions in Germany": *New York Post*, February 2, 1935.

49 "We want to see Max Schmeling!": *8 Uhr-Blatt*, March 1, 1935.

49 "We would hardly know our youth": *Angriff*, March 9, 1935.

50 "television enthusiasts"; "non-political hero": *San Francisco Examiner*, March 10, 1935.

50 "a bodyguard of four very husky-appearing fellows": *International Herald Tribune*, March 11, 1935.

50 "some of the people whom we as National Socialists easily could have done without": *Westdeutscher Beobachter*, March 11, 1935.

51 the "gay" armlets of the storm troopers: *Daily Mail* (London), March 11, 1935.

51 "Any barked order": *Daily Express* (London), March 19, 1935.

51 "Nearest the ring are gaunt-faced": Ibid., March 11, 1935.

51 "What happens now is not a mere welcome": Ibid.

51 Schmeling "like a tiger," "merciless," "controlled," "imperturbably calm": Arno Hellmis broadcast for German Radio Corporation, Deutsches Rundfunkarchiv, DRA 2743222

52 "into a hurricane": *Angriff*, June 15, 1938.

52 "silence that could almost be felt": Trevor C. Wignall, *Ringside* (London: Hutchinson and Co., 1941), p. 53.

52 "the most beautiful tenor voice"; "Hitler's favorite": Ibid.

53 "in all crudeness": *L'Auto*, March 11, 1935.

53 "German men with their eyes tight": *Daily Express* (London), March 18, 1935.

53 "They knew that Hamas, for all his poor showing": *New York Times*, March 11, 1935.

54 "locals with sausages covered": *L'Auto*, March 12, 1935.

54 "Germany has outstripped the seemingly undefeatable America": *Box-Sport*, March 11, 1935.

54 "That's a real fine thing for a politician to do": *New York Mirror*, March 11, 1935.

54 "The superiority of the ex–world champion": *Angriff*, March 11, 1935.

54 "Now we get Baer": *Chicago Tribune*, March 11, 1935.

54 "Among the amusing sidelights of Germany today": *Daily Express* (London), March 16, 1935.

54 "altars to manliness": *Angriff*, March 11, 1935.

55 "When Schmeling Won . . . And Yussel 'Heiled'": *New York Daily News*, March 21, 1935.

55 "just to carry out the Nazi motif": *New York World-Telegram*, March 22, 1935.

55 "In the Broadway delicatessens and nighteries": *New York Daily News*, March 22, 1935.

55 "In the sports world, it is being considered a big joke": *Morgn-zhurnal*, March 22, 1935.

55 "What the 'ell would you do?": *New York Post*, March 22, 1935.

55 "When in Rome, eat pasta fazoole": *New York Mirror*, March 22, 1935.

55 "500 percent Jewish": *Forverts*, April 27, 1940.

55 "What did these birds expect Yussel to do": *New York Daily News*, March 28, 1935.

56 "well and courteously treated": Ibid., February 12, 1935.

56 "punch his way right off the printed page": *New York Sun*, April 14, 1937.

56 "A hard-hitting 'Nordic' meets Max Baer": *New York American*, March 12, 1935.

56 "As always occurs when religion is used": *New York Daily News*, March 28, 1935.

56 "Schmeling Gives Yussel the Ozone": *New York Mirror*, March 28, 1935.

56 "Managers are only the means to the end": Ibid., April 10, 1935.

57 "I really need Joe Jacobs": Schmeling, *Erinnerungen*, p. 298.

57 "the Swastika vs. the Star of David": *Fränkische Tageszeitung*, March 28, 1935.

57 "Who *iss* Chim Braddock?": *New York Journal-American*, July 2, 1938; *Washington Post*, December 8, 1935.

58 "The Negro mixed-breed [*Negermischling*] from Alabama": *Box-Sport*, June 24, 1935; "*Halbneger*": *12 Uhr-Blatt*, July 24, 1935; "Joe Clay Face": *Box-Sport*, April 22, 1935.

58 "Within a short period of time": *Box-Sport*, February 4, 1935.

Chapter Three: A Star Rises in the Midwest

60 "This boy should be able to do something": Edward Van Every, *Joe Louis, Man and Super-Fighter* (New York: Frederick A. Stokes Co., 1936), p. 48.

60 "All my life my hands felt important to me": "In This Corner . . . Joe Louis," produced and written by Mel Baily, directed by Arthur Forrest. WNEW-TV, July 21, 1963, in Museum of Television and Radio, New York.

60 "the white boys make it too tough": *Los Angeles Examiner*, February 14, 1935.

60 "Lewis": *Detroit Free Press*, February 23, 1933.

61n "clever Negro lawyer": *New York Sun*, June 27, 1935.

61n "Neither Roxborough nor Black": *Life*, June 17, 1940.

61n "I figured this way": *New York Times*, November 8, 1948.

61 "the Detroit colored lad with the frozen face": *Chicago Daily News*, March 10, 1933.

62 "The coloreds are on average better": *Box-Sport*, October 28, 1935.

63 "A colored fighter": *Lincoln (Nebraska) Evening Journal*, August 18, 1937.

63 "When the colored brother is capable in sports": Gallico, *Farewell to Sports* (New York: Alfred A. Knopf, 1938), p. 299.

63 "is generally a magnificent physical specimen": Ibid., p. 306.

63 "The Negro is regarded as pure cattle": Ibid., p. 306.

63 "The reason they fight so well": *Los Angeles Times*, February 1, 1935.

63 "Negro fighters are used merely": *Norfolk Journal and Guide*, June 9, 1934.

64 "We've got to wait until somebody can produce a half-clown and half-gorilla": *Chicago Defender*, June 30, 1934.

64 "Take him away": *Life*, June 17, 1940.

64 "You were born with two strikes on you": *Liberty*, November 23, 1935.

64 "just a funny-looking boy": *New York Sun*, June 19, 1937.

64 "very good outside the ring"; "You've got to be a killer, otherwise I'm getting too old"; "I ain't goner waste any of your time": *Ring*, September 1937.

64 "Let your fists be your referee": *New York Sun*, June 11, 1936.

64 "too easygoing—too nice a fella"; "didn't have any blood in his eye": United Press International, June 18, 1936.

64 "You can't show no pity in this game"; "When you get a man in distress": *Chicago American*, July 5, 1938.

64 "You just gotta throw away your heart"; "Joe Louis ain't no natural killer": Ronald K. Fried, *Corner Men: The Great Boxing Trainers* (New York: Four Walls Eight Windows, 1991), p. 121–23.

65 "fool nigger dolls": Joe Louis, with Edna and Art Rust, Jr. *Joe Louis: My Life* (New York: Harcourt Brace Jovanovich, 1978), p. 39.

66 "If he isn't the hardest punching heavyweight": *New York World-Telegram*, June 10, 1937.

66 "hung like a sack of wheat": *Chicago Tribune*, December 1, 1934.

67 *"The Ring* welcomes Louis": *Ring*, February 1935.

67 "If Louis stops the clever Californian": *Chicago American*, December 12, 1934.

67 "already has most of the contenders for the championship": *Chicago Tribune*, December 14, 1934.

67 "the jaw-crashing, sleep-producing blow": Ibid., December 15, 1934.

68 "wrap it up" or "go to town": Interview, Eddie Couzins.

68 "Who's going to stop this new 'black peril'": *Chicago Tribune*, December 15, 1934.

68 "seeping out of the 'black belt'": *Collyer's Eye*, July 27, 1935.

68 "It wasn't arranged in the European sense": Interview, Truman Gibson.

68 "a little girl back in Detroit": *Chicago Tribune*, June 23, 1935.

69 "A pretty good-looking young heavy": Van Every, *Joe Louis*, pp. 11–12.

69 "Colored people usually reason": *Philadelphia Tribune*, June 27, 1935.

69 "I noticed he couldn't flick that arm with the same alacrity": *Philadelphia Tribune*, August 29, 1935.

69 HEAVYWEIGHTS DUCKING JOE LOUIS: *New York Post*, December 4, 1934.

69 "a voodoo to hoodoo": *Philadelphia Tribune*, December 27, 1934.

69 "he will find the color line facing": *Chicago Defender*, January 26, 1935.

69 "Hard rights and lefts, coupled with real economic need": *Pittsburgh Courier*, January 5, 1935.

70 "The ease with which such an abstract idea": *Philadelphia Tribune*, January 24, 1935.

70 "Jack Johnson put the kibosh": *Boxing*, March 20, 1935.

70 "When the color line is used as a subterfuge": *Ring*, May 1935.

70 "He's a bomber": Barney Nagler, *Brown Bomber: The Pilgrimage of Joe Louis* (New York: World Pub., 1972), p. 42.

71 "One of these days several thousand": *Los Angeles Examiner*, February 22, 1935.

71 "California women from domestic service": *Baltimore Afro-American*, March 9, 1935.

71 "It should please the fearful modern Vardamans and Tillmans": *Chicago Defender*, July 6, 1935.

71 "The Colored Comet": *Norfolk Journal and Guide*, May 18, 1935.

72 "Well, you understand he's a nigger": Nagler, *Brown Bomber*, p. 42.

72 "He's ready for New York, but New York ain't ready for him": Louis, *Joe Louis*, p. 47.

73 "Overnight, Jacobs will become the most powerful": *Ring*, May 1935.

73 "the pugilist-infested stretch": *Los Angeles Times*, May 28, 1936.

73 "It seems that their duties": *Bang*, October 3, 1936.

73 "New York is eager to see him go": *Detroit Times*, March 29, 1935.

73 "I don't want him to have anything on his mind": *Detroit Times*, March 29, 1935.

74 "The greatest young heavyweight": *New York American*, March 31, 1935.

74 "Every time he sweeps an opponent": *Washington Post*, March 31, 1935.

74 "we don't want any great big house": *Pittsburgh Sun-Telegraph*, August 23, 1935.

74 SOLID SOUTH DECIDES JOE LOUIS MUST BE SOMEBODY: *Chicago Defender*, April 13, 1935.

75 "I'd get up": *Dayton Daily News*, April 22, 1935.

75 "All the while you're in training": *Baltimore Afro-American*, June 15, 1935.

Chapter Four: New York Falls in Love

76 "Big Brown Bomber Hits Town": *New York Post*, May 16, 1935.

76 "Travelers threading their way": *New York Herald Tribune*, May 16, 1935.

76 "like the Empire State Building": *Pittsburgh Courier*, April 20, 1935.

77 "New Knockout Sensation": *Amsterdam News*, May 18, 1935.

77 "I've seen punches thrown this afternoon": *New York Mirror*, May 26, 1935.

77 "We're gonna have a lot of fun with that third strike": *In This Corner*, Museum of Television and Radio.

77 "I ain't ever had to yet": *New York Evening Journal*, June 6, 1935.

77 "a throwback": Ibid., May 16, 1935.

77 "There never was such a dead pan": *New York Sun*, May 17, 1935.

78 "gaudy extravagances": *New York Herald Tribune*, June 23, 1935.

78 "This unfortunate pituitary case": Gallico, *Farewell to Sports*, p. 56.

78 "the stupidest move in the history": *New York World-Telegram*, May 17, 1935.

78 "the race angle intruding": *Variety*, July 3, 1935.

79 "strong race people": Letter, Charles Roxborough to Walter White, May 11, 1935, in NAACP I, C-335, NAACP Papers, Library of Congress.

79 "One wonders where Pegler": Walter White to *New York World-Telegram*, May 21, 1935, in NAACP Papers, Library of Congress.

79 "I'd be a mean sucker": *Pompton Lakes* (New Jersey) *Bulletin*, May 30, 1935.

79 "nothing of the show-off, comedy coon here": Van Every, *Joe Louis*, p. 126.

79 "Mistah, I'se leavin'": *Detroit News*, June 25, 1935.

79 "What a spectacle"; "a healthy dark beige youth": *New York Age*, June 21, 1935.

80 "Louis may not be as perfect": *Baltimore Afro-American*, May 25, 1935.

80 The "Cinderella Man": Jeremy Schaap, *Cinderella Man: James J. Braddock, Max Baer, and the Greatest Upset in Boxing History* (Boston and New York: Houghton Mifflin, 2005), p. xiii.

80 "Did you ever see?": *New York Herald Tribune*, June 17, 1937.

81 "Do you mean those are the two best fighters": Ibid., June 16, 1938.

81 "Next Tuesday night the most historic event": *Philadelphia Tribune*, June 20, 1935.

81 "he will have definitely qualified as the foremost American": *New York World-Telegram*, May 16, 1935.

81 "See the Next World's Heavyweight Champion": *Detroit Tribune*, June 22, 1935.

82 "skyrocketing grosses": *Chicago Defender*, July 13, 1935.

82 "every ham-hock, fish-fry, and liquor joint": *New York Herald Tribune*, June 23, 1935.

82 "Your race . . . has been misrepresented": *Pittsburgh Courier*, June 29, 1935.

82 "you come across a lot of guys named Elmer": *New York World-Telegram*, June 25, 1935.

82 "I don't want him to beat him": *Norfolk Journal and Guide*, June 8, 1935.

82 "and a great deal of the skimmed milk": *New York Evening Journal*, June 26, 1935.

83 "as if he were waiting for a street car": *Cleveland Press*, June 28, 1935.

84 "Ladies and gentlemen, before proceeding": *Boxing World Record*, 1938; *Ring*, February 1946.

84 "did more good than the army": *Pittsburgh Courier*, July 6, 1935.

84 "Oh, my goodness, Louis looks like a little boy beside him": Interview, Jim Clark.

84 "transformed into a sleek and tawny animal": *New York Sun*, June 26, 1935.

84 "a red smile that didn't make sense": *Knockout*, January-February 1937, p. 69.

84 "ready that guy for the big splash": *New York Sun*, June 26, 1935.

84 "You have this boy right where you want him"; "You just drop old Betsy on that fellow's chin, and we will start the parade for home": Ibid.

84 "heavy, menacing, brutish, dumb": *New York Daily News*, June 26, 1935.

85 "You're the greatest fighter": Ibid., June 26, 1935.

85 "a second Jack Dempsey": International News Service, June 26, 1935.

85 "impromptu insanity" of "gargantuan proportions": *Detroit News*, June 26, 1935.

85 "Bootblacks blacked brown shoes": *Detroit Times*, June 26, 1935.

85 "They're happier over Louis": *Detroit News*, June 26, 1935.

85 "The ring has a new marvel": *New York Mirror*, June 27, 1935.

86 "As orderly an assemblage": *New York Evening Journal*, June 26, 1935.

86 "all but arm-in-arm": *Washington Tribune*, June 29, 1935.

86 "first chance in ten years": *Norfolk Journal and Guide*, July 6, 1935.

86 "Go Down, Moses": *Detroit News*, June 26, 1935.

86 "Look-a-here, folks"; "Eat Joe Louis peanuts": *Baltimore Afro-American*, July 6, 1935.

86 "gaudily meatish": *San Francisco Examiner*, March 7, 1935.

86 "You are as safe as at 42nd and Broadway": *Chicago Tribune*, June 26, 1935.

86 "I'm tired of this handshakin' business anyway": *New York Evening Journal*, June 26, 1935.

87 "all the noise that had preceded": *Detroit News*, June 26, 1935.

87 "Joe Louis is a fighter, not a talker": *New York Post*, June 26, 1935.

87 "a sort of lame-duck": Ibid., June 27, 1935.

87 "The American Negro is a natural athlete": *New York Sun*, June 27, 1935.

87 "In Africa there are tens of thousands": *New York Mirror*, June 27, 1935.

87 "like comparing Lou Gehrig with Al Capone": *New York Herald Tribune*, June 30, 1935.

87 "You see him awake in bed": *Binghamton News*, June 28, 1935.

88 "a healthy Negro boy": *Detroit Times*, June 27, 1935.

88 "colored champion of the world": *Baltimore Afro-American*, August 10, 1935.

88 "a secret New York conclave": *Collyer's Eye*, July 6, 1935.

88 "Louis deserves the right": *Boston Post*, July 8, 1935.

88 "vitamins C, A, S and H": *Chicago Tribune*, June 28, 1935.

89 "Max isn't interested in the title": *Detroit Free Press*, June 27, 1935.

89 "If the *Daily Worker* really wanted": *Amsterdam News*, July 6, 1935.

89 "Each victory of Louis": Associated Negro Press, July 6, 1935.

89 "hot cha brown-skin girls": *New York Evening Journal*, June 27, 1935.

89 "lets things inside of bottles STAY INSIDE OF BOTTLES": *Chicago Defender*, July 6, 1935.

89 "The white world of sports": *Norfolk Journal and Guide*, July 13, 1935.

90 "Harlem's got some money today": *New York Herald Tribune*, June 27, 1935.

90 German culture "negrified": Johnpeter Horst Grill and Robert L. Jenkins, "The Nazis and the American South in the 1930s: A Mirror Image?" *Journal of Southern History* 58 (1992), p. 671.

90 "out of a healthy spirit": *Angriff,* November 25, 1930.

90 "In every Negro, even in one of the kindest disposition": *Nationalsozialistische Monatshefte,* No. 1/1933 (Munich: F. Eber Nachf., 1933), pp. 12–13.

91 "Negroes don't have anything to grin about": Hans Massaquoi, *Destined to Witness: Growing Up Black in Nazi Germany* (New York: William Morrow, 1999), p. 108.

91 "This law is not inhumane": *Berliner illustrierte Nachtausgabe,* May 3, 1933.

91 "uniquely and colossally dangerous": *Box-Sport,* July 1, 1935.

91 "*Lehmgesicht*": Ibid., April 22, 1935.

92 "ever-grinning and sneering": Ibid., November 29, 1933.

92 "I had rather live in the Rhineland": *Crisis,* February 1935.

92 "with hatred in their eyes": Martin Duberman, *Paul Robeson* (New York: Alfred A. Knopf, 1988), pp. 184–85.

93 "The Americans again have all the trump cards": *Völkischer Beobachter,* September 7, 1935.

93 "twelve slow and thrill-less rounds": Universal Service, July 8, 1935.

93n "jüdische Börsenjobber"; "very close to treason"; "Jewish behavior": Bundesarchiv, *Auszug aus dem Stenographischen Verhandlungsbericht über die Beratung der Ratsherren am 27. März 1936:* Landesarchiv Berlin, LAB A Rep. 001-02, Nr. 953.

93 "One word from Joe, and Max does as he pleases": *New York Evening Journal,* July 26, 1935.

94 "Schmeling! Schmeling! Who's got Max Schmeling?": *New York Times,* July 16, 1935.

94 "never saw the day": *Ring,* October 1935.

94 "I am convinced he's been giving us all": *Chicago Tribune,* July 28, 1935.

94 "He talks like he was Dempsey": Ibid.

94 "Who in hell does he think he is anyway?" *New York Herald Tribune,* July 27, 1935.

94 "They always say that he is black": *Box-Sport,* August 20, 1935.

94 HAIL, JOE LOUIS: *Der Kicker,* October 10, 1935.

95 "the body of a caribou": *Paterson Evening News,* August 7, 1935.

95 "the glorified fish peddler of Maxwell Street": *Chicago Daily News,* August 3, 1935.

95 "Boy, I bet that dawg": *Chicago Tribune,* August 8, 1935.

95 "at the rail of ocean liners": *Chicago Herald and Examiner,* August 8, 1935.

95 "Don't let him hit me again, Mister!": *New York Daily News,* August 9, 1935.

95 "I must have been in a transom": *New Orleans Item,* June 18, 1936.

95 "the gayest jubilee Chicago's Negroes have ever enjoyed": *Chicago Herald and Examiner,* August 8, 1935.

95 "You can kill me": *Baltimore Afro-American,* September 27, 1935.

96 "His personality is more impressive": *Amsterdam News,* August 24, 1935.

96 Sportscaster calling Louis a "nigger": *Chicago Defender,* August 17, 1935.

96 "Dodge him?": *New York Sun,* August 9, 1935.

96 "I don't care who's in the other corner": *New York Times,* September 19, 1935.

Chapter Five: Champion in Waiting

97 "epitome of Negro progress": *Washington Post,* August 29, 1935.

97 "get a peek at Joe": *Washington Star,* August 29, 1935.

98 "Just to see him": *Washington Daily News,* August 28, 1935.

98 "How you, Mr. President?" *Chicago Defender,* August 31, 1935.

98 "Joe, you certainly are a fine looking young man": *Baltimore Afro-American,* September 7, 1935.

98 "whether it was Joe Louis who greeted the President": *Amsterdam News*, August 31, 1935.

98n "Joe, we need muscles like yours": *New York Times*, November 10, 1948.

98 "Impossible": *12 Uhr-Blatt*, September 24, 1935.

98 "The Punch Without the Smile": *Baltimore Afro-American*, August 24, 1935.

98 "smooth and full of punch": Ibid., June 22, 1935.

99 "Send me some money so that I won't be put out": *Baltimore Afro-American*, June 15, 1935.

99 "You really is my kind of man": *Chicago Defender*, August 24, 1935.

99 "Joe Louis Is the Man": Rounder Records Corp., Rounder 82161-1106-2.

99 "He's in the Ring (Doin' the Same Old Thing)": Ibid.

99 "a worth while [sic] addition to the library": *Chicago Defender*, September 21, 1935.

100 "When white children want to be called": *Norfolk Journal and Guide*, August 17, 1935.

100 "Aren't the papers wonderful about Joe Louis?" Carl Van Vechten to James Weldon Johnson, September 27, 1935, James Weldon Johnson Collection, Beinecke Rare Book and Manuscript Library, Yale University.

100 "The last thing I wanted Joe and Jesse": *Pittsburgh Courier*, July 6, 1935.

100 "usually no good for a year": *Baltimore Afro-American*, June 13, 1935.

100 "where our beauticians are prepared": *Amsterdam News*, July 27, 1935.

100 "not overlong making up her mind": *Baltimore Afro-American*, September 24, 1935.

100 "Miss Trotter, who had been employed": *Chicago Defender* September 7, 1935.

100 "so massive and sparkling": *Amsterdam News*, September 28, 1935.

100 "Marva is an old-fashioned girl": *Baltimore Afro-American*, September 14, 1935.

100 "Sure, she can cook southern fried chicken": *Chicago Tribune*, August 8, 1935.

101 "Louis' mind will be on the girl friend": *Chicago Daily News*, September 6, 1935.

101 "representing all walks of life": *Pittsburgh Courier*, September 21, 1935.

101 "He'd go for coffee": Interview, Truman Gibson.

101 "She is a mixed-blood": *Box-Sport*, September 24, 1935.

101 "become pestiferous and interfere": Ibid.

101 "If they can learn to put as many punches into their sermons": *Baltimore Afro-American*, September 21, 1935.

101 "Joe Louis impressed me as a quiet": *Kansas City Call*, September 20, 1935.

102 "He lives like an animal, untouched by externals": *New York Daily News*, September 24, 1935.

102 "The Ring Robot": *New York Sun*, September 4, 1935.

102 "He can fight, sure": September 5, 1935, in Julian Black Scrapbook, Library of Congress.

102 "Among ofays, who seem to bewilder him": *Amsterdam News*, September 14, 1935.

102 "The statue was a social sort of fellow": *Baltimore Afro-American*, May 30, 1935.

102 "paper chins": *New York World-Telegram*, September 9, 1935.

102 "Joe Louis: Will This Black Moses": *Fortune*, October 1935.

103 "All those who, because of their grandmothers' illness or death": *Box-Sport*, October 15, 1935.

103 "bride-elect": *Amsterdam News*, September 28, 1935.

103 "winsome lass": *Baltimore Afro-American*, September 28, 1935.

103 "New York was the delta, and towns": *Pittsburgh Courier*, September 21, 1935.

103 "The entire colored population of greater New York": *Box-Sport*, September 3, 1935.

103 "a first-class funeral": *Angriff*, September 24, 1935.

104 "I haven't seen bills like that since 1928": *New York Morning Telegraph*, September 25, 1935.

104 "Up to just a few months ago, no one believed the fistic game": *New York American*, September 23, 1935.

104 "something Roman": *New York Daily News*, September 24, 1935.

104 "an array of palookas": *Atlanta Journal*, September 23, 1935.

104 received a shot of "cocaine": *Ring*, December 1935.

104 "the loudest suit even Broadway": *Daily Express* (London), September 25, 1935.

104 "If my heart ain't just right": *New York American*, September 25, 1935.

104 "You could fight twice": Ibid.

105 "To hell with the foreman": *New York Daily News*, September 26, 1935.

105 "real ermine": *Amsterdam News*, September 28, 1935.

105 "any more than you could take a broom": *Wichita Beacon*, September 23, 1935.

106 "the outer fringes of the stadium looked": *Chicago Tribune*, September 25, 1935.

107 "I dreamed about the fight not long ago": *Norfolk Journal and Guide*, September 21, 1935.

107 "Kill him, Joe! Kill him!"; "Please don't do that": *New York Daily News*, September 25, 1935.

107 "the Negro who came here all the way from Alabama": *Macon Telegraph*, September 25, 1935.

107 "Through it all, the fleeting action of a second": *Chicago Tribune*, September 25, 1935.

108 "There were so many Joe Louises": *Boston Globe*, September 26, 1935.

108 "I wonder if his new bride's heart": *New York Daily News*, September 25, 1935.

108 "I guess I could have got up again": *New York Mirror*, September 26, 1935.

108 "When I get executed": *Look*, December 20, 1938.

108 "That's a great fighter": *Boston Globe*, September 25, 1935.

108 "If you folks is all through": *Chicago Herald and Examiner*, September 26, 1935.

109 "Why attempt to describe it?": *Amsterdam News*, September 28, 1935.

109 "Forget repeal. Forget Prohibition": *New York World-Telegram*, September 25, 1935.

109 "With one hand on the horn button": *Detroit Evening Times*, September 25, 1935.

109 "Joe Louis has driven the blues away from Beale Street": Associated Press, September 25, 1935.

109 "noisy canyons of romping humanity": *Norfolk Journal and Guide*, September 28, 1935.

109 "They seeped out of doorways": *New Masses*, October 8, 1935.

110 "Some young fellow now playing marbles": *New York Sun*, September 26, 1935.

110 "too good to be true, and absolutely true": *Esquire*, December 1935.

110 "To my friend Max Schmeling": *New York Daily News*, September 26, 1935.

110 "Mr. Louis, what makes you happier": VA 8259, Hearst Metrotone Newsreel Collection, UCLA Film and Television Archive.

110 "Joe will be the kingpin as long": *New York Morning Telegraph*, September 26, 1935.

111 "In deepest Mississippi as well as in highest Harlem": *Crisis*, November 1935.

111 someone "could go down to Washington": *Amsterdam News*, October 5, 1935.

111 "All sportsmen, more especially the Coloured races of the world": *Bantu World* (Johannesburg), September 28, 1935.

111 "might tend to arouse racial animosity": *Baltimore Afro-American*, October 19, 1935.

111 "a promising young savage of 17 or 18": *New York American*, September 26, 1935.

111 "sweet recompense for a degrading past": *New York Post*, September 27, 1935.

112 "Gypsies, Negroes, and their bastards": *Gesetz zum Schutz des deutschen Blutes und der deutschen Ehre. Gesetz vom 15. September 1935,* RGB1 I, 1935, S. 1146f., clarified by Wilhelm Frick, Reich Minister of the Interior, in *Deutsche Juristenzeitung,* December 1, 1935.

112 "a purebred white European": *8 Uhr-Blatt,* September 26, 1935.

112 "Negroid-Jewish matters": Deutsche Presse, no. 42/1935, p. 519.

112 "In America, once so full of racial pride": *Fränkische Tageszeitung,* September 26, 1935.

112 "Joe is very delicate": Associated Negro Press, October 2, 1935.

112 "Isn't it superb the way the press and public": Letter, Walter White to John Roxborough, September 26, 1935, in NAACP I, C-335, NAACP Papers, Library of Congress.

113 "Mr. and Mrs. James McDonald": Ibid., October 12, 1935.

113 "You busy businessmen, who crowd everything into your heart": *Chicago Defender,* August 17, 1935.

113 "in fighting pose": *Philadelphia Tribune,* September 12, 1935.

113 "We only hope that he will be as clean a sportsman": *Baltimore Afro-American,* October 19, 1935.

113 "streaked pell-mell across the field": Ibid., October 26, 1935.

114 "She's nice to look at": *Norfolk Journal and Guide,* October 12, 1935.

114 "Marva is sweet": *Pittsburgh Courier,* December 7, 1935.

114 "Instead of beautiful headlines of interest": *Chicago Defender,* October 5, 1935.

114 "I found him charming": Letter, Eslanda Robeson to Mr. and Mrs. Carl Van Vechten, November 21, 1935, Van Vechten Papers, Beinecke Rare Book and Manuscript Library, Yale University.

114 "just about the toughest darky we ever had in these parts": *New York Daily News,* October 9, 1935.

114 "big and strong as an ox": *Camden (New Jersey) Courier-Post,* September 28, 1935.

115 "could easily pass for Indian braves": Ibid., September 27, 1935.

115 "None of them is dark-skinned like the average southern Negro": Ibid.

115 "coolness and cunning": *Radio Guide,* June 20, 1936.

115 "If Schmeling wants gold he can get": *Daily Mail* (London), September 26, 1935.

115 "an ambitious, determined fighter": *Box-Sport,* November 18, 1935.

116 Louis no "*Überboxer*": *Angriff,* October 19, 1935.

116 "loamface"; "masterpiece of bluffing": *Völkischer Beobachter,* October 19, 1935.

116 "This Negro is no champion": *Box-Sport,* October 21, 1935.

116 "exert a positive influence on the right people": Schmeling, *Erinnerungen,* p. 322.5,367

116 "white hope": *Box-Sport,* December 2, 1935.

117 "knight in shining armor": Ibid.

117 "New York's Jewish Mayor" and his "wire pullers": *New York Times,* July 27, 1935.

117 "ten degrees colder than the weather": *New York Daily News,* December 7, 1935.

117 "a joke" to quit Olympics: *New York Herald Tribune,* December 7, 1935.

117 "I'd like to fight this Bomber": *New York Times,* December 7, 1935.

117 "A million and a half": *New York Sun,* December 7, 1935.

117 "The first time I get him alone": *New York Daily News,* December 7, 1935.

118 "In retrospect, it was incredibly naïve": Schmeling, *Erinnerungen,* p. 324.

118n "But Joe, that would hardly be fair to your wife": Van Every, *Joe Louis,* p. 176.

118 "See how he stands in front, and open": *New York Daily News,* December 9, 1935.

118 "I can report faithfully": Ibid.

118 JOE LOUIS LOOKS LIKE JOE PALOOKA: *New York Herald Tribune*, December 9, 1935.

119 "all we heard was Louis": *Washington Post*, December 8, 1935.

119 "I've got him sewed up like a sweater": North American News Service, September 12, 1935.

119 "through as gentlemanly conduct": *New York Morning Telegraph*, December 17, 1935.

120 "hurt everyone sitting within": *Washington Post*, December 15, 1935.

120 "the swiftest and most explosive": *New York American*, December 14, 1935.

120 "I no queet!": *New York Daily News*, December 14, 1935.

120 "He dropped his chin": *New York Morning Telegraph*, December 15, 1935.

120 "I don't want to kill anybody in this business": *Chicago Defender*, December 21, 1935.

120 "No mere words are adequate": *New York Herald Tribune*, December 15, 1935.

121 "Grins at Start": *Washington Post*, December 15, 1935.

121 "I vill tell you something, Choe": *Topical Times*, July 9, 1938.

121 "If Schmeling is as smart as I think he is": *New York Daily News*, December 15, 1935.

122 "best indication that the race problem in the United States is still alive": *Box-Sport*, December 23, 1935.

122 "When did this 'palooka' appoint himself": *Pittsburgh Courier*, January 4, 1936.

122 "Do you know how long": *New York Daily News*, December 17, 1935.

122 "I have discovered that Louis can be hit by a right hand": *New York Herald Tribune*, December 14, 1935.

122 "what you would call a good investment": *Saturday Evening Post*, August 29, 1936.

Chapter Six: The Condemned Man

123 "Sho' 'nuff if I'm dead": *New York Mirror*, December 22, 1935.

123 "first million": *Pittsburgh Courier*, January 11, 1936.

123 "Do you think I'm crazy": *New York Daily News*, February 20, 1936.

123 "Boxers, managers, promoters, manufacturers": *Ring*, January 1936.

124 "One man—Joe Louis—has done more for boxing": Ibid., May 1936.

124 "Tall men, skinny men, fat men, roly-poly men": Ibid., January 1936.

124 "It's a commercial affair with me": Ibid.

124 "a worse whipping than Mrs. Barrow ever gave him": *New York Age*, January 11, 1936.

124 "Benedict Arnold": *Chicago Defender*, February 22, 1936.

124 "'Uncle Tom' Johnson": *Pittsburgh Courier*, March 2, 1936.

124 "A jimsonweed in the nostrils": *Norfolk Journal and Guide*, June 13, 1936.

124 "Johnson down in his heart doesn't believe": *New York Age*, January 11, 1936.

124 "Say, I like Joe": *Ring*, April 1936.

125 "the N.A.A.C.P. would blow up in despair": Letter, Walter White to Russ Cowans, January 13, 1936, NAACP Papers, Library of Congress.

125 "For heavens sake": *Washington Post*, February 13, 1936.

125 "What I Think About Joe Louis and His Future Fights": *Pittsburgh Courier*, March 21, 1936.

126 "With the Brown Bomber present": *Amsterdam News*, March 14, 1936.

126 "Caesar's triumphant entry into Rome": *Pittsburgh Courier*, April 11, 1936.

126n "Not God, not government": Martin Luther King, Jr., *Why We Can't Wait* (New York: Harper & Row, 1963), pp. 119–20; *Daily Worker*, February 16, 1936; "Only six more weeks to go": *Chicago Daily News*, September 6, 1935.

126n "half-crazy": Records, Board of Parole, State of North Carolina.

126 "report" that England, France, and Holland had sent "secret suggestions": *Daily Worker*, February 16, 1936.

127 "darling of the Americans": *Box-Sport*, April 6, 1936.

127 "fine suits and a splendid car": Ibid., June 22, 1936.

127 "no understanding for the honor and dignity": Ibid., April 27, 1936.

127 "surely no unintelligent fellow": 12 *Uhr-Blatt*, June 4, 1936.

127 "one cannot think of any man": *Box-Sport*, June 22, 1936.

127 "seemed disturbed and somewhat angry": Schmeling, *Erinnerungen*, p. 327.

127 "predestined" to fight with their fists; "A better fighting morale can move mountains": *Box-Sport*, March 23, 1936.

127 "This great commercial enterprise": *Reichssportblatt*, April 8, 1936.

127 nonpolitical sportsmen were "unthinkable": *Chicago Tribune*, February 4, 1936.

128 "In my heart I view this day": 12 *Uhr-Blatt*, March 27, 1936.

128 "Max Schmeling will remain Hitler's hero": *Neue Volkszeitung*, June 13, 1936.

128 "I expect to bring home": *Denver Post*, April 13, 1936.

128 "You see, Louis didn't make": 12 *Uhr-Blatt*, April 15, 1936.

128 "For me there exists no racial dividing line": *Denver Post*, April 13, 1936.

129 "Schmeling is the most famous and best loved athlete": *Sheboygan (Wisconsin) Press*, March 3, 1936.

129 "The Schmelings are quite open": Elke Fröhlich (ed.), *Die Tagebücher von Joseph Goebbels*, T.I, Bd. 3/II: März 1936–Februar 1937 (Munich: K.G. Saur, 2001): April 15, 1936, p. 61.

129 "shabby" sendoff: *New York Times*, April 16, 1936.

129 "If the mood at Schmeling's departure is an omen": *Box-Sport*, April 20, 1936.

129 "my mere participation in this bout": 12 *Uhr-Blatt*, April 15, 1936.

130 "I guarantee you, if Louis makes the same mistakes with me": *New York Daily News*, April 22, 1936.

130 "Why should he? He's a politician and I am a sportsman": *New York Evening Journal*, April 21, 1936.

130 "Against it? That is all they talk about": *New York Sun*, April 22, 1936.

130 "you'll lick this guy and lick him good": *New York World-Telegram*, April 22, 1936.

130 "How much enjoyment can Schmeling": *Washington Post*, April 24, 1936.

131 "This is the life": *New York American*, May 9, 1936.

131 "I know a way, but I better not tell it": *New York American*, May 2, 1936.

131 "I couldn't understand him most of the time": Ibid.

131 "a vest pocket edition of Lenox Avenue": *Lakewood Daily Times (New Jersey)*, June 19, 1936.

132 "not only a great admirer of the Brown Bomber": *Norfolk Journal and Guide*, June 6, 1936.

132 "visions of Barnum and Bailey": *Asbury Park Press*, May 13, 1936.

132 "What's the matter with you, fella": *New York Post*, May 14, 1936.

132 "Black Moses"; "something in the nature of a miracle": Van Every, *Joe Louis*, pp. 1–2.

133 "You notice his mouth first": *New York American*, May 8, 1936.

133 "my friend": *New York Sun*, June 15, 1936.

133 "Mike Jacobs' pet pickaninny": *New York Evening Journal*, June 12, 1936.

133 "Joe Louis Takes": *Chicago American*, June 15, 1936.

133n "Ah ain't afraid": *Chicago Tribune*, June 14, 1938.

133 "In his native, untrained way": *New York World-Telegram*, June 13, 1936.

133 "These are good colored folks": *Charlotte Observer*, June 17, 1936.

133 "Don't think Joe isn't intelligent": *Champion of Youth*, June 1936.

133 "perfect coordination of mind and muscle": *New York American*, May 5, 1936.

134 "silky," "snaky": Ibid., May 8, 1936.

134 "I'm Sorry I Made You Cry"; "Let's Call It a Day": Ibid., May 18, 1936.

134 "An enterprising salesman could catch": *Baltimore Afro-American*, May 30, 1936.

134 "Park Avenue has its Newport": *Pittsburgh Courier*, June 6, 1936.

134 "The whole atmosphere here": *Amsterdam News*, May 30, 1936.

134 "Now the place is as genuinely democratic": *Norfolk Journal and Guide*, June 13, 1936.

135 "The only thing they give the Race freely": *Chicago Defender*, May 30, 1936.

135 "As she walks the streets": *Amsterdam News*, May 30, 1936.

135 "With her around all Louis wanted": *Richmond Planet*, June 20, 1936.

135 "exhibitionistically frivolous": *New York American*, June 1, 1936.

135 "His admirers say not to worry": Ibid., May 28, 1936.

135 "grave error of looking too dangerous": *New York Daily News*, June 6, 1936.

136 "housemaid's knee, leaping dandruff": Ibid., June 8, 1936.

136 "I've got to make Louis look bad": *New York World-Telegram*, June 18, 1937.

136 "plain ordinary anti-Negro propaganda": *Daily Worker*, May 31, 1936.

136 "Throughout his brief professional career": *Collyer's Eye*, May 30, 1936.

136 "as accurate and as rhythmical as a Beethoven sonata": *Norfolk Journal and Guide*, June 13, 1936.

136 "If you've got the stuff": *Baltimore Afro-American*, June 13, 1936.

136 "Its attitude seems to be": *Newark Star-Eagle*, June 9, 1936.

136 "the same as if he were a janitor": *Baltimore Afro-American*, June 20, 1936.

136 "We don't have to rush him": *Boston Post*, June 13, 1936.

136 "Chappie, what's wrong with your fighter?": Fried, *Corner Men*, pp. 138–39.

137 "Gosh, how worried he is about Schmeling!": Letter, Walter White to John Roxborough, June 12, 1936, NAACP Papers, Library of Congress.

137n "when you have gotten the [Schmeling] fight out of the way": Ibid.

138 "A good right hand will beat Louis": *Liberty*, June 20, 1936.

138 "Why don't you ask Louis what he plans to do?": *Middletown (New York) Times*, June 11, 1936.

138 "So! I see you give me a chance to win, after all": *New York Daily News*, June 5, 1936.

138 "If confidence were music": Ibid., May 24, 1936.

138 "fistic senility": *Newark Star-Eagle*, June 12, 1936.

138 "Today he seems so vitally alive": *New York Herald Tribune*, June 13, 1936.

138 "Reich sports idol" and "spectacularly non-Aryan" manager: *New Yorker*, June 13, 1936.

138n "constant upbeat chatter made me nervous": Schmeling, *Erinnerungen*, p. 335.

139 "I'm telling you something: That Louis has lost it": *Atlanta Journal*, June 21, 1936.

139 "so-called greatness": *Ellenville (New York) Journal*, May 28, 1936.

139 "Them guys have been making a plaster cast": *Los Angeles Times*, June 21, 1936.

139 "It was he who made Schmeling a champion": *New York World-Telegram*, June 15, 1936.

139 "By now [Jacobs] knew he was dealing with a Grade A rat": Ibid., June 20, 1947.

139 "Dere will be no war": *Boston Traveler*, June 14, 1936.

140 "In sport, the Negro and white": *Champion of Youth*, June 1936.

140 "A sweaty hog of a man": *New York Journal-American*, November 30, 1946.

140 "He knows very well": Arno Hellmis, *Max Schmeling: Die Geschichte eines Kämpfers* (Berlin: Deutscher Verlag, 1937) p. 100.

140 "Reklame"; Mike Jacobs as "a very smart boy": *Angriff*, June 17, 1936.

140 "Some woolly head of a Negro": Ibid., June 19, 1936.

140 "absolutely not to be broached": Hans Bohrmann (ed.), *NS-Presseanweisungen der Vorkriegszeit*, Bd. 4/II: 1936 (Munich: K.G. Saur, 1993): June 18, 1936.

141 "Well, it won't go fifteen rounds": *Newark Star-Eagle*, June 17, 1936.

141 "a nice piece of dough": *Collyer's Eye*, May 30, 1936.

141 "As between Schmeling the German and Joe Louis": *Atlanta Journal*, June 19, 1936.

141 "In the face of this one waits for the pyramids to crumble": *Philadelphia Tribune*, May 21, 1936.

141 "One can only ask ourselves with what sauce": *L'Auto*, June 17, 1936.

142 "a killing is still the best show on earth": *New York Sun*, June 18, 1936.

142 "City of Suckers": *Montreal Herald*, June 17, 1936.

142 "greater than me or anybody else the game has ever had": *Boston Post*, June 16, 1936.

142 "They won't even bet he has black hair": *New York World-Telegram*, June 18, 1936, in Julian Black scrapbooks, Library of Congress.

142 "What's going to happen to Schmeling": *New York Mirror*, May 25, 1936.

142 "There is nothing so uncertain as a dead sure thing": *New York Sun*, June 17, 1936.

142 "man who came back": *The Boxing News*, June 1936.

142 "Everyone knows Louis is going to win!": *Newark Sunday News*, March 13, 1960.

142 "a personal friend of Hitler and Goebbels": *Saturday Evening Post*, September 5, 1936.

143 "too sure of himself for his own good": *Boston Globe*, June 17, 1936.

143 "This guy Schmeling is no chump": *Atlanta Georgian*, June 19, 1936.

143 "an undercurrent of distant fear": *Norfolk Journal and Guide*, June 27, 1936.

143 "The trouble with Joe is that you newspapermen": Fried, *Corner Men*, p. 140.

143 "It is not our place to predict a defeat": *Box-Sport*, June 15, 1936.

143 "fresher, younger, stronger": *Hamburger Anzeiger*, June 18, 1936.

143 "Most likely he'll manage": *12 Uhr-Blatt*, June 18, 1936.

143 "Possibly the town has come to the conclusion": *New York Morning Telegraph*, June 16, 1936.

144 "tripe"; "one of Herr Hitler's representatives": *New York Mirror*, June 16, 1936.

144 "Why let a German": *Mobile Press*, June 18, 1936.

144 "The boss told me": *Indianapolis Recorder*, June 20, 1936.

144 "The biggest fight of all": *Daily Herald* (London), June 18, 1936.

144 "It's the silliest thing I ever heard": *Indianapolis Recorder*, June 20, 1936.

144 "While condemning Hitler": *Amsterdam News*, July 27, 1936.

145 "Joe is so handsome": *Los Angeles Evening Herald and Express*, June 18, 1936.

145 "Stage parties, banquets and dances EVERYWHERE": *Philadelphia Tribune*, June 18, 1936.

145 "When and If Joe Louis Loses": *Amsterdam News*, June 20, 1936.

145 "The white world has long believed": *Amsterdam News*, June 13, 1936.

145 "just about the greatest heavyweight you've ever seen": *Newark Star-Eagle*, June 17, 1936.

Chapter Seven: Victor and Vanquished

146 "What round?": *Newark Evening News*, June 18, 1936.

146 "Bad day, eh?": *New York American*, June 19, 1936.

147 "You gentlemen know each other": *New York Herald Tribune*, June 19, 1936.

147 "Now on the scales: Joe Louis!": *New York Sun*, June 18, 1936.

147 "Thank you, General": Ibid.

147 "Good luck this evening, Joe!": Schmeling, *Erinnerungen*, p. 336.

147 "As the condemned man and the executioner stood": *New York Herald Tribune*, June 19, 1936.

147 "too normal, too perfect": Dr. Vincent Nardiello, *The World of Nardiello* (Unpublished; property of David Nardiello), chap. 11, p. 153.

148 "That ain't no way to spell my name": *New York World-Telegram*, June 18, 1936.

148 "How's about it, Uncle Mike?": Ibid.

148 "Go to bed now and don't get run over by a truck": *New Orleans Item*, June 19, 1936.

148 "You can see them guys all summer long": *New York Daily News*, June 19, 1936.

148 "raining pitchforks"; "dead fish on his hands": *New York Sun*, June 19, 1936.

148 "He worried off four pounds": *Los Angeles Times*, June 20, 1936.

148 "The stay the heavens gave him": *New York Post*, June 19, 1936.

149 "Max will weather Louis' early assault": *New York Evening Journal*, June 19, 1936.

149 *"Heute sieg swelft runde"*: *Spur*, September 1936.

149 "all golf, stances and grips and hooks and slices": *Detroit Free Press*, June 20, 1936.

149 "That was the biggest 39,000 I ever saw": *New York Sun*, June 20, 1936.

149 "yawned in the darkness like divots on a fairway": *New York Herald Tribune*, June 21, 1936.

150 "Unlike the American Negro, Jews do not believe": *Richmond Planet*, June 27, 1936.

150 "illuminated bulletin board": *Boston Post*, June 18, 1936.

150 "was just something for the fans to look at": *Newark Star-Eagle*, June 20, 1936.

151 "Chatted and laughed with her": Fröhlich (ed.), *Die Tagebücher von Joseph Goebbels*, T.I, Bd.3/II, June 11, 1936, p. 104.

151 "We're anxious the entire evening": Ibid., T.I, Bd. 3/II, June 20, 1936, p. 112.

151 "Night of the Boxers": *Berliner illustrierte Nachtausgabe*, June 18, 1936.

151 "We will broadcast the Louis-Schmeling fight": *Nemzeti Sport* (Budapest), June 21, 1936.

151 "a true symphony of rattling alarm clocks": *NS-Kurier*, June 20–21, 1936.

152 "Good luck, Max!" Schmeling, *Erinnerungen*, p. 337.

152 "I know you can win, Max": Ibid.

152 *"Tot"*; "cold as ice": *New York Mirror*, September 15, 1937.

152 "I want to see him": *New York Evening Journal*, June 20, 1936.

153 "A sort of premonition": *Norfolk Journal and Guide*, June 27, 1936.

153 "I wish good health to all my friends": Hellmis, *Max Schmeling*, p. 110.

153 "one of the greatest heavyweights in the annals of Fistiana"; "Let us cast aside all prejudism"; "Let us say 'Ring the bell, let 'er go, and may the best man be the winner'": *New York Post*, June 20, 1936.

154 "sneeringly confident and patronizingly bored": *New Orleans Times-Picayune*, June 21, 1936.

154 "Nervous conversation popped on all sides like firecrackers": *New Republic*, June 27, 1936.

154 "an almost insolent confidence": Ibid.

154 "filling in": *Connecticut Nutmeg*, June 2, 1938.

154 "This baby is easier than either Carnera or Baer": *New York Sun*, August 15, 1936.

154 "he iss going to fall for it": *Topical Times*, July 9, 1938.

154 "sort of deadened everything": *New York World-Telegram*, August 6, 1936.

155 "fairy-tale city": This and subsequent quotes from the German radio broadcast of June 19, 1936, come courtesy of Mr. Ralf Klee, a German sports scholar, who owns what appears to be the only complete audio recording of the 1936 fight, contained on twenty-seven Decelith sound foils. He hopes to include them in his own sports museum.

155 "You fetched him a pretty good one"; "I think I knock him out"; "I have him where I want him": *Saturday Evening Post*, September 5, 1936.

155 "Joe, honey, get up! *Get up!*"; "Kill him, Max! Kill him!": *New York Evening Journal*, June 20, 1936.

156 "young cub who had been roundly cuffed": *Richmond Times-Dispatch*, June 21, 1936.

156 "The gasps that went up": Wignall, *Ringside*, p. 59.

156 "Those far back . . . cannot see the stupor": *San Francisco Examiner*, June 20, 1936.

156 "Now I got him": *Topical Times*, July 9, 1938.

156 "*So. Den Übermensch haben wir*": *Saturday Evening Post*, September 5, 1936.

157 "I just remember one pop, a sort of sudden blaze of lights": *Boston Post*, June 17, 1937.

157 "like a man on stilts": *Washington Post*, June 20, 1936.

157 "*Der Übermensch hat ja Gummibeine*": *Saturday Evening Post*, September 5, 1936.

157 "Finally, a blue, the color of lapis lazuli, rimmed his eyes brightly": *Boston Post*, June 20, 1936.

158 "*Der wird frech. Nehm's ihm wieder ab*": *Saturday Evening Post*, August 29, 1936.

158 "Go on, Maxieboy, kill that nigger, kill him!": Hellmis, *Max Schmeling*, p. 117.

158 "A ship in a storm without a rudder or a mast": *New York Sun*, June 20, 1936.

159 "like a tired child at bed-time prayer": *New York Evening Journal*, June 20, 1936.

159 "And Louis is down again": *New Orleans Times-Picayune*, January 25, 1937.

159 "Up Chappie! Up, boy! Steady!": *New York Evening Journal*, June 20, 1936.

160 "there was a miserable, frightened look": *Norfolk Journal and Guide*, June 27, 1936.

160 "a terrific burst of acclaim": *Columbus (Georgia) Enquirer*, June 20, 1936.

160 "For a fraction of a moment, the crowd seemed unable to cheer": *Macon Telegraph*, June 20, 1936.

160 "Sixty thousand people stood": *New York Herald Tribune*, June 20, 1936.

160 "the white gentile section": *Amsterdam News*, June 27, 1936.

160 "You, yourself are still trembling and shaken": *Pittsburgh Courier*, June 18, 1938.

161 "There lay Joe Louis in an abject heap": *Los Angeles Evening Herald and Express*, June 20, 1936.

161 "He's hurt bad": *San Francisco Examiner*, June 20, 1936.

161 "Her face streaming with tears": *New York Evening Journal*, June 20, 1936.

161 "a blocky young man": *Boston Post*, June 20, 1936.

161 "beaten his way back over the rough trail from Hasbeenville": *San Francisco Examiner*, June 20, 1936.

161 "We never saw a gamer fighter": *New York World-Telegram*, June 29, 1941.

162 "I guess I fooled you guys": *The People* (London), June 21, 1936.

162 "a world full of pinwheels": *Boston Globe*, June 20, 1936.

162 "a grotesque Stepin' Fetchit type of a tired Negro": *Washington Post*, June 20, 1936.

162 "Wrapped in his garish red and blue ring robe": *Boston Post*, June 20, 1936.

162 "There goes one of them supermen": *Newark Star-Eagle*, June 20, 1936.

162 "in vast and amazing plenitude": *Boston Post*, June 20, 1936.

163 "Don't fool me, Mister": *New York Evening Journal*, June 20, 1936.

163 "They wouldn't believe their eyes": *Amsterdam News*, June 27, 1936.

163 "Some day the sphinx will talk": *New York World-Telegram*, June 20, 1936.

163 "Had I found God himself": *L'Auto*, June 21, 1936.

163 "For your wonderful victory": *Völkischer Beobachter*, June 21, 1936.

163 "In the twelfth round, Schmeling knocks out the Negro": Fröhlich (ed.), *Die Tage-bücher von Joseph Goebbels*, T.I, Bd.3/II, June 20, 1936, p. 112.

164 "For the wonderful victory of your husband": *Völkischer Beobachter*, June 21, 1936.

164 "What joy, what deliriousness": *L'Auto*, June 20, 1936.

164 "All of Berlin is joyful": Ibid., June 21, 1936.

164 "at a million-dollar angle": *Newark Star-Eagle*, June 20, 1936.

164 "Where's all dem guys?": United Press International, June 20, 1936; "Youse newspaper guys, youse experts": *New York World-Telegram*, June 20, 1936.

165 "I'm even with the world! I'm even with the world!": *New York Herald Tribune*, June 20, 1936.

165 "I'm so happy"; "I leave here three years ago": *New York Herald Tribune*, June 20, 1936.

165 "I am a proud man": *Boston Herald-Traveler*, June 20, 1936.

165 Fighting is a profession: United Press International, June 20, 1936.

165 "Please, tell my countrymen at home": *Berliner Lokal-Anzeiger*, June 20, 1936.

165 "*Heil Hitler*": *Boston Herald-Traveler*, June 20, 1936.

165 "I'm Dreaming with Open Eyes": *Deutsche Allgemeine Zeitung*, June 20, 1936.

165 "wall of people": *Der Mitteldeutsche*, June 21, 1936.

166 "We knocked out that Brown Bomber": *New York Post*, June 20, 1936.

166 "I was the only one in Hollywood": *New York Herald Tribune*, June 21, 1936.

166 "We could not stand him, either": Ibid.

166 "Germany—it vas going crazy": *New York Post*, June 20, 1936.

166 "You could understand better": Ibid.

166 "Youse guys don't know nothin'": Ibid.

166 "Cover up yo' face, Chappie": *New York Journal-American*, February 3, 1938.

166 "Is he hurt much?": *Los Angeles Evening Herald and Express*, June 20, 1936.

167 "You just got tagged, Chappie": *New York World-Telegram*, June 20, 1936.

167 "You can't get to him nohow": *New York Herald Tribune*, June 20, 1936.

167 "Everything was in a fog": *Detroit Free Press*, June 20, 1936.

167 "I sure didn't mean to hit him low": *Los Angeles Evening Herald and Express*, June 20, 1936.

167 "Say, don't forget that one Max hit": Ibid.

167 "No, I ain't going to retire": *Detroit Free Press*, June 20, 1936.

167 "That knockout was the best thing"; "Yes, maybe we can tell him sumthin' from now on": Ibid.

167 "I don't want to resort to alibis": Ibid.

168 "Joe Jacobs outsmarted us": *Los Angeles Times*, December 21, 1937.

168 "This fight will make him a great fighter": *New York Post*, June 20, 1936.

168 "Louis vs. Schmeling would draw": *Detroit Evening Times*, June 20, 1936.

168 "You mark my words": United Press International, June 20, 1936.

168 "Fighting's a nailing business": *New York Sun*, August 15, 1936.

168 "Joe, your head looks like a watermelon": Nagler, *Brown Bomber*, p. 68.

168 "Poor thing, he is sleeping": *Paris Soir*, June 21, 1936.

168 "She covered her face with her handkerchief": *Amsterdam News*, July 4, 1936.

168 "Schmeling made the chocolate drop": Augusta Wallace Lyons to author, November 2001.

169 "every man you met had a five or six-to-one wager": *Philadelphia Record*, June 21, 1936.

169 "Nothing can take the place of experience": *New York Herald Tribune*, June 23, 1936.

169 "Max smashed that nigger!": Willie Smith with George Hoefer, *Music on My Mind: The Memoirs of an American Pianist* (New York: De Capo, 1975), p. 247.

169 MAX SCHLÄGT JOE LOUIS IN DER 12 RUNDE K.O.: *Mobile (Alabama) Press*, June 20, 1936.

169 "Big black, brown and yellow feet": *Philadelphia Tribune*, June 20, 1936.

169 "weeping desperately and wearing": *California Eagle*, June 26, 1936.

170 "Joe didn't land a single good punch": *New York Evening Journal*, June 20, 1936.

170n "Schmeling has done boxing a service": *Daily Mail* (London), June 22, 1936; "outrageous"; "should be made the means of national uprising and revolt": *Boxing*, June 24, 1936.

170 "tap-tap-tapped his way": *New York Post*, June 23, 1936.

170 "as though his heart would break": Walter White to Joe Louis, June 23, 1936, in NAACP papers, Library of Congress.

170 "Not even the worst days of the Depression": *Boston Chronicle*, June 27, 1936.

170 "The musician who usually thumps": Ibid., July 4, 1936.

171 "there was a deathly silence": *Buffalo Evening News*, June 20, 1936.

171 "That Louis let me down": *New Orleans Item*, June 20, 1936.

171 "just another Negro getting beaten by a white man": Lena Horne and Richard Schickel, *Lena* (Garden City, N.Y.: Doubleday, 1975), p. 75.

171 GLOOM ENGULFING THE CITY'S HARLEM: *Chicago Defender*, July 4, 1936.

171 "The blow came all the harder": *The Friend* (Bloemfontein, South Africa), June 22, 1936.

171 "surged back onto the floor": *Mobile Register*, June 20, 1936.

172 "The people know now": *Norfolk Journal and Guide*, June 27, 1936.

172 "political Max Schmeling": *Daily Herald* (London), June 22, 1936.

172 "a one hour's wonder": *Social Justice*, June 29, 1936.

172 "paraded in bedlamic pilgrimages": *New York American*, June 21, 1936.

172 "resembled midnight of New Year's Eve": *Macon Telegraph*, June 20, 1936.

172 "Max the Great": Interview, Max Wiley.

172n "talked at a rate": *Rand Daily Mail*, June 20, 1936.

172 "the limitless aversion of the colonial English": *Box-Sport*, August 10, 1936.

172 "What the race lost in money": *Chicago Defender*, June 27, 1936.

172 "An idol representing everything": *New York Post*, June 20, 1936.

173 "the Negro race went around": *Boston Guardian*, July 23, 1936.

173 "draped like a vulture's wings": *Baltimore Afro-American*, July 2, 1938.

173 "From a conquering fistic idol": *Buffalo Evening News*, June 20, 1936.

173 "jungle cunning": *New York Sun*, June 22, 1936.

173 "reign of terror": *New Orleans Times-Picayune*, June 21, 1936.

173 "Joe Louis is just a legend today": *Chicago Daily News*, June 20, 1936.

173 "I-Told-You-So Day": *New York Mirror*, June 21, 1936.

173 "Pet Pickaninny": *Atlanta Journal*, June 20, 1936.

173 "Louis did what all the negro": *Memphis Commercial Appeal*, June 22, 1936.

173 "nigger," "darkie," "coon," and "Sambo": *Chicago Defender*, July 4, 1936.

173 "that hinterland of barbarism": *Richmond Planet*, June 27, 1936.

174 "Americans are interested in money": *New York American*, June 23, 1936.

174 "Maybe the people in Germany": *Boston Globe*, June 21, 1936.

174 "the victorious German boxer raised his arm": *Angriff*, June 21, 1936.

174 "I will liberate Schmeling": Fröhlich (ed.), *Die Tagebücher von Joseph Goebbels*, T.I, Bd.3/II, June 24, 1936, p. 115.

174 "the swarthy brunet with the narrow black eyes": *New York World-Telegram*, September 2, 1937.

174 "Germany, the land of the fastest race cars": *Dresdner Neueste Nachrichten*, June 21, 1936.

174 "An achievement like that of Max Schmeling": *Der Führer*, June 23, 1936.

175 "My sacrificial lamb": *Bayerische Ostmark*, June 22, 1936.

175 "You know, the money is in this country": *New York Post*, June 24, 1936.
175 "a new Germany . . . a Germany that has faith in itself again": *Fränkischer Kurier*, June 22, 1936.
175 "saved the reputation of the white race": *Das Schwarze Korps*, June 25, 1936.
175 "confirmed the supremacy of a race": *Il Messaggero*, June 20, 1936.
175 "The Negro is of a slave nature": *Der Weltkampf*, August 1936.
175 "made a one-sided and primitive impression": *Kreuz Zeitung*, June 21, 1936.
175 "Beaten is not the right word": *Box-Sport*, July 1, 1936.
175 "When an acquaintance said 'The mind is just better' ": *Völkischer Beobachter*, July 8, 1936.
176 "Take good care of that": *Boston Sunday Post*, June 21, 1936.
176 "Joe's all right": *New York Times*, June 21, 1936.
176 "I don't think Louis is through": *Washington Post*, June 21, 1936.
176 "beaming like a school kid": *New York Daily News*, June 22, 1936.
176 "Should clean up": *Variety*, June 24, 1936.
176 "The End of the Reign": *Oshkosh Northwestern*, June 23, 1936.
176 "The Fight So Thrilling": *Zanesville (Ohio) Times-Recorder*, June 27, 1936.
176 "All this turning of coats": *New Republic*, July 8, 1936.
176 "Daddy, I could kill": Walter White to Joe Louis, June 23, 1936, in NAACP papers.
177 "If it were not for the deep tragedy beneath": *Norfolk Journal and Guide*, June 27, 1936.
177 "Was not that a surprise": *Chicago Tribune*, June 22, 1936.
177 "Brown Bouncer": *New York Times*, June 22, 1936.
177 "If a German": *The People* (London), June 21, 1936.
178 "two marvels of the Twentieth Century": *Lakewood (New Jersey) Daily Times*, June 24, 1936.
178 "I just want to touch him!": Ibid.
178 "Get Braddock ready!": *New York Daily News*, June 24, 1936.

Chapter Eight: Climbing Back

179 "lap of honor": *Box-Sport*, July 1, 1936.
179 "It seemed as if a hurricane were let loose": Ibid.
179 "the greatest spokesman for Germany": *Hamburger Fremdenblatt*, June 27, 1936.
180 "We want to see our Schmeling!": *Box-Sport*, July 1, 1936.
180 "Frankfurt couldn't have been more excited": *Paris Soir*, June 28, 1936.
180 "Even those of us who bet": Transcript of radio broadcast, June 21, 1938, in Walter Winchell Papers, New York Public Library.
180n "Schmeling Knocks Out Jewish Horror Press": *Die Brennessel*, July 7, 1936.
180 "clobbered by a mulatto"; "loudmouthed manner": *Angriff*, June 28, 1936.
181 "And [Schmeling] says that he alone": Ibid.
181 special "lighting car": *Berliner Lokal-Anzeiger*, June 27, 1936.
181 "*Lieber Max, sei Willkommen*": *Völkischer Beobachter*, June 28, 1936.
182 "gave a running commentary and every time I landed a punch": Schmeling, *Erinnerungen*, pp. 363–64.
182 "Dramatic and thrilling": Fröhlich (ed.), *Die Tagebücher von Joseph Goebbels*, T.I, Bd.3/II, June 28, 1936, p. 119.
182 "the most worthless kitsch": *Süddeutsche Zeitung*, September 27, 1975.
182 "a white man must not be beaten": *Los Angeles Times*, June 25, 1936.
182 "Heil Hitler!"; "Heil Germany!"; "Heil Schmeling!": *New York Times*, July 5, 1936.

182 "A Film That Concerns All Germans": *Box-Sport*, July 6, 1936.
183 "Long before the fight he was in excellent form"; "In every one of his movements"; etc.: *Max Schmelings Sieg—ein deutscher Sieg*, directed by Hans H. Zerlett, narrated by Arno Hellmis, edited by Albert Baumeister, Syndikat-Film Berlin (Tobis-Gruppe), 1936.
184 "as if they hadn't known about the outcome of the fight before": *Dresdner Neueste Nachrichten*, July 10, 1936.
184 "downright life-threatening": *Der Film-Kurier*, July 10, 1936.
185 "Hollywood scarcely could have outdone the scene": Associated Press, June 13, 1938.
185 "joy-groggy": *Der Film-Kurier*, July 10, 1936.
185 "the audience was literally shivering out of excitement": *Leipziger Beobachter*, Nos. 15–16/1936, July 10, 1936.
185n "An atmosphere of tension spread": *Box-Sport*, July 19, 1937; "the biggest box office attraction of the season": *Chicago Defender*, July 25, 1936.
185 "decorated with red, swastika-ed ribbons": *Saturday Evening Post*, August 29, 1936.
186 offered a "dagger of honor" and the title of "Honorary Commander of the SA": Schmeling, *Erinnerungen*, pp. 382–83.
186 "Nazi Max": *Daily Worker*, December 20, 1936.
187 "champion chasers": *New York World-Telegram*, June 29, 1936.
187 "When he went back to Germany and tossed himself": *Daily Worker*, June 20, 1937.
187 "It would seem that Schmeling made a mistake": International News Service, January 9, 1937.
187 "One nice thing about Joe": *Detroit Free Press*, June 22, 1936.
187 "hiding behind everything except a set of false whiskers": Ibid.
188 "I saw the fight": *New York Journal-American*, December 24, 1953.
188 "the most outstanding athlete in the country": *Chicago Defender*, July 11, 1936.
188 "No angels sang": *New York World-Telegram*, June 22, 1936.
188 "Detroit and its people still believe in you": *Detroit Tribune*, June 25, 1938.
188 "What happened last Friday night": Walter White to Joe Louis, June 23, 1936, in NAACP papers.
188 "I wanted him to know": Walter White to John Roxborough and Julian Black, June 24, 1936, in NAACP papers.
188 "literally ill": Walter White to John Dancy, June 24, 1936, in NAACP papers.
189 "Joe is human and is just a kid yet": *Palmetto Leader*, June 27, 1936.
189 "Louis-Schmeling Fight": Rounder Records Corp., Rounder 82161-1106-2.
189 "maelstrom of flattery": *Chicago Defender*, June 27, 1936.
189 "Coney Island trimmings": *Ring*, September 1937.
190 "We wish Joe well": *Black Man*, July/August 1936.
190 "would not have been worth": *Baltimore Afro-American*, June 27, 1936.
190 "Too much Mrs."; "He should have married sooner": *New York Post*, June 20, 1936.
190 "professional jinxer": *New York Age*, April 16, 1938.
191 "slickster" had dropped a "deadening pill": *Amsterdam News*, July 2, 1938.
191 "daze producing chemical": *California Eagle*, July 3, 1936.
192 "specially prepared by a friend": *Pittsburgh Courier*, July 11, 1936.
192 "What kind of dope was used": *Indianapolis Record*, July 11, 1936.
192 "There was nothing wrong": *Kansas City Call*, July 3, 1936.
192 "Mr. Schmeling is a fine gentleman and a clean sportsman": *New York Sunday Mirror*, July 5, 1936.
192 "The town is gabbing about Joe Louis": *New York Daily News*, June 26, 1936.

192 "The mere fact that those back of": *Collyer's Eye*, June 27, 1936.

192 "One thing I'm not going to write about": *Amsterdam News*, June 27, 1936.

192 "Joe Louis will be licked": *New York Morning Telegraph*, June 21, 1936.

193 "the Negro is all right": *Greensboro (North Carolina) Daily News*, July 9, 1936.

193 "Young or old, two hundred right hands": *New York Sun*, June 23, 1936.

193 "We think he will become": *New York American*, August 15, 1936.

193 "Negroes are now defiling": *Atlanta Daily World*, June 21, 1936.

193 "Don't be a Joe Louis": *Amsterdam News*, August 15, 1936.

193 "I have nothing but pity and sympathy": *Philadelphia Tribune*, June 25, 1936.

193 "Joe Louis is not through!": *Pittsburgh Courier*, July 4, 1936.

193 "Joe Louis We Are with You": *Louisville Defender*, June 27, 1936.

193 "the thunder of boos": *Amsterdam News*, September 26, 1936.

193 "Guess I got a bit swell-headed": *Chicago Defender*, August 8, 1936.

194 "A carload of Jesse Owenses": *Baltimore Afro-American*, July 18, 1936.

194 "After a long, difficult, and unprecedentedly": *Völkischer Beobachter*: August 4, 1936.

194 "Pfennig über Alles": *Ken*, June 18, 1938.

194 "Max Schmeling's business conferences": *New York Mirror*, August 21, 1936.

195 "only with the greatest difficulty": *Box-Sport*, August 2, 1936.

195 "I've heard lots about you!": *New York American*, July 30, 1936.

195 "Inwardly, many of us were trying to atone for Joe's loss": William J. Baker, *Jesse Owens: An American Life* (New York: Free Press, 1986), p. 84.

195 "exalted pews": *Daily Express* (London), January 28, 1938.

195n "popular justice to expiate"; "The white audience is cheering": *Angriff*, December 12–13, 1936; "The people expected to see us eat": *Amsterdam News*, August 22, 1936.

195 "How was the zeppelin thing?": *New York World-Telegram*, August 10, 1936.

196 "A tractable Joe Louis"; "Now you are watching the real Joe Louis": *Pittsburgh Courier*, August 15, 1936.

196 "Chappie heah got believin' all you newspapah": *New York Evening Journal*, August 14, 1936.

196 "He has tried to cram ten years of boxing lessons": *New York Daily News*, August 18, 1936.

196 "go in for thinking on an extensive scale": *New York Times*, August 18, 1936.

196 "After they are through teaching him": Associated Negro Press, August 10, 1936.

196 "a washed up old man and an overballyhooed": *New York Daily News*, August 18, 1936.

197 A "burlesque": *New York Daily News*, August 19, 1936.

197 "very capable opponent": *New York Herald Tribune*, August 19, 1936.

197 "Schmeling was the luckiest man in the world": Ibid.

197 "Joe's mad at Schmeling, but Sharkey paid for it": Nagler, *Brown Bomber*, p. 69.

197 "one long sustained guttural chant of victory": *Pittsburgh Courier*, August 22, 1936.

197 "they" were letting Louis be Louis again: *Chicago Defender*, August 22, 1936.

197 "Youth must be served": *Detroit Evening Times*, August 19, 1936.

197 "I want Max Schmeling next": *New York Herald Tribune*, August 19, 1936.

197 Louis was "alright"; Sharkey had fought a "stupid" fight; "I could beat him every time I fought him": *New York Sun*, August 20, 1936.

197 "Not fifteen minutes before, Harlem was as quiet": *Baltimore Afro-American*, August 22, 1936.

198n "nice little Frankenstein monster": *Daily Worker*, August 26, 1937.

198 "I hope the twenty-one doctors": *New York American*, August 22, 1936.

198 "By next June, some convenient excuse": *New York Mirror*, September 6, 1936.

198 "dreadfully and gnawingly": *Saturday Evening Post*, August 29, 1936.

198 "A Red Mob in Dinner Jackets": *New York Herald Tribune*, August 23, 1936.

198 "men in the background": 12 *Uhr-Blatt*, August 19, 1936.

199 "best friend among writers": *Saturday Evening Post*, August 22, 1936.

199 "Maxie stepped out from under again": *New York Mirror*, December 13, 1936.

199 "wanted a revenge that money": *Baltimore Afro-American*, July 2, 1938.

199 "I suppose there were close to 500,000 Ettore": *Amsterdam News*, September 26, 1936.

199 JOE LOUIS UNDER KNIFE: *Baltimore Afro-American*, November 7, 1936.

199 "Now, one presumes": *New York Mirror*, September 27, 1936.

200 "I don't believe it": Ibid. November 13, 1936.

200 "Schmeling's only defense is Joe Jacobs": *New York World-Telegram*, December 1, 1936.

200 "Such things cannot be!": Ibid. December 11, 1936.

200 "Imagine Promoter Mike Jacobs or Manager Yussel Jacobs": *New York Mirror*, December 13, 1936.

200 "The heavyweight champion of the world a Nazi!" *New York World-Telegram*, December 15, 1936.

200 "goose-stepped with Schmeling": *Amsterdam News*, December 19, 1936.

200 "superannuated geezers": *Daily Worker*, December 12, 1936.

201 "I'm sorry it had to be like that": *Baltimore Afro-American*, December 19, 1936.

201 "What a superb job Joe, Jack and you have done": Letter, Walter White to John Roxborough, December 17, 1936, NAACP Papers, Library of Congress.

201 "knocked one more nail in the coffin": *Daily Worker*, December 20, 1936.

201 "Whether you like Hitler or the Nazis or Germans or spinach": *New York Sun*, September 24, 1936.

Chapter Nine: A German Commodity

202 "an unprecedented event in the annals of Detroit": *Life*, June 17, 1940.

202 "the greatest money-making athlete": *New York Evening Journal*, December 21, 1936.

202 "Nordic" boxing powers decided against title shot: *Chicago Defender*, January 16, 1937.

203 "tranquil progress": *Commentator*, February 1937.

203 "a long, long way": Letter, Walter White to Lowell Thomas, January 29, 1937, NAACP Papers, Library of Congress.

203 "the stench of the old slave market": *Daily Worker*, February 1, 1937.

203 "That bust on the chin Max gave Louis": *New York American*, January 26, 1937.

203 "all records for retreating since Napoleon": *New York Mirror*, January 30, 1937.

203 "The legend of 'American sportsmanship'": *Amsterdam News*, February 6, 1937.

203 "Thank God! I've seen him at last": *Baltimore Afro-American*, February 27, 1937.

204 "They say I can't take a punch": *Los Angeles Times*, April 2, 1937.

204 "a penny a throw": *New York Evening Journal*, April 2, 1937.

204 "the brown wizard of Galveston": *Lincoln (Nebraska) Evening Journal*, January 6, 1939.

204 "a hundred dollars to five": *Boxing News*, September 1937.

204 "His clean living and high-minded morals": *Chicago Defender*, May 1, 1937.

204 "Patriotic American": Letter, May 16, 1933, in Papers of the Non-Sectarian Anti-Nazi League, Rare Book and Manuscript Library, Butler Library, Columbia University.

205 "make all others seem pale and pointless by contrast": *New York Evening Journal*, January 9, 1937.

205 "which he willingly or unwillingly represents": *Anti-Nazi Economic Bulletin*, February 1937.

206 "Why should Americans boycott the Schmeling-Braddock fight?": *New York Daily News*, January 12, 1937.

206 "God help the Jews in Germany": Ibid., January 23, 1937.

206 "almost stupid beyond belief boycott": Letter, Citizens Protective League to the NAACP, January 12, 1937, NAACP Papers, Library of Congress.

206 "Must we allow these most loathsome and despicable": Letter, undated, Papers of the Non-Sectarian Anti-Nazi League, Columbia University.

206 "is forced to be a Nazi if he doesn't want": *Boston Post*, January 11, 1937.

206 "one of the most hated organizations": Letter, Samuel Untermyer to J. G. Fredman, January 12, 1937, Papers of the Non-Sectarian Anti-Nazi League, Columbia University.

206 "Schmeling might just as well remain in Germany": *New Orleans Times-Picayune*, January 12, 1937.

207 "Even without the aid of any other organizations": *Minneapolis Journal*, January 10, 1937.

207 "easy-going Max": *Jewish Examiner*, January 15, 1937.

207 "People tell stories about Schmeling 'Heiling Hitler'": *Jewish Advocate*, January 12, 1937.

207 "leaped at the excuse like a speckled trout": *New York Herald Tribune*, January 10, 1937.

207 "draw flies": *New York Mirror*, January 9, 1937.

207 "I want to be fair to Schmeling": *Chicago Tribune*, February 1, 1937.

208 "anti-Nazi front men": *Bang*, January 16, 1937.

208 "There is a powerful aroma of larceny": *Boston Globe*, January 12, 1937.

208 "We don't owe the Horst Wessel muzzler": *New York Daily News*, January 10, 1937.

208 "akin to boycotting smallpox": *New York World-Telegram*, January 18, 1937.

208 "Hitler's boyfriend"; "Storm Trooper Moxie"; "Hitler's emissary to America": *Daily Worker*, March 7, 1937.

208 "He should have known": Ibid., January 17, 1937.

208 SCHMELING HECKLED IN UNBELIEVABLE WAY: *New York Herald Tribune*, January 9, 1937.

208 "racially conscious Americans": *New York Herald Tribune*, January 10, 1937.

208 IF YOU LOVE YOUR CHILDREN: *Angriff*, January 10, 1937.

208 "traditions of fairness": *New York Times*, January 10, 1937.

208 "100 per cent Americans": *American Israelite*, January 21, 1937.

209 "the Hitler-Heiling Joe Jacobs": *Anti-Nazi Economic Bulletin*, March 1937.

209 "Schmeling is a hero": *Daily Worker*, February 17, 1937.

209 BOYCOTT BROKEN!: *Völkischer Beobachter*, January 20, 1937.

209 "The Jews don't help us": *Crisis*, February 1936.

209 "Negro-Jew-Catholic-hating Nazis": *Amsterdam News*, January 16, 1937.

209 "Maybe they have some Negro servant": Ibid.

210 "certain individuals in the boxing game": Letter, Walter White to Bill Nunn, February 19, 1937, NAACP Papers, Library of Congress.

210 "promotional stooge": *Chicago Tribune*, June 22, 1937.

210 "Why should Jim, who was on relief for years": *New York Evening Journal*, February 22, 1937.

210 "a clique that has nothing to do with sports": *Box-Sport*, February 22, 1937.

211 "It is understood that Chancellor Hitler": Memo, Douglas Jenkins, American consul general in Berlin, February 1, 1937, to secretary of state, State Department Archives.

211 "This fight will be the greatest sporting event of the year 1937": Herman Esser to Hans Heinrich Lammers, February 10, 1937, in Bundesarchiv, BA Rk43 II/810a.

211 "This still needs to be discussed with Göring": Fröhlich (ed.), *Die Tagebücher von Joseph Goebbels*, T.I, Bd.3/II, February 27, 1937, p. 395.

212 "You know, they do me an honor": Associated Press, March 2, 1937.

212 "ghost battle": *Daily Worker*, March 3, 1937.

212 "chamber of horrors"; "brown-shirted fanatic": *New York Daily News*, March 4, 1937.

212 "shameless Jew lout"; "New York's chief gangster": Ibid., March 5, 1937.

212 "a dwarf with a grotesque belly": Ibid., March 6, 1937.

212 "un-American city in the country"; "Jews-York": *Berliner illustrierte Nachtausgabe*, March 5, 1937.

212 "No less than three million members of this race": *Fränkische Tageszeitung*, March 5, 1937.

212 "a product of the lower east-side of New York": *Deutscher Weckruf und Beobachter*, March 11, 1937.

212 "real culture": quoted in *New York Herald Tribune*, March 6, 1937.

213 "All posts are requested not to diminish vigilance": *Jewish Veteran*, March 1937.

213 "since in American boxing the Jews play a great role": Bohrmann (ed.), *NS–Presseanweisungen der Vorkriegszeit*, Bd.5/I:1937: March 12, 1937.

213 "the most boot-licking contract ever advanced": *Daily Worker*, March 14, 1937.

213 "What else?": *Washington Post*, February 10, 1938.

214 "Joe Louis is colored": *Baltimore Afro-American*, March 27, 1937.

214 "the sports pages are for sports": *Bang*, May 29, 1937.

214 "The Führer doesn't want soft mamma's boys": *12 Uhr-Blatt*, April 20, 1937.

215 "the wonderful style of his victory over Louis": *Berliner Zeitung am Mittag*, April 16, 1937.

215 "Max Schmeling has long": *Box-Sport*, April 19, 1937.

215 "storms of applause": *Angriff*, April 17, 1937.

215 "Braddock is a coward, and continually searching for new excuses": Fröhlich (ed.), *Die Tagebücher von Joseph Goebbels*, T.I, Bd.4: März–November 1937, April 13, 1937, p. 93.

215 "I'm not going to sacrifice": *Boston Post*, June 21, 1937.

215 "a longshoreman who proudly carries": *Daily Worker*, May 18, June 20 and 21, 1937.

215 "Braddock looks upon Louis": Associated Negro Press, May 7, 1937.

215 "If the heavyweight champion can't protect himself": *New York Sun*, June 8, 1937.

215 "The ugly monster of race prejudice": *Norfolk Journal and Guide*, May 15, 1937.

216 "journey into the unknown": *Box-Sport*, May 4, 1937.

216 "I've told you again and again": *Berliner Zeitung am Mittag*, May 25, 1937.

216 "the shadow-boxing championship of the universe": *New York Mirror*, May 11, 1937.

216 "Evidently Max is trying to fathom": *New York Herald Tribune*, May 19, 1937.

216 "If I make excuses this time": *Boston Traveler*, June 18, 1938.

217 "a fair indication": *New York Herald Tribune*, June 2, 1937.

217 "mediocre boxer": *New York Daily News*, May 29, 1937.

217 "Kid Ghost": *Daily Worker*, June 3, 1937.

217 broadcast going "ghost to ghost": *New York American*, June 3, 1937.

217 "If the sports injustice": *Box-Sport*, June 1, 1937.

217 "With the Führer this afternoon": Fröhlich (ed.), *Die Tagebücher von Joseph Goebbels*, T.I, Bd.4, May 27, 1937, p. 153.

217 "This fight for the fight has maybe been harder": Arno Hellmis radio interview with Max Schmeling and Max Machon, recorded on June 2, 1937, at the NBC Studios at Rockefeller Center, New York, for shortwave transmission to Germany. Museum of Television and Radio, New York, Program No. A 593.

217 "the most popular man in America": *Völkischer Beobachter*, June 3, 1937.

218 "a singular song of praise": Hellmis, *Max Schmeling*, p. 6.

218 "a block of wood": Ibid., p. 89.

218 "The greatest injustice": 12 *Uhr-Blatt*, June 3, 1937.

218 "We set our date last winter": *New York American*, May 25, 1937.

218 "the most titanic farce": *New York Herald Tribune*, June 4, 1937.

218 "This here business is sorta nutty": *New York Evening Journal*, June 4, 1937.

218 "the consummation of as complete": *New York Sun*, June 4, 1937.

218 "phantom manager": *New York Mirror*, May 25, 1937.

219 "Bitterness is strictly a new act": *Wichita Beacon*, June 5, 1937.

219 "Who cares about being suspended?": *New Yorker Staats-Zeitung*, June 4, 1937. "What is the decision—noddings!": *Newark Star-Eagle*, June 4, 1937. "They make a joke of the title": *New York Herald Tribune*, June 4, 1937. "It's all my fault": *Milwaukee Journal*, June 4, 1937.

219 "The sense of justice in every civilized man": *New York Sun*, June 5, 1937.

219 "Severe diarrhea?" 8 *Uhr-Blatt*, June 4, 1937.

220 "the Mt. Everest of all dudgeons": *New York Sun*, June 25, 1937.

220 "Schmeling being given the run-around by Braddock": Fröhlich (ed.), *Die Tagebücher von Joseph Goebbels*, T.I, Bd.4, June 5, 1937, p. 169.

220 "must continue to write in the sharpest manner": Bohrmann (ed.), *NS-Presseanweisungen der Vorkriegszeit*, Bd.5/I:1937: June 7, 1937.

220 "seduced from the path of contract duty": *Madison Square Garden Corporation v. Braddock*, 90 F. 2d 924, 929 (1937).

220 "world championship of the old world": Franz Metzner to Hauptmann Wiedmann, June 7, 1937, in Bundesarchiv, BA NS 10/538.

220 "the greatest interest": Ibid.

220 "as a counterweight against the American methods of deception": Metzner to District Finance Office, June 7, 1937, in Bundesarchiv, BA R 1501/5099.

220 "The incredible enthusiasm with which the fair Englishmen": *Berliner Zeitung am Mittag*, June 17, 1937.

220 "moral" world champion: *Box-Sport*, June 15, 1937.

220 "the arrogant monopoly": Franz Metzner to Falony et al., June 23, 1937, in Bundesarchiv, BA R 1501/5098.

221 "The European front of unity against American gangsterism": Metzner to Tschammer, July 1, 1937, in Bundesarchiv, BA R 1501/5101.

221 "You can bet all the tea in China he is": *New York World-Telegram*, June 18, 1937.

Chapter Ten: Banishing Jack Johnson's Ghost

222 "Joe Louis was a great fighter": *New York Sun*, June 17, 1937.

222 "living argument against the hypocrisy": *Amsterdam News*, June 12, 1937.

223 "just a cheap and sleazy road company": *New York Daily News*, June 15, 1937.

223 "will ever be able to pound anything": Ibid., June 22, 1937.

223 "going the way of nearly all negro gladiators": *Collyer's Eye*, June 5, 1937.

223 "This is Joe's first romance": *Amsterdam News*, March 6, 1937.

223 "I can think of a million things wrong": *New York Daily News*, June 22, 1937.

223 "Youth, speed, strength, reflexes": *New York Sun*, June 22, 1937.

224 "One guy is getting old": *New York American*, May 19, 1937.

224 "mild contusions and abrasions": quoted in *Amsterdam News*, February 13, 1937.

224 "there should be a minimum of exultation": *Baltimore Afro-American*, June 19, 1937.

224 "might be taken in its stride": *Baltimore Afro-American*, June 19, 1937.

224 "Louis will be the last colored man": *Baltimore Afro-American*, June 19, 1937.

224 "Race pride is one thing": *Long Island Review*, undated, in L. S. Alexander Gumby Collection on the American Negro, Rare Book and Manuscript Library, Butler Library, Columbia University.

224 "a white man can say a lot more": *Houston Informer*, June 23, 1937.

224 "Red," "Lefty," "Good Time Charley," "One-Eye": *Daily Express* (London), June 23, 1937.

225 "Chicago is one of those places": *New York American*, June 23, 1937.

225 "Why pay $27.50": *New York World-Telegram*, June 24, 1937.

225 "They ain't educated": *New York Evening Journal*, June 21, 1937.

225 "Black and White Sox Park": *New York World-Telegram*, June 22, 1937.

225 "and among all of these you find": *Norfolk Journal and Guide*, June 26, 1937.

225 "Joe Louis Special": *Houston Informer*, June 8 and 19, 1937.

226 "Germany isn't interested": *New York Herald Tribune*, June 22, 1937.

226 "The outcome of the fight": Bohrmann (ed.), *NS-Presseanweisungen der Vorkriegszeit*, Bd.5/I:1937, June 22, 1937.

226 "a primitive man, a boxing machine": *Box-Sport*, June 22, 1937.

226 "Gee, Joe, you sure are light for this fight": *New York American*, June 23, 1937.

226 "There is no legend of world domination": *Chicago Tribune*, June 22, 1937.

226 "armed to the molars": *New York World-Telegram*, June 22, 1937.

227 "completely alabastered": *Boston Post*, June 23, 1937.

227 "widely known mortician": Associated Negro Press, July 3, 1937.

227 "a sheepish-faced boy in a long bathrobe": *Chicago Daily News*, June 23, 1937.

227 "Chappie, this is it": Nagler, *Brown Bomber*, p. 73.

227 "Every man, woman and child": *Norfolk Journal and Guide*, June 26, 1937.

228 "You throw that towel in there": *New York Mirror*, March 30, 1938.

228 "Braddock fought a more relentless foe": *Chicago Tribune*, June 23, 1937.

228 "Get your hands up, Jimmy!": *New York World-Telegram*, June 23, 1937.

229 "in a halo of gleaming particles": *Philadelphia Tribune*, June 30, 1938.

229 "Braddock went over stiffly": *New York Mirror*, June 23, 1937.

229 "Get up, Jim!": *Memphis Commercial Appeal*, June 23, 1937.

229 "Chappie! Chappie! Let's cut the title in two and celebrate!": Associated Press, June 23, 1937.

229 "Ol' glove, you shoa had dynamite in you tonight": *New York Evening Journal*, June 23, 1937.

229 "I guess them years jes' crept up on him"; "Nice to be young, ain't it?": Associated Press, June 23, 1937.

229 "It don't feel no different": *New York Sun*, June 24, 1937.

229 "the fightingest champion there ever was": *Louisville Times*, June 23, 1937.

229 "Just give me one more shot at that Schmeling": *Atlanta Daily World*, June 17, 1938.

229 "I guess the poor guy hasn't come to": *New York World-Telegram*, June 24, 1937.

230 "Swirling, careening, madly dashing": *Pittsburgh Courier*, June 26, 1937.

230 I TOLD YOU SO: *Chicago Defender*, June 26, 1937.

230 "They threw that party": *Chicago Tribune*, June 23, 1937.

230 "His right really was pretty good": *Chicago Herald & Examiner*, June 24, 1937.

230 "One moment there wasn't nobody": *New York World-Telegram*, June 23, 1937.

230 "We want Schmeling!"; "We want the Nazi man!": *Daily Worker*, June 24, 1937.

230 "How do you like that, white man?": *New York Sun*, June 23, 1937.

230 "One thousand policemen fingered clubs": *Daily Worker*, June 23, 1937.

230 "kayoed the same barrier of discrimination": Ibid., June 27, 1937.

231 "darktown Baltimore"; "Christmas Eve in darkest Africa": Alistair Cooke, *One Man's America*, (New York: Knopf, 1952), p. 73.

231 "a tumult of joyous celebration": Russell Baker, *Growing Up* (New York: Congdon & Weed, 1982), pp. 203–6.

231 "wildly happy with the greatest celebration": *The Autobiography of Malcolm X*, p. 23.

231 "I guess the better man won": *Boxing News*, June 1937.

231 "The cynical philosopher": *Norfolk Journal and Guide*, June 26, 1937.

231 "into the brightest limelight": *California Eagle*, June 25, 1937.

231 "If this same Joe Louis": *Black Dispatch (Oklahoma City)*, July 3, 1937.

231 "That letter should have been sent": *New York Age*, July 3, 1937.

231 "flat-footed nigger": Box 55, Folder 20 in NBC papers, Wisconsin Historical Society.

232 "England trembles every time": *Baltimore Afro-American*, July 10, 1937.

232 "Negro entertainment in a theater for white persons": *Pittsburgh Courier*, July 3, 1937.

232 "utter lack of restraint": *Durham (North Carolina) Sun*, June 23, 1937.

232 "Driven by jealousy and the 'Can't Take It' mood": *Louisiana Weekly*, July 3, 1937.

232 "there are none so blind as those who will not see": *New York Age*, March 5, 1938.

232 "quiet, inoffensive personality": *Birmingham News*, June 24, 1937.

232 "Powder Town": Associated Press, June 23, 1937.

233 "an old, sad-eyed, gray-pated Negro": *Chicago Sunday Times*, June 27, 1937.

233 "dementia praecox of the recurring type": *Montgomery Advertiser*, July 18, 1937.

233 "If he rests too long, he gets fat and lazy": *New York Daily News*, July 16, 1937.

233 "If white champions can loaf": *Pittsburgh Courier*, July 3, 1937.

233 "as natural as young love": International News Service, June 24, 1937.

234 "merely wanted Rockefeller Center": *Norfolk Journal and Guide*, August 7, 1937.

234n "One leaves the theater a little ashamed": *Box-Sport*, July 19, 1937.

234n "I see no improvement in Louis": *New York Journal-American*, August 18, 1937.

234 "That's What America's Boxing World Champion Looks Like": *8 Uhr-Blatt*, June 23, 1937.

234 "Europe steps in"; a "historic event": *12 Uhr-Blatt*, June 23, 1937.

234 "We will box in September": *Angriff*, June 24, 1937.

235 "The Schmeling fight against the Englishman": Bohrmann (ed.), *NS-Presseanweisungen der Vorkriegszeit*, Bd.5/I: 1937: June 24, 1937.

235 "The sour-grapes edition": *Daily Worker*, June 25, 1937.

235 "The Reich is the first state in the world": *New York World-Telegram*, June 23, 1937.

235 "Nothing should be carried about the reports in the English press": *NS-Presseanweisungen der Vorkriegszeit*, Bd.5/I: 1937: July 1, 1937.

235 "would amount to a lack of self-respect": *NS-Presseanweisungen der Vorkriegszeit*, Bd.5/I: 1937: August 26, 1937.

235 "One beaten by Schmeling": *Berliner illustrierte Nachtausgabe*, July 28, 1937.

235 "Promoter Jacobs' plans call for stalling Max": *New York Mirror*, July 10, 1937.

235 "The longer they postpone the fight": International News Service, July 6, 1937.

236 "with mouths wide open": *Baltimore Afro-American*, September 18, 1937.

236 "the back and forth record": *Deutsches Volksecho*, August 28, 1937.

236 "In Germany they call me the champion": *New York World-Telegram*, August 19, 1937.

236 "if poor old Chim can knock down Louis"; "laughed with all the cheery good humor": *New York Mirror*, August 19, 1937.

236 "a clear dislike": *Norfolk Journal and Guide*, August 28, 1937.

236 "Everybody has a chance": *New York Post*, August 23, 1937.

236 "would tolerate no further gypping of the German": *New York Mirror*, January 15, 1938.

236 "If that spontaneous demonstration for Maxie": Ibid., September 2, 1937.

237 "He is not more": *Clearfield (Pennsylvania) Progress*, August 31, 1937.

237 "Joe Louis lost everything": *New York Herald Tribune*, August 31, 1937.

237 "His footwork is atrocious; his headwork, nil": *New York Daily News*, September 1, 1937.

237 "would hardly knock over": *New York Mirror*, September 1, 1937.

237 "The Alabama-born darky": *New York World-Telegram*, August 31, 1937.

237n "We note that you at no time": Letter, Walter White to Harry Grayson, September 9, 1937, NAACP Papers.

237 "Bomber Without Bombs": *Reichssportblatt*, September 6, 1937.

237 AND THEY CALL THAT A WORLD CHAMPIONSHIP! *Hamburger Anzeiger*, August 31, 1937.

237 "Instead of the milling, man-eating panther of old": *Chicago Defender*, September 4, 1937.

237 "If he knocks his man out in a jiffy": *Ring*, November 1937.

238 "It would be better for the fight game": *Amsterdam News*, September 11, 1937.

238 "You done me half a million dollars'": *New York Journal-American*, September 2, 1937.

238 "Too much teaching": *New York Age*, September 11, 1937.

238 "had taken the glamour away": *Chicago Tribune*, September 20, 1937.

238 "Champions often come up with broken bones": *New York World-Telegram*, September 1, 1937.

239 "bad stage management"; "disgraceful theater": 12 *Uhr-Blatt*, September 2, 1937.

239 "They'll be in a line, from here": *New York World-Telegram*, April 25, 1938.

239 "You could see them breaking": Barney Nagler, "Joe Louis's Finest Hour," *Saga*, September 1955.

239 "That's the best thing I've ever heard you say yet!": *Pittsburgh Courier*, September 11, 1937.

239 "I do not think I will get what you call the run-around": *Cleveland Plain Dealer*, September 5, 1937.

239 "placed the sport above the money": *Box-Sport*, September 6, 1937.

239 "any other opponent for the glorious 'world champion'": *Völkischer Beobachter*, September 8, 1937.

Chapter Eleven: The Rematch Becomes Reality

241 "bevy of the comeliest stars": *New York Times*, September 26, 1937.

241 "Schmeling has suffered extraordinary financial losses": letter, Metzner to Tschammer, November 4, 1937, in Bundesarchiv, BA R 1501/5101.

241 "as big as Central Park": *New York Sun*, May 30, 1941.

241 "To find an opponent for Schmeling": *Angriff*, October 21, 1937.

241 "with open arms and with joy": *Box-Sport*, November 29, 1937.

242 "The League is not willing to feed": *New York Post*, December 1, 1937.

242 "They do not want me to have easy fights": *New York Journal-American*, December 9, 1937.

242 "wrangling endlessly": Ibid.

243 "the willing whetstone": Associated Press, December 12, 1937.

243 "I haven't the slightest doubt": *New York Mirror*, December 12, 1937.

243 "The passersby smile, if they look at all": *Angriff*, December 10, 1937.

243 "particular racial character": *Box-Sport*, December 14, 1937.

243 "We're all fighting": Ibid.

243 SCHMELING IS A GERMAN COMMODITY: *New York Daily News*, December 14, 1937.

243 "Don't send money": *New York Sun*, December 14, 1937.

243 "Jacobs would sell out": *New York Daily News*, December 14, 1937.

243 "Jacobs would sell out his own mother!": *New York Sun*, December 14, 1937.

243 "Well, I hope them boycotters don't feel hurt": Associated Press, December 14, 1937.

243 "the champion who fears no man": *Brooklyn Daily Eagle*, December 14, 1937.

244 "the crowd almost tore his ear off"; "one of those old Dempsey ovations": *New York World-Telegram*, December 14, 1937.

244 "Max's rooters rattled the windows": *New York Daily News*, December 14, 1937.

244 "Schmeling desoives all the credit": *New York Mirror*, December 15, 1937.

244 "My nerves are shot": *New York World-Telegram*, December 14, 1937.

244 "Max, you were wonderful!": *New York Mirror*, December 15, 1937.

244 "Emotionally, Louis probably took": *New York World-Telegram*, December 14, 1937.

245 Schmeling "looked terrible"; "he ought to go back": *Washington Post*, December 15, 1937.

245 "contained in a prodigious yawn": *Amsterdam News*, December 18, 1937.

245 "to see another pair of gloves": *Brooklyn Eagle*, December 14, 1937.

245 "go messin' roun' in no fog": *New York Journal-American*, December 14, 1937.

245 "Some of my friends": *New York Times*, December 15, 1937.

245 "Max Schmeling's popularity, particularly with the Brown Shirts": *New York Times*, December 15, 1937.

245 "he would have knocked out any other heavyweight": *Angriff*, December 15, 1937.

245 "Schmeling Also KO'd the USA Jews": *8 Uhr-Blatt*, December 14, 1937.

245 "Samuel Untermyer & Co.": Ibid., December 15, 1937.

245 "the circle of Jewish boycott agitators": *Völkischer Beobachter*, December 15, 1937.

246 "an audience of appreciative storm troopers": *Anti-Nazi Bulletin*, December 1937.

246 "I'll get rid of all those headaches": *New York Journal-American*, December 15, 1937.

246 "not only over a strong opponent": *12 Uhr-Blatt*, December 22, 1937.

246 "a small clique of sleazy Jewish agitators"; "never learned to kiss up to the newspaper Jews": H.J.: *Das Kampfblatt der Hitler-Jugend*, December 4, 1937; February 5, 1938.

247 "To Our German World Champion": Ibid., February 26, 1938.

247 "Joe Louis hadn't hung up his 'sock'": *Pittsburgh Courier*, December 25, 1937.

247 "I'll show him the next time": Ibid., July 2, 1938.

247 Louises were "definitely apart": *Pittsburgh Courier*, January 8, 1937.

247 "a Harlem night club chorine": *New York Daily News*, January 10, 1938.

247 "sepia songstress": *Baltimore Afro-American*, January 15, 1938.

247 "Wherever she goes, she is the object of all eyes": *Chicago Defender*, January 22, 1938.

247 "Despite all of the upsetting rumors": *Pittsburgh Courier*, January 22, 1938.

248 "the sweetest little wife": *Pittsburgh Courier*, January 22, 1938.

248 "meddled and meddled and meddled"; "will defend my title": *Chicago Defender*, February 12, 1938.

248 "a dud, with a capital D": *Baltimore Afro-American*, January 8, 1938.

248 "His awkwardness will remind them": Ibid.

249 "One had expected more": Elke Fröhlich (ed.), *Die Tagebücher von Joseph Goebbels*, T.I, Bd.5: Dezember 1937–Juli 1938 (Munich: K.G. Saur, 2000), January 31, 1938, p. 126.

249 "He tirades a lot against America": Ibid., T.I, Bd.5, February 2, 1938, p. 131.

249 "Thrilling and dramatic": Ibid., T.I, Bd.5, February 4, 1938, p. 135.

249 "real American" fashion: *8 Uhr-Blatt*, February 5, 1938.

250 "I'm kinda sorry today's fight happened": *New York Herald Tribune*, January 31, 1938.

250 "Tab this—Louis over Schmeling": *Ring*, April 1938.

250 "I only hope that Hitler": *Boston Globe*, February 4, 1938.

250 "Under his leadership, German boxing": *12 Uhr-Blatt*, March 30, 1938.

251 "sports-world gangsterism": *Box-Sport*, January 31, 1938; "World Jewry": *12 Uhr-Blatt*, April 16, 1938.

251 "It won't be long tonight": *New York Herald Tribune*, February 25, 1938.

251 "a snarling, fighting man of the jungle": *Philadelphia Tribune*, March 3, 1938.

251 "Sitting there on his dinky little stool": *New York Mirror*, February 25, 1938.

252 "I guess it was too cold": *Chicago Tribune*, April 2, 1938.

252 "Although it takes long residence": *New York Mirror*, April 16, 1938.

252 "He really is a brave lad": Fröhlich (ed.), *Die Tagebücher von Joseph Goebbels*, T.I, Bd.5, April 17, 1938, p. 263.

252 "Schmeling is expecting you": *Reichssportblatt*, May 17, 1938.

253 All the talk of war was "crazy": *Reichssportblatt*, April 26, 1938.

253 "as homeless as Orphan Annie": *New York Mirror*, April 7, 1938.

253 "His main and valid": *Ken*, June 18, 1938.

253 "Boxing's oldest gate gag": *New York World-Telegram*, April 4, 1938.

253 "For every customer who stays away": *Amsterdam News*, April 23, 1938.

253 "a Nazi tool": *Brooklyn Eagle*, April 27, 1938.

253 "Unless Schmeling shows himself": *New York World-Telegram*, April 28, 1938.

254n "It's too bad": *New York Mirror*, May 11, 1938.

254 "Most of the trouble with the Jews": *Lincoln Evening Journal*, April 29, 1938.

254 "Jacobs said he did not see any": *Nation*, June 18, 1938.

254 "It is unfortunate that such as he": *Jewish Veteran*, May 1938.

254 a set of brochures: The brochure is in the papers of the Non-Sectarian Anti-Nazi League, Columbia University.

255 "six attractive women": Memo, May 4, 1938, Papers of the Non-Sectarian Anti-Nazi League.

255 "Those folks are crazy": *New York Times*, May 9, 1938.

255 "Every time these boycotts get under way": *Brooklyn Eagle*, May 16, 1938.

255 boycott "silly": *New York Herald Tribune*, May 10, 1938.

255 "Herr Schmeling may be a Nazi": *New York Times*, May 9, 1938.

255 "A representative of a government?": Ibid., May 13, 1938.

255 "I didn't make this trip for fun": *Brooklyn Eagle*, May 9, 1938.

255 "How is it already, the gate?": *New York Mirror*, May 10, 1938.

256 "like a blue mountain"; "Tell 'em about the Boy Scouts": Ibid.

256 "This is—how you say": International News Service, May 11, 1938.

256 the "most photographed head": *Box-Sport*, May 23, 1938.

256 "Here's your stamp, my good young man": Ibid.

256 "You won't need six weeks": *Brooklyn Eagle*, May 10, 1938.

256 "You see, he's a Negro": Associated Press, May 10, 1938.

256 "Louis may not even know it himself": *New York Times*, May 10, 1938.

256 "That is the psychological aftermath": *New York Journal-American*, May 10, 1938.

256 "an Aryan Show Horse"; "In small groups I would try to explain": Schmeling, *Erin-nerungen*, p. 423.

256 "completely heartfelt and friendly": *Box-Sport*, May 16, 1938.

257 "The contents of the flyers are too stupid": Ibid., May 23, 1938.

257 "All I have to do will be to cut down on my ice cream": *New York Times*, May 11, 1938.

257 "When I get in the ring": *New York Sun*, May 12, 1938.

257 "You can bet all de money you got": *Indianapolis Recorder*, May 14, 1938.

257 "Hah'ya, Max": *New York Journal-American*, May 12, 1938.

257 "Joe, we want two words from you"; "Louis handed him what must have felt like": *New York Mirror*, May 12, 1938.

257 "as you would if a friendly": Ibid.

258 "His eyes shine in proud delight": *8 Uhr-Blatt*, May 20, 1938.

258 "A master stroke of diplomatic strategy": *New York World-Telegram*, May 13, 1938.

258 "Jews are once again trying to sabotage": Fröhlich (ed.), *Die Tagebücher von Joseph Goebbels*, T.I, Bd.5, May 18, 1938., p. 306.

Chapter Twelve: Pompton Lakes and Speculator

259 "The world heavyweight championship is making": *Box-Sport*, June 13, 1938.

259 "tornadic" start: *New York Journal-American*, June 3, 1938.

259 "Last time Chappie f'ot jus'": *Boston Post*, June 14, 1938.

260 Louises together "only about sixty-six" days: *Baltimore Afro-American*, June 25, 1938.

260 "men in sports clothes": *Richmond Afro-American Planet*, June 18, 1938.

260 "jeweled octoroons from the Cotton Club": *Chicago Daily News*, June 2, 1938.

260 "There's wire netting": London *Sunday Pictorial*, June 19, 1938.

260 "just another fighter he was going to stop": Fried, *Corner Men*, p. 148.

260 "with all the savage vigor": *Memphis Commercial Appeal*, June 16, 1938.

260 "that started in Albany": *New York World-Telegram*, June 8, 1938.

261 "hit hard enough to dent a cake frosting": *New York World-Telegram*, June 10, 1938.

261 BROWN BOMBER LOOKS LIKE TAN TARGET: *New York Post*, June 10, 1938.

261 "Louis has never been accused of being erudite": *New York Herald Tribune*, June 16, 1938.

261 "Schmeling will make no mistake": *New York World-Telegram*, June 16, 1938.

261 "They tried Shufflin' Joe": *New York Times*, June 17, 1938.

261 "Experimentation to him": *New York Mirror*, June 3, 1938.

261 "There can be no question": *Los Angeles Times*, June 21, 1938.

261 "I don't know that Cy what-you-calls-him": *New York Journal-American*, June 20, 1938.

261 "They are saying Joe Louis": *Atlanta Journal*, June 21, 1938.

261 "I don't think he has changed a lick": *New York Sun*, June 20, 1938.

262 "feeding time at the zoo": *Boston Sunday Advertiser*, June 5, 1938.

262 "vastly improved mentally": *New York Post*, June 8, 1938.

262 "In Joe's trade a well-delivered clout": *New York Mirror*, June 21, 1938.

262 "Keep Joe from thinking": *New York Journal-American*, April 16, 1938.

262 "that remarkable sense of rhythm": Ibid., June 7, 1938.

262 "chauvinism and backwardness": *Daily Worker*, June 18, 1938.

263 "inflicted an inferiority complex": *New York Sun*, June 8, 1938.

263 "Joe Louis never will admit it": *Charleston (South Carolina) News & Courier,* June 22, 1938.

263 "The psychology is true": *Daily Texan,* June 19, 1938.

263 "Joe Louis is as much an American": *Richmond News-Leader,* June 22, 1938.

263 "For the first time in the history": *New York Daily News,* June 22, 1938.

263 "The public, even in the deep South": Walter White to Lowell Thomas, June 20, 1938, in NAACP papers.

264 "You fight him the way": *New York World-Telegram and Sun,* May 1, 1957.

264 "the greatest right": *Port Arthur (Texas) News,* December 8, 1937.

264 "One of the most liberal and genuine": *Pittsburgh Courier,* June 11, 1938.

264 "ridiculous": *Atlanta Daily World,* June 15, 1938.

264 "Gene, he not only never fought": *New York Sun,* June 11, 1938.

264 Schmeling's "spiritual fortification": *Connecticut Nutmeg,* May 26, 1938.

264 "did not have to dance": *Angriff,* June 10, 1938.

265 "he would be awkward": *Chicago American,* June 15, 1938.

265 "His burning desire for revenge": *Pittsburgh Courier,* June 25, 1938.

265 "I don't like Schmeling": *New York Journal-American,* May 18, 1954.

265 "The old drowsiness is gone": *New York Journal-American,* June 17, 1938.

265 "I know how to fight Max, now": *New York Daily News,* June 14, 1938.

265 "Sheer youthful exuberance": *New York World-Telegram,* June 22, 1938.

265 "a fit subject for the psychiatric ward": *Atlanta Daily World,* June 15, 1938.

265 "My rheumatics will give me": *New York Mirror,* June 15, 1938.

265 "They've finally got that boy mad": Associated Press, June 16, 1938.

265 "All of his work leaves the impression": *Box-Sport,* June 13, 1938.

266 "the dollar assets of Herr Mike Jacobs": *Box-Sport,* May 30, 1938.

266 "as close to perfection": *New York Sun,* June 17, 1938.

267 "He is planning to right-cross you": *Chicago Defender,* June 18, 1938.

267 "the merest shadow of embonpoint": *Amsterdam News,* June 18, 1938.

267 "We were the center of attraction": Ibid.

267 "The black dynasty of pugilism": *Chicago American,* June 2, 1938.

267 the white press hid Schmeling's racism: *Gary American,* June 17, 1938.

267 "Make no mistake, Max Schmeling": *Chicago Times,* June 7, 1938.

267 "Ve haff no strikes": Ibid., June 17, 1938.

267 "Both he and Machon sincerely believe": *Chicago Times,* June 14, 19, and 20, 1938.

268 "floating sports hotel": *8 Uhr-Blatt,* June 9, 1938.

268 "Only the sporting side of the contest": Bohrmann (ed.), *NS-Presseanweisungen der Vorkriegszeit,* Bd. 6/I: 1938: June 10, 1938.

268 "preludes and omens": *Frankfurter Volksblatt,* June 23, 1938.

268 "like stepping from this enlightened": *New York Mirror,* June 18, 1938.

268 "Nasty Adolph's oaf-ficial observer": *St. Louis Star-Times,* June 13, 1938.

268 "spirit of Horst Wessel": *Atlanta Georgian,* June 18, 1938.

269 "Little wonder that he dashes back": *New York Mirror,* June 18, 1938.

269 "He made Max what he is today": *New York Times,* May 28, 1938.

269 "Jews will not forget": *Forverts,* June 22, 1938.

269 "the absolute low-down": *Atlanta Georgian,* June 19, 1938.

269 "In Germany, we still believe": *Chicago Tribune,* June 21, 1938.

270 "This fellow isn't a sportsman": *Daily Worker,* June 23, 1938.

270n Hamburg would be renamed "Schmeling": *Hamburger Tageblatt,* June 22, 1938.

270 "Look, Max, you're a nice guy": *Boston Globe,* June 21, 1938.

270 "If this dirty nigger Joe Louis": *Amsterdam News*, June 25, 1938.

270 "an old Jewish trick": Ibid.

270 "under orders to speak arrogantly": *New York World-Telegram*, June 24, 1938.

271 "He's willing to gab about food": *New York Herald Tribune*, June 15, 1938.

271 "He made his prediction": *New York Sun*, June 15, 1938.

271 "May the best man win, for you are the best": *Chicago Defender*, June 25, 1938.

271 "attired in regalia that made Hollywood look positive dowdy": *Atlanta Georgian*, June 20, 1938.

271 "as wide open as Boston Common": *Boston Post*, June 19, 1938.

271 "You can bet all the marijuana in Harlem": *Brooklyn Eagle*, June 20, 1938.

272 "I think in our first round we will feel each other out": *Liberty*, June 25, 1938.

272 "Harlemites who daily risk 600 to 1 odds": *New York Post*, June 22, 1938.

272 "Everything I could beg"; "I think Schmeling": *Amsterdam News*, June 18, 1936.

272 "Honest Opinion Poll": *New York Post*, June 22, 1938.

272 "Kay, O.": *Birmingham News*, June 22, 1938.

272 "I think he will whip the nigger again": Associated Negro Press, July 18, 1938.

273 "A young Christian Science lady": *Daily Worker*, July 1, 1938.

273 "Come early and don't drop your program": *Atlanta Georgian*, June 19, 1936.

273 "hits harder than any man alive": *Chicago Tribune*, June 22, 1938.

273 "Now, let's see": *Daily Worker*, June 21, 1938.

274 "a revolting pandering to racial prejudice": *New York Daily News*, June 20, 1938.

274 "it is understood the 'proper arrangements'"; "The cards are stacked": *Collyer's Eye*, June 4 and 18, 1938.

274 "as stiff and cold as a stalactite": *Brooklyn Eagle*, June 22, 1938.

274 "Herr Hitler has our title": *Boston Post*: June 22, 1938.

274 "the Joe Louis of old": *Chicago Defender*, June 18, 1938.

275 "There are a few things of which we may be reasonably certain": *New York Sun*, June 21, 1938.

275 "The fight may not go more than six": *Atlanta Constitution*, June 22, 1938.

275 "Joe Louis has a big mouth": *Der Kicker*, June 21, 1938.

275 "On this point we can agree": *Il Popolo d'Italia*, June 22, 1938.

275 "150 Million Will Listen to the Schmeling-Louis Bout Tonight": *Berliner Zeitung am Mittag*, June 22, 1938.

276 "full of confidence without bragging like the Negro": *Fränkische Tageszeitung*, June 22, 1938.

276 "To feel that the homeland is standing behind me": *Berliner Zeitung am Mittag*, June 22, 1938.

276 "Have correct fighting weight": *Hamburger Anzeiger*, June 21, 1938.

276 "screams of terror" outside jewelry store: *New York Daily News*, June 21, 1938.

276 "In Jewish homes there is a fresh pang": *Daily Herald* (London), June 20, 1938.

276 "a doomed people": *New York Sun*, June 18, 1938.

276 "Mr. Joe Jacobs must think": *Chicago Tribune*, June 18, 1938.

277 "New York City has been overrun": *Indianapolis Star*, June 19, 1938.

277 "For humanity's sake": *New York World-Telegram*, June 20, 1938.

277 "We have kept Schmeling waiting": *New York Times*, June 1, 1938.

277 "a quarter of every dollar": *Daily Express* (London), June 15, 1938.

277 "The alleged anti-German attitude of the New York audience": *Berliner Lokal-Anzeiger*, June 21, 1938.

277 had "ballyhooed the fight": *Nation*, June 16, 1938.

278 "As long as people are boobs enough": *Roanoke Times*, June 22, 1938.

278 "Max Schmeling will fly to New York": *New York Mirror*, June 23, 1938.

279 The German was "Sphinx-like" as he emerged: *New York Sun*, June 22, 1938.

279 "Next time we'll speak, you'll be world champion": *12 Uhr-Blatt*, June 22, 1938.

279 "We find this all a little strange, exaggerated": *Box-Sport*, July 11, 1938.

279 "We sink into the asphalt": *Paris Soir*, June 23, 1938.

279 "city of wash-house air": *Box-Sport*, July 11, 1938.

280 "You've traveled 1,500 miles to see me": *Newark Evening News*, June 14, 1938.

280 "something somehow turns off": *Box-Sport*, June 20, 1938.

280 "In him, too, the wanderlust of the typical German": *Angriff*, June 22, 1938.

280 "National-Socialist Germany, the sports people": *Königsberger Zeitung*, June 21, 1938.

280 "Germany's best-known radio announcer": *8 Uhr-Blatt*, June 20, 1938.

280 "Nothing but a dumb accident": *Angriff*, June 23, 1938.

280 "the primitive nature-boy": *Der Kicker*, June 21, 1938.

281 "I'm just afraid that Schmeling"; "Schmeling will do it": *Angriff*, June 23, 1938.

281 "Not a train pulled to a stop": United Press, June 20, 1938.

281 "Who's he gonna fight?": *Associated Press*, June 20, 1938.

281 "Louis Victory Special": *Associated Negro Press*, May 25, 1938.

281 "I can count on the fingers of one hand": *Atlanta Daily World*, June 20, 1938.

281 attendance at Aqueduct racetrack was of "holiday proportions": *New York Sun*, June 23, 1938.

281 "As jittery as a bridegroom": *Washington Post*, June 22, 1938.

282 "Not even General Washington": *Associated Negro Press*, June 20, 1938.

282 "From her bag, she drew an old": *New York World-Telegram*, June 21, 1938.

282 "Of course, after the fight, there will be a rush": *Norfolk Journal and Guide*, June 25, 1938.

282 "It is a grab in the dark": *New York Sun*, June 22, 1938.

282 "the fight nobody knows anything about": *Richmond Times-Dispatch*, June 22, 1938.

Chapter Thirteen: The Fight

283 "To the next world's champion": *Chicago Tribune*, June 23, 1938.

283 "Creole fashion plate": *New York Mirror*, June 23, 1938.

284 "I ain't going to take my pants off": *New York Sun*, June 23, 1938.

284 "as emotionless as the corner of a house": *New York Daily News*, June 23, 1938.

284 "I'm gonna finish this one in a hurry": *Pittsburgh Courier*, July 2, 1938.

284 "not only a menace to his fighter": *Knickerbocker News*, June 17, 1938.

285 "We'd better let the champ rest": *Chicago Daily News*, September 11, 1964.

285 "I'm goin' out and fight three rounds": *New York Daily News*, July 1, 1938.

285 "I did all I could": Fried, *Corner Men*, p. 148.

285 June 22 would be "very disappointing": *Knickerbocker News*, June 16, 1938.

285 JOE LOUIS, WORLD'S CHAMPION; "We were in the land": *Richmond Times-Dispatch*, June 23, 1938.

285 "step on it": Roy Wilkins, *Standing Fast: The Autobiography of Roy Wilkins* (New York: Viking Press, 1982), p. 164.

285 "The crowd simply carried you through the gates": *Afro-American and Richmond Planet*, June 25, 1938.

286 "Usually a sports event": Original flyer, collection of author.

286 "I'd like to see Joe Louis blast": *Daily Worker*, June 22, 1938.

287 "seemed electrically charged": Interview, Lester Rodney.

287 "A Gatsby sort of atmosphere": Interview, Babs Simpson.

288 "rich Harlem Negroes": *Dresdner Neueste Nachrichten,* June 23, 1938.

288 "A sea of faces": *Afro-American and Richmond Planet,* June 25, 1938.

288 "in an unreal gray haze": *Box-Sport,* July 11, 1938.

289 the largest radio audience: *Radio Guide,* June 25, 1938.

289 "listened in at car doors, trucks, stores, hotels": *Pacific,* January 1946.

289 "Let's not have speaking now": *Richmond Times-Dispatch,* June 23, 1938.

290 "To my father": *Mobile Register,* June 13, 1938.

290 "to show she was absolutely composed": *Pittsburgh Courier,* July 2, 1938.

290 "could come and root for Joe": *Chicago Defender,* July 2, 1938.

290 "championship ball" for blacks in Brooklyn: *New York Age,* June 25, 1938.

291 "The world will hold you responsible": Emilio Azcarraga to John F. Royal, June 18, 1938, in NBC papers, Wisconsin Historical Society.

291 "should a Negro defeat a Fascist": *Chicago Daily News,* June 6, 1938.

291 "There was no doubt whatsoever": *Haynt* (Warsaw), June 24, 1938.

291 "Shvartser Bombardier": *Sport-tsaytung* (Warsaw), June 28, 1938.

291 "Behind the windows in almost every apartment": *Angriff,* June 24, 1938.

291 "the murderous American heat": Ibid., June 22, 1938.

292 "*Hallo Berlin . . . Hallo Deutschland*": All Hellmis quotes from the 1938 fight are taken from the English-language translation found in the NBC papers at the Wisconsin Historical Society. No version of the German original survives; the German used in this and subsequent quotations is my best guess of what Hellmis said.

292 "You'll need only one": *Indianapolis Recorder,* July 2, 1938.

292 "Don't make a sucker out of me": *Ring,* March 1950.

292 "a Nazi son-of-a-bitch": Richard Bak, *Joe Louis: The Great Black Hope* (Da Capo Press: New York, 1998), p. 163.

292 "prancing and dancing as a Man O' War": *Philadelphia Tribune,* June 23, 1938.

293 "No challenger in memory": *New Orleans Item,* June 27, 1938.

293 "the picture of suavity": *Boston Post,* June 23, 1938.

294 "Do you hear the booing?": Hellmis transcript, NBC papers, Wisconsin Historical Society.

294n "Listen to this booing": Herbert Swope to David Sarnoff, June 24, 1938, in NBC papers, Wisconsin Historical Society.

294 "the biggest Bronx cheer": Associated Press, June 21, 1938.

295 "saw fit to give Schmeling": *Chicago Defender,* July 2, 1938.

296 "wrinkled his forehead like a washboard": *News of the World* (London), June 26, 1938.

296 "Unchain them!"; "Kill that Nazi, Joe!": *Pittsburgh Courier,* June 25, 1938.

296 "It seemed that each man and woman": *New Masses,* July 5, 1938.

296 "nervous and jumpy as a doped race horse": *Ken,* July 28, 1938.

296 "They've got that guy hopped up": *New Orleans Item,* June 23, 1938.

296 "This is the million-dollar thrill of sports": *Newark Star-Eagle,* June 22, 1938.

296 "One hundred and sixty thousand knees": *Amsterdam Recorder,* June 23, 1938.

297 "a silence, like the calm of Heaven": *Philadelphia Tribune,* June 30, 1938.

297 "Fourteen million brown men, women and children": *Pittsburgh Courier,* July 2, 1938.

297 "Look out, Joe!": *Atlanta Constitution,* June 23, 1938.

297 "bobbed up and down": *New York Mirror,* June 23, 1938.

297 "These folks at once sensed another victory": *Chicago Defender,* July 2, 1938.

298 "The Negro swung, hooked": *Ken,* July 28, 1938.

298 "Oh! oh!": *New York Sun*, June 23, 1938; "Genug! Genug!": *New York Daily News*, June 24, 1938.

298 "I thought in my mind": *New York Times*, November 10, 1948.

298 "Did you hear that?": Interview, Larry Kent.

298 "half human, half animal": Wilson, *Boxing's Greatest Prize* (London: S. Paul, 1980), p. 25.

298 "Sweetest music I ever heard": *Philadelphia Tribune*, June 30, 1938.

298 "Hitler's wilted pet": *Daily Worker*, June 24, 1938.

299 "like a spinning wheel": *Haynt* (Warsaw), June 24, 1938.

299 "like the shrieking of a mother": *Prager Mittag*, June 23, 1938.

299 "Impossible!": *New York World-Telegram*, June 23, 1938.

300 "With each blow": Ibid.

300 "Laughter roared through the land": *Pittsburgh Courier*, July 2, 1938.

300 "A red drool dribbled": *Boston Evening American*, June 23, 1938.

300 "to smash it like a baseball bat": *New York Herald Tribune*, June 23, 1938.

300 "a pale study in vicarious suffering": *Boston Post*, June 23, 1938.

300 "like a seagull": *Sunday Pictorial* (London), June 26, 1938.

300 "Schmeling was no longer": *Liberty*, May 23, 1942.

301 "water ran past the corners": *New York World-Telegram*, June 23, 1938.

301 "He was—for the first time": *New Orleans Item*, June 27, 1938.

301 "I told you so": Denis Brian, *Tallulah, Darling: A Biography of Tallulah Bankhead* (New York: Macmillan, 1980), p. 84

301 "The happiest people I saw": Associated Negro Press, June 29, 1938.

302 "Wasn't it swell?": *Baltimore Afro-American*, July 2, 1938.

302 "My daddy told me": *Chicago Defender*, June 25, 1938.

302 "Beat the hell out of the damn": Rayford W. Logan, "William Edward Burghardt Du Bois," speech delivered at Howard University, June 5, 1968, Rayford W. Logan Papers, Moorland-Spingarn Research Center, Howard University. For this, I am indebted to Professor Kenneth Janken of the University of North Carolina.

302 "Everybody danced and sang": *Pacific*, January 1946.

302 "dusky maids in evening gowns": *Macon Telegraph*, June 23, 1938.

302 "Then our visitors walked silently": Jimmy Carter, *An Hour Before Daylight* (New York: Simon & Schuster, 2001), pp. 32–33.

302 "It was hard to explain": *Midwest Daily Record*, June 29, 1938.

303 "did a fandango": *Philadelphia Inquirer*, June 23, 1938.

303 "Fighting Fury . . . Forked Lightning": *Pittsburgh Courier*, June 25, 1938.

303 "Horror, dynamite, mayhem": *Philadelphia Tribune*, June 23, 1938.

304 "In every land and in myriad tongues": *Pittsburgh Courier*, June 25, 1938.

304 "Listen to this, buddy": *New York Mirror*, June 23, 1938.

304 "Mox kept a bold front": *New Orleans Item*, June 27, 1938.

304 "Bang": *Charlotte News*, June 23, 1938.

304 "I told you I sent out": *Baltimore Afro-American*, July 2, 1938.

305 "Donovan could have counted": *New York Times*, June 23, 1938.

305 forty-one blows, thirty-one of them "serious": *Ring*, May 1946.

305 "I was in a hurry": *Hep*, February 1957.

305 "Artie, that was the softest": *New York World-Telegram*, June 23, 1938.

305 "Joe, you are a real champion": *New York Journal-American*, June 23, 1938.

305 "He wept softly at first": *New York Daily News*, June 23, 1938.

306 "Reduced to dithering bewilderment": *Time*, July 4, 1938.

306 "Some of the noble 72,000": *Philadelphia Record,* June 25, 1938.

306 "a little addled": Letter, R. H. White to Roy Witmer, July 1, 1938, NBC Papers, Wisconsin Historical Society.

306 "What round is it?": Interview, Richards Vidmer.

306 *"Unser Max!":* American Israelite, June 30, 1938.

306 "the shortest, sweetest minute": Wilkins, *Standing Fast,* p. 164.

307 "We might just as well": *New York Herald Tribune,* June 26, 1938.

307 "I'm willing to eat": *Chicago Defender,* July 2, 1938.

307 "Lift up the hand that did it": *New York World-Telegram,* June 23, 1938.

308 "Ah sho 'nuff": *Newark Star-Eagle,* June 23, 1938.

308 "What for? Didn't he just have his chance and lose?": Ibid.

308 "You must have felt different tonight": Ibid.

308 "Ah just felt stronger": Ibid.

308 "He never hurt me": *Pittsburgh Courier,* June 25, 1938.

308 "I got what folks call revenge": Associated Press, June 23, 1938.

308 "Ah don't know how many": *Newark Star-Eagle,* June 23, 1938.

308 "Levinsky was pretty easy": *New York World-Telegram,* June 23, 1938.

308 "I was sore at some of the things": *Daily Worker,* June 23, 1938.

308 "Well, he didn't deny them": Ibid.

308 "Now man, you know 'ah ain't": *Brooklyn Eagle,* June 23, 1938.

308 "Why, you old son of a gun!": *Providence Journal,* June 23, 1938.

308 "exactly like a wool-gathering youngster": *New York Times,* June 23, 1938.

308 "Nice work, Joe!": *Daily Worker,* June 24, 1938.

308 "This is our anniversary tonight": *Bronx Home News,* June 23, 1938.

309 "Nice work, Bomber": *Pittsburgh Courier,* June 25, 1938.

309 "How's that for our old boy?": Ibid.

309 "giving Father Time time": Associated Press, June 24, 1938.

309 "Sportsmanship, I suppose": *Bronx Home News,* June 23, 1938.

309 *"Heil Louis!":* Newark Star-Eagle, June 23, 1938.

309 "He is a pugilistic old man": *New York Mirror,* June 23, 1938.

309 "To put it bluntly": *New York World-Telegram,* June 23, 1938.

Chapter Fourteen: Aftermath

310 *"aus":* Angriff, June 24, 1938.

310 "That was the last word in the ether": *Prager Mittag,* June 23, 1938.

310 "That was the last word from the receiver": *Nasz Przeglad* (Warsaw), June 23, 1938.

310 "as if someone had suddenly": *Box-Sport,* June 27, 1938.

311 "Shaking our heads silently": *Angriff,* June 24, 1938.

311 "a breathless, half-loud crossfire": Ibid.

311 "We looked at each other silently": *Dresdner Neueste Nachrichten,* June 23, 1938.

311 "Go back to Germany! You Nazi bum, you never could fight!": *Atlanta Georgian,* June 23, 1938.

311 "woebegone and tragic figure": *New York Daily News,* June 23, 1938.

311 "Too bad, Max": Ibid.

311 "When he got in his dressing room": *New York Mirror,* June 24, 1938.

312 "Yah, he hit me such a terrible blow": *New York Daily News,* June 23, 1938.

312 "Such terrible pain. I can't move": *New York World-Telegram,* June 1938.

312 "A kidney blow is a foul": *New York Daily News,* June 23, 1938.

312 "Max! Max!": *Philadelphia Bulletin*, June 23, 1938.

312 "It wasn't vare, it wasn't": Ibid., June 23, 1938.

312 "strictly legal": *New York World-Telegram*, June 23, 1938.

312 "But Max, how was dot possible?": *Newark Star-Eagle*, June 23, 1938.

312 "What's clear is that his version": *Paris Soir*, June 23, 1938.

312 "Jacobs could not have done": *New Orleans Times-Picayune*, June 23, 1938.

312 "wondered if Louis had hit": *Newark Star-Eagle*, June 23, 1938.

312 "What will Hitler think?": *New York Daily News*, June 23, 1938.

312 "Nothing. Dot's foolish": *New York World-Telegram*, June 23, 1938.

313 "Yah, I fight again": *New York Daily News*, June 23, 1938.

313 "You Go to My Head": *Chicago Tribune*, June 24, 1938.

313 "No, sah, dat was no foul": *Newark Star-Eagle*, June 23, 1938.

313 "That's for German consumption": *New York Times*, June 23, 1938.

313 "make good stuff for the home trade": *New York Mirror*, June 23, 1938.

313 "It must have been a kidney punch to the chin": *New York Journal-American*, June 23, 1938.

314 "This is their night": *New York Daily News*, June 23, 1938.

314 "Too bad it ended so early": *New York Post*, June 23, 1938.

314 "aflame in happiness": Interview, Babs Simpson.

314 "Had you been in Harlem": *Pittsburgh Courier*, July 2, 1938.

314 "There never was a Harlem": *Daily Worker*, June 24, 1938.

314 "They wanted to make a noise": *New Masses*, July 5, 1938.

314 THE BLACK RACE IS SUPREME: *Milwaukee News*, June 23, 1938.

314 "their Broadway": Associated Press, June 23, 1938.

314 "looked like clusters of black ripe grapes": *New Masses*, July 5, 1938.

314 "The Lord is a good Man": *New York World-Telegram*, June 23, 1938.

314 "I remember for a while": Interview, Evelyn Cunningham.

314 LOUIS WINS, HITLER WEEPS: *New York World-Telegram*, June 23, 1938.

314 "Read about the big fight!": *Amsterdam (New York) Recorder*, June 23, 1938.

315 "Seventh Ave. looked": *New York World-Telegram*, June 23, 1938.

315 "clear off the excess baggage": *Milwaukee News*, June 23, 1938.

315 "the type of stuff": *Baltimore Afro-American*, July 2, 1938.

315 "Joe Louis! Joe Louis!": *New York Journal-American*, June 23, 1938.

315 "I bet all of 'em are on relief": *Philadelphia Tribune*, June 30, 1938.

315 "Joe Louis doesn't knock out": *Chicago Defender*, July 2, 1938.

315 "repeated wild shooting like in the jungle": *8 Uhr-Blatt*, June 24, 1938.

315 "There wasn't no nighttime then": Interview, Wilmer Cooper.

315 "a well of weltschmerzen": *New York Post*, June 23, 1938.

315 "I wonder what they think": *New York Journal-American*, June 23, 1938.

316 "I made it as quick as possible": International News Service, June 23, 1938.

316 "Joe Louis shine": Interview, Irwin Rosee.

316 "Joe is on top of the proverbial heap": *New York Age*, July 2, 1938.

316 "Joe knocked old Hitler cold": *Daily Worker*, June 25, 1938.

316 "Louder! Louder!": *Chicago Tribune*, June 24, 1938.

316 "police making an attempt": *Philadelphia Tribune*, June 23, 1938.

317 "Little children rushed by my house": *Pittsburgh Courier*, July 2, 1938.

317 "thousands of Negroes and many Jews": *Indianapolis News*, June 23, 1938.

317 "On the grass on the Paradeway": *Kansas City Call*, June 24, 1938.

317 "the mellow voice of a Negro Paul Revere": *Cincinnati Post*, June 23, 1938.

317 "plain old cheap": *California Eagle*, June 30, 1938.

317 "Boy, am I glad": *Newark Evening News*, June 23, 1938.

317 "To de ring, to de ropes, to de flo!" *Memphis Post-Scimitar*, June 23, 1938.

317 "Joe Louis ball": *LaFayette Sun*, June 29, 1938.

317 "That's my little Joe": *Baltimore Afro-American*, July 2, 1938.

317 "That boy must be worth": *Mobile Register*, June 23, 1938.

317 "began to scream in all directions": *Pittsburgh Courier*, July 16, 1938.

317 "joy-mad Race members": *Chicago Defender*, July 23, 1938.

318 "The gathering thereupon cheered": *Daily Gleaner* (Kingston, Jamaica), June 23, 1938.

318 "Throwing garbage, tin containers": *Atlanta Daily World*, June 26, 1938.

318 "hugging and street fighting": *Newark Evening News*, June 23, 1938.

318 "Where is Max Schmeling?": *Charlotte News*, June 28, 1938.

318n "Lynch the nigger!": *Gary Post-Tribune*, June 23, 1938.

318n "Prizefights between white men and Negroes": Ibid., June 24, 1938.

318n "We have, as a whole": *Gary American*, July 8, 1938.

318 "Henry Street is the only place": *Roanoke Times*, June 25, 1938.

319 "teeming mass of joyful humanity": *Norfolk Journal and Guide*, July 2, 1938.

319 "When colored people are filling streets": *Baltimore Afro-American*, July 2, 1938.

319 "the tragic aspect": *Afro-American and Richmond Planet*, June 25, 1938.

319 "We want Joe!": *New York World-Telegram*, June 24, 1938.

319 "I remembered my first fight with him": *New York Daily News*, June 24, 1938.

320 "feminine draw is nil": *Variety*, June 29, 1938.

320 "The one round isn't giving the fans": *Philadelphia Tribune*, June 30, 1938.

320 "The champ hasn't got a scratch": *Amsterdam News*, July 2, 1938.

320 "I think Louis'll be the champion": *New York Mirror*, June 25, 1938.

320 "a full-fledged man": *New York Times*, June 25, 1938.

320 "We congratulate him": *New York World-Telegram*, June 24, 1938.

321 "The Nazis stacked their political all": *Amsterdam News*, July 9, 1938.

321 "It was as if each had been in that ring himself": *Pittsburgh Courier*, July 2, 1938.

321 "a great fight by a great champion": Ibid., June 25, 1938.

321 "He is one of the worst": *Baltimore Afro-American*, July 2, 1938.

321 "Champ Joe Louis": Rounder Records Corp., Rounder 82161-1106-2.

322 "his spirit will stalk the world": *Chicago Defender*, June 25, 1938.

322 DUKE ELLINGTON RATED: *Pittsburgh Courier*, July 16, 1938.

322 "I have been a reader": *Baltimore Afro-American*, July 23, 1938.

322 "even the tiniest hint": *New York World-Telegram*, June 24, 1938.

322 "not so much that Schmeling himself": *Montreal Herald*, June 23, 1938.

322 "With the defeat of the boxing Hitler envoy": *Deutsches Volksecho*, July 2, 1938.

322 "Grandfather wouldn't have believed": *Philadelphia Record*, June 24, 1938.

323 "Our sympathies on the disgraceful showing": Bundesarchiv, Pol. Archiv AA R 104981.

323 "like a tiger": *Charleston (South Carolina) News and Courier*, June 24, 1938.

323 "Joe Louis, the lethargic, chicken-eating": *Washington Post*, June 23, 1938.

323 "It is nothing for us to weep about": *Chicago Daily News*, June 24, 1938.

323 "Somebody'll beat him": *New York Journal-American*, June 23, 1938.

323 "the greatest exhibition of punching": *Philadelphia Record*, June 23, 1938.

323 "Probably he punches faster": *Ken*, July 28, 1938.

323 "The ring may have seen a greater fighter": *New York Sun*, June 23, 1938.

323 "Schmeling was worse": *New York Daily News*, June 23, 1938.

323 "just pathetic": *Connecticut Nutmeg*, July 7, 1938.

323 "he'll find that he had a grandfather": *Washington Post*, July 1, 1938.
324 "our fastest runners are colored boys": *Atlanta Journal*, June 24, 1938.
324 "The colored people do not win": *Charleston (South Carolina) News and Courier*, June 24, 1938.
324 "No intelligent person": *Huntsville Times*, June 24, 1938.
324 "lost all of their courage": *Morgn-zhurnal*, June 24, 1938.
324 Führer had taken it straight in the "philosophy": *Forverts*, June 24, 1938.
324 "If only Schmeling's collapse": *Jewish Times*, July 1, 1938.
324 "they stuck the whole stupid myth": *Daily Worker*, September 16, 1938.
324 "The Negro sent the 'pureblooded Aryan'": Ibid., June 25, 1938.
324 "Let's not disrespect good fists": *Nasz Przeglad* (Warsaw), June 24, 1938.
324 *"Hey Louis!":* Ibid.
325 "special fight edition": *Rand Daily Mail*, June 26, 1938.
325 HITLER'S RACISM KNOCKED OUT: *La Nación* (Buenos Aires), June 23, 1938.
325n "It simply bears out": *New York Daily News*, June 26, 1938.
325 "A terrible defeat": Fröhlich (ed.), *Die Tagebücher von Joseph Goebbels*, T.I, Bd.5, June 24, 1938, p. 358.
325 "extremely depressed": *News Chronicle* (London), June 23, 1938.
325 received the news "philosophically": *New York Journal-American*, June 23, 1938.
325 "triumphal entry": *News Chronicle* (London), June 23, 1938.
325 "It seemed as if everyone": *Jacksonville Times-Union*, June 24, 1938.
326 "It was impossible": *Angriff*, June 25, 1938.
326 "It's terrible that punches like that": *New York Times*, June 24, 1938.
326 'MAX' INJURY A RUSE: *Chicago Times*, June 24, 1938.
326 "Max didn't go out of his way": *Bronx Home News*, June 24, 1938.
326 "Disowned by his race": *New York Mirror*, June 26, 1938.
326 "the sorriest figure in sportdom": *B'nai B'rith Messenger*, July 8, 1938.
327 "He is his own manager": *New York Journal-American*, June 26, 1938.
327 "No, I ain't going over to see him": *New York Herald Tribune*, June 24, 1938.
327 "Wishing you good luck": *Boston Globe*, June 24, 1938.
327 "The newspapers now only have themselves": Bohrmann (ed.), *NS-Presseanweisungen der Vorkriegszeit*, Bd.6/I: 1938: June 23, 1938.
327 "Yes, Schmeling may have been almost killed": *New York Times*, June 24, 1938.
327 Berlin as "dumbfounded": *Friend* (Johannesburg), June 24, 1938.
327 *"Neger und Elefanten":* Interview, Walter Wohlfeiler.
328 "proud and happy": *Boersen Zeitung*, quoted in *New York Daily News*, June 23, 1938.
328 "Schmeling seems not to have reckoned": *Philadelphia Daily News*, June 24, 1938.
328 "certain American profiteers": 12 *Uhr-Blatt*, June 23, 1938.
328 "attacked like an animal": *Box-Sport*, June 27, 1938.
328 "To be beaten by such means": *Der Alemanne*, June 24, 1938.
328 "It is time to have the subject": Bohrmann (ed.), *NS-Presseanweisungen der Vorkriegszeit*, Bd. 6/I: 1938: June 24, 1938.
329 "Two minutes determine the work": *Box-Sport*, June 27, 1938.
329 "keep his place in the heart": *HJ: Das Kampfblatt der Hitler-Jugend*, July 2, 1938.
329 "it is now time to stop": Bohrmann (ed.), *NS-Presseanweisungen der Vorkriegszeit*, Bd. 6/I: 1938: June 29, 1938.
329 "even if he looks like a Norwegian sailor": *Reichssportblatt*, July 26, 1938.
329 "I got even": *New York Journal-American*, February 24, 1965.
330 "A man who had been run over": *Chicago Defender*, July 9, 1938.

330 "He could have hit me": *New York World-Telegram*, June 29, 1938.
330 "a lyrical enthusiasm": Ibid., July 2, 1938.
330 left eye still "in mourning": *New York Journal-American*, July 3, 1938.
330 "There is vork to be done": Ibid., July 2, 1938.
330 "anozzer chance": Ibid., July 3, 1938.
330 "Since Schmeling's future": Bohrmann (ed.), *NS-Presseanweisungen der Vorkriegszeit*, Bd. 6/I: 1938: July 1, 1938.
330 "We traveled seven thousand miles": *New York Herald Tribune*, June 23, 1938.
331 "The Nazis will break down no doors": *Washington Post*, June 24, 1938.
331 "that would never have done": *New York Daily News*, July 10, 1938.
331 "A few intimates": International News Service, July 16, 1938.
331 "That's certainly one thing": Letter, Louis Lochner to Betty Lochner, July 10, 1938, in Louis Lochner Papers, Box 6, Folder 38, Wisconsin Historical Society.
331 "Today, Schmeling has more friends": *Box-Sport*, July 18, 1938.
331 "burning curiosity": Ibid., June 27, 1938.
331 "the all-powerful Mike Jacobs": Ibid., July 11, 1938.
332 "[Schmeling] is brutally beaten": Fröhlich (ed.), *Die Tagebücher von Joseph Goebbels*, T.I, Bd.5, July 13, 1938, p. 378.
332 arrived "too late": *New York Times*, July 31, 1938.
332 "The hunt is on": *Ring*, September 1938.
332 "No champion was ever": Ibid., March 1939.

Epilogue

333 "I thought that would be": *Los Angeles Times*, October 23, 1938.
333 "It may be impossible": *Life*, June 17, 1990.
333 "laid a rose": *Washington Post*, January 23, 1942.
333 "We'll win": *New York Times*, March 16, 1942.
334 "There's a lot wrong": *Los Angeles Times*, June 26, 1962.
334 "this time in a far greater arena": Richard Bak, *Joe Louis: The Great Black Hope* (Dallas: Taylor Publishing, 1996), p. 226.
334 "as happy and gay as one can be": *Reichssportblatt*, September 13, 1938.
334 "as popular as ever": *Box-Sport*, October 3, 1938.
335 "I am Joe Louis's master": *Chicago Tribune*, January 29, 1939.
335 "provides boxing with its best puzzle": *Chicago Tribune*, February 2, 1939.
335 "the strangest and perhaps": *Washington Post*, March 3, 1939.
335 "The fact that Schmeling is allowed": *Aufbau*, January 27, 1939.
335 "I am not what you say": Associated Press, February 15, 1939.
336 "The reporters looked at each other": Ibid.
336 "chicken feed and a million": *Reno Evening Gazette*, July 8, 1938.
336 "had done everything except": *Reno Evening Journal*, November 3, 1939.
336 "considered that he had squared": Ibid.
336 "a wish of the Führer is an order": Metzner to Schmeling, March 13, 1939, in Bundesarchiv, BA R 1501/510.
336 "supposedly no longer good enough": Schmeling to Metzner, March 28, 1939, in Bundesarchiv, BA R 1501/5101.
336 "lack of trust in your abilities": Metzner to Schmeling, undated, in Bundesarchiv, BA R 1501/5101.
337 "Y'know, he looked so natural": *New York Mirror*, April 28, 1940.

337 "It is too bad": *New York Times*, April 26, 1940.

337 "Why, I made Max rich": *Boxing and Wrestling*, December 1953.

338 "Max Schmeling, Germany's most popular boxer": *Die Deutsche Wochenschau*, February 26, 1941.

338 "As an athlete, he is a role model": *Angriff*, February 27, 1941.

338 "a great fighter and a great fellow": *New York Times*, May 29, 1941.

338 "not at all the fellow": *New York Journal-American*, June 10, 1941.

338 "fetch Joe Louis' scalp": International News Service, August 28, 1941.

339 "Right now he wouldn't be": *Washington Post*, August 29, 1941.

339 "*Maxe! Maxe!*": *Box-Sport*, November 3, 1941.

339 "We are thinking": *Wisconsin Rapids Daily Tribune*, August 1, 1944.

340 "An aroused American": *Liberty*, February 27, 1943.

340 "I'd kill him . . . with a gun": *Washington Post*, May 27, 1944.

340 "desperate attempt to save his skin": *Fight Facts*, July 27, 1945.

340n "destroyed the nigger Louis": Interview, Bob Jagoda.

341 "Here comes Joe!": Letter, R. J. Peterson to author.

341 "He's a Nazi through and through": *Stars and Stripes*, May 17, 1945.

341 "He may, indeed"; "Schmeling wouldn't act": *Washington Post*, May 18, 1945.

342n "Göring became very animated": Werner Bross, *Gespräche mit Hermann Göring während des Nürnberger Prozesses* (Flensburg: C. Wolff, 1950), pp. 33–34.

342 "It was all psychological": United Press International, January 25, 1946.

343 "The people who used to know": *Newsweek*, February 11, 1946.

343 "Time out for those who feel nauseated": clipping, undated, in morgue of the *New York Journal-American*, Harry Ranson Humanities Research Center, Austin, Texas.

343 "With Schmeling, nothing was haphazard": *Ring*, May 1946.

343 "That's one more reason why I don't like": *New York Times*, November 10, 1948.

344 "They should have called him": *American Legacy*, Winter 2002.

344 "The rules of arithmetic": North American News Association, September 12, 1935.

345 "Joe Louis punch"; "Joe Louis Kentucky straight bourbon": *Washington Post*, August 17, 1952.

345 "I don't believe the people": Ibid., May 20, 1954.

345 "Twenty-five thousand soldiers": *Milwaukee Journal*, May 21, 1954.

345 "Max, there is nothing to explain": *New York World-Telegram*, April 14, 1962.

345 "It wasn't a bit like old times": *Chicago Daily News*, May 17, 1954.

346 "The years have softened": *New York Journal-American*, May 18, 1954.

346 "Maybe a few decadent democrats": *New York Post*, May 28, 1954.

346 "Is it less reprehensible": *New York Post*, May 28, 1954.

346 "Joe, here is a friend of yours!": Schmeling, *Erinnerungen*, p. 251.

346 "crowning rejection": *Walla-Walla (Washington) Union-Bulletin*, June 1, 1954.

347 "What about this fellow?": *This Is Your Life*, October 23, 1960.

347 "There is an aura of unreality": *New York Post*, December 6, 1960.

347 "Max Schmeling invaded Miami Beach": *New York Herald Tribune*, March 14, 1961.

348 "He's done enough for me": Interview, Irwin Rosee.

348 "Uncle Tom": *New York Times*, October 12, 1980.

348n "Joe, you really think": *Time*, April 27, 1981.

348 "There's no more tough guys": *New York Times*, February 8, 1959.

348 "The golden age of prizefighting": Ibid., July 26, 1959.

348 "like poor Joe Louis": *Las Vegas Sports Form*, December 9, 1978.

348 "No one said it out loud": *New York Times*, November 11, 1978.

349 "For that alone": Remarks prepared by Rabbi Joshua Haberman, collection of the author.

349n "almost unanimously"; "simply disappeared": The relevant portions of Schmeling's memoirs are in *Erinnerungen*, pp. 425–33.

350 "Mr. Schmeling doesn't answer": Interview, Professor Hans Joachim Teichler.

351 "The embodiment of the decent German": *Frankfurter Allgemeine*, February 5, 2005.

351 "Our last hero is dead": *Welt am Sonntag*, February 6, 2005.

351 "a simple, modest": *Die Tageszeitung*, March 1, 2005.

351 "I didn't only like him": *Los Angeles Times*, December 28, 1988.

Photo Insert 1

Page 1, top; page 10, top right: The Granger Collection, New York

Page 1, bottom: Lusha Nelson/*Vanity Fair*, © 1935 Conde Nast Publications Inc.

Page 2, top left, bottom left; page 3, top and bottom; page 6, top left and bottom; page 7, top, middle, and bottom; page 8, middle and bottom; page 9, top left and right; page 10, top left and bottom; page 15, top: Corbis

Page 4, top: *New York Telegram*, front page, Sport Section © Scripps-Howard Foundation Wire

Page 4, bottom; page 10, top middle: © 1933 *The New York Times*

Page 5, top: General Research Division, The New York Public Library, Astor, Lenox, and Tilden Foundations

Page 5, bottom; page 11, top; page 12, top; page 13, bottom: *New York Daily News*

Page 6, middle: Courtesy of the Burton Historical Collection, Detroit Public Library

Page 8, top: Reprinted with permission from the *New York Post*, May 16, 1935. Copyright, NYP Holdings, Inc.

Page 9, bottom: *The Ring*

Page 11, bottom; page 12 middle; page 13 top; page 16, top: AP/WIDE WORLD PHOTOS

Page 12, bottom: Cover, *Berliner illustrierte Zeitung*, Nr. 26, June 25, 1936

Page 14, top: Front page used by permission, *Atlanta Daily World*

Page 14, bottom: Used with permission, *Chicago Defender*

Photo Insert 2

Page 1, top: The Granger Collection, New York

Page 1, middle: Bavarian State Library, Munich, Germany

Page 1, bottom; page 2, bottom; page 3, bottom; page 10, top; page 11; page 12, top; page 15, bottom: Corbis

Page 3, top: Reprinted with the permission of the Estate of Willard Mullin and Shirley Mullin Rhodes

Page 3, middle; page 7, top: Harry Ransom Humanities Research Center/The University of Texas at Austin

Page 4, top: Afro-American Newspapers Archives and Research Center

Page 4, middle left: From the Collections of the Alabama Department of Archives and History

Page 4, middle right, bottom: *The Ring*

Page 5, top: Used with permission, *Chicago Defender*

Page 5, middle; page 6, bottom; page 10, bottom: AP/WIDE WORLD PHOTOS

Page 5, bottom; page 14, bottom: *8 Uhr-Blatt/Abendzeitung* Nürnberg

Page 9, top, bottom; page 12, bottom; page 13, bottom; page 14, top: *New York Daily News*

Page 13, top: *The San Francisco Examiner*

Page 16: Courtesy of the Gropper family

INDEX

Schmeling, Max (*continued*)
balancing of German and American
interests, 8, 9–10, 17–18, 23, 31–3,
35–6, 39, 43, 128–9, 139–40, 186–7,
240–1, 341–2
biography of, 26, 28, 46
Braddock's aborted 1937 match with,
138, 187
British arrest of, 341–2
career ups and downs of, 8, 9, 10, 16, 19,
25–7, 40–1, 43–8, 116–17, 161
celebrity of, 16, 19, 32, 174–6, 179–87,
195, 351
character and personality of, 9, 15,
16–17, 18–19, 23, 25, 26, 32, 129, 219,
236, 267, 270–4, 280, 334, 341, 346, 351
Coca-Cola distribution of, 346, 350
country homes of, 32, 182, 241, 341, 344
criticism of, 19, 25–6, 28, 29, 31, 44–5,
93*n*
death and burial of, 350–1
democratic leanings seen in, 28
European light heavyweight
championship of, 19
exhibition tours of, 26, 31, 34, 35
extraordinary longevity of, 350, 351
failed exhibition tour of, 209–10, 211–12,
213
fans of, 16, 19, 23, 25, 47–53, 268, 279–80
farming of, 344
financial concerns of, 19, 20, 93, 194–5,
241, 266, 327, 330, 331
as first European to win heavyweight
title, 15
German heavyweight championship of,
19
German pogroms denied by, 32–3, 35
German statue of, 27
German support of, *see* Goebbels,
Joseph, Schmeling and; Hitler,
Schmeling's relationship with
German troops entertained by, 339
heavily accented English of, 16, 31–3,
118, 166, 176, 256, 257, 267, 313
injuries of, 19, 20, 22, 313, 325–7, 329–30,
334, 338
Iron Cross awarded to, 338
Jewish friends of, 32, 33, 35, 41, 47
Jewish opposition to, 31, 35, 39, 143–4,
149–50, 187, 205–15, 238–9, 242–3,
245–7, 253–5, 285–6
on JL, 117, 118, 121, 128, 130, 173–4, 193,
197, 198–9, 256, 257
JL compared with, 261–2
JL's reunion with, 345–6
JL's threatened lawsuit of, 199

JL studied by, 115–16, 118, 119, 121, 165,
197, 244
latter-day righteous Gentile role of,
350
managers of, *see* Bülow, Arthur;
Fleischer, Nat; Jacobs, Joe
marriage of, *see* Ondra, Anny
memoirs of, 47, 55
methodical boxing style of, 16, 18, 19,
51–2, 93, 154–9, 272, 297
motorcycle accident of, 19
Nazi Germany represented by, 7, 9, 39,
42–3, 45–54, 161–2, 163–4, 174–5,
179–87, 189, 214–15, 234–5, 241, 246–7,
264, 276, 321, 322, 345
patrons of, 20
personal chef of, 269, 279
physical appearance of, 9, 16, 27
physical fitness of, 17, 138, 267
political involvement denied by, 9, 32–3,
35, 118, 139–40, 186, 206, 347
post-defeat German status of, 313, 325,
326, 327–8, 329, 334–42
post-war rehabilitation attempted by,
342–4, 347
pre-fight air flight of, 278–9
retirement of, 343–4
right hand punch of, 18
rumored death of, 325–6, 331, 335, 338,
339
theatrical films made by, 48, 151
as "The Black Uhlan of the Rhine," 22,
32, 158, 346–7
three autobiographies of, 349
training of, 17, 18, 26, 31, 36, 41, 49, 79,
130–1, 136–41, 147, 183, 216
wealth of, 346
as Wehrmacht paratrooper, 334, 336–8,
339, 346
world heavyweight championship of, 15,
16, 24–6, 28, 32, 57
Schmeling's Victory: A German Victory
(*Schmelings Sieg*), 9, 291, 312
Schröder, Gerhard, 351
Schultz, Sigrid, 43
Schutzstaffel (SS), 78, 175, 249, 250
Schwarze Korps, Das, 175
Schweinau, 311
Scottsboro boys, 89, 111, 133, 137*n*
Seabiscuit, 7
Seamon, Manny, 260, 293, 344
Searcy State Hospital for the Negro
Insane, 233, 290
Seelig, Erich, 28, 29
segregation, 10, 61, 63, 67, 79, 101, 112, 177,
233, 320